Presidential Leadership
Politics and Policy Making

Second Edition

Presidential Leadership

Politics and Policy Making

Second Edition

George C. Edwards III
Texas A & M University

Stephen J. Wayne
Georgetown University

St. Martin's Press   **New York**

To Carmella and Cheryl

Senior Editor: Don Reisman
Development Editor: Michael Weber
Project Editor: Joyce Hinnefeld
Production Supervisor: Alan Fischer
Editorial Assistant: Rob Skiena
Graphics: G&H Soho
Cover Design: Tom McKeveny

For information, write:
St. Martin's Press, Inc.
175 Fifth Avenue
New York, NY 10010

ISBN: 0-312-01880-0

Preface

The presidency is a much praised, much damned institution. During the early 1960s it was seen as the major innovative force within the government. People looked to the president to satisfy an increasing number of their demands. Presidential power was thought to be the key to political change.

By the late 1960s and early 1970s, this power was seen as a serious problem. Scholars blamed presidents and their excesses for involvement in the war in Southeast Asia and for Watergate and other scandals. Restrain the "imperial" presidency became the cry.

Presidents Ford and Carter responded to this plea by attempting to deimperialize the office. Ford opened the White House to opposing views; Carter initially reduced the size, status, and perquisites of presidential aides. Both were careful not to exceed their constitutional and statutory powers.

Growing institutional conflict between Congress and the presidency and within the executive branch raised questions about the possibility of effective governance. Worsening economic conditions, increasingly scarce resources, and a series of foreign policy crises produced a desire for more assertive, more directive leadership. The presidency was seen as imperiled; weakness, not strength, its problem. Disappointment in presidential performance replaced fear of presidential abuses.

The Reagan presidency led scholars once again to reevaluate the workings of the system and the role of the president within it. Reagan's ability to achieve some of his major policy goals indicated that stalemate need not paralyze the government. But it also gave rise to fears, particularly after the Iran-Contra affair, of the dangers that improperly exercised power can produce.

Obviously, presidential leadership cuts two ways. It is desirable yet potentially harmful. It is necessary but difficult, perhaps more difficult today than in the past. Even though the president has limited influence over the environment in which he must operate, he is expected to solve most of the major problems that affect a significant portion of the American population. While expectations of the presidency remain as great as ever, the costs of meeting these expectations have increased. To make matters worse, presidents regularly receive more blame and credit for external conditions than they deserve. All of this has complicated the president's leadership task and, at the same time, made that task more critical.

This book, the text's second edition, is about presidential leadership, about the obstacles to that leadership, and about the skills necessary to overcome those obstacles. It focuses on the nature of executive leadership in the American political system.

We posit in this edition two models of leadership: the president as director of change and the president as facilitator. In the director of change model, the president leads the nation by dominating other political actors; in the facilitator model, he works, bargaining and pleading, at coalition building to further the attainment of his and his constituency's goals. These models provide the framework within which we assess leadership in the modern presidency.

In this second edition, we focus more heavily on the human elements of presidential leadership. Chapter 8, "The Personalized Presidency," is new. It evaluates the importance of social, physical, and psychological factors in determining the chief executive's performance. It seeks to explain how cognitive skills, interactive behavior, and psychological dimensions affect, directly or indirectly, the perceptions, judgments, and actions of presidents. To make room for this new chapter, we have shortened and made an appendix out of the first edition's chapter on studying the presidency.

We offer in this book no simple formula for presidential success, but we do assess the costs and consequences of presidential leadership in a pluralistic system where separate institutions are forced to share powers. We believe that effective, responsible presidential leadership can play a vital role in providing the coherence, direction, and support necessary to articulate and achieve national policy and political goals.

One of the difficulties we faced in writing this book was choosing a pronoun to represent the president. Traditionally, the male pronoun has been used, since only men have held this office. Reluctantly, we have adopted this convention because always pluralizing the word is inappropriate and always using the "he or she" combination is awkward. We apologize if we have offended anyone by the use of this convention. We trust that in the near future women (as well as members of minority groups) will be elected president and vice president (and thereby complicate our task as authors even more).

We wish to thank our friends at St. Martin's Press for the help they have provided us in the development, editing, and marketing of the second edition of this work. Developmental editor, Michael Weber, in particular, contributed significantly to the improvement of the manuscript. We also wish to thank Professors Eric Davis of Middlebury College, Richard K. Sher of the University of Florida, and Earl Shaw of the University of Minnesota for their insightful critiques. Finally, and most importantly, we want to acknowledge and thank our respective wives, Carmella Edwards and Cheryl Beil, for their patience, encouragement, and help. It is to them that we dedicate this book.

George C. Edwards III
Stephen J. Wayne

Contents

1

Presidential Leadership: An Introduction

No office within American government, or for that matter most other systems, has commanded the attention, stirred the imagination, and generated the emotions that the presidency has. Considered the first among equals, it has become the dominant institution in a system designed for balanced government, the prime initiator and coordinator among separate and independent institutions, the foremost mobilizer among disparate and, often, competing interests, and the principal communications link from and to a multitude of groups and individuals. It is a many-faceted, dynamic office—with a plethora of responsibilities, a variety of roles, and a large range of powers.

Within it, the president is clearly the chief. Executive officials look to him for direction, coordination, and general guidance in the implementation of policy; members of Congress look to him for establishing priorities, exerting influence, and providing services; the heads of foreign governments look to him for articulating positions, conducting diplomacy, and flexing muscle; the general public looks to him for enhancing security, solving problems, and exercising symbolic and moral leadership—a big order to be sure.

Unfortunately for the president, these expectations often exceed his abilities to meet them. It is not simply a question of his skill or personality, although both contribute to his capacity to do the job and to do it well. The problem is the system, particularly its constitutional, institutional, and political structures. The Constitution divides authority; institutions share power; and parties lack cohesion and often a sustained ideological thrust.

Despite the president's position and status, he has difficulty overcoming these constraints. Nor can he easily ignore or reduce what is expected of him. As a consequence, disappointment is frequent regardless of who occupies the Oval Office.

To some extent, this has always been the case. But in recent times, the gap between expectations and performance seems to have widened. Disenchantment has increased; confidence has declined; the popularity of many presidents has plummeted during the course of their administrations. Effective presidential leadership has thus become more diffcult but no less vital if the American system is to work.

This book addresses these problems and the ability of presidents to surmount them. First and foremost, this is a book about presidential leadership, about the capacity of chief executives to fulfill their tasks, to exercise their powers, and to utilize their organizational structures. It is a book about political leadership, about public opinion, group pressures, media coverage, and presidential salesmanship before, during, and after elections. It is also a book about policy leadership, about institutions and processes, about priority setting, coalition building, and governmental implementation. Finally, it is a book about personal leadership, about incumbents in office, about their goals, national needs, and the formal and informal ways of accomplishing their objectives.

In order to understand the problems of contemporary presidential leadership, it is necessary to gain perspective on the institution and its development. The first two parts of this chapter provide that perspective. In them we present an overview of the creation of the office and its evolution. We place particular emphasis on the growth of its policy-making roles, its advisory and administrative structures, and its political and public dimensions. In the third part of the chapter we examine recent changes in the political and policy environment and the impact of those changes on the president's job performance. We assess the sources of the institution's problems and present the dilemmas for contemporary leadership. In the final section we discuss how we will go about exploring these dilemmas.

THE ORIGINAL PRESIDENCY

The Creation of the Institution

The contemporary presidency bears little resemblance to the one the framers of the Constitution artfully designed in 1787 in Philadelphia. Their executive had more limited authority, less functional responsibility, and no explicit institutional structure or operating procedures. The times, of course, were different.

Although the Constitution's framers saw the need for an independent executive empowered with its own authority, they did not begin with a consensus on the form this executive should take nor the powers it should possess. At the outset of their deliberations, two basic questions had to be answered: Should the office be entrusted to one person or to several individuals? and What combination of functions, responsibilities, and powers would yield an energetic yet safe executive?

The first of these questions was resolved early in the convention after a short but pointed discussion. James Wilson, delegate from Pennsylvania, had proposed that only a single individual could combine the characteristics of "energy, dispatch, and responsibility." Critics immediately responded that such an executive would be dangerous—"the foetus of monarchy," in the words of Edmund Randolph.

In denying the allegation that what they really wanted was a king, Wilson and James Madison sought to contrast their more limited executive with the powers of a king. As the debate intensified, Madison proposed that the institution's authority be established before the number of executives was decided. This constituted one of the most astute parliamentary moves of the Constitutional Convention. Wilson had previously declared that the prerogatives of the British monarch were not a proper guide for determining the executive's domain. They were too extensive. The American executive, he argued, should possess only executive authority, the power to execute laws and make those appointments that had not otherwise been provided for. The Convention accepted Wilson's delineation, a delineation that made it safe to entrust the office to a single individual. This was promptly done. Only later were those powers expanded through enumeration.

Wilson was primarily responsible for this enumeration as well. As a member of the committee charged with taking propositions approved by the Convention and shaping them into a constitution, he detailed the executive's powers with phraseology taken from the New York and Massachusetts constitutions. Surprisingly, his enumeration engendered little debate. The powers were not particularly controversial. Couching them in the language of two state constitutions made them more palatable to the delegates. Most were quickly and quietly adopted.

Agreement on the checks to secure and restrain the executive was a little more difficult. Abuses of past executives—particularly British monarchs and colonial governors—combined with the excesses of contemporary legislatures made the maintenance of an institutional balance essential. The problem was how to preserve the balance without jeopardizing the independence of the separate branches or impeding the lawful exercise of their authority. In the end the framers resolved this problem by checking those powers that they believed to be most dangerous, the ones which historically had been subject to greatest abuse (appointments, treaty making, and declarations of war), while protecting the general spheres of authority from encroachment (in the executive's case by a qualified veto).

Presidential responsibility was also encouraged by the provisions for reeligibility and a short term of office. Reappointment was the great motive to good behavior. For those executives who flagrantly abused their authority, impeachment was the ultimate recourse.

The traditional weapon to defend executive authority was the veto. Theoretically, it could function to protect those executive prerogatives that were threatened by the legislature. In practice, it had frequently been employed to preclude the enactment of laws that the executive opposed. Herein lay its danger. The compromise was to give the president the veto but allow two-thirds of both houses to override it.

In summary, the relative ease with which the presidency was empowered indicates that a consensus developed on the bounds and substance of executive authority. Not only had certain traditional prerogatives been rejected but others had been readily accepted. In deciding which of these powers should be given to the new institution, the framers turned to the tenets of balanced government as articulated by the French theorist Charles de Montesquieu in his well-quoted treatise, *The Spirit of the Laws,* and practiced to some extent in the states of Massachusetts and New York.[1] Those powers which conformed to the basic division of authority were accepted; those which actually or potentially threatened the institutional balance were rejected.

Fears of potential abuse led to differing opinions on how best to constrain the branches without violating the principle of separate spheres of authority. The majority of the delegates opted for sharing powers, particularly in foreign affairs, and principally with the Senate. Their decision, reached toward the end of the convention when the pressures to compromise were greatest, exacerbated the fears of those who believed that the Senate would come to dominate the president and control the government.

Many of the opponents of the Constitution saw the sharing of powers as far more dangerous than the general grant of executive authority that was specified in Article 2. While each of the president's powers engendered some objection during the ratification debate, the most sustained criticism was directed at the relationship with the upper chamber. In the end, the proponents of the Constitution prevailed, but the debate over the efficacy of shared powers between executive and legislative branches has continued through the years.

The Scope of Article 2

In one sense what the framers did is obvious. It is written in Article 2. In another sense, however, their deliberations and decisions have been subject to constant interpretation. Unlike Article 1, where the Constitution detailed the legislative powers that were given to Congress, Article 2 stated executive authority in a more general way: "The executive power shall be vested in a President of the United States of America." For years scholars have debated whether this designation provides the president with an undefined grant of authority or simply confers on him the title of the office.

Although the answer to this question remains in doubt, the executive portion of the president's responsibilities is relatively clear. The framers charged the president with the administration of government. He was given the task of faithfully executing the law and the capacity to do so by overseeing the executive departments. The departments were not designated by the Constitution. They were established by legislation during the first Congress and later Congresses. The president, however, was to have a hand in choosing the people who ran them.

The need to provide the executive with some discretion to respond to emergency or extraordinary situations was also considered essential. Heading the only institution with continuous tenure and the only one with a national perspective, the president was thought to be able to respond to events more quickly and decisively than the Congress. Traditionally this type of emergency power resided in the executive.

In his *Second Treatise of Civil Government*, the British philosopher John Locke had written of the need for such a power, which he termed a prerogative.[2] The framers agreed. Having themselves experienced under the Articles of Confederation a legislature unable to respond to emergencies, they desired to provide such a capacity in their constitutional arrangement and gave it to the president.

The debate over the war powers illustrates their dilemma as well as their solution. Initially, the Congress was given the authority to make war. Fearing that the word "make" might preclude the executive from responding to an attack if Congress were not in session, the framers agreed to substitute the word "declare." This provided the president with flexibility but did not alter the basic intent—to have Congress decide whether or not to go to war. Even after making that decision, Congress retained powers that affected the conduct of hostilities. These powers serve to limit the president's discretion as commander in chief.

Similarly in foreign affairs, the president was limited in what he could do alone without the approval of the Senate or both houses. He did, however, share the treaty-making role with the upper chamber. The president exercised the initiative. But even here, the wording of the Constitution suggested that the Senate was to have a role in the negotiation of treaties as well as in their ratification.

Although executive powers were expected to expand during emergencies, they were never without limits. The exercise of discretionary powers by the executive was always tied to legislation. The president could summon Congress into special session; he was obligated to report to it on the state of the union; he could recommend necessary and expedient legislation; but it was the Congress that in the end had to decide what laws, if any, to enact. Even in the case of the veto, two-thirds of both houses would have the last word.

In short, the relatively general grant of executive authority gave the president broad discretion in the exercise of his principal responsibility— the execution of the law. Some of his powers were exclusive but others were shared. Some of them were enumerated but that enumeration was not exhaustive. The president had considerable freedom to oversee subordinates of his own choosing in his administration of government. On the other hand, his discretion in formulating policy was extremely limited. Congress, not the executive, was expected to assume that role in the normal course of events.

THE EVOLUTION OF THE PRESIDENCY

Policy-Making Roles

Although the president's constitutionally designated authority has not been formally amended, the scope of that authority has been expanded by law and precedent. Over the years, the president's policy-making powers have grown dramatically. Chief executives, starting with Washington, set the contours of foreign policy. Beginning with Jefferson, they shaped it to the point of actually defining what the war policy would be. There were other early examples of presidential initiatives in foreign affairs, notably Monroe's famous doctrine that pledged United States protection of the independent states on this side of the Atlantic.

Crisis situations expanded the president's powers still further, as Lincoln's actions during the Civil War demonstrated. Lincoln justified his exercise of power by the gravity of the situation. "Was it possible to lose the nation and yet preserve the Constitution?" he asked. To his own question, he replied, "I felt that measures otherwise unconstitutional might become lawful by becoming indispensable to the preservation of the Constitution through the preservation of the nation."[3]

Lincoln was not challenged by Congress during the war, but after it Congress reasserted its authority. Throughout the remainder of the nineteenth century, Congress, not the president, dominated the relationship between the branches. In fact, when, as a professor of politics, Woodrow Wilson wrote his perceptive study on the American political system in the mid-1880s, he titled it *Congressional Government.*

Wilson wrote at the end of an era. By the time he became chief executive, the president's roles in both foreign and domestic affairs had expanded, and Wilson revised his book. Demands for a more activist government had encouraged Presidents McKinley and Theodore Roosevelt to work more closely and harmoniously with Congress to fashion major policy initiatives. Roosevelt was responsible for much of this activity.

Assuming an assertive posture in both foreign and domestic affairs, Roosevelt expanded the president's policy-making roles. He sent the navy halfway around the world (and then requested appropriations from Congress to return it home); he announced a corollary to the Monroe Doctrine, further involving the United States in hemispheric activities; he helped instigate a revolution in Colombia, quickly recognized the independence of insurgents on the Isthmus of Panama, and promptly entered into an agreement with them to build a canal. He was the first president to travel outside of the United States (to Mexico and Panama) and the first to help settle a war, for which he won the Nobel Peace Prize. Within the domestic sphere, Roosevelt busted trusts, crusaded for conservation, and mediated a major coal strike. He was also instrumental in getting Congress to enact important legislation, including the Pure Food and Drug Act, the Meat Inspection Act, and the Hepburn (railroad) Act.

Roosevelt's theory of the presidency justified and accommodated his activism. Writing in his autobiography after his political career had ended, Roosevelt stated:

> My view was that every executive officer, and above all every executive officer in high position, was a steward of the people bound actively and affirmatively to do all he could for the people, and not to content himself with the negative merit of keeping his talents undamaged in a napkin.[4]

In contrast, William Howard Taft, Roosevelt's successor, expressed a much more restrained conception:

> The true view of the executive function is, as I conceive it, that the president can exercise no power which cannot be fairly and reasonably traced to some specific grant of power or justly implied and included within such express grant as proper and necessary to its exercise. Such specific grant must be either in the federal Constitution or in an act of Congress passed in pursuance thereof. There is no undefined residuum of power which he can exercise because it seems to him to be in the public interest.[5]

Roosevelt's *stewardship* theory has prevailed. With the exception of the three Republican presidents of the 1920s, occupants of the Oval Office in the twentieth century have assumed active political and policymaking roles. Woodrow Wilson and Franklin Roosevelt, in particular, expanded Theodore Roosevelt's initiatives in international and domestic matters.

Wilson was the first president to propose a comprehensive legislative program and the first to be involved in summitry. He was the architect of the proposal to establish a League of Nations, although he was unable to persuade the Senate to accept his plan.

Franklin Roosevelt enlarged the president's role in economic affairs. Coming into office in the midst of the Great Depression, he initiated a series of measures to deal with the crisis and succeeded in getting Congress to enact them. He maintained the posture of an international leader, maneuvering the country's entrance into World War II and participating in summit conferences to win the war and plan the peace. He also made the critical decision to develop the atomic bomb.

The modern presidency is said to have begun in the era of Franklin

Roosevelt. It is characterized by presidential activism in a variety of policy-making roles. Many of the practices which Roosevelt initiated or continued have been institutionalized by his successors and/or required by Congress.

Organizational Structure

The structure of the modern presidency also developed during the Roosevelt period. In 1939 the Executive Office of the President was created. Prior to that time presidents had depended largely on their department heads for administration and advice.

The Constitution did not explicitly provide for an administrative structure. It did, however, contain oblique reference to one. There was a provision in Article 2 that the president could demand in writing the opinions of subordinate officials. It was up to the first Congress to establish the executive departments as the principal administrative units of government. It created three departments (Foreign Affairs, Treasury, and War) and appointed an attorney general and a postmaster general. Since then, ten more departments and more than one hundred agencies have been established.

Throughout most of the nineteenth century it was Congress, not the president, who dominated the administration of government. Statutes specified many organizational details of the departments, including their jurisdiction, staffing levels, and even operating procedures. For the most part, there was little oversight from the president.

The autonomy of the departments contributed to the influence of their secretaries, who headed them. Since the department heads were the president's principal advisers, they exercised considerable leverage in helping to design administration goals and in mobilizing congressional support. With the exception of the Jefferson, Jackson, and Lincoln administrations, strong department secretaries and weak presidents characterized executive advisory relationships.

This began to change at the outset of the twentieth century as a consequence of the president's growing influence in Congress. As that increased, the potency of the department secretaries, individually and collectively, began to decline. They lost their privileged position between president and Congress. Their support of administration proposals became less critical than it had been to the president's legislative success.

The concern that Theodore Roosevelt and, particularly, William Howard Taft evidenced toward the organization of government also contributed eventually to the president's enhanced status and power within the executive branch. Taft appointed a Committee on Economy and Efficiency to recommend improvements. Reporting in 1913, the committee urged the creation of a more hierarchial structure with the president assuming a larger administrative role.

Initially, Congress was reluctant to comply. However, sizable budget deficits, inflated by United States involvement in World War I, provided the legislature with a financial (and political) incentive to do so. Unable to control the deficits, Congress turned to the president for help. It enacted the Budget and Accounting Act of 1921, which made it a presidential responsibility to estimate the financial needs of the individual departments and agencies on a yearly basis and provided the president with an institutional mechanism to do so, the Bureau of the Budget.

When Franklin Roosevelt took office and expanded the president's domestic policy role, he needed more information, more expertise, and more staff. At first he depended on personnel provided by the executive departments. When that did not prove satisfactory, he turned to a small group of experts to advise him on how to make the organizational structure of the executive more responsive to his needs. The group, headed by Louis Brownlow, issued a report that said:

> The President needs help. His immediate staff assistance is entirely inadequate. He should be given a small number of executive assistants who would be his direct aides in dealing with the managerial agencies and administrative departments of government.[6]

The Brownlow committee urged the creation of a separate presidential office. In 1939 Congress approved the act that established the Executive Office of the President. Initially the office consisted of five units: the White House, Bureau of the Budget, and three World War II agencies (the National Resources Planning Board, the Liaison Office for Personnel Management, and the Office of Government Reports). Eventually over forty different councils, boards, and offices have been housed at one time or another in this office.

The creation of the Executive Office provided the president with a structure directly responsive to his interests. The White House became his personal office. Presidential aides performed political tasks that were dictated by the president's immediate needs, actions, and goals. Having no constitutional and statutory authority of their own and no political base other than the president's, their influence was dependent on their access to him. They did his calling.

Whereas the White House functioned as a personal extension of the president, the Budget Bureau became an institutional extension of the presidency. It coordinated the policy-making functions of the department and agencies, imposing a presidential perspective on the executive branch in the process.

During subsequent administrations, the duties of the Executive Office have been expanded and its organizational structure redesigned. Staffed by civil servants and run by political appointees, it continues to perform a variety of critical tasks. It is considered essential for an activist presidency, but its large size, its many roles, and its organizational autonomy make it difficult for the president to oversee, much less to control.

Public Dimensions

In addition to the development of the presidency as an institution and the growth of its policy-making roles, the public dimension of the office has expanded as well. This too has been a relatively recent phenomenon. Franklin Roosevelt was the first to use the mass media (radio) to communicate directly with the American people on a regular basis. His successors have used television to the same end.

For most of the nineteenth century the presidency was not a particularly visible office, although the president received his share of critical commentary. Jefferson was the first to claim a partisan mandate and Jackson the first to claim a public one.[7]

A variety of factors contributed to a more active public posture by presidents toward the beginning of the twentieth century. The growth of news-gathering organizations and newspaper chains made it possible to communicate with more people more quickly. The advent of yellow journalism combined with the increased activism of government generated more interest in the opinions and behavior of public officials, particularly the president.

Theodore Roosevelt, more than any of his predecessors, took advantage of these developments to focus attention on himself, his policies, and his activities. He was the first president to give reporters a room in the White House and the first to hold regular meetings with the press. Using his position as "a bully pulpit," Roosevelt rallied public support for his positions and proposals.

Roosevelt's presidency prompted Professor Woodrow Wilson to revise his view that the governmental system was dominated by Congress. The president could be as big a man as he wanted, Wilson asserted in 1908. He could use his position as party and national leader to enhance his political power and thereby exert influence on Congress:

> His capacity will set the limit; and if Congress be overborne by him, it will be no fault of the makers of the Constitution—it will be from no lack of constitutional powers on its part, but only because the President has the nation behind him, and Congress has not. He has no means of compelling Congress except through public opinion.[8]

Wilson attempted to heed his own words. The enactment of his legislative program can be attributed in large part to his political leadership and public oratory. His greatest disappointment, however, his inability to persuade the Senate to ratify the Treaty of Versailles ending World War I, stemmed from his failure to exercise these skills successfully. Wilson, who went on a public-speaking tour to build support for his position, overestimated his ability to lead public opinion and underestimated his opponents' capacity to do so.

While Theodore Roosevelt and Woodrow Wilson used the presidency as a podium, neither of them was as skillful at manipulating the press as was Franklin Roosevelt. In his first term, Franklin Roosevelt held more press conferences than any of his predecessors. Meeting frequently with small groups of reporters in the Oval Office, he used these sessions to articulate his views and float trial balloons. He also made extensive and productive use of radio in his fireside chats.

By the end of the Roosevelt era, the presidency had been permanently altered by the media. It had become the most visible national office. Coverage of the White House was constant. The president was always in the news.

The intensive and extensive media focus on the president has had three principal effects. First, it has permanently added a new role to the president's job, that of communicator in chief, and has required that skills commensurate with this role be exercised. Second, it has heightened public expectations of presidential performance. Advances in communications have enabled organized groups to promote the desires of their membership more effectively. The president has become the focal point for many of these increased demands on government. Third, media coverage has linked public approval more closely to the exercise of presidential power. Now more than ever, presidents need to build support outside of government to gain support within it. Taken together, these factors indicate why increased public exposure for the president has, at best, been a mixed blessing.

PROBLEMS OF CONTEMPORARY LEADERSHIP

These changes, singularly and together, have created new demands on the president which, as a consequence, have generated new roles and obligations for him and new criteria by which he is to be judged. These new roles and criteria, in turn, have affected perceptions of leadership. In the past, the people did not look to the president to solve most national economic, social, and political problems. Today they do. The president is expected to be a chief policymaker. He is expected to exercise a wide range of powers. Ancillary coordination, communication, and co-optation functions have followed from these expanded roles and powers.

Institutional growth has been another consequence of a more activist presidency. The size of the office has increased enormously. Prior to 1939 the president was assisted by a few aides, most of whom were detailed from executive departments and agencies. The total budget for the salaries and expenses of those working for the president was $125,804.98 in 1925. In 1939 when the Executive Office was created, it was about $250,000. Today it is about $28 million for the White House alone, and that does not include the one hundred or so detailees paid from other executive budgets. The first Executive Office of the President consisted of five agencies, including the White House; fifty years later it has ten agencies and a combined staff of approximately 1,500.

The larger staff has increased the president's capacity to perform added responsibilities and to do so with less dependence on executive departments and agencies. But the enlargement of that staff has also worked to extend the very functions and responsibilities that the staff was designed to serve. This expansion has limited the president's personal influence over what functions his presidency performs and to a lesser extent how his administration is organized to perform them.

Not only has the presidential office grown in size and solidified in organization but its policy processes have become institutionalized. Mechanisms for preparing the budget, formulating a program, building support in Congress, and advising the president whether to sign or veto legislation have developed and continued from administration to administration. These routines have also worked to shape the functions and processes they serve.

There have been significant changes in the public dimensions of the office as well. The selection process has become more individualized. Parties do not organize and mediate between candidates and the voters as they did in the past. Public expectations have increased as a consequence of longer campaigns, more personalized appeals, and many specific promises made to organized groups. Yet, the electoral coalition needed to win no longer provides the basis for governing. New coalitions have to be formed on an issue-by-issue basis.

The national media seemingly are more critical of the president than in the past. Communications from and to the public are more direct and immediate. Such communications enable the White House to measure the pulse of public opinion more accurately, but also condition responses, shorten the time frame, and ultimately, constrain the president's options.

Interest groups have proliferated and professionalized. They have become more sophisticated at influencing their members and mobilizing them behind specific policy positions. No institution or individual, not the Executive Office of the President, the White House, or even the president, is immune from these pressures.

Lobbying increases the political impact of many presidential decisions. It can force the president's hand, making him compromise for political reasons when he would rather not do so for policy reasons. The proliferation of professionalized interest groups makes the redistribution of resources more difficult. Over time, it increases levels of dissatisfaction among different sectors of the public. It adversely affects the president's relations with Congress.

Changes within the legislature have reinforced this organized pluralism. Congress has decentralized law making, shifting power to a large number of subcommittee chairs. Ironically, more members of Congress must now be consulted, coordinated, and cajoled at the very time when Congress has involved itself in more issues of executive policy making and policy implementation. The president must work harder than in the past to achieve his administration's legislative goals.

He is similarly constrained within the executive branch. The continuing orientation of the bureaucracy to outside groups plus its ongoing relationships with Congress work to limit presidential influence. Most presidential appointees in the departments and agencies soon find themselves with divided loyalties.

And that is not all. External factors within the environment have enlarged policy expectations of the president but at the same time made those expectations less subject to presidential control than they were in the past. The president is expected to manage the economy, but the increasing interdependence of nations limits his ability to do so; the scarcity of some natural resources no longer permits unlimited development and forces decisions that have important political consequences; the vulnerability of the United States to nuclear attack shortens the president's reaction time and broadens the effect of national security decisions. It also contributes to the public's psychological dependence on the president and the security needs that the office serves.

Finally, events from the late 1960s to the present—United States involvement in Vietnam, the Watergate cover-up, the Iran–Contra affair, and various congressional scandals—have impugned the motives and integrity of high officials, including the president's. He no longer enjoys the benefit of the doubt many of his predecessors had. This makes it more difficult for him to rally and maintain public support despite the expectation that he do so.

ORIENTATION AND ORGANIZATION OF THIS STUDY

Thinking about Leadership: Two Perspectives

This book is titled *Presidential Leadership* because it focuses on just that—leadership. The exercise of influence is central to our concept of leadership, as it is to most political scientists. We want to know whether the president can influence the actions and attitudes of others and affect the output of government. It is important to distinguish between attempts to lead and leadership itself. Both are of primary interest in this book, and we devote much of our effort to exploring the relationship between the two.

Presidential leadership typically involves obtaining or maintaining the support of other political actors for the chief executive's political and policy stances. In the American political system, most political actors are free to choose whether or not to follow the chief executive's lead; the president cannot force them to act, presenting a challenge to his political leadership.

Although thinking of leadership in terms of influence is useful for the study of presidential leadership, the concept remains somewhat nebulous. To guide our examination, we consider it useful to refine the concept of leadership by contrasting two broad perspectives on the presidency. In the first the president is the *director* of change. Through his leadership he creates opportunities to move in new directions, leading others where they otherwise would not go. In the role of director he is out in front, establishing goals and encouraging others to follow.

A second perspective is less heroic but nonetheless important. Here the president is primarily a *facilitator* of change. He exploits opportunities to help others go where they want to go anyway. In the role of facilitator the president reflects and perhaps intensifies widely held views, using his resources to achieve his constituency's aspirations.

The director creates a constituency to follow his lead, whereas the facilitator endows his constituency's views with shape and purpose by interpreting and translating them into legislation. The director shapes the contours of the political landscape to pave the way for change, whereas the facilitator exploits opportunities presented by a favorable configuration of political forces.

The director moves mountains and influences many independent actors. He has the more formidable task because he establishes the agenda and persuades a perhaps reluctant public or Congress to support his policies. In contrast, the facilitator works at the margins, influencing a few critical actors and taking advantage of the opportunities for change already present in his environment. In both cases the president exercises leadership, yet the scale of the leadership is clearly different. The range and scope of the director's influence are broad, whereas those of the facilitator are more narrow.

The two perspectives are not neat categories: we employ them simply to increase our understanding of presidential leadership by exploring its possibilities. The issue is not whether leadership matters, but rather how much and under what conditions. It is not sufficient to conclude, however, that sometimes the environment is receptive to change and at other times not. This viewpoint simply begs the question of whether presidents are able to influence the environment so as to create the opportunity for change. Understanding the possibilities of leadership permits an assessment of the performance of presidents.

The notion of the dominant president who moves the country and the government by means of strong, effective leadership has deep roots in our political culture. Those chief executives whom Americans revere, such as Washington, Jefferson, Jackson, Lincoln, Wilson, and both Roosevelts, have taken on mythic proportions as leaders. Even though the public is frequently disillusioned with the performance of presidents and recognizes that stalemate is common, Americans eagerly accept what appears to be effective presidental leadership, as in the case of Ronald Reagan in 1981, as evidence on which to renew faith in the potential of the presidency. After all, if presidential leadership works some of the time, why not all of the time?

This perception directly influences expectations and evaluations of presidents. If it is reasonable to expect successful leadership from the White House, then failures of leadership must be personal deficiencies. If problems arise because the leader lacks the proper will, skills, or understanding, then the solution to the need for leadership is straightforward and simple: elect a president willing and able to lead. Because the system is responsive to appropriate leadership, it will function smoothly with the right leader in the Oval Office. The public can indulge in high expectations of the president and freely criticize him if he fails, for example, to bring around Congress or the public to his point of view. The blame lies clearly in the leader rather than the environment. Americans need not concern themselves with broader forces in American society that may influence presidential leadership. Because these forces are complex and perhaps even intractable, to focus on the individual as leader simplifies analysis and evaluation of the problems of governing.

On the other hand, what if presidential leadership is not preeminent in American government? What if presidential leadership has less potential than holders of the conventional wisdom believe and the president actually operates at the margins in leading the country? What if the national preoccupation with the chief executive is misplaced and belief in the impact of the individual leader is largely a myth—a product of a search for simple solutions in an extremely complex, purposefully inefficient system in which the founders' handiwork in decentralizing power defeats even the most capable leaders?

If this is the case, the public should expect less of the president and be less disappointed when he is not successful in leading. In addition, the focus should be less exclusively on the president and more on the context in which the president seeks to lead. Major changes in public policy may then require more than just the "right" person in the job and may not turn on a president's leadership qualities. It does not, of course, follow that failures of presidential leadership may never be attributed to the White House or that the president has no control over the outcome of his relations with other political actors. It does mean that a better understanding of presidential leadership is necessary to think sensibly about the role of the chief executive in the nation's political system.

Conceptual Focus

This book will explore the president's leadership problems and the attempts by recent chief executives to overcome them. It will do so by examining multiple facets of the presidency within the context of its political and policy-making roles. Our orientation will be eclectic. Instead of adopting a particular perspective, the book will present several. Instead of imposing a single thesis, it will discuss many of the hypotheses, generalizations, and conclusions which have been advanced by students of the presidency.

The reason for utilizing a variety of approaches and presenting a body of research findings is that there is no one generally accepted theory of the presidency, no one conceptual framework within which to study the office, no one thesis, other than perhaps Richard Neustadt's on presidential power,[9] that has commanded the attention and acceptance of most presidency scholars.

Despite an abundant literature on the presidency, our understanding of how that institution works is not nearly as sophisticated as our understanding of Congress or even the Supreme Court. Much of the presidency still operates behind closed doors.

What factors have conditioned the methodology, shaped the content, and limited the findings of so much of the presidency literature? Three stand out: (1) the view that each president and administration is relatively unique; (2) the difficulty of obtaining first-hand information on the operation of the institution; (3) the absence of a comprehensive theory. Together these factors have impeded the ability to do rigorous, analytic, empirical research on the presidency.

The personalities of individual presidents and their staffs, the particular events and circumstances of their time in office, and the specific problems and actions of their administrations have led scholars to treat each presidency as if it were unique. Emphasizing the differences between presidencies rather than the similarities between them makes the identification of patterns and relations more difficult and, in turn, makes it harder to generalize. Description rather than analysis and speculation rather than generalization have become the standard fare.

The relatively closed character of the institution has contributed to the problem. The presidency is not easy to observe from a distance. Public pronouncements and actions tell only part of what happens and why it happens—usually the part that the people in power wish to convey. Inside information is difficult to obtain. Decision makers, particularly those at the top of the executive bureaucracy, are not readily accessible. Their busy schedules combined with their natural reluctance to reveal information that may be embarrassing, sensitive, or in other ways controversial often make them unwilling and unresponsive sources.

Nor is dependence on journalistic accounts usually satisfactory. Journalists tend to be event oriented. They do not usually employ a time frame or perspective that is sufficiently comprehensive to permit generalizations, particularly on the institutional and behavioral aspects of the office.

The third factor that contributes to the problem is the absence of an overall theory that explains presidential behavior. Unlike other areas in political science such as individual voting behavior, in which there is a body of theory that explains and predicts who votes and why, the presidency literature has not produced an explanation of why presidents do what they do or what consequences their actions have. Nor has it been able to predict what they will do or what consequences their actions will have in the future. There are, however, many prescriptions of what presidents should do.

The nature of these problems suggests that we should cast our net as broadly as possible when examining the institution and exploring the president's leadership opportunities and problems. This is why we have decided not to focus on a single theme (which might exclude important information) but to examine a set of critical relationships. These relationships are between the president and those whose support he needs to do his job.

To function effectively an occupant of the Oval Office must be elected, build and maintain popular support, make decisions, and present, promote, and implement policies. Each of these requirements involves reciprocal relationships in which presidents influence and are influenced by others. That is why we must examine both sides of these relationships rather than focus exclusively on the president.

Relationships provide a conceptual framework for studying presidential leadership. They enable us to explain the behavioral causes and consequences of presidential activities. By stressing relationships, however, we do not suggest that legal powers, informal roles, institutional structures, and psychological factors are unimportant. Indeed, we firmly believe one cannot understand the presidency without an extensive knowledge of these matters, and we provide such a background. Our point of departure is that we discuss these matters within the context of presidential relationships rather than vice versa. Powers, roles, structures, and personality should not be viewed as ends in themselves. They are important to us for what they contribute to the president's ability to formulate, establish, and implement policies.

Outline

This book is organized into four broad sections. They deal with politics and public relations, with the person in the institution, with the presidency's interaction with the rest of the government, and with the policy-making process.

The next four chapters concern the relationship between the president and the public. In Chapters 2 and 3 we discuss nomination politics and the general election. Here we focus on the interaction between presidential candidates and the electorate. In Chapter 4 we turn to the president in office and his relations with the general public, and in Chapter 5 we examine the communications link between the incumbent and the media. In each of these chapters we explore leadership problems. Obviously, winning electoral support, gaining public approval, and obtaining favorable media coverage are critical to a president's success.

In Chapters 6, 7, and 8 we analyze the relationship between the institution and the people in it. Specifically, we examine the interaction among the president, his White House advisers, and others who wish to affect his decisions. Here attention is directed toward presidential decision making. The institutional environment combined with the president's personal style condition his discretion and ultimately affect his choices.

In the third part of the book we turn to the interaction that the president must have with the executive branch, Congress, and the judiciary to achieve his policy objectives. Promoting programs in Congress, implementing them in the bureaucracy, and adjudicating them in the courts are necessary if presidential leadership is to be effective.

After scrutinizing presidential relations, we then discuss the formulation of public policy in and by the presidency. Individual chapters concern domestic, budgetary and economic, and foreign and defense policy making. In each chapter we identify and assess expectations of presidential leadership and the resources that are available for meeting these expectations.

Having explored the critical relationships between the president and the public, the president and the presidency, the president and the other branches, and the president and the policy-making process, we end with an appendix that discusses another important but different kind of relationship—that of the president and political science. Our object is to demonstrate how various perspectives on the office and methods of studying it can affect what we know about the president. We conclude where we began. If the presidency is a multifaceted institution (as we claim it is), then it can best be understood only by adopting a variety of approaches and techniques. That is why our orientation is eclectic, why we have introduced a number of themes, and why we have chosen critical presidential relationships as the conceptual framework for this study.

NOTES

1. Charles de Montesquieu, *The Spirit of the Laws,* vol. 1 (New York: Hafner, 1949).
2. Locke wrote: "Where the legislative and executive power are in distinct hands, as they are in all moderated monarchies and well-framed governments, there the good of the society requires that several things should be left to the discretion of him that has the executive power. For the legislators not being able to foresee and provide by laws for all that may be useful to the community, the executor of the laws, having the power in his hands, has by the common law of Nature a right to make use of it for the good of the society, in many cases where the municipal law has given no direction, till the legislative can conveniently be assembled to provide for it" (John Locke, "Second Treatise of Civil Government," in Thomas I. Cook, ed., *Two Treatises of Government* [New York: Hafner, 1956], p. 203).
3. Abraham Lincoln, "Letter dated April 8, 1964," reprinted in Harry A. Bailey, Jr., ed., *Classics of the American Presidency* (Oak Park, Ill.: Moore Publishing Co., 1980), p. 34.
4. Theodore Roosevelt, *The Autobiography of Theodore Roosevelt* (New York: Scribner's, 1913), p. 197.
5. William Howard Taft, *Our Chief Magistrate and His Powers* (New York: Columbia University Press, 1916), p. 138.
6. President's Committee on Administrative Management, *Report with Special Studies* (Washington, D.C.: U.S. Government Printing Office, 1937), p. 5.
7. It was during the 1820s that the electorate began to choose presidential electors directly rather than have them selected by state legislatures. This increased the value of obtaining and maintaining public support for the president. Tradition, however, required that this be done in a manner that befitted the dignity of the office. Public addresses were permitted; personal campaigning was discouraged. The party was expected to shoulder the electoral burden for its candidates. Not until William Jennings Bryan's quest for the nation's highest office in 1896 did candidates take to the stump themselves.
8. Woodrow Wilson, *Constitutional Government* (New York: Columbia University Press, 1908), pp. 70–71.
9. Richard E. Neustadt, *Presidential Power: The Politics of Leadership from FDR to Carter* (New York: Wiley, 1980).

SELECTED READINGS

Cronin, Thomas E., ed. *Inventing the American Presidency* (Lawrence, KS: University Press of Kansas, 1989).
Robinson, Donald L. *"To the Best of My Ability."* New York: W. W. Norton, 1987.

2

The Nomination
Process

Every four years there are two presidential selection processes: the first to nominate candidates, the second to choose between them. Both require considerable time, money, and effort.

The nominating system has evolved significantly in recent years. Rules governing delegate selection, laws regulating contributions and spending, communications controlled and uncontrolled by the candidates have all changed dramatically within the last thirty years. These changes have literally revolutionized the nomination process. They have affected the types of candidates who seek their party's nomination, the qualifications they demonstrate as criteria for their selection, and the leadership they are able to exert on their party and, ultimately, within the presidency. Today, aspirants for their party's nomination are more on their own. They have greater opportunity to articulate their own priorities and shape their own issue agenda, to develop their own style, and to build their own political coalitions. In this sense, if successful, they are in a good position to bring new ideas, new people, and new leadership to the presidency.

The nomination process, however, contributes to the difficulty presidential aspirants may encounter in exercising this leadership. This process heightens public expectations but weakens partisan support, usually accentuating divisions within the party. It encourages personality politics by focusing on personal characteristics, a threatrical style, and a "sound-bite mentality," rather than on a more substantive discussion of the critical goals and issues that lie ahead. What it provides to the candidate who wins the nomination is a label, but not necessarily a tight organization and coherent policy consensus to rely on during the general election campaign and to provide direction and support in the presidency.

In this chapter we will discuss these changes and their impact on those seeking the presidency. The chapter is organized into four parts. First we present a historical overview of the nomination process, describing its evolution from congressional caucus to brokered national conventions to popular selection of the delegates through primaries and caucuses. In the second part we examine the factors that condition that selection: party rules, finance laws, and public relations. Emphasizing the changes that have occurred within each of these areas, we describe their impact on parties and their standard bearers. Next, we turn to the strategy and tactics of seeking the nomination. We discuss the principal components of that strategy for front runners and non–front runners. Finally, in the last part of the chapter, we take this quest to the national convention and describe the unofficial and official business of these large, semipublic extravaganzas: drama and staging; rules, credentials, and platforms; and the nominations themselves. We also present a brief characterization of the successful candidates. In conclusion, we summarize changes in this process and their implications for winning the general election and governing the country.

THE EVOLUTION OF THE SYSTEM

The nominating system began to evolve after the Constitution was written and the first two presidential elections were conducted. The framers had not concerned themselves with nominations, because there were no parties to nominate candidates. Assuming that well-qualified individuals would comprise the pool from which the president and vice president would be selected, the convention delegates directed their efforts toward encouraging an independent judgment by the electors. They considered such a judgment essential if the two *most* qualified persons were to be chosen.

Once political parties emerged, however, the notion of making an independent decision was constrained by the party's desire to choose an individual whose views were consistent with its own. This required a mechanism by which the parties could designate their nominees.

In 1796 party leaders met informally to agree on their tickets. Four years later partisan congressional caucuses met for the purposes of recommending candidates. "King Caucus," as it came to be known, constituted the principal mode of nomination until the 1820s, when factions developed within Jefferson's Republican party, the only viable party at the time. These factions eventually led to the demise of the caucus and the development of a more decentralized mode of nomination that was consistent with the increasingly sectional composition of the parties. By the 1830s national nominating conventions became the principal means for brokering those interests and uniting the party for a national campaign.

The first convention was held in 1831 by the Anti-Masons, a small but relatively active third party. Having virtually no congressional representation of its own, this party could not use a caucus of legislators to decide on its candidates. Instead, it organized a general meeting in which delegates from the state parties would choose its nominees as well as determine the party's positions on the important issues of the day. The two major parties followed suit in 1832. Thereafter conventions became the standard method for selecting nominees and for articulating policy positions.

These early conventions were informal and rowdy by contemporary standards. The delegates themselves decided on the procedures for conducting the meetings. Choosing the delegates was left to the state party and, more specifically, to its leadership. In most cases, public participation was minimal.

Nineteenth-century conventions served a number of purposes. They provided a forum for party bosses. They constituted a mechanism by which agreements could be negotiated and support mobilized. By brokering interests, they helped unite disparate elements within the party, converting a conglomeration of state organizations into a national coalition for the purpose of electing a president and vice president.

The nominating system buttressed the position of party officials, but it did so at the expense of the rank-and-file party members. The influence of the leadership depended in large part on its ability to deliver the votes. To ensure loyalty, the bosses handpicked their delegations.

Demands for reform began to be heard at the beginning of the twentieth century. A number of states changed their mode of selection to primary elections to permit greater public participation. This movement, however, was short-lived. Low voter turnout in primary states, the costs of holding such an election, and the opposition of party leaders to rank-and-file involvement persuaded several state legislatures to make their primaries advisory or discontinue them entirely. As a consequence, the number of primaries declined after World War I as did the percentage of delegates selected in them (see Table 2-1).

Strong candidates avoided primaries. Running in too many of them was interpreted as a sign of weakness, not strength. It indicated lack of national recognition and/or failure to obtain the support of party leaders.

Those who did enter these public contests did so mainly to test their popularity rather than to win convention votes. Dwight D. Eisenhower in 1952, John F. Kennedy in 1960, and Richard M. Nixon in 1968 had to demonstrate that being a general, a Catholic, or a once-defeated presidential candidate would not be fatal to their chances. In other words, they needed to prove they could win the general election by doing well in some primaries.

With the possible exception of John Kennedy's victories in Wisconsin and West Virginia in 1960 and Barry Goldwater's in California in 1964, primaries were neither crucial nor decisive for winning the nomination until the 1970s.[1] When there was a consensus within the party on a single candidate, primaries helped confirm it; when there was not, primaries were not able to produce it. They had little to do with whether the party was united or divided at the time of the convention.

Table 2-1. Number of Presidential Primaries and Percentage of Convention Delegates from Primary States, by Party, Since 1912

| Year | Democratic | | Republican | |
	Number of Primaries	Percentage of Delegates	Number of Primaries	Percentage of Delegates
1912	12	32.9%	13	41.7%
1916	20	53.5	20	58.9
1920	16	44.6	20	57.8
1924	14	35.5	17	45.3
1928	17	42.2	16	44.9
1932	16	40.0	14	37.7
1936	14	36.5	12	37.5
1940	13	35.8	13	38.8
1944	14	36.7	13	38.7
1948	14	36.3	12	36.0
1952	15	38.7	13	39.0
1956	19	42.7	19	44.8
1960	16	38.3	15	38.6
1964	17	45.7	17	45.6
1968	17	37.5	16	34.3
1972	23	60.5	22	52.7
1976	29*	72.6	28*	67.9
1980	31*	74.7	35*	74.3
1984	26	62.9	30	68.2
1988	34	66.6	35	76.9

*Does not include Vermont, which held nonbinding presidential preference votes but chooses delegates in state caucuses and conventions.

Sources: 1912–1964, F. Christopher Arterton, "Campaign Organizations Face the Mass Media in the 1976 Presidential Nomination Process" (paper delivered at the Annual Meeting of the American Political Science Association, Washington, D.C., September 1–4, 1977); 1968–1976, Austin Ranney, *Participation in American Presidential Nominations, 1976* (Washington, D.C.: American Enterprise Institute, 1977), table 1, p. 6. The figures for 1980 were compiled by Austin Ranney from materials distributed by the Democratic National Committee and the Republican National Committee; 1984 and 1988 figures were supplied by the Democratic and Republican National Committees.

CHANGES IN THE POLITICAL ARENA

Party Reforms

By the end of the decade of the 1960s that situation was to alter dramatically. Largely as a result of the tumultuous Democratic convention of 1968 whose nominee, Hubert Humphrey, had not competed in the primaries, demands for a larger voice for the party's rank and file increased. In response to these demands, the party appointed a series of commissions to examine its rules for delegate selection and to propose changes. The commissions had two basic goals: to encourage greater participation in party activities and to make the convention more representative of typical Democratic voters.

To achieve these objectives, the party in the 1970s attempted to tune delegate selection more closely to popular sentiment. Delegates had to be chosen in the calendar year of the convention. In the past they had been selected up to two years prior to the convention. Fees for entering primaries were lowered or abolished. In the past, the high costs of registration had discouraged some candidates from running. Three-fourths of the delegates had to be chosen at levels no larger than congressional districts. In the past some states had elected all of their delegates at the state level, underrepresenting minorities in the process. The allocation of the delegates to candidates had to reflect fairly the popular vote which the candidates received within the state. Previously, the party had permitted winner-take-all voting by which all the delegates could be awarded to the candidate with the most votes.[2]

In nonprimary states the meetings for choosing the delegates had to be publicly announced with adequate time given for campaigning. The old system of proxy voting, whereby a state party leader would cast a large number of votes for the delegates of his or her choice, was abolished. State central committees were no longer permitted to appoint more than 10 percent of the delegates.

The other major objective of the reforms was to promote more equal representation of the rank and file in the delegations themselves. To achieve this aim the party required states to implement affirmative action plans for specific groups which had been subject to discrimination in the past. Native Americans, African-Americans, and youth were singled out, and states were required to set goals for representation in their delegations based on the proportion of the group's population within the state. With respect to women, the Democrats went one step further, requiring its conventions, beginning in 1980, to be equally divided between men and women.

One consequence of these reforms was to make primaries the preferred method of delegate selection. To avoid having their delegations challenged, many state legislatures simply had the voters choose them (see Table 2-1). A second result was to tie the popular vote more closely to the allocation of convention delegates. This made the process more open and more participatory.

In 1984 almost 19 million people participated in the Democratic primaries. In 1988 the number was over 23 million for the Democrats and over 12 million for the Republicans; in addition, the caucuses of both parties attracted an estimated 1 million people. Twenty years earlier only 12 million people participated in the preconvention nomination process of both parties.

Efforts to make convention delegates more representative of their party as a whole have had mixed results. Demographic representation has improved (see Table 2-2); however, ideological and issue differences

Table 2-2. The Demography of the Delegates, 1968–1988

National Convention Delegates

	1968		1972		1976		1980		1984		1988	
	Dem	*Rep*	*Dem*	*Rep*	*Dem*	*Rep*	*Dem*	*Rep*	*Dem*	*Rep*	*Dem*	*Rep*
Women	13%	16%	40%	29%	33%	31%	49%	29%	49%	44%	48%	33%
Black	5	2	15	4	11	3	15	3	18	4	23	4
Under thirty	3	4	22	8	15	7	11	5	8	4	4	3
Lawyer	28	22	12	—	16	15	13	15	17	14	16	17
Teacher	8	2	11	—	12	4	15	4	16	6	14	5
Union member	—	—	16	—	21	3	27	4	25	4	25	3
Attending first convention	67	66	83	78	80	78	87	84	78	69	65	68
Protestant	—	—	42	—	47	73	47	72	49	71	50	69
Catholic	—	—	26	—	34	18	37	22	29	22	30	22
Jewish	—	—	9	—	9	3	8	3	8	2	7	2
Liberal	—	—	—	—	40	3	46	2	48	1	43	0
Moderate	—	—	—	—	47	45	42	36	42	35	43	35
Conservative	—	—	—	—	8	48	6	58	4	60	5	58
Median age	49	49	42	—	43	48	44	49	43	51	46	51

Source: CBS News Delegate Surveys, 1968 through 1988. Characteristics of the public are average values from seven CBS News/*The New York Times* polls, 1988. Reprinted from Martin Plissner and Warren J. Mitofsky, "The Making of the Delegates, 1968–1988," *Public Opinion* 11 (September/October 1988): 47. © 1988 American Enterprise Institute for Public Policy Research, Washington, D.C. 20036.

between the delegates and the rank-and-file are still apparent. Those who have attended conventions as delegates have displayed greater ideological consistency than average party voters. Democratic delegates have indicated that they were more liberal and Republican delegates have indicated they were more conservative than the rank-and-file members of their respective parties. Table 2-3 presents their differences with fellow party members on key policy issues in 1988.

In addition to affecting the composition of the delegates, the rules changes had other effects. They lengthened the process and inflated its costs. Candidate fatigue and public boredom increased. The influence of the media also grew, particularly in the early critical stages. The party became more factionalized with its state and local leadership less able to affect presidential nominations within their own areas. Party leaders were not even guaranteed a place on their own delegations. Initially, the number of party officials attending the national meetings declined.

To offset these unintended results, the Democrats reformed their

Table 2-3. Views of the Convention Delegates and Voters, 1988 (in percentages)

	Delegate Survey		CBS/NYT Poll July 1988	
	Rep.	*Dem.*	*Reg. Rep.*	*Reg. Dem.*
Ideology				
—Liberal	0%	43%	11%	26%
—Moderate	36	43	44	42
—Conservative	59	5	40	28
Size of govt.*				
—Small	81	14	59	33
—Big	4	56	30	56
Fedl. funding abortion				
—Favor	16	57	28	32
—Oppose	69	22	62	56
Gay rights law				
—Favor	26	65	28	43
—Oppose	58	18	57	40
Sympathy for Palestinians				
—More sympathy	28	50	22	26
—No more	46	22	53	49
Government spending				
—Defense	72	10	53	34
—Social programs	13	75	39	55

reforms after their unsuccessful 1980 general election campaign. They tried to shorten the process by tightening the time frame in which the nominating process could occur. Only a few states were given permission to hold their contests prior to the second Tuesday in March. The effect of imposing this "window period" during which states could choose their convention delegates was to compress and frontload the schedule. States moved their contests toward the beginning of the time frame in order to maximize their influence on the results. In 1988 the entire southern region along with eight other states chose to hold their primaries or the initial round of their caucuses during the second week of March, most of them on the second Tuesday (so-called Super Tuesday). Approximately one-third of the Democratic delegates and 42 percent of the Republican delegates were selected by mid-March. Choosing so many delegates so early forced the candidates to organize and campaign early, primarily via the mass media.

Democrats also tried to increase the influence of elected and ap-

Table 2-3. (continued)

	Delegate Survey		CBS/NYT Poll July 1988	
	Rep.	*Dem.*	*Reg. Rep.*	*Reg. Dem.*
Death penalty				
—Favor	88%	49%	79%	64%
—Oppose	6	38	15	27
School prayer[†]				
—Favor	51	22	72	67
—Oppose	34	65	25	26
E.R.A.[†]				
—Favor	34	86	68	80
—Oppose	51	4	25	11
Bal. budget amendment[†]				
—Favor	77	38	80	77
—Oppose	13	47	11	9
Top tax rate				
—Increase	19	67	61	63
—No change	64	14	32	27

*CBS/NYT poll May 1988.
[†]CBS/NYT poll August 1988.

Source: Martin Plissner and Warren J. Mitofsky, "The Making of the Delegates, 1968–1988," *Public Opinion* 11 (September/October 1988): 46.

pointed party officials. Each state was allocated additional delegates to be selected from its members of Congress, elected officials, and party officials. These delegates, known as superdelegates, were not formally committed to a particular candidate and could have held the balance of power in an otherwise divided convention. Finally, the Democrats gave states some flexibility in determining the formula by which delegates would be allocated. The party also reduced the minimum percentage of the vote needed by candidates to obtain delegates to fifteen percent in 1988.

In 1984 and again in 1988 the allocation of delegates caused controversy during the preconvention process. Jesse Jackson in particular alleged that the rules were biased against lesser-known minority candidates such as himself. In support of his position, Jackson pointed to discrepancies between his delegate totals and his popular vote. In states in which the delegates were elected directly, Jackson's proportion of the delegates was less than his proportion of the vote (see Table 2-4). To rectify these inequalities (and gain Jackson's support for the 1988 general election campaign), the Democratic Rules Committee agreed to support changes in the rules for 1992 that would promote proportionality and reduce the number of nonelected delegates.

The Democratic party's continuous attempts to fine-tune its rules stem from the advantages and disadvantages these rules bestow on different groups and candidates within the party. The initial reforms in the early and mid-1970s benefitted candidates who were outsiders and who appealed to party activists primarily on the basis of their liberal orientation. The exception was Jimmy Carter, who rode a wave of popularism and a promise of good government to the nomination. In the 1980s the rules favored better-known national candidates, who were able to generate a broader appeal but one that was generally consistent with the party's traditional economic and social policy positions.

In both cases the beneficiaries of the nomination process found themselves in a much less advantageous position in the general election campaign. The competitiveness of the process created and maintained divisions within the party. The need to appeal to specific groups saddled the nominees with images, positions, and affiliations which they could

Table 2-4. Allocation Formulas and Delegate Support in 1988

	Popular Vote		Delegates	
	Dukakis	*Jackson*	*Dukakis*	*Jackson*
Direct Election Primary	46%	29%	56%	12%
Bonus System Primary	43	28	54	30
Proportional Representation Primary	40	30	43	34

Source: Percentages calculated on the basis of vote reported in *Congressional Quarterly* 46 July 9, 1988, p. 1892.

not easily shed. Also, the promises made to different groups to promote unity created additional baggage to carry in the presidential campaign. The tendency of the Democratic party to tinker with its rules for delegate selection is apt to continue so long as specific groups within the party perceive that the rules are unfair to them and so long as Democrats believe that their nomination process hurts their candidates' chances in the general election.

The Republicans have not been nearly as divided over their rules for choosing delegates. One reason is that the party is more homogeneous than the Democrats. Another is that the Republicans have not mandated national guidelines for the states as the Democrats have. Nonetheless, they have also been affected by many of the changes. The impact on the party has been felt in two ways: through public pressure to broaden participation and improve the representation of minorities and through new state laws, designed to conform to Democratic rules, laws which affect the scheduling and structure of caucuses and primaries.

States are free to determine how and when nominating elections are to be conducted. However, two Supreme Court decisions, *Cousins* v. *Wigoda* (419 U.S. 477, 1975) and *Democratic Party of the U.S.* v. *LaFollette* (449 U.S. 897, 1981), give the party the right to reject delegates to its national convention that are not selected in conformity with its rules. These decisions have put pressure on states, particularly those whose legislature is controlled by the Democrats, to abide by its mandatory rules in order to prevent challenges to the state delegation at the national convention.

Finance Laws

While the reforms in party rules have had a profound effect, they are not the only major changes to affect the nomination process. New finance laws have had a major impact as well. They have altered the way in which money is raised and spent and the amount that is available.

Throughout most of American history candidates of both parties depended almost exclusively on large contributions to finance their campaigns. This dependence, combined with spiraling costs, secret and sometimes illegal contributions, and little public information about giving and spending, raised serious questions about the conduct of elections in a democratic society. Could officials be responsive to national needs as well as to those of their individual benefactors? Had the presidency become an office that only the wealthy could afford—or, worse yet, that only those with wealthy support could seek?

In the 1970s Congress began to address some of these issues. It enacted legislation to limit skyrocketing expenses, especially in the media, to control the influence of large contributors, and to bring them out in the open. Limits were placed on the amount of money presidential and vice presidential candidates and their families could contribute to their own campaigns and the amount that could be spent. Other legislation established a fund to subsidize the presidential nomination process and support the general election.

Faced with a threatened veto of this legislation by the Republican president Richard Nixon, the Democrats in Congress agreed to a compromise whereby the law would not take effect until after the 1972 election, in which Nixon planned to run for reelection. In that election a number of large corporations were pressured into making contributions to the Nixon reelection committee in violation of the law. The spending of campaign funds on dirty tricks and other unethical and illegal activities, including the break-in of the Democratic National Committee's headquarters at the Watergate, further aroused public ire and resulted in new and more stringent legislation.

Passed in 1974, the new law provided for public disclosure, contribution ceilings, campaign spending limits, and federal subsidies for the nomination process. Some of its provisions were highly controversial. Critics immediately charged a federal giveaway, a robbery of the Treasury. Opponents of the legislation also argued that the limits on contributions and spending violated the constitutionally guaranteed right to freedom of speech. In the landmark case of *Buckley* v. *Valeo* (424 U.S. 1, 1976), the Supreme Court agreed in part. It upheld the right of Congress to regulate the contributions and expenditures of campaign organizations but not the independent spending of individuals and groups during the campaign. The Court's decision forced Congress to enact new legislation in 1976, which it subsequently amended in 1979. The major provisions of this legislation are as follows:

- *Public Disclosure.* All contributions of $200 or more must be identified. All expenditures of $200 or more must be reported. Campaign committees are also required to file periodic reports before the election and a final report after it.

- *Contribution Limits.* In any election, contributions from individuals cannot exceed $1,000 to a single candidate, $20,000 to a national political party committee, and $5,000 to other political committees, with the total not to exceed $25,000 in any one year. Personal contributions from a candidate or that candidate's immediate family are limited to $50,000 if the candidate accepts federal funds. Candidates who do not accept federal funds are not limited in what they can contribute to their own campaign. Table 2-5 summarizes the contribution limits. Individuals and political action committees (PACs) can spend an unlimited amount on their own for candidates of their choice provided they do not consult or communicate in any way with the candidate's campaign organization.

Table 2-5. Contribution Limits

	To Each Candidate or Candidate Committee per Election	To National Party Committee per Calendar Year	To Any Other Political Committee per Calendar Year	Total per Calendar Year
Individual may give	$1,000	$20,000	$5,000	$25,000
Multicandidate committee* may give	5,000	15,000	5,000	No limit
Party committees may give	1,000 or 5,000[+]	No limit	5,000	No limit
Other political committees may give[†]	1,000	20,000	5,000	No limit

*A multicandidate committee is a political action committee with more than fifty contributors which has been registered for at least six months, and, with the exception of state party committees, has made contributions to five or more federal candidates.
†Limit depends on whether or not the party committee is a multicandidate committee.

Source: Federal Election Commission, "The FEC and the Federal Campaign Finance Law" (Washington, D.C.: Government Printing Office, 1978), p. 4.

- *Campaign Expenses.* Candidates who accept public funding are limited in the amount they can spend. During the the preconvention period there is an overall ceiling as well as individual state limits. In 1988 the ceiling was $23.05 million. The state limits, based on the size of the voting-age population and a cost-of-living adjustment, ranged from approximately $446,600 in the smaller states to over $7 million in the largest. Fund-raising expenses up to 20 percent of expenditures and accounting and legal fees are exempt from these spending limits.

  During the general election, the federal grant cannot be exceeded. In 1988 it was $46.1 million. Candidates who do not accept federal funds have no limit on their expenditures.

- *Matching Funds.* Major party contenders who raise $5,000 in each of twenty states in contributions of $250 or less, a total of $100,000, are eligible to receive matching grants during the prenomination period, which begins January 1 of the year in which the election occurs. Only the first $250 of each contribution will be matched.

- *Communication Notices.* All authorized advertisements by candidates' organizations must state the name of the candidate or agent who authorized them. All nonauthorized advertisements must identify the person who made or financed the ad and his or her organizational affiliation, if any.

• *Compliance Procedures.* The Federal Election Commission has authority to investigate possible violations, hold hearings, and assess certain civil penalties. Its decision may be appealed to United States district courts. The Justice Department retains the authority for criminal investigation and prosecution.

Congress had a number of objectives in enacting campaign finance legislation. It had hoped to reduce the dependence on large donors, discourage illicit contributions, broaden the base of public support, and curtail spiraling costs at the presidential level.

While all these objectives have not been achieved, the law has had a significant impact on nomination politics. It has substantially reduced secret contributors and unexplained expenses, although it has not eliminated violations, overpayments, and improper reporting procedures. For campaign expenditures which he paid from his own credit card in 1984, Senator Gary Hart was fined $15,000.

Dependence on large contributors has also been reduced. However, the $1,000 limit on individual donations, the $250 ceiling on matching grants, and the eligibility requirements to get federal funds have all made the solicitation of a large number of small contributions essential during the preconvention phase.

Although the law has decreased the importance that a handful of large donors had in previous campaigns, it has increased the impact of organized nonparty groups. By forming political action committees, these groups can contribute up to $5,000 to individual candidates in their primary campaigns. Direct contributions by PACs to aspirants for their party's nomination have not been that significant. They constitute only a small percentage of the funds candidates receive. Independent expenditures are another matter. They have increased enormously in recent years.

At the presidential level, PACs exercise influence by virtue of their independent spending more than by their direct contributions to candidates. With media expenses constituting a larger proportion of the total campaign budget, the kinds of help PACs can best provide—operating telephone banks, distributing promotional material, holding newsworthy events, and mobilizing their own membership—can have a significant impact on close contests, particularly at the beginning of the nomination process. PACs can be so helpful that candidates frequently create their own in the years before the official start of the campaign.

Despite PACs, independent expenditures, and creative ways to circumvent the restrictions of the law, the campaign finance legislation has produced greater equity. The matching-fund provision has given lesser-known candidates of the major parties a better opportunity to gain public support. Previously, candidates without national visibility found it harder than their well-known counterparts to raise the money necessary to run an effective campaign. Democrat Michael Dukakis is a good example of a lesser-known candidate who raised "big bucks" to run a national nominating campaign.

However, by increasing the number of candidates and their ability to run in more primaries, the Federal Election Campaign Act has had the effect of factionalizing the national parties and ultimately weakening their structure. The organization of the successful candidate is not dismantled after the nomination; it is expanded, often competing with the regular party organization.

Finally, the number of candidates vying for each party's nomination has significantly increased the amount of money spent in preconvention politics. In 1976 the expenditures of both parties totaled almost $67 million. In 1980 that figure was almost double, $128 million. Even without competition the Reagan-Bush campaign in 1984 raised and spent close to the legal limit. In 1988 these figures were significantly higher.

Public Relations

The third major change in the nomination process has been the enlargement of its public dimension. In the past, the quest for the nomination was a relatively private affair. Candidates made their case primarily to state party leaders. There was little need to discern public attitudes, project public appeals, or build public support. Now there is.

The cast of characters is also different. In the past, preconvention campaign organizations consisted of a relatively small group of party regulars. Today that organization numbers in the hundreds at its headquarters and in the thousands in the field. Jesse Jackson's army of volunteers numbered in the hundreds of thousands. Moreover, most of the principals do not hold important party positions but are professional campaigners with a partisan tinge: pollsters, media consultants, grassroots organizers, direct mailers, accountants and attorneys specializing in electoral politics. No candidate can be without these wizards of modern campaign technology.

Even the traits the candidates must demonstrate are different. They need less political experience but more public exposure. They need to be good actors and good orators. They should be reasonably photogenic. They must be willing to campaign continuously in the public eye through the mass media and primarily on radio and television, often for over two years. Nominations are no longer obtained behind closed doors. Support is acquired by personal appeals to the party's electorate.

To be credible, these appeals must be in tune with public opinion. The pulse of the voters conditions the message that is presented and the image that is created. Thus, a critical early step for any serious candidate is to have that pulse taken. A pollster must be hired and a private poll commissioned.

POLLS.   John F. Kennedy was the first candidate to engage a pollster in his quest for the nomination. Preconvention surveys conducted by Louis Harris in 1960 indicated that Hubert Humphrey, Kennedy's principal rival, was vulnerable in Wisconsin and West Virginia. On the basis of this information, the Kennedy campaign wisely decided to concentrate time, effort, and money in these states. Victories in both helped demonstrate Kennedy's popularity, thereby improving his chances for the nomination enormously.

Private polls are important for several reasons. They provide information about the opinions, beliefs, and attitudes of voters; they identify perceptions people have of the candidates and their positions; they suggest the kinds of appeals that are apt to be most persuasive and the groups to whom these appeals should be made. Armed with this information, media campaigns can be designed and targeted. Periodic polling allows them to be monitored over the course of the nomination process. Pollster Pat Caddell's reading of public moods in 1983 had a major impact on Gary Hart's redesigning his appeal in 1984. Similarly, skillful polling by the Dukakis campaign in 1988 provided information on which locations in the South to target for direct appeals on Super Tuesday.

Poll results are also used to build momentum, increase morale, raise money, and affect media coverage. By indicating who can win and who should be taken seriously, polls affect the amount of attention candidates receive. In general, the more coverage they have, particularly during the early months, the more volunteers they can attract, and the more money they can raise.

MEDIA.   After polls have been taken, appeals can be made. The mass media have become the principal vehicles for accomplishing this objective. This was not always the case.

When party leaders exercised the most influence, personal contact was most effective. When a relatively small number of primaries were held, personal appearances at rallies, speeches before clubs, and press conferences for local media energized rank-and-file supporters. When people received most of their information from print media, newspaper coverage (supplemented by campaign literature) educated and influenced those who were interested in politics and who would take part in the nomination process.

All this has changed. The electorate has grown in size and diversity. Primaries and multistaged caucuses have proliferated. With twenty states holding Democratic contests and seventeen holding Republican ones on Super Tuesday in 1988, candidates had no choice but to depend on the mass media to reach potential voters.

The use of visual and audio media has revolutionized campaigning. It has made image creation more important, brought public relations specialists into candidate organizations, and siphoned off a relatively large proportion of the campaign budget for television and radio. In 1988 over half was devoted to television alone. Ironically, it has also made the candidates less spontaneous. Fearful that their words and actions might be misinterpreted or misconstrued, they now tend to play it safe. They ad lib less and follow a script more. In debates, press conferences, and interviews, candidates tend to repeat their "stump" speeches. They sound more and more like their commercials. Even events are staged for home video consumption. During campaign trips, candidates often get no further than the airport tarmac. The purpose of their visits is to get media exposure. Since local television crews will be at the airport, going further is usually unnecessary to receive coverage on the local news. Candidates can also buy satellite time and be interviewed by one station after another in different parts of the country without having to leave the studio.

The media, particularly television, have influenced the nomination process in several other respects. The early contests have become more important because of the attention they are given. New Hampshire, traditionally the first state to hold a presidential primary, produces a lot of media coverage. Until 1988, it ranked first in the amount of attention it received.[3] Naturally, the candidate who did surprisingly well in this primary benefitted enormously. Eugene McCarthy in 1968, George Mc-Govern in 1972, Jimmy Carter in 1976, Gary Hart in 1984, and George Bush in 1988 all gained visibility and credibility from their New Hampshire performances, even though none had a majority of the vote. The initial round of the Iowa caucuses, held before the New Hampshire primary, received even more extensive attention in 1988. In total the coverage of nomination contests in these two states accounted for 34 percent of *all* the nomination in 1988.[4]

Early victories help establish front-runner status. They can provide an important psychological boost. Being declared a winner improves one's standing in the polls, makes fund raising easier, and aids in attracting backers who contribute to later primary success.

But media publicity can have a negative consequence as well—even for the winner. When Bob Dole defeated George Bush in the 1988 Iowa caucus, he jumped 12 percent in tracking polls conducted over the next several days in New Hampshire. His subsequent loss to Bush in that state by only 9 percent of the popular vote was magnified by the exposure accompanying his Iowa victory. Dole was never able to regain the momentum.

Moreover, the media treat front runners more harshly than challengers. There is more investigative reporting and more implicit criticism of their candidacies. Being a front runner guarantees not only greater coverage but also greater scrutiny.[5]

Another way in which the media affect delegate selection is in their interpretation of the results of primaries and caucuses. The winners are not necessarily those who do best but those who do better than expected. When performance exceeds expectations or does not meet them, that is news. When performance meets expectations, it is less newsworthy. Candidates therefore tend to underestimate their vote in public in order to be able to indicate how satisfied they are with the results when those results are announced. Eugene McCarthy's ability to do this was a key factor in his primary challenge first of Lyndon Johnson and then of Robert Kennedy in 1968. McCarthy contested nine primaries and won two but minimized the impact of his seven losses using this low-prediction posture. Similarly, Jimmy Carter in 1976 purposely kept his predictions low. In the words of his campaign manager Hamilton Jordan:

> It has already been established in the minds of the national press that Mo Udall is going to do well in New Hampshire. He has established that expectation. If he does not win in New Hampshire, I think now by the measuring criteria that the press is going to apply, he will have underperformed. Well, we'd never talk about winning in New Hampshire. We never talk about winning anywhere. We talk about doing well.[6]

Michael Dukakis used the same tactic in Iowa in 1988, making his third place finish seem less newsworthy than it would have been had he been expected to do better.

Not only is the outcome of the primaries subject to interpretation, but so is the importance attached to particular contests. Generally speaking, the media give primaries more attention that caucuses, close elections more emphasis than one-sided ones, and statewide contests better coverage than district elections. The New York and Wisconsin primaries were catalysts for the Democrats in 1988.

Candidates can affect the coverage they receive. The importance they place on individual primaries, for example, especially when a number of them occur on the same day, can affect the impact that those primaries have in the public's eye. Other tactics used to influence the media include the timing and staging of events, the release of information, and even access to the candidate and his senior aides. Major announcements are made in sufficient time to get on the evening news. Speeches are scheduled to maximize the viewing audience. Quiet periods, such as Saturday, are considered a good time to hold a press conference or schedule interviews. In addition to receiving same-day coverage by television, a Saturday event usually gets prominent treatment in the Sunday papers.

Access is another valuable commodity. At the beginning of the nomination process, access is cheap, especially for lesser-known candidates who need media attention. As the campaign progresses, access becomes more important and, at the same time, more difficult to obtain. There is more competition among journalists, the candidates have a more demanding schedule, and a larger public relations staff stands between the correspondents and the nominees. Granting interviews under these circumstances can do much to affect the quantity and quality of coverage received.

To a large extent those who repoort the news are dependent on this material. Many news stories come directly from the candidates themselves. A study of the 1980 election by Michael Robinson and Margaret Sheehan reported:

> On UPI, just over 40 percent of the Carter news came directly from Carter, his press office, his staff, or his administration. Fewer than 10 percent came via the investigative route. On CBS, it was the same story, so to speak, only more so. A full two-thirds of the "official" news about Carter came via a Carter-controlled news source.[7]

Advertising is another way to shape and, if need be, change public perceptions. Its principal advantage is the amount of control that can be exercised over it by the candidate and advisers. The message can be designed to create a certain effect. It also can be aired as often as money permits. Not only can advertising reach a potentially large population, but it also can be targeted to specific groups within it. Take Democratic candidate Michael Dukakis' pitch to organized labor in the 1988 Democratic primaries. One of his ads featured labor leader Thomas McIntyre talking to would-be Dukakis supporters:

> I've known Mike a long time, and I gotta say Dukakis is not your 'shot 'n' beer' kind of guy, but working people around here love him. . . . You want somebody to drink with? Call your buddy. You care about your job? Vote for Mike Dukakis.

In contrast, an Al Gore commercial shown in New York before its Democratic primary appealed to highly educated, affluent voters. With teenagers playing basketball in the background, a relaxed Gore states:

> If America's going to remain competitive in business, science and technology, we have to give our children a first-rate education, and we're just not doing that today. We're losing too many kids to drugs and an inadequate education. We need a president who is not just going to talk tough, but who's willing to show some strength. And if that means saying that education is important to national security and if that means using the military to help stop drugs at our borders, let's do it.

Political ads are not without their limitations, however. Like all commercials, they are blatantly partial, usually expensive, and require the services of skilled personnel to buy time, produce the spot, and act in it. To overcome the problem of partiality, political advertisers have gone to great lengths to project an image of authenticity and spontaneity in their commercials. To minimize costs, they have concentrated on local, less expensive media during the preconvention period. To reach a smaller but specific audience, they have used radio. To appeal to a large, more general population, they have employed television. The need for experts is reflected in the hiring of media consultants early in the campaign, often many months before the first contest. Candidates are now regularly coached, made up, and scripted before appearing on camera.

The increasing importance of the media has had a major effect on the conduct of campaigns. It has made radio and television the critical communication links between candidates and the voters. Advertising in these media has become a major component of campaign strategy, although its utility varies with several factors. It is generally considered more significant in the larger states that hold primaries and at the beginning of the nomination process when less is known about the candidates than at the end.

FIELD WORK.   Despite the importance of media, candidates still need to organize at the grass roots. They need advance people to arrange for their appearances and to assemble their crowds, other politicians, and the media. They need schedulers to plan their days and decide which invitations to accept. They need local organizers to run phone banks to identify voters, and they need volunteers to ring doorbells, circulate literature, and get would-be supporters to the polls. Eugene McCarthy and George McGovern recruited thousands of college students to help them in their primary efforts. In 1976 Carter's "peanut brigade," a group of Georgians who followed their candidate from state to state, was particularly effective in canvassing and organizing; the support the Reverend Jesse Jackson received from the African-American community had a similar effect in 1984 and 1988. In caucus states, such as Michigan, Jackson's army overwhelmed the less effectively organized efforts of his opponents.

THE QUEST FOR THE NOMINATION

Greater public involvement in the nomination process has changed the strategy and tactics of those seeking the nomination. Campaigns begin much earlier than in the past. They are more broad-based. They require more money up front, an organization in place, and a game plan that targets an appeal and constructs a winning coalition. The game plan in turn is predicated on certain fundamental assumptions about the nomination:

1. That sufficient time and energy be devoted to personal campaigning in the preprimary and early preconvention period. Only an incumbent can remain in the White House and even he can remain there too long.
2. That a strong, in-depth organization for the initial caucuses and

primaries be built. Television advertising is important, but it is not possible to win by it alone.

3. That a firm financial base be established early and a spending strategy devised. All caucuses and primaries are not equal; the first ones are more important and, hence, require the allocation of greater resources.

4. That the order of events and the rules of the game be understood and, if possible, manipulated. Magnifying victories and minimizing defeats usually require that strong states be isolated and weak ones paired with strong ones.

5. That groups within the party be targeted and appeals to them be made. Over the course of the campaign, however, these appeals must be moderated and broadened. If the overall constituency is too narrow, it is difficult to win the nomination and even more difficult to win the general election.

The actual strategy that candidates adopt depends on their status at the beginning of the campaign. If they are not well known, their initial goal must be to establish their credibility. Publicly announcing their intentions, establishing a campaign headquarters, qualifying for matching funds, and obtaining political endorsements are necessary but not sufficient conditions to do so. At the outset, the key is recognition. Over the long haul, it is momentum and the acquisition of delegates.

Recognition is bestowed by the media on those who do better than expected in the early primaries and caucuses; momentum is achieved by a series of prenomination victories, which increases the amount of delegate support. Together, recognition and momentum compensate for what the non–front runners lack in reputation and appeal. That is why non–front runners concentrate their time, efforts, and resources in the first few contests. They have no choice. Winning will provide them with opportunities later on; losing will confirm their secondary status.

Jimmy Carter's 1976 quest for the Democratic nomination is a good example of a successful non–front runner approach. Carter began his campaign as a relatively unknown southern governor with limited financial resources and organizational support. He concentrated his efforts in Iowa and New Hampshire with the aim of doing well in these early contests. By attracting media attention, he hoped to establish his credibility as a viable candidate. Early success, he anticipated, would facilitate fund raising, organization building, and continued media coverage. Here's how Hamilton Jordan, Carter's principal strategist, described the game plan in a 1974 memo to the candidate:

> The prospect of a crowded field coupled with the new proportional representation rule does not permit much flexibility in the early primaries. No serious candidate will have the luxury of picking or choosing among the

early primaries. To pursue such a strategy would cost that candidate dele-gate votes and increase the possibility of being lost in the crowd. I think that we have to assume that everybody will be running in the first five or six primaries.

A crowded field enhances the possibility of several inconclusive prima-ries with four or five candidates separated by only a few percentage points. Such a muddled picture will not continue for long as the press will begin to make "winners" of some and "losers" of others. The intense press coverage which naturally focuses on the early primaries plus the decent time inter-vals which separate the March and mid-April primaries dictate a serious effort in all of the first five primaries. Our "public" strategy would probably be that Florida was the first and real test of the Carter campaign and that New Hampshire would be just a warm-up. In fact, a strong, surprise show-ing in New Hampshire should be our goal, which would have a tremen-dous impact on successive primaries.[8]

The goal was achieved. Dubbed the person to beat after his victories in the Iowa caucus and New Hampshire primary, Carter's defeat of George Wallace in Florida enabled him to overcome a disappointing fourth-place finish in Massachusetts a week earlier and become the ac-knowledged front runner and delegate leader.

The Carter strategy became the model for most Democratic aspi-rants in 1984 and 1988. With the exception of Senator Gore, who concen-trated his initial efforts on the southern regional primaries, all the other Democratic candidates focused their attention and resources on the early contests.

For the front runners—like Walter Mondale in 1984 for the Demo-crats and George Bush in 1988 for the Republicans—the task is different. They have to maintain credibility, not establish it. This provides them with a little more flexibility at the outset. Front runners can announce their candidacy later, although their organization should still be in place early. Particular primaries and caucuses may be targeted, some can be avoided, but the first ones have to be contested. A broad-based cam-paign can be planned, but resources still have to be front-loaded.

The principal advantages that front runners have are greater name recognition and a larger resource base. Status and position make it easier to raise money, establish an organization, and obtain endorsements. This enhances the front runner's potential but it also creates expecta-tions which may be difficult to meet. A front runner can overcome a single defeat, but will find it more difficult to survive a string of setbacks.

Ronald Reagan's preconvention campaign in 1980 is a good example of the front-runner approach. He raised and spent a lot of his money in the early primaries and caucuses. He built in-depth organizations in many states, obtained political endorsements, and benefitted from a large staff of professionals and volunteers. George Bush followed a simi-lar strategy eight years later. By the beginning of the election year, he had raised over $11 million and built large field organizations in the states that were to hold the first contests. He had a sophisticated media operation already in place. His overwhelming defeat of Senator Dole in the South all but ensured his nomination by the end of the second week in March.

Although Michael Dukakis did not begin as the front runner, parts of his strategy resembled George Bush's. Like Bush he also had organized effectively and raised funds early. Unlike Bush, he did not enjoy high name recognition, many political endorsements, and large numbers of volunteers. He had to pay organizers, earn endorsements, and gain public credibility and national standing by victories in the early contests. Moreover, he had to target his appeal carefully to specific groups within the Democratic party's electoral coalition. He was particularly successful in the South, an area of the country where he did not enjoy broad national support, by winning 26 percent of the votes and almost 32 percent of the delegates. As the nomination contests moved into the North and West, Dukakis was in the driver's seat with more delegates, more money, and more potential supporters than any of his rivals. His opposition dwindled. Only Jesse Jackson remained until the end.

The Jackson campaign did not fit the typical strategic models. Lacking Dukakis' financial base, Jackson mobilized an army of volunteers in a massive grass-roots effort which was most effective in states with a large minority population and those with caucus-type elections. Although Jackson could not afford to buy as much media as the other principal candidates, he did attract considerable media attention by virtue of his personal magnetism, his liberal political perspective, and his passionate supporters and detractors. Passion plays well on television.

In the end Jackson was successful in articulating his appeal and energizing his constituency but not in winning the nomination. The distinctiveness of his message and his personality, the very liberal policy positions he advocated, and his lack of governmental experience made him less acceptable and perhaps more risky in the eyes of a majority of Democratic voters than the more traditional, less exciting, centrist governor of Massachusetts, Michael Dukakis.

NATIONAL CONVENTIONS

Theoretically, the party chooses its standard bearers at its national convention in the summer preceding the presidential election. In practice the nominees have usually been decided upon well before the convention meets. Since most of the delegates are publicly committed, their decisions are readily predictable. Television networks and wire services provide a running total of delegate preferences throughout the nomination period.

Theoretically, the delegates make policy decisions when formulating their party's platform. In practice, platform decisions have been hammered out by representatives of the principal candidates prior to the convention.

Theoretically, conventions unify the delegates for the forthcoming election. In practice, candidate and policy disagreements are highlighted by the media, making unity more difficult to achieve.

What purpose, then, do conventions serve? They are part of American folklore. They ratify decisions of the voters during the primaries and the caucuses. In the event that no candidate emerges with a clear majority, they select the nominee. In the event different groups are unhappy with provisions of the platform, they serve as a court of last resort, as a final arbiter and judge. Finally, they draw attention to the parties and their nominees. They excite the faithful and implore the public to support their candidates in the general election.

It is this public dimension that has gained importance in recent years. From the perspective of the party, the real function of the conventions is to show off its nominees and its policy positions; from the perspective of the candidates, it is to start building a broad-based electoral coalition; from the perspective of organized groups, it is to gain visibility and support for their positions and causes; from the perspective of the media, it is to capture the excitement and ritual of an extravaganza and to spotlight whatever drama and suspense it produces.

Public Dimensions

Television broadcasting of national conventions began in 1952. Almost immediately, a sizable audience was attracted. According to the Nielsen ratings, 20 to 30 percent of the potential audience watched the conventions between 1952 and 1968, with the number swelling during the most significant events.

The large number of viewers is significant because of the potential effect conventions have on those who watch them. The conventions heighten interest, thereby potentially increasing turnout; they arouse latent feelings, thereby raising partisan awareness; and they color perceptions, thereby affecting the public's evaluation of the candidates and their stands.[9]

Party leaders assume that the more unified the convention, the more favorable its impact on the electorate. That is why they take the media, particularly television, into account when planning, staging, and scheduling their national meetings.

Television has changed conventions. They have become faster paced than in the past. Tedious reports and roll calls have been reduced.

There are fewer candidates placed in nomination, and the speeches themselves are shorter. The length of the sessions has also been reduced. In 1988 the major networks carried them only during and after eastern prime time, forcing convention managers to compress their major events into shorter segments.

Not only do convention planners wish to capture an audience by providing entertainment and a fast-paced meeting, they also desire to put their candidates and party in the most favorable light. To do this they have scripted the meetings, placing the major unifying events such as the keynote address and acceptance speeches during prime viewing hours and potentially discordant situations such as debate on gay rights, abortion, and busing late in the evening or in the afternoon.

Although party officials try to present a united front favoring their nominee and platform, the television networks do not. They try to generate interest by emphasizing variety, maximizing suspense, and exaggerating conflict. This attempt often requires them to focus less on the official proceedings and more on other activities, including those outside the convention hall. The vice presidential selection frequently receives much attention, although in recent years, the likely nominee has been identified before the convention has gotten under way. Still, in 1988, Bush's choice of Senator Dan Quayle attracted considerable scrutiny from the media, much of it negative. Information about the senator's background and qualifications counterbalanced some of the favorable coverage Bush received, although it did have the beneficial effect of monopolizing the news for the Republican ticket. The media also tend to play up disputes over the rules, delegate credentials, and the party platform.

Official Business

Conventions still make or at least ratify major decisions. They adopt rules, accept credentials, determine platforms, and choose the standard bearers.

Rules govern the manner in which the meetings are conducted. They can spark heated controversy, particularly if they affect the outcome of the nomination. In 1952, Dwight Eisenhower's supporters at the Republican convention challenged the credentials of a sizable number of delegates for Robert Taft from southern states. Before deciding on the challenges, however, the convention adopted a "fair play" rule that prohibited these contested delegates from voting on any question, including their own credentials. This effectively prevented many Taft delegates from voting and enabled Eisenhower to win the challenges and eventually the nomination.

An even more acrimonious division over party rules occurred in 1980 at the Democratic convention. At issue was a proposed requirement that delegates vote for the candidate to whom they were publicly pledged at the time they were chosen to attend the convention. Trailing Jimmy Carter by about six hundred delegates, Edward Kennedy, who had previously supported the requirement, urged an open convention in which delegates could vote their consciences rather than merely exercise their commitments. This would have required rejection of the pledged delegate rule. Naturally, the Carter organization favored the rule and strenuously lobbied for it. Carter was successful. The vote in support of the rule effectively clinched his nomination.

Disputes over the credentials of delegates have also divided conventions and influenced their outcomes. In 1912 and again in 1952, grass-roots challenges to old-line party leaders generated competing delegate claims at Republican conventions. In each case the result of the challenge affected the outcome of the nomination: William Howard Taft won in the first instance and Dwight Eisenhower in the second. Approximately 7 percent of all Republican delegates were challenged between 1872 and 1956.[10]

The Democrats have also had their share of delegate disputes, particularly in the early 1970s when the party was making major changes in its rules for delegate selection. A case in point was the California challenge at the 1972 Democratic convention. According to state law, George McGovern, winner of the primary, was entitled to *all* the delegates. However, a commission, which McGovern had initially chaired, recommended that Democratic delegates be awarded in *proportion* to the popular vote a candidate received. Opponents of McGovern challenged the winner-take-all result of the California primary on the basis of the proportional rule. The party's credentials committee upheld this challenge. McGovern, now arguing in favor of a state law against proportional voting, took his case to the convention floor and won. His victory assured him of sufficient delegates to win the nomination. State-wide, winner-take-all primaries were subsequently banned by the Democrats.

Another function of conventions is to draft a platform. It too has been the subject of considerable controversy. Changes in the selection process seem to have produced more issue-oriented delegates who tend to gravitate to the platform committee, and specifically, to the subcommittee considering "their" issues. This has tended to exaggerate rather than minimize the policy differences among the delegates. Television has also magnified the problem by providing publicity for platform challenges. As a consequence of these factors, the platform-drafting process has become more open and more divisive. The Republicans have suffered less than the Democrats. Being the more homogeneous and smaller of the two parties, they have been subjected to fewer and less intense pressures from organized interest groups.

Two often conflicting aims lie at the heart of the platform-drafting process. One has to do with winning the election and the other with pleasing the party's coalition. In order to maximize the vote, platforms cannot alienate. They must permit people to see what they want to see. This is accomplished by increasing the level of vagueness and ambiguity on the most controversial and emotionally charged issues. In 1988 the Democrats went so far as to present a statement of principles in lieu of their usual laundry list of promises for each group comprising their electoral coalition. The Republicans continued to emphasize traditional images and positions in their 1988 platform.

While platforms contain rhetoric and self-praise, they also consist of goals and proposals that differentiate them from one another. In an examination of the Democratic and Republican platforms between 1944 and 1976, Gerald Pomper found that most of the differences were explained by planks made by one party but omitted by the other.[11] Over the years the Republicans have emphasized defense and general governmental matters, while the Democrats have stressed economic issues, particularly those of labor and social welfare. Significant differences have emerged in recent years over the role of government. The Democrats have been more supportive of the federal government's involvement in domestic matters, while the Republicans have placed more emphasis on the private sector to solve the nation's economic woes.

Finally, the convention must select the nominees. The decision is usually predictable and generally occurs on the first ballot. Since 1924, when the Democrats took 103 votes before they agreed on John W. Davis, there have been only four conventions (two in each party) in which more than one ballot was needed. For the Republicans this last occurred in 1948, for the Democrats in 1952.

Despite the tendency to develop a consensus well before the convention meets, there have still been attempts to defeat the front runner at the convention itself. Two strategies for doing this have been employed. One is to release polls showing the strength of the non–front runner and the weakness of the convention leader in the general election. The objective here is to play on the delegates' desire to nominate a winner. Rockefeller tried this in 1968 but to no avail.

A second tactic, one that has been used in more recent conventions, is to create an issue prior to the presidential balloting and win on it, thereby showing the vulnerability of the leader and raising doubts about whether he can be nominated. If the issue affects rules which have an impact on the vote, so much the better. Ronald Reagan in 1976 and Ted Kennedy in 1980 tried this ploy but also without success. Their defeats on key votes confirmed their status as also-rans but did not end their campaigns. With the nomination out of reach, both concentrated on the platform. For the most part, the front runners did not accept these platform challenges, choosing instead to concede policy positions in order to obtain their opponents' backing in the forthcoming campaign.

Having effectively wrapped up the nomination, they could afford to be magnanimous and were.

Characteristics of the Nominees

The nomination of small-state governors by the Democrats in 1976 and 1988 and a former movie actor, ex-California governor by the Republicans in 1980 indicate that changes in the preconvention process may have affected the kind of people chosen by their parties. In theory, many are qualified. In practice, a number of informal qualifications limit the pool of potential nominees. Successful candidates have usually been well known prior to the delegate selection process. Most have had promising political careers and have held high government positions.

Of all the positions from which to seek the presidential nomination, the presidency is clearly the best. Only five incumbent presidents (three of whom were vice presidents who succeeded to the office) failed in their quest for the nomination. It should be noted, however, that several others, including Harry Truman and Lyndon Johnson, were persuaded to retire rather than face tough challenges.

Over the years, there have been a variety of other paths to the White House. When the caucus system was in operation, the position of secretary of state within the administration was regarded as a stepping stone to the nomination if the incumbent chose not to seek another term. When national conventions replaced the congressional caucus, the Senate became the incubator for most successful presidential candidates. After the Civil War, governors emerged as the most likely contenders, particularly for the party that did not control the White House.

In the 1960s Washington-based officials, particularly the vice president and members of the Senate, reemerged as the most viable candidates. They enjoyed the advantage of national media coverage in an age of television and national political experience at a time when the role of the government was greatly expanding. The nominations of Jimmy Carter in 1976, Ronald Reagan in 1980, and Michael Dukakis in 1988 are exceptions to this recent trend. Both Carter and Reagan benefitted from the antigovernment, anti-Washington mood of the electorate following Watergate.

There are other informal criteria, although they have less to do with qualifications for office than with public prejudices. Only white males have ever been nominated by the two major parties for president. Until 1960, no Catholic had been elected, although Governor Al Smith of New York was nominated by the Democrats in 1928. Michael Dukakis, of Greek ancestry, was the first candidate without a northern European heritage, a surprising commentary on a country that has regarded itself as a melting pot.

Personal matters, such as health, finance, and family life, can also be factors. After George Wallace was crippled by a would-be assassin's bullet, even his own supporters began to question his ability to withstand the rigors of the office. Today, presidential candidates are expected to release medical reports and financial statements. Michael Dukakis' hesitancy to do so in 1988 was soundly criticized and fueled rumors that he had seen a psychiatrist.

Family ties have also affected nominations and elections. There have been only two bachelors elected president, James Buchanan and Grover Cleveland. During the 1884 campaign, Cleveland was accused of fathering an illegitimate child. Taunted by his opponents: "Ma, Ma, Where's my Pa? / Gone to the White House / Ha! Ha! Ha!" Cleveland admitted responsibility for the child, even though he was not certain he was the father.

In more recent times, candidates have been hurt by marital problems and allegations of sexual misconduct. The dissolution of Nelson Rockefeller's marriage and his subsequent remarriage seriously damaged his presidential aspirations in 1964, and Senator Edward Kennedy's marital problems and the Chappaquiddick incident were serious detriments to his presidential candidacy in 1980 and contributed to his decision not to seek his party's nomination in 1984. Reagan's election in 1980, however, suggests that having been divorced is no longer a relevant factor, at least for those who have been happily remarried for some time. Sexual misconduct is still a factor, though. In 1988 Senator Gary Hart was forced to withdraw from the race after reporters revealed that he had spent time with a woman who was not his wife. He later reentered the race but could not overcome charges of womanizing.

Finally, most recent presidential nominees have tended to be wealthy. Dwight Eisenhower, Gerald Ford, and, to a lesser extent, Richard Nixon, and Walter Mondale were exceptions. Although government subsidies have somewhat lessened the impact of personal wealth, they have not eliminated it entirely. Having a secure financial base contributes to one's ability to seek and win the nomination.

Most of the characteristics of the presidential nominee apply to the vice presidential candidate as well. However, that choice has also been affected by the perceived need for geographic, ideological, and most recently, sexual balance. Presidential aspirants have tended to select vice presidential candidates primarily as running mates and only secondarily as governing mates. Despite statements to the contrary, most attention is given to how the prospective nominee would help the ticket. Like the presidential nominee, parties have also insisted that the vice presidential aspirant possess all-American traits, including being of sound mind and body. In 1972 Senator Thomas Eagleton was forced to withdraw as the Democratic vice presidential nominee when his past psychological illness became public. In 1988 the Republican vice presidential nominee, Senator Dan Quayle, was hounded by charges that his father, a wealthy

Indiana newspaper publisher, used his influence to get young Quayle into the National Guard and thus reduce his chances of serving in the Vietnam War.

CONCLUSION

The nominating process has evolved significantly over the years. Developed initially to enable the parties to influence electoral selection, it now permits the public to affect that selection as well. With broader rank-and-file participation has come expanded activities by candidates, expanded coverage by the mass media, and expanded public appeals by the parties.

When the presidency was created, the nomination of candidates for the office was not distinguished from the election of the president himself. The development of political parties at the turn of the century led to an informal modification of the electoral plan. At first, congressional caucuses performed the nominating function. As the parties acquired a broader, more decentralized base, the caucus system broke down and was replaced by national nominating conventions. These conventions have continued to operate, although power within them has shifted from political leaders within the states to a broader segment of the political party. The growth of primaries, the increasing impact of the mass media, and eventually the changes in party rules, finance laws, and campaign technology accelerated the movement toward more participatory nominating politics in which public support became the critical element.

On balance, these changes in the public dimension of contemporary politics have made the nomination process more democratic. They have encouraged greater rank-and-file participation in the selection of the party's nominees. They have also generated greater sensitivity by the candidates to the desires of groups within the party and to the opinions and attitudes of the general electorate.

But the costs of democracy have been high. They have adversely affected opportunities for winning and governing. Parties are now more factionalized; their leadership is weaker; they exercise less control over their own nominees. Unity in the general election is more difficult to achieve.

Campaigns are more onerous and more expensive. Candidates have to spend years seeking the nomination. The public is subjected to a barrage of appeals, images, promises, and positions. It is numbed by the campaign.

Not only is it more difficult to win the nomination, but it is also more difficult to govern. Contemporary campaigns hype expectations;

they make agendas more difficult to define and make alliances more fragmentary and more personal; they decrease the president's political power while they increase demands on his job. All of this has made strong presidential leadership more difficult. It would be nice to find a way out of this dilemma, but most contemporary presidents have had difficulty doing so.

NOTES

1. In 1968 dissent within the Democratic party, as evidenced by Senator Eugene McCarthy's surprising showing in the New Hampshire primary, indicated that the incumbent, President Lyndon Johnson, would have difficulty securing renomination, much less reelection.

2. Since an object of these changes was to make delegate selection more indicative of the preferences of the voters, the party tried to prohibit those who did not consider themselves Democrats from participating in its primaries. It was only partially successful. Because many states did not require or even permit voters to register by party, the Democrats were forced to accept an oral affirmation of party preference, one that permitted independents and even Republicans to cross over and vote in Democratic primaries in certain states.

3. Michael J. Robinson and Margaret A. Sheehan, *Over the Wire and on TV: CBS and UPI in Campaign '80* (New York: Russell Sage Foundation, 1983), p. 174.

4. Robert Lichter, Daniel Amundson, and Richard Noyes, *The Video Campaign: Network Coverage of the 1988 Primaries* (Washington, D.C.: American Enterprise Institute, 1988), p. 12.

5. Robinson and Sheehan, *Over the Wire and on TV*, p. 243.

6. Hamilton Jordan, quoted in F. Christopher Arterton, "Campaign Organizations Face the Mass Media in the 1976 Presidential Nomination Process" (paper delivered at the Annual Meeting of the American Political Science Association, Washington, D.C., September 1–4, 1977), p. 23.

7. Robinson and Sheehan, *Over the Wire and on TV*, p. 184.

8. Hamilton Jordan, "Memorandum to Jimmy Carter, August 4, 1974," in Martin Schram, *Running for President, 1976* (New York: Stein and Day, 1977), pp. 379–80.

9. Thomas E. Patterson, *The Mass Media Election* (New York: Praeger, 1980), pp. 72–74.

10. Paul T. David, Ralph M. Goldman, and Richard C. Bain, *The Politics of National Party Conventions* (Washington, D.C.: Brookings Institution, 1960), p. 263.

11. Gerald M. Pomper, "Control and Influence in American Politics," *American Behavioral Scientist* 13 (1969): 223–28; Gerald M. Pomper with Susan S. Lederman, *Elections in America* (New York: Longman, 1980), p. 161.

SELECTED READINGS

Alexander, Herbert E., and Brian A. Haggerty. *Financing Politics.* Lexington, Mass.: D. C. Heath, 1988.

——————. "Misinformation on Media Money." *Public Opinion* 11 (May/June 1988): 5 ff.

Bartels, Larry M. "Candidate Choice and the Dynamics of the Presidential Nomination Process." *American Journal of Political Science* 31 (1987): 1–30.

Crotty, William, and John S. Jackson III. *Presidential Primaries and Nominations*. Washington, D.C.: Congressional Quarterly, 1985.

Cook, Rhodes. "The Nominating Process." In Michael Nelson, ed. *The Elections of 1988*. Washington, D.C.: The Congressional Quarterly, 1989. Pp. 25–61.

Davis, James W. *National Conventions in an Age of Party Reform*. Westport, Conn.: Greenwood, 1983.

Greer, John G. "Rules Governing Presidential Primaries." *Journal of Politics* 48 (1986): 1006–25.

Lichter, S. Robert. "Misreading Momentum." *Public Opinion* 11 (May/June 1988): 15 ff.

Lichter, S. Robert, Daniel Amundson, and Richard Noyes, *The Video Campaign: Network Coverage of the 1988 Primaries*. Washington, D.C.: American Enterprise Institute, 1988.

Orren, Gary R., and Nelson W. Polsby. *Media and Momentum: The New Hampshire Primary and Nomination Politics*. Chatham, N.J.: Chatham House, 1987.

Plissner, Martin, and Warren J. Mitofsky, "The Making of the Delegates, 1968–1988." *Public Opinion* 11 (September/October 1988): 45–47.

Pomper, Gerald M. "The Presidential Nominations." In Gerald Pomper, ed., *The Election of 1988*. Chatham, N.J.: Chatham House, 1989, pp. 33–77.

Sabato, Larry J. *PAC Power*. New York: W. W. Norton, 1985.

Sorauf, Frank J. *Money in American Elections*, Glenview, Ill.: Scott, Foresman, 1988.

3

The Presidential Election

Winning the nomination is only half the battle. The real prize comes from being elected. For the candidate the general election campaign is at least as arduous as the nomination struggle. Shorter in length but with a larger and more heterogeneous electorate, it requires similar organizational skills but different strategic plans and public appeals to build a majority coalition. For the party, the quest for the presidency is only one election among many in which it has an interest and an involvement. Like the other elections, however, the campaign is subject to its influence but not to its control. For the voter the effective choice is narrower but the criteria for judgment are more extensive. Personal evaluation alone is not the only factor that affects the decision whether to vote and, if so, for whom.

For the presidency the campaign has significant implications. Not only does it designate which team and what party will direct activities for the next four years, but it highlights the key policy issues at the beginning of the president's term. It provides the contours of the administration's initial agenda and contributes to the components of its governing coalition. Moreover, it sets the tone for the next few years and indicates the kind of leadership that the public expects and desires. In this sense the campaign defines the president's leadership tasks and opportunities—whether he needs to direct change or can simply facilitate it by keeping the machinery of government going.

In this chapter we will explore these factors and their implications for our electoral and governing systems. We will do so by examining the strategic environment in which presidential elections occur, the critical factors that must be considered when planning and conducting the campaign, and the meaning of the election for the voters and new administration.

The chapter is organized into three parts. In the first we focus on the environment of the election: the Electoral College, voter attitudes, public financing, and media coverage. We assess the impact of each of these factors on the election. We then turn to the strategy and tactics of the campaign itself. We discuss how organizations are constructed, how appeals are designed, projected, and targeted, and how coalitions are built. In the third part we evaluate the election outcome from two perspectives: what it suggests about the moods, opinions, and attitudes of the electorate and what it portends for the president and his governing responsibilities. Does it guide the president, give him a mandate, and increase or decrease his capacity for leadership?

THE STRATEGIC ENVIRONMENT

Every election occurs within an environment that shapes its activity and affects its outcome. For the presidency the Electoral College provides the legal framework for this environment, while public attitudes and group loyalties condition the political climate. Money and media constitute the principal resources and instruments by and through which campaign objectives may be achieved. Each of these factors must be considered in the design and conduct of a presidential campaign and in assessing its impact on the election.

The Electoral College

Of these critical elements only the Electoral College is unique. It was designed by the framers of the Constitution to solve one of their most difficult problems—how to protect the president's independence and, at the same time, have a technically sound, politically efficacious system that would be consistent with a republican form of government. Most of the delegates at the Philadelphia convention were sympathetic to a government based on consent but not to one based on direct democracy. They wanted a mechanism that would choose the most qualified person but not necessarily the most popular. And they had no precise model to follow.

Two methods had been proposed originally: selection by the legislature and election by the voters. Each, however, had its drawbacks. Legislative selection posed a potential threat to the institution of the presidency. How could the executive's independence be preserved if election and reelection hinged on the president's popularity with Congress?[1] Popular election was seen as undesirable and impractical. Not only did most of the delegates lack faith in the public's ability to choose the best-qualified candidate, but they also feared that the size of the country and the poor state of its communication and transportation would preclude a national campaign. Sectional distrust and rivalry aggravated this problem, since the states were obligated to oversee the conduct of such an election. A third alternative, some type of indirect election, was proposed a number of times during the convention, but it was not until near the end that election by electors was seriously considered as a possible compromise solution.

According to the terms of the Electoral College compromise, presidential electors were to be chosen by the states in a manner designated by their legislatures. In order to ensure their independence, the electors could not simultaneously hold a federal government position. The number of electors was to equal the number of senators and representatives from each state (see Appendix C). Each elector had two votes but could not cast both of them for inhabitants of his or her own state.[2] At a designated time the electors would vote and send the results to Congress, where they were to be announced in a joint session by the president of the Senate, the vice president. The person who received a majority of votes cast by the Electoral College would be elected president, and the one with the second highest total would be vice president. In the event that no one received a majority, the House of Representatives would choose from among the five candidates with the most electoral votes, with each state delegation casting one vote. The Senate was to determine the vice president in the event that there was a tie for second place.

The new mode of selection was defended on two grounds: (1) it allowed state legislatures to establish the procedures for choosing electors but permitted the House of Representatives to decide if there were no Electoral College majority; and (2) it gave the larger states an advantage in the initial voting for president in accordance with the principle of majority rule but provided the smaller states with an equal voice if the electoral vote was not decisive, in accordance with the principle of equal representation for each of the states. These compromises placated sufficient interests to get the proposal adopted and subsequently ratified as part of the Constitution.

EVOLUTION.   Only in the first two elections, when Washington was the unanimous choice, did the electors exercise a nonpartisan and presumably independent judgment. Within ten years from the time the federal government began to operate, the party system had developed and electors became its political captives. Nominated by their party, they were expected to vote for the party's candidates, and they did. In 1800 all of the Republican electors voted for Thomas Jefferson and Aaron Burr. Since the procedure for casting ballots did not permit electors to distinguish between their presidential and vice presidential choices, the result was a tie, which the House of Representatives, controlled by the Federalist party, had to break. To avoid such problems in the future, the Constitution was amended in 1804 to provide for separate balloting for president and vice president.

The next nondecisive presidential election occurred in 1824 when four candidates received votes for president: Andrew Jackson (99 votes),

John Q. Adams (84), William Crawford (41), and Henry Clay (37). The new amendment required the House of Representatives to choose from among the top three, not the top five as the Constitution had originally prescribed. Eliminated from the competition was Henry Clay, the Speaker of the House. Clay threw his support to Adams, who won. It was alleged that Clay did so in exchange for appointment as secretary of state, a charge that he vigorously denied. After Adams became president, however, he did appoint Clay secretary of state.

Jackson, the winner of the popular vote, was outraged at the turn of events and urged the abolition of the Electoral College. Although his claim of a popular mandate in 1824 is open to question,[3] opposition to the system mounted, and a gradual democratization of the election process occurred. More and more states began to elect their electors directly on the basis of their partisan leanings. By 1832, only South Carolina retained the old practice of having its legislature do the selecting.

There was also a trend toward statewide election of the entire slate of electors. In the past some states had chosen their electors within legislative districts. Choosing the entire slate of electors on the basis of the popular vote produced a bloc of electoral votes. Whichever candidate received the most popular votes in a state got all the electoral votes of that state. This had two principal effects. It maximized the state's voting power, but it also created the possibility of a disparity between the popular and electoral vote in the nation as a whole. It became possible for the candidate with the most popular votes to lose in the Electoral College if that candidate lost the big states by small margins and won the smaller states by large margins.

This occurred in 1876, the next disputed election, when Democrat Samuel J. Tilden received 250,000 more popular votes and 19 more electoral votes than his Republican rival, Rutherford B. Hayes. However, Tilden was one short of a majority in the Electoral College. Twenty electoral votes were in dispute. Dual returns had been received from three southern states. Charges of fraud and voting irregularities were made by both parties.

Three days before the Electoral College vote was to be officially counted, Congress established a commission to resolve the dilemma. Consisting of eight Republicans and seven Democrats, the commission validated all of the Republican claims by a strictly partisan division, thereby giving Hayes a one vote victory. Tilden could have challenged the results in court but chose not to do so.

The only other election in which the popular vote winner was beaten in the Electoral College occurred in 1888. Democrat Grover Cleveland had a plurality of 95,096 popular votes but only 168 electoral votes compared with 233 for the Republican, Benjamin Harrison. Cleveland's loss of Indiana by about 3,000 votes and New York by about 15,000 led to his defeat.

Although all other popular vote leaders have won a majority of electoral votes, shifts of just a few thousand popular votes in a few states could have altered the results. Thomas E. Dewey could have denied Harry S. Truman a majority in the Electoral College in 1948 with 12,487 more California votes. In 1960, a change of less than 9,000 votes in Illinois and Missouri would have meant that John F. Kennedy lacked an Electoral College majority. In 1968, a shift of only 55,000 votes from Richard M. Nixon to Hubert H. Humphrey in three states (New Jersey, Missouri, and New Hampshire) would have thrown the election into a Democratic House of Representatives. In 1976, a shift of only 3,687 in Hawaii and 5,559 in Ohio would have cost Jimmy Carter the election. The potential for the popular will to be thwarted remains.

POLITICS.   The Electoral College is not neutral. No system of election can be. In general, it works to the benefit of the very largest states (those with more than fourteen electoral votes) and the very smallest (those with less than four). It helps the largest states not only because of the number of electoral votes they cast but because the votes are normally cast in a bloc. The smallest states are also aided because they are overrepresented in the Electoral College. By having three electoral votes, regardless of size, a sparsely populated state such as Alaska will have more of an advantage than it would have in a direct popular vote.

The winner-take-all system also gives an edge to pivotal groups within the larger and more competitive states. Those groups that are geographically concentrated and have cohesive voting patterns derive the most benefit. Part of the opposition to changing the system has been the reluctance of these groups to give up what they perceive as their competitive advantage.

The Electoral College also works to the disadvantage of third and independent parties. The winner-take-all system within states, when combined with the need for a majority within the college, makes it difficult for third parties to accumulate enough votes to win an election. To have any effect, third-party support must be geographically concentrated, as George Wallace's was in 1968 and Strom Thurmond's was in 1948, rather than evenly distributed across the country, as Henry Wallace's was in 1948 and John Anderson's was in 1980.

Periodically, proposals to alter or abolish the Electoral College have been advanced. Most of these plans would eliminate the office of elector but retain the college. One would allocate a state's electoral vote in proportion to its popular vote; another would determine the state's electoral vote on the basis of separate district and statewide elections; a third would use the winner-take-all system within the states but add a bonus to the popular vote winner in the nation as a whole. Only one plan, direct election, would abolish the Electoral College entirely. The popular vote winner would be elected provided that person received at least 40 percent of the popular vote. Thus far, Congress has been reluctant to approve any of these changes and seems unlikely to do so until some electoral crisis or unpopular result occurs.

Political Attitudes and Groupings

As the constitutional framework structures presidential elections, so political attitudes and group loyalties affect the conduct of campaigns. Voters do not come to the election with completely open minds. They come with preexisting views. They do not see and hear the campaign in isolation. They observe it and absorb it as part of their daily lives. In other words, their attitudes and associations affect their perceptions and influence their behavior. This is why it is important for students of presidential elections to examine public attitudes and patterns of social interaction.

Considerable research has been conducted on these subjects.[4] It suggests that people develop political attitudes early in life. Over time these attitudes become more intense and more resistant to change and therefore more important influences on voting behavior. Attitudes affect perceptions of the campaign and evaluations of the parties, the candidates, and the issues.

Of all the factors that contribute to the development of a political attitude, how an individual identifies with a political party is the most important. Party identification operates as a conceptual filter, providing clues for interpreting the issues, for judging the candidates, and for deciding if and how to vote. The stronger this identification, the more compelling the cues. Conversely, the weaker the identification, the less likely it will affect perceptions during the campaign and influence voting.

The amount of information that is known about the candidates also affects the influence of partisanship. In general, the less that is known, the more likely the people will follow their partisan inclinations when voting. Since presidential campaigns normally convey more information than do other elections, the influence of party is apt to be weaker in these higher-visibility contests.

When identification with party is weak or nonexistent, other factors, such as the personalities of the candidates and their issue positions, will be correspondingly more important. In contrast to party identification, which is a long-term stabilizing factor, candidate and issue orientations are short-term, more variable influences that change from election to election. Of the two, the image of the candidate has been more significant.

Candidate images turn on personality and policy dimensions. People tend to form general impressions about candidates on the basis of what is known about their leadership potential, decision-making capabilities, and personal traits. For an incumbent president seeking reelection, accomplishments in office provide much of the criteria for evaluation. For the challenger, experience, knowledge, confidence, and assertiveness substitute for performance. Other characteristics, such as trustworthiness, integrity and candor, may also be important, depending on the times.

The candidates' positions on the issues, however, seem less important than their partisanship and performance or experience. Candidates themselves contribute to this effect by fudging their positions on issues during the general election campaign so as to broaden their appeal and not alienate potential supporters. Staying in the mainstream tends to place the major party candidates close to one another on a variety of issues.

The low level of information and awareness that much of the electorate possesses also tends to downgrade the impact of issues on voting behavior. To be important, issues must stand out from campaign rhetoric. They must attract attention; they must hit home. Without personal impact, they are unlikely to be primary motivating factors in voting. To the extent that positions on issues are not discernible, personality considerations become the critical short-term variable.

Ironically, that portion of the electorate that can be more easily persuaded—weak partisans and independents—tends to have the least information. Conversely, the most committed tend to be the most informed. They use their information to support their partisanship.

In recent years the percentage of the population identifying with a party has declined, as has the intensity of that identification. This has resulted in a more volatile electorate that decides later in the campaign whether and how to vote. In 1988 about two-thirds of the electorate identified with one or the other of the major parties, compared with three-fourths thirty years earlier.[5]

TURNOUT.   The weakening of party identification has also contributed to the decline in turnout in recent years by decreasing the partisan motivation for voting. In 1988 just slightly over 50 percent of those eligible to vote actually did so (see Table 3-1).

Party identification is not the only factor that affects whether people vote. Interest in the election, concern over the outcome, feelings of civic responsibility, and a sense of political efficacy also contribute. Naturally the person who feels more strongly about the election and its consequences is more likely to vote.

In addition to attitudinal factors, demographic characteristics that relate to turnout include education, income, and occupational status. As people become more educated, as they move up the socioeconomic ladder, as their jobs gain in status, they are more likely to vote. Education is the most important of these variables. It has the greatest bearing on whether people vote.[6]

Finally, state laws influence voting. In order to cast a ballot on election day, a citizen must be registered to vote. Within broad federal guidelines, the states prescribe the rules for registration. In recent years an

Table 3-1. Participation in Presidential Elections

Year	Total Adult Population (including Aliens)*	Total Presidential Vote	Percentage of Adult Population Voting
1824	3,964,000	363,017	9%
1840	7,381,000	2,412,698	33
1860	14,676,000	4,692,710	32
1880	25,012,000	9,219,467	37
1900	40,753,000	13,974,188	35
1920	60,581,000	26,768,613	44
1932	75,768,000	39,732,000	52.4
1940	84,728,000	49,900,000	58.9
1952	99,929,000	61,551,000	61.6
1960	109,672,000	68,838,000	62.8
1964	114,090,000	70,645,000	61.9
1968	120,285,000	73,212,000	60.9
1972	140,777,000	77,719,000	55.5
1976	152,308,000	81,556,000	53.5
1980	164,595,000	86,515,000	52.6
1984	174,447,000	92,653,000	53.1
1988	182,600,000	91,602,291	50.2

*Restrictions based on sex, age, race, religion, and property ownership prevented a significant portion of the adult population from voting in the nineteenth and early twentieth centuries. Of those who were eligible, however, the percentage casting ballots was often quite high, particularly during the last half of the nineteenth century.

Source: Population figures for 1824 to 1920 are based on estimates and early census figures that appear in Neal R. Pierce, *The People's President* (New York: Simon and Schuster, 1968), p. 206. Population figures from 1932 to 1988 are from the U.S. Department of Commerce, Bureau of the Census, *Statistical Abstract of the United States* (Washington, D.C., 1987), p. 250. Figures for 1988 were compiled from official election returns.

increasing percentage of the eligible population has not been registered. The failure to register accounts for a significant portion of the nonvoting. In 1988 the actual rate of registration among the population decreased by 2.2 percent.[7] Two political scientists, Raymond Wolfinger and Steven Rosenstone, estimated that simplifying the procedures to permit election day registration could increase turnout by as much as 9 percent, although their conclusions have been challenged.[8]

The magnitude of the turnout problem is indicated in Table 3-1. The percentage of adults who vote has declined steadily since 1960. In 1988 it dropped to its lowest level in over 60 years. The decline in turnout in recent years seems to have hurt the Democrats more than the Republicans. Democratic registration has declined while Republican registration has increased, although the Democrats still outnumber the Republicans in states that require registration by party.[9]

Candidates and their advisers must take these factors into account when planning their campaign. They must also be conscious of the social basis of contemporary American politics—the racial, ethnic, religious, and even sexual groupings that comprise each party's electoral coalition.

PARTISAN COALITIONS.   It was during the depression that the Democrats became the majority party. They built their coalition primarily along economic lines with the bulk of it coming from those in the lower socioeconomic strata. In addition, the party maintained the support of white southerners who had voted Democratic since the Civil War.

Today the Democrats still form the dominant party, but their coalition is much more fragile than in the 1930s. White southern support has eroded within the last three decades, white labor support has also declined, and the party has barely maintained the backing of Catholic voters (see Table 3-2). On the other hand, it has increased its support from African-Americans and Hispanics, retained its Jewish constituency, and cut into the Republican vote in the Northeast. In recent years the Democrats have also been the beneficiaries of a female vote, particularly from younger, working women.

The Republicans were the majority party before the 1930s. During the depression the GOP lost the support of much of the working class and was unable to attract new groups to its coalition. Business and professional people, however, maintained their Republican affiliation, as did nonsouthern, white Protestants. Today, the Republican party receives much of its support from white-collar workers, professional workers and managers, and those primarily in the upper-middle classes. The party has increased its popularity in the Sunbelt, Rocky Mountain areas, and Far West but has lost popularity in the so-called Rust Belt of the Northeast and Midwest. Recently men have given GOP candidates at the national level more support than they have given their Democratic challengers.

Although the Republican coalition has not grown significantly, the party's potential for winning presidential elections has. One of the reasons for this seeming contradiction is that the socioeconomic bases of the parties are eroding. The coalitions have become frayed. Although class, religion, and geography are still related to party identification and voting behavior, they are not as strongly related as they were in the past. Voters are less influenced by the groups with which they associate. They exercise a more independent judgment on election day, and one that is less predictable. That is why the Republicans' chances have improved even though their party has not become dominant.

Financial Considerations

A third factor that affects the strategic environment of presidential campaigns is the funding provided by the federal government. In the past, candidates were dependent on the generosity of their backers and

Table 3-2. Party Identification of Selected Groups (in percentages)

	Rep.	Dem.	Ind.	Number of Interviews
National	*30%*	*40%*	*30%*	*1,864*
Sex				
Men	31	35	34	930
Women	28	44	28	934
Age				
18–29 years	33	31	36	413
18–24 years	39	27	34	213
25–29 years	26	36	38	200
30–49 years	25	42	33	735
50 & older	32	43	25	710
50–64 years	32	40	28	347
65 & older	31	47	22	363
Region				
East	28	44	28	476
Midwest	28	35	37	482
South	33	40	27	565
West	28	40	32	341
Race				
White	32	36	32	1,659
Non-whites	10	68	22	205
Blacks	11	74	15	173
Hispanics	26	47	27	120
Education				
College graduates	34	33	33	375
College incomplete	34	33	33	473
High school graduates	27	43	30	635
Not high school graduates	26	47	27	371
Occupation				
Professional & Business	35	30	35	541
Other white collar	25	42	33	146
Blue collar	26	41	33	691
Skilled workers	30	32	38	286
Unskilled workers	23	48	29	405
Household Income				
$40,000 & over	38	32	30	363
$25,000–$39,999	33	33	34	433
$15,000–$24,999	28	40	32	396
Under $15,000	25	49	26	549
Religion				
Protestants	34	38	28	1,068
Catholics	26	45	29	516
Labor Union				
Labor union families	24	48	28	356
Non-union families	31	38	31	1,508

Source: *Gallup Opinion Index*, January 1988. Reprinted by permission.

the support of their party. And considerable generosity was needed to finance these national efforts.

In 1860, Lincoln spent an estimated $100,000 on his presidential campaign. One hundred years later, Kennedy and Nixon were each spending one hundred times that amount. In the twelve years following the 1960 election, expenditures quadrupled. Inflation, air travel, and particularly television advertising contributed to the sharp rises. Table 3-3 lists the costs of the major party candidates in presidential elections from 1860 to 1972.

Table 3-3. Costs of Presidential General Elections, 1860–1972 Major Party Candidates

Year	Republican		Democratic	
1860	$100,000	Lincoln*	$50,000	Douglas
1864	125,000	Lincoln*	50,000	McClellan
1868	150,000	Grant*	75,000	Seymour
1872	250,000	Grant*	50,000	Greeley
1876	950,000	Hayes*	900,000	Tilden
1880	1,100,000	Garfield*	335,000	Hancock
1884	1,300,000	Blaine	1,400,000	Cleveland*
1888	1,350,000	Harrison*	855,000	Cleveland
1892	1,700,000	Harrison	2,350,000	Cleveland*
1896	3,350,000	McKinley*	675,000	Bryan
1900	3,000,000	McKinley*	425,000	Bryan
1904	2,096,000	T. Roosevelt*	700,000	Parker
1908	1,655,518	Taft*	629,341	Bryan
1912	1,071,549	Taft	1,134,848	Wilson*
1916	2,441,565	Hughes	2,284,590	Wilson*
1920	5,417,501	Harding*	1,470,371	Cox
1924	4,020,478	Coolidge*	1,108,836	Davis
1928	6,256,111	Hoover*	5,342,350	Smith
1932	2,900,052	Hoover	2,245,975	F. Roosevelt*
1936	8,892,972	Landon	5,194,741	F. Roosevelt*
1940	3,451,310	Willkie	2,783,654	F. Roosevelt*
1944	2,828,652	Dewey	2,169,077	F. Roosevelt*
1948	2,127,296	Dewey	2,736,334	Truman*
1952	6,608,623	Eisenhower*	5,032,926	Stevenson
1956	7,778,702	Eisenhower*	5,106,651	Stevenson
1960	10,128,000	Nixon	9,797,000	Kennedy*
1964	16,026,000	Goldwater	8,757,000	Johnson*
1968†	25,402,000	Nixon*	11,594,000	Humphrey
1972	61,400,000	Nixon*	30,000,000	McGovern

*Indicates winner.
†George Wallace spent an estimated $7 million as the candidate of the American Independent party in 1968.

Source: Herbert E. Alexander, *Financing Politics* (Washington, D.C., Congressional Quarterly, 1980), p. 5.

The spiraling costs of campaigning in the 1960s and early 1970s made candidates increasingly dependent on large donors. The number of individuals who contributed $10,000 or more grew dramatically during this period.

The rapidly rising donations and expenditures created even greater inequalities than had existed in the past. In 1964, 1968, and 1972 the Republican nominees were able to spend more than twice as much as their Democratic counterparts. This became a bone of contention, since it was assumed that money contributed to electoral success.

A cursory look at total expenditures in presidential elections lends some support to this thesis. In general elections between 1860 and 1972, the winner outspent the loser twenty-one out of twenty-nine times (see Table 3-3). Republican candidates have spent more than their Democrat opponents in twenty-five out of the twenty-nine elections during this period. The four times they did not, the Democrats won. These figures would suggest that the potential for winning is affected by and affects the capacity to raise money.

The high costs of campaigning, the dependence on large donors, and the inequities in the amounts candidates received and could spend prompted a Democratically controlled Congress in the 1970s to enact legislation for public funding of presidential elections.

The funding provision went into effect in 1976. At that time the federal contribution to the major party candidates was set at $20 million plus a cost-of-living adjustment. In 1988, when that adjustment was taken into account, each of the major candidates received $46.1 million.

The nominees of the major parties are automatically eligible for funds. Third-party candidates do not qualify until they receive 5 percent of the presidential vote. Thereafter, they are eligible to get funds equal to their proportion of the popular vote until that vote drops below 5 percent. John Anderson, a third-party candidate in 1980, received $4.2 million for his 6.6 percent of the vote, enough to pay off his debts but not enough to have mounted a vigorous campaign.

The law permits the national parties to spend two cents per citizen of voting age in support of their presidential nominees. In 1988 this amounted to $8.3 million.

A 1979 amendment also allows state and local political parties to spend an unlimited amount of funds on voluntary efforts to turn out the vote. The printing and distribution of literature, the operation of phone banks, and the coordination of registration and get-out-the-vote drives are all included. This is referred to as "soft money."

The campaign finance legislation has had a major impact on the conduct of presidential elections. It has equalized spending between the major party candidates. Theoretically, this should work to the Democrats' and to the incumbent's benefit. Equal spending denies the Republicans their traditional financial edge. It also makes it more difficult for a challenger, who lacks the news-making capacity of an incumbent, to get equal public attention.

In 1976 these advantages seemed to offset one another. In subsequent elections they did not. Superior Republican resources at the national, state, and local levels enabled the GOP to mount national media campaigns and selective grass-roots efforts for many of its candidates for national and state office including president and vice president. In contrast, the Democrats , who have suffered from a weaker financial and organizational position, could not benefit their tickets nearly as much, although they were more successful in 1988 than in previous years, raising $68 million and spending $58 million (approximately double their 1984 figures). The Republican totals for 1988 were $171 million raised and $152 million spent.

Independent efforts by political action committees, protected by the First Amendment to the Constitution, have also assumed increasing importance in presidential contests. In 1976, Democrat Carter was greatly aided by labor's efforts on his behalf in several key states. In the 1980s it was Republican candidates who were the principal benefactors of independent spending by individuals and groups.

Finally, the law has affected and will continue to affect the major parties. Here, however, the law may be more destructive than supportive. It is not the major parties, however, but the major party candidates who receive the bulk of government support. Moreover, the prohibition against private contributions has enlarged the role and impact of PACs, further weakening the national parties' influence over the campaigns of their candidates. Limited funding has also prompted the candidates to utilize the mass media, not old-style party organizations, to reach the largest number of voters in the most cost-effective way.

News Coverage

News coverage also affects the strategic environment. Today most people follow presidential campaigns on television. It is the prime source of news for approximately two-thirds of the population. Newspapers are a distant second, being the major source for only about 20 percent. Radio and magazines trail far behind.

Since it is an action-oriented, visual medium, television reports the drama and excitement of the campaign. It does so by emphasizing the contest. Who is ahead? How are the candidates doing? Is the leader slipping? It is this horse-race aspect of the campaign that provides the principal focus during the nomination phase, and with a close contest, during the general election as well.

The need to stress the contest affects which issues are covered when issues are covered. The medium focuses on those that provide clear-cut differences between the candidates, those that provoke controversy, and those that can be presented in a simple, straightforward manner. These are not necessarily the issues that the candidates have stressed during their campaigns. In general, substantive, policy questions of what the government should do tend to receive little in-depth coverage.[10] In 1988 it was "campaign" issues about the candidates, their organizations, and their strategies and tactics that received the most emphasis.[11] Much of this coverage was negative. According to one analysis, media criticism on the three major television networks was more prevalent than praise by about two to one.[12]

Although candidates may influence their news coverage, they cannot control it. Try as they may to counter an uncomplementary evaluation and project a favorable image, it is very difficult to divert the media's focus or blunt the effect on the voters.

The time, money, and energy spent on image building suggests that it has a major impact on electoral behavior. Although there is little tangible evidence that the media campaign changes attitudes, it does generate interest, increase awareness, and affect perceptions of the candidates by the electorate. In this way, it can influence voting.

Studies of presidential campaigning in the 1940s indicated that the principal impact of the print media was to activate predispositions and reinforce attitudes rather than to convert voters. Newspapers and magazines provided information but primarily to those who were most committed. The most committed, in turn, used the information to support their beliefs. Weeding out opposing views, they insulated themselves from unfavorable news and opinions that conflicted with their own.[13]

Television might have been expected to change this because it exposes the less committed to more information and the more committed to other points of view. Avoidance is more difficult, since viewers are more captive of the picture than readers are of the printed page. Moreover, television news tends to be "more mediating, more political, more personal, more critical, [and] more thematic than old-style print."[14] Whereas newspapers describe events, indicating what candidates say and do, television presents the dramatic elements. It provides a visual slice of reality, not a compendium of people, places, and things.

Television compartmentalizes the news, fitting a large number of stories into a thirty-minute broadcast. Of necessity, this restricts the time that can be devoted to each. Campaign stories average one and a half minutes on the evening news, the equivalent of only a few paragraphs of a printed account. This helps explain why viewers do not retain much information from it.

Two political scientists, Thomas E. Patterson and Robert D. McClure, studied how television reported the news during the 1972 campaign and found:

1. Most election issues are mentioned so infrequently that viewers could not possibly learn about them.

2. [M]ost issue references are so fleeting that they could not be expected to leave an impression on viewers.

3. [T]he candidates' issue positions generally were reported in ways guaranteed to make them elusive.[15]

"Television news adds little to the average voter's understanding of election issues," they wrote. "Network news may be fascinating. It may be highly entertaining. But it is simply not informative."[16]

From what sources, then, do people receive information? One of the most interesting findings of the Patterson and McClure study is that people actually get more information from the advertisements they see on television than from the networks' evening news programs. The reason seems to be that ads are more repetitive and more compact. When placed with other commercials in popular shows, they are difficult to avoid. In fact, television watchers pay about twice as much attention to political advertisements as they do to other kinds of commercials.

What effect does this have on the election? Who is influenced and how? Students of the electoral process suggest three principal effects for three different groups of voters.

1. *Strong Partisans.* The media tend to reinforce their feelings and loyalties. Acting as a catalyst, television, radio, and newspapers move members of this group in the direction of their inclinations. In other words, they make them more Democratic or more Republican and thus more likely to exercise their partisan judgment on election day.

2. *Weak Partisans* (including those who claim they are independent but lean in a partisan direction). The campaign is too short to change their beliefs or attitudes, but it is long enough to affect their perceptions of the candidates. By providing them with more information about the candidates and their stands, the media raise doubts or remove them. By so doing either they produce cross-pressures that lead to uncertainty and may ultimately cause partisan defections or nonvoting, or they may actually reduce pressure, thereby generating a partisan response.

3. *Independents* (those with no partisan affiliation and sometimes little interest in politics). The media bring them into contact with the campaign, which, in turn, may excite interest, arouse concern, improve knowledge, and in the end, affect judgment. In this way the media increase the likelihood of voting and the influence of candidate evaluation on the voting decision itself.

THE PRESIDENTIAL CAMPAIGN

Campaigning by presidential candidates is a relatively recent phenomenon. For much of American history, personal solicitation by the party nominees was viewed as demeaning and unbecoming of the dignity and status of the presidency. It was not until 1860 that this tradition of nonparticipation by the candidates themselves was broken when Senator Stephen A. Douglas, Democratic nominee for president, spoke out on the slavery issue. Douglas did not set an immediate precedent. Presidential candidates remained on the sidelines for most of the nineteenth century. Party supporters made appeals on their behalf.

The second nominee who personally campaigned was William Jennings Bryan. Gaining the Democratic nomination following his famous "cross of gold" speech, Bryan pleaded his case for free silver to groups around the country. By his own account, he traveled more than eighteen thousand miles, made more than six hundred speeches, and, according to press estimates, spoke to almost five million people.[17] In contrast, Bryan's opponent of that year, William McKinley, campaigned from the front porch of his home.

Republican candidates did little more than front porch oratory until the 1930s, but Democrats Woodrow Wilson and Al Smith took their campaigns to the public in 1912 and 1928, respectively. By 1932 active campaigning by the nominees became the rule rather than the exception. Franklin Roosevelt crisscrossed the country by railroad, making it possible for thousands of people to see him.[18] He employed radio to reach millions of others. Roosevelt's skillful use of this communication medium demonstrated the potential that a personal appeal can have for winning and leading.

Television accelerated this potential, making it easier for a candidate to reach millions of voters. But television also created new obstacles for the nominees and their parties. The physical appearance of the candidates became more important. Attention focused on the images they presented. New game plans had to be designed. These plans contained broad public appeals, appeals that were candidate oriented, appeals that were projected by sophisticated marketing techniques, appeals that were carefully targeted to specific groups within the electorate. Additionally, large, multitiered, functionally differentiated campaign organizations had to be developed.

Running an Organization

A large, specialized political organization is essential to coordinate the myriad of activities which must be performed in any presidential campaign. These include advance work, scheduling, press arrangements, issue research, speech writing, polling, advertising, grass-roots organizing, accounting, budgeting, legal activities, and liaison with state and local party committees and other "friendly" groups.

Organizations vary in structure and style. Some have been very centralized, with a few individuals making most of the major decisions; others have been more decentralized. Some have worked through or in conjunction with national and state party organizations; others seem to have disregarded these groups entirely and created their own field organizations. Some have operated from a comprehensive game plan; others have adopted a more incremental approach. The Goldwater organization in 1964, the Nixon operation in 1972, and the Reagan and Bush efforts in 1984 and 1988 exemplified the tighter, hierarchical structure, in which a few individuals control decision making and access to the candidate. The Humphrey campaign in 1968 and Mondale's effort in 1984 were run by looser, more fluid organizational structures.

There are tensions in every campaign, tensions between the candidate's organization and the party's, between the national headquarters and the field staff, between the research and operational units. Some of these tensions are the inevitable consequence of personnel operating under severe time constraints and pressures. Some are the result of the need to coordinate a large, decentralized party system for a national campaign. Some result from limited resources and the struggle over who gets how much.

Some of these tensions were evident in the early stages of the Dukakis campaign. Democratic leaders who had experience in other national presidential campaigns were not actively recruited or even encouraged to join the Dukakis effort. Not only did this produce ill will among Democrats, but it resulted in costly delays in addressing the critical strategic needs of the campaign: articulating consistent messages, targeting them to potential supporters, scheduling the nominee and his vice presidential running mate, and arranging for debates with the opposition.

In contrast, the Bush organization was the model of efficiency. Its campaign left nothing to chance. Using the experience of the Reagan and Bush efforts in 1980 and 1984, the Bush organization serially presented its themes based on careful survey research and in-depth group studies, controlled the media focus, put its presidential candidate on the offensive, and thereby shifted the debate over issues to its turf.

Designing a Presidential Image

To become president it is necessary to act like one, to display the traits of an ideal president. Strength, boldness, and decisiveness are intrinsic to the public's image of the office. During times of crisis or periods of social anxiety these leadership characteristics are considered absolutely essential. The strength that Franklin Roosevelt was able to convey by virtue of his successful bout with polio and that Eisenhower imparted by his military command in World War II contrasted sharply with the perceptions of Stevenson in 1956, McGovern in 1972, and Carter in 1980 as weak, indecisive, and vacillating. Mondale in 1984 and Bush in 1988 also suffered from the general perception that they lacked these leadership traits, although Bush was able to overcome his "wimp" image during the general election campaign. Bush was also able to demonstrate that he understood the economic needs and desires of the average citizen despite his upper-class background.

In addition to seeming strong enough to be president, it is also important to appear competent, to exhibit sufficient knowledge and skills for the job. In the public's mind, personal experience testifies to the ability to perform.

The advantage of incumbency is obviously important in maintaining a presidential image. Being president produces recognition, esteem, and clout. Presidents have an organization and mechanism through which they can affect events or at least influence their timing, help certain individuals, groups, and areas of the country, and promote certain policies and programs where it is to their political benefit to do so. The announcement of grants and appointments, the support of legislation, even the use of White House and cabinet officials as surrogates enhance the president's position at the expense of a challenger. It also helps to provide a record, which in turn fosters an image of leadership. To a lesser extent, these incumbency advantages can also extend to the vice president so long as the vice president can demonstrate leadership qualities of his own.

While incumbency contributes to a perception of leadership, it does not guarantee it. In the 1970s the gap between expectations and performance widened in the public mind. Even presidents had to demonstrate that they were sufficiently presidential to justify being returned to office. Ford tried to show that he had sufficient knowledge and grasp of the issues in his campaign against Carter in 1976. Similarly, Carter had to contrast favorably his knowledge, decision-making abilities, and personal skills with Reagan's in 1980, largely to overcome the perception that his presidency had not been very effective.

In contrast, the challenger must appear as presidential as possible. Carter in 1976, Reagan in 1980, and Dukakis in 1988 had to provide the electorate with information about their leadership abilities, particularly as governors. Mondale had a more difficult task—to demonstrate that he was an influential congressional leader and vice president, yet not responsible for the problems of the Carter years.

Projecting an Appeal

Once a presidential image is established, it must be projected. This can be done in a variety of ways: in speeches and news conferences, in press releases and interviews, and in print, radio, and television advertising. Of all these methods, advertising, particularly on television, reaches the largest audience, has the most sustained impact, and is least subject to interference by media representatives. That is why recent presidential campaigns have allocated about two-thirds of their budgets to this method of reaching the voters.

ADVERTISING.   To be effective, advertising must be presented in an interesting and believable way. It must maintain interest. For television, this frequently means action. The ad must move. For Reagan the need in 1980 was different. Advisers, fearful that a slick presentation would bring attention to the candidate's career as an actor, presented Reagan in that election as a talking head with as few gimmicks and diversions as possible. In contrast, his 1984 advertising used the trappings of the presidency to demonstrate his leadership of the country.

Advertising tends to be targeted to different sections of the country and to different groups within the electorate. The objective of targeting is to bring the campaign home, to influence specific groups of voters who share many of the same concerns. This requires that issues and positions be relevant to the audience. The candidate's appearance, message, and language must mesh. Media buyers will normally code stations by their viewers and their program format so that the messages fit the audience both demographically and regionally. They will also keep abreast of the content, timing, and placements of their opponents' ads in order to be in a position to reply quickly or divert resources to other media markets.

Frequently, a candidate works as hard to destroy his opponent's image as he does to build his own. This is known as confrontational advertising and has been used with regularity in presidential campaigns since 1964. That year perhaps the most famous (or infamous) negative ad was created for the Democrats. Called daisy girl, it was designed to reinforce the impression that Republican candidate Barry Goldwater was a trigger-happy zealot who would not hesitate to use nuclear weapons against a Communist foe.

The advertistment began with a little girl in a meadow plucking petals from a daisy. She counted to herself softly. When she reached eleven, her voice faded and a stern-sounding male voice counted down from nine. When he got to zero, there was an explosion, the little girl disappeared, and a mushroom-shaped cloud covered the screen. President Johnson was heard saying, "These are the stakes, to make a world in which all of God's children can live or go into the dark. . . . The stakes are too high for you to stay at home." The ad ended with a plea to vote for Johnson.

The commercial was run only once. Goldwater supporters were outraged and protested vigorously. Their protest kept the issue alive. In fact, the ad itself became a news item, and parts of it were shown on television newscasts, thereby reinforcing the impression the Democrats wished to leave in the voters' minds.

The emphasis given confrontational, or negative, advertising has increased in recent years. In 1988 both candidates ran more ads that were critical of their opponents than ones that lauded their own accomplishments and qualifications for the office. Bush attacked Dukakis for his positions on defense, the environment, and crime. One of his hardest-hitting commercials featured a Massachusetts prison furlough program which Dukakis supported as governor. The ad pictured tough-looking inmates in prison garb walking through a revolving door. It suggested that Dukakis was soft on crime. An even more poignant and sensational spot, sponsored by a PAC that was supporting Bush, showed a picture of Willie Horton, a convicted murderer who stabbed a man and raped his female companion after escaping while on a furlough from a Massachusetts prison. Amid gruesome commentary about Horton's criminal acts, the ad contrasted the positions of Dukakis and Bush on crime—much to Dukakis's disadvantage.

The extent of the negative advertising by the Bush campaign and groups that supported his candidacy led Dukakis to run antinegative ads about Bush's negative advertising. In one, the governor was seen sitting in front of a television showing a Bush commercial that accused Dukakis of being against virtually every new weapons system for the military. An angry Dukakis turns off the set and says: "I'm fed up with it. Haven't seen anything like it in twenty-five years of public life, George Bush's negative TV ads: distorting my record, full of lies, and he knows it."

The amount of negative advertising itself became an issue in 1988 and contributed to the lack of enthusiasm and negative perceptions about both candidates, and some believe, to the lower voter turnout. Nonetheless, the negative personal references are consistent with a trend in the media's presentation of candidates that emphasizes their character and judgment and deemphasizes a detailed discussion of their positions on issues.

From the perspective of the candidates and their managers, political advertising works. It affects voter perceptions and reinforces attitudes and opinions. The environment can be predetermined, the words and pictures can be created and coordinated, and the candidate can be rehearsed to produce the desired effect.

In contrast, news is more difficult to influence. The candidate's message is mediated partially by the structure of the event and partially by how the media choose to cover it. Remarks may be edited for the sake of the story. A candidate can be interrupted, his comments interpreted, and his policies evaluated. Major statements can even be ignored—if, for example, the candidate makes some goof or if hecklers are present. Antiabortion protesters dogged Geraldine Ferraro in 1984, making abortion an issue wherever she spoke. Under these circumstances, aspirants for the presidency and vice presidency exercise much less leverage. They are not powerless, however.

Campaign organizations work very hard to affect the coverage they receive. Speeches for presidential candidates are now scripted for their

THE MAKING OF THE PRESIDENT, 1988

Source: Copyright © 1988 by Herblock in *The Washington Post*.

sound bites, the nine to fifteen seconds that will be shown on the evening news. Events are staged with television in mind. Placing candidates in uncontrollable situations is avoided whenever possible, particularly by front runners. Reagan in 1984 and Bush in 1988 held few press conferences and limited access by media representatives.

Contemporary campaigns lack spontaneity but are designed for maximum public impact. Symbols are used to convey images: themes are presented on a weekly or biweekly basis. Press releases, advertisements, and candidate statements are carefully synchronized to maintain the campaign's focus. Even seemingly off-the-cuff remarks are usually prepared and timed to contribute to the overall thematic effect.

DEBATES.   Debates are another good example of events which candidates go to great lengths to influence. More than any other single campaign event, presidential debates have gained public attention. It is estimated that more than half of the adult population in the United States watched all of the 1960 Kennedy-Nixon debates and almost 90 percent saw one of them.[19] The first Ford-Carter debate in 1976 attracted an estimated viewing audience of 90 million to 100 million; the 1980 Carter-Reagan debate was seen by approximately 150 million viewers, while the 1984 and 1988 debates attracted in the neighborhood of 125 million viewers.

With so many people watching, meticulous planning goes into each debate. Representatives of the candidates study the locations, try to anticipate the questions, and brief and rehearse the candidates. Mock studios are built and the debate environment simulated. In 1980 this elaborate preparation took a bizarre twist. Those who readied Ronald Reagan for his debate obtained the briefing material which Carter's aides had prepared for him. Knowing the questions that Carter anticipated and the answers he was advised to give helped Reagan counter Carter's responses. The debate made him look good.

Candidates have viewed presidential debates as vehicles for improving their images and/or damaging their opponents. In 1960, Kennedy wanted to counter the image of being perceived as too young and inexperienced. Nixon, on the other hand, sought to maintain his stature as Eisenhower's knowledgeable and competent vice president and the obvious person to succeed his "boss" in office. In 1976, Ford saw the debates as an opportunity to appear presidential while Carter saw them as a means of shoring up his Democratic support. In 1980 the rationale from Reagan's perspective was to reassure voters about himself and his qualifications for office while for Carter, it was another chance to exaggerate the differences between himself and his opponent. In 1984 and again in 1988 the candidates sought to establish their leadership credentials (or in Reagan's case, maintain his) and critique their opponent's position (or in Reagan's case, defend his administration's policies).

The media assess debates in terms of winners and losers. Their evaluation conditions how the public judges the results. Since most people do not follow the content very closely and do not put much faith in their own judgment, media commentary can have a considerable impact on public opinion following the debate. It can even modify the immediate impressions people have, moving them in the direction of the acknowledged winner. This happened in 1976 and again in 1980.

In theory, debates tend to help challengers more than incumbents. Since they are less well known, challengers have more questions raised about them, their competence, and their capacity to be president. The debates provide an opportunity to satisfy some of these doubts in a believable setting and on a comparative basis. By appearing to be at least the equal of their incumbent opponents, challengers enhance their presidential image. There are fewer reasons for voting against them. The impact of debates tends to be greater in a close election, where the perceptions of the candidates are more fluid.

In practice, debates tend to reinforce predispositions and attitudes.

Those who are inclined toward a particular candidate tend to see that candidate in a more favorable light in the debate. Even a weak performance, such as Reagan's in his first debate with Mondale in 1984, is not apt to change many voting decisions. Thus debates tend to be decisive only in very close elections where influencing the perceptions of a relatively small proportion of voters could make a difference. In 1960 and again in 1976, the debates may have affected who won and who lost. In 1980 the one presidential debate probably contributed to Reagan's margin of victory. In 1984 and 1988 the debates had less discernible impact on the results.

Building a Winning Coalition

Once appeals are designed and projected they must be targeted to potentially receptive voters. When doing this, candidates must consider their political bases of support as well as the geographic foundations of the Electoral College. The goal is to build a coalition that results in winning a majority of the electoral votes, not necessarily a huge popular victory.

For the Democrats this translates into two strategic objectives: rekindle partisan loyalties and turn out a sizable vote. The two are related in that partisanship is a motivation for voting. This is why Democratic candidates make the link between their party and themselves explicit: "McGovern, Democrat for the people"; "Carter, Democrat, a leader for a change"; "Dukakis, he's on your side." They direct their appeal toward the rank and file who comprise their electoral coalition.

The task for any Democratic standard bearer is to maintain the loyalty of party supporters. To achieve this, appeals must be directed toward the major groups that make up the party's electoral coalitions. These special interest and demographic groups tend to be more highly organized and politically potent in the Democratic party than in the Republican party. Thus, Democratic candidates tend to be more issue-specific, particularly with respect to domestic economic concerns around which their coalition was originally built.

In contrast, Republicans tend to make a more general appeal: "He's (Ford) making us proud again"; "The time is now for Reagan." As members of the more homogeneous of the two major parties, Republican candidates have less of a problem with partisan defections but need the votes of Democrats and independents to win. Thus, it is the partisans of the dominant party and, increasingly, the expanding group of independents to whom much of the campaign is directed. In 1980 Reagan focused his criticism of the Carter administration and directed it to those who were adversely affected by its policies: blue-collar workers, ethnic and religious minorities, and middle- to lower-income families. In 1984 his campaign again targeted blue-collar workers and ethnic groups. In

1988 both Bush and Dukakis appealed to Reagan Democrats who had defected four and eight years earlier, as well as to a growing number of white-collar, middle-income voters.

The Republicans have been particularly effective in recent years with their use of symbols. Bush's use of the Pledge of Allegiance in 1988 is a case in point. Criticizing Governor Dukakis for vetoing a bill enacted by the Massachusetts legislative that would have disciplined teachers for not requiring all school children to recite the Pledge, Bush appealed to a basic feeling of patriotism. Similarly his positions on abortion and pornography generated an emotional response, particularly from parents with young children. The prison furlough and Willie Horton ads were designed to evoke a fear of threats to personal security that is evident among much of the population.

In addition to group appeals, campaigns also have a geographic thrust consistent with the Electoral College. The large states always receive attention.

In the last three decades the Democrats have focused on the Northeast, Midwest, and Pacific Coast because of their party's declining support at the presidential level in the South, Far West, and Rocky Mountain areas. In 1976, and initially in 1988, their strategic goal was different—to regain the South in order to reduce pressure on the party's effort in the large industrial states. Carter succeeded in large part because of his southern heritage, but Dukakis, even with Texan Lloyd Bentsen on the ticket, was unable to close the gap and had to devote his resources increasingly to areas of traditional Democratic strength.

The Republican support in the Sunbelt and Rocky Mountain areas has given that party an important advantage. It has enabled the GOP to concentrate its efforts and resources in states the Democrats must win. A narrow victory in several of these key states can effectively doom the Democrats' chances. Whether the Republicans' recent victories indicate that they have a lock on the Electoral College remains to be seen. It does seem clear, however, that the Democrats would improve their chances by choosing a southerner or westerner to head their ticket.

THE MEANING OF THE ELECTION

Polling the People

From the candidate's perspective the name of the game is to win. From the voter's perspective, it is to decide who will govern for the next four years. Naturally, throughout the campaign there is considerable interest in what the probable results will be.

Prior to the election, pollsters take the pulse of the electorate. Those who work for the candidates do so to help the campaigns adjust and target appeals. Those who work for the media do so to provide news on the horse race and to forecast the results.

Since 1916 there have been nationwide surveys of public sentiment during the campaign. However, some of the early polls did not accurately forecast the results. The most notable gaffes occurred in 1936 and 1948, when major surveys predicted that Alfred M. Landon and Thomas E. Dewey would win. The principal reasons that these surveys were incorrect were that they concluded their polling too far before election day and that the people interviewed were not randomly selected. These problems were subsequently corrected, and more recently preelection polls at the end of the campaign have closely reflected the popular vote (see Table 3-4).

The final surveys are published before the election. They indicate the likely outcome, but they are not the final forecast. That comes on election night and is done by the major news networks. They, too, survey voters but do so after they cast their ballots. The networks have two principal objectives in conducting these final exit polls: to forecast accurately the winner of the election ahead of the other networks and to explain the principal reasons for the result.

Here's how they work. A large number of precincts across the country are randomly selected. Representatives of the media, often college students, interview voters as they leave the polls. The interview is intended to measure the beliefs and attitudes of the electorate. In the course of the interview, each voter is asked to complete a printed ballot and deposit it into a sealed box. Throughout the day, these ballots are collected and tabulated and the results are telephoned to a central computer bank. After the election in a state has been completed, the findings of the poll are broadcast.

These early forecasts have engendered considerable controversy. Since the country is divided into separate time zones, projections of the results in the East and Midwest are known before voting is concluded in the Rocky Mountain and Pacific Coast states and in Alaska and Hawaii. At issue is whether these early projections affect that late voting. Although the evidence is not conclusive, it does suggest a slight decline in turnout but little vote switching as a consequence of these forecasts.[20]

The issue was raised in 1980 but with a slightly different twist. When the early returns and private polls indicated a Reagan landslide, President Carter appeared before his supporters at 8:30 P.M. Eastern Standard Time, while polls were still open in most parts of the country, and acknowledged defeat. His concession speech, carried live on each of the major networks, incurred extensive criticism, particularly from defeated West Coast Democrats. They alleged that the president's remarks discouraged many Democrats from voting, thereby contributing to their defeat as well. However, it is difficult to substantiate this claim. In gen-

Table 3-4. Final Preelection Polls and Results, 1948–1988

Year	Gallup Poll	Roper, CBS/NYT Polls[†]	Harris Poll	Actual Results*
1948				
Truman	44.5	37.1		49.6
Dewey	49.5	52.2		45.1
Others	6.0	4.3		5.3
1952				
Eisenhower	51.0			55.1
Stevenson	49.0			44.4
1956				
Eisenhower	59.5	60.0		57.4
Stevenson	40.5	38.0		42.0
1960				
Kennedy	51.0	49.0		49.7
Nixon	49.0	51.0		49.5
1964				
Johnson	64.0		64.0	61.1
Goldwater	36.0		36.0	38.5
1968				
Nixon	43.0		41.0	43.4
Humphrey	42.0		45.0	42.7
Wallace	15.0		14.0	13.4
1972				
Nixon	62.0		61.0	60.7
McGovern	38.0		39.0	37.5
1976				
Carter	48.0	51.0	46.0	50.1
Ford	49.0	47.0	45.0	48.0
Others	3.0	2.0	3.0	1.9
Undecided			6.0	
1980				
Reagan	47.0		46.0	50.7
Carter	44.0		41.0	41.0
Anderson	8.0		10.0	6.6
Others				1.7
Undecided	1.0		3.0	
1984				
Reagan	59.0		56.0	59.0
Mondale	41.0		44.0	41.0
Others/Undecided			2.0	
1988				
Bush	53.0	48[†]	51.0	53.4
Dukakis	42.0	40	47.0	45.6
Others/Undecided	5.0	12	2.0	1.0

*Except in 1948, 1976, and 1980 the percentage of votes for minor candidates is not noted.
[†]For 1988, figures are from CBS/New York Times Poll; other figures are from Roper Polls.
Source: Final Gallup poll, "Record of Gallup Poll Accuracy," *Gallup Opinion Index*,
December 1988, p. 44.

eral, turnout declined more in the East and Midwest than it did in the Far West in 1980. Even if there was a decline after Carter's concession, there is little evidence to suggest that Democrats behaved any differently from Republicans and independents. Hawaii, the last state to close its polls, voted for Carter. Similarly, in 1988, despite the forecasts aired on all the major networks that Bush had won, three of the last four states to close their polls voted for Dukakis. Nonetheless, Congress is likely to establish a uniform time for the termination of voting in the continental United States for 1992.

Despite the criticism they have received, television networks are likely to continue to depend on exit polling because it provides a portrait of the electorate and usually contains a wealth of information about its political and ideological preferences, positions on issues, and evaluations of the candidate. This information may be correlated with demographic data to discern voting patterns and to infer the reasons for the vote (see Table 3-5, pages 80–82, for data on the 1988 electorate).

The problem with this type of analysis is that it is time-bound (election day) and limited to a portion of the electorate (those who vote before a certain hour in the key states). It does not permit inferences about the effect of the campaign on the electorate nor about changing patterns of public opinion. To make such inferences it is necessary to interview and reinterview the same voters. Since 1948, researchers of the University of Michigan have been collecting and analyzing data collected in this manner. Their studies have provided the most sophisticated understanding of voting behavior.

Analyzing the Results

The Michigan analysis is premised on the concept of a normal vote, the vote that could be expected if partisanship were the only influence on the voting decision. Of course, it is not the only influence. Short-range factors, such as the evaluation of the candidates and their ideology and positions on issues, interfere, reinforce, or supplement the electorate's partisan judgment. The object of the Michigan analysis is to identify these factors and their impact. In this way deviations from the expected or normal vote can be explained.

Beginning in the 1960s, partisan attitudes of the electorate began to weaken. Candidate and issue orientations became more important influences on the vote. According to the Michigan analysts, it was Kennedy's religion in 1960 that seemed to account for the closeness of the election. They estimate that he lost approximately 1.5 million popular votes because he was Catholic, although he might actually have benefitted in the Electoral College because of the concentration of Catholics in the large industrial states with the most electoral votes.[21]

In 1964, it was Goldwater's uncompromising ideology and positions on issues that helped provide Johnson with an overwhelming victory in all areas but the Deep South.[22] Moderate Republicans and independents voted more Democratic than usual that year. Four years later, however, it was defections from the Democratic party that spurred the Wallace third-party candidacy and contributed to Nixon's triumph. In 1972, the Democrats were again divided. Over 40 percent of those who identified with the Democratic party voted for Nixon as did 66 percent of the independents and most of the Republicans. The perception of McGovern as incompetent as well as ideologically to the left of his party contributed to the larger than normal Republican vote.[23]

Short-range factors regarding issues and candidates were also evident in 1976; but they were not of sufficient magnitude to offset the longer-term partisan inclinations of the electorate. Carter won in 1976 primarily because he was the majority party nominee and secondarily because he was from the South, the first Democrat to win the South since 1960.[24] He was also perceived as having greater potential for strong and effective leadership than his Republican opponent, President Gerald Ford.

In 1980, however, Carter lost despite the fact that he was a Democrat and because he was no longer seen as having that potential. His record as president doomed his candidacy. Reagan, in contrast, won in 1980 primarily because he was the option who had become acceptable. He did not win because of his ideology, his policy positions, or his personal appeal.[25] In the words of two election analysts, "[Reagan] was the least positively evaluated candidate elected to the presidency in the history of the national election studies which date back to 1952."[26] Nonetheless, it was Reagan who offered the potential for change. When judged against Carter's performance, this potential seemed more appealing to the electorate.

Four years later the voters rewarded President Reagan for what they considered to be a job well done. His 1984 victory was even more impressive. With 59 percent of the popular vote and 525 (out of 538) electoral votes, Reagan won in a referendum on his performance in office. The electorate voted *for* him in 1984 just as they had voted *against* Carter in 1980. He won not because he was a conservative, not because the public agreed with his policy positions on most issues, but because they approved of his leadership and wanted him to continue.

The 1988 election constituted still another referendum on the Reagan presidency, although obviously not on President Reagan. Vice President Bush benefitted from the public's perception of good times and greater national security. He won an impressive victory, receiving 53 percent of the popular vote and 426 electoral votes. His support was broad-based. Although he obtained majorities in all areas of the country, he did particularly well in the South, winning 58 percent of the vote there (see Table 3-5). Most of those who cast ballots for Reagan in 1984 continued to support Bush in 1988. The exceptions were Reagan Democrats, who preferred Dukakis by a slight margin.

As Table 3-5 indicates, ideology and party worked to reinforce voting patterns in 1988, with the Republican candidate, Bush, winning overwhelmingly among Republicans and conservatives and the Democratic candidate, Dukakis, doing almost as well among Democrats and as well among liberals. The problem for Dukakis, however—and any liberal Democrat for that matter—is that the Democratic proportion of the two-party vote has declined substantially since 1960, as has the percentage of the electorate that considers itself liberal. Among self-declared independents, Bush enjoyed a solid lead (12 percent).

In addition to ideology and party, the 1988 vote (as reflected in the CBS News–N.Y.Times exit poll) also evidences clear class distinctions. Bush did better among the more privileged, establishment groups, among white-collar workers, and among those who were better educated (except for people with postgraduate education). Dukakis maintained the traditional support Democrats receive from those in the lower economic, educational, and social groupings.

Finally, race and gender differences continued to persist in presidential politics, although generational differences were somewhat muted. The Republican candidate received a predominantly white vote with substantially more support from men than from women. Youth, however—who preferred Reagan by substantial margins in 1984—divided their votes more evenly in 1988, with Bush enjoying a modest advantage. The Democratic candidate did best with the oldest age group, a legacy of the Roosevelt Revolution when the Democrats became the majority party. He also did well among minority racial groups, particularly African-Americans and Hispanics.

The voting patterns in 1988 suggest a continuation of the trends that have characterized presidential voting in the last two decades. They show the declining influence of partisanship. No longer is a unified dominant party sufficient to dictate the outcome. For the presidency, the critical factors remain economic, social, and national security conditions and how those conditions reflect on the demonstrated or potential leadership qualifications of the candidates. In 1988 those conditions in the aggregate were seen as favorable by a majority of the voters. Over the course of the campaign they helped shape the perception that the incumbent vice president, Bush, was more experienced, competent, and personally caring than his Democratic challenger, Dukakis, and more likely to maintain the perceived gains of the previous eight years. For most Republican and many independent voters, for most of those who had prospered during the Reagan presidency, for those who believed in the values that the Republicans and their candidates articulated—personal security; individual economic freedom; and God, family, and country—the Bush campaign struck a responsive cord. That is why Bush won the election.

Table 3-5. Portrait of the Electorate

% of 1988 Total		Vote in 1980			Vote in 1984		Vote in 1988	
		Reagan	Carter	Anderson	Reagan	Mondale	Bush	Dukakis
—	TOTAL	51%	41%	7%	59%	40%	53%	45%
48	Men	55	36	7	62	37	57	41
52	Women	47	45	7	56	44	50	49
85	Whites	55	36	7	64	35	59	40
10	Blacks	11	85	3	9	89	12	86
3	Hispanics	35	56	8	37	61	30	69
69	Married	—	—	—	62	38	57	42
31	Not married	—	—	—	52	46	46	53
20	18–29 years old	43	44	11	59	40	52	47
35	30–44 years old	54	36	8	57	42	54	45
22	45–59 years old	55	39	5	59	39	57	42
22	60 and older	54	41	4	60	39	50	49
8	Not a high school graduate	46	51	2	49	50	43	56
27	High school graduate	51	43	4	60	39	50	49
30	Some college education	55	35	8	61	37	57	42
35	College graduate or more	52	35	11	58	41	56	43
19	College graduate	—	—	—	—	—	62	37
16	Postgraduate education	—	—	—	—	—	50	48

Table 3-5. (continued)

% of 1988 Total		Vote in 1980			Vote in 1984		Vote in 1988	
		Reagan	Carter	Anderson	Reagan	Mondale	Bush	Dukakis
—	TOTAL	51%	41%	7%	59%	40%	53%	45%
48	White Protestant	63	31	6	72	27	66	33
28	Catholic	49	42	7	54	45	52	47
4	Jewish	39	45	15	31	67	35	64
9	White fundamentalist or evangelical Christian	63	33	3	78	22	81	18
25	Union household	43	48	6	46	53	42	57
12	Family income under $12,500	42	51	6	45	54	37	62
20	$12,500–$24,999	44	46	7	57	42	49	50
20	$25,000–$34,999	52	39	7	59	40	56	44
20	$35,000–$49,999	59	32	8	66	33	56	42
24	$50,000 and over	63	26	9	69	30	62	37
19	$50,000–$100,000	—	—	—	—	—	61	38
5	Over $100,000	—	—	—	—	—	65	32
25	From the East	47	42	9	52	47	50	49
28	From the Midwest	51	40	7	58	40	52	47
28	From the South	52	44	3	64	36	58	41
19	From the West	53	34	10	61	38	52	46
35	Republicans	86	8	4	93	6	91	8
37	Democrats	26	67	6	24	75	17	82
26	Independents	55	30	12	63	35	55	43

Table 3-5. (continued)

% of 1988 Total		Vote in 1980			Vote in 1984		Vote in 1988	
		Reagan	Carter	Anderson	Reagan	Mondale	Bush	Dukakis
—	TOTAL	51%	41%	7%	59%	40%	53%	45%
18	Liberals	25	60	11	28	70	18	81
45	Moderates	48	42	8	53	47	49	50
33	Conservatives	72	23	4	82	17	80	19
31	Professional or manager	57	32	9	62	37	59	40
11	White-collar worker	50	41	8	59	40	57	42
13	Blue-collar worker	47	46	5	54	45	49	50
4	Full-time student	—	—	—	52	47	44	54
5	Teacher	46	42	10	51	48	47	51
5	Unemployed	39	51	8	32	67	37	62
10	Homemaker	—	—	—	61	38	58	41
2	Agricultural worker	36	59	4	—	—	55	44
16	Retired	—	—	—	60	40	50	49

Note: 1988 data based on questionnaires completed by 11,645 voters leaving polling places around the nation on election day. 1984 data based on questionnaire from 9,174 voters; 1980 data based on questionnaires from 15,201 voters. Those who gave no answer are not shown. Dashes indicate that a question was not asked in a particular year.

Family income categories in 1980: Under $10,000, $10,000–14,999, $15,000–24,999, $25,000–49,999 and $50,000 and over. "Fundamentalist or evangelical Christian" was labeled "born-again Christian" in 1980 and 1984. Male and female college graduates include postgraduate education.

Source: "Portrait of the Electorate," from *The New York Times*, November 10, 1988, p. B6.

Assessing the Mandate

Despite the many postelection analyses conducted by political scientists, journalists, and politicians, the meaning of the election results often remains unclear. The reasons that people vote for a president vary. Some do so because of his party, some because of his stands on issues, some because of their assessment of his potential or his performance. For most, a combination of factors contributes to their voting decision. This combination makes it difficult to discern exactly what the electorate means, desires, or envisions by its electoral choice. The president is rarely given a clear mandate for governing.

Assuming that party is a principal influence on voting behavior, what cues can a president cull from his political connection? Party platforms frequently contain a laundry list of positions and proposals, but there are problems in using them as a guide for the new administration. The presidential candidate may not agree with all the positions taken.

THE MANDATE

Source: Copyright 1988 *The Times*. Reprinted by permission of Los Angeles Times Syndicate.

He may have had to accept certain compromises in the interests of party unity. Platforms are not prioritized. Yet, presidents must assert priorities if they are to govern successfully.

Besides the platform, are there any other partisan indicators to which a president might look for guidance? The parties' electoral images—the Democrats' in domestic affairs and the Republicans' in foreign affairs—suggest broad emphases but not precise directions. The positions on issues and voter evaluations of the candidates are also important, but neither offers detailed guides to agenda building. While pollsters can discern a mood or even a range of views, they have difficulty assessing the intensity of public opinions, much less evaluating what it all means. Not only do people with similar attitudes and beliefs vote for a candidate for different reasons, but people with very different attitudes and beliefs vote for the same candidate. In short, the campaign may identify problems, but the vote rarely points to specific solutions.

Instead of looking to the electorate for direction, successful candidates tend to look to themselves and their campaigns. They should. Throughout the election period they set the tone and make the appeals they wish to present to the voters.

Unfortunately, the promises and positions of the candidates generate diverse expectations which are difficult to fulfill. Kennedy pledged to get the country moving again; Johnson to continue the momentum and create a Great Society; Nixon to bring a divided nation together; Carter to provide a more honest, open, responsive leadership; Reagan to assume a new, steadier course in economic and foreign affairs; and Bush to maintain peace and prosperity. Moreover, by their ambiguity candidates encourage voters to see what they want to see and believe what they want to believe. This naturally results in disillusionment once a new president begins making decisions. The broader the electoral coalition, the more likely that some will be disappointed.

Finally, the campaign's emphasis on personal and institutional leadership also inflates expectations. By creating impressions of assertiveness, decisiveness, and potency, candidates help shape public expectations of their performance in office. Jimmy Carter contributed to the decline in his own popularity by promising more than he could deliver. Carter's problem was not unique to his presidency.

Converting the Electoral Coalition for Governance

Not only does the selection process inflate performance expectations and create a set of diverse policy goals, it also lessens the president's power to achieve them. His political muscle has been weakened by the decline in the power of party leaders and the growth of autonomous state and congressional electoral systems.

In the past, the state party organizations were the principal units for conducting the general election campaign. Today, they are not. In the past, partisan ties united legislative and executive officials more than they currently do.

Today, the process has become highly personalized. Candidates create their own organizations and mount their own campaigns, but they pay a price for this independence. To put it simply, it makes governing more difficult. The electoral process provides the president with fewer political allies in the states and in Congress. It makes his partisan appeal less effective. It fractionalizes the bases of his support.

The establishment of candidate campaign organizations and the use of out-of-state coordinators have weakened the parties, creating competition, not cooperation, within them. The competition cannot help but deplete the natural reservoir of partisan support a president needs to tap once in office.

Moreover, the democratization of the selection process has also resulted in the separation of state, congressional, and presidential elections. In the aftermath of Watergate, Jimmy Carter made much of the fact that he did not owe his nomination to the power brokers within his party or his election to them or to members of Congress. But the same can be said for members of Congress and, for that matter, governors and state legislators. Presidents are not indebted to them nor are they indebted to presidents. The increasing independence of Congress decreases legislators' political incentives to follow the president's lead.

The magnitude of the president's problem is compounded by public expectations of his leadership. Yet that leadership is difficult to achieve because of the constitutional and political separation of institutions. Thus, the weakening of party ties during the electoral process carries over to the governing process, with adverse consequences for the president.

Finally, personality politics has produced factions within the parties. It has created a fertile environment for the growth of interest group pressures. Without strong party leaders to act as brokers and referees, groups vie for the candidate's attention and favor during the campaign and for the president's after the election is over. This group struggle provides a natural source of opposition and support for almost any presidential action or proposal. It enlarges the arena of policy making and contributes to the multiplicity of forces that converge on most presidential decisions.

What is a president to do? How can he meet public expectations in light of the weakening of partisanship and the increased sharing of policy-making powers? How can a president lead, achieve, and satisfy pluralistic interests at the same time?

Obviously, there is no set formula for success. Forces beyond the president's control may affect the course of events. Nonetheless, the president must exercise as strong political leadership as possible. He must establish his own priorities and thereby shape public expectations of what he hopes to do. He must take advantage of opportunities, particularly in the period following the election. He must construct his own policy alliances and thereby actualize potential supporters. In doing so he must articulate his appeal clearly and convey it effectively to the general and specialized publics.

With fewer natural allies, declines in popularity are practically inevitable and usually more serious. They detract from the president's ability to accomplish his goals. The growing influence of personality on people and events makes the president's job much tougher. As a consequence, during ordinary times he is forced to be a facilitator even though he might prefer to be a director of change.

CONCLUSION

The system of election designed by the framers of the Constitution has been substantially modified over the years. Theoretically the Electoral College continues to select the president, but in practice the popular vote, aggregated by states, decides the outcome.

During much of America's electoral history political parties were the principal link between candidates and the voters. They chose the nominees, organized their campaigns, mobilized their support, and stood to gain if they were elected. Moreover, partisan attitudes conditioned the perceptions and voting behavior of much of the electorate.

This has changed. Today there are more mediators and more mediums. Party professionals are less important but campaign professionals are more important. Pollsters, grass-roots organizers, and media experts now plan and run the campaigns. They discern attitudes, design and project appeals, target voters, and mobilize what they hope will be a winning coalition. They utilize the techniques of market research and the vehicles of the modern electronic age. Radio, television, direct mail, and phone banks have become the principal ways to reach voters. The influence of the party has suffered as a consequence.

The presidential campaign has become more candidate oriented. It is the candidates who now create their organizations, receive federal funds, and mount highly personalized appeals. Moreover, the electorate's personal evaluation of the candidates plays an increasingly important role in their voting decision.

This personalization of the presidential selection process has serious implications for the exercise of presidential leadership. It tends to inflate public expectations yet reduce the capacity to achieve them. The president is more on his own. His electoral coalition is not easily converted into a governing coalition. This, in turn, has forced presidents and their staffs to devote more time, energy, and resources to mobilizing and maintaining outside support, to controlling the media's focus, and to worrying about reelection.

The relationship between president and public has more influence on the presidency and the policy-making process than it has had in the past. We will examine that influence in the next two chapters.

NOTES

1. The initial solution to this problem was to grant the president a long term of office but make him ineligible for reelection. This, however, created an additional dilemma. It provided little incentive for the president to perform well and denied the country the possibility of reelecting a person whose experience and success in office might make him better qualified than anyone else. Reflecting on these concerns, delegate Gouverneur Morris urged the removal of the ineligibility clause on the grounds that it "intended to destroy the great motive to good behavior, the hope of being rewarded by a reappointment" (Gouverneur Morris, *Records of the Federal Convention*, ed. Max Farrand [New Haven: Yale University Press, 1921], 2: 33).

2. So great was the sectional rivalry, so parochial the country, so limited the number of people with national reputations, that it was feared that electors would tend to vote primarily for those from their own states. To prevent the same states, particularly the largest ones, from exercising undue influence in the selection of both the president and vice president, this provision was included. It remains in effect today.

3. The most populous state at the time, New York, did not permit its electorate to participate in the selection of electors. Moreover, in three of the states in which Jackson won the electoral vote but lost in the House of Representatives, he had fewer popular votes than Adams. He captured the majority of electoral votes in two of these states because the electors were chosen on a district rather than statewide basis (William R. Keech, "Background Paper," in *Winner Take All: Report of the Twentieth Century Fund Task Force on Reform of the Presidential Election Process* [New York: Holmes and Meier, 1978], p. 50).

4. Much of this research has been under the direction of the Center for Political Studies at the University of Michigan. Starting in 1952, it began conducting nationwide surveys during presidential elections. The object of these surveys was to identify the major influences on voting behavior. A random sample of the electorate was interviewed before and after the election. Respondents were asked a series of questions designed to reveal their attitudes toward the parties, candidates, and issues. On the basis of the answers, researchers constructed a model to explain voting behavior and presented it in a book entitled *The American Voter.* Published in 1960, this very important work contained both theoretical formulations and empirical findings. See Angus Campbell et al., *The American Voter* (New York: Wiley, 1960).

5. Data for 1988 are from combined surveys for Americans Talk Security, from January to June 1988, as published in *Public Opinion* 11 (September/October 1988): 34.

6. Raymond E. Wolfinger and Steven J. Rosenstone, *Who Votes?* (New Haven: Yale University Press, 1980), pp. 13–26.

7. Ruy A. Teixeira, "Registration and Turnout" *Public Opinion* 11 (January/February 1989): 57.

8. Wolfinger and Rosenstone. *Who Votes?*, p. 73; see Ruy A. Teixeira, "Will the Real Voter Please Stand Up?" *Public Opinion* 11 (July/August 1988): 41–44 for the challenge.

9. Richard L. Berke, "Study Finds Marked Drop in Voter Registration Since 1984," *The New York Times*, November 4, 1988, p. A20.

10. Thomas Patterson, "Television and Election Strategy," in Gerald Benjamin, ed., *The Communications Revolution in Politics* (New York: Academy of Political Science, 1982), pp. 27–28.

11. S. Robert Lichter, Daniel Amundson, and Richard E. Noyes, "Election 88: Media Coverage," *Public Opinion* 11 (January/February 1989): 18.

12. Ibid.: 19.

13. Paul Lazarsfeld, Bernard Berelson, and Hazel Goudet, *The People's Choice* (New York: Columbia University Press, 1948); Bernard Berelson, Paul Lazarsfeld, and William McPhee, *Voting: A Study of Opinion Formation in a Presidential Campaign* (Chicago: University of Chicago Press, 1954).

14. Michael J. Robinson and Margaret A. Sheehan, *Over the Wire and on TV: CBS and UPI in Campaign '80* (New York: Russell Sage Foundation, 1983), p. 9.

15. Thomas E. Patterson and Robert D. McClure, *The Unseeing Eye* (New York: Putnam, 1976), p. 58.

16. Ibid., p. 54.

17. William J. Bryan, *The First Battle* (Port Washington, N.Y.: Kennikat Press, 1971), p. 618.

18. One reason that Roosevelt initiated the whistle-stop tour in 1932 was to overcome the whispering campaign about his physical condition. Roosevelt had been crippled by polio. To demonstrate that he was not confined to a wheelchair, he appeared standing up when he addressed groups.

19. Elihu Katz and Jacob J. Feldman, "The Debates in the Light of Research: A Survey of Surveys," in Sidney Kraus, ed., *The Great Debates* (Bloomington: Indiana University Press, 1962), p. 190.

20. In a 1964 survey of approximately 1,700 registered voters in California, Harold Mendelsohn found that few watched the early broadcasts and then voted. Most voted first. The impact of the early broadcasts on those who saw them and then cast ballots was about the same for supporters of Johnson and Goldwater (Harold Mendelsohn and Irving Crespi, *Polls, Television, and the New Politics* [Scranton, Pa.: Chandler, 1970], pp. 234–36). A similar study of the 1968 election conducted by other researchers arrived at a similar conclusion. (Sam Tuchman and Thomas E. Coffin, "The Influence of Election Night Television Broadcasts in a Close Election," *Public Opinion Quarterly* 35 [1971]: 315–26). However, in the 1972 election, political scientists Raymond Wolfinger and Peter Linquiti concluded that there was a small decline in the West Coast vote after the Nixon victory had been predicted (Raymond Wolfinger and Peter Linquiti, "Tuning In and Tuning Out," *Public Opinion* 4 [1981]: 57–59).

21. Philip E. Converse et al., "Stability and Change in 1960: A Reinstating Election," in Angus Campbell et al., *Elections and the Political Order* (New York: Wiley, 1966), p. 92.

22. Philip E. Converse, Aage R. Clausen, and Warren E. Miller, "Electoral Myth and Reality: The 1964 Election," *American Political Science Review* 59 (June 1965): 321–36.

23. Arthur H. Miller et al., "A Majority Party in Disarray: Policy Polarization in the 1972 Election" (paper presented at the Annual Meeting of the American Political Science Association, New Orleans, Louisiana, September 4–8, 1973).

24. Arthur H. Miller and Warren E. Miller, "Partisanship and Performance: Rational Choice in the 1976 Presidential Elections" (paper presented at the Annual Meeting of the American Political Science Association, Washington, D.C., September 1–4, 1977).

25. Arthur H. Miller and Martin P. Wattenberg, "Policy and Performance Voting in the 1980 Election" (paper delivered at the annual meeting of the American Political Science Association, New York, September 3–6, 1981), p. 15.

26. Ibid., p. 6.

SELECTED READINGS

Campbell, Angus, Philip E. Converse, Warren E. Miller, and Donald E. Stokes. *The American Voter.* New York: Wiley, 1960.

"Election '88." *Public Opinion* 11 (January/February 1989).

Garand, James C. "Localism and Regionalism in Presidential Elections: Is There a Home State or Regional Advantage?" *Western Political Quarterly* 41 (March 1988): 85–104.

Goldman, Peter, and Tony Fuller. *The Quest for the Presidency, 1984.* Toronto: Bantam, 1985.

Ladd, Everett Carll. "The 1988 Elections: Continuation of the Post–New Deal System." *Political Science Quarterly* 104 (1989): 1–18.

Ladd, Everett Carll, with Charles D. Hadley. *Transformations of the American Party System.* New York: Norton, 1975.

Marcus, George E. "The Structure of Emotional Response: 1984 Presidential Candidates." *American Political Science Review* 82 (1988): 737–761.

Miller, Arthur H., Martin P. Wattenberg, and Oksana Malanchuk. "Schematic Assessments of Presidential Candidates." *American Political Science Review* 80 (1986): 521–540.

Nelson, Michael, ed. *The Elections of 1988.* Washington, D.C.: Congressional Quarterly, 1989.

Nie, Norman H., Sidney Verba, and John R. Petrocik. *The Changing American Voter.* Cambridge, Mass.: Harvard University Press, 1976.

Patterson, Thomas E. *The Mass Media Election: How Americans Choose Their President.* New York: Praeger, 1980.

Pomper, Gerald M., et al. *The Election of 1988: Reports and Interpretations.* Chatham, N.J.: Chatham House, 1989.

Robinson, Michael J., and Margaret A. Sheehan. *Over the Wire and on TV: CBS and UPI in Campaign '80.* New York: Russell Sage Foundation, 1983.

Wayne, Stephen J. *The Road to the White House.* 3rd ed. New York: St. Martin's Press, 1988.

Wolfinger, Raymond E., and Steven J. Rosenstone. *Who Votes?* New Haven, Conn.: Yale University Press, 1980.

4

The President
and the Public

"Public sentiment is everything. With public sentiment nothing can fail, without it nothing can succeed." These words, spoken by Abraham Lincoln, pose what is perhaps the greatest challenge to any president: to obtain and maintain the public's support. As every student of the presidency quickly learns, the president is rarely in a position to command others to comply with his wishes. Instead, he must rely on persuasion. A principal source of influence for the president is public approval of his performance and his policies.

Presidents want both to please the public and to avoid irritating it. They also want to lead public opinion. Accomplishing these goals is premised to a large degree on knowing what the public is thinking. Gauging public opinion is a difficult task, however. Citizens' opinions on policy are often uncrystallized and lacking in coherence. Moreover, the tools available to measure public opinion, such as polls, the mail, and election results, are far from perfect and make it difficult to infer opinion on specific issues.

The president is in the limelight of American politics, and citizens come quite naturally to organize their political thinking and focus their hopes for the future around the White House. Although this attention provides the potential for presidential leadership of the public, it is purchased at a high cost. The public's expectations of the chief executive's policy performance, personal characteristics, and private behavior tend to be high. They are also often contradictory with regard to both policy and leadership style. It is quite clear that no leader can fully meet these expectations, yet they provide the context within which the president struggles to gain and maintain public support.

Probably the most visible political statistics in American life are the frequent measurements of the public's approval of the president. Political commentators duly note whether the president is doing better or worse than in the last poll (sort of a political batting average). But on what bases do people arrive at their evaluations of the president? Certain predispositions in the public, such as party affiliation and the positivity bias (a proclivity to evaluate people favorably), provide an important component of the explanation of presidential approval. Job-related personal characteristics and the president's handling of, and stands on, the issues are also important. On the other hand, the president's personality and the personal effects and short-run success of policies play a less important role.

Presidents are not passive followers of public opinion. In the words of Franklin Roosevelt, "All our great Presidents were *leaders* of thought at times when certain historic ideas in the life of the nation had to be clarified." His cousin, Theodore Roosevelt, had earlier observed: "People used to say of me that I . . . divined what the people were going to think. I did not 'divine.' . . . I simply made up my mind what they ought to think, and then did my best to get them to think it."[1] Throughout almost the entirety of Ronald Reagan's tenure in office, polls showed that the public wanted to lower the federal deficit and did not want to cut social programs. They were willing to decrease planned military spending to accomplish these goals. The president refused to go along.

Presidents offer several rationales for not following public opinion. President Nixon claimed he was not really acting contrary to public opinion at all but rather he represented the "silent majority" that did not express its opinion in activist politics. Similarly, presidents may argue that their actions are on behalf of underrepresented groups, such as the poor or an ethnic minority. The extreme case of this technique, of course, is for a president to say that he is representing a future (probably unborn) generation. This kind of rationale is used today on behalf of environmental and energy policies designed to save natural resources for the future population. Presidents have also wrapped themselves in the mantle of the courageous stateman following his principles and fighting the tides of public opinion.

Whatever the reasons given, presidents have generally not been content only to follow public opinion on issues or to let their approval ratings reach some "natural" level. Instead, they usually have engaged in substantial efforts to lead the public. Sometimes their goals have been to gain long-term support for themselves, while at other times they have been more interested in obtaining support for a specific program. Often both goals are present.

Moving the public provides one of the clearest tests of presidential leadership. The president as director establishes the national agenda and creates a constituency to follow his lead. The president as facilitator, on the other hand, reflects and perhaps intensifies widely held views. His challenge is to channel an already existing tide of public opinion to achieve his goals.

In this chapter we explore the president's attempts to understand public opinion and the public's expectations and evaluations of him. We are interested in both the nature of the attitudes the public has and, even more important, *why* it holds them. Such study will deepen our understanding not only of expectations and evaluations but of the obstacles the White House faces in measuring public opinion. We also examine presidential efforts to influence public opinion, including appealing directly to the public, controlling information, employing symbols, and engaging in public relations activities. We do not assume, of course, that presidents are always successful in influencing the public. Thus, we are equally concerned with the effectiveness of the various techniques of opinion leadership presidents use.

UNDERSTANDING PUBLIC OPINION

Presidents need public support, and understanding public opinion can be a considerable advantage to them in gaining and maintaining it. At the very least, presidents want to avoid needlessly antagonizing the public. Thus, presidents need reliable estimates of public reactions to the actions they are contemplating. It is equally useful for presidents to know what actions and policies, either symbolic or substantive, the public wants. No politician wants to overlook opportunities to please constituents and, perhaps even more significant, to avoid frustrating them. By knowing what the public desires, a president may use his discretion to gain its favor when he feels the relevant actions or policies are justified.

In addition, presidents often want to lead public opinion to support them and their policies. To do this they need to know the views of various segments of the public, whom they need to influence and on what issues, and how far people can be moved. Presidents usually do not want to use their limited resources on hopeless ventures. Nor do they want to be too far ahead of the public. If they are, they risk losing their followers and alienating segments of the population.

Americans' Opinions

Before a president can understand what opinions the public holds, citizens must have opinions. Although Americans are usually willing to express opinions on a wide variety of issues, we generally cannot interpret their responses as reflecting crystallized and coherent views. Citizens' opinions are often rife with contradictions, because they fail to give their views much thought and do not consider the implications of their policy stands for other issues. For example, national polls show consistently that the American people place a very high priority on balancing the budget. At the same time, majorities favor maintaining or increasing spending on virtually every component of public policy, but they also oppose increasing taxes.[2]

Policy making is a very complex enterprise, and most voters do not have the time, expertise, or inclination to think extensively about most issues, especially those as distant from their everyday experiences as federal regulations, nuclear strategy, and bureaucratic reorganizations. After years of fighting and political controversy, a majority of Americans still do not know which side the United States supports in Nicaragua.[3] The major domestic policy initiative of Ronald Reagan's second term was tax reform. Yet as the bill was nearing the end of its legislative path in the Senate, only 40 percent of the people had heard or read even "some" about it.[4]

In short, anyone attempting to understand American public opinion operates under the handicap that many people do not have opinions on issues of significance to the president, and many of the opinions that the public expresses are neither crystallized, coherent, nor informed. Nevertheless, sometimes opinions are widely held, such as on issues that touch the public directly like economic conditions and civil rights. Moreover, the president may desire to know the distribution of the opinions that do exist. Under these circumstances, what means can the president rely upon to measure public opinion?

Public Opinion Polls

One common tool for measuring public attitudes is public opinion polls. Whether they are commissioned on behalf of the White House or by various components of the mass media, they allow the president to learn how a cross section of the population feels about a specific policy, conditions in their lives, or his performance in office.

In an attempt to understand public opinion on matters of special concern to them, recent presidents have commissioned their own polls. Franklin D. Roosevelt was the first president to pay much attention to polls, which were just being scientifically developed during his tenure in office. Presidents Johnson, Nixon, Ford, Carter, and Reagan all retained private polling firms to provide them with soundings of American public opinion. In the last three administrations, pollsters have also played a large role as high-level political advisers. President Bush went so far as to offer his campaign pollster, Robert Teeter, the position of deputy White House chief of staff.

Despite their widespread use in the modern White House, public opinion polls are not completely dependable instruments for measuring public opinion. An important limitation of polls is that questions usually do not attempt to measure the intensity with which opinions are held. People with intense views will probably be more likely to act on those views to reward or punish politicians than people who state a preference but for whom the issue is incidental and a matter of indifference.

A related problem with polls is that the questions asked of the public seldom mesh with the decisions that a president faces. He rarely considers issues in the "yes/no" terms presented by most polls. Evidence of widespread support for a program does not indicate how the public stands on most of the specific provisions under consideration. Yet such details do not lend themselves to mass polling, because they require specialized knowledge that few Americans possess.

Another problem with polls is that responses may reflect the particular wording of the choices presented to citizens, especially for those people who lack crystallized opinions on issues. If questions are of the "agree/disagree" variety, there is a bias toward the "agree" alternative. If the "official" government position is indicated in a question, this often elicits a bias toward that position, especially on foreign policy issues. Public attitudes toward China softened considerably after the president began making overtures toward establishing relations with the People's Republic.

On policies that are very controversial, it may be impossible to ascertain public attitudes without some "contamination" by the use of "loaded" symbols in the questions. When people were asked in a poll whether federal "welfare" programs should be turned over to state and local governments, 39 percent replied in the affirmative. In a survey the following month only 15 percent favored turning over federal programs for "aid to the needy" to state and local governments.[5]

A final limitation of polls from the president's perspective is that, unless he or his party pays for them, polls are not taken at his convenience. If opinion on an issue is measured at all, it is likely to be a one-time measurement, so the president will not be able to learn of changes in public opinion. Thus, the president cannot rely upon public polls to inform him of what the public is thinking on a given issue at a particular time.

Questions that inevitably arise when discussing presidents and polls include the following: How should presidents use public opinion data? Does use of these data constrain presidents rather than indicate where their persuasive efforts should be focused? Do presidents, in effect, substitute followership for leadership?

Presidents ritually deny that their decisions are influenced by polls. According to President Carter's chief media adviser, Gerald Rafshoon, "If we ever went into the president's office and said, 'We think you ought to do this or that to increase your standing in the polls,' he'd throw us out." Instead of using polls to determine his policies, Carter used them to measure how effective he was in getting his message across to the public and to determine the obstacles in his path.[6]

Other presidents have also claimed that they have not been captives of public opinion polls, but all recent presidents have used polls in their efforts to lead. More than any other administration, the Reagan White House used polling in its decision-making process. Reagan's pollster, Richard Wirthlin, took polls every three or four weeks for the president (more often during a crisis) and met regularly with him and his top aides. Wirthlin's goal was to determine when the nation's mood was amenable to the president's proposals and what its reactions were to the president's actions. Bush's pollster, Robert Teeter, is performing similar functions. The White House wants the timing of the presidential agenda to be compatible with the political climate to maximize the probabilities of achieving the president's objectives.[7]

Presidential Election Results

If presidents cannot always rely on polls to inform them about public opinion, theoretically they can gain valuable insights through interpretation of their own electoral support. In other words, perhaps they can learn what voters are thinking when they cast their ballots for president. Before such an approach can be useful for a president seeking to understand public opinion, the following conditions must be met:

1. Voters must have opinions of policies.
2. Voters must know candidates' stands on the issues.
3. The candidates that voters support must offer them the alternatives they desire.
4. There must be a large turnout.
5. Voters must vote on the basis of issues.
6. The president must be able to correlate voter support with voters' policy views.

As we saw in Chapter 3, these conditions rarely occur, making presidential election results a tenuous basis for interpreting public opinion.

Mail from the Public

The mail is another potential means for the president to learn about public opinion. Although estimates vary and record keeping is inconsistent, there can be no doubt that the White House receives a tremendous volume of communications from the public. President Reagan received more than 4,500 letters daily.[8] Naturally, a president can read only a negligible percentage of this avalanche of messages. The White House staff screens the mail and keeps a log that summarizes opinion on critical issues. Correspondence that requires a response is forwarded to relevant agencies.

The president usually reads only a few items from a day's mail, and these are communications from personal friends, prominent and influential citizens, and interest group leaders. He may answer a few letters from ordinary citizens, primarily as a public relations gesture. President Reagan received a handful of letters every couple of weeks and the overall numbers, pro and con, on relevant issues. Mail from important individuals and organizations the president wants to rebuff is usually answered by his top assistants.

Even if the president could read more mail, it would not necessarily provide a useful guide to what the public is thinking about policy issues, since most of the mail does not focus on the issues with which the president must deal. In addition, those who communicate with the White House are not a cross section of the American people. They overrepresent the middle and upper classes and people who agree with the president.

Understanding Public Opinion in Perspective

Presidents find it difficult to understand public opinion. There is potential for slippage between what the public wants, what it is understood to want, and what it receives. There is also the possibility that the president will exceed the boundaries of what the public finds acceptable. There is no lack of examples of the White House being surprised by public reaction to events and presidential actions. These range from President Nixon's decision to invade Cambodia in 1970 to Ronald Reagan's efforts to halt increases in social security benefits in 1981.[9]

Even if presidents feel (or at least *say*) they understand public opinion on a particular issue, they do not necessarily follow it. A typical line in a presidential address to the nation on a specific issue goes something like, "Although the action I am taking may be unpopular, I am doing what I feel is in the best interests of the country." For example, in a speech on the invasion of Cambodia in 1970, President Nixon stated:

> I would rather be a one-term president and do what I believe is right than to be a two-term president at the cost of seeing America become a second-rate power and to see this nation accept the first defeat in its proud 190-year history.[10]

As we said earlier, presidents often feel, with good reason, that they know more about policy than most members of the public and that they sometimes have to lead public opinion instead of merely following it. Gerald Ford expressed this view:

> I do not think a President should run the country on the basis of the polls. The public in so many cases does not have a full comprehension of a problem. A President ought to listen to the people, but he cannot make hard decisions just by reading the polls once a week. It just does not work, and what the President ought to do is make the hard decisions and then go out and educate the people on why a decision that was necessarily unpopular was made.[11]

PUBLIC EXPECTATIONS OF THE PRESIDENT

When a new president assumes his responsibilities as chief executive, he enters into a set of relationships, the contours of which are largely beyond his control. The nations with which he will negotiate, the Congress he must persuade, and the bureaucracy he is to manage, for example, have well-established routines and boundaries within which they function. These set the context of the president's relationships with them.

Public evaluations of the president also occur within an established environment: public expectations. The public has demanding expectations of what the president should be, how he should act, and what his policies should accomplish. It is up to him to live up to these expectations. Although some presidents may succeed over time in educating the public to alter their expectations, the public's views change slowly and usually the changes that take place only create additional burdens for the president. In addition, the static nature of the president's personal characteristics and leadership style and the American political system's inherent constraints on his power and capacity to choose the most effective policies limit his ability to meet the public's expectations. Frustration on the part of both the president and the public is inevitable in such a situation.

High Expectations

The public's expectations of the president in the area of policy are substantial and include his ensuring peace, prosperity, and security. Table 4-1 shows the results of polls taken in December 1976 and 1980 following the elections of Presidents Carter and Reagan, respectively.

Table 4-1. Early Expectations of Presidents Carter and Reagan

	% Feel Can Expect	
Policy	Carter	Reagan
Reduce unemployment	72%	69%
Reduce inflation	*	66
Reduce cost of government	59	70
Increase government efficiency	81	89
Deal effectively with foreign policy	79	77
Strengthen national defense	81	76

'Not available.

Source: "Early Expectations: Comparing Chief Executives," *Public Opinion*, February/March 1981, p. 39.

Performance expectations of each president are quite high and cover a broad range of policy areas. We want the good life, and we look to the president to provide it.

Later in this book we will see that the president's influence on public policy and its consequences is quite limited most of the time. Nevertheless, the public holds the president responsible for them anyway. To quote President Carter: "When things go bad you [the president] get entirely too much blame. And I have to admit that when things go good, you get entirely too much credit."[12] Since conditions emphasized in the press seem to be bad more than good, it is usually blame that presidents receive.

In addition to expecting successful policies from the White House, Americans expect their presidents to be extraordinary individuals. (This, of course, buttresses the public's policy expectations). The public desires the president to be honest, intelligent, cool in a crisis, caring, competent, and to possess a sense of humor. Substantial percentages also want him to have imagination and charisma. Obviously, it is not easy to meet these expectations, and, as we have seen, presidents are watched very carefully to see whether they do.

The public not only has high expectations for the president's official performance but also lofty expectations for his private behavior. Substantial percentages of the population strongly object if the president engages in behavior that is very common in American society. For example, when the Watergate tapes revealed that President Nixon frequently used profane and obscene language in his private conversations, many Americans were outraged. The public demands that the president's public and private life be exemplary.

In addition, there is a substantial gap between the expectations the public has of what the president should accomplish (and for which it will hold him accountable) and the degree of success the public expects the president to have in meeting its expectations. For example, at the time George Bush took office, half the people expected him to be an "outstanding" or "above average" president, and 68 percent were optimistic about the next four years with him in the White House (almost exactly the same results found in 1977 and 1981 for Carter and Reagan, respectively). At the same time, over 70 percent of the people felt he would not keep his campaign promise not to raise taxes, 75 percent did not expect him to balance the budget within four years, and majorities did not expect him to reduce homelessness or the drug problem significantly.[13] The fact that the juxtaposition of these views might be unfair to the president does not seem to disturb many of his constituents.

The tenacity with which Americans maintain high expectations of the president may be due in large part to the encouragement they receive from presidential candidates to do so. The extremely lengthy process by which Americans select their presidents lends itself to political hyperbole. For one year out of every four, the public is enticed to expect more from the president than it is currently receiving. Evidently they take this rhetoric to heart and hold presidents to ever higher standards, independent of the reasonableness of these expectations.

High expectations of presidents are also supported by political socialization; schoolchildren are often taught American history organized by presidential eras. Implicit in much of this teaching is the view that great presidents were largely responsible for the freedom and prosperity Americans enjoy. From such lessons it is a short step to presuming that contemporary presidents can be wise and effective leaders and, therefore, that the public should expect them to be so. Furthermore, commentators may compare contemporary presidents to an ideal president, compounded out of the strongest attributes of their predecessors.

Yet another factor encouraging high expectations of the White House is the prominence of the president. He is the nation's spokesman, the personification of the nation—the closet thing Americans have to a royal sovereign. Upon his election he and his family dominate the news in America. The president's great visibility naturally induces people to focus attention, and thus demands and expectations, upon him.

Related to the president's prominence is the tendency to personalize. Issues of public policy are often extremely complex. To simplify them, Americans tend to think of issues in terms of personalities, especially the president's. It is easier to blame a specific person for personal and societal problems than it is to analyze and comprehend the complicated mix of factors that really causes these problems. Similarly, it is easier to project frustrations onto a single individual than it is to deal with the contradictions and selfishness in people's own policy demands. At the midpoint of his term in office President Carter reflected: "I can see why it is difficult for a President to serve two terms. You are the personification of problems and when you address a problem even successfully you become identified with it."[14]

Part of the explanation for the public's high expectations of the president probably lies in its lack of understanding of the context in which the president functions. We shall see in later chapters that the president's basic power situation in the nation's constitutional system is one of weakness rather than strength. Yet this is widely misperceived by the public. In 1979, for example, only 36 percent of the people felt the president had too little power, and 49 percent felt his power was "just right."[15]

Do high expectations of the president affect the public's evaluations of his performance? Although we lack sufficient data to reach a definitive conclusion, there is reason to believe that they do. Sometimes the negative impact of high expectations in the public's support for the president is of the chief executive's own making. Jimmy Carter provides a good example of a president who was his own worst enemy in this regard. Both before and after taking office, he set very high standards for himself and his administration and assured the public that he would live up to them. Unfortunately, he was unable to keep many of his promises, such as balancing the budget and keeping his administration free from scandal.

We have, of course, no way to calculate precisely the influence of such unkept promises on the president's standing with the public, and none of them alone is probably of much significance. Yet their collective impact undoubtedly depresses the president's approval ratings because they help to undermine the aura of statesmanship and competence that attracted support in his election campaign. According to Richard Wirthlin, President Reagan's pollster, expectations are the ultimate source of public frustration.[16] Perhaps presidents should lower expectations, especially at the beginning of their terms, so they will not mortgage their reputation and prestige to nuances of governing they have not yet learned.

Contradictory Expectations

The contradictions in the public's expectations of the president present an additional obstacle to presidents in their efforts to gain public support. With contradictory expectations it is very difficult to escape criticism and loss of approval—no matter what they do.

Contradictory expectations of the president deal with either the content of policy or his style of performance. Our expectations of policy are confused and seemingly unlimited. We want low taxes and efficient government, yet we do not want a decrease in public services. We desire plentiful gasoline, but not at a higher price. We wish inflation to be controlled, but not at the expense of higher unemployment or interest rates. We yearn for a clean environment, yet we are anxious to have industrial development.

It is true, of course, that the public is not entirely to blame for holding these contradictory expectations. Presidential candidates often enthusiastically encourage voters to believe that they will produce the proverbial situation in which the people can have their cake and eat it, too. In the 1980 presidential campaign Ronald Reagan promised, among other things, to slash government expenditures, substantially reduce taxes, increase military spending, balance the budget, and maintain government services. In 1988 George Bush promised to reduce and eventually eliminate the budget deficit. He also promised not to raise taxes, weaken national defense, or reduce social services.

Expectations of the president's leadership style are also crucial in the public's evaluation of the president. People want a president who embodies a variety of traits, some of which are contradictory.

1. We expect the president to be a *leader*, an independent figure who speaks out and takes stands on the issues even if his views are

unpopular. We also expect the president to preempt problems by anticipating them before they arise. Similarly, we count on the president to provide novel solutions to the country's problems. To meet these expectations the president must be ahead of public opinion, acting on problems that may be obscure to the general populace and contributing ideas that are different from those currently in vogue in discussions of policy.

In sharp contrast to our expectations for presidential leadership are our expectations that the chief executive be *responsive* to public opinion and that he be constrained by majority rule as represented in Congress. The public overwhelmingly desires Congress to have final authority in policy disagreements with the president, and it does not want the president to be able to act against majority opinion.[17]

The contradictory expectations of leadership versus responsiveness place the president in a no-win situation. If he attempts to lead, he may be criticized for losing contact with his constituents and being unrepresentative. Conversely, if he tries to reflect the views of the populace, he may be reproached for failing to lead and for not solving the country's problems.

2. We expect our presidents to be open-minded politicians in the American tradition and thus exhibit *flexibility* and willingness to compromise on policy differences. At the same time we also expect the president to be *decisive* and to take firm and consistent stands on the issues. These expectations are also incompatible, and presidents can expect to be criticized for being rigid and inflexible when they are standing firm on an issue. Presidents will also be disparaged for being weak and indecisive when they do compromise.

3. A large majority of the public wants the president to be a *statesman*, to place the country's interests ahead of politics. Yet a majority of the same public also desires their president to be a skilled *politician*, and a substantial minority favors the president's exercising loyalty to his political party. If the president acts statesmanlike, he may be criticized for being too far above the political fray, for being an ineffective idealist and insufficiently solicitous of his party supporters. Jimmy Carter began his term on such a note when he attempted to cut back on "pork barrel" water projects. If he emphasizes a party program, however, the president may be criticized for being a crass politician, without concern for the broader national interest.

4. Americans like their presidents to run *open* administrations. They desire a free flow of ideas within the governing circles in Washington, and they want the workings of government to be visible to them and not sheltered behind closed doors. At the same time

they want to feel that the president is *in control* of things and that the government is not sailing rudderless. If a president allows internal dissent in White House decision making and does not try to hide or succeed in hiding this dissent from the public, he will inevitably be reproached for not being in control of his own aides. But if he should attempt either to stifle dissent or to conceal it from the public, he will be accused of being isolated, undemocratic, unable to accept criticism, and of attempting to muzzle opposition.

5. Finally, Americans want their presidents to be able to *relate* to the average person in order to inspire confidence in the White House and to have compassion and concern for the typical citizen. Yet, as we have shown throughout our discussion of expectations, the public also expects the president to possess characteristics far *different* from their own and to act in ways that are beyond the capabilities of most people. To confuse the matter further, the public also expects the president to act with a special dignity befitting the leader of this country and the free world and to live and entertain in splendor. In other words, presidents are not supposed to resemble the common man at all.

If a president seems too common, he may be disparaged for being just that—"common." One only has to think of the political cartoons of Harry Truman and Gerald Ford, implying that they were really not up to the job of president. On the other hand, if a president seems too different, appears too cerebral, or engages in too much pomp, he will likely be denounced as snobbish and isolated from the people and as being too regal for Americans' tastes. Again, one has to think back only to the Nixon White House to recall such criticisms.

PUBLIC APPROVAL OF THE PRESIDENT

The most visible and significant aspect of the president's relations with the public is his level of approval. The president's efforts to understand and lead public opinion and his efforts to influence the media's portrayal of him are aimed at achieving public support. This support is related to his success in dealing with others, especially the Congress. The higher the public's level of approval of the president, the more support Congress gives his programs.[18]

Whether they are based on perceptions encouraged by the White House, the media, or other political actors, or based on detached and careful study, opinions about the president and his policies are formed. People are also affected, sometimes quite directly, by the impact of foreign and domestic policies. In this section we examine the economy, war, stands on issues, the president's personality and personal characteristics, and international events as possible explanations for presidential approval. Regarding specific policies, we are concerned with whether evaluations of the president's performance, the success of the president's policies, or people's personal experiences of those policies are most influential in determining presidential approval.

In addition, there are certain less dynamic factors in the form of predispositions that citizens hold, such as political party identification and the positivity bias, that may strongly influence their evaluations of the president. Party in particular not only directly affects opinions of the president but also mediates the impact of other variables. Thus it is important that we examine predispositions as well as more specific opinions about the president and his policies.

Party Identification

Evaluations of the president's performance reflect the underlying partisan loyalties of the public. Members of the president's party are predisposed to approve of his performance and members of the opposition party are predisposed to be less approving. Independents, those without explicit partisan attachments, fall between the Democrats and Republicans in their levels of approval of the president. The average difference in support between Democrats and Republicans in the period 1953–1988 was 39 percentage points, a very substantial figure. Independents fall in between, averaging a difference of 18 percentage points from Democrats and 21 percentage points from Republicans.

The impact of partisanship on evaluations of the president can also be seen by examining presidential approval at a cross section of time. In July of 1974, shortly before he resigned, Richard Nixon registered overall support of 25 percent. Approval among Democrats had diminished to a meager 13 percent, and among independents he received only a 23 percent approval rating. Yet even at the height of the Watergate crisis, 52 percent of Republicans gave the president their approval. Five years later, at the end of July 1979, Jimmy Carter, a Democratic president, saw his approval fall to an overall 29 percent. Republican approval stood at only 18 percent. Democrats, on the other hand, were more than twice as likely to support Carter, giving him 37 percent approval. Independents were in the middle at 27 percent.

The public was polarized along party lines during Ronald Reagan's tenure more than under any of the last seven presidents. Between 1953 and 1980 the absolute difference in approval levels between Democrats and Republicans was 35 percentage points, itself a substantial figure. During Reagan's time in office, the gap between Democrats and Republicans widened to 52 percentage points.

Positivity Bias

Another predisposing factor is the "positivity bias," which one authority defines as the tendency "to show evaluation of public figures and institutions in a generally positive direction."[19] Americans have a general disposition to prefer, to learn, and to expect positive relationships more than negative relationships and to perceive stimuli as positive rather than negative. They tend to have favorable opinions of people.

The causes of the positivity bias are not well known, but it seems to have the greatest potential for influence in ambiguous situations, such as the beginning of a president's term, when new occupants of the White House are unknown to the public as chief executives. There is a coming together after presidential campaigns. People want their new presidents to succeed and usually give them the benefit of the doubt.

Although positivity should encourage presidential approval throughout a president's tenure, it is especially important at the beginning of a new president's term, when he lacks a track record. One way to see the impact of positivity bias is to compare the electoral percentages by which presidents first won election with their approval in the first Gallup poll taken after their inauguration. Such a comparison is made in Table 4-2. (President Ford is excluded because he never won an election for the presidency.) The figures clearly show that, with the exception of Ronald Reagan and George Bush, a substantially larger percentage of the people are willing to give new presidents their approval at the beginning of their terms than were willing to vote for them two months earlier. Whether the lack of early support for Presidents Reagan and Bush constitutes a trend remains to be seen.

As presidents perform their duties, they become better known to citizens, who have more basis for judgments about them. Moreover, the public may begin to perceive greater implications of presidential policies

Table 4-2. Comparison of Electoral Percentages and Postinaugural Approval (in percentages)

President	Popular Vote in First Election	Approval in First Postinaugural Poll
Eisenhower	55%	69%
Kennedy	50	72
Johnson	61	71
Nixon	43	60
Carter	50	66
Reagan	51	51
Bush	53	51

Source: Gallup Poll.

for their own lives as time passes. If these are viewed unfavorably, people may be more open to, and pay more attention to, negative information about the president.

A related factor may be at work in affecting presidents' approval by the public early in their terms. As the people have little basis on which to evaluate the president, they may turn to others for cues. A new chief executive is generally treated favorably in the press. Moreover, there is excitement and symbolism inherent in the peaceful transfer of power, inaugural festivities, and "new beginnings." All of this creates a very positive environment in which initial evaluations of elected presidents take place and buttresses any tendency toward the positivity bias.

Several studies have found evidence of what some authors term a *fait accompli*, or bandwagon effect. In other words, after an election people, especially those who voted for the loser, tend to view the winner more favorably than they did before the election. The depolarization of politics following an election and the positivity bias itself probably help to create an environment conducive to attitude change.[20]

The Persistence of Approval

We have seen that presidents typically begin their initial terms with the benefit of substantial support from the public. But how long does this honeymoon last? Conventional wisdom seems to indicate that presidents soon have to begin making hard choices that inevitably alienate segments of the population. Additional support for this view comes from a revealing response of President Carter in 1979 to a reporter's question concerning whether it was reasonable to expect the president to rate very highly with the American people. The president answered:

> In this present political environment, it is almost impossible. There are times of euphoria that sweep the Nation immediately after an election or after an inauguration day or maybe after a notable success, like the Camp David Accords, when there is a surge of popularity for a President. But most of the decisions that have to be made by a President are inherently not popular ones. They are contentious.[21]

Source: B.C. by Johnny Hart, by permission of Johnny Hart and Creators Syndicate, Inc.

Despite the reasonableness of these expectations, presidential honeymoons are not always short-lived. Examining shifts in presidents' approval ratings reveals that although declines certainly do take place, they are neither inevitable nor swift. Eisenhower maintained his standing in the public very well for two complete terms. Kennedy and Nixon held their public support for two years, as did Ford, once he suffered his sharp initial decline. Johnson's and Carter's approval losses were steeper, although Johnson's initial ratings were inflated by the unique emotional climate at the time he assumed office. The same was true, of course, for Ford. Reagan's approval ratings were volatile, but he stood at 64 percent approval at the time of his second inauguration, 13 percentage points higher than when he began.

Thus, honeymoons are not necessarily fleeting times during which new occupants of the White House receive a breathing period from the public. Instead, the president's constituents seem to be willing to give a new chief executive the benefit of the doubt for some time. In January 1982 over 70 percent of the public felt it would not be fair to judge President Reagan's economic program passed in mid-1981 until at least the end of 1982.[22] It is up to each president to exploit this goodwill and build solid support for his administration in the public. This is why the first few months are often critical for setting the tone of the administration and shaping the reputation of the president.

Long-Term Decline

In addition to examining approval levels within presidential terms, we also need to look for trends in public support across presidents. As we can see in Figure 4-1, from 1953 through 1965, with the single exception of 1958, at least 60 percent of the public approved the president on the average. Support from two out of three Americans was not unusual. Starting in 1966, approval levels changed dramatically. Since that time, support from even half the public has been the exception rather than the rule.

What happened? We cannot provide a definitive answer to this question, but it seems reasonable to argue that the war in Vietnam, a highly divisive policy following an era of peace, had a destructive effect on President Johnson's approval levels. Although Richard Nixon rebounded somewhat from his predecessor's low standing in the polls from 1966 to 1968, he did not rise back to pre-1966 levels, and Watergate sent his approval levels to new lows.

Just how much residual effect the factors of Vietnam and Watergate have had on the approval levels of the presidents that followed is impossible to determine with certainty. We do know that President Ford's pardon of Nixon tied him to Watergate and that his public support plummeted immediately following his announcement. Moreover, a 1974

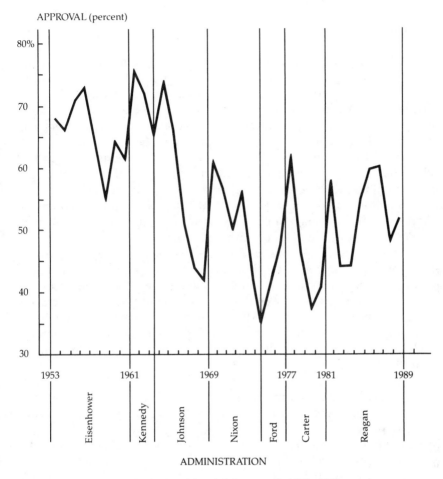

APPROVAL (percent)

ADMINISTRATION

Figure 4-1. Average Yearly Presidential Approval, 1953–1988
Source: Gallup Polls.

survey of Wisconsin residents found that 55 percent of the respondents agreed that Watergate had reduced their confidence in the office of president.[23]

We also know that President Carter did not enjoy high levels of approval, and Ronald Reagan's approval varied considerably over the course of his presidency. Contrary to accounts in the popular media, Reagan sustained high levels of approval only for a two-year period beginning near the end of his first term. Although the generally low level of support for some presidents may be purely a product of their individual actions and characteristics, it is difficult not to conclude that the events of the late 1960s and early 1970s have weakened the predispositions of many Americans to support the president.

Personality or Policy?

A factor that we commonly associate with someone's being approved is personality. The focus on presidents or other public figures, may create a tendency to evaluate them more on style than substance. The fact that Americans pay relatively little detailed attention to politics and policy adds further support to the view that the president's personality plays a large role in the public's approval of him.

Dwight Eisenhower was unique among modern presidents in that his public standing preceded and was independent of his involvement in partisan politics. He was a likeable war hero who had recently been a principal leader in the highly consensual policy of defeating Germany in World War II. His image following the war was so apolitical that both parties approached him about running for president.

Nevertheless, Eisenhower was evaluated by the public as a partisan figure. Republicans were much more likely to approve his handling of the presidency than were Democrats. Moreover, the differences between the approval levels of the two groups of party identifiers are typical of those for other presidents. Thus, the personal component of Eisenhower's public support may have kept his overall level of approval high, but it did not protect him from evaluations as a partisan figure or from fluctuations in approval related to other conditions and events in the public's environment.

Personality may buttress presidential approval, but it is not a dynamic factor. In other words, it cannot explain shifts in the president's standing with the public. Sharp changes in approval have occurred for presidents whose public manners have remained unaltered. Although impressions the public holds of the president's personality form early and change slowly, what the public feels ought to be and the way people evaluate what they see can change more rapidly. "Cleverness" can soon be viewed as "deceit," "reaching down for details" as "a penchant for the trivial," "evaluating all the alternatives" as "indecisiveness," "charm" as "commonness" or, even worse, "vulgarity," "staying above politics" as "naivete." The contradictory expectations the people hold of the president help to set the scene for these changing interpretations of presidential behavior, allowing the public to switch emphasis in what it looks for in a president and how it evaluates what it sees.

In addition, the public may "like" presidents but still disapprove of the way they are handling their jobs. A poll near the middle of President Carter's term found that almost twice as many people liked the president as approved of the manner in which he was handling the presidency.[24] Several years later the Gallup Poll found that 74 percent of the public approved of President Reagan as a person, but only 49 percent approved of his performance as president.[25]

Thus, although we cannot specify the contribution of personality to presidential approval, we do know that policy matters play a large role in evaluations of presidents. Changes in presidential approval are in large part a response to what people see happening in the world and not merely a reaction to a particular personality. And, as we should expect in light of the findings in the previous section, the president's approval is affected whether or not he is responsible for these policy outcomes.

The Economy

The state of the economy has a pervasive influence on our lives. The conventional view is that people's evaluations of the president are affected strongly by their personal economic circumstances. That is, people are more likely to approve of the president if they feel they are prospering personally than if they feel they are not. Lyndon Johnson, for example, believed that "the family pocketbook was the root-and-branch crucial connection to all his plans and hopes for the future."[26]

Yet there is plenty of reason to be skeptical of the role of short-term self-interest in evaluations of the president.[27] People differentiate their own circumstances from those of the country as a whole. In 1988 a Gallup poll found that although only 56 percent of the public was satisfied with the way things were going in the country, 87 percent were satisfied with the way things were going in their personal lives.[28] People may evaluate the president in terms of the state of the economy as a whole, rather than its effect on them personally, or they may simply evaluate how well the president is handling economic policy, regardless of the short-term impact of his actions. In fact, the public may approve of a president who is struggling with a difficult situation even if he is not meeting with great tangible success. Franklin Roosevelt in 1933 and 1934 seems to be such a case.

This reasoning regarding the public's evaluation of the president applies to other factors besides the economy. The Vietnam War may have influenced citizens' evaluations of the president because of how they viewed it as a general policy rather than how it affected them personally. Jimmy Carter's standing in the public may have benefitted for several months from favorable public perceptions of his handling of the Iranian hostage crisis, despite the fact the hostages were not freed during this period.

Examining survey data shows results in lines with this theorizing.[29] Whether people and their families feel financially better or worse off over the past year or expect to be in the coming year, whether they or their families have experienced unemployment, or whether they have been hurt by inflation has little or no bearing on their approval of the president. The same is true when we ask people their views about the state of the economy itself, including evaluations of past and future conditions, price levels, unemployment, and the economy in general. When we turn to the public's evaluation of the president's *handling* of the economy, however, we find a different picture. Citizens' evaluations of the president's handling of unemployment, inflation, and the economy in general are related strongly to overall presidential approval. In sum, the public evaluates the president's role in the economy more on the basis of his performance than on its view of the state of the economy.

War

War is frequently discussed as a factor in presidential approval. The reasons for this attention are obvious: wars disrupt and sometimes polarize society and are very costly in terms of lives and money. The president, moreover, in his role as commander-in-chief, is inevitably closely identified with war policy. Unlike the economy, war, fortunately, is not always with us. We do have some relevant data from polls taken during the Vietnam War, however.

As in the case of the impact of the economy on presidential approval, the personal circumstances of individuals do not seem to affect their evaluations of the president. Persons who had a member of their immediate family or close friends or relatives in the armed services as a result of the Vietnam War did not evaluate the president differently from those who were not as directly touched by the war. We find, however, that the public's evaluations of the president's handling of the war strongly influenced overall presidential approval.

Other Issues

When we examine public opinion on other issues, ranging from national health insurance to federal aid to minorities, we find that citizens' policy differences with the president are modestly related to their evaluations of his performance in office. Once again, however, people's direct evaluations of the president's actions in policy areas such as energy and crime control exert the strongest influence on their overall evaluations of his performances.

Personal Characteristics

Much of the commentary on the president in the press and in other forums focuses on his personal characteristics, especially integrity, intelligence, and leadership abilities. When the public is asked about such job-related characteristics, its responses are clearly related to its evaluations of the president. Assessments of characteristics such as the president's integrity, reliability, and leadership ability may change as new problems arise, or in relation to the president's past performance. Certain characteristics may become more salient in response to changing conditions. When the Iran–Contra affair became news, President Reagan's decision-making style became a prominent issue. Many people came to evaluate his focus on the "big picture" and detachment from the details of governing in a less positive light.

Rally Events

To this point we have examined factors that may affect presidential approval systematically over time, but sometimes public opinion takes sudden jumps. One popular explanation for these surges of support are "rally events." John Mueller, in his seminal definition of the concept, defined a rally event as one that is international, directly involves the United States and particularly the president, and is specific, dramatic, and sharply focused. Such events confront the nation as a whole, are salient to the public, and gain public attention and interest.[30]

The preponderance of evidence indicates that the rally phenomenon rarely appears and that the events that generate it are highly idiosyncratic and do not seem to differ significantly from other events that were not followed by surges in presidential approval. Moreover, the events that cause sudden increases in public support are not restricted to international affairs, and most international events that would seem to be potential rally events fail to generate much additional approval of the president.

Summary

Public approval of the president is the product of many factors. At the base of evaluations of the president is the predisposition of many people to support the president. Political party identification provides the basic underpinning of approval or disapproval and mediates the impact of other factors. The positivity bias and the bandwagon effect buttress approval levels, at least for a while.

Changes in approval levels appear to be due primarily to the public's evaluation of how the president is handling policy areas such as the economy, war, energy, and foreign affairs. Citizens seem to focus on the president's efforts and his stands on issues rather than on his personality or how his policies affect them personally or even whether his policies are successful in the short run. Job-related personal characteristics of the president also play an important role in influencing the degree of presidential approval. Conversely, rally events may provide an occasional increment of support, but in general they do not seem to be very significant.

LEADING THE PUBLIC

Direct Opinion Leadership

If public support can be a useful leadership resource for the president, is he in a position to call upon it when he needs it? Commentators on the presidency often assume that the White House can persuade or even mobilize the public if the president is a skilled enough communicator. Before accepting this premise, however, a critical examination of the chief executive's efforts at leading the public is needed.

The most visible and obvious technique employed by presidents to lead public opinion is to seek the public's support directly. Presidents frequently attempt to influence public opinion with speeches over television or radio or in person to large groups. Recent presidents have averaged one public appearance every day. Not all presidents are effective speakers, however, and not all look good under the glare of hot lights and the unflattering gaze of television cameras. Moreover, the public is not always receptive to the president's message.

All presidents since Truman have had media advice from experts on lighting, makeup, stage settings, camera angles, clothing, pacing of delivery, and other facets of making speeches. Despite this aid and despite the experience that politicians inevitably have in speaking, presidential speeches aimed at directly leading public opinion have typically not been very impressive. Only Kennedy and Reagan have mastered the art of speaking to the camera.

No matter how effective a president might be as a speaker, he still must contend with the predisposition of his audience. As we noted in our discussion of the campaign, members of the public screen his messages through their own views and values, posing a formidable challenge to persuasion. The president also cannot depend upon an attentive audience. Most people are not very interested in politics. The relative importance the typical person attaches to a president's address is illustrated by the attention presidential staffs give to setting the date for the president's annual State of the Union message. They have to be careful to avoid preempting prime time on the night that offers the current season's most popular shows while at the same time trying to maximize their national viewing audience.

The public's general lack of interest in politics constrains the president's leadership of public opinion in the long run as well as on a given day. Although he has unparalleled access to the American people, the president cannot make too much use of this situation. If he does, his speeches will become commonplace and will lose their drama and interest. That is why presidents do not make appeals to the public, particularly on television, very often. Some presidents, such as Reagan and Nixon, have turned to radio and midday addresses to reserve prime-time televised addresses for important speeches.

Television is a medium in which visual interest, action, and conflict are most effective. Presidential speeches are unlikely to contain these characteristics. Although some addresses to the nation, such as President Johnson's televised demand for a voting rights act before a joint session of Congress in 1965, occur at moments of high drama, they do not typically do so.

Presidents not only have to contend with the medium but they also must concern themselves with their messages. The most effective speeches seem to be those whose goals are general support and image building rather than specific support. They focus on simple themes rather than complex details. Calvin Coolidge used this method successfully in his radio speeches, as did Franklin Roosevelt in his famous "fireside chats." The limitation of such an approach, of course, is that general support cannot always be translated into public backing for specific policies.

SUCCESS OF APPEALS.   We should not be surprised, then, that direct appeals to the public often fail. Ronald Reagan was certainly interested in policy change and went to unprecedented lengths to influence public opinion. Nevertheless, numerous national surveys of public opinion have found that support for regulatory programs and spending on health care, welfare, urban problems, education, environmental protection, and aid to minorities increased rather than decreased during Reagan's tenure. On the other hand, support for increased defense expenditures was decidedly lower at the end of his administration than when he took office. In the realm of foreign policy, near the end of 1986 only 25 percent of the public favored the president's cherished aid to the Contras in Nicaragua. Finally, Americans did not move their general ideological preference to the right.[31]

Despite the limitations of their abilities to exercise direct opinion leadership over the public, presidents are aided by the willingness of Americans to *follow* their lead, especially on foreign policy. Foreign policy is more distant from the lives of most Americans than is domestic policy and is therefore seen as more complex and based on specialized knowledge. Thus people tend to defer more to the president on foreign issues than on domestic ones that they can relate more easily and directly to their own experience. Studies have shown public opinion undergoing changes in line with presidents' policies on the invasion of Grenada, testing nuclear weapons, relations with the People's Republic of China, and both the escalation and deescalation of the war in Vietnam.[32]

One scholar ascertained public opinion on six potential responses to the 1979–1980 hostage crisis in Iran. Then he asked those who opposed each option if they would change their view "if President Carter consid-ered this action necessary." The policy options and the public's re-sponses to them are shown in Table 4-3.[33] In each case a substantial percentage of the public changed its opinion in deference to the sup-posed opinion of the president. Similarly, a poll of Utah residents found that two-thirds of them opposed basing the deployment of MX missiles in Utah and Nevada. But an equal number said they would definitely or probably support President Reagan if he decided to go ahead and base the missiles in those states.[34]

Not all results are so positive, however. In one study different sam-ple groups were asked whether they supported a domestic policy pro-posal dealing with welfare and a proposal dealing with foreign aid. One of the groups was told President Carter supported the proposals. The authors found that attaching the president's name to either proposal not only failed to increase support for them but actually had a negative effect because those who disapproved of Carter reacted very strongly against proposals they thought were his.[35] The limited evidence available indi-cates that presidents are much more likely to be successful in influencing public opinion when they have high approval ratings themselves.[36]

As we learned earlier, the public generally does not have crys-tallized opinions on issues and is therefore often easy to sway in the short run. But this volatility also means that any opinion change is subject to slippage. As issues fade into the background or as positions on issues confront the realities of daily life, opinions that were altered in response to presidential leadership may quickly be forgotten. This is especially likely to occur where the president's influence on public opin-ion seems to be greatest: foreign policy.

A balanced view of the president's ability to lead public opinion directly must take into consideration both the potential for and the obsta-cles to leadership. As in so many other presidential relationships, the

Table 4-3. Reconsidering Policy Opinions in Response to the President
(in percentages)

Policy	Original Approval	Approval after Reconsideration	Change Due to President
Wait and see	58%	83%	25%
Return Shah to Iran	21	53	32
Send Shah elsewhere	74	87	13
Naval blockade	62	85	23
Threaten to send troops	43	73	30
Send troops	29	62	33

Source: Lee Sigelman, "Gauging the Public Response to Presidential Leadership," *Presidential Studies Quarterly* 10 (Summer 1980): 431.

direct leadership of public opinion provides opportunities, especially in foreign policy, but no guarantees of success. It is for this reason that presidents often rely on more subtle methods of opinion leadership.

Information Control

A technique for influencing public opinion that is less direct than appeals to the public is information control. This comes in many forms, ranging from withholding information from the public to lying. If the public is unaware of a situation or has a distorted view of it, then the president may have more flexibility in achieving what he desires. Often the president desires public passivity as much as he wants public support.

WITHHOLDING INFORMATION.   The classification of information under the rubric of "national security" is a frequently used means of withholding information. Most people support secrecy in handling national security affairs, especially in such matters as defense plans and strategy, weapons technology, troop movements, the details of current diplomatic negotiations, the methods and sources of covert intelligence gathering, and similar information about the defense, negotiations, and intelligence gathering of other nations. However, there has been controversy over the amount of information classified and whether classification is used by the president and other high officials to influence public opinion. When officials withhold information that might aid the public in evaluating their performance in office and in answering general questions of public policy but that might embarrass them if made public, they may provide a distorted view of reality and increase or maintain support for themselves.

DEEMPHASIS OF INFORMATION.   A president can also employ more subtle methods of manipulating information in an effort to influence public opinion. He can, for example, order that information collected by the goverment be deemphasized. When the economy was not doing well in 1971, the White House ordered the Bureau of Labor Statistics to discontinue its monthly briefing of the press on prices and unemployment. Similarly, during the Vietnam War the Defense Department gave much more attention in its public announcements to deserters from enemy forces than to deserters from the armed forces of our South Vietnamese allies. In each case the government possessed information that might negatively influence public perceptions of the president and his administration. It chose not to emphasize this "bad news."

COLLECTION OF INFORMATION.   Going a step further, a president can simply not order that information on a policy be collected. This, of course, prevents the public from fully evaluating his performance. President Johnson had invested a great deal in his Great Society domestic programs and did not want to cut back on them when large amounts of funds were needed for the Vietnam War. Although warned by the Council of Economic Advisers at the end of 1965 of the need for a tax increase to avoid the inflation that would result from having *both* "guns and butter," he refused to request one. Instead Johnson kept the precise expenditures on the war from Congress and the public. No serious effort was ever made to determine the true costs of United States involvement in the war, and Americans felt the ravages of inflation for years to come.

TIMING OF THE RELEASE OF INFORMATION.   Sometimes information is provided, but the timing of its release is used to try to influence public opinion. On November 2, 1970, the White House announced the most recent casualty figures from Vietnam. They were a five-year low and their announcement was made on Monday instead of Thursday as usual, presumably because the 1970 congressional elections were being held the next day. The Carter administration revealed that the Pentagon had developed a new technology that made aircraft virtually invisible to enemy detection devices. This disclosure coincided with an administration effort during the 1980 presidential election campaign to show that it was working to strengthen national defense. Taking the opposite tack, the Ford administration announced that the country was in a recession one week after the 1974 congressional elections. The Reagan administration knew that its economic forecasts had been too optimistic, but it did not change them until after the crucial vote on the president's tax cut proposal in 1981.

OBFUSCATION OF INFORMATION.   Presidents and their aides may also attempt to obscure or distort the truth in order to confuse or mislead the public. President Eisenhower regularly gave purposefully ambiguous answers at his press conferences.[37] A classic example of this technique is an answer Nixon's press secretary Ron Ziegler gave to a reporter's questions about the Watergate tapes.

> I would feel that most of the conversations that took place in those areas of the White House that did have the recording system would, in almost their entirety, be in existence, but the special prosecutor, the court, and I think, the American people are sufficiently familiar with the recording system to know where the recording devices existed and to know the situation in terms of the recording process, but I feel, although the process has not been undertaken yet in preparation of the material to abide by the court decision, really, what the answer to that question is.[38]

Distortion comes in many forms. One of the most common is to provide impressive statistics without going into the details of how they were compiled. Reagan's budget director, David Stockman, admitted "rigging the [budget] numbers to the point that even we couldn't understand them."[39] In 1982 President Reagan told the American people more than half the stores investigated by the government were selling items that were prohibited for purchase with food stamps. He omitted the fact that the stores that were investigated were ones already suspected of abuse.

Presidents have also used tricks to make budgets appear smaller. In his last year in office President Johnson introduced the "unified budget," which included trust funds previously *excluded* from the budget, such as those for social security, unemployment benefits, highway construction, and retirement pensions of railroad workers. The fact that the trust funds were running a surplus allowed him to cut the size of the projected federal deficit—at least on paper, because these surplus trust funds cannot be used to cover the deficit in the regular budget. President Nixon introduced the "full employment" budget in fiscal 1972. His ruse was to calculate the federal revenues not at what was expected but at what they would be if there were full employment (which there was not). This subterfuge allowed him to show a smaller overall deficit. In more recent times presidents (and Congress) have used what are termed "off-budget" expenditures to reduce the size of the budget—on paper.[40]

It is not only what goes into compiling a "fact" that is important for the public's evaluation of it, but also the context of events in which the "fact" occurs. In 1964 Lyndon Johnson went before Congress to ask for a resolution supporting retaliation against North Vietnam for two attacks on United States ships in the Gulf of Tonkin. The Gulf of Tonkin Resolution was subsequently passed with only two dissenting votes and marked a watershed in the nation's military actions in Vietnam. As the president desired, it was passed in the context of strong public support for retaliating against "unprovoked" attacks against Americans.

The public might have been less enthusiastic in its backing of military reprisals, however, if it had known what the president knew about the context in which the North Vietnamese actions took place. First, the United States had secretly been gathering intelligence and supporting covert South Vietnamese operations against North Vietnam for several years before the incidents in the Gulf of Tonkin. Some of these activities were going on in the vicinity at the time of the attacks on United States ships, and the North Vietnamese might have thought our ships were involved.

The second piece of crucial contextual information that was withheld from the American people was that there was considerable reason to doubt that the second attack ever occurred! As President Johnson later said (in private, of course), "For all I know, our Navy was shooting whales out there."[41] Although it is possible that at the time the president had honestly concluded that the attack had in fact occurred, there is little doubt that the public's approval of retaliatory actions would have been more restrained if it had had this information.

Attempts to distort information are not always successful. By 1967 two-thirds of the American people felt the Johnson administration was not telling them all it should know about the Vietnam War. In 1971 a similar percentage felt the same way about the Nixon administration.[42] Out of such attitudes emerged a credibility gap and low levels of popular standing for these presidents.

PREVARICATION.   The most extreme form of information control is lying. Do presidents lie? The answer is yes. The range of subjects of lies is great and includes the topics of the country's military situation in Vietnam; its role in the 1954 coup in Guatemala; the U-2 incident; the nation's role in the Bay of Pigs invasion; the presence of missiles in Cuba in 1962; the United States role in the overthrow of President Diem of South Vietnam; the attempted bribery by the United States of the prime minister of Singapore; the motivations behind the American invasion of the Dominican Republic in 1965; the reasons that the USS *Liberty* was sunk by our Israeli allies in the 1967 Six-Day War; the nation's attempts to prevent the election of Marxist Salvador Allende as president of Chile; the Watergate cover-up; the invasion of Grenada; trading hostages with terrorists; presidential plans for appointments, travel, and policies; and even the president's review of requests to use the White House tennis courts.[43]

In his press conference on September 28, 1982, President Reagan responded to questions on the economy with descriptions of the growth of the gross national product, the rate of increase in the unemployment rate under his predecessor, the proportion of the population in the work force, and the increase in the purchasing power of the average family. All of these were assertions about the economy's performance, and all of them were motivated by a desire to put it in the best possible light. Unfortunately, all of these statements were also untrue![44] Whether the president's responses were carefully planned or the result of his misunderstanding of the statistics is unclear.

One thing is clear. The American people resent being lied to. A poll near the end of 1986 found that 72 percent of the sample did not agree that it was acceptable for the government to lie—even to achieve foreign policy goals.[45] At the same time the Reagan administration was losing credibility on a wide range of issues: substantial majorities of the public, for example, did not believe its claims concerning the secret sale of arms to Iran, its denial of a trade of a captured Soviet spy for the release of an American newsman detained in Moscow, and its denial that an American pilot shot down over Nicaragua was a CIA agent.[46] It was also criticized for releasing false reports that Libya was planning new terrorist attacks.

INFORMATION CONTROL IN PERSPECTIVE.   What can we conclude from our discussion of information control? Perhaps the most obvious pattern that we have found is that it is most common in the national security area. The reason is simple: it is difficult for the public to challenge official statements about events in other countries, especially military activities, which often are shrouded in secrecy. It is much easier to be skeptical about domestic activities that American reporters can scrutinize and to which they can provide alternative views. In addition, the public can relate many domestic policies to their own experiences more easily than they can relate most foreign and military policies. When officials' statements do not correspond to people's experiences, they have a built-in basis for skepticism.

Information control is employed to deny information not only to a foreign adversary but also to the American public. In virtually all of the examples involving national security policy, from the U-2 flight over the Soviet Union to the secret bombing of Cambodia, the "enemy" knew the truth. Only the American public was left in the dark.

Information control is an unfortunate and, regrettably, a common technique used by presidents. Their goal is to influence public opinion by controlling the information upon which the public bases its evaluations of chief executives and their policies and upon which it determines if there is cause for concern. Although we have no way to measure the impact of these efforts, it is probably safe to say that some are successful and some lead to embarrassment and a loss of credibility for the president and his administration.

The Use of Symbols

The language used in political discourse may have an influence on public opinion independent of the subject under discussion. One important aspect of political language is the use of symbols, things that are simple or familiar that stand for things complex or unfamiliar. Symbols are frequently used to describe politicians, events, issues, or some other aspect of the political world. Naturally, symbols are not synonyms for what they describe. The choice of symbols inevitably highlights certain aspects of an issue or event and conceals others. Thus, if presidents can get a substantial segment of the public to adopt symbols favorable to them, they will be in a position to influence public opinion.

Because of the potential power of symbols in shaping public opinion, presidents have encouraged the public to adopt certain symbols as representative of their administrations. Franklin Roosevelt dubbed his administration the "New Deal," and Harry Truman termed his the "Fair Deal." Each symbol was an oversimplification for new and extremely complex policies, but each served to reassure many Americans that these policies were for their good. Similarly, John Kennedy's "New Frontier" and Lyndon Johnson's "Great Society" served as attractive symbols of their administrations.

Symbols are also used to describe specific policies. President Johnson declared a "War on Poverty" despite the fact that many saw the "war" as more of a skirmish. President Nixon went to considerable efforts to have the public view the January 1973 peace agreement ending the involvement of American troops in Vietnam as "peace with honor," clearly a controversial conclusion. He also claimed his administration represented "law and order," a claim that is especially ironic in light of the Watergate debacle.

Perhaps the most important and effective televised address President Reagan made to the nation in 1981 was his July 27 speech seeking the public's support for his tax-cut bill. In it he went to great lengths to present his plan as "bipartisan." It was crucial that he convince the public that this controversial legislation was supported by members of both parties and was therefore, by implication, fair. Despite the fact that House Democrats voted overwhelmingly against the president's proposal two days later, he described it as "bipartisan" *eleven* times in the span of a few minutes! No one could miss the point.

As these examples indicate, symbols can be manipulated in attempts not only to lead public opinion but also deliberately to mislead it. During the Watergate controversy Richard Nixon repeatedly referred to his unwillingness to cooperate fully with Congress and the special prosecutor as necessary to protect the office of the presidency (a powerful symbol), not himself as a particular president. This is an argument frequently used by presidents when they oppose legislation that would limit their power.

The White House tries to label opponents as well as policies. President Nixon's chief of staff, H. R. Haldeman, accused critics of Nixon's Vietnam peace plan of being traitors, and the president made no disclaimer. Vice President Agnew classified administration critics as "radical-liberals" and "effete snobs."

The presidency uniquely lends itself to symbolic manipulation. In his role as chief of state the president personifies the government and our nation's heritage. Presidents use this opportunity to enhance their public standing. They are frequently seen on television welcoming heads of state or other dignitaries to the White House, dedicating federal projects, speaking before national groups, or performing ceremonial functions, such as laying a wreath at the Tomb of the Unknown Soldier in Arlington National Cemetery.

Foreign travels provide even greater opportunities for the president to be viewed as the representative of America and as a statesman above partisan politics. As he deals with the leaders of other nations on matters of international importance and as he is greeted by cheering crowds of Egyptians, Poles, or Italians, Americans naturally take pride in him as the representative of our country, the embodiment of our goals, and the bearer of our goodwill. As we shall see, presidents are aware of this and may schedule activities so they will be covered on prime-time television.

The president also participates in many ceremonial roles dealing with domestic matters. These include having his picture taken with the winner of the national spelling bee, the teacher of the year, or the March of Dimes poster child; lighting the national Christmas tree; and issuing proclamations celebrating national holidays such as Thanksgiving and Veterans Day and lesser-known celebrations such as National Pickle Week.

All of this activity as chief of state, the president hopes, will help foster the view that he is a fitting head of state and competent to run the country and make important and difficult decisions. He wants to try to relieve some of the fears and anxieties of the public and provide hope for and confidence in the future. If he is successful in projecting an image of dignity and ability, which may or may not be accurate, he will make it easier for people to vest their allegiance in him as a visible, human source of authority and to accept decisions they might otherwise oppose.

While engaging in these and other functions, the president often makes appeals to patriotism, traditions, and our history (and its greatness) to move the public to support him, reminding people of their common interests. He also frequently invokes the names of revered leaders of the past, such as Lincoln or Truman, who made difficult decisions on the basis of high principles, and relates himself or his decisions to them.

Presidents also make gestures to show that they are really "one of the people." President Carter made considerable use of this technique, desiring to be seen as a people's president. At his inauguration he walked (instead of rode) down Pennsylvania Avenue from the Capitol to the White House after taking the oath of office. He conducted a "fireside chat" over national television, seated before a blazing fire and dressed casually in a sweater instead of a suit. He also staged a press conference in which private individuals could call in from around the country and directly ask him questions.

Despite the considerable efforts presidents make to manipulate symbols, they are not always successful. The Nixon administration tried to find a slogan that captured its essence, including the "New Federalism," the "New American Revolution," the "Generation of Peace," and the "Open Door," but none of these metaphors caught on with the press or the public. Gerald Ford wore a WIN (for "Whip Inflation Now") button to represent his economic priorities during a televised address before a joint session of Congress, but it only became an object of derision.

Many observers feel that a president's failure to lead the public to adopt broad symbols for his administration can cause severe problems in relations with the public. Jimmy Carter faced a great deal of criticism for lacking a unifying theme and cohesion in his programs, for failing to inspire the public with a sense of purpose, an idea to follow. Instead of providing the country with a sense of his vision and priorities, he emphasized discrete problem solving. In other words, he had an analytic but not synthetic approach to government.

On the other hand, Ronald Reagan was able to project a simple, coherent vision for his presidency that served him well in attracting adherents and in countering criticism when the inevitable contradictions in policy arose. He continually invoked symbols of his vision of America, which critics saw as disguising serious flaws in his policies. According to Pat Buchanan, who served as the White House director of communications, "For Ronald Reagan the world of legend and myth is a real world. He visits it regularly and he's a happy man there."[47] The president obtained political as well as personal rewards for his use of symbols. For example, he maintained his identification with balanced budgets although he never submitted a budget that was even close to being balanced and his administration was responsible for more deficit spending than all previous administrations combined.

Public Relations

In its efforts to mold public opinion, the White House employs public relations techniques modeled after those of commercial advertising firms. One indicator of the importance of public relations to contemporary presidents is the presence of advertising specialists in the White House. Michael Deaver, one of the three aides forming the "troika" at the top of the White House hierarchy in Ronald Reagan's first term, was a public relations specialist. His role was that of a general adviser with special responsibilities for developing and coordinating public relations. These responsibilities included orchestrating the president's public appearances and scheduling and coordinating public appearances by other administration officials to help ensure that they publicized the president's policies and had maximum impact and that their public postures were consistent and not distracting.

The use of public relations specialists has become customary. One of President Johnson's closest aides, Jack Valenti, came to the White House from the advertising business and went into the motion picture industry when he left. Richard Nixon carried the hiring of public relations experts even further. His chief of staff, H. R. Haldeman, his press secretary and later close adviser, Ron Ziegler, and several other aides came to the White House from advertising firms. President Carter put Gerald Rafshoon, the advertising director for his 1976 campaign, on the White House staff.

Aside from serving as an indicator of the importance presidents place on public relations, the presence of these aides may influence the substance and especially the timing of policy. Being human, all presidents are subject to the temptation to do the most popular thing. For example, an analysis of President Johnson's public statements on Vietnam shows that he varied their content—that is, their "hawkishness"—with the audience he was addressing.[48] The potential for subordinating substance to style is clearly present. This is especially true when presidents hire public relations aides like Michael Deaver, who freely admitted that he had little interest in matters of public policy and argued that "image is sometimes as useful as substance."[49]

There is also the potential for running the White House like an advertising agency. A close observer of the Reagan administration found that one matter permeated staff meetings of top White House officials: how the topic under discussion would play in the media.[50] In addition, since an advertising specialist's orientation is to stress a uniform image, the power of such persons can be a centralizing force in an administration. Emphasis on "team play" inevitably leads to the discouragement of dissent and irregularity because they blunt the impact of the president's image. The parallels between this description and the Nixon White House are especially striking.

SPREADING THE WORD.   The primary goal of White House public relations efforts is to build support for the president and his policies. Part of this job is "getting the word out" about the president, his views, and his accomplishments. Lyndon Johnson constantly sought more publicity and even arranged to have favorable articles placed in the *Congressional Record* with prefatory remarks provided by the White House. Richard Nixon took a special interest in public relations. His office of communications tried to stimulate books on Nixon, suggested ideas for feature articles about the president and his family, wrote speeches for leading administration officials, attempted to exercise more control over the public relations of the executive branch, held regional press briefings to publicize younger members of the administration, stacked a televised press conference with Nixon supporters, and pressured the Bureau of Labor Statistics to issue announcements of the number of new jobs created in the economy (as the unemployment rate failed to fall). The office also placed representatives of the administration on television shows and lecture platforms and dispersed information to editors, commentators, and reporters and to ethnic, religious, geographic, professional, and other types of groups interested in particular policies.

Reaching the enormous television audience of about 50 million viewers of the evening news is especially important to the White House, and the president's staff builds his schedule around efforts to do so. As President Ford's deputy press secretary put it: "Whenever possible, everything was done to take into account the need for coverage. After all, most of the events are done for coverage. Why else are you doing them?"[51]

Public relations efforts may focus on certain presidential characteristics. Photographs portraying the president as a family man or pet owner are common. Reagan White House aides ghost-wrote, under the president's name, a story on keeping physically fit and had it published in a popular Sunday newspaper magazine supplement. The idea was to subtly make the point that Ronald Reagan was not too old for the job. In January 1976 President Ford held a special budget briefing so he could display that he was "competent," a subject over which there had been considerable debate in the press.[52]

Many aspects of public relations were employed in the early days of the Reagan administration. The president focused on his priority item: the economy. Publicity was carefully planned at the time of his first speech urging budgetary reductions. Press briefings were held, and administration officials appeared on all three Sunday interview shows— "Issues and Answers,""Meet the Press," and "Face the Nation"— "Nightline," the "MacNeil-Lehrer Report," and one of the morning news shows. Throughout, the White House paid close attention to the image of the president as well, trying to portray him as busy and engaged in important decision making, not remote and passive.

The president and his aides tailor messages they wish to transmit to the public to the needs of the press. President Carter emphasized short two- or three-minute statements to the White House press over longer addresses, because he knew that is all that would be shown on the evening news broadcasts. Similarly, announcements are timed so that reporters can meet their papers' deadlines. Those made too late in the evening will not appear in the next morning's newspapers and those made too late in the afternoon will miss publication in the evening papers.

If the White House wants to decrease the coverage of an event, it can wait until after the evening news programs to announce it. Then it might be buried among the next day's occurrences. It can also pass the word to administration officials to avoid appearing on interview programs or holding press conferences. The White House tries to avoid having the president announce bad news. Better to let a subordinate serve as the lightning rod. When the United States pulled the marines out of Lebanon, it was announced as President Reagan was flying to his California ranch for a vacation. Conversely, the White House loves good news, so it is careful to spread it out over time so each incident receives full coverage.

MEDIA EVENTS   In addition to general efforts to publicize the president, the White House often stages "media events" in hope of obtaining additional public support. President Nixon's trip to China in 1972 was a great media event. The White House obtained agreement from the Chinese to allow live television coverage, and the networks sent three large cargo planes of equipment and more than one hundred technicians, producers, and executives to do the job. Of course, the White House was not passive in obtaining media coverage. The president's plane arrived in Peking and returned to Washington during prime time. The latter was accomplished only by sitting on the ground in Anchorage, Alaska, for nine hours! The president was very much aware of the huge viewing audience. In his opening remarks at the first banquet in Peking, he referred to the fact that "more people are seeing and hearing what we say than on any other occasion in the whole history of the world."

President Carter engaged in most of the public relations activities of his predecessors and added a few innovations of his own. In addition to staging a call-in and several town meetings, Carter traveled to New York City to sign the bill authorizing federal aid to the city. The White House signing of the Camp David Accords between Egypt and Israel on prime-time television was a spectacular media event.

No administration was more attentive to the potential of media events than Ronald Reagan's. As Michael Deaver put it, "You get only forty to eighty seconds on a given night on the network news, and unless you can find a visual that explains your message you can't make it stick."[53] Deaver carefully scripted every second of the president's public appearances, right down to placing tape on the floor telling Reagan where to stand for the best camera angles.[54]

Some of the staged events in the Reagan administration were quite spectacular. In the election year of 1984, for example, the president followed Nixon's precedent and toured China. Later that spring, not coincidentally when the Democratic primaries were reaching their climax, Reagan attended an economic summit meeting in Europe. His aides felt the subject matter of the summit was too dry to attract much attention in the public, so they had him engage in a folksy visit to Ireland (the town of Ballyporeen was selected for the presidential visit only after it was checked for visual charm), some stately hobnobbing with Queen Elizabeth (filled with colorful pageantry), and the delivery of an emotional speech at an American cemetery in Normandy commemorating the fortieth anniversary of D-Day. The visuals were superb, and they later appeared in campaign commercials.

At times media events can be used quite cynically. When Reagan was under fire for not supporting civil rights, he paid a visit to a black family that had had a cross burned in its front yard. The White House did not mention that the cross burning had occurred five years earlier. When the president's pollster found that the public overwhelmingly disapproved of the administration's reductions in aid to education, Michael Deaver arranged for Reagan to make a series of speeches emphasizing quality education. As Deaver later gloated, public approval of the president regarding education "flip-flopped" without any change in policy at all.[55]

Some of the emphasis on media events is the White House's response to the nature of the media, which we examine in the next chapter. According to Larry Speakes, the White House press spokesman during most of Ronald Reagan's tenure in the White House,

> We knew that television had to have pictures to present its story. . . . So when Reagan was pushing education, the visual was of him sitting at a little desk and talking to a group of students, or with the football team and some cheerleaders, or in a science lab. Then we would have an educators' forum where the president would make a noteworthy statement. We learned very quickly that the rule was no picture, no television piece, no matter how important our news was.[56]

CONCLUSION

The president's relations with the public are complex. He needs its support in order to play an effective leadership role, yet he has a difficult time obtaining it. Expectations are high and contradictory and the public's desires are hard to ascertain. Although the public appears to award or withhold its support of the chief executive largely on job-performance grounds, its perceptions of issues and the president's actions are hazy. Just how the public reaches its conclusions about the president's performance is not well understood. In theory, however, there is ample opportunity for the president, directly and through the press, to influence public perceptions.

Given this environment, presidents are not content to follow public opinion. In their search for public support they invest substantial amounts of time, energy, ingenuity, and personnel in techniques that include direct appeals to the public, use of symbols, information control, and public relations. Some of this activity is quite legitimate, and some is not. Some of it follows Richard Nixon's view that "It's not *what* Presidents do but how they do it that matters."[57]

There is no guarantee of success in these efforts, however, and they often fail to achieve their desired effects. The president, even a "great communicator," is not able to move the public much on his own. The chief executive is not a director who leads the public where it otherwise would not go, reshaping the contours of the political landscape. Instead, he is a facilitator who reflects and perhaps intensifies widely held views and endows his constituency's views with structure and purpose through his interpretations of them. As President Carter's press secretary, Jody Powell, put it:

> [With] Communications and the management of them, the impact is marginal. The substance of what you do and what happens to you over the long haul is more important, particularly on the big things like the economy. . . .

Poor communications comes up after a problem is already there, if an economic program doesn't work, if it is ill-conceived, or if circumstances
change. . . . The ability to turn a sow's ear into silk purses is limited. You
can make it into a silkier sow's ear, that's all.[58]

Nevertheless, presidents continue to employ these tactics, adding their
own wrinkles to those of their predecessors as they seek public support.

NOTES

1. Franklin Roosevelt and Theodore Roosevelt, quoted in Emmett John Hughes,
"Presidency vs. Jimmy Carter," *Fortune*, December 4, 1978, pp. 62, 64; our italics.

2. See, for example, "Opinion Outlook," *National Journal*, February 6, 1988, p. 348.

3. See, for example, *CBS News/The New York Times Poll*, April 15, 1986, table 16.

4. *CBS News/The New York Times Poll*, June 24, 1986, table 9.

5. Advisory Commission on Intergovernmental Relations, *Changing Public Attitudes
on Governments and Taxes* (Washington, D.C.: Advisory Commission on Intergovernmental
Relations, 1981), pp. 1–4.

6. See Dom Bonafede, "Carter and the Polls—If You Live by Them, You May Die by
Them," *National Journal*, August 19, 1978, pp. 1312–13.

7. Interview with Richard Wirthlin, West Point, N.Y., April 19, 1988.

8. Donald T. Regan, *For the Record: From Wall Street to Washington* (San Diego: Harcourt Brace Jovanovich, 1988), p. 274.

9. See, for example, Saul Pett, "Interview Draws Rare Portrait of Carter," *New
Orleans Times-Picayune*, October 23, 1977, sec. 1, p. 13; Richard M. Nixon, *RN: The Memoirs
of Richard Nixon* (New York: Grosset and Dunlap, 1978), pp. 935, 945; and Herbert G. Klein,
Making It Perfectly Clear (Garden City, N.Y.: Doubleday, 1980), p. 341.

10. Richard M. Nixon, "Addresses to the Nation on the Situation in Southeast Asia,"
Public Papers of the President of the United States: Richard Nixon, 1970 (Washington, D.C.: U.S.
Government Printing Office, 1971), p. 410.

11. Gerald R. Ford, "Imperiled, Not Imperial," *Time*, November 10, 1980, p. 31.

12. President Carter, quoted in Godfrey Hodgson, *All Things to All Men: The False
Promise of the Modern American Presidency* (New York: Simon and Schuster, 1980), p. 25.

13. *The Polling Report* 5 (January 30, 1989): 2–4.

14. "Carter Interview," *Congressional Quarterly Weekly Report*, November 25, 1978, p.
3354.

15. Gallup poll, *Attitudes toward the Presidency*, January 1980, p. 21.

16. Interview with Richard Wirthlin, West Point, N.Y., April 19, 1988.

17. Jack Dennis, "Dimensions of Public Support for the Presidency" (paper presented at the Annual Meeting of the Midwest Political Science Association, Chicago, April
1975), tables 4, 8; Hazel Erskine, "The Polls: Presidential Power," *Public Opinion Quarterly*
37 (Fall 1973): 492, 495.

18. George C. Edwards III, *At the Margins* (New Haven: Yale University Press, 1989),
chap. 6.

19. David O. Sears, "Political Socialization," in Fred I. Greenstein and Nelson Polsby,
eds. *Micropolitical Theory*, vol. 2 of *Handbook of Political Science* (Reading, Mass.: Addison-
Wesley, 1975), p. 177.

20. See George C. Edwards III, *The Public Presidency* (New York: St. Martin's, 1983),
p. 261, n. 13.

21. "Remarks of the President at a Meeting with Non-Washington Editors and Broad-
casters," White House Transcript, pp. 11–12.

22. *CBS News/The New York Times Poll, Part 1*, January 1982, table 34.

23. "Institutions: Confidence Even in Difficult Times," *Public Opinion*, June/July 1981,
p. 33.

24. *Gallup Opinion Index*, November 1978, pp. 8–9.

25. "Reagan: A Likeable Guy," *Public Opinion*, December/January 1981, p. 24.

26. Jack Valenti, *A Very Human President* (New York: Norton, 1975), p. 151.

27. On this subject see Edwards, *The Public Presidency*, p. 227, and sources cited therein.

28. Michael Kagay, "Personal Satisfaction Rises in U.S., Poll Shows," *The New York Times*, December 25, 1988, Sec. A, p. 10.

29. For a more in-depth analysis of presidential approval, see Edwards, *The Public Presidency*, chap. 6; George C. Edwards III, *Presidential Approval* (Baltimore: Johns Hopkins University Press, 1990).

30. John E. Mueller, *War, Presidents, and Public Opinion* (New York: Wiley, 1970), pp. 208–13.

31. See Edwards, *At the Margins*, chap. 7, fns. 48–51.

32. Eugene J. Rossi, "Mass and Attentive Opinion on Nuclear Weapons Test and Fallout, 1954–1963," *Public Opinion Quarterly* 29 (Summer 1965): 280–97; Robert S. Erikson, Norman R. Luttbeg, and Kent L. Tedin, *American Public Opinion: Its Origins, Content, and Impact*, 2nd ed. (New York: Wiley, 1980), p. 144; Mueller, *War, Presidents, and Public Opinion*, pp. 69–74.; *CBS News/The New York Times Poll*, October 28, 1983, p. 2; and Barry Sussman, "Reagan's Talk Gains Support for Policies," *Washington Post*, October 30, 1983, sec. A, pp. 1, 18.

33. Lee Sigelman, "Gauging the Public Response to Presidential Leadership," *Presidential Studies Quarterly* 10 (Summer 1980): 427–33. See also Pamela Johnston Conover and Lee Sigelman, "Presidential Influence and Public Opinion: The Case of the Iranian Hostage Crisis," *Social Science Quarterly* 63 (June 1982): 249–64.

34. "Most Utah Residents Say 'No' to MX Missile Deployment," *Bryan-College Station Eagle*, September 15, 1981, p. 5A.

35. Lee Sigelman and Carol K. Sigelman, "Presidential Leadership of Public Opinion: From 'Benevolent Leader' to Kiss of Death?" *Experimental Study of Politics* 7, no. 3 (1981): 1–22.

36. Benjamin I. Page and Robert Y. Shapiro, "Presidential Leadership through Public Opinion," in George C. Edwards III et al., eds., *The Presidency and Public Policy Making* (Pittsburgh: University of Pittsburgh Press, 1985), pp. 22–36.

37. Fred I. Greenstein, "Eisenhower as an Activist President: A Look at New Evidence," *Political Science Quarterly* 94 (Winter 1979–1980): 588–90.

38. Israel Shenker, "Obfuscation Foes against Ziegler and an Air Attache," *The New York Times*, November 28, 1974, sec. 1, p. 35.

39. David Stockman, *The Triumph of Politics* (New York: Harper and Row, 1986), p. 173. See also pp. 132, 353.

40. These expenditures are primarily federal loans to the public for specified investment and assistance projects, federal guarantees of loans made by private issuers, and lending activities of federally sponsored enterprises, such as the Farm Credit Administration, Federal Home Loan Bank system, Student Marketing Association, and the Federal National Mortgage Association. Although they involve billions of dollars of outlays, these funds are not included in the regular budget.

41. Joseph C. Goulden, *Truth Is the First Casualty* (Chicago: Rand McNally, 1969), p. 160.

42. Mueller, *War, Presidents, and Public Opinion*, pp. 112–13.

43. For a more complete discussion see Edwards, *The Public Presidency*, pp. 60–64. See also Larry Speakes, *Speaking Out* (New York: Scribner's, 1988), pp. 141, 160–62, 172.

44. Dick Kirschten, "Reagan and Reality," *National Journal*, October 16, 1982, p. 1765.

45. *CBS News/The New York Times Poll*, October 30, 1986, table 29.

46. William Schneider, "Opinion Outlook," *National Journal*, November 29, 1986, pp. 2908–09.

47. Steven V. Roberts, "Return to the Land of the Gipper," *The New York Times*, March 9, 1988, p. A28.

48. Lawrence C. Miller and Lee Sigelman, "Is the Audience the Message? A Note on LBJ's Vietnam Statements," *Public Opinion Quarterly* 42 (Spring 1978): 71–80. See also Malcolm Goggin, "The Ideological Content of Presidential Communications," *American Politics Quarterly* 12 (July 1984): 361–84.

49. Michael K. Deaver, *Behind the Scenes* (New York: William Morrow, 1987), p. 73. See also pp. 126–27, 135.

50. Laurence I. Barrett, *Gambling with History* (New York: Penguin, 1983), p. 442.

51. Michael Baruch Grossman and Martha Joynt Kumar, *Portraying the President: The White House and the News Media* (Baltimore: Johns Hopkins University Press, 1981), p. 29.

52. Ibid., p. 234.

53. Deaver, *Behind the Scenes*, p. 141.

54. See Regan, *For the Record*, pp. 247–49.

55. Rich Jaroslovsky, "Manipulating the Media Is a Specialty for the White House's Michael Deaver," *The Wall Street Journal*, January 5, 1984, p. 44.

56. Speakes, *Speaking Out*, p. 220.

57. John Ehrlichman, *Witness to Power: The Nixon Years* (New York: Simon and Schuster, 1982), p. 267.

58. Jody Powell, quoted in Michael Baruch Grossman and Martha Joynt Kumar, "Carter, Reagan, and the Media: Have the Rules Changed or the Poles of the Spectrum of Success?" (paper presented at the Annual Meeting of the American Political Science Association, New York, September 3–6, 1981), p. 18. See also p. 26.

SELECTED READINGS

Cronin, Thomas E. "The Presidency and Its Paradoxes." In Thomas E. Cronin and Rexford G. Tugwell, eds., *The Presidency Reappraised*, 2nd ed. (New York: Praeger, 1977).

——————. "The Presidency Public Relations Script." In Rexford G. Tugwell and Thomas E. Cronin, eds., *The Presidency Reappraised*. New York: Praeger, 1974.

Edwards, George C., III. *Presidential Approval*. Baltimore: Johns Hopkins University Press, 1990.

——————. *The Public Presidency*. New York: St. Martin's, 1983.

Graber, Doris, ed. *The President and the Public*. Philadelphia: Institute for the Study of Human Issues, 1982.

Kernell, Samuel. *Going Public*. Washington, D.C.: Congressional Quarterly, 1986.

Kinder, Donald R. "Presidents, Prosperity, and Public Opinion," *Public Opinion Quarterly* 45 (Spring 1981): 1–21.

Klein, Herbert G. *Making It Perfectly Clear*. Garden City, N.Y.: Doubleday, 1980.

Lau, Richard, and David O. Sears. "Cognitive Links between Economic Grievances and Political Responses." *Political Behavior* 3, no. 4 (1981): 279–302.

Miller, Lawrence C., and Lee Sigelman. "Is the Audience the Message? A Note on LBJ's Vietnam Statements." *Public Opinion Quarterly* 42 (Spring 1978): 71–80.

Miroff, Bruce. "The Presidency and the Public: Leadership as Spectacle." In Michael Nelson, ed., *The Presidency and the Political System*. Washington, D.C.: Congressional Quarterly, 1988.

Mueller, John E. *War, Presidents, and Public Opinion*. New York: Wiley, 1970. Chaps. 9–10.

Sigelman, Lee. "Gauging the Public Response to Presidential Leadership." *Presidential Studies Quarterly* 10 (Summer 1980): 427–33.

Sigelman, Lee, and Carol K. Sigelman. "Presidential Leadership of Public Opinion: From 'Benevolent Leader' to Kiss of Death?" *Experimental Study of Politics* 7, no. 3 (1981): 1–22.

Tulis, Jeffrey K. *The Rhetorical Presidency.* Princeton, N.J.: Princeton University Press, 1987.

Wayne, Stephen J. "Great Expectations: What People Want from Presidents." In Thomas E. Cronin, ed., *Rethinking the Presidency.* Boston: Little, Brown, 1982.

Wise, David. *The Politics of Lying: Government Deception, Secrecy, and Power.* New York: Vintage, 1973.

5

The President and the Media

Despite all their efforts to lead public opinion, presidents do not directly reach the American people on a day-to-day basis. It is the media that provide people with most of what they know about the chief executive, his policies, and the consequences of his policies. The media also interpret and analyze presidential activities, even the president's direct appeals to the public.

The media, or press, is the principal intermediary between the president and the public, and relations with the press are an important aspect of the president's efforts to lead public opinion. If the press portrays the president in a favorable light, he will face fewer obstacles in obtaining public support. If, on the other hand, the press is hostile toward his administration, the president's task will be more difficult.

Because of the importance of the press to the president, the White House goes to great lengths to encourage the media to project a positive image of the president and his policies. These efforts include coordinating the news, holding press conferences, and providing a range of services such as formal briefings, interviews, photo opportunities, background sessions, travel accomodations, and daily handouts.

In addition to the chief executive's efforts to influence the media, there is another side of this relationship we must examine: the content of the news. Ultimately, it is the written and spoken word that concerns the president. Leaks of confidential information and what is seen in the White House as superficial and biased reporting exacerbate the tensions inherent in relations between the president and the press. Presidents commonly view the press as a major obstacle to their obtaining and maintaining public support. Criticism of media coverage as being trivial and distorted and as violating confidences is a standard feature of most administrations. The White House feels that this type of reporting hinders its efforts to develop public appreciation for the president and his policies.

In this chapter we examine the nature and structure of presidential relationships with the press, emphasizing both the context of these relationships and the White House's attempts to obtain favorable coverage through holding press conferences and providing services for the press. We also focus on the substance of the media's coverage of the president, discussing the controversial issues of leaks to the press and superficiality and bias in the news. Finally, we consider the evidence regarding the important but generally overlooked question of the effects of press coverage of the White House on public opinion.

If the president fits the model we have termed director, he will receive favorable press coverage of his administration and reliably use the press to advance his interests. In contrast, a facilitator president will experience a more adversarial relationship, one characterized by more neutral coverage and a constant struggle by the White House to obtain both space and sympathetic treatment in the media.

THE EVOLUTION OF MEDIA COVERAGE

Today we are accustomed to turning to our newspapers or television sets to learn conveniently about what the president has said or done. Things have not always been this way. Before the Civil War, newspapers were generally small, heavily partisan, and limited in circulation. Between 1860 and 1920 a number of changes occurred that permanently altered the relationships between the president and the press.

Several technological innovations, including the electric printing press, the telegraph, the typewriter, the telephone, linotype, and wood-pulp paper, made it both possible and economical to produce mass-circulation newspapers carrying recent national news. Aside from the sales efforts of the newspapers themselves, the increasing literacy of the population helped to create a market for these papers.

The growing interest in national affairs as a result of the new importance of the national government also helped newspapers. The government began to regulate the economy with the Interstate Commerce Commission and its antitrust efforts. It expanded its role in world affairs during the Spanish-American War and World War I. Both of these events kindled support for and great interest in the activities of the government in Washington. The increased interest in national affairs was also caused by the renewed prominence of the presidency following an era of congressional ascendancy. Theodore Roosevelt took an activist view of the presidency and exploited the new opportunities to reach the public provided by the mass-circulation press. He used the White House as a "bully pulpit" to dramatize himself and the issues in which he was interested. He sought and gained extensive access to the press in order to forge a more personal relationship with the American people.

Ever since the first Roosevelt occupied the White House, news about the president has played an increasingly prominent role in the printed press, both in absolute terms and relative to coverage of Congress or the national government as a whole. Research on the contemporary presidency has found that almost three-fourths of national government news focuses on the president.[1]

Presidents have found that they need the press because it is their primary link to the people. The press, in turn, finds coverage of the president indispensable in satisfying its audience and in reporting on the most significant political events. The advent of radio and television has only heightened these mutual needs.

The history of relations between the president and the press has not involved unlimited goodwill. President George Washington complained that the "calumnies" against his administration were "outrages of common decency" motivated by the desire to destroy confidence in the new goverment.[2] John Adams was so upset at criticism in the press that he supported the Sedition Act and jailed some opposition journalists under its authority.

Thomas Jefferson, certainly one of our greatest defenders of freedom, became so exasperated with the press as president that he argued that "even the least informed of the people have learned that nothing in a newspaper is to be believed." He also felt that "newspapers, for the most part, present only the caricature of disaffected minds. Indeed, the abuses of freedom of the press have been carried to a length never before known or borne by any civilized nation." These observations, it should be noted, come from the man who earlier had written that "were it left to me to decide whether we should have a government without newspapers or newspapers without a government, I should not hesitate to prefer the latter."[3]

Almost two centuries later things have not changed very much. Although all presidents have supported the abstract right of the press to criticize them freely, most have not found this criticism very comfortable while in office. They have viewed some of the press as misrepresenting (perhaps maliciously) their views and actions, failing to perceive the correctness of their policies, and dedicated to impeding their goals. As the Iran–Contra scandal unfolded, Ronald Reagan complained of the press circling the White House like "sharks."

No matter who is in the White House or who reports on him, presidents and the press tend to be in conflict. Presidents are inherently policy advocates and want to be able to define a situation and receive favorable coverage. They will naturally assess the press in terms of its aiding or hindering their goals. The press, on the other hand, has the responsibility for presenting reality. While the press may fail in its efforts, it will assess itself on that criterion. The president wants to control the amount and timing of information about his administration, while the press wants all the information that exists without delay. As long as their goals are different, presidents and the press are likely to be adversaries.

RELATIONS BETWEEN THE PRESIDENT AND THE PRESS

The White House Press Corps

Who are the reporters that regularly cover the White House? The regulars represent diverse media constituencies. These include daily newspapers like the *Washington Post* and *The New York Times;* weekly newsmagazines like *Time* and *Newsweek;* the wire services like the Associated Press (AP) and United Press International (UPI); newspaper chains like Hearst, Scripps-Howard, Newhouse, and Knight; the television and radio networks; the foreign press; and "opinion" magazines like the *New Republic* and the *National Review.* In addition, photographers, columnists, television commentators, and magazine writers are regularly involved in White House–press interactions. More than seventeen hundred persons have White House press credentials. Fortunately, not everyone shows up at once. About sixty reporters and fifteen photographers regularly cover the White House, and the total of both increases to more than one hundred when an important announcement is expected. Attendance at a presidential press conference may number about three hundred.

The great majority of daily newspapers in America have no Washington correspondents, much less someone assigned to cover the White House. The same can be said for almost all of the country's individual television and radio stations. These papers and stations rely heavily upon the AP and UPI wire services, each of which covers the White House continuously and in detail with three full-time reporters.

The Presidential Press Operation

The White House's relations with the media occupy a substantial portion of the time of a large number of aides. About one-third of the high-level White House staff is directly involved in media relations and policy of one type or another, and most staff members are involved at some time in influencing the media's portrayal of the president.

The person in the White House who most often deals directly with the press is the president's press secretary. Probably the central function of press secretaries is to serve as conduits of information from the White House to the press. They must be sure that clear statements of administration policies have been prepared on important policy matters. The press secretaries usually conduct the daily press briefings, giving prepared announcements and answering questions. In forming their answers they often do not have specific orders on what to say or not to say. They must be able to think on their feet to ensure that they accurately reflect the president's views. Sometimes these views may be unclear, however, or the president may not wish to articulate his views. Therefore, press secretaries may seem to be evasive or unimaginative in public settings. They also hold private meetings with individual reporters, where the information provided can be more candid and speculative.

To be effective in the conduit role the press secretary must maintain credibility with reporters. Credibility rests on at least two important pillars: (1) truth and (2) access to and respect for the president and senior White House officials. If a press secretary is viewed as not telling the truth or as not being close to top decision makers (and therefore not well informed), he will not be an effective presidential spokesman, because the press will give little credence to what he says. Credibility problems have arisen for several press secretaries as a result of these perceived deficiencies.

Press secretaries also serve as conduits from the press to the president. They must sometimes explain the needs of the press to the president. For example, all of Lyndon Johnson's press secretaries tried to persuade the president to issue advance information on his travel plans to the press. When he refused, they provided it anyway and then had it expunged from the briefing transcript so the president would not see it. Press secretaries also try to inform the White House staff of the press's needs and the rules of the game, and they help reporters gain access to staff members.

Press secretaries are typically not involved in substantive decisions, but they do give the president advice, usually on what information should be released, by whom, in what form, and to what audience. They also advise the president on rehearsals for press conferences and on how to project his image and use it to his political advantage.

Since the time of William Loeb, Theodore Roosevelt's press secretary, the White House has attempted to coordinate executive branch news. Presidents have assigned aides to clear the appointments of departmental public affairs officials, to keep in touch with the officials to learn what news is forthcoming from the departments, and to meet with them to explain the president's policy views and try to prevent conflicting statements from emanating from the White House and other units of the executive branch. Specialists have had responsibility for coordinating national security news.

Of course, such tactics do not always work. President Ford wanted to announce the results of the *Mayaguez* operation from the White House, but he found to his disappointment that the Pentagon had already done so, making any presidential announcement anticlimactic. At the beginning of his second year in office, President Reagan issued an order that required advance White House approval of television appearances by cabinet members and other top officials, but it soon lapsed.

Coordinating the news from the White House itself has also been a presidential goal. Presidents have sometimes monitored and attempted to limit the press contacts of White House aides, who have annoyed their bosses by using the media for their own purposes. President Reagan, for example, instituted a policy midway through his administration that required his assistant for communications to approve any interview with any White House official requested by a member of the media. All requests were monitored and entered on a computer so the White House could keep tabs on whom reporters wanted to see. Since even the White House press cannot wander through the East or West wings on their own, the only way to speak to aides without administration approval was to call them at home, a practice discouraged by presidential assistants and generally avoided by the media. Such efforts to limit press access are exceptional, however, and have proved to be largely fruitless.

Recent administrations have also made an effort to coordinate publicity functions within the White House, attempting to present the news in the most favorable light, such as preventing two major stories from breaking on the same day, smothering bad news with more positive news, and timing announcements for maximum effect.

All recent presidents, including Eisenhower, who had a reputation to the contrary, have read several newspapers each day, especially *The New York Times* and the *Washington Post*. Kennedy, Johnson, and Reagan were also very attentive to television news programs. Johnson had a television cabinet with three screens so he could watch all three networks at once. But even this was not enough to satisfy his thirst for news. He also had teletypes that carried the latest reports from the AP and UPI wire services installed in the Oval Office, and he monitored them regularly.

President Nixon rarely watched television news and did not peruse large numbers of newspapers or magazines, but he was extremely interested in press coverage of his administration. He had his staff prepare a daily news summary of newspapers, magazines, television news, and the AP and UPI news wires. Often this summary triggered ideas for the president, who gave orders to aides to follow up on something he read. The news summary also went to White House assistants. Subsequent presidents have continued the news summary, altering it to meet their individual needs, and have circulated it to top officials in their administrations. The Carter White House instituted a separate magazine survey and even a weekly summary of Jewish publications when it became concerned about a possible backlash within the American Jewish community against the administration's Middle East policy.

Presidential Press Conferences

The best-known direct interaction between the president and the press is the presidential press conference. The frequency of press conferences has varied. Franklin Roosevelt held about seven a month; Truman cut this figure in half. Eisenhower further reduced their frequency, holding about two press conferences each month, a rate maintained by Kennedy and Johnson. Carter and Ford averaged closer to one press conference per month, while Nixon and Reagan held only about one press conference every two months. Such figures should not be accepted at face value, however. What presidents count as press conferences varies considerably, and the figures for average frequency of press conferences may conceal wide fluctuations in the time between conferences. The trend is clearly in the direction of fewer formal press conferences, however, especially for chief executives like Reagan who do not perform well in unstructured settings. President Bush held only one in his first six months in office.

Naturally, the more time that has elapsed between press conferences, the more events and governmental actions that will have transpired since the last press conference. The more that has transpired, the more wide-ranging the questions asked of the president are likely to be. And the more wide-ranging the questions, the more superficial the coverage of any one topic is likely to be.

Another factor that has perhaps reduced the utility of the press conferences for eliciting useful information about government has been their increasing size. Modern presidents have generally employed a large room (such as the State Department auditorium or the East Room in the White House) for press conferences, usually relying upon public address systems. The increased number of reporters covering press conferences and the setting in which they take place have inevitably made them more formal. More reporters mean more persons with different concerns and thus less likelihood of follow-up questions to cover a subject in depth. Spontaneity in questions and answers has largely been lost.

Presidents have taken other steps that have contributed to the formalization of press conferences. Beginning with Truman, they have undergone formal briefings and "dry runs" in preparation for questions that might be asked. Presidents have asked their aides and the departments and agencies to submit to them possible questions and suggested answers, and sometimes they call for further information. In 1982 President Reagan began holding full-scale mock news conferences. Guessing at questions is not too difficult. There are obvious areas of concern, and questions raised at White House and departmental briefings and other meetings with reporters provide useful cues. The president also can anticipate the interests of individual reporters, and he has discretion over whom to recognize. In Reagan's news conferences, reporters were assigned seats, and the president, using a seating chart, called them by name. In one case Reagan called a reporter only to discover that he was not even attending the conference. The reporter, watching the news conference in his living room at home, asked a question anyway but only his family heard it. The next day the newspapers had a field day reporting the incident.

The change in the nature of the presidential press conferences from semiprivate to public events has diminished their utility in transmitting information from the president to the press. Since every word they say is transmitted verbatim to millions of people, presidents cannot speak as candidly as, say, Franklin D. Roosevelt could. Nor can they speculate freely about their potential actions or evaluations of persons, events, or circumstances. Instead, they must choose their words carefully, and their responses to questions are often not terribly enlightening.

Presidents since Truman have frequently begun their press conferences with carefully prepared opening statements. Examples include President Kennedy's 1962 blast at the steel companies for raising their prices (eventually leading to the increases being rescinded) and President Carter's five-minute monologue on his administration's accomplishments in a televised press conference during the 1980 presidential election. Lyndon Johnson was especially likely to deliver an opening statement. These statements have given presidents an opportunity to reach the public on their own terms. Opening statements may also further reduce the opportunities for questions while at the same time they may focus questions on issues of the president's choosing (contained in the statement).

Because presidents are in control of their press conferences, they can state that they will not entertain questions on certain topics. They may also evade questions with clever rhetoric or simply answer with a "no comment." Or they can use a question as a vehicle to say something they planned ahead of time. If necessary they can reverse the attack and focus on the questioner, or conversely, they can call on a friendly reporter for a "soft" question. Eisenhower used a skilled evasiveness and impenetrable syntax to avoid direct answers to embarrassing or politically sensitive questions, something not unusual among presidents.

Presidents and their staffs have sometimes found it convenient to plant questions with the press. In other words, they end up asking themselves questions. This practice started at least as early as Franklin Roosevelt, and Eisenhower and Johnson often made use of it.

Many of the questions asked the president involve trivial topics. One reason for this is deference to the president. Reporters meet the president on his territory, not theirs, and dutifully rise when he enters the room. An adversarial relationship may exist outside the press conference, but it is rarely reflected during the sessions themselves. The author of a study of press conferences found only two occasions in fifteen years when the number of hostile questions asked by reporters at any press conference exceeded three.[4]

The artificial nature of press conferences, especially on television, may lead to distortions. On the one hand, a truly spontaneous answer to a question may be candid, but it also may be foolish or expose the president's ignorance of an area. Generalizations based on such a reply may be inaccurate because the president may actually be well informed but require more than a few seconds to think about a complex problem. On the other hand, some presidents may be glib, charming, and attractive, and therefore perform well in a spontaneous press conference but really not be very competent. The advent of television has further increased the potential for distortion, since a president's physical attractiveness, delivery, and flair for the dramatic may leave more of an impression on the public mind than the substance of his answers.

In sum, presidential press conferences are often not very informative. In the more formal and less spontaneous press conferences that characterize the more recent era, the president has a substantial opportunity to control the image he projects. He often begins with a prepared announcement, his answers to most questions are equally prepared, and he has leeway on when he will hold the conference and whom he will call upon. While the press conference does provide the president an opportunity to focus national attention upon himself, stimulate public opinion, and criticize or support various political actors, and while the preconference briefing may serve as a useful device for informing the president across a broad spectrum of issues, we cannot depend upon the conference to reveal the real president, and the nature of television may distort more than it reveals.

Services for the Press

In order to get their messages across to the American people and to influence the tone and content of press presentation of those messages, presidents have provided services for the press. One of the most important is the backgrounder. The president's comments to reporters may be "on the record" (remarks may be attributed to the speaker); "on background" (a specific source cannot be identified but the source's position and status can—such as a "White House source"); "deep background" (no attribution); or "off the record" (the information reporters receive may not be used in a story). For purposes of convenience we shall term all sessions between White House officials (including the president) and the press that are not "on the record" as "backgrounders." All recent presidents, especially Johnson and Ford, have engaged in background discussion with reporters, although President Nixon's involvement was rare. Some presidents, especially Eisenhower and Nixon, have relied heavily upon their principal foreign policy advisers to brief reporters on foreign affairs.

The most common type of presidential discussion with reporters on a background basis is a briefing. In these sessions the president typically explains a policy's development and what it is expected to accomplish. Interestingly, the president does not appear to stress the substance of policy. He seldom makes "hard" news statements in background briefings, because this would irritate absent members of the press. The reporters watch the president perform, and since the president controls the conditions of these briefings, the chances of making a favorable impression are good.

Reporters tend to view middle-level aides as the best information sources. They have in-depth knowledge about the substance of programs, and they are generally free from the constraints of high visibility, so they are in a good position to provide useful backgrounders. Backgrounders are particularly important for these officials because presidents are generally intolerant of staff members who seek publicity for themselves, and most interviews with White House staff are on this basis. Sometimes aides say more than their superiors would like in order to prod the president in a particular policy direction.

Backgrounders have a number of advantages for the White House. Avoiding direct quotation allows officials to speak on sensitive foreign policy and domestic policy matters candidly and in depth, something domestic politics and international diplomacy would not tolerate if speakers were held directly accountable for their words. The White House hopes such discussions will help it communicate its point of view more clearly and serve to educate journalists, perhaps preparing them for future policies, and make them more sympathetic to the president's position in their reporting. An impressive performance in a background session can show the White House to be competent and perhaps elicit the benefit of the doubt in future stories. Moreover, background sessions can be used to scotch rumors and limit undesirable speculation about presidential plans and internal White House affairs.

On the other hand, backgrounders may be aimed at the public (in the form of trial balloons that the White House can disclaim if they meet with disapproval) or at policymakers in Washington. They may also be directed at other countries. To discourage the Soviet Union's support of India in its war with Pakistan, Henry Kissinger told reporters in a backgrounder that the Soviet policy might lead to the cancellation of President Nixon's trip to Moscow. Since the statement was not officially attributed to Kissinger, it constituted less of a public threat to the Soviet Union, while at the same time it communicated the president's message.[5]

Reporters have generally been happy to go along with protecting the identities of "spokesmen" and "sources" (although an experienced observer can identify most of them), because the system provides them more information than they would have without it. This increase of information available to reporters adds to the information available to the public, and it probably helps advance journalistic careers as well.

Backgrounders, of course, have also provided the White House opportunities to disseminate misleading or self-serving propaganda anonymously. Sometimes such propaganda concerns intramural warfare, an especially common theme in the Ford administration but also appearing in the Nixon and other administrations.

In addition to the more informal sessions, briefings are held each weekday for the White House press (they were held twice daily in the Reagan administration). In the daily briefings reporters are provided with information about appointments and resignations, decisions of the president to sign or not to sign routine bills and explanations for his actions, and the president's schedule (whom he will see that day, what meetings he has, what his future travel plans are, and when the press can see him). More significantly from the standpoint of the press, the briefing provides presidential reactions to events, the White House "line" on issues and whether it has changed, and a reading of the president's moods and ideas. This information is obtained through prepared statements or answers to reporters' queries. Responses to the latter are often prepared ahead of time by the White House staff. The daily briefings, of course, also provide the press with an opportunity to have the president's views placed on the public record, which eases the burdens of reporting.

Usually the president's press secretary or his deputy presides over these briefings, although sometimes the president participates. White House staff members and executive branch officials with substantial expertise in specific policy areas such as the budget or foreign affairs sometimes brief the press and answer questions at the daily briefing or at special briefings, especially when the White House is launching a major publicity campaign.

Interviews with the president and top White House staff members are a valuable commodity to the press, and sometimes the White House uses them for its purposes. President Nixon traded an exclusive interview to Hugh Sidney of *Time* for a cover story on him. In order to obtain an interview with President Ford, even the venerable Walter Cronkite agreed to use only questions the president could handle easily. At other times the White House may give exclusives to a paper like *The New York Times* in return for getting a story in which it is interested a prominent place in the paper.[6]

Providing the press exclusive information may be as ingratiating as an exclusive interview and may be used to distract reporters from more embarrassing stories. At other times the White House may trade advance notice of a story for information reporters possess about developments elsewhere in the government that are not clear to the president and his staff.

Recent presidents, with the exception of Richard Nixon, have regularly cultivated elite reporters and columnists, the editors and publishers of leading newspapers, and network news producers and executives with small favors, social flattery, and small background dinners at the White House. (Nixon turned these chores over to top aides.) The first call ABC anchorperson Peter Jennings received after winning his job was from Ronald Reagan.[7] Since the 1960s the White House has had first a special person and then an office for media liaison to deal directly with the representatives of news organizations, such as editors, publishers, and producers, in addition to the press office that deals with reporters' routine needs.

There are many additional services that the White House provides for the press. It gives reporters transcripts of briefings and presidential speeches and daily handouts announcing a myriad of information about the president and his policies, including advance notice of travel plans and upcoming stories. Major announcements are timed to accommodate the deadlines of newspapers, magazines, and television networks.

Photographers covering the president are highly dependent on the White House press office, which provides facilities for photographers on presidential trips and arranges photo opportunities, making sure they will produce the most flattering shots of the president (such as Johnson's left profile). President Reagan even prohibited impromptu questions from reporters at photographing sessions. Moreover, the official White House photographers provide many of the photographs of the president that the media use. Naturally, these are screened so that the president is presented favorably.

When the president goes on trips, at home or abroad, extensive preparations are made for the press. These preparations include arranging transportation and lodging for the press, installing equipment for radio and television broadcasting, obtaining telephones for reporters, erecting platforms for photographers, preparing a detailed account of where and with whom the president will be at particular times, providing elaborate information about the countries the president is visiting, forming pools of press members to cover the president closely (as in a motorcade), and scheduling the press plane to arrive before the president's so the press can cover his arrival.

As many of these services suggest, the press is especially dependent upon the White House staff in covering presidential trips, particularly foreign trips. The number of sources of information is generally reduced, as is the access of the press to the principal figures it wishes to cover. Thus the president's aides are in a good position to manipulate press coverage to their advantage. Coverage of foreign trips is generally favorable, although perhaps less so than in the past now that reporters with expertise in foreign affairs accompany the president, and the press points out the relationship of the trip and its goals and accomplishments to the president's domestic political problems.

Even in Washington, however, reporters are very much in a controlled environment. Reagan aides went so far as to have the motor of the president's helicopter revved so he could not hear questions shouted by the press as he left for a weekend at Camp David. Similarly, the president held no press conferences at all during the 1984 presidential campaign. Reporters may not freely roam the halls of the White House, interviewing whomever they please. They are highly dependent upon the press officer for access to officials, and about half their interviews are with the press secretary and his staff. Much of their time is spent waiting for something to happen or watching the president at formal or ceremonial events. Since most news stories about such occurrences show the president in a favorable light, the press office does everything possible to help reporters record these activities. Similarly, the White House is happy to provide photographs featuring the president's "warm," "human," or "family" side. These please editors and the public alike.

Briefings, press releases, and the like can be used to divert the media's attention from embarrassing matters. The Reagan White House adopted a strategy of blitzing the media with information to divert its attention after the press raised questions about the president's sleeping through Libyan attacks on United States forces off the coast of Africa.[8] More frequently, the White House, by adopting an active approach to the press, gains an opportunity to shape the media's agenda for the day. Through announcements and press releases it attempts to focus attention on what will reflect positively on the president. Such information frequently generates questions from reporters and subsequent news stories. Representatives of the smaller papers, who have few resources, are more heavily dependent upon White House–provided news than are the larger news bureaus, including the major networks. They are the most likely to follow the White House's agenda. Moreover, since White House reporters, especially the wire services, are under pressure to file daily "hard news" reports, the White House is in a strong position to help by providing information, much of it trivial and all of it designed to reflect positively on the president. As a Ford official put it: "You can predict what the press is going to do with a story. It is almost by formula. Because of this they are usable."[9]

Many observers, including journalists, feel that the press tends to parrot the White House line, so conveniently provided at a briefing or in a press release, especially early in a president's term. The pressure among journalists to be first with a story increases the potential for White House manipulation inherent in this deferential approach, as concerns for accuracy give way to career interests.

Presidents have undoubtedly hoped that the handouts, briefings, and other services they and their staffs provide for reporters will gain them some goodwill. They may also hope that these services will keep the White House press from digging too deeply into presidential affairs. In addition, they want to keep reporters interested in the president's agenda, because bored journalists are more negative in their reporting and may base their stories on trivial incidents like the president's stumbling on a plane.

In addition, the White House controls a commodity of considerable value to the press: information on the president's personal life. Most reporters are under pressure to provide stories on the minutiae of the president's life, no matter what he does. Some White House aides have found that the provision of such information can co-opt journalists or sidetrack them from producing critical stories. Some reporters will exploit the opportunity to please their editors instead of digging into more significant subjects; others reciprocate their favorable treatment by the White House with positive stories about the president.

Seeing yet another opportunity to influence the press, the White House has provided services for the local as well as the national and Washington-based media. Relations with the local media took a significant step forward in the Nixon administration. In an effort to bypass the more liberal national press and to develop goodwill, President Nixon held briefings for local news executives or had senior administration officials give them. He also sent administration briefing teams around the country to discuss his legislative proposals with local media representatives. The local press, they found, was very responsive to this attention, often giving the president substantial publicity and using the White House story ideas and sometimes even the background materials it provided. Special mailings of news releases and documents to newspapers, television and radio stations, journal writers, citizens groups, and private individuals were also made.

Subsequent presidents learned that dealing directly with the non-national press was very useful in obtaining coverage of the president's message in the local and specialty media. Once the Washington press reports an issue, it tends to drop it and move on to the next one, yet repetition is necessary to convey the president's views to the generally inattentive public. Moreover, the Washington press tends to place more emphasis on the support of or opposition to a program than on its substance, although the White House wants to communicate the latter.

The Nixon administration's efforts at dealing with the local press were continued and expanded. Gerald Ford invited local news announcers to the White House for taped personal interviews to be used exclusively in their home stations. He also held press conferences for reporters from the local press. Every other week President Carter had local newspapers and broadcast journalists come to Washington to meet him and be briefed by administration officials. The information provided in these meetings was not released to the general press for twenty-four hours so that the out-of-town journalists could file their exclusive stories. At the end of 1978 the White House began to provide thirty- and forty-second taped radio spots free of charge to radio stations that called a toll-free White House number. All White House press releases and texts are now available by computer to anyone subscribing to the service. Top officials can also do interviews with local television stations through satellite hookups.

Presidents who engage in servicing (and lobbying) the local media undoubtedly hope that they will receive a sympathetic hearing from journalists grateful to be invited to the White House and perhaps susceptible to presidential charm. They also hope that by providing information directly to the local media they can evade the closer scrutiny of the Washington- and New York–based national media, with its greater resources to challenge White House versions of events and policies and to investigate areas of government not covered by briefings or press releases. Naturally, they hope they can create some goodwill that will be reflected in news stories on the local level.

PRESS COVERAGE OF THE PRESIDENT

Leaks

In early 1982 President Reagan read the riot act to his cabinet, denouncing the release of confidential information to the press by anonymous sources as one of the major problems facing his administration. He was particularly concerned about leaks regarding his upcoming budget proposals for defense spending, a number of foreign policy matters, and the urban enterprise zones proposal that he wanted to save for his State of the Union message.[10] The president's frustration is evident in the quip with which he opened a press conference held at about the same time: "I was going to have an opening statement, but I decided that what I was going to say I wanted to get a lot of attention so I'm going to wait and leak it."

Ronald Reagan was hardly the first president to be upset by leaks. Sometimes they can be potentially quite serious, as when the United States negotiating strategy of the first SALT talks was disclosed during the Nixon administration. When the *Pentagon Papers* were leaked to the public, President Nixon felt that there was a danger that other countries would lose confidence in our ability to keep secrets and that information on the delicate negotiations then in progress with China might also be leaked, endangering the possibility of rapprochement.[11] At other times they are just embarrassing, as when internal dissent in the administration is revealed to the public. President Johnson feared leaks would signal what he was thinking, and he would lose his freedom of action as a result.

Who leaks information? The best answer is "everybody." Presidents themselves do so, sometimes inadvertently. As Lyndon Johnson once put it: "I have enough trouble with myself. I ought not to have to put up with everybody else too."[12] Top presidential aides may also reveal more than they intend. When a leak regarding President Reagan's willingness to compromise on his 1981 tax bill appeared in *The New York Times*, White House aides tracked down the source of the story and found it was budget director David Stockman.[13] A year earlier a leak revealing secret CIA arms shipments to Afghan rebels was attributed to the office of the president's chief national security adviser.[14] Lt. Col. Oliver North charged that members of Congress had leaked the fact that the United States had intercepted Libyan radio messages, which in turn enabled it to capture the hijackers of the *Achille Lauro* cruise liner. But *Newsweek* magazine reported that the source of the leak was none other than Oliver North himself.

Most leaks, however, are deliberately planted. As one close presidential aide put it, "99 percent of all significant secrets are spilled by the principals or at their direction."[15] Presidents are included in those who purposefully leak. *Newsweek* used to hold space open for the items John Kennedy would phone to his friend Benjamin Bradlee right before the magazine's deadline.[16] There are many reasons for leaks. They may be used as trial balloons to test public or congressional reaction to ideas and proposals or to stimulate public concern about an issue. Both the Ford and Carter White House used this technique to test reaction to a tax surcharge on gasoline. When the reaction turned out to be negative, they denied ever contemplating such a policy. At other times information is leaked to reporters who will use it to write favorable articles on a policy.

Diplomacy is an area in which delicate communications play an important role. Leaks are often used to send signals to other nations of our friendship, anger, or willingness to compromise. For example, during negotiations with the Japanese regarding restricting imports, the Reagan administration leaked a story that the talks were going badly to pressure Japan into moderating its position. At the same time leaks provide the president with the opportunity to disavow publicly or to reinterpret what some might view as, for example, an overly "tough" stance or an unexpected change in policy.

Leaks may also be used to influence personnel matters. The release of information letting a stubborn official know that the official's superiors wish him or her to leave may force a resignation and thus save the problem of firing the official, or, conversely, make the official's position a public issue, increasing the costs of such a firing. Similarly, the release of information on an appointment before it is made places the president in an awkward position and can help ensure that he follows through on it or prematurely denies he has such plans.

Some leaks are designed to force the president's hand on policy decisions. During the Indian–Pakistani War, President Nixon maintained a publicly neutral stance but was really favoring Pakistan. When this was leaked there was inevitably pressure to be neutral in action as

" I HAD To SWITCH YOUR LIE DETECTOR TEST THIS AFTERNOON FROM 3 TO 1
   BECAUSE YOU'RE SCHEDULED To LEAK·SOME INFORATION AT 2 ! "

Source: Reprinted by permission of Tribune Media Services.

well as in rhetoric. Conversely, in the case of Lyndon Johnson, a leak
that he was thinking about a decision could ensure that he would take
no such action.

Leaks may serve a number of other functions for individuals. They
may make one feel important or help one gain favor with reporters.
Leaks may also be used to criticize and intimidate personal or political
adversaries in the White House itself or protect and enhance reputations. In the Ford administration, White House counsel Robert Hartmann and the chief of staff Richard Cheney often attacked each other
anonymously in the press. Several members of the White House staff
attacked Press Secretary Ron Nessen in an effort to persuade the president to replace him. When negotiations with North Vietnam broke
down in late 1972, White House aides employed leaks to dissociate the
president from his national security adviser.

Presidents sometimes leak information for their own political purposes. Lyndon Johnson leaked information on nuclear weapons to answer Barry Goldwater in the 1964 presidential election. A Nixon aide
leaked a false story to *The Wall Street Journal* that the president was
considering seeking legislation to reduce the independence of the Federal Reserve Board and that the board's chairman, Arthur Burns, was a
hypocrite because he sought a personal salary increase while he was
asking the rest of the country to dampen its demands. The UPI received

a somewhat similar story. These leaks were attempts to make Burns more responsive to White House demands. The Nixon White House often employed leaks as a political tactic.

In all of these cases government officials were using the press for their purposes and not vice versa. Although reporters may well be aware of being used, the competitive pressure of the news business makes it difficult for them to pass up an exclusive story. Nevertheless, most good reporting, even investigative reporting, does not rely heavily upon leaks. Instead, reporters put together stories by bits and pieces.

It is generally fruitless to try to discover the source of a leak. The Reagan administration tried everything from lie detector tests to logging every journalist's interview on a computer, but nothing stopped the leaks. According to White House chief of staff Donald Regan, "In the Reagan Administration the leak was raised to the status of an art form. Everything, or nearly everything, the President and his close associates did or knew appeared in the newspapers and on the networks with the least possible delay."[17]

Superficiality

Early in this century Woodrow Wilson complained that most reporters were "interested in the personal and trivial rather than in principles of policies."[18] Things have not changed much in the ensuing generations. In a background briefing in 1979 President Carter complained to reporters: "I would really like for you all as people who relay Washington events to the world to take a look at the substantive questions I have to face as a president and quit dealing almost exclusively with personalities."[19] In this section we examine the question of the superficiality of the coverage of the presidency and the reasons for it.

Today media coverage of national news is characterized by brevity and simplicity. Editors do not want to bore or confuse their viewers, listeners, or readers. They often resort to the use of themes ("another example of rivalries within the White House"), symbols (a supermarket checkout line may represent inflation), and personification (an unemployed mother of five) to simplify issues. Moreover, most reporting is about events, actions taken or words spoken by public figures, especially if the events are dramatic and colorful, such as ceremonies and parades. Conflicts between clearly identifiable antagonists (the president versus the Speaker of the House) is highly prized, particularly if there is something tangible at stake, such as the passage of a bill.

The amount of information transmitted under such conditions is very limited. This type of news coverage is ill-equipped to deal with the ambiguities and uncertainties of most complex events and issues. Moreover, it provides little in the way of the background and contextual information that is essential for understanding political events. Although the electronic media, especially television, are the most typical source of news for Americans, they do the poorest job of providing information to the public. According to CBS anchorman Dan Rather, "You simply cannot be a well-informed citizen by just watching the news on television."[20]

Human interest stories, especially those about the president and his family, are novel and easier for the public to relate to than are complex matters of public policy. They are always in high demand. Nancy Reagan's new White House china received more attention in the press than most issues. Scandals involving public persons of all kinds receive high-priority coverage. Disasters and incidents of violence make for excellent film presentations, are novel, contain ample action, and are portrayed in easily understood terms. The intricacies of a presidential tax proposal are not so fortunate.

Studies show that coverage of presidential election campaigns is basically trivial, especially on television. Coverage of issues is spotty and superficial. The stands candidates take on issues are usually old news to reporters, who must suffer through hearing the same speech, with slight variations added for local audience appeal, again and again. The candidates' stands are not viewed as news. In general, substantive issues are reported in terms of their impact on politics rather than in terms of their merits.[21]

Clear-cut differences on issues between candidates have the potential for confrontation, even if the drama results from skillful tape editing, and these differences are emphasized within the space allotted to coverage. Such issues are not typical, however. Media coverage does not reflect the blend of issues advocated by the candidates. Moreover, the press generally ignores issues that the candidates neglect, even though they may be significant to the typical citizen. What does receive extensive coverage, as we saw in Chapter 3, is the "horse race"—the campaign as opposed to what the campaign is ostensibly about. Stories feature conflict, make brief points, are easily understood (often in either/or terms), and, especially on television, have film value.

Superficial news coverage is not limited to elections. Most of the White House press activity comes under the heading of the "body watch." In other words, reporters focus on the most visible layer of the president's personal and official activities and provide the public with a step-by-step account. They are interested in what the president is going to do, how his actions will affect others, how he views policies and individuals, how he presents himself, and whose stars are rising and falling, rather than in the substance of policies or the fundamental processes operating in the executive branch.

Editors expect this type of coverage, and reporters do not want to risk missing a story. As the Washington bureau chief of *Newsweek* said: "The worst thing in the world that could happen to you is for the President of the United States to choke on a piece of meat, and for you not to be there."[22] The emphasis of news coverage is on short-run, "instant history." Perspective on the events of the day is secondary. Thus, embarrassing items such as blunders and contradictions made by the president and his staff are widely reported, especially if the president is low in the polls (providing a consistent theme). Similarly, major presidential addresses are often reported in terms of how the president looked, how he spoke, and the number of times he received applause as much as in terms of what he had to say.

Presidential slips of the tongue or behavior are often blown out of all proportion. In the second debate between Gerald Ford and Jimmy Carter during the 1976 presidential campaign, Ford made a slip and said that Eastern Europe was "free from Soviet domination." Everyone, including the president, knew that he had misspoken. Unfortunately for Ford, he refused to admit his error for several days while the press had a field day speculating about his basic understanding of world politics. Similarly, when Richard Nixon described the persons "blowing up the campuses" as "bums," the press extended the adjective to all students, something the president had not meant. The uproar following this "news" can well be imagined.

In its constant search for "news," the press, especially the electronic media, is reluctant to devote repeated attention to an issue, although this might be necessary to explain it adequately to the public. As a deputy press secretary in the Carter administration said: "We have to keep sending out our message if we expect people to understand. The Washington Press corps will explain a policy once and then it will feature the politics of the issue."[23] This is one incentive for the president to meet with the non-Washington press.

One of the causes of superficial press coverage of the presidency is the demands of news organizations for information that is new and different, personal and intimate, revealing and unexpected. According to the White House correspondent for a major newspaper chain: "It's a lot easier for me to get [my stories] into several newspapers in the chain with a story about Amy [President Carter's daughter] than with a story about an important policy decision."[24] ABC White House correspondent Sam Donaldson commented, in much the same vein, "A clip of a convalescent Reagan waving from his window at some circus elephants is going to push an analytical piece about tax cuts off the air every time."[25]

Given the emphasis on the short run and the demand for details of the president's activities, reporters face continual deadlines. There is little time for reflection, analysis, or comprehensive coverage.

A related factor contributing to the trivialization of the news is the great deal of money and personnel needed to cover the president, including following him around the globe and on vacations. Because of this investment and because of the public's interest in the president, reporters must come up with something every day. Newsworthy happenings do not necessarily occur every day, however, so reporters either emphasize the trivial or blow events out of proportion. While covering a meeting of western leaders on the island of Guadeloupe, Sam Donaldson faced the prospect of having nothing to report on a slow news day. Undaunted, he reported on the roasting of the pig the leaders would be eating that evening, including "an exclusive look at the oven in which the pig would be roasted."[26] Similarly, the White House press often focuses on the exact wording of an announcement in an effort to detect a change in policy. Frequently it finds significance where none really exists.

There are more than organizational imperatives at work in influencing coverage of the president, however. Reporters' backgrounds and personal interests also underlie the trivialization of the news. They are often ill at ease with abstractions, and when they talk to each other about politics, they emphasize the superficial aspects—who will be elected, what bills will pass, what personalities the principal actors have, who has power.

The typical White House reporter lacks special background on the presidency. Moreover, the White House press frequently lacks policy expertise relevant to understanding the issues with which the president deals. Thus, its focus on politics and personalities rather than on issues is not surprising.

To delve more deeply into the presidency and policy requires not only substantial expertise but also certain technical skills. Washington reporters in general and White House reporters in particular do little documentary research. They are trained to do interviews and transmit handouts from press secretaries and public information officials rather than to conduct research. Moreover, in-depth research requires a slower pace and advance planning, and journalists tend to be comfortable with neither.

Sometimes several factors influence coverage of the presidency at the same time. Despite the glamour attached to investigative reporting following the Watergate scandal, not much of it takes place. Most reporters are unwilling or unable to take the time necessary for investigative work and the coordination required with other reporters and news bureau staff to cover all leads successfully. The ethic of journalism is to go it alone, and the incentives are generally to get news out fast. Similarly, the slowness of the process of using the Freedom of Information Act to force the release of documents inhibits its use. A final hinderance to investigative reporting is the reluctance of many editors to publish analyses sharply divergent from the president's position without some confirmation from what they consider to be an authoritative source who would be willing to go on the record in opposition to the president.

Not only does the press provide superficial coverage of the stories it reports, but many important stories about the presidency are missed altogether because of the emphasis of the media. Implementation of policy, the predominant activity of the executive branch, is very poorly covered because it is not fast-breaking news; it takes place mostly in the field, away from the reporters' natural territory, and it requires documentary analysis and interaction with civil servants who are neither famous nor experts at public relations. Similarly, the White House press misses most of the flow of information and options to the president from the rest of the executive branch.

Bias

Bias is the most politically charged issue in press relations with the president. Bias is also an elusive concept with many dimensions. Although we typically envision bias as news coverage favoring identifiable persons, parties, or points of view, there are more subtle and more pervasive forms of bias that are not motivated by the goal of furthering careers or policies.

Many studies covering topics such as presidential election campaigns, the Vietnam War, and local news conclude that the news media are not biased *systematically* toward a particular person, party, or ideology, as measured in the amount or favorability of coverage. The bias found in such studies is inconsistent; the news is typically characterized by neutrality.[27] After six years as President Reagan's press secretary, Larry Speakes concluded that the news media had generally given the administration "a fair shake" and that "they probably gave us a longer honeymoon than we deserved."[28]

Some people may equate objectivity with passivity and feel that the press should do no more than report what others present to it. This simple passing on of news is what occurs much of the time, and it is a fundamental reason for the superficiality of news coverage. Sometimes, however, reporters may feel the necessity of setting the story in a meaningful context. The construction of such a context may entail reporting what was *not* said as well as what was said; what had occurred before; and what political implications may be involved in a statement, policy, or event. If the press is passive, it can be more easily manipulated, even representing fiction as fact.

This discussion of the general neutrality of news coverage in the mass media pertains most directly to television, newspaper, and radio reporting. Columnists, commentators, and editorial writers usually cannot even pretend to be neutral. Newspaper endorsements for presidential candidates overwhelmingly favor Republicans.[29] Newsmagazines are sometimes less neutral than newspapers or television. In the 1940s, 1950s, and 1960s Henry Luce used *Time* to criticize Harry Truman, to campaign for his view of a China policy, to help elect Dwight Eisenhower as president, and to support the Vietnam War, and the magazine has continued to favor Republican presidents. Unfair but picturesque adjectives are often used in newsmagazines to liven up stories. So are cartoons and drawings, which are generally unflattering to the president.

A number of factors help to explain why most mass-media news coverage is not biased systematically toward a particular person, party, or ideology. Reporters tend not to be partisan or strong ideologues; nor are they politically aligned or holders of strong political beliefs. Journalists are typically not intellectuals or deeply concerned with public policy. Moreover, they share journalism's professional norm of objectivity. The organizational processes of story selection and editing also provide opportunities for softening judgments of reporters. The rotation of assignments and rewards for objective news gathering are further protections against bias. Local television station owners and newspaper publishers are in a position to apply pressure regarding the presentation of the news, and, although they rarely do so, their potential to act may restrain reporters.

Self-interest also plays a role in constraining bias. Individual reporters may earn a poor reputation if others view them as biased. The television networks, newspapers, newsmagazines, and the wire services, which provide most of the Washington news for newspapers, have a direct financial stake in attracting viewers and subscribers and do not want to lose their audience by appearing biased, especially when multiple versions of the same story are available to major news outlets. Slander and libel laws and the "political attack" rule, providing those personally criticized on the electronic media with an opportunity to respond, are formal limitations on bias.

To conclude that the news contains little explicit partisan or ideological bias is not to argue that the news does not distort reality in its coverage. It does! Even under the best of conditions, some distortion is inevitable due to simple error or such factors as lack of careful checking of facts, the efforts of the news source to deceive, and short deadlines.

In a very important sense, values are pervasive in the news, and it is difficult to imagine how it could be otherwise. As members of our society, journalists are imbued with such values as democracy, capitalism, and individualism, and these unconsciously receive positive treatment in the media. Similarly, journalists have concepts of what is "new," "abnormal," and "wrong" and notions of how the world works (e.g., how power is distributed) and how to draw inferences that guide them in their efforts to gather and present the news.

Journalism also contains a structural bias. Selecting, presenting, editing, and interpreting the news inevitably require judgments about what stories to cover and what to report about them, because there is simply not enough space for everything. Thus the news can never mirror reality. In addition, the particular ways in which the news is gathered and presented have consequences for distortion in news coverage.

We have already seen that the news is fundamentally superficial and oversimplified and is often overblown, all of which provides the public a distorted view of, among other things, presidential activities, statements, policies, and options. The emphasis on action and the deviant (and therefore "newsworthy" items) rather than on patterns of behavior and the implication that most stories represent more general themes of national significance contribute further to this distortion. Personalizing the news downplays structural and other impersonal factors that may be far more important in understanding the economy, for example, than individual political actors.

We have also seen that the press prefers to frame the news in themes, which both simplify complex issues and events and provide continuity of persons, institutions, and issues. Once these themes are established, the press tends to maintain them in subsequent stories. Of necessity, themes emphasize some information at the expense of other data, often determining what information is most relevant to news coverage and the context in which it is presented.

Once a stereotype of President Ford as a "bumbler" was established, every stumble was magnified in coverage of him. He was repeatedly forced to defend his intelligence, and many of his acts and statements were reported as efforts to "act" presidential. Once Ford was typecast, his image was repeatedly reinforced and was very difficult to overcome.

Sometimes themes are established by the press to attract an audience for coverage of an event. A study of television coverage of the 1972 Democratic National Convention found that, although the networks were neutral as to partisanship, they portrayed the convention as more disorderly and conflictual than it actually was. Television's requirements for themes and conflict encouraged reporters to focus on differences between delegates, and the technique of switching from camera to camera gave the impression of rapidly shifting action.[30]

Reporters often fail to alert readers and viewers about the tentativeness of much of what the press reports. Although sources may be unreliable, motives obscure, facts disputed or confused, and meanings unclear, the news is presented in a straightforward manner that communicates little notion of uncertainty. Similarly, reporters often do not make it clear that they have made inferences in their reporting. Such presentations enhance the credibility of journalists who deliver the news, but they provide the potential for distortion in the process.

Some observers feel that the press is biased against whomever holds office at the moment and that reporters want to expose them in the media. Reporters, they argue, hold disparaging views of most politicians and public officials, finding them self-serving, lacking in integrity and competence, hypocritical, and preoccupied with reelection. Thus it is not surprising that journalists see a need to expose and debunk them through general derogation. This orientation may be characterized as neither liberal nor conservative, but reformist.[31]

White House reporters are always looking to expose conflicts of interest and other shady behavior of public officials. Moreover, many of their inquiries revolve around the question, "Is he up to the job?" Reporters who are confined in the White House all day may attempt to make up for their lack of investigative reporting with sarcastic and accusatory questioning. Moreover, the desire to keep the public interested and the need for continuous coverage may create a subconscious bias in the press against the presidency that leads to critical stories.

News coverage of the presidency often tends to emphasize the negative (although the negative stories are typically presented in a neutral manner). In the 1980 election campaign the press portrayed President Carter as mean and Ronald Reagan as imprecise rather than Carter as precise and Reagan as nice. The emphasis, in other words, was on the candidates' negative qualities. As the following excerpt from Jimmy Carter's diary regarding a visit to Panama in 1978 illustrates, "objective" reporting can be misleading:

> I told the Army troops that I was in the Navy for 11 years, and they booed. I told them that we depended on the Army to keep the Canal open, and they cheered. Later, the news reports said that there were boos and cheers during my speech. I reckon that was an accurate report![32]

On the other hand, one could argue that the press is biased *toward* the White House. Their general respect for the presidency is often transferred to individual presidents. Framed at a respectful distance by the television camera, the president is typically portrayed with an aura of dignity working in a context of rationality and coherence on activities benefitting the public. Word selection often reflects this orientation as well. In addition, at least until recently, journalists followed conventions that protected politicians and public officials from revelations of private misconduct.

The White House enjoys a consistent pattern of favorable coverage in newspapers, magazines, and network news. The most favorable coverage comes in the first year of a president's term, before he has a record to criticize and critics for reporters to interview. Coverage focuses on human interest stories of the president and his appointees and their personalities, goals, and plans. The president is pictured in a positive light as a policymaker dealing with problems. Controversies over solutions arise later. Newspaper headlines also favor the president, and news of foreign affairs provides basic support for the policies and personalities of the administration.[33]

Ultimately, the issue of bias may hang on questions of nuance. As Bill Moyers, public affairs analyst and former presidential press secretary, put it, "Depending on who is looking and writing, the White House is brisk or brusque, assured or arrogant, casual or sloppy, frank or brutal, warm or corny, cautious or timid, compassionate or condescending, reserved or callous."[34] Given the limitations of language and the lack of agreement on the exact nature of reality, it is almost impossible for the media to please everyone.

MEDIA EFFECTS

The most significant question about the substance of media coverage, of course, is about the impact it has, if any, on public opinion. Unfortunately, we know very little about this subject. Most studies on media effects have focused on attitude changes, especially in voting for presidential candidates, and have typically found little or no evidence of influence. Reinforcement of existing attitudes and opinions has been the strongest effect of the media.[35] There are other ways to look for media effects, however. The public appears to be a fairly passive audience and usually does not do a great deal of perceptual screening of the news. Repeated coverage of an issue or person by all the media, television's use of themes and simple story lines, and the vividness of live coverage of visually exciting events can buttress the media's effect on the public.

The media are more likely to influence perceptions than attitudes. The press can influence the perceptions of what public figures stand for and what their personalities are like, what issues are important, and what is at stake. If the media raise certain issues or personal characteristics to prominence, the significance of attitudes that people already hold may change and thus alter their evaluations of, say, presidential performance, without their attitudes themselves changing. In other words, the media can influence the criteria by which the president is judged.

The public's information on and criteria for evaluating candidates parallel what is presented in the media: campaign performance, personality traits, mannerisms, and personal background rather than positions on issues, ability to govern, and relevant experience. Moreover, what the press emphasizes about elections (the horse race) is what the people say is important about them, what they discuss about them in private conversations, and what they remember about them.[36]

While it cannot be conclusively proven that media coverage contributes to the public's deemphasis of the professional capacities and policy plans of candidates, it is reasonable to speculate that press emphasis on the horse race and personality traits encourages the public to view campaigns in these terms. Thus, although the press may not directly influence voters to support a particular candidate, it probably amplifies the public's predispositions to view public affairs through personalities rather than more complex factors.

Earlier we saw that the press gave substantial coverage to President Ford's misstatement about Soviet domination of Eastern Europe. This coverage had an impact on the public. Polls show that most people did not realize the president made an error until they were told so by the press. After that, pro-Ford evaluations of the debate declined noticeably as voters' concerns for competence in foreign policy making became salient.[37] A somewhat similar switch occurred after the first debate between Walter Mondale and Ronald Reagan in 1984.[38]

The press probably has the greatest effect on public perceptions of individuals and issues between election campaigns, when people are less likely to activate their partisan defenses. The prominant coverage of Gerald Ford's alleged physical clumsiness was naturally translated into suggestions of mental ineptitude. In the president's own words:

> Every time I stumbled or bumped my head or fell in the snow, reporters zeroed in on that to the exclusion of almost everything else. The news coverage was harmful, but even more damaging was the fact that Johnny Carson and Chevy Chase used my "missteps" for their jokes. Their antics—and I'll admit that I laughed at them myself—helped create the public perception of me as a stumbler. And that wasn't funny.[39]

Once such an image is established in the mass media, it is very difficult to change, as reporters continue to emphasize behavior that is consistent with their previously established themes.

During the Iranian hostage crisis ABC originated a nightly program entitled "America Held Hostage," Walter Cronkite provided a "countdown" of the number of days of the crisis at the end of each evening's news on CBS, many feature stories on the hostages and their families were reported in all the media, and the press gave complete coverage to "demonstrations" in front of the United States embassy in Tehran. The latter were often artificially created for consumption by Americans. This crisis gave President Carter's approval rating a tremendous boost, at least for a while. Conversely, when the American ship *Pueblo* was captured by North Korea, there were many more American captives, but there were also no television cameras and few reporters to cover the situation. Thus the incident played a much smaller role in American politics.

Those with only marginal concern for politics may be especially susceptible to the impact of the media because they have few alternative sources of information and less-developed political allegiances. Thus, they have fewer strongly held attitudes to overcome. Similarly, coverage of new issues that are removed from the experiences of people and their political convictions is more likely to influence public opinion than coverage of continuing issues.

Almost all citizens are basically ignorant of such areas of the world as Central America, Afghanistan, and Poland. The press plays a pivotal role in shaping perceptions of the personalities and issues involved in conflicts abroad (generally only conflicts receive coverage) and the nation's stake in the outcomes of the disputes. In such situations we have seen that there is substantial potential for distortion. The public is heavily dependent on the media for information and has little basis for challenging what it reads and sees in the news. The illustrations of the conflict—scenes of combat or demonstrations, for example—may become the essence of the issue in the public's mind. The underlying problems, which the president must confront, may be largely ignored.

The president needs public understanding of the difficulty of his job and the nature of the problems he faces. The role of the press here can be critical. Watching television news seems to do little to inform viewers about public affairs; reading the printed media is more useful. This may be because reading requires more active cognitive processing of information than watching television, and there is more information presented in newspapers.

We have seen that press coverage of the president is superficial, oversimplified, and often overblown, providing the public a distorted picture of White House activities. This trivialization of the news drowns out coverage of more important matters, often leaving the public ill-informed about matters with which the president must deal, ranging from the renegotiation of the Panama Canal Treaty to funding social security benefits. The preoccupation of the press with personality and the results of policies does little to help the public appreciate the complexity of presidential decision making, the trade-offs involved in policy choices, and the broad trends outside the president's control.

In the previous chapter we saw that the president's access to the media is at least a potential advantage in influencing public opinion. Press focus on the president has disadvantages as well. It inevitably leaves the impression that the president *is* the federal government and crucial to our prosperity and happiness. This naturally encourages the public to focus its expectations on the White House. So does the national frame of reference provided by a truly mass media and the media's penchant for linking coverage of even small matters with responses from the president or presidential spokesmen.

Moreover, the extraordinary attention the press devotes to the president magnifies his flaws. Even completely unsubstantiated charges against the president may make the news because of his prominence. Familiarity may not breed contempt, but it certainly may diminish the aura of grandeur around the chief executive.

Similarly, commentary following presidential speeches and press conferences may influence what viewers remember and may affect their opinions.[40] Although the impact of commentary on presidential addresses and press conferences is unclear, it is probably safe to argue that it is a constraint on the president's ability to lead public opinion. In the words of two observers:

> Critical instant analysis undermines presidential authority by transforming him from presentor to protagonist. . . . Credible, familiar, apparently disin-

terested newsmen and -women, experts too, usually agreeing with each other, comment on the self-interested performance of a politician. Usually the president's rhetoric is deflated, the mood he has striven to create dissipated.[41]

While reviewing evidence of the impact of the media on public opinion concerning the president, it is important to keep in mind the significant limitations on this influence. Characteristics of readers and viewers—including short attention spans, lack of reading ability, selective perception (especially for those who have well-developed political views), general lack of interest in politics, lack of attentiveness to the media when exposed to it, and forgetfulness—limit the impact of the media.

The nature of the news message also affects the impact of the media. The great volume of information available in the news; the limited time available in which to absorb it (especially for television viewers); the superficial coverage of people, events, and policies; the presentation of the news on television and in most newspapers in disconnected snippets; and the lack of guidance through the complexities of politics all constrain the influence of the media on public opinion. As a result, people often do not understand the news and actually learn little in the way of specifics from it. The lack of credibility of news sources among some readers and viewers further limits the impact of the media.

Visuals may also distract from verbal messages. Leslie Stahl of CBS News did a long report on Ronald Reagan during the 1984 presidential campaign, criticizing him for deceiving the American people with public relations tactics. Instead of the complaints she expected from the White House, however, she received thanks. Reagan's press aides appreciated the pictures of the president campaigning and were not concerned with the journalist's scathing remarks.[42]

CONCLUSION

The mass media play a prominent role in the public presidency, providing the public with most of its information about the White House and mediating the president's communications with his constituents. Presidents need the press in order to reach the public, and relations with the press are an important complement to the chief executive's efforts at leading public opinion. Through attempting to coordinate news, holding press conferences, and providing a wide range of services for the press, the White House tries to influence its portrayal in the news.

The president's press relations pose many obstacles to his efforts to obtain and maintain public support. Although it is probably not true that press coverage of the White House is biased along partisan or ideological lines or toward or against a particular president, it frequently presents a distorted picture to the public and fails to impart an appropriate perspective from which to view complex events. Moreover, presidents are continuously harassed by leaks to the press and are faced with superficial, oversimplified coverage that devotes little attention to substantive discussion of policies and often focuses on trivial matters. This type of reporting undoubtedly affects public perceptions of the president, usually in a negative way. It is no wonder that chief executives generally see the press as a hindrance to their efforts to develop appreciation for their performance and policies in the public.

It is clear that the president is a facilitator rather than a director in relation to the press. He is in a constant struggle with the press and cannot depend on it to stress what he feels is most important about his administration or to provide favorable coverage in the stories it produces. Presidents vary in their success in using the media to promote their goals, but they all are limited in doing so by the nature and independence of the "fourth branch" of government.

Before leaving this chapter, we feel it is important to put the subject in perspective. Americans benefit greatly from a free press. This should not be forgotten as we examine the media's flaws. The same press that provides superficial coverage of the presidency also alerts people to abuses of authority and to attempts to mislead public opinion. It is also much less biased than the heavily partisan newspapers that were typical early in the nation's history. The press is an essential pillar in the structure of a free society.

Moreover, perhaps the fundamental reason that press coverage is much less than its critics would like it to be is that it must appeal to the general public. When the public, or a sizable segment of it, demands more of the mass media, it undoubtedly will receive it. In short, although mass-media coverage of the presidency is often poor, it could be much worse and it is probably about what the public desires. The media reflect as well as influence American society.

NOTES

1. Elmer E. Cornwell, Jr., "Presidential News: The Expanding Public Image," *Journalism Quarterly* 36 (Summer 1959): 275–83; and Alan P. Balutis, "The Presidency and the Press: The Expanding Presidential Image," *Presidential Studies Quarterly* 7 (Fall 1977): 244–51.

2. Richard Harris, "The Presidency and the Press," *New Yorker*, October 1, 1973, p. 122; Dom Bonafede, "Powell and the Press—A New Mood in the White House," *National Journal*, June 25, 1977, p. 981.

3. Harris, "The Presidency and the Press," p. 122; and Peter Forbath and Carey Winfrey, *The Adversaries: The President and the Press* (Cleveland: Regal Books, 1974), p. 5.

4. Jarol B. Manheim, "The Honeymoon's Over: The News Conference and the Development of Presidential Style," *Journal of Politics* 41 (February 1979): 60–61.

5. Doris A. Graber, *Mass Media and American Politics*, 3rd ed. (Washington, D.C.: Congressional Quarterly Press, 1989), p. 252.

6. Michael Baruch Grossman and Martha Joynt Kumar, *Portraying the President: The White House and the Media* (Baltimore: Johns Hopkins University Press, 1981), pp. 59–60, 63–64, 280–81.

7. Interview with Peter Jennings, New York, N. Y., October 18, 1987.

8. Dom Bonafede, "The Washington Press—It Magnifies the President's Flaws and Blemishes," *National Journal*, May 1, 1982, pp. 267–71.

9. David L. Paletz and Robert M. Entman, *Media—Power—Politics* (New York: Free Press, 1981), pp. 55–56.

10. "Reagan Outburst on Leaks," *Newsweek*, January 18, 1982, p. 23; and Walter S. Mossberg, "Reagan Prepares Curbs on U.S. Officials to Restrict News Leaks on Foreign Policy," *The Wall Street Journal*, January 13, 1982, p. 7.

11. William Safire, *Before the Fall: An Inside View of the Pre-Watergate White House* (New York: Doubleday, 1975), p. 373; and Henry Kissinger, *Years of Upheaval* (Boston: Little, Brown, 1981), p. 116.

12. Lyndon Johnson, quoted in George Christian, *The President Steps Down: A Personal Memoir of the Transfer of Power* (New York: Macmillan, 1970), p. 203.

13. "The U.S. vs. William Colby," *Newsweek*, September 28, 1981, p. 30.

14. "The Tattletale White House," *Newsweek*, February 25, 1980, p. 21.

15. Robert T. Hartmann, *Palace Politics: An Inside Account of the Ford Years* (New York: McGraw-Hill, 1980), p. 38.

16. William J. Lanouette, "The Washington Press Corps—Is It All That Powerful?" *National Journal*, June 2, 1979, p. 898.

17. Donald T. Regan, *For the Record: From Wall Street to Washington* (San Diego, Calif.: Harcourt Brace Jovanovich, 1988), p. xiv.

18. Woodrow Wilson, quoted in William Small, *To Kill a Messenger: Television News and the Real World* (New York: Hastings, 1970), p. 221.

19. President Carter, quoted in Michael Baruch Grossman and Martha Joynt Kumar, "Carter, Reagan, and the Media: Have the Rules Really Changed or the Poles of the Spectrum of Success?" (paper presented at the Annual Meeting of the American Political Science Association, New York, September 3–6, 1981), p. 8.

20. Dan Rather, quoted in Hoyt Purvis, ed., *The Presidency and the Press* (Austin, Tex.: Lyndon B. Johnson School of Public Affairs, 1976), p. 56.

21. See George C. Edwards III, *The Public Presidency* (New York: St. Martin's, 1983), p. 149, and sources cited therein.

22. Quoted in Grossman and Kumar, *Portraying the President*, p. 43.

23. Quoted in ibid., p. 26.

24. Quoted in ibid., p. 231.

25. Sam Donaldson, quoted in "Washington Press Corps," *Newsweek*, May 25, 1981, p. 90.

26. Sam Donaldson, *Hold On, Mr. President* (New York: Random House, 1987), pp. 196–97.

27. See Edwards, *The Public Presidency*, p. 156, and sources cited therein.

28. Larry Speakes, quoted in Eleanor Randolph, "Speakes Aims Final Salvos at White House Practices," *Washington Post*, January 31, 1987, p. A3.

29. John P. Robinson, "The Press as King-Maker: What Surveys from Last Five Campaigns Show," *Journalism Quarterly* 51 (Winter 1974): 587–94, 606.

30. David L. Paletz and Martha Elson, "Television Coverage of Presidential Conventions: Now You See It, Now You Don't," *Political Science Quarterly* 91 (Spring 1976): 109–31.

31. See Edward Jay Epstein, *News from Nowhere* (New York: Vintage, 1973), pp. 215–20; Herbert J. Gans, *Deciding What's News* (New York: Vintage, 1979), pp. 68–69, 187; and Stephen Hess, *The Washington Reporters* (Washington, D.C.: Brookings Institution, 1981), p. 88.

32. Jimmy Carter, *Keeping Faith: Memoirs of a President* (New York: Bantam, 1982), pp. 179–80.

33. On this topic, see Edwards, *The Public Presidency*, p. 162, and sources cited therein.

34. Bill D. Moyers, "The Press and Government: Who's Telling the Truth?" in Warren K. Agee, ed., *Mass Media in a Free Society* (Lawrence, Kan.: University Press of Kansas, 1969), p. 19.

162   PRESIDENTIAL LEADERSHIP

35. For an overview, see Cliff Zukin, "Mass Communication and Public Opinion," in Dan D. Nimmo and Keith R. Sanders, eds., *Handbook of Political Communication* (Beverly Hills, Calif.: Sage, 1981), pp. 359–90.

36. Thomas E. Patterson, *The Mass Media Election: How Americans Choose Their President* (New York: Praeger, 1980), pp. 84–86, 98–100, 105, and chap. 12; Doris A. Graber, "Personal Qualities in Presidential Images: The Contribution of the Press," *Midwest Journal of Political Science* 16 (February 1972): 295; and Graber, *Mass Media and American Politics*, p. 223.

37. Frederick T. Steeper, "Public Response to Gerald Ford's Statements on Eastern Europe in the Second Debate," in George F. Bishop, Robert G. Meadow, and Marilyn Jackson-Beeck, eds., *The Presidential Debates: Media, Electoral, and Public Perspectives* (New York: Praeger, 1978), pp. 81–101.

38. Michael J. Robinson, "News Media Myths and Realities," in Kay Lehman Schlozman, ed., *Elections in America* (Boston: Allen and Unwin, 1987), p. 149.

39. Gerald R. Ford, *A Time to Heal: The Autobiography of Gerald R. Ford* (New York: Harper and Row, 1979), p. 289; see also pp. 343–44.

40. Dwight F. Davis, Lynda Lee Kaid, and Donald Singleton, "Information Effects of Political Commentary," *Experimental Study of Politics* 6 (June 1977): 45–68; Lynda Lee Kaid, Donald L. Singleton, and Dwight Davis, "Instant Analysis of Televised Political Addresses: The Speaker versus the Commentator," in Brent D. Ruben, ed., *Communication Yearbook I* (New Brunswick, N.J.: Transaction Books, 1977), pp. 453–64; and John Havick, "The Impact of a Televised State of the Union Message and the Instant Analysis: An Experiment" (unpublished paper, Georgia Institute of Technology, 1980, typescript).

41. Paletz and Entman, *Media—Power—Politics*, p. 70.

42. Interview with Leslie Stahl, West Point, N. Y., 1986.

SELECTED READINGS

Abel, Elie, ed. *What's News: The Media in American Society*. San Francisco: Institute for Contemporary Studies, 1981.

Braestrup, Peter. *Big Story*. Garden City, N.Y.: Anchor, 1978.

Edwards, George C., III. *The Public Presidency*. New York: St. Martin's, 1983. Chaps. 3 and 4.

Epstein, Edward Jay. *News from Nowhere: Television and the News*. New York: Vintage, 1973.

Gans, Herbert J. *Deciding What's News*. New York: Vintage, 1979.

Grossman, Michael Baruch, and Martha Joynt Kumar. *Portraying the President: The White House and the News Media*. Baltimore: Johns Hopkins University Press, 1981.

Hess, Stephen. *The Washington Reporters*. Washington, D.C.: Brookings Institution, 1981.

Hofstetter, Richard C. *Bias in the News: Network Television Coverage of the 1972 Election Campaign*. Columbus, Ohio: Ohio State University Press, 1976.

Iyengar, Shanto, and Donald R. Kinder. *News That Matters*. Chicago: University of Chicago Press, 1987.

Kaid, Lynda Lee, Donald L. Singleton, and Dwight Davis. "Instant Analysis of Televised Political Addresses: The Speaker versus the Commentator." In Brent D. Ruben, ed., *Communication Yearbook I*. New Brunswick, N.J.: Transaction Books, 1977.

Lammers, William W. "Presidential Press Conference Schedules: Who Hides and When?" *Political Science Quarterly* 96 (Summer 1981): 261–78.

Manheim, Jarol B. "The Honeymoon's Over: The News Conference and the Development of Presidential Style." *Journal of Politics* 41 (February 1979): 55–74.

Minow, Newton, John B. Martin, and Lee M. Mitchell. *Presidential Television.* New York: Basic Books, 1973.

Paletz, David L., and Robert M. Entman. *Media—Power—Politics.* New York: Free Press, 1981.

Patterson, Thomas E. *The Mass Media Election: How Americans Choose Their President.* New York: Praeger, 1980.

Porter, William E. *Assault on the Media: The Nixon Years.* Ann Arbor, Mich.: University of Michigan Press, 1976.

Robinson, Michael Jay. "The Impact of Instant Analysis." *Journal of Communication* 27 (Spring 1977): 17–23.

Robinson, Michael Jay, and Margaret A. Sheehan. *Over the Wire and On TV: CBS and UPI in Campaign '80.* New York: Russell Sage Foundation, 1983.

Safire, William. *Before the Fall: An Inside View of the Pre-Watergate White House.* New York: Doubleday, 1975.

Steeper, Frederick T. "Public Response to Gerald Ford's Statements on Eastern Europe in the Second Debate." In George F. Bishop, Robert G. Meadow, and Marilyn Jackson-Beeck, eds., *The Presidential Debates: Media, Electoral, and Public Perspectives.* New York: Praeger, 1978.

6

The Presidential Office

A president's tasks are many and varied. The job is too big for any one person to perform. Presidents need help. They need help in making, promoting, and implementing their decisions. They need help in attending to the symbolic and ceremonial functions of the office. They need help in articulating their beliefs, communicating their policy, and responding to public moods, opinions, and expectations.

The executive departments and agencies were obviously intended to provide such help, but they alone have not been sufficient. Their interests, needs, and ongoing responsibilities have not been synonymous with the president's all the time or even most of the time. Besides, they serve a number of masters. In addition to the chief executive, they must look to Congress for their programs and budgets and to their clientele for policy requests and political support. With an increasing number of issues overlapping departmental jurisdictions and an increasing number of matters requiring presidential attention, presidents need their own advisory bodies and institutional structures for assistance.

They need them for three principal reasons: to obtain information on people and policies; to maintain linkage to the constituencies with whom they must interact; and to ensure that their priorities are clear, their decisions are implemented, and their interests are protected. Only if these needs are satisfied can presidents exercise effective leadership.

Although presidents cannot lead alone, their dependence on others creates potential problems for them. The information they receive on people or policy can be incorrect, biased, or simply too narrow. Their link to the community can be severed or overloaded by too much or too little activity. Overzealous behavior by their staff can result in a loss of perspective, a failure to consider all options or consult with a range of people, and unwise or even illegal behavior. None of this serves the president's interests. In short, presidents need good staff support. But good staff support, in turn, requires telling presidents what they may not want to hear, being sensitive to diverse and often critical political forces, and operating according to recognized and accepted rules and procedures.

In this chapter we will examine the institutional components of presidential leadership and their operation within the governmental system: the cabinet, the Executive Office, and the president's personal office, the White House. Beginning with the oldest of these advisory bodies, the cabinet, we briefly describe its creation, evolution, and its demise. We then explore the institutionalization of advisory responsibilities in the Executive Office. Here the emphasis is on the growth of this bureaucracy within a bureaucracy and its impact on the president and the performance of his presidential responsibilities. After a historical sketch of the evolution of the White House, we examine patterns of staffing and their relationship to the style and objectives of the president. In the final section we assess the increasing importance of the vice presidential office.

ORGANIZING EXECUTIVE ADVICE

The Evolution of the Cabinet

The Constitution did not create a separate advisory council for the president. The framers had discussed the idea but rejected it largely out of the fear that the president might try to sidestep responsibility for his own actions by using his council as a foil. In order to avoid the fiction, popular in England at the time, that the king could do no wrong, that any harmful action he committed was always the result of poor or even pernicious advice from his counselors, the Constitution designated that the president could demand written opinions of his subordinates. Having these in writing, it was hoped, would pinpoint responsibility.

Although presidents had been expected to use their department secretaries in both administrative and advisory capacities, there was no expectation that the secretaries would function as the principal body of advisers. However, in 1791, when George Washington prepared to leave the capital city, he authorized his vice president, secretaries of state, treasury, and war, and the chief justice to consult with each other on governmental matters during his absence. The following year, the president began to meet more frequently with the heads of the executive departments but without the vice president and the chief justice. During the undeclared naval war with France, these meetings became more frequent. It was James Madison who referred to this group as the president's cabinet. The name stuck. Jefferson's resignation as secretary of state in 1794 in protest over the administration's policies fixed the partisan nature of the group. Members were expected to provide counsel as well as support.

For the next 140 years, the cabinet functioned as the president's principal advisory body for both foreign and domestic affairs. Administrative positions on controversial proposals were often thrashed out at cabinet meetings. Presidents also turned to their cabinets for help in supporting them on Capitol Hill. The personal relationships between the individual secretaries and members of Congress frequently put the cabinet officials in a better position than the president to obtain this support. Strong cabinets and weak presidents characterized executive advisory relationships during most of the nineteenth century.

The president's position began to change as his capacity for exerting personal influence improved. The ability to shape public opinion and mobilize partisan support, evident during the administrations of Theodore Roosevelt and Woodrow Wilson, strengthened the president's hand in dealing with Congress and with his own department heads. Beginning in 1921, the power to affect department and agency decision making through the budget process also contributed to a stronger presidency.

As a consequence of these changes, cabinet meetings became more of a forum for discussion than a mechanism for making decisions. Franklin Roosevelt even trivialized the forum. His practice was to go around the table asking each participant what was on his or her mind. Frequently after the session, several secretaries remained to discuss their important business with him without other secretaries in attendance.

Although Truman emphasized the importance of the cabinet upon taking office (as have all of his successors), he did not meet with it regularly. Rather than utilizing his department secretaries as an advisory body, he turned to them individually as Roosevelt had done and relied on a few senior staff aides in the White House for help in formulating policy.

The cabinet enjoyed a resurgence under Eisenhower, meeting some 230 times during his eight years in office. The president personally presided over most of these meetings and used his presence to achieve consensus on policy. The sessions themselves often featured elaborate presentations of proposals by individual department heads and their staffs. These presentations, replete with visual aides and supporting materials, were the prelude to final decisions on the administration's legislative program prior to its presentation to Congress.

Johnson also met with his cabinet frequently, more so as his administration progressed. According to Professor James E. Anderson, Johnson used it as a management tool: to exchange information and ideas, to develop a sense of group-mindedness, a team approach; and to promote internal coordination and oversight of key presidential initiatives.[1] The president dominated the sessions, sometimes employing them as a sounding board for new proposals and sometimes as a vehicle for issuing directives to his department heads.[2] Unlike Eisenhower and Johnson, other contemporary presidents have not turned to the cabinet as a collectivity for advice or administration.

Kennedy rarely met with his cabinet, and Nixon, despite his announced intention to revert to a cabinet system, held few meetings and relegated department heads to positions of lesser importance in his administration. Ford and Carter held cabinet meetings at the beginning of their administrations and then slowly discontinued them. Carter, for example, met with the cabinet every week during his first year in office, every other week during his second year, once a month during his third year, and sporadically during his final year. Neither used their cabinets as key advisory bodies.

Although Reagan met less frequently with the full cabinet as his presidency progressed, he employed a cabinet model of decision making. Known as a cabinet council system, it was organized on the basis of broad policy areas. The councils, composed of various departmental secretaries, performed some of the same advisory functions that the cabinet as a group did during and before the Eisenhower administration. They deliberated policy recommendations, developed administration positions, and helped coordinate the implementation of key presidential decisions. Staff support was provided by the White House. Nominally chaired by the president, the councils were run in his absence by one of the department heads who had been designated as chairman *pro tempore*. In Reagan's first term there were seven cabinet councils; in the second there were three. The frequency with which the councils met to discuss administration policy was also reduced in the second term as the number of administration policy initiatives declined.

The Cabinet's Demise

While the cabinet council system has not been an unqualified success (see Chapter 12), it has addressed and partially overcome some of the principal weaknesses of the contemporary cabinet—notably its size and its diversity. Table 6-1 lists the departmental components of the contemporary cabinet. In addition to the secretaries, the vice president, senior White House aides, and other executive officials of cabinet rank may attend its sessions. The increasingly technical nature of policy making and the need for highly specialized information also made it difficult for secretaries to be sufficiently versed in the intricacies of issues outside of their own areas to carry on an intelligent discussion. At best this limited participation at cabinet meetings to the few who were informed and competent; at worst it reduced the level of the discussion and extended the time of debate.

There are other reasons for the cabinet's decline. Increasing pressure from outside groups forced secretaries to assume more of an advocacy role for their respective departments (referred to as "going native"), particularly in meetings in which they had to go on the record or even in closed sessions which could be leaked to the press. The tendency to advocate department interests increased over the course of an administration. The cabinet meetings thus became more confrontational and less

Table 6-1. The Cabinet, 1990

Department	Year Created	President	Fiscal 1990 Rankings	
			Budget	*Civilian Personnel Authority*
State	1789	Washington	12	10
Treasury	1789	Washington	3	3
Interior	1849	Polk	14	8
Agriculture	1862	Lincoln	4	5
Justice	1870	Grant	11	7
Commerce (formerly part of Department of Commerce and Labor, 1903)	1913	Wilson	13	6
Labor (formerly part of Department of Commerce and Labor, 1903)	1913	Wilson	8	11
Defense (consolidated Department of War, 1789, and Department of Navy, 1798)	1947	Truman	1	1
Housing and Urban Development	1965	Johnson	9	13
Transportation	1966	Johnson	6	9
Energy	1977	Carter	10	12
Health and Human Services (formerly part of Department of Health, Education, and Welfare, 1953)	1980	Carter	2*	4
Education (formerly part of Department of Health, Education, and Welfare, 1953)	1980	Carter	7	14
Veteran Affairs	1988	Reagan	5	2

*Includes social security; without social security, HHS would rank third and Treasury second.

useful as a device for reaching a consensus or building one after policy decisions had been made. The cabinet council system helped to avoid this "going native" problem by keeping the focus on the president's agenda and by effectively integrating the policy-making operations of the White House and the executive departments.

Moreover, the need and desire to extend personal influence discouraged department secretaries from discussing their concerns in a group setting. Cabinet members usually prefer the president's ear alone, and contemporary presidents have tended to encourage one-on-one situations to maximize their own flexibility, increase their own bargaining power, and conserve their own time. Reagan and Eisenhower have been the exceptions.

These factors help explain why recent presidents have met with their cabinets less as their administrations have progressed.[3] They also suggest why presidents have increasingly differentiated among their secretaries in seeking advice. The heads of certain departments have tended to exercise closer and more collaborative relationships with the president. These tend to be the most influential secretaries, those who comprise the so-called inner cabinet. According to political scientist Thomas E. Cronin, they include the heads of the State, Treasury, Justice, and Defense Departments.[4]

In contrast, the other secretaries, who are considered members of the outer cabinet, tend to have a more distant relationship with the president because of the nature of their departments and clientele. "These departments experience heavy and often conflicting pressures from clientele groups, from congressional interests, and from state and local governments, pressures that often run counter to presidential priorities."[5] Advocating departmental interests and exercising administrative responsibilities make it more difficult for secretaries to perceive problems from the president's perspective and recommend solutions that accord with his needs rather than theirs. This has given presidents little choice but to develop their own institutional and personal staffs.

The Executive Office

The Executive Office of the President (EOP) was established by executive order in 1939. Its title, however, is a misnomer. Its functions are not primarily executive, nor is it (or was it ever) a single office.

The principal objective of the EOP has always been to help the president perform central, nondelegable tasks, including those involved in his expanded policy-making roles. For the most part, administrative responsibilities have been avoided. The various offices in the EOP have not taken over the ongoing responsibilities of the departments and agencies, although they have helped coordinate some interagency projects.

Nor is the Executive Office a single monolithic agency. It has always consisted of a number of specialized staffs. The first EOP was composed of five separate units, including the Bureau of the Budget and the White House. Over the years forty-six different boards, offices, and councils have been placed within its purview. Figure 6-1 lists its current units.

While the EOP has evolved in size and function, it has not done so in a systematic, carefully planned way. Rather, its development has been a product of historical accident, the needs of different administrations, and the goals of different presidents. Most chief executives have changed the Executive Office in some way, adding or deleting some of its units. Some have attempted to overhaul it entirely. The most extensive reorganization occurred during the first term of the Nixon presidency.

Unhappy with the piecemeal expansion of the executive that had

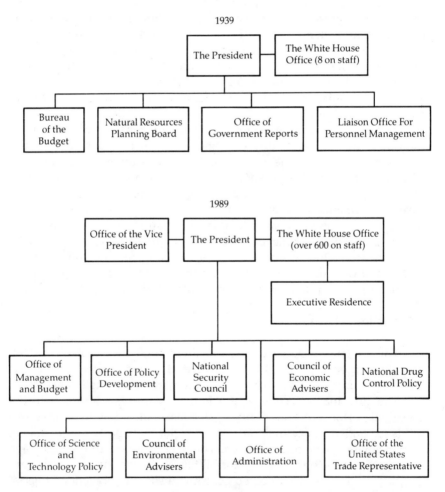

Figure 6-1. Executive Office of the President—At Its Inception and Today

occurred prior to 1968, President Nixon appointed a council at the beginning of his administration to review the entire executive branch structure including the organization and operation of the EOP. Meeting over a fourteen-month period, this advisory council proposed recommendations to centralize and streamline the executive branch, thereby making it more responsive to the president's political needs. Included was a recommendation to create a separate domestic policy-making staff, and another to reorganize and retitle the Bureau of the Budget.

The changes not only affected the composition of the Executive Office but decision making within it. More political positions, filled by presidential nominees, were created. This had the effect of decreasing the role and influence of civil servants. It also shifted power from the departments and agencies to the presidency. Political appointees in the upper echelon of the White House and the Office of Management and Budget (OMB) dominated activities, ran the processes, advised the president, and made sure that his wishes were carried out.

Criticism of the hierarchical structure of the Nixon presidency, the heavy-handed tactics of his principal aides, and the inaccessibility of the president to others in the executive branch and Congress led to a moderating effect and less-centralized control during the Ford and Carter presidencies. Ford was more accessible to department and agency heads and more receptive to their input than was his predecessor. He did not use the EOP to impose a perspective on them as the Nixon administration attempted to do. Carter, too, gave his department secretaries considerable latitude in articulating and promoting their positions and in administering their own departments.

Carter also reorganized the EOP, decreasing the number of offices and reducing its personnel. The smaller office, however, did not increase the president's capacity to manage the government. Unable to impose discipline on the various departments and agencies, Carter was eventually forced to fire two cabinet secretaries who consistently undercut his position on Capitol Hill and in their own departments. President Reagan did not make major structural changes in his Executive Office.

Consequences of Structural Change

The transformations that have occurred in the EOP have made the structure of that office more consistent with the personal styles of individual presidents. This has resulted in short-term advantages for the president, but long-term disadvantages for the presidency. Together, they have produced instability in organization, irregularity in operations, and turnover in personnel. Relations between the president and executive branch agencies have been subject to continuing uncertainty with each new administration. Transitions between administrations have been made more arduous. The wheel has to be reinvented constantly.

Despite the initial objective of the office to help the president oversee the operational responsibilities and policy-making efforts of the executive departments and agencies, not to substitute for them, separate policy-making units have been established. Despite the initial desire to staff the EOP with civil servants, political appointees have increased in number and particularly in influence. Despite the initial goal to keep the Executive Office small in size and general in capabilities, it has become a larger, more highly specialized, presidential bureaucracy.

This growth, differentiation, and politicization has worked at cross-purposes. On one hand, it has increased the political sensitivity of the president; on the other, it may have decreased his capacity to obtain neutral policy advice. Discontinuities in policy between and even within administrations have resulted.

There is another problem. Politicization has caused the presidency's institutional memory to fade. Turnover among its political appointees and career officials has increased, often placing the president's people at a competitive disadvantage when dealing substantively with officials from other departments and agencies.

Although the establishment of a presidential bureaucracy has increased the presidency's discretion and extended its influence, it has also generated internal rivalry and competition. Senior presidential aides enjoy considerable status by virtue of their access to and influence on the president. They also exercise considerable authority within their functional areas. This status and that authority have contributed to tension between department and agency heads and the White House which, in turn, has accentuated problems of maintaining loyalty and mobilizing support within an administration. Information leaks are now a perennial problem for every president.

While the establishment of an institutional mechanism within the presidency has increased the president's ability to meet the multiple demands of his office, it has also helped perpetuate those demands. Bureaucracies have a self-perpetuating character. By performing functions and meeting expectations, these structures encourage those expectations to persist. Subsequent presidents who do not meet them are criticized.

Finally, the development of the presidency has enhanced the institution's power, but it has probably decreased the president's personal influence on that institution. A chief executive is either forced to immerse himself in the details of administration, consuming valuable time and energy in the process, or to delegate that responsibility to others. If he chooses to delegate, as most presidents have done, then he faces the danger of having key operational and policy decisions shaped by others acting on his behalf. His presidency becomes theirs. His failure to delegate, on the other hand, can cloud his perspective. It can prevent him from seeing the big picture as he tries to set national goals and devise national policy. Ronald Reagan fell victim to the first of these dangers, and Jimmy Carter to the second.

PROVIDING A PRESIDENTIAL STAFFING SYSTEM

In addition to the support the institution requires, presidents need assistants to help them perform their personal duties and responsibilities. Until the creation of an official White House staff in 1939, that help was mainly clerical and frequently in short supply.

The Early Years

For the first seventy years, Congress did not even provide the president with secretarial support. Early presidents were expected to write their own speeches and answer their own correspondence. Most employed a few aides and paid them out of their own salary. These assistants tended to be young and undistinguished. Frequently, they were related to the president. They were paid low wages and generally performed menial tasks.

In 1857 Congress enacted a separate appropriation for a personal secretary, but the position did not assume great importance or even much potential at the time. If anything, the quality of the secretaries actually employed by presidents declined. Andrew Johnson's aide, his son Robert, was an alcoholic; Grant's secretary, General Orville E. Babcock, was indicted for fraud; Hayes's assistant, William Rogers, was generally regarded as incompetent.[6]

The secretary's role and influence began to expand with the administration of Chester Arthur. Daniel G. Rollings, who had assisted Arthur as vice president, helped him draft speeches and legislative messages.[7] Grover Cleveland's chief aide, Dan Lamont, performed a variety of political and personal tasks. His influence was attested by the press corps' labeling him "assistant president"; he was the first presidential assistant to receive such an appellation.

In the twentieth century, the secretary's functions were gradually increased. Theodore Roosevelt's principal aide, William Loeb, Jr., began to deal with the press on a regular basis. Wilson's secretary, Joseph Tumulty, controlled access to the Oval Office and functioned as an appointments secretary, political adviser, administrative manager, and public relations aide.

The number of presidential assistants also began to increase during this period. Whereas Benjamin Harrison could house his entire staff on the second floor of the White House near his own living quarters, in McKinley's administration, a separate group of offices had to be constructed outside the mansion for the president's staff. When the West

Wing was completed in 1909, the president's aides occupied an even larger space near the president's office.

Hoover doubled the number of his administrative aides from two to four and was also helped by more than forty others: clerks, typists, messengers, and so on. Franklin Roosevelt expanded presidential support still further. In addition to a small administrative staff, he had key aides, budgeted to the executive departments but available for White House work. The creation of a separate White House unit as part of the Executive Office enabled Roosevelt to move several of these individuals to the official White House staff, but it did not end the practice of using detailees for presidential tasks.

The Personalized White House, 1939 to the Mid-1960s

In establishing the first White House office, Roosevelt designed a highly personal staff system. Six key administrative aides performed action-forcing assignments for the president, ones that were dictated by Roosevelt's immediate needs and activities. The president ran the staff operation himself, making assignments, receiving reports, and generally coordinating activities. Presidential assistants were expected to be anonymous. They were given general responsibilities. No one exercised exclusive jurisdiction over "their" function or program. On the contrary, lines of authority were purposely blurred and assignments overlapped. Roosevelt even encouraged competition among his aides to maximize his information and extend his influence. According to Professor Richard E. Neustadt, he enjoyed "bruised egos."[8]

The organization of Roosevelt's White House was a prescription for personal control. It satisfied Roosevelt's needs. It was not, however, a model his successors could easily follow, because it conformed to Roosevelt's style, not theirs. The increasing responsibilities of the presidency dictated a larger, more specialized staff structure.

The White Houses of Truman and Eisenhower were more hierarchial in form and more carefully differentiated in function than Roosevelt's, although senior aides in both administrations continued to operate with a great deal of informality with one another and enjoyed easy access to the president. Of the two staffs, Eisenhower's was the larger and more formal. Areas of responsibility were more clearly designated.

Eisenhower had a penchant for organization and adopted a system along the lines of the one he experienced in the military. A chief of staff oversaw the operation and regulated the flow of visitors and memoranda to the Oval Office. Unlike Roosevelt and Truman, who desired to maximize their information and involvement, Eisenhower preferred a system that relieved him of numerous detailed decisions. He desired to set general policy and then work behind the scenes to build political support for it. To some extent he used his staff as a shield to enhance his own flexibility.

While the Roosevelt, Truman, and Eisenhower operations differed somewhat in size, structure, and style, they had much in common. By contemporary standards they were relatively small and operated more as a personal extension of the president than as an institutional extension of the presidency. With the exception of Eisenhower's chief of staff, Sherman Adams, presidential aides did not possess the status and clout of department secretaries. Their influence stemmed from their mediating role, their ability to obtain information, and their proximity to the president. When the White House called, the president's personal interests were usually the reason.

The Institutionalized White House, 1960s–

Changes began to occur in the 1960s. They had a profound effect not only on the way the White House was structured and how it worked but on the operation of the entire executive branch itself. Presidential aides became better known, exercised more power, and tended to monopolize the president's attention and his time. The White House grew in size, specialization, and responsibilities. It has between 500 and 600 people on its staff or detailed to it and a budget of $28.6 million for the fiscal year, 1990.

The most notable change during the Kennedy–Johnson period was the institutionalization of policy-making functions by and in the White House. Senior presidential aides became the principal policy advisers. They supervised their own staffs, which were based in the Executive Office. These staffs competed with the departments and agencies for influence. The institutionalization of policy making in the White House had three major effects. First, it gave the president more discretion and allowed him to take more personal credit for policy developed by his administration. Second, it gave the presidency a capacity to formulate policy distinct from and independent of the departments and agencies. Third, it accelerated the shift of power from the departments and agencies to the White House. Cabinet secretaries were no longer the president's only advisers within their respective spheres. In some cases they were not even primary advisers. Their status declined accordingly while that of the president's assistants increased.

The growth of the White House naturally affected the relationship between the president and his aides, particularly at the middle and lower levels of the White House. Informality was replaced by a more formal arrangement. Personal interaction with the president became more difficult and less frequent for more members of the staff. The president's time became an even more precious and closely guarded commodity.

176 PRESIDENTIAL LEADERSHIP

How the president related to his senior aides was still a matter of personal style. Kennedy consciously attempted to emulate Franklin Roosevelt's model but without the internal competition that Roosevelt generated. Senior Kennedy staffers, many of whom had worked together on the 1960 election campaign, were a close-knit group. They operated in an ad hoc, collegial manner. Many of the recommendations for major presidential decisions and actions were the product of group decisions.

Lyndon Johnson inherited Kennedy's staff structure and did little to change it initially beyond the addition of several of his long-time aides. Over the course of his administration, however, the jurisdiction of those who worked in the White House became more clearly defined. Policy advisers, in particular, exercised considerable influence within their respective spheres in developing recommendations and options for the president.

Nixon gave his senior policy aides even greater power and enlarged their functions accordingly. His White House was hierarchically structured and centrally managed. Ironically, Nixon had begun his presidency by announcing a return to a cabinet form of government in which the heads of the principal executive departments would be the prime initiators and implementors of administration policy. He contemplated a small White House staff composed of a handful of senior advisors. Nixon's personal style, however, clashed with this type of staffing system.

After a relatively short time, Nixon instituted changes that resulted in a larger, more specialized White House staff that numbered in excess of five hundred people, with sizable policy staffs in the national security and domestic areas supporting presidential activities.

The Nixon White House had clear lines of authority and vertical patterns of decision making. From a managerial perspective it operated smoothly. From a political perspective there were problems which impeded the president's ability to make and implement policy. The system insulated Nixon from the departments and agencies, members of Congress, and even from many of his own staff. Access to him was limited to a few top aides. The difficulty of communicating with the president produced dissatisfaction with White House decision-making procedures, although in the short run it also enhanced the clout of the White House aides who coordinated the processes and saw the president on a regular basis.

After his reelection in 1972, Nixon sought to expand his personal and political influence by transferring trusted White House officials to important positions in the departments and agencies. The events of Watergate aborted the plan, immobilized the White House, and raised doubts about the wisdom of having a large personal staff whose blind loyalty to the president impaired their judgment and his.

Ford and Carter both reacted to the Nixon experience in slightly different ways. Ford improved access to the president; Carter cut down on the size and status of the White House and the perquisites of those working there.

At first, both presidents also tried to structure their White House like the spokes of a wheel with themselves at the hub. Theoretically, top aides, operating autonomously within their own offices but collegially as a staff, were to have direct and easy access to the president. There was to be no chief of staff.

In practice, the system did not work well. Turf battles quickly erupted within the White House and between it and other executive agencies. These internal disputes plagued both administrations for most of their time in office.

Presidential advising was also adversely affected. The presentation of a wide range of options to the president was not assured. Each administration had difficulty establishing and articulating priorities. Presidential interests were not always protected or promoted.

Eventually, a more efficient operating structure emerged in each administration. Coordination between the White House and the departments improved. Better organization for dealing with outside groups was created. Lines of authority were more clearly designated. A chief of staff was appointed. Each president began to use his own time more wisely.

The lessons of the Ford and Carter experiences were not lost on Ronald Reagan and those who advised him. What were these lessons? First, the White House had grown too large and too specialized during the 1970s to operate effectively without a tight administrative structure and efficient operating procedures. Second, while considerable autonomy was necessary for those engaged in policy making and consensus building, the individual offices in the White House that dealt with these activities had to be coordinated if the administration was to speak with a single voice and act in a unified manner. Third, although White House involvement in a host of presidential activities could not be easily reduced, the activities and initiatives of the president could be more carefully marshalled.

The Reagan approach was to maintain a large, structurally differentiated White House staff, even expanding it in the first term to include more outreach efforts. However, a more centralized management orientation was imposed. Attempts to coordinate the input of departments more effectively into the policy-making process were also made. The trick was to foster department initiatives without reducing presidential influence or abdicating White House responsibilities. The Reagan administration used its cabinet council system to achieve this objective (see Chapter 9).

The functional differentiation of the Reagan White House resembled that of previous administrations. The traditional policy-making and constituency-building offices that had come to be regarded as necessary were maintained. What was different in the first term was the attempt to distinguish between operational and policy responsibilities in the White House organization. An operational division, charged with mobilizing support for the president's program, reported to the chief of staff. The policy division, charged with developing the program, was coordinated by a counsellor to the president.

The system worked well largely because of the personal interaction of the three principal aides who coordinated the White House and linked it to the president. James Baker, chief of staff, oversaw the political offices; Edwin Meese, counsellor to the president, supervised the policy councils; and Michael Deaver, deputy chief of staff, handled public relations as well as the needs of the president and his wife. Together they orchestrated the staff's activity, monitored the operation of the different White House units, briefed the president on a daily basis, and acted on his behalf.

Personnel changes at the beginning of Reagan's second term produced a very different environment for White House decision making. Instead of a triumvirate coordinating policy, a single chief of staff dominated it. Instead of adjusting policy objectives to the political realities of the times, a more consistent ideological perspective was imposed. The result was a White House operation that eased the president's load as it shielded him from external opinions. The machinations of several members of the national security staff that culminated in the Iran–Contra affair as well as the president's unprepared and disengaged reaction to the affair illustrate the dangers for presidents of delegating too much power and providing too little supervision of the White House. In its final two years, the Reagan White House returned to a more collaborative, coordinated, politically sensitive operation.

The early Bush White House followed the pattern established during the final Reagan years. A chief of staff, John Sununu, oversaw White House operations as well as monitored the flow of people and papers to the president. Senior staff aides for the most part reported through Sununu to the president. Bush's hands-on style and high energy level, however, facilitated more direct contact with his principal White House advisers than his immediate predecessor desired or had. The principal structural units of the contemporary White House are illustrated in Figure 6-2.

Trends in White House Staffing

Since its creation, the White House has undergone significant growth. It has become more specialized. Greater presidential needs and responsibilities have resulted in a larger and more functionally differentiated office. Every recent president has added to the structure. Eisenhower established a congressional liaison office; Kennedy created a

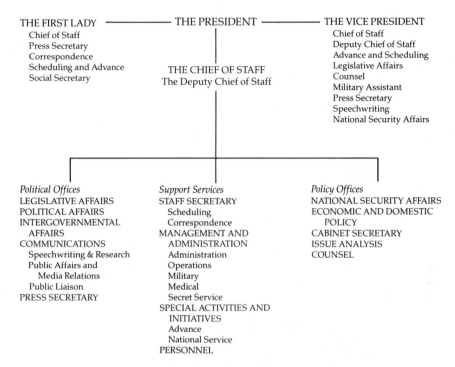

THE FIRST LADY ─────── THE PRESIDENT ─────── THE VICE PRESIDENT

THE FIRST LADY
  Chief of Staff
  Press Secretary
  Correspondence
  Scheduling and Advance
  Social Secretary

THE CHIEF OF STAFF
The Deputy Chief of Staff

THE VICE PRESIDENT
  Chief of Staff
  Deputy Chief of Staff
  Advance and Scheduling
  Legislative Affairs
  Counsel
  Military Assistant
  Press Secretary
  Speechwriting
  National Security Affairs

Political Offices
LEGISLATIVE AFFAIRS
POLITICAL AFFAIRS
INTERGOVERNMENTAL
  AFFAIRS
COMMUNICATIONS
  Speechwriting & Research
  Public Affairs and
    Media Relations
  Public Liaison
PRESS SECRETARY

Support Services
STAFF SECRETARY
  Scheduling
  Correspondence
MANAGEMENT AND
  ADMINISTRATION
  Administration
  Operations
  Military
  Medical
  Secret Service
SPECIAL ACTIVITIES AND
  INITIATIVES
  Advance
  National Service
PERSONNEL

Policy Offices
NATIONAL SECURITY AFFAIRS
ECONOMIC AND DOMESTIC
  POLICY
CABINET SECRETARY
ISSUE ANALYSIS
COUNSEL

Figure 6-2. Principal Offices in the White House

national security adviser and staff; Johnson instituted a domestic coun-
terpart; Nixon expanded both policy staffs as well as the press and
communications offices; Ford added an economic assistant and a modest public liaison operation; Carter vastly enlarged the public liaison
function as well as created an office for intergovernmental affairs; Reagan added a political affairs office and a secretariat for cabinet administration in addition to a short-lived office of planning and evaluation.
Many of these units have remained. Although the number of officials
budgeted to the White House has been reduced, largely for reasons of
politics and public relations, the functions and capabilities of the office
are larger than ever.

The institutional components reflect these functions. There is little a
president can do to alter them as long as the expectations and obligations he inherits remain large. He may tinker with the structure, but he
cannot radically change it.

Over time, the White House becomes more important to the president. Over time, his need for a more centrally managed and efficiently
run staff becomes obvious in large part because a president finds that he
has to depend more and more on his assistants for information, advice,
and liaison activities in addition to the servicing of his own needs.

White House staffs tend to expand over the course of an administration, and presidents come to rely increasingly on their staffs as leaks and loyalty problems surface and as press and public criticism mounts. Ironically, the larger and more powerful the staff becomes, the more resistant it is to the president's personal control. Like any large organization, it develops a structure and a routine of its own.

Moreover, the staff operation tends to exhibit self-perpetuating tendencies. These tendencies may even be reinforced as personnel leave and subordinates are promoted to replace them. Turfs are established and protected. Standard operating procedures evolve. The White House achieves greater autonomy over priority decision making. It begins to engulf the president as he depends increasingly on it.

The president exerts the most influence on his staff at the top among his senior aides. His style affects their interaction with him, their priorities, and to a lesser extent, their operation of their offices. Whether he chooses to overlap their jurisdiction or carefully delineate their authority, to have them compete or operate in a collegial manner, to delegate decision making or get involved in the details himself is his prerogative, although there are consequences for each of these ways of doing business.

Evaluating the Staffing System

There have been three basic models which presidents have employed to organize their White Houses: the *collegial* model that Kennedy used and Carter attempted to employ; the *competitive* system which Franklin Roosevelt engineered; and the *central management* model that characterized the Nixon presidency, and to a lesser extent, the Eisenhower and Reagan White Houses. Each of these staffing arrangements has its pros and cons.

The collegial system is characterized by a relatively small group of senior aides who work informally together to advise the president and plan and coordinate administration positions and responses. The key ingredient is their working together. The system is predicated on the ability of the president's top assistants to adopt a team approach and generate loyalty and to do so without centralized direction and control.

One danger is that the team will be too cohesive, their perceptions too uniform, and their advice too complementary. The psychologist Irving Janis refers to this problem as "groupthink" and suggests that it is most apt to occur in crisis situations. What happens, according to Janis, is that the crisis generates a desire for unity among policy advisers. Critical opinions are suspended and a consensus is produced.[9]

A number of high-level administration decisions may have been influenced by this groupthink effect. The reaction to Pearl Harbor, the response to North Korean aggression, and the escalation of the Vietnam War are three modern examples. The ill-fated decision by almost all of Kennedy's advisers to support an invasion of the Bay of Pigs in

Cuba in 1961 is another. When that mission failed, President Kennedy took steps to avoid a repetition of this groupthink mentality. He would constantly question his advisers and frequently absent himself from their deliberations.

Other presidents have also tried to ensure candor and encourage dissent among their aides. Ford would request opposing points of view in meetings he attended. Carter insisted that he be presented with a wide range of options.

To coordinate advisers and relieve the president from being overburdened with detailed decisions, a central management structure with clear lines of authority has been used. In such a system senior aides are given authority within their functional areas but report through a hierarchy that organizes and coordinates the entire operation.

The problem with such an arrangement is that it can be too efficient. Important decisions can get made before they reach the Oval Office. At the top, presidential assistants can become assistant presidents. Down the line, middle-level officials operate outside of the president's purview. If carried to an extreme, such a system can imprison the chief executive for whom it was designed to serve.

And that is not all. A centrally managed system aggravates the proclivity toward isolation that White Houses usually evidence over time. It can work to insulate the president and those around him from public as well as private criticism. The risk, similar to the groupthink effect, is that sufficient weight will not be given to countervailing views. Bad policy decisions and poor political judgments can result.

What is a president to do? Which structural model in whole or part would best facilitate the achievement of his policy objectives and political goals and do so at the least cost? The answer depends on the president's personal style and the kinds of decisions that need to be made during his administration.

In general, those presidents who wish to maximize their involvement, their discretion, and their influence benefit more from a fluid advisory relationship. On the other hand, those who prefer to make the final decision themselves, leaving the burden of soliciting and coordinating advice to others, are better served by a more formal arrangement. Kennedy, Johnson, and Carter fall into the first category; Nixon, Ford, and Reagan into the second, although in each case too much fluidity or too much structure can be dangerous.

Presidents who wish to depart from existing policy, particularly that which is based on strong outside interests, would tend to gain from the flexible advisory arrangement. The less formal the structure, the more quickly it can respond to changing conditions and the more easily it can produce innovative policy. Kennedy is an example of a president who had these objectives, who desired new and creative policy. Johnson is another. Nixon and Carter, in contrast, were less interested in innovation and more interested in obtaining the careful analysis that a well-staffed White House policy operation could produce.

To use the leadership dichotomy we have presented, if the president wishes to exert leadership as a *facilitator,* then the office can tolerate more open discussion, produce more options, and provide more interactive patterns than if the president wishes to be a *director* of change. There is no one formula for good presidential staffing, but good presidential staffing is a critical component of the formula for effective presidential leadership. Although presidents may be more dependent on others than they were in the past, they can still affect the staffing they receive. They can and do influence the personnel, organization, and operation of their own office. That is why, if they are victimized by their own staff, they usually have themselves at least partially to blame.

INVOLVING THE VICE PRESIDENT

Presidential support has been supplemented in recent years by the activities of the vice president and his staff. These activities range from providing policy advice and making political appeals to performing a variety of ceremonial functions. It was not always this way.

For years the vice presidency was regarded as a position of little importance. It was the brunt of jokes and laments. The nation's first vice president, John Adams, complained, "My country has in its wisdom contrived for me the most insignificant office that ever the invention of man contrived or his imagination conceived."[10] Thomas Jefferson, the second person to hold the office, was not quite as critical. Describing his job as "honorable and easy," he added, "I am unable to decide whether I would rather have it or not have it."[11]

Throughout most of the nineteenth century, the vice president performed very limited functions. Other than succeeding to the presidency, the holder of this position had only one designated constitutional responsibility—presiding over the Senate and voting in case of a tie. Nor did presidents enlarge these responsibilities very much. Vice presidents played only a peripheral role within their respective administrations, so much so that when Professor Woodrow Wilson wrote his treatise on American government in the 1880s, he devoted only one paragraph to the vice president. "The chief embarrassment in . . . explaining how little there is to be said about it," Wilson concluded, is that "one has evidently said all there is to say."[12] John Nance Garner, Franklin Roosevelt's first vice president, offered perhaps the most earthy refrain in his much-quoted comment that the office was "hardly worth a pitcher of spit."

Were Adams, Jefferson, and Garner alive today, they would have to reevaluate their assessments. The position has increased enormously in importance. Roosevelt's sudden death, Eisenhower's illness, and Kennedy's assassination cast attention on the vice president and generated support for clarifying succession during presidential disability and for filling the vice presidency should it become vacant. These events also contributed to the enhancement of the office by encouraging presidents to do more to prepare their vice president for the number one job.

Eisenhower was the first of the modern presidents to upgrade the vice president's role. He invited Richard Nixon, his vice president, to attend cabinet, National Security Council, and legislative strategy meetings. During his illness, Nixon presided over these sessions. According to Bradley H. Patterson, Jr.:

> Nixon was present at over 171 Cabinet meetings and chaired at least 20 of them in Ike's absence. He attended more than 217 NSC meetings and presided at some 26 of those, joined 173 legislative leaders' meetings, chairing two of them. The Cabinet and the National Security Council papers were sent to Nixon; his policy assistant attended both the post-Cabinet debriefings at the White House and the meetings of the NSC Planning Board. Eisenhower's privileged daily Staff Notes information memoranda were also taken to the vice president.[13]

In addition, as vice president, Nixon was sent on a number of well-publicized trips for the administration.

Lyndon Johnson was also involved in a variety of activities. As John Kennedy's vice president, he helped coordinate administration efforts to eliminate racial discrimination and promote exploration of outer space. He participated in legislative lobbying efforts, joining Kennedy at the White House breakfasts for congressional leaders. He also traveled abroad on behalf of the administration. Nonetheless, Johnson was not enamored with the job. To biographer Doris Kearns he stated:

> Everytime I came into John Kennedy's presence, I felt like a goddamn raven hovering over his shoulder. Away from the Oval Office, it was even worse. The Vice Presidency is filled with trips around the world, chauffeurs, men saluting, people clapping, chairmanships of councils, but in the end, it is nothing. I detested every minute of it.[14]

Despite their own experiences, neither Johnson nor Nixon added new responsibilities to the office, although both continued to have their vice presidents perform a variety of ceremonial, diplomatic, and political roles, such as chairing committees, making speeches, and representing the administration at international and national events. Hubert Humphrey and Spiro Agnew were not influential presidential advisers. Humphrey was not invited to the Tuesday lunch group strategy sessions for the Vietnam War, and Agnew found his access to the president more and more limited as the administration progressed. Neither exercised major influence on the formulation of important policy initiatives within their administrations.

Nelson Rockefeller, Gerald Ford's vice president, had the opportunity to do so. He was given good personal access to the president and an important policy-making role—to oversee the development of domestic programs. Quickly, however, his priorities clashed with those of others within the administration. Coming under increasing criticism from conservative Republicans, he announced his intention not to seek the vice presidency in the 1976 election and subsequently removed himself from an active policy-making and advisory role.

Whereas Rockefeller did not realize the vice president's potential as a presidential adviser, Walter Mondale, and, to a lesser extent, George Bush, did. Both had an office in the West Wing of the White House and a staff that was integrated with the president's.

Mondale saw Carter on a regular basis. While he had no ongoing administrative responsibilities, he was given *carte blanche* to be included in any conference, see any paper, and participate in any study that he desired. Carter writes in his memoirs that Mondale ". . . received the same security briefings I got, was automatically invited to participate in all my official meetings, and helped to plan strategy for domestic programs, diplomacy, and defense."[15] Carter also provided opportunities for Mondale to shape policy, and he did. He was also instrumental in improving congressional relations for the administration, heading a priority-setting mechanism, facilitating administration lobbying on key bills, helping to establish a public liaison operation in the White House, and using his own political connections to groups outside the government to improve coalition building for the president.

When President Reagan wished to demonstrate his concern with crisis management, drug enforcement, and government relations, he appointed Bush to head committees studying these issues. Bush also served as a personal envoy of the president in visits to North Atlantic Treaty Organization (NATO) countries, on a fact-finding trip to Lebanon, and by attending the funeral of several foreign policy leaders. His aides represented him at the senior staff, legislative strategy group, and other key meetings in the White House.

The expanded role for the vice president has resulted in an enlarged budget and supporting staff for the office. In 1961 Lyndon Johnson had only twenty professional and clerical aides. Today the vice president has approximately sixty with a budget in the neighborhood of $2 million. That staff is divided into two groups, one charged with helping the vice president perform his legislative functions and the other, his executive responsibilities. The legislative office, the smaller of the two, arranges meetings with members of Congress and aids the vice president in his role as president of the Senate. It is located in the Senate chamber. The executive office, housed in the Executive Office Building next to the White House, handles domestic and international policy questions, administrative responsibilities, and media coverage, as well as appointments, travel, and scheduling.

One reason for Mondale's and Bush's success was their willingness to exercise power behind the scenes and not become the focus of public attention. They let the president take the credit. According to political scientist Paul C. Light, these experiences suggest four rules that should be followed by vice presidents if they are to be influential:

1. Never complain to the press. One of Rockefeller's continuing problems in the Ford administration was his high profile in the press. Leaks were easily traced to the Vice President's office.
2. Never take credit from the President. The Vice President must remember who is President and who is not. According to Mondale, once Carter made a decision, "I wouldn't rag him."
3. Fall in line. No matter how much the Vice President opposes a presidential decision, he or she must support the final policy. The Vice President does not have to become a vocal supporter or lobbyist, but must fall in line like any other staffer.
4. Share the dirty work. Though the Vice President may not like endless travel (and nights in Holiday Inns, as Mondale once complained), it is all part of being a team player. Mondale, for example, was on the road 600 days during his term.[16]

The growth of the vice presidency has not only benefitted the vice president, but it has also worked to the president's advantage. It has provided him with additional resources for the performance of his ceremonial and symbolic functions, additional personal resources for the exercise of his political and public opinion roles, and additional policy advice from an official who shares his national and political perspective.

Each of these advantages, however, can become a disadvantage if the vice president rivals the president for political influence, policy direction, or personal power. Presidents want strong and loyal support, but they do not relish internal opposition, particularly from those who are a heartbeat or an election away from replacing them. That is why the vice president's influence is still dependent to a much larger extent on the president's personal needs than on the institutional responsibilities of his office.

Finally, the evolution of the vice president indicates why the criteria for filling the office should evolve as well. In the past, vice presidential candidates have been selected primarily for their electibility, for their contributions to the ticket. If presidents are to obtain maximum benefit from their vice presidents today, then they must choose their running mates on the basis of their capacity to govern as well.

CONCLUSION

Today the president's tasks are far too numerous, require too much knowledge, and may be fraught with too many obstacles for the president to undertake them alone. He needs the information and advice of others; he needs to build and maintain political alliances; and he needs to increase the credit and reduce the blame for his actions. All of these needs are serviced by his presidential office.

The founders undoubtedly would have been surprised and probably dismayed by the growth and institutionalization of that office. They conceived of the president in narrower terms, as a chief executive with subsidiary responsibilities. They also envisioned his need for subordinates and advisers. Still, nothing in their deliberations suggests an institution as large, complex, and influential as the presidential office has become.

Most of this growth has occurred in the twentieth century, much of it since World War II. The office has become larger, more specialized, and increasingly politicized. It has developed an independent capacity to advise and inform the president, to formulate and prioritize policy, to orchestrate and oversee department and agency input, and to build public and congressional support.

As a result of this growth, senior presidential aides have become more important, more prestigious, and more visible. They occupy more of the president's time. In contrast, department secretaries have lost some of their status, their access to the president, and their exclusive influence over policy within their department's primary spheres.

Not only has the creation and maintenance of a presidential office occurred at the expense of the departments and agencies, but it may also have occurred at some cost to the president. While the influence of the presidency and its capacity to affect policy have undoubtedly been enhanced, the president's personal ability to oversee his staff on an ongoing basis has not. In fact, it has been made more difficult by the large size of the office and the number of functional responsibilities it performs.

This has placed the contemporary president in a dilemma. He needs a large, functionally differentiated staff to exercise leadership, yet his leadership is frequently at the mercy of this staff. Thus, the expansion of the presidential office has been a mixed blessing. Created to meet increased expectations, it has generated new ones. Designed to coordinate and facilitate executive branch decision making, it has produced serious tensions between the White House and the departments. Tailored to systematize advice to the president, it has proliferated that advice and sometimes has worked to isolate the president from his advisers.

Yet, its expansion has obviously been necessary. It has been both a cause and effect of the growth of government, of the executive branch, and of the president's leadership responsibilities.

NOTES

1. James Anderson, "A Revised View of the Johnson Cabinet," *Journal of Politics* 48 (1986): 531.
2. Ibid.: 534–35.
3. The need to develop a team approach and produce new policy is most acute at the beginning of an administration, when cabinet input is desired. Toward the end, the implementation of that policy, often the prerogative of a single department, consumes more time. The increasing constraints on a president's time resulting from periods of extended foreign travel or the quest for reelection also make it difficult for presidents to continue to meet with their cabinet on a regular basis.
4. Thomas E. Cronin, *The State of the Presidency* (Boston: Little, Brown, 1980), p. 276.
5. Ibid., p. 283.
6. William C. Spragens, "White House Staffs (1789–1974)," in Bradley D. Nash et al., eds., *Organizing and Staffing the Presidency* (New York: Center for the Study of the Presidency, 1980), pp. 20–21.
7. Ibid., p. 21.
8. Richard E. Neustadt, "Approaches to Staffing the Presidency," *American Political Science Review* 54 (December 1963): 857.
9. Irving Janis, *Groupthink* (Boston: Houghton Mifflin, 1982).
10. John Adams, *The Works of John Adams*, ed. C. F. Adams (Boston: Little, Brown, 1850), 1: 289.
11. Thomas Jefferson, *The Writings of Thomas Jefferson*, ed. P. L. Ford (New York: Putnam 1896), 1: 98–99.
12. Woodrow Wilson, *Congressional Government* (New York: Meridian Books, 1956; originally printed in 1885), p. 162.
13. Bradley H. Patterson, Jr., *The Ring of Power* (New York: Basic Books, 1988), p. 287.
14. Lyndon Johnson, quoted in Doris Kearns, *Lyndon Johnson and the American Dream* (New York: Harper and Row, 1976), p. 164.
15. Jimmy Carter, *Keeping Faith* (New York: Bantam Books, 1982), p. 39.
16. Quoted from Paul C. Light, "Second Counts: Filling the New Vice Presidency" (paper presented at the Brookings Institution, Washington, D.C., 1984), pp. 20–21.

SELECTED READINGS

Anderson, James E. "A Revised View of the Johnson Cabinet." *Journal of Politics* 48 (1986): 529–37.

Campbell, Colin. *Managing the Presidency.* Pittsburgh: University of Pittsburgh Press, 1986.

Cohen, Jeffrey E. *The Politics of the U.S. Cabinet: Representation in the Executive Branch, 1789–1984.* Pittsburgh: University of Pittsburgh Press, 1988.

Goldstein, Joel K. *The Modern American Vice Presidency.* Princeton, N.J.: Princeton University Press, 1982.

Hart, John. *The Presidential Branch.* New York: Pergamon, 1987.

Hess, Stephen. *Organizing the Presidency.* Washington, D.C.: Brookings Institution, 1988.

Janis, Irving. *Groupthink.* Boston: Houghton Mifflin, 1982.

Kernell, Samuel, and Samuel L. Popkin, eds. *Chief of Staff: Twenty-Five Years of Managing the Presidency.* Berkeley, Calif.: University of California Press, 1986.

Kessel, John H. "The Structures of the Carter White House." *American Journal of Political Science* 27 (1983): 431–63.

——————. "The Structures of the Reagan White House." *American Journal of Political Science* 28 (1984): 231–58.

Light, Paul C. *Vice Presidential Power.* Baltimore: Johns Hopkins University Press, 1984.

Patterson, Bradley H., Jr. *The Ring of Power.* New York: Basic Books, 1988.

Pfiffner, James P. "White House Staff Versus the Cabinet: Centripetal and Centrifugal Roles." *Presidential Studies Quarterly* 16 (1986): 666–90.

Pika, Joseph A. "Management Style and Organizational Matrix." *Administration and Society* 20 (1988): 3–29.

Reedy, George. *The Twilight of the Presidency.* New York: New American Library, 1987.

Riddlesperger, Jr., James W., and James D. King. "Presidential Appointments to the Cabinet, Executive Office, and White House Staff." *Presidential Studies Quarterly* 16 (1986): 691–99.

Rockman, Bert A. "The Style and Organization of the Reagan Presidency." In Charles O. Jones, ed. *The Reagan Legacy.* Chatham, N.J.: Chatham House, 1988. Pp. 3–29.

Rose, Richard. *The Post-Modern President: The White House Meets the World.* Chatham, N.J.: Chatham House, 1988.

Walcott, Charles, and Karen M. Hult. "Organizing the White House: Structure, Environment, and Organizational Governance." *American Journal of Political Science* 31 (1987): 109–25.

7

Presidential
Decision Making

The essence of the president's job is making decisions—about foreign affairs, economic policy, and literally hundreds of other important matters. The task is a difficult one, and many obstacles to rational decision making are present. Leadership in the area of decision making is of a different nature than in the other arenas of presidential activity we examine in this book. The president needs to ensure that he has before him a full range of options and the appropriate information necessary for evaluating them.

The president's leadership in decision making requires both that he establish a working relationship with his subordinates and have an organization in the White House that serves his decision-making needs. Often he will have to persuade his own appointees in the White House and the bureaucracy to provide him with the options and information he requires. As we will see, they have many incentives not to do so.

There are other obstacles as well. Lack of time to consider decisions and previous commitments of the government may constrain a president's decision making. So may the president's own personal experiences and personality.

The director president will have a full range of options and information at his disposal, and he will be relatively unencumbered by environmental constraints on his range of choices. More subject to the influence of contextual factors, the facilitator president will be more dependent on his environment for options and information and more constrained in his decision making.

Figure 7-1 is a graphical representation of the influences on presidential decision making. In the outer circles are the broad contexts in which decisions take place; in the inner circles are the more immediate influences. In this chapter we examine the influence the factors represented in the outer five rings have on presidential decision making. In the following chapter we consider the impact of the president's personal characteristics.

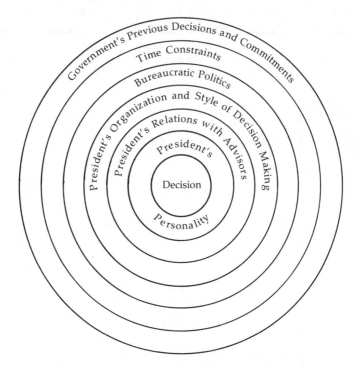

Figure 7-1. Influences on Presidential Decision Making

PREVIOUS COMMITMENTS

The first step in understanding presidential decision making is to recognize that the president operates under severe constraints in his decision making, no matter what his approach to making decisions. As Kennedy aide Theodore Sorensen has observed:

> We assume that the President makes decisions. . . . Presidents rarely, if ever make decisions . . . in the sense of writing their conclusions largely on a clean slate. They make choices. They select options. They exercise judgments. But the basic decisions, which confine their choices, have all too often been previously made by past events or circumstances, by other nations, by pressures or predecessors or even subordinates.[1]

Thus, the president's decisions usually fall within parameters set by prior commitments of the government that obligate it to spend money, defend allies, maintain services, or protect rights.

For example, when George Bush took office in January 1989, the American people were in general agreement that the federal deficit was the most important matter for the new president to tackle. Bush was not able to start from scratch and consider how best to allocate federal expenditures, however. As we discuss in Chapter 13, almost the entire federal budget was already committed before Bush took the oath of office. A president could propose to save money by, say, eliminating the navy or ending the provision of health care for the indigent, but such solutions would receive little support. Bush's decision making was restricted to marginal changes in the budget.

TIME CONSTRAINTS

The diverse obligations of the president and his top aides impose severe constraints on the amount of time they can devote to generating and evaluating options and information. According to a Carter aide:

> When the President asks to see all the potential alternatives, it is an impossible request. Not only do we have to limit the range to the few that just might work but we have to cut back to save on time. The staff already has too much to do without attempting that kind of analysis—it involves too much time.[2]

Overloaded advisers may rely on others, equally overloaded, to bring crucial information to the attention of the president. Several of President Truman's advisers believed there was a serious danger of Chinese intervention in the Korean War if the president attempted to reunite all of Korea under a non-Communist government. However, no one went to him to argue that he should reverse his decision allowing General MacArthur to invade Communist North Korea. Each person thought that someone else would do it.[3]

The president and his advisers rarely have the luxury of anticipating new issues. According to Zbigniew Brzezinski, President Carter's national security adviser, at the time the fateful revolution in Iran began,

> our decision making circuits were heavily overloaded. The fall of 1978 was the time of the Camp David process and its aftermath. This was also the time of the stepped-up SALT negotiations, and during the critical December days we would literally rush from one meeting, in which the most complex positions on telemetry encryption or cruise missile definition would be hammered out, to another meeting on the fate of Iran. The fall . . . was also the period of the critical phase in the secret U.S.–Chinese negotiations. . . . In addition, the crisis in Nicaragua was beginning to preoccupy and absorb us. Finally, [Secretary of State] Cy Vance was heavily involved in key negotiations abroad, notably in the Middle East, while for [Secretary of Defense] Harold Brown this was the period of most difficult battles with the President over the defense budget. . . . It was unfortunately not a time in which undivided attention could be focused easily and early on what became a fatal strategic and political turning point.[4]

Sometimes deadlines make it necessary for the president and his aides to cease the consideration of information and options and make a decision. In the words of President Reagan's budget director, David Stockman:

> I just wish that there were more hours in the day or that we didn't have to do this so fast. I have these stacks of briefing books and I've got to make decisions about specific options. . . . I don't have time, trying to put this whole package together in three weeks, so you just start making snap judgments.[5]

Because of such time limits, the less controversial parts of elaborate policies often receive too little attention and contain too much logrolling.

If a study about an issue is not available when policymakers must make a decision, the report will go unread. If the report is required by a certain date and more than one person has been engaged to produce it, there is an incentive for the participants to "soften" their views in order to reach a consensus. This, in turn, can mask problems inherent in the policies they recommend. Moreover, the pressure of hammering together a report under a strict deadline may make it quite incoherent.

ORGANIZATION AND STYLE OF DECISION MAKING

Each president is unique and has broad discretion in structuring his decision making in the White House. There are many ways to do this, and each has consequences for the effectiveness of the advisory system. In this section we explore the ways in which the organization and style of the presidential advisory process can affect the president's consideration of options and information.

White House Organization

Many commentators on the presidency stress the formal aspects of White House organization, but they may be overemphasized, at least as they relate to presidential decision making. As Kennedy aide Theodore Sorensen has commented, "To be preoccupied with form and structure—to ascribe to . . . reform and structure a capacity to end bad decisions—is too often to overlook the more dynamic and fluid forces on which presidential decisions are based."[6]

There is virtual unanimity among observers of the presidency that one cannot develop an ideal organization for the White House that is appropriate for every president. The organization of the White House will inevitably reflect the personality and work habits of the incumbent. Moreover, the chief executive's personal style will dominate any organizational scheme. If a president has a penchant for acting without adequate study, he will defeat any advisory system that he has established in the White House. According to an experienced presidential aide, "The nature of the *man* is absolutely crucial and decisive, altogether overriding the issue of organization."[7]

As discussed in Chapter 6, White House structure may also reflect the goals of presidents. Those like Franklin Roosevelt, John Kennedy, and Lyndon Johnson who were concerned with producing innovative policies have displayed a tendency toward flexible staff arrangements.

Presidents may simultaneously use several approaches to organizing their decision making, depending on the president's level of interest in a policy area, his policy priorities, and the strengths and limitations of his principal advisers in each policy area. For example, President Ford employed a hierarchical model of centralized management for foreign policy in which he concentrated responsibility in Henry Kissinger's hands. In economic policy, he employed a managed multiple advocacy system in which collegial discussions among a wider range of advisers occurred. In the area of domestic policy, where he did not want to undertake policy initiatives, he delegated responsibility to Vice President Rockefeller and dealt with issues on an ad hoc basis.

Organizational charts may be misleading. When asked by a fellow White House assistant about drawing up an organization chart of the Johnson White House, Bill Moyers replied:

> Such an exercise is a gross misuse of a good man's time; nothing useful can come from it since the White House staff reflects the personal needs of the President rather than a structural design. . . . There is no pattern to it that can be fitted to a chart.[8]

Henry Kissinger adds that the influence of a presidential assistant "derives almost exclusively from the confidence of the President, not from administrative arrangements."[9]

We should not be surprised, then, that top Carter aides sometimes "walked" their memos into the president's office when he was gone, circumventing the prescribed system for the circulation of memoranda to the president (to ensure that all relevant views were gathered), and then made sure that their memos were on top of the president's pile. President Eisenhower's decision-making process was really much more fluid than the rigid hierarchy that would appear on an organization chart. Nixon adviser John Connally regularly bypassed the White House chain of command.

Sometimes what appears to be crucial presidential consultation with his advisers is actually much less. One of the crucial moments in America's involvement in Vietnam came in July 1965 when President Johnson committed the United States to large-scale combat operations. In his memoirs Johnson goes to considerable lengths to show that he considered very carefully all the alternatives available at the time. The detailed account by one of his aides of the dialogue between Johnson and some of his advisers shows the president probing deeply for answers, challenging the premises and factual bases of options, and playing the devil's advocate. Yet a presidency scholar has argued persuasively that this "debate" was really a charade, staged by the president to lend legitimacy to the decision he already had made.[10] Richard Nixon has been accused of similar behavior.

After analyzing sources of decisional problems in foreign policy, political scientist Alexander George concluded

> There appears to be no single structural formula by which the chief executive and his staff can convert the functional expertise and diversity of viewpoints of the many offices concerned with international affairs into consistently effective policies and decisions.[11]

We may confidently add that this is also true for domestic policy decisions.

On the other hand, organization does make a difference. As we saw in the previous chapter, the two most common White House organizational schemes are the hierarchical and the "spokes of the wheel." Recent presidents have found that they require a chief of staff to coordinate the flow of White House business and to give them time to focus on priorities and reflect on questions of basic strategy.

Both Gerald Ford and Jimmy Carter began their tenures trying to employ the spokes-of-the-wheel approach, but both had to alter their organizational scheme to establish more of a hierarchical system headed by a chief of staff. The following comments by President Ford explain why this was necessary and also indicate the significance of organization:

> Initially, when I became President, I did not want to have a powerful chief of staff. . . . I was aware of the trouble . . . top assistants had caused my predecessors. I was determined to be my own chief of staff. . . . I would have five or six senior assistants with different areas of responsibility . . . and they would be able to see me at regular intervals during the day. . . . But as I was to discover soon enough, it simply didn't work. Because power in Washington is measured by how much access a person has to the President, almost everyone wanted more access than I had access to give. I wanted to have an "open" door, but it was very difficult; my working days grew longer and longer, and the demands on my time were hindering my effectiveness. Someone . . . had to be responsible for scheduling appointments, coordinating the paper flow, following up on decisions I had made and giving me status reports on projects and policy development. I didn't like the idea of calling this person chief of staff, but that in fact was the role he would fill.[12]

Hierarchical staff organizations save the president's time and promote thorough evaluation of options. Yet many observers of the presidency are concerned with such arrangements because the hierarchy that screens information may also distort it. This does not occur because presidential aides "capture" the president, however. Even in the Nixon administration, with its famed "palace guard" around the president, whatever isolation occurred in the Oval Office was with the full concurrence and encouragement of the president. The president used his staff to serve his own needs and to keep out those whom he did not want to see. Moreover, we lack systematic evidence that Nixon's chiefs of staff provided Nixon with a distorted view of the issues with which he desired to deal.

The president's staff also needs to sift issues so that only those requiring his involvement will be presented to him. If he attempts to solve all the problems that come to the White House, he will spread his and his advisers' attention too thinly, wasting time and scarce resources. In addition, the more the president does, the more problems for which others will hold him accountable. Presidents Ford and Carter had tendencies toward becoming involved in relatively minor matters and both have been criticized, even by their own aides, for lacking the appropriate breadth of vision and understanding necessary to shape and guide the government.

Presidents—Eisenhower, Nixon, Ford, and Reagan are examples— often want their advisers to reach a consensus on an issue and make a recommendation to them before it receives much consideration in the Oval Office. This does not mean that they will accept the recommendation, however. Gerald Ford's description of his approach is typical:

> I myself liked to have consensus developed before a problem came to my desk for decision, but then I reserved the right to go behind that consensus to find out what the differing views were in the process. In that way I got a feel as to whether it was just a weak compromise or whether it was a legitimate one that provided the best answer.[13]

The Form of Advice

Different presidents prefer to receive advice in different forms. Presidents Nixon and Carter preferred to reach their decisions on the basis of written memoranda on the pros and cons of various options. In contrast, Presidents Eisenhower, Kennedy, Johnson, Ford, and Reagan used memos to focus discussion but frequently discussed issues with advisers in relatively open settings.

There are advantages and disadvantages of both the verbal and paper approaches. The latter requires that options that go to the president be thoroughly "staffed out," that is, that relevant officials comment upon them after careful analysis. As Henry Kissinger explains, if this does not occur,

> the danger is real that plausibility is confused with truth and verbal fluency overwhelms cool analysis. . . . in the absence of staff work, decisions may be made which the facts do not support, where individuals talk to impress and

not to elucidate at a time when precision is crucial. The temptation . . . is . . . to allow a fleeting and superficial consensus to ratify unexamined assumptions. There are the simultaneous risks of paralysis and recklessness. Principals cannot really know the consequences of their recommendations unless those recommendations have been translated into specific operational terms.[14]

Reviewing advice on paper also saves the president time and protects the confidentiality of communications. It may also provide an outlet for those who find it difficult to express themselves directly to the president in order to articulate their views. The most vociferous critic out of the president's presence can become the meekest lamb when meeting the president personally. This inhibition in speech is not unusual. President Carter found that people's oral skills often deserted them when they were in the Oval Office. He had a somewhat similar experience of his own in his first debate with President Ford in 1976.

On the other hand, the requirement that communications to the president be written and thoroughly researched may deny the chief executive access to some useful information and ideas. Some aides simply resist writing memos, as did Jody Powell, one of President Carter's closest advisers. Face-to-face discussions with advisers may also provide the president with information that is not reflected in the written word. Direct confrontation between advocates of diverse positions allows the participants to pinpoint their critiques of each other's positions and raise relevant follow-up points. Oral discussions also provide opportunities for advisers to highlight the most important points and crucial nuances in arguments and for presidents to learn the intensity of officials' views and the confidence with which they hold them. This may alert the chief executive to the level of support he may expect from officials who oppose his ultimate decision. In addition, some ideas, especially those that are highly sensitive, can be best or perhaps only advanced personally and informally in the give-and-take of conversation, and some may not be ready for memoranda but deserve mention so the president will be aware of the fullest range of options.

In order for face-to-face discussions among advisers and the chief executive to be useful, the president must be able to accommodate the interpersonal tensions inherent in an advisory system of close give-and-take. Yet not all presidents possess this tolerance. Richard Nixon's personality was not amenable to dealing with oral confrontations. He dreaded meeting new people, especially if they were in a position to rebuff or contradict him. To avoid tension, he spoke elliptically and had a tendency to agree with whomever he was speaking (only to disavow it later). Thus, the president conducted as much business as possible by memos, in which he was more likely to express his true views and less likely to meet with opposition. To avoid confrontations he sometimes called carefully constructed meetings that included one dissenter and began by agreeing with that person and then allowed himself to be talked out of that position, leaving the holdout isolated and more likely to join in a consensus view.

Nixon's aversion to open disagreement both affected the quality of his decision-making process and led him to alter policy decisions to achieve consensus. According to national security adviser Henry Kissinger:

> So much time, effort, and ingenuity were spent in trying to organize a consensus of the senior advisers that there was too little left to consider the weaknesses in the plan or to impose discipline on the rest of the government. There was no role for a devil's advocate. At every meeting, to gain the acquiescence of the potential recalcitrant, Nixon would offer so many modifications that the complex plan he was seeking to promote was eventually consumed. . . . Each of these steps may have been minor; the cumulative impact was considerable.[15]

The oral approach also carries the danger that the president will decide on the basis of the last person he talked to instead of on the basis of careful consideration of alternatives. President Ford sometimes did this, as when he agreed to support Secretary of Labor John Dunlap on a labor relations bill, only to face the opposition of the rest of his cabinet and top advisers when the bill passed. The president vetoed the bill amidst embarrassing publicity on his policy reversal, angering labor interests, which felt betrayed, and undercutting his secretary of labor, who resigned over the matter.

Another requirement for the oral approach to be effective is that the president must not dominate the discussion. If he does, he may not devote sufficient attention to the advice he receives and may influence that advice by his comments. According to Hamilton Jordan, Jimmy Carter's White House chief of staff:

> I had learned when Jimmy Carter was Governor that if I wanted to change his mind or challenge him on something that was important or complicated, it was best to do it in writing. If I went into his office to argue with him, armed with five reasons to do something, I would rarely get beyond point one before he was aggressively countering it. I seldom got to the second or third point.[16]

Similarly, another Carter aide found that the president was formidable in face-to-face encounters and often persuaded him to his view, even though upon reflection he concluded the president was actually wrong on the matter. When personally confronted, the president may be on the defense; written differences of opinion may be easier to accept.

Multiple Advocacy

Closely related to the form in which the president receives advice is the range of options he receives and the effectiveness with which they are presented. The president should not be dependent upon a single channel of information, as occurred, for example, when the president and other high officials, including the Joint Chiefs of Staff, relied upon the CIA's estimates of the success of the 1961 invasion of Cuba at the Bay of Pigs. It occurred again in 1965 when the president relied upon the American embassy in the Dominican Republic for the information that led to this country's invasion of the island. Moreover, the key assumptions of alternatives should be evaluated by officials who did not develop them and thus have no personal stake in them. Only the CIA evaluated the Bay of Pigs plan, with disasterous consequences.

Quality decision making requires more than that the president be presented with a diversity of views. It is also necessary that each point of view be represented by an effective advocate. This is not always the case, however, because differences exist among advisers in persuasive skills, intellectual ability, policy expertise, power, status, standing with the president, and analytical staff support. These disparities may distort the decision-making process by giving some viewpoints an undue advantage. As Kennedy aide Theodore Sorensen has observed, "The most formidable debater is not necessarily the most informed, and the most reticent may sometimes be the wisest."[17]

Multiple advocacy also forces a larger number of issues to the top, that is, to the president; debate and give-and-take on them require a substantial commitment of time on the part of both the president and his staff, and time is a scarce commodity in the White House. According to a Ford assistant, "Multiple advocacy is very nice on paper. It just can't work in the White House. We don't have time to make sure all the advisors have access to the President. This is not day-care; it is survival of the fittest."[18] In addition, the president may not be interested in all his advisers have to offer on a policy about which he cares little.

Multiple advocacy also runs a considerable risk of increasing staff conflict. The president must engage in the delicate balancing act of being in firm control of the process of decision making while encouraging free and open discussion. This is difficult enough to accomplish while he is considering options. It is even more of a challenge after he decides on a course of action, because it is not uncommon for both winners and losers among presidential advisers to be less than gracious and turn to back stabbing and leaks to the press. Some political scientists have suggested that the president needs a process manager to balance the resources of his advisers and strengthen the weaker advocates, ensure that all options are articulated and have effective advocates, set up additional channels of information, arrange for independent evaluations of decisional premises and options when necessary, and generally monitor the decision-making process and identify and correct any malfunctions. This delicate role can easily be undermined if the custodian is also a policy adviser, presidential spokesman, enforcer of decisions, administrative operator, or watchdog for the president's power stakes. He or she must remain an "honest broker" concerned with the process of advising the president. This adviser must also keep his or her own staff small so that it will not become specialized and circumvent established channels of advice.

In some decision-making situations an adviser may adopt the role of "devil's advocate" in order to provide a challenge to the dominant point of view. The devil's advocate may relieve some of the stress of decision making because officials feel they have considered all sides of an issue, and there may be some public relations benefits for the president when the word is spread that he considered the full range of views. Decision makers may also benefit from listening to and rebutting challenges to their course of action, and those least enthusiastic about a decision may be more willing to join in a consensus view if there has been debate before it is reached.

Nevertheless, the devil's advocate does not necessarily improve the quality of White House decision making. Since the devil's advocate is playing a role and is not a true dissenter, he or she is unlikely to persist in opposition or try to form coalitions or employ all resources to persuade others. Such an advocate is not really engaged in a truly competitive struggle. Moreover, officials may discount ahead of time the comments of one who persistently plays the devil's advocate role. Yet if devil's advocacy is not routinized, there is no assurance it will be operating when it is needed to provide balance to an argument.

Even if a president chooses to consider a range of viewpoints, he may not benefit fully from them. For example, Gerald Ford has been criticized for falling back on his experience as a legislator and reaching decisions by weighing the views of others and then leaning in the direction of the consensus opinion. Presidential authority is diluted when the chief executive bases decisions on the number of advisers on a side rather than on his own informed judgment.

Presidential Involvement

In his classic study of presidential power, Richard Neustadt alerted future presidents that they would need information, including tangible details, to construct a necessary frame of reference for decision making.[19] As we have seen, the president cannot assume that any person or advisory system will provide him the options and information he requires. Thus, presidents must reach out widely for them.

If a president fails to actively oversee his decision-making system and insist that it provide him the options and information he requires, the consequences may be profound. On January 17, 1986, President Ronald Reagan signed a document, technically called a "finding," that paved the way for the United States to sell arms secretly to Iran in hopes of obtaining the release of American hostages held in the Middle East.

The finding also created the opportunity to generate profits on the arms sales that could be, and were, diverted covertly to the Contras fighting the Nicaraguan government.

The finding was presented to the president by his national security adviser, Vice Admiral John Poindexter. It had a cover memo, prepared by Lt. Col. Oliver North, but the president did not read the memo. Although the memo pointed out that the plan was opposed by the secretaries of state and defense, the memo presented neither their views nor justifications for the assertions of success the memo made. Yet the president did not insist that better staff work be done. Eleven days earlier, before the National Security Council meeting he called to discuss it took place, the president had signed a similar finding that also had not been fully staffed, not realizing that the paper was only a proposal for discussion.

The arms sale policy was a failure and undermined the nation's strongly asserted position of not trading arms, or anything else, for hostages. When details of this policy decision began to emerge later in the year, there was a loud public outcry. The president's standing fell substantially in the polls, and his political clout was diminished. Things got even worse when the diversion of funds to the Contras came to light. At this point the president fired North, accepted the resignation of Poindexter, and had to endure a year of congressional hearings and a critical investigation by a special commission he appointed to examine his handling of the matter.

A spate of books written by top officials in the Reagan administration (detractors term them "kiss and tell") revealed that Ronald Reagan was a peculiarly detached decision maker. As we noted in Chapter 6, he had strong views on the basic goals of public policy but left it to others to implement his broad vision. Aides prepared detailed scripts on index cards for his use in meetings. His detachment and lack of mastery of the details of policy hindered his evaluation of policy options.

PRESIDENTIAL RELATIONSHIPS WITH ADVISERS

The president requires the services of personal aides to carry out his duties. Since he must rely so heavily upon his aides and work so closely with them, he naturally chooses persons of similar attitudes and compatible personalities. Moreover, strong personalities, which typically characterize presidents, create environments to their liking and weed out irritations.

Many, perhaps most, people find it difficult to stand up to the president and disagree with him. There is evidence that President Reagan's aides had growing doubts about his economic policies even in 1981 but did not relay them to the president until after the program was enacted.

"All those in favor say 'Aye.'"
"Aye."   *"Aye."*   *"Aye."*
          "Aye."   *"Aye."*
Source: Drawing by H. Martin; © 1979 The New Yorker Magazine, Inc.

At times advisers are strong advocates of a position before a meeting with the president and then completely switch their arguments during the meeting after they learn the president has accepted the opposite view. It was because of this phenomenon that President Kennedy often absented himself from meetings of his advisers during the Cuban missile crisis. He wanted everyone to feel free to speak his mind.

Sometimes advisers find it difficult to disagree with the president because of the latter's strong, dynamic, or magnetic personality. These traits are certainly not unusual in successful politicians, especially presidents. Former White House assistant Chester Cooper has written that President Johnson often polled his foreign policy advisers one at a time to discover their views on the Vietnam War. Each would respond "I agree," although Cooper, and undoubtedly others, did *not* agree. Cooper even dreamed of answering no, but he never did.[20] Other Johnson administration officials report of a similar tendency of those around the president to tell him what they thought he wanted to hear about the war rather than what they really thought.

One reason for the reluctance of presidential aides to challenge the president is that they are completely dependent upon him for their jobs, their advancement, and the gratification of their egos. Cabinet members are nearly as dependent, although they may have support in Congress or from interest groups. Because aides usually desire to perpetuate their positions, they may refrain from giving the president "unpleasant" information or from fighting losing battles on behalf of their principles. Even Nixon's White House chief of staff, H. R. Haldeman, felt that he had to survive in his own job and therefore failed to fight sufficiently the dark side of the president's character.

Thus, the president often finds it difficult to evoke critical responses from those around him. Gerald Ford observed:

> Few people, with the possible exception of his wife, will ever tell a President that he is a fool. There's a majesty to the office that inhibits even your closest friends from saying what is really on their minds. They won't tell you that you just made a lousy speech or bungled a chance to get your point across. . . . You can tell them you want the blunt truth; you can leave instructions on every bulletin board, but the guarded response you get never varies.
>
> And yet the President—any President—needs to hear straight talk. He needs to be needled once in a while, if only to be brought down from the false pedestal that the office provides. He needs to be told that he is, after all, only another human being with the same virtues and weaknesses as anyone else. And he needs to be reminded of this constantly if he's going to keep his perspective.[21]

All of these tendencies may be reenforced by a president who "punishes" aides who present options and information he does not like. Lyndon Johnson was such a person. He forced top aides and officials who dissented on Vietnam to leave his administration, and he went so far as to reduce contact with such key people as Secretaries of Defense Robert McNamara and Clark Clifford and Vice President Hubert Humphrey.

Johnson's press secretary George Reedy observed that the White House had an inner political life of its own. Thus, the staff carefully studied the president's psyche to gain and maintain access to him. They wanted to be around when there was good news to report and discreetly absent when the news was bad, hoping someone else would receive the blame. Naturally, this gamesmanship helped to distort Johnson's view of reality.

Richard Nixon had little interest in critiques of his weak points, and those who attempted to criticize him did not maintain their influence very long. Even as secure and personable a president as Franklin Roosevelt is reported to have allowed only those who did not challenge him to remain around.

The dampening effect that behavior like Johnson's or Nixon's can have on discussions even outside the Oval Office can be substantial. Office of Congressional Relations chief Lawrence O'Brien and Vice President Hubert Humphrey were in constant contact for months before they became aware of each other's views on Vietnam. Because President

Johnson equated criticism with disloyalty, even the highest officials in the White House kept their dissent to themselves.

Strong presidents may also, in effect, tell their advisers what advice to offer them. In 1965 President Johnson complained to the army chief of staff that he needed solutions other than bombing to stop the Communists from taking over South Vietnam and sent the general, who was reluctant to escalate the war, to Vietnam. When he returned, the president urged the Joint Chiefs of Staff to propose measures "to kill more VC" (Viet Cong). It is not surprising that five days later the chiefs submitted their first recommendation for direct use of American troops in combat.

Richard Nixon sometimes sought out advisers who would tell him what he wanted to hear. He turned to John Connally for "tough" advice, such as when he wanted someone to urge him to mine the harbor at Haiphong, North Vietnam. A Nixon aide once observed the president and Connally cruising down the Potomac on the presidential yacht, the *Sequoia*, as Nixon was trying to talk his adviser into recommending that he institute wage and price controls on the economy.

A president with heightened fears of security leaks may place loyalty above competence, independence, or openness as a criterion for evaluating and relying upon advisers. He may also control the information flow tightly and keep even insiders in the dark. One of the reasons President Johnson relied so heavily on a group of five or six high officials (called the Tuesday lunch group) to advise him on the Vietnam War was that he felt the larger National Security Council leaked too much information. According to Secretary of State Dean Rusk, "The Tuesday luncheons were where the really important issues regarding Vietnam were discussed in great detail. This was where the real decisions were made. And everyone there knew how to keep his mouth shut."[22]

Ironically, one inhibition on freedom of dissension in the White House and in the upper levels of the bureaucracy is public opinion. If the president allows open discussion of policy views, then there will inevitably be disagreement. This disagreement is often then presented in the press as evidence that the president is not in control and that the White House lacks a sense of direction. Thus, by being open the president may lose some public support but by being closed to options and information he may make poor decisions.

Feuding and infighting for power and access to the president among ambitious aides are also obstacles to rational decision making. This rivalry takes several forms. One of the most common techniques is to attack rivals through leaks to the press that they are out of favor with the president or not competent to carry out their duties. Sometimes the leaks place competitors for power in a favorable context but one that will displease the president, who may value credit and publicity for himself rather than his aides.

In recent years the Nixon, Ford, and Reagan administrations stand out for the extent of their internal feuding and infighting. One high-level Reagan aide disclosed how he and other White House officials tried to undercut Secretary of State Alexander Haig. "In a classic case of Washington infighting, we threw virtually every booby trap in his way that we could, planted every story, egged the press on to get down on him."[23]

All of this feuding encourages self-interested behavior by presidential advisers that may distort their vision and cause them to overextend their arguments and present unbalanced discussions of options and their consequences to the president. There is also a tendency for competing advisers to seek to aggrandize influence and monopolize the counsel on which presidential decisions are based, providing insufficient information, analysis, and deliberation for decisions. Staff rivalry also detracts from the efficiency of White House operations as it wastes time and lowers staff morale. Moreover, publicity on feuding in the White House can embarrass the president when it is covered in the press, which it inevitably is.

High officials in Washington know that their ability to function effectively with the bureaucracy depends on being known for their effectiveness with the president. Dean Rusk, former secretary of state, argues that "the real organization of government at higher echelons is . . . how confidence flows down from the President."[24] To maintain their reputations for effectiveness with the president, officials may not strongly advocate positions that they consider sound if they feel the president is unlikely to adopt their proposals. An official does not usually want to be known as one whose advice the president rejected.

An additional potential hindrance to sound advice for the president is the loss of perspective by White House aides. Because working in the White House is a unique experience, a narrowing of viewpoint may easily occur. Especially for top aides, the environment is luxurious, secure, and heady, and the exercise of power is an everyday experience. The potential for isolation is real, and the chief executive must fight these insulating tendencies. President Johnson was very sensitive about his aides losing perspective, and thus he closely controlled the use of White House perks and stripped his staff of pretensions with a "merciless persistency."[25]

An adviser's conception of his job influences his delivery of information and options. President Eisenhower's secretaries of defense, Charles Wilson and Neil McElroy, considered themselves managers of the department and did not become heavily involved in disputes over foreign policy or strategic doctrine. By contrast, Secretary of Defense Robert McNamara adopted an aggressive stance as an adviser. But McNamara's colleague, Secretary of State Dean Rusk, did not consider it his job to participate in policy disputes with his colleagues or the president. In fact, many observers thought he did not effectively present State Department views on Vietnam or other foreign policy issues.

BUREAUCRATIC POLITICS AND DECISION MAKING

A primary source of options and information for the president is the bureaucracy. Yet it is not a neutral instrument. Individuals and the agencies they represent have interests of their own to advance and protect and do not necessarily view issues from the president's perspective. Moreover, the structure of the flow of information and the development of options may also hinder decision making in the White House.

Organizational Parochialism

Government agencies have a tendency toward inbreeding. The selective recruitment of new staff helps to develop homogeneous attitudes. Those attracted to work for government agencies are likely to support the policies carried out by those agencies, whether they be in the fields of social welfare, agriculture, or national defense. Naturally, agencies prefer hiring like-minded persons. Within each agency the distribution of rewards creates further pressure to view things from the perspective of the status quo. Personnel who do not support established organizational goals and approaches to meeting them are unlikely to be promoted to important positions. Moreover, all but a few high-level policymakers spend their careers within one agency or department. Since people want to believe in what they do for a living, this long association strongly influences the attitudes of bureaucrats.

Related to long-time service in an agency is the relatively narrow range of each agency's responsibilities. Officials in the Department of Education, for example, do not deal with the budget for the entire national government but only with the part that pertains to their programs. It is up to others to recommend to the president what is best for national defense, health, or housing. With each bureaucratic unit focusing on its own programs, there are few people to view these programs from a wider, national perspective.

Influences from outside an agency also encourage parochial views among bureaucrats. When interest groups and congressional committees support an agency, they expect continued bureaucratic support in return. Since these outsiders generally favor the policies the bureaucracy has been carrying out all along (which the outsiders probably helped initiate), what they really want is "more of the same."

All of these factors result in a relatively uniform environment in which policy making takes place. Intraorganizational communications pass mainly among persons who share similar frames of reference and who reinforce bureaucratic parochialism by their continued association.

The influence of parochialism is strong enough that even some presidential appointees, who are in office for only short periods of time, adopt the narrow views of their bureaucratic units. The Nixon White House felt that even close associates of the president were "captured" by the bureaucracy. The dependence of such officials on their subordinates for information and advice, the need to maintain organizational morale by supporting established viewpoints, and pressures from their agencies' clienteles combine to discourage high-ranking officials from maintaining broad views of the public interest.

President Nixon observed that "it is inevitable when an individual has been in a Cabinet position or, for that matter, holds any position in Government, [that] after a certain length of time he becomes an advocate of the status quo; rather than running the bureaucracy, the bureaucracy runs him."[26] Thus, parochialism can lead officials to see different faces on the same issue. In 1977 President Carter asked Congress for an authorization for a 20 percent cutback in wheat acreage and the placing of several million tons of food and feed grains in reserve. This proposal followed an intense internal debate in which the Department of Agriculture, reacting to the demands of farmers, wanted an even bigger cutback; the Treasury Department and the Council of Economic Advisers opposed any cutback out of concern for future consumer prices and the export potential of the United States should food shortages develop; and the State Department was concerned about the proposal's effect on international negotiations regarding an international grain reserve. In other words, policymakers in different bureaucratic units with different responsibilities saw the same policy in a different light and reacted differently to it.

It was to combat this parochialism that President Reagan went to considerable lengths to insulate his new cabinet appointees from the traditional agency arguments in defense of programs the White House had slated for cuts. They received their initial briefings from the president, the OMB director, and citizens groups rather than from the bureaucracy; were often assigned deputies with close personal and ideological ties to the White House; and were given little time to react to the president's proposals.

Maintaining the Organization

As a result of parochialism in the bureaucracy, career officials come to believe that the health of their organization and its programs is vital to the national interest. In their eyes, this well-being depends in turn on the organization's fulfilling its missions, securing the necessary resources (personnel, money, authority), and maintaining its influence. Organizational personnel can pursue their personal quests for power and prestige, the goals of their organization, and the national interest all at the same time without perceiving any role conflicts. Moreover, policymakers in different organizational units are prone to see different faces on the same issues because of their different organizational needs.

The single-mindedness of policymakers attached to various agencies causes them to raise options and gather information that support the interests of their organization and avoid or oppose options and information that challenge those interests. In this way, the goals of maintaining an organization may displace the goals of solving the problems for which the organization was created. As one former high White House official has written, "For many cabinet officers, the important question was whether their department would have the principal responsibility for the new program—not the hard choices that lay hidden within it."[27]

Within most organizations there is a dominant view of the *essence* of the organization's mission and the attitudes, skills, and experience employees should have to carry out that mission. Organizations usually propose options they believe will build upon and reinforce the essential aspects of their organizations. Although its bombing campaigns had not had unqualified success in previous wars, the air force lobbied for strategic bombing and deep interdiction in the Vietnam War. One way to do this was to argue for bombing as a central feature of United States policy in order to show its utility. The lack of success only reinforced the air force's efforts to step up bombing even further; the air force never admitted it was not accomplishing its objectives. An organization will also vigorously resist efforts of others to take away, decrease, or share its essence and the resources deemed necessary to realize that essence.

In their struggles over roles and missions, bureaucrats may distort the information and options provided to senior officials. In Vietnam the air force and navy were each concerned that the other might encroach on its bombing missions: the navy was also concerned about justifying the high cost of its aircraft carriers. Thus, they competed in their efforts at air warfare. The aspect of this interservice competition that was most damaging to the accuracy of the perceptions high-level decision makers had of American success in the war was the battle over the relative effectiveness of each service's air warfare. Each was concerned for future budgets and missions and could not let the other get the upper hand. Thus, each exaggerated its own performance, expecting the other to do likewise.

Budgets are another vital component of strategies to maintain an organization. This is true for grant-awarding agencies, as well as for agencies with large operational capabilities like the military services and the Department of Agriculture. Because staff within governmental organizations generally believe their work is vital to the national interest, and because conventional wisdom stipulates that a larger budget enables an organization to perform its functions more effectively, units normally request an increase in funding and fight decreases. The size of a group's budget not only determines the resources available for its services but also serves as a sign of the importance others attach to the organization's functions.

Agency personnel also examine any substantive proposal to ascertain its impact on the budget. They rarely suggest adding a new function to their responsibilities if it must be financed from monies already allocated for ongoing activities. Moreover, components of large organizations, like units in the military or the Department of Health and Human Services, are concerned about maintaining or increasing their percentage of the larger unit's budget.

An organization's staff members are likely to raise and support options that give them autonomy. In their view they know best how to perform their essential mission. They resist options that would place control in the hands of higher officials or require close coordination with other organizations. This desire for autonomy helps explain why several agencies independently gather and evaluate national security intelligence from their own perspective. As Richard Nixon complained when he was disappointed in the intelligence reports he received, "Those guys spend all their time fighting each other."[28]

Because organizations seek to create and maintain autonomous jurisdictions, they rarely oppose each other's projects. This self-imposed restraint reduces the conflict between organizations and correspondingly reduces the options and information available to the president. In dealing with their superiors, the leaders of an organization often guard their autonomy by presenting only one option for a new program. The rationale is that if higher officials cannot choose among options, they cannot interfere with the organization's preference.

Once an agency of government has responsibility for a program, it has a tendency to evaluate it positively. Thus,

> After the American presence in Vietnam was increased and the programs enlarged . . . each bureaucratic organization then had its own stakes. The military had to prove that American arms and advice could succeed. The Foreign Service had to prove that it could bring about political stability in Saigon and build a nation. The CIA had to prove, especially after the Bay of Pigs fiasco, that it could handle covert action and covert paramilitary operations lest it chance having its operational missions in general questioned. The Agency for International Development (AID), like the State Department and the military, had to prove that pacification could work and that advice and millions of dollars in assistance could bring political returns. . . . by 1965 almost all career professionals became holier than the Pope on the subject of U.S. interests in Vietnam.[29]

Organizational and Personal Influence

To achieve the policies they desire, organizations and individuals seek influence. In pursuing power, officials often further distort the processes of generating options and gathering information for the president. One way for organizations to increase their influence is to defer to one another's expertise. The operations of all large-scale organizations, including governments, require a considerable degree of specialization and expertise. Those who possess this expertise, whether within executive agencies or congressional committees, naturally believe they know best about a subject in their field, and they therefore desire primary influence over the resolution of issues in their subject area. Because each set of experts has a stake in deference to expertise (they each receive benefits from it), reciprocal deference to expertise becomes an important theme in policy making. One result of this reciprocity is that fewer challenges to expert views are aired than might otherwise be the case.

For several decades there has been an implicit agreement between the Departments of State and Defense that each would stay out of the other's affairs. During the Vietnam War the State Department often took no part in shaping war policies and refrained from airing its views on many of them. Contributing to this restraint was Secretary of Defense McNamara's adamant belief that the State Department should not challenge the military's appraisal of the actual progress of the war. Once when the director of the State Department's Bureau of Intelligence and Research attempted to do so, McNamara forcefully elicited a promise from Secretary of State Dean Rusk that such a challenge would not recur. He thus deliberately blocked the flow of information on the war. This meant that policymakers had to defer to Defense Department assessments that were often inaccurate and biased toward military rather than political solutions.

Although deference to expertise is not always a satisfactory way of resolving conflicts in policy making, it is often the only possible course of action. Governmental agencies are the sole source of data and analysis on many issues. As their work becomes more and more specialized, it becomes more and more difficult to check their information and evaluations. This problem is exacerbated by a need for secrecy on most national security policies, which makes it necessary to limit even further the number of participants in the policy-making process.

To take full advantage of deference to expertise and to increase their influence further, organizations seek to prevent their own experts from disseminating conflicting information and options. Contrary information and evaluations undercut the credibility of a unit's position. Moreover, by presenting several real options, a unit increases the range of possible policy decisions and commensurately decreases the probability that the option favored by the unit's leaders will be selected. Thus, the Joint Chiefs of Staff rarely disagree in their recommendations. The relevant departments never really presented President Carter options on welfare reform, in part because they were afraid he would select an alternative they opposed. No one would insist to the president that reform would be costly, because they feared he would then reject reform efforts.[30]

If there are disagreements among the experts in an organizational unit, efforts to produce an appearance of unanimity can reduce the experts' recommendations to broad generalizations. A record of agreement on the least disputed common denominators usually fails to mention many controversial points that may be crucial to the ultimate success of the policy at issue. When compromise positions reach the president in a form that suggests a unified consensual judgment, they can give him a false sense of security because he may lack an awareness of the potential problems buried within the recommendations.

For bureaucrats interested in their own careers, the prospect of a deferred promotion or even dismissal makes them reluctant to report information that undercuts the official stands of their organizations. The example of the Foreign Service officers who frankly (and accurately) reported on the strength of the Communists in China during the late 1940s was not quickly forgotten in the bureaucracy. They were driven from the Foreign Service for allegedly pro-Communist sympathies. Twenty years later, the Foreign Service's memory of these incidents may have inhibited candid reporting on the weakness of the South Vietnamese regime and the strength of the Viet Cong. In addition, senior officials at the State Department are still complaining about the Foreign Service's lack of creativity.

Some officials anticipate sanctions even in the absence of their being exercised. One of the most embarrassing incidents of Jimmy Carter's early presidency was the scandal surrounding Bert Lance, his close friend and the director of the Office of Management and Budget. Lance eventually resigned under pressure after details of his business and personal financial dealings were made public. For our purposes the question is, why did the president not know of these problems?

At least a large part of the answer seems to be that officials responsible for reviewing Lance's background soft-pedaled the reports in an effort to cultivate the goodwill of the new administration. The deputy comptroller general (who was acting comptroller) later testified that he knew of Lance's problems but downplayed them to avoid losing his job. Indeed, he hoped to be appointed comptroller general. It also appears that the relevant United States attorney closed his investigation of Lance early, over the objections of several of his subordinates, hoping not to irritate the new president so that he could keep his job and qualify for a federal pension.

At times an illusion of competition conceals a basic consensus. Rivalry among the military organizations has reached legendary proportions, but much of it is superficial. Interorganizational competition among the armed services has primarily been over jurisdictional matters (which service should do what) rather than over questions of substantive policy.

Experts also create an illusion of competition when they agree to compare their preferred action to unfeasible alternatives. Lyndon Johnson's advisers have been criticized for juxtapositioning in 1964 their favored option of bombing North Vietnam against two phony options: in effect, blow up the world or scuttle and run.

Bureaucratic Structure

The structure of administrative organizations is one of the factors that impedes the flow of options and information to higher-level decision makers. Most bureaucracies have a hierarchical structure, and the information on which decisions are based usually passes from bottom to top. At each step in this ladder of communication, personnel screen the information from the previous stage. Such screening is necessary because the people at the top—presidents—cannot absorb all the detailed information that exists on an issue and must have subordinates summarize and synthesize information as it proceeds upward. The longer the communication chain, the greater the chance that judgments will replace facts; nuances or caveats will be excluded; subordinates will paint a positive face on a situation to improve their own image or that of their organization; human error will distort the overall picture; and the speculations of "experts" will be reported as fact.

Screening, summarizing, and human error are not the only pitfalls in the transmission of information. When subordinates are asked to transmit information that can be used to evaluate their performance, they have a tendency to distort information in order to put themselves in the most favorable light. Body counts of killed enemy soldiers in Vietnam, made by the troops who had faced them in combat, were notoriously unreliable and became even more so as they were padded at each higher level of the military hierarchy to demonstrate successful operations. Equally inaccurate were the estimates of bombing damage, made by the pilots flying the bombing missions.

Subordinates sometimes distort facts by not reporting those that indicate danger. President Kennedy was not apprised of the following problems with the contingency plan for the Bay of Pigs: the men participating in the invasion had not been told to go to the mountains if the invasion failed; between the beach and the mountains which supposedly offered refuge was a large swamp; and only one-third of the men had received guerrilla training. Instead, he was simply informed that if the invasion failed, the men would go to the mountains and carry out guerrilla warfare. At other times subordinates may exaggerate the evidence in support of their favored alternative in order to increase the probability of its being chosen.

Even in the hierarchical executive branch, the president cannot depend on information being centralized. There was a great deal of information pointing to the Japanese attack on Pearl Harbor, for example, but it was never fully organized. No one brings forward all the political, economic, social, military, and diplomatic considerations of a policy in a recognizable manner for the president's deliberation because the bureaucracy relevant to any policy is too decentralized and too large and produces too much paper to coordinate information effectively.

The president may attempt to compensate for the problems of hierarchy by sending personal aides or outsiders to assess a situation directly and propose options. However, the person assigned to the task may determine the nature of the report more than the situation itself. When President Kennedy sent General Maxwell Taylor and Walt Rostow on a fact-finding mission to South Vietnam, their recommendations for military action could have been predicted on the basis of their views before they left on the trip. Moreover, the president cannot bypass senior officials very often without lowering their morale and undercutting their operational authority.

President Kennedy's chief White House national security adviser, McGeorge Bundy, ordered that cables to the State Department, the Central Intelligence Agency (CIA), and the Pentagon be sent directly to the White House and not just to the Washington headquarters of those departments where they could be summarized and analyzed for transmittal to the president. But this practice could not correct the distortion that may have gone into the cables in the first place, and someone had to summarize and synthesize the tremendous volume of information before it reached the president.

Organizations use routines or standard operating procedures (SOPs) to gather and process information in a methodical fashion. However, the character of the SOPs may delay the recognition of critical information, distort the quality of information, and limit the options presented to policymakers.

In the case of the Cuban missile crisis, several weeks before the president was aware of the missiles there was a good deal of information in the United States intelligence system pointing to their presence. But the time required by SOPs to sort out raw information and double check it delayed recognition of the new situation. Organizational routines also masked signs forecasting the 1974 leftist coup in Portugal. Officials from the intelligence services of the CIA, the Defense Department, and the State Department testified after the event that their routines did not focus much attention on Portugal, and they could not shift personnel rapidly to a new area of concern.

SOPs affect not only *if* and *when* information is collected but also the substance of the information. In Vietnam the military's concentration on the technical aspects of bombing caused it to substitute a set of short-run physical objectives for the ultimate political goals of the war. Military reports emphasized physical destruction per se rather than the political impact of such destruction. The enemy's capacity to recruit more men or rebuild a structure never seemed to enter into the calculations.

Standard operating procedures give disproportionate weight to information entering the system from regular channels. For example, the United States was highly dependent on the Shah of Iran and Savak, the Shah's secret police organization, for information about Iran. Until a few months before the Shah was deposed, they reported to the CIA and President Carter that there was no likelihood of revolution. The White House rejected more pessimistic reports from journalists and others outside the regular flow of information.

SOPs structure the process of decision making by preselecting those who will be asked for advice and predetermining when they will be asked. There are routine ways of invading foreign countries and of determining agency budgets. Some persons will be involved at earlier stages than others, and some will be viewed as having more legitimate and expert voices in policy discussions. When Lyndon Johnson limited his circle of personal advisers on the Vietnam War to a half-dozen top officials, those at a lower rung in the foreign policy hierarchy found it harder to have their dissents heard. In addition, there was little opportunity for others in the cabinet to challenge the war policy because they were not in the right decision-making channels.

Purely analytic units often have problems in being heard. According to Henry Kissinger:

> I can think of no exception to the rule that advisers without a clear-cut area of responsibility eventually are pushed to the periphery by day-to-day operators. The other White House aides resent interference in their spheres. The schedulers become increasingly hesitant in finding time on the President's calendar.[31]

Thus, information is most likely to influence policy making if the position of those who have it ensures they must be consulted before a decision is made.

Standard operating procedures also affect the nature of the alternatives proposed by bureaucratic units. Bureaucracies typically propose their standard ways of doing things rather than innovative solutions to problems. These standard policies may not be appropriate for the problem at hand.

As a result of problems with established routines, presidents often create special task forces of "outside" experts to develop new programs. Such bodies, brought together for a new purpose, are less likely than established agencies to be blinded by SOPs.

Because only decision makers directly responsible for a policy are normally consulted on "secret" matters, fewer advisers contribute to secret deliberations than to debate on more open issues. This reduces the range of options that are considered in a secret decision and limits the analysis of the few options that are considered. The secrecy of President Johnson's Tuesday lunch group, which made the important decisions on the Vietnam War, prevented an advance agenda. Thus, decisions were made without a full review of the options beforehand. Secrecy also makes it easier for those directly involved to dismiss (intentionally or unintentionally) the dissenting or offbeat ideas of outsiders as the products of ignorance, which is unfortunate because secret information is often inaccurate or misleading. President Kennedy wished he had not been successful in persuading *The New York Times* not to publish the plans for the Bay of Pigs invasion; he afterward felt that publicity might have elicited some useful critiques.

CONCLUSION

The president faces an enormously difficult and complex task in making decsions on a wide range of issues. He must work within the parameters of the national goverment's prior commitments and is further constrained by the limited time he can devote to considering options and information on any one policy. In addition, the president faces a number of other potential hazards in reaching decisions. The struggling facilitator, not the dominating director, is the description that matches the process of presidential decision making most of the time.

There are a variety of ways for the president to organize the White House and acquire advice. Not all of them are equally useful in ensuring that he is presented with a full range of options, each supported with effective advocacy. Moreover, the president may experience problems with his aides' reluctance to present candid advice, which may be aggravated by the president himself, and with their efforts to increase their influence.

Bureaucratic politics also play a role in determining the options and information the president receives and the form in which he receives it. Agencies and their personnel inevitably have narrower perspectives than the White House and desire to maintain and expand their programs, status, and influence. Those ambitions often bias the options and information presented to the White House. The ways in which bureaucratic units collect, process, and transmit options and information and the secrecy that sometimes accompanies them may add further distortion to what the president sees.

It is important that the president be sensitive to the many obstacles to effective decision making and attempt to avoid or compensate for them as best he can, realizing that perfectly rational decision making is unattainable.

NOTES

1. Theodore Sorensen, quoted in John C. Donovan, *The Politics of Poverty*, 2nd ed. (Indianapolis: Pegasus, 1973), p. 111.
2. Quoted in Paul C. Light, *The President's Agenda: Domestic Policy Choice from Kennedy to Carter* (Baltimore: Johns Hopkins University Press, 1982), p. 179.
3. Richard E. Neustadt, *Presidential Power: The Politics of Leadership from FDR to Carter* (New York: Wiley, 1980), pp. 106–07.
4. Zbigniew Brzezinski, *Power and Principle: Memoirs of a National Security Adviser, 1977–1981* (New York: Farrar, Straus, and Giroux, 1983), p. 358; see also p. 396.
5. David Stockman, quoted in William Greider, "The Education of David Stockman," *Atlantic*, December 1981, p. 34.
6. Theodore C. Sorensen, *Decision-Making in the White House: The Olive Branch or the Arrows* (New York: Columbia University Press, 1963), p. 3.
7. Bryce Harlow, quoted in Emmet John Hughes, *The Living Presidency: The Resources and Dilemmas of the American Presidential Office* (Baltimore: Penguin, 1973), p. 345.
8. Bill Moyers, quoted in Larry Berman, "Political Scientists in Presidential Libraries: How Not to Be a Stranger in a Strange Land" (paper presented at the Annual Meeting of the American Political Science Association, Washington, D.C., September 1979), n. 52.
9. Henry Kissinger, *White House Years* (Boston: Little, Brown, 1979), p. 47; see also p. 1455.
10. Larry Berman, *Planning a Tragedy: The Americanization of the War in Vietnam* (New York: Norton, 1982).
11. Alexander L. George, "The Case for Multiple Advocacy in Making Foreign Policy," *American Political Science Review* 66 (September 1972): 766.
12. Gerald R. Ford, *A Time to Heal: The Autobiography of Gerald R. Ford* (New York: Harper and Row, 1979), p. 147; see also p. 186.
13. Gerald R. Ford, "Imperiled, Not Imperial," *Time*, November 10, 1980, p. 31.
14. Kissinger, *White House Years*, p. 602; see also p. 40.
15. Ibid., p. 996.
16. Hamilton Jordan, *Crisis: The Last Year of the Carter Presidency* (New York: Putnam, 1982), p. 42.
17. Sorensen, *Decision-Making in the White House*, p. 62.
18. Quoted in Light, *The President's Agenda*, p. 200.
19. Neustadt, *Presidental Power*, chaps. 6 and 7.
20. Chester L. Cooper, *The Lost Crusade: America in Vietnam* (New York: Dodd, Mead, 1970), p. 223.
21. Ford, *A Time to Heal*, pp. 187–88.
22. Dean Rusk, quoted in Leon V. Sigal, *Reporters and Officials: The Organization and Politics of Newsmaking* (Lexington, Mass.: Heath, 1973), p. 147.
23. Larry Speakes, *Speaking Out* (New York: Scribner's, 1988), p. 244–45.
24. "Mr. Secretary: On the Eve of Emeritus," *Life*, January 17, 1969, p. 62B.
25. Jack Valenti, *A Very Human President* (New York: Norton, 1975), pp. 115–16.
26. Richard M. Nixon, *Public Papers of the Presidents: Richard Nixon, 1972* (Washington, D.C.: U.S. Government Printing Office, 1974), p. 1150.
27. Harry McPherson, *A Political Education* (Boston: Little, Brown, 1972), p. 298.
28. H. R. Haldeman, *The Ends of Power* (New York: Times Books, 1978), p. 107.
29. Leslie H. Gelb with Richard K. Betts, *The Irony of Vietnam: The System Worked* (Washington, D.C.: Brookings Institution, 1979), p. 239.
30. Laurence E. Lynn, Jr., and David def. Whitman, *The President as Policymaker: Jimmy Carter and Welfare Reform* (Philadelphia: Temple University Press, 1981), pp. 116, 269.
31. Henry Kissinger, *Years of Upheaval* (Boston: Little, Brown, 1982), p. 74.

SELECTED READINGS

Allison, Graham. *Essence of Decision: Explaining the Cuban Missile Crisis*. Boston: Little, Brown, 1971.

Anderson, Paul A. "Decision Making by Objection and the Cuban Missile Crisis," *Administrative Science Quarterly* 28 (June 1983): 201–22.

Berman, Larry, *Planning a Tragedy: The Americanization of the War in Vietnam.* New York: Norton, 1982.

Destler, I. M. *Presidents, Bureaucrats, and Foreign Policy: The Politics of Organizational Reform.* Princeton: Princeton University Press, 1972.

Downs, Anthony. *Inside Bureaucracy.* Boston: Little, Brown, 1967.

Edwards, George C., III, and Ira Sharkansky. *The Policy Predicament: Making and Implementing Public Policy.* San Francisco: Freeman, 1978.

Gelb, Leslie H., with Richard K. Betts. *The Irony of Vietnam: The System Worked.* Washington, D.C.: Brookings Institution, 1979.

George, Alexander L. *Presidential Decisionmaking in Foreign Policy: The Effective Use of Information and Advice.* Boulder, Colo.: Westview Press, 1980.

Halperin, Morton H. *Bureaucratic Politics and Foreign Policy.* Washington, D.C.: Brookings Institution, 1974.

Kessel, John H. "The Structures of the Reagan White House." *American Journal of Political Science* 28 (May 1984): 231–58.

March, James G., and Herbert A. Simon. *Organizations.* New York: Wiley, 1958.

Neustadt, Richard E. *Presidential Power: The Politics of Leadership from FDR to Carter.* New York: Wiley, 1980.

Porter, Roger. "Gerald R. Ford: A Healing Presidency." In Fred I. Greenstein, ed., *Leadership in the Modern Presidency.* Cambridge, Mass.: Harvard University Press, 1988. Pp. 199–227.

Simon, Herbert A. *Administrative Behavior: A Study of Decision-Making Processes in Administration Organization.* 2nd ed. New York: Free Press, 1957.

Sorensen, Theodore C. *Decision-Making in the White House: The Olive Branch or the Arrows.* New York: Columbia University Press, 1963.

8

The Personalized Presidency

In Chapter 6 we discussed the office of the presidency. The size of that office, its structures and modes of operation, and its patterns of communication, coordination, and decision making all affect what the president does and how effectively he does it. Presidential decisions and actions are also influenced by the environment in which they occur. We focused on that environment in Chapter 7 and listed a variety of factors that impinge on decision making either directly or indirectly. These included advisory patterns, organizational structures, bureaucratic politics, and standard operating procedures as well as longer-term external forces and events such as the political climate, economic and social conditions, and public attitudes and opinions.

But presidents are not robots. Nor do we believe that all their decisions are fated. They have choice and exercise it. It matters how skilled they are, how smart they are, and how quickly they absorb information and make decisions. Their attitudes and values, their view of their roles and tasks, and their long- and short-term goals can all affect their decisions and conduct in office. Moreover, how they feel on a particular day, whether they are sick or healthy, tired or rested, sad or happy, frustrated or contented, may also have an impact. Beneath these feelings, their personality, cognitive skills, and interactive behavior will affect either directly or indirectly their perceptions, evaluations, and ultimately their judgments and actions as president.

The type of leadership role presidents desire and the one they usually pursue (whether they try to direct or facilitate change) and to some extent whether they are successful at it follow in large part from their personal needs and abilities. Theodore Roosevelt needed to maintain a strong, public presence as president; Calvin Coolidge preferred to operate in a low-key manner outside of public view; Lyndon Johnson had to dominate personal relations; both he and Richard Nixon wanted to exercise strategic control; Ronald Reagan was more laid back and willing to delegate.

Whether presidents are successful in the role they choose to pursue depends in large part on the fit between their personality and the public mood, on their capacity to influence people and shape events, and on their ability to make the right choices and avoid problems and decisions that can be dealt with by others. This chapter will discuss these personalized aspects of the presidency. After treating the purely formal, constitutional requirements for office, it will examine factors that affect presidents' preferences and, ultimately, their ability to lead: their social and political background, their physical attributes and general health, their psychological character and style of doing business, and their cognitive skills and perceptions. Additionally, patterns of interaction within the White House that directly or indirectly impinge on presidential priorities and their implementation will also be discussed. In this manner the chapter will address the critical question that the American electorate faces and must answer every four years—what difference does it make *who* is elected president?

QUALIFICATIONS FOR OFFICE

The framers of the Constitution were naturally aware that personal factors could and would affect presidential performance. Although they hoped that presidents would have altruistic motives and set exemplary standards in their public and private behavior, they could not predicate the powers and responsibilities of the office on this assumption. Rather they had to take precautions against the potential abuse of power by the executive, abuses they believed they had experienced during the colonial period under the reign of George III.

Thus, they devised a constitutional structure to constrain the president and other federal officials from exceeding their authority and provided a mechanism for removing them if they did. Reeligibility was seen as a motive for good behavior. Moreover, they envisioned the indirect selection process in the Electoral College as more likely to achieve an informed, intelligent, national judgment than a direct election by the general public. Presumably the electors could spot dangerous character problems more readily than the average voters, or so the framers believed.

Conceiving that character was more a product of personality than position, the delegates at the Philadelphia Convention did not impose a long list of qualifications for the office. On the contrary, they listed only three requirements in the Constitution. The president must be a natural-born citizen who has been a resident in the United States for fourteen years and is at least thirty-five years old. The citizenship and residence qualifications were designed to prevent those with allegiances to other countries, by virtue of their birth or residential preference, from becoming president and thereby being in a position to subvert the national interests of the United States. The age requirement was imposed because the delegates at the Philadelphia Convention believed that the presidency demanded a higher level of maturity than any other position in the United States government. Minimum age for the House of Representatives was set at twenty-five and for the Senate at thirty.

With the possible exception of age, those formal requirements have precluded few who might otherwise be considered qualified from seeking the presidency. However, a set of informal requirements, as noted in Chapter 2, has in practice restricted eligibility to a much smaller subset of the population. Despite the notion, so appealing in democratic theory, that the nation's highest position should be one to which any citizen can aspire and achieve, the fact is that presidents as a group have not represented a microcosm of American society.

SOCIAL AND POLITICAL BACKGROUND

To put it simply, American presidents have not been typical Americans. They have been advantaged by virtue of their wealth, the professional positions they have held, and the personal contacts they have made. Born into families of high social status and considerable economic means, they have benefitted from greater educational and professional opportunities than their peers have enjoyed.

Despite the log cabin myth, perpetuated by Abraham Lincoln's rise to political prominence, most presidents have not had humble origins. In fact, Lincoln did not either.[1] The early presidents in particular were men of high social class. Eight of our presidents were the product of only four families: John Adams and John Quincy Adams (father and son), William Henry Harrison and Benjamin Harrison (grandfather and grandson), Theodore Roosevelt and Franklin Roosevelt (cousins), and James Madison and Zachary Taylor (common grandparents). At least half of those who have served in the White House during the twentieth century had backgrounds of social or political prominence (see Tables 8-1 and 8-2). Only Calvin Coolidge, Richard Nixon, and Ronald Reagan might be said to have suffered from poverty in their youth.

The advantages that higher income and social status can provide can be seen in the educational levels and professional activities that presidents as a group have attained. Most have been well educated. Of those who held office in the twentieth century, only Harry S Truman did not attend a university. Most, in fact, have undergraduate and graduate degrees (see Table 8-1).

Education has been used as a springboard for professional careers that have culminated in public service. Most presidents held elective office prior to being president. Eisenhower was the last not to have done so, although he did run and defeat Senator Robert A. Taft in the Republi-

Table 8-1. Social and Political Background of Twentieth-Century Presidents

Presidents	Years Served	Father's Occupation	Own Occupation	Undergraduate College
William McKinley	1897–1901	Businessman	Lawyer	Allegheny College
Theodore Roosevelt	1901–1909	Businessman	Lawyer	Harvard
William H. Taft	1909–1913	Lawyer	Lawyer	Yale
Woodrow Wilson	1913–1921	Minister	Educator	Princeton
Warren G. Harding	1921–1923	Physician	Journalist	Ohio Central
Calvin Coolidge	1923–1929	Storekeeper	Lawyer	Amherst
Herbert Hoover	1929–1933	Blacksmith	Engineer	Stanford
Franklin D. Roosevelt	1933–1945	Businessman	Lawyer	Harvard
Harry S Truman	1945–1953	Farmer	Businessman	None
Dwight D. Eisenhower	1953–1961	Mechanic	Military	U.S. Military Academy
John F. Kennedy	1961–1963	Businessman	Journalist	Harvard
Lyndon B. Johnson	1963–1969	Farmer	Educator	Southwest Texas Teachers College
Richard Nixon	1969–1974	Streetcar Motorman	Lawyer	Whittier College
Gerald Ford	1974–1977	Businessman	Lawyer	University of Michigan
Jimmy Carter	1977–1981	Farmer	Farmer, Businessman	U.S. Naval Academy
Ronald Reagan	1981–1989	Shoe Salesman	Actor	Eureka College
George Bush	1989–	Businessman, Politician	Businessman, Politician	Yale

can presidential primaries. The increasing public dimensions of the office have also put a premium on communication skills, which contributed to actor Ronald Reagan's rise to political prominence and success in office.

Whereas social and political position have given certain individuals an advantage in winning the presidency, they may have also contributed to their success in governing, or at least that is what two sociologists have concluded. E. Digby Baltzell and Howard G. Schneiderman correlated the social class origins of presidents with recent evaluations of those who have served as president by historians and political scientists. They found that presidents from higher social classes tended to be more favorably evaluated than those from lower social classes (as indicated in Table 8-2).[2]

Why presidents from higher social classes tend to perform more effectively is difficult to say. Baltzell and Schneiderman suggest that high standards of performance and emphasis on public service may be traced to the fact that "our best aristocratic traditions have stressed *doing* a better job rather than the prevalent, middle-class ideology which has always stressed *getting* a better job."[3]

Of course, higher-class origins do not guarantee a successful presidency any more than lower-class origins preclude it. The correlation between class and effectiveness is itself suspect without a theoretical basis for believing the two are related. In warning of these dangers, Baltzell and Schneiderman note, tongue in cheek (we think), that height is also related to presidential greatness.[4] Others have found a correlation between height and electoral success.[5]

PHYSICAL ATTRIBUTES AND GENERAL HEALTH

Although height may be only indirectly related to presidential performance (through its psychological impact), other physical conditions and personal attributes may have a more direct effect. Take personal feelings, for example. Few would deny that people's feelings affect their job performance. For presidents these feelings could increase or decrease their willingness to listen to options, their capacity to weigh alternatives and make the best decision, and their ability to persuade others to support their choice. They could also affect their energy level, their capacity to withstand the rigors of the office, their concentration, even their tolerance.

Despite the importance of health, information about the medical pathologies of presidents has been extremely limited. Even today, the medical diagnoses and treatments of presidents are presented in a sketchy way, particularly at the onset of a health problem. The reason that health problems are understated is that administrations want to prevent precipi-

Table 8-2. Murray-Blessing's Ranking of Presidential Performance Related to Pessen's Ranking of Social-Class Origins†

	Upper Class	Upper-Middle Class	Middle and Lower Class
GREAT			
1. Lincoln			Middle
2. F. Roosevelt	Upper Upper		
3. Washington	Upper Upper		
4. Jefferson	Upper Upper		
NEAR GREAT			
5. T. Roosevelt	Upper Upper		
6. Wilson	Lower Upper		
7. Jackson		Upper Middle	
8. Truman		L. Upper/U. Middle	
ABOVE AVERAGE			
9. J. Adams	Lower Upper		
10. L. Johnson		Upper Middle	
11. Eisenhower			Middle
12. Polk	Middle Upper		
13. Kennedy	Middle Upper		
14. Madison	Upper Upper		
15. Monroe	Lower Upper		
16. J. Q. Adams	Upper Upper		
17. Cleveland		L. Upper/U. Middle	
AVERAGE			
18. McKinley		Upper Middle	
19. Taft	Upper Upper		
20. Van Buren		Upper Middle	
21. Hoover		Upper Middle	

tous public reactions and maintain continuity of policy both within the government and between it and other governments. Thus, it was not revealed until weeks after Ronald Reagan left the hospital following the attempt on his life how close he had actually come to death. Similarly, Grover Cleveland's two cancer operations, Woodrow Wilson's incapacity after a stroke, Franklin Roosevelt's worsening health, and John F. Kennedy's affliction with Addison's disease were not made known to the public during their presidencies.

Presidents seem to have had more than their share of illnesses and poor health while in office. George Washington had pneumonia, rheumatism, and a persistent back problem; Andrew Jackson was sick during much of his eight years as president; William Henry Harrison died in office after a bout with viral pneumonia, which he contacted on Inauguration Day; Zachary Taylor also died in office, succumbing to gastroenteritis early in his presidency; Lincoln suffered from headaches and depression which may have been an indication that he suffered from

Table 8-2 (continued).

	Upper Class	Upper-Middle Class	Middle and Lower Class
AVERAGE			
22. Hayes		L. Upper/U. Middle	
23. Arthur		Upper Middle	
24. Ford		Upper Middle	
25. Carter		Upper Middle	
26. B. Harrison	Upper Upper		
BELOW AVERAGE			
27. Taylor	Upper Upper		
28. Tyler	Upper Upper		
29. Fillmore			Lower Middle
30. Coolidge		L. Upper/U. Middle	
31. Pierce		L. Upper/U. Middle	
FAILURE			
32. A. Johnson			Upper Lower
33. Buchanan		Upper Middle	
34. Nixon			Lower Middle
35. Grant		Upper Middle	
36. Harding		L. Upper/U. Middle	

Note: W. H. Harrison and Garfield are not included because both served less than one year in office.

†Study conducted in 1981 by Robert K. Murray and Tim H. Blessing of Pennsylvania State University.

Source: E. Digby Baltzell and Howard G. Schneiderman, "Social Class in the Oval Office," *Society* 25 (September/October 1988): 46. Copyright © 1988 by Transaction Publishers.

Marfan syndrome, a genetic disease that affects joints and connective tissues; Wilson had a debilitating stroke; Harding had heart disease, a weak stomach, and died from a misdiagnosed seizure; Garfield and McKinley were shot and probably lost their lives from improper and inept medical treatment.

In the modern era, Franklin Roosevelt's health deteriorated as president, and he died in office from a coronary. Eisenhower had three major illnesses: coronary thrombosis in 1955, acute ileitis in 1956, and a minor stroke in 1957. In addition to Addison's disease, Kennedy aggravated a back problem he had had since college and treated it throughout his presidency with special braces, exercises, and a chair designed to alleviate pressure. He also took a cortisone-based medicine to relieve his back pain. Lyndon Johnson had both a gall bladder and hernia operation while in office and caught pneumonia on at least one occasion. The burdens of Vietnam and Watergate put both Johnson and Richard Nixon under severe mental strain, although in general Richard Nixon, Gerald

Ford, and Jimmy Carter enjoyed relatively good health as president. Ronald Reagan had operations for the removal of malignant growths in his colon and on his face, as well as suffering serious injury during the assassination attempt in 1981.

The effects of these medical problems on presidential performance, of course, vary. In general, the more serious the illness or injury is, the longer the recovery period, the more removed the president becomes from the day-to-day functioning of the office, and the more likely that critical decisions are delayed or delegated to others. What is more difficult to discern is how decision making is affected when presidents are not up to speed, when their judgment is affected by medication or pain.

Health issues are related to the aging process. Presidents are older than most Americans. Their mean age upon assuming office has been fifty-four. Reagan was the oldest, first elected at sixty-nine, while Theodore Roosevelt and Kennedy have been the youngest, inaugurated at forty-three. The reason that the framers set a minimum age was their assumption that maturity, wisdom, and experience were products of age, but so is infirmity. Furthermore, older people may be less able to engage in vigorous activities, and at a certain point tend to become slower mentally, have shorter attention spans and reduced memory, and, sometimes, are less able to handle stress.[6] The nation's oldest president, Ronald Reagan, joked about his dozing off at cabinet meetings; he frequently forgot names, dates, and other pertinent details and carried index cards to remind him of information he needed to know. In his first debate with challenger Walter Mondale in 1984, Reagan's poor recall and rambling answers prompted concern about his mental capacity at seventy-three. His age became a campaign issue, one that Reagan effectively dealt with by his performance in the second debate and subsequent campaign.

Obviously, the electoral success of presidents, particularly in the contemporary period in which much personal campaigning is frequently required, testifies to some extent to their physical fitness and may auger well for their fitness as president. On the other hand, every campaign takes its toll. Moreover, skillful media consultants and campaign organizers can create an impression of activity and vigor when the reality may be much less compelling. In 1944 Franklin Roosevelt's aides staged a series of public appearances for the president to refute rumors that his health was declining. In 1984 Ronald Reagan's manager projected the impression of much campaign activity by getting the president on the evening news every night in another campaign-related event. During much of the campaign, the evening news event was his *only* one of the day.

In addition to their lower energy levels, older people are also more prone to sickness and disability than are those in their younger and middle years.[7] The onerous duties and awesome responsibilities of the office have aggravated these manifestations of the aging process. Typically, before and after pictures of the president reveal the physical signs of aging: thinning, receding, and graying hair; facial wrinkles and blemishes; double chins; and the like. Take Lyndon Johnson, for example. Historian Eric Goldman, who worked in the Johnson White House, commented on the changes in Johnson's appearance during the five years that he was president:

> On March 31, 1968, I and the millions of others sat at our television sets for a speech of President Johnson's that he had labeled as especially important. I had not seen LBJ on television for quite a while and I was shocked. My mind went back over the changes in his appearance and manner during his five years in the White House. There were the days immediately after the assassination—the rangy, rugged figure, every antenna alert, trailed by edgy aides, looking around him with those hard, piercing eyes, always as if he were sniffing out a friend and foe, always as if he were remembering that a smile or a handshake might be needed here or there. . . .
>
> Now, in March 1968 an old, weary, battered man was on the television screen. The face was deeply lined and aging; the drawl occasionally cracked and wavered. His manner gave no intimation of FDR, and little of the LBJ of 1964. Rather it suggested a lecturish, querulous schoolmaster.[8]

Although the Johnson experience may not be typical, it is suggestive of the physical toll that the presidency can exact.

Statistics on the longevity of those who have served in the nation's highest office tend to support the "killing" nature of the job. As a group, presidents have had shorter life spans than their contemporaries.[9] Excluding the four presidents who were assassinated at a relatively young age, the longevity of the thirty-one others who have died is shorter than that of their peers, particularly if other demographic variables such as race, gender, sex, educational level, and professional background are taken into account. Presidents also live shorter lives than the average member of Congress or the Supreme Court.[10]

Although the numbers are small and generalizations hazardous, these statistics lend support to the conventional wisdom that the presidency is a very arduous and stressful position. In their conversations and writings, presidents have referred to the constant pressures they were under. In the words of President Johnson:

> The work of the President is demanding and unrelenting. It is always there to be done. Of all the 1886 nights I was President, there were not many when I got to sleep before 1 or 2 A.M., and there were few mornings when I didn't wake up by 6 or 6:30. It became a question of how much the physical constitution could take. I frankly did not believe in 1968 that I could survive another four years of the long hours and unrelenting tensions I had just gone through.[11]

One of the difficulties of being president is that there is no escape. Presidents cannot go on vacation and forget about their work. They are always on duty, always the center of attention. In his memoirs, *Mandate for Change*, President Eisenhower wrote:

> a President is President no matter what his location. For example, during eight weeks in Denver 1954 my staff and I worked every day other than Sundays, including six that I spent in the mountains at Fraser, Colorado. . . . During those weeks I saw 225 visitors, not including my own immediate staff, made four official trips out of Denver, delivered six speeches, made three television appearances, attended five official luncheons or dinners, considered 513 bills from Congress, signing 488 into law and vetoing 25. Finally, I signed 420 other official papers or documents—all of the business of direct concern to the running of the Executive Branch.[12]

Medical studies link long hours, persistent pressures, and a stressful environment to a variety of physical and mental illnesses: high blood pressure, cardiovascular disease, stroke, and, generally, lower resistance to communicable diseases. Perhaps this explains why presidents who have served more than four years in office have had more serious health problems and shorter life spans than those who completed one term or less. Similarly, presidents judged less successful and who, as a consequence, may have encountered more frustration and difficulty have lived shorter lives than those who were evaluated as more successful.

PSYCHOLOGICAL ORIENTATION

Common sense suggests that personality affects behavior, but scientifically, it is difficult to prove. Personality is not directly observable. It must be inferred from observable behavior. That inference, in and of itself, is likely to be based on unverifiable assumptions such as those postulated by Sigmund Freud, Carl Jung, Alfred Adler, or more contemporary psychological theorists.

Although discerning the precise effect of personality on behavior and thereby distinguishing its impact from other variables may be beyond the scope of contemporary social science, it is still important to focus on personality and examine it within the context of the contemporary presidency. The increasing emphasis given to personal character by the media, by candidates, and by those in office demands that it receive scholarly attention as a critical component of political leadership.

Two basic types of studies focus on the relationship between personality and performance. One, known as psychobiography, seeks to explain a single president's behavior on the basis of a comprehensive psychological analysis of his life. Frequently beginning with his youth, adolescence, and early political experiences, the study progresses through his career as a public official. Examples of presidential psychobiographies that have been frequently cited include Alexander George and Juliette L. George, *Woodrow Wilson and Colonel House;* Fawn Brodie, *Thomas Jefferson;* Doris

Kearns, *Lyndon Johnson and the American Dream;* Bruce Mazlish, *In Search of Nixon;* and Betty Glad, *Jimmy Carter: In Search of the Great White House.*[13]

The other type of analysis, more comparative in scope, seeks to generalize about presidential behavior on the basis of certain psychological dimensions. It seeks to discern the ways in which personality may affect seeking the presidency and then exercising power within it—how personality shapes, motivates, conditions responses, and influences judgments in decision making. One of the most stimulating and influential studies that addresses these questions is James David Barber's book, *The Presidential Character.*[14]

Presidential Character

Originally published in 1972, Barber's study seeks to explain, and under certain conditions, predict generalized responses on the bases of several dimensions of personality. His objective is to create a framework that can be used to categorize a president's psychological tendencies and then use that categorization as an explanatory and predictive tool. Since psychological orientation per se is not discernible to the naked eye, it must be inferred from behavior that is. Three manifestations of that behavior are words, work, and personal interaction. Together, they provide clues to aspects of an individual's personality.

Which aspects are most relevant? From the standpoint of presidential performance, Barber suggests three: character, style, and world view.

Character is the least discernible but most basic of these components. In Barber's words, it "is the way the President orients himself toward life"—how he views himself.[15] Self-esteem underlies character. Naturally, the better a president feels about himself, the more easily he will be able to accept criticism, think rationally, and learn on the job.

If character is the inner core, style is the outer garb. It constitutes the way a "President goes about doing what the office requires him to do—to speak, directly or through media, to large audiences; to deal face to face with other politicians, individually and in small, relatively private groups; and to read, write, and calculate by himself in order to manage the endless flow of details that stream onto his desk. No President can escape doing at least some of each."[16] Style varies with the president and with the times. It is important because it is a predictable coping mechanism, a way of handling people, tasks, and communication.

The third component is world view. Barber defines it as "how he [the president] sees the world and his lasting opinions about what he sees."[17] It consists of "his primary, politically relevant beliefs, particularly his conceptions of social causality, human nature, and the central moral conflicts of the time."[18]

According to Barber, these three psychological components form a pattern of motives, habits, and beliefs that result in behaviors that are evident throughout life. Moreover, these behaviors and the psychological foundation upon which they rest are not easily changed. Once developed, they tend to persist. Thus, while politicians shift and may even reverse their stands on policy usually to resonate better with changes in public opinion, their personality and its manifestations remain more stable; as a consequence, they are better predictors of how politicians will perform in public office. This makes the study of personality important not only to those who wish to understand the "whys" of presidential behavior but also to those who must decide which candidates have the temperament, style, and vision that is most likely to succeed in office. Helping the American electorate in its voting decisions is an important objective of Barber's work.

To provide some analytic tools that the average citizen can use to make this evaluation, Barber develops a typology based on two observable personality dimensions: activity and affect. Activity is the level of energy that is devoted to the job—whether a person is basically active or passive. Affect concerns the level of satisfaction that is obtained from the work—whether a person's political life is a positive or negative experience. In Barber's words, "The activity baseline refers to what one does, the affect baseline to how one feels about what he does."[19] There are four possible combinations, which are summarized in Table 8-3.

Of these four character types, the active-positive is clearly the one Barber believes is best suited for the presidency. Such a person brings to the office the level of activity needed to sustain the multiplicity of roles the president must assume. Moreover, the positive attitude toward work generates its own psychological and physical benefits. It contributes to energy level; it eases the inevitable interpersonal conflicts that result from competing perspectives, interests, policy goals, and ambitions; and it increases tolerance. Presidents who enjoy their work tend to be more eager to take on new and difficult challenges. Each of the other personality types has built-in weaknesses that could impede them in the performance of their presidential duties—perhaps affecting their vision, impairing their judgment, or causing decisions or actions that may not be in their best interests.

Barber's model assumes that type casting can provide a valuable clue to the potential difficulties that might develop in the presidency. Although Barber cannot predict these difficulties with certainty, or anticipate particular reactions to particular events, he can indicate general tendencies and reactions to which certain personality types are prone. One problem, however, with making electoral judgments on the basis of this type of analysis is that those presidents who have been characterized as most psychologically qualified have not always turned out to be the most effective. Table 8-4 lists Barber's categorization of twentieth-century presidents, beginning with William Howard Taft.

Table 8-3. Presidential Character Types

Active-Positive	*Active-Negative*
This presidential type is characteristic of an energetic president who enjoys his work and who tends to be productive and capable of adjusting to new situations. Such a person generally feels confident and good about himself.	This type describes a president who works hard but does not gain much pleasure from it, and who tends to be intense, compulsive, and aggressive. He may pursue his public actions in a self-interested manner. Such a person generally feels insecure and uses his position to overcome these feelings of inadequacy and even impotency.
Passive-Positive	*Passive-Negative*
This type describes a relatively receptive laid-back individual who wants to gain agreement and mute dissent at all costs. Such a person is apt to feel pessimistic and unloved on a deep psychological level. As president, the passive-positive individual attempts to compensate for these feelings by being overly optimistic and by continually trying to elicit agreement and support from others.	This presidential type can be said to abhor politics and withdraw from interpersonal relationships. Such an individual is ill-suited for political office, much less the nation's highest one. He or she suffers from low self-esteem and a sense of uselessness and is apt to take refuge in generalized principles and standard procedures.

Source: Adapted from James David Barber, *The Presidential Character*, 3rd ed. (Englewood Cliffs, N.J.: Prentice-Hall, 1985), pp. 9–10.

Table 8-4. The Personality Types of Contemporary Presidents

Active-Positive	*Active-Negative*
Franklin D. Roosevelt	Woodrow Wilson
Harry S Truman	Herbert Hoover
John F. Kennedy	Lyndon B. Johnson
Gerald Ford	Richard M. Nixon
Jimmy Carter	
George Bush	
Passive-Positive	*Passive-Negative*
William Howard Taft	Calvin Coolidge
Warren G. Harding	Dwight D. Eisenhower
Ronald Reagan	

Source: James David Barber, *The Presidential Character*, 3rd ed. (Englewood Cliffs, N.J.: Prentice-Hall, 1985).

Franklin Roosevelt is an example of an active-positive type who is generally regarded as a great president, while Woodrow Wilson, who is also well regarded by historians, is active-negative. Two recent, extremely popular presidents, Dwight Eisenhower and Ronald Reagan, are not even active (and in Eisenhower's case not positive either, according to Barber), while Gerald Ford and Jimmy Carter, who were much less popular (and many would argue much less successful), are both active and positive, as is George Bush (see Box 8-1 on pages 232–233). Among the nineteenth-century presidents, Abraham Lincoln, generally considered one of America's greatest presidents, has been categorized as active-negative by political scientist Jeffrey Tulis.[20]

What is the problem? Has Barber made a major methodological error or has he merely miscategorized some presidents? Much controversy has surrounded these and other questions. Barber's critics have alleged that his categories are too broad and ambiguous, that his activity and affect dimensions are too crude because they are dichotomous, and that psychological tendencies themselves do not neatly fit into one and only one box. Moreover, Barber's explanation tends to be tautological. Categories are defined first rather than being derived from empirical evidence, and the definitions are then used to explain empirical phenomena. Finally, according to Alexander George, Barber's predictions are self-fulfilling.[21] If they turn out to be correct, as they did in the case of Nixon, then Barber can claim that the psychological explanation is a valid one; if the predictions do not occur, then he could assert that the environment was not ripe for the psychological tendencies to produce their expected reaction. None of these criticisms invalidates the model, but they do question its scope, application, and general utility as an explanatory and predictive tool.

In addition to the methodological problems, there may be another reason that psychological types and presidential success do not always mesh. Barber himself alludes to this reason when he discusses the interaction of personality, the power situation in which presidents find themselves, and the national climate of expectations. Presidents must make decisions and take actions within a potent political environment over which they have limited influence. Thus, although their character, style, and world view are relatively constant, the power mix and public moods are not. The environment that may have contributed to the election or success in office of one personality type may change.

Mood Cycles

In a fascinating sequel to his analysis of personality, Barber examines mood in a book entitled *The Pulse of Politics*.[22] There, he proposes a typology of electoral periods based on three basic public moods:

1. *Conflict*. Barber defines this period as a battle for power, a clash of competing interests in which "candidates mobilize their forces for showdowns and shoot-outs, blasting each other with rhetorical volleys. . . . It is the myth of the fighting candidate . . . Harry S Truman battling through to victory against overwhelming odds."[23]

2. *Conscience*. In this period, an appeal to principle, to good and honest American values, is made: "Attention focuses on the dangers of blind ambition, corruption, even tyranny. . . . The call goes out for a revival of social conscience . . . the cleansing of the temple of democracy."[24] People look for the candidate whose life and character symbolize decency, honor, and virtue—such as Jimmy Carter after Watergate.

3. *Conciliation*. This period is characterized by a desire for tranquility, goodwill, compromise, and cooperation. According to Barber, "Righteousness turns to self-righteousness . . . disagreement becomes disruption. . . . The public turns for solace, for domestic tranquillity." The electorate wants a president it can like such as Warren G. Harding.[25]

For Barber, each of these periods generates the next. The cycle is continuous and recurs every twelve years. The most successful presidents are likely to be those whose personalities best fit the mood of the period and can adapt to changes in that mood over the course of their presidencies (see Table 8-5 on page 234).

A variety of reasons may explain why some personality types do not fit the times. The public may make a poor judgment on election day; they may not have had viable options; partisan or other factors may affect the outcome. However, Barber believes that the more the public knows about the personalities of the nominees, the more likely they will make a wise voting decision.

The dynamics of the public pulse combined with the stability of personality provide a potential down-the-road problem for the president. Selected in part because his personality may have coincided with the public mood at the time of the election, the president may have difficulty adjusting when that mood changes. As a consequence, he may be more apt, particularly under stress, to react impulsively on the basis of his own psychological needs rather than in a manner that more rationally calculates public costs and benefits. That is why the active-positive type has an advantage. The psychological orientation of this type facilitates adjustment to changing conditions. Moreover, the active-positive president is more apt to listen to reason.

Despite the advantages that active-positive presidents have, success is not assured by their personality alone. For one thing, all such presi-

BOX 8-1.   GEORGE BUSH: IN SEARCH OF A MISSION
by James David Barber

Candidate Bush turned out to be a surprise. President Bush may be a bigger one. . . .

Mr. Bush's Presidential style was defined in his first independent political success, in Texas in 1962, when as local party chairman he defused a conflict between the John Birch Society and establishment Republicans. Bush the negotiator took that on as his main talent, and so it remains.

His rhetoric is coachable, as the '88 campaign brought out. He speaks about as well as Gerry Ford. His homework falls short of B-plus, as demonstrated by his lack of knowledge about such heavy issues as abortion and defense. When it comes to curiosity about reality, George Bush is no Jack Kennedy, no Harry Truman. He inherits from Mr. Reagan a practical prejudice for the rich, masked by "conservatism," and a readiness to manipulate the media.

Why expect from President Bush anything other than a continuation of the Reagan mythologic politics? . . .

Mr. Bush wants a mission. It is important that he likes normal, ordinary politics and that he invests much energy in that work. His character is active-positive, a pattern that means he is ready to learn, to change, to develop in office, as distinct from the fixated types, such as Richard Nixon or Lyndon Johnson.

In his convention acceptance speech he declared that "I am a man who sees life in terms of missions . . . missions defined and missions completed." Could George Bush not take on a mission to build a system of peace and justice in this world?

That could happen. Mr. Bush's life has been dramatized time and again, from his viewpoint, by his taking on major missions. Going off on his 18th birthday in 1942 to be the youngest Navy pilot in World War II—which he now cites as his first mission—was a thrill. He put himself up for duty, as his father kept preaching and practicing, and for devotion to others, as his mother kept demanding. He got far away from the fear of father and interference by mother. We won the war. He won the Distinguished Flying Cross. Mission accomplished.

After Yale and marriage, he took on a second big mission in 1948, changing his life by moving to Texas. To be sure, the suggestion came from a family friend and he did not have to provide his own finances. But from George Bush's viewpoint, moving to West Texas was a move to another world. There, from Mr. Bush's perspective, they developed a life of their own, demonstrating that he could shape his own existence far from Greenwich, Conn.

BOX 8-1 *(continued)*.

Years later, in 1975, President Ford asked Republican National Committee Chairman Bush to come over and "discuss the future." Mr. Ford mentioned that the Ambassadorships to Britain and France were open. To Mr. Ford's surprise, Mr. Bush asked to be envoy to China, having "come to a decision much like the one we made in 1948. Back then we had decided not to do the traditional thing, but to head for the West."

The pattern strongly suggests that George Bush sees himself as enlivened and inspired by a mission into a new, different, distant, unknown land. Could he move out into the real world and take on the challenge of forging peace and justice, not in the failed Reagan manner but in a new and different way? Given Mr. Bush's past, this is conceivable. He is not stuck with consistency.

On the other hand, Mr. Bush's hunger for mission could carry us all over the brink of disaster. To whom will he look for the mission? Some spin doctors like those who drove his campaign? His right-wing Chief of Staff, John H. Sununu? His managerial Secretary of State–designate, James A. Baker 3d? Sir Lancelot has become King Arthur. Who knows to whom he will look for guidance?

The ultimate danger is war. That was Mr. Bush's first big mission. The inevitable frustration Mr. Reagan's left-over debt imposes on any new domestic programs could make him angry. So could the natural desire of the press to avoid being spun as it was before, and thus to criticize him as weak. Congressional Democrats may well stand tall against his administration's recommendations.

Economic realities, even beyond the deficit, pose a most difficult obstacle to any major political mission. One of Mr. Nixon's in-house conspirers, H. R. Haldeman, noted that Mr. Bush would "do anything for the cause." Turning to a military cause, even beyond the dimension of the Grenada invasion that Mr. Bush helped to orchestrate, is always going to be a temptation for this President. That could confirm his recent reaction to the story that Mr. Baker would use him as a puppet: "I am not a damned piece of meat."

The Bush potential is there, as it turned out to be for Harry S Truman, who fostered the Marshall Plan. Or as it turned out to be for Lyndon Baines Johnson, who fostered the Vietnam disaster. We cannot assume he will just sit still and shut up. If he does believe in what he says he does—including reality—the better turn could happen.

Source: The New York Times, January 19, 1989, p. A31. Copyright © 1989 by The New York Times Company. Reprinted by permission.

Table 8-5. Public Moods and Presidential Types

Year	Mood	President	Character Type
1900	Conflict	William McKinley	Passive-
1904	Conscience	Theodore Roosevelt	Active-
1908	Conciliation	William Howard Taft	Passive-Positive
1912	Conflict	Woodrow Wilson	Active-Negative
1916	Conscience	Woodrow Wilson	Active-Negative
1920	Conciliation	Warren G. Harding	Passive-Positive
1924	Conflict	Calvin Coolidge	Passive-Negative
1928	Conscience	Herbert Hoover	Active-Negative
1932	Conciliation	Franklin D. Roosevelt	Active-Positive
1936	Conflict	Franklin D. Roosevelt	Active-Positive
1940	Conscience	Franklin D. Roosevelt	Active-Positive
1944	Conciliation	Franklin D. Roosevelt	Active-Positive
1948	Conflict	Harry S Truman	Active-Positive
1952	Conscience	Dwight D. Eisenhower	Passive-Negative
1956	Conciliation	Dwight D. Eisenhower	Passive-Negative
1960	Conflict	John F. Kennedy	Active-Positive
1964	Conscience	Lyndon B. Johnson	Active-Negative
1968	Conciliation	Richard M. Nixon	Active-Negative
1972	Conflict	Richard M. Nixon	Active-Negative
1976	Conscience	Jimmy Carter	Active-Positive
1980	Conciliation	Ronald Reagan	Passive-Positive
1984	Conflict	Ronald Reagan	Passive-Positive
1988	Conscience	George Bush	Active-Positive

Source: James David Barber, *The Pulse of Politics* (New York: W. W. Norton, 1980).

dents may not achieve their potential or successfully adapt to new situations. For another, external factors beyond the president's control may exercise so much influence that they dictate the outcome, despite what the president might do or wish to do. It is difficult in this type of analysis to pinpoint the extent to which personality is the principal explanatory variable, much less how it interacts with others to affect the final outcome. For many social scientists this reduces the validity of psychologically based explanations and renders the prescriptions which follow from them less compelling.

There is another problem with using psychological models for making voting decisions. The public usually lacks the information and expertise with which to make sophisticated judgments. Evaluations of character are apt to be superficial.

Despite its limitations (and they are substantial), Barber's model continues to frame much of the debate on personality and the presidency. Although he has not succeeded in providing a comprehensive theory or an air-tight explanation of why presidents function as they do in office, he has focused attention on the obvious importance of personality and has identified certain facets of it that must be considered when explaining and anticipating presidential performance.

COGNITIVE DIMENSIONS

If Barber is correct, there is a link between character and world view. Beliefs are shaped by how individuals view themselves and others within the environment in which they live. Personal needs, in short, affect perceptions, beliefs, and values. They condition the processing of information, the consideration of options, and the making of decisions.

Utilizing a World View

Presidents and their aides bring to office sets of beliefs about politics, policy, human nature, and social causality—or, in other words, beliefs about how the world works and why it does so. These beliefs serve decision makers by providing a frame of reference for raising and evaluating policy options, filtering information and giving it meaning, establishing potential boundaries of action, and supplying an approach to decision making itself. Beliefs also help busy officials cope with complex decisions to which they can devote limited time, and they predispose them to act in certain directions.

During the Cuban missile crisis President Kennedy precluded diplomatic and nonmilitary responses to the situation at the outset and actually considered a fairly narrow range of military options (contrary to much conventional wisdom). Kennedy believed that the presence of Soviet missiles in Cuba greatly increased the threat to the national security of the United States and that the Soviet Union would remove the missiles only if forced to do so by the threat of American military sanctions. His decisions followed naturally from those premises.

Although sets of beliefs are inevitable and help to simplify the world, they can be dysfunctional as well. This is perhaps most dramatically illustrated in the case of surprise attacks by one country on another. In these situations beliefs often interfere with effective analysis when they filter information and give it meaning because "the primary problem in major strategic surprise is not intelligence but political disbelief."[26]

Let us turn to the October 1973 war in the Middle East as an illustration. Months before it occurred, American (and Israeli) foreign policy officials had plenty of information pointing to an attack on Israel by Egypt and Syria, but they dismissed this evidence and concluded that war was improbable. Even as military operations were taking place, intelligence agencies discounted them as indicators of full-scale war. The fundamental problem in analysis was the preconceptions of officials, which led them to misinterpret the available facts. Since they knew

Egypt and Syria could not win such a war, their definition of rationality led them to conclude that the two countries would not initiate one. They ignored the possibility of the two countries starting an unwinnable war for psychological reasons, that is, to restore their self-respect.

Another way that presidents influence decision making is by establishing the objectives for public policies. Decisions about U.S. participation in the Vietnam War were molded by the views of top officials. The premises they shared included the contentions that a non-Communist Vietnam was important to the security and credibility of the United States; the war-torn country was a critical testing ground of the ability of this country to counter Communist support for wars of national liberation; communism was a world conspiracy; South Vietnam would fall to the North without American aid; and if South Vietnam fell to communism, other countries would shortly follow. When these views were coupled with President Johnson's more general premises that all problems were solvable and that the United States could do anything, this country's intervention was a foregone conclusion.

The doctrinal consensus on Vietnam made it difficult to challenge United States policy. Defining doctrine in terms of necessity foreclosed policy options. As a result, "no comprehensive and systematic examination of Vietnam's importance to the United States was ever undertaken within the executive branch. Debates revolved around how to do things better and whether they could be done, not whether they were worth doing."[27]

Similarly, Robert McFarlane, President Reagan's former national security adviser, testified before the special congressional committee investigating the Iran–Contra affair that no government-wide analysis of American interests in Nicaragua was ever made. Answers to the most important questions were assumed.

A president's view of a problem and proposed response to it is especially likely to foreclose consideration of alternatives in a crisis when there is a premium on rapid and decisive action. The North Korean invasion of South Korea in 1950 and the civil war in the Dominican Republic in 1965 were seen by Presidents Truman and Johnson, respectively, as threats to the United States, and they decided virtually immediately that American armed forces would be employed in those countries.

Managing Inconsistency

The environment in which the president operates is complex and uncertain. Yet the human mind is not comfortable with these characteristics. It has certain cognitive needs and prefers stable views to a continuous consideration of options.

The problem of inconsistency in decision making is persistent. Lyndon Johnson became obsessed with the correctness of his views on the

Vietnam War. He simply had to feel he was right or else he would have to open himself to the pain of reliving his old decisions and options.

It does not follow that the president should not continue to consider options and information once a policy decision has been made. The decision may have been a poor one. Yet busy aides are typically reluctant to risk irritating an even busier president by attempting to reopen a question he thought was settled. In the words of two close observers of decision making:

> Once a president sets policy, it becomes a herculean task for senior officials and bureaucrats to argue against it. Presidents have to make clear up and down the line that they want to hear criticisms and alternatives from their subordinates before they read them in the press, and that dissenters will be rewarded as well as team players. They should press for agreement on coherent policies but also leave the door open to revising judgment.[28]

It is especially difficult to review decisions regarding national security while fighting is taking place. Speaking from experience, Vice President Hubert Humphrey wrote: "Once a wartime decision has been made and men's lives have been lost, once resources are committed—and most dangerously, once a nation's honor has been committed—what you are doing becomes almost Holy Writ. Any division, dissension, or diversion is suspect."[29]

Decision makers often experience stress as they try to cope with the complexity of decisions, especially in times of crisis. In a revealing incident President Warren G. Harding explained to a friend:

> John, I can't make a damn thing out of this tax problem. I listen to one side and they seem right, and then God! I talk to the other side and they seem just as right, and there I am where I started. I know somewhere there is a book that would give me the truth, but hell, I couldn't read the book. I know somewhere there is an economist who knows the truth, but I don't know where to find him and haven't the sense to know him and trust him when I did find him. God, what a job![30]

Fortunately, most of those occupying the Oval Office have had greater confidence in their intellectual capacity than Harding.

The mind simplifies in order to deal with the complexities of the world and resolves uncertainty by ignoring or deemphasizing information that contradicts existing beliefs. These mental activities occur through unconsciously operating inference mechanisms that function to some extent in everyone's mind. Those mechanisms may have as great an influence on a person's beliefs as objective evidence. Consequently, most policymakers remain unreceptive to a major revision of their beliefs in response to new information, especially if they have had success in the past with applying their general beliefs to specific decisions or if they have held their beliefs for a long time. Moreover, they are unlikely to search for information that challenges their views or for options contrary to those they advocate. Instead, they tend to incorporate new information in ways that render it comprehensible within their existing frames of reference. In other words, they rationalize it to support their previously held beliefs.

One relatively simple technique for managing inconsistency consists in attaching very negative consequences to alternatives, as top policymakers did to the option of "scuttle and run" from Vietnam. By concluding that the role of the United States in international relations would be seriously diminished by such action, decision makers dismissed an alternative that was widely advocated outside the government.

Realted to this mechanism of predicting undesirable consequences is that of making inferences based on selected indicators to show that a particular situation could not possibly occur. If policymakers accept this inference of impossibility, there is no need for them to consider information pointing to the "impossible" situation, alternatives to prevent or respond to it, or what effect it would have on the alternatives that *are* being considered. Before the massive North Vietnamese Tet offensive in early 1968, planning regarding the war was based on the assumption that no such offensive was possible; top American officials paid little heed to information that contradicted this assumption. Data on the size and fire power of South Vietnamese forces, the number of hamlets pacified, and the number of Communists killed provided welcomed positive feedback on this nation's policy and were accepted as signs of progress; policymakers never realistically weighed those indicators against the size of the task at hand. Another, classic example of the inference of impossibility was the belief that the Japanese could not attack Pearl Harbor. Because they were not expecting an attack, American officials did not notice the signs pointing toward it. Instead, they paid attention to signals supporting their current expectations of enemy behavior.

Another means of reducing inconsistency and thereby decreasing the pressure to consider alternatives is similar to what we commonly term "wishful thinking." Information inconsistent with ongoing policy may be deemphasized by believing that undesirable conditions are only temporary and will ameliorate in response to current policy. Officials used this type of reasoning to garner support for the continued escalation of the Vietnam War. All that was needed to force the enemy to succumb, they argued, was to keep up the pressure. More generally, in the face of contradictory or ambiguous indicators of the progress of the war, they listened most carefully to the optimistic rather than the pessimistic reports or the caveats to positive assessments and hoped for the best. As two authorities on decision making in the Vietnam War have written, "The human mind's capacity to perceive and balance evidence with perfect rationality is limited, and men are peculiarly able to combine pessimism and optimism, doubt and confidence, recognition of negative evidence and persistence in positive assumptions, all at the same time."[31]

Yet another means of resolving uncertainty and simplifying decision making is reasoning by analogy. The conclusions supported by this type of reasoning seem to have strength independent of the available evidence, probably because the analogies simplify and provide a coherent framework for ambiguous and inconsistent information.

Metaphors and similes simplify a complex and ambiguous reality by relating it to a relatively simple and well-understood concept. If one is then used as the basis of an analogy, the possibilities for error are considerable. Part of the theoretical underpinning for the Vietnam War was often characterized as the "domino theory" of international relations, which holds that the United States must prevent countries from falling to the Communists because once one country falls, the one next to it will fall, and then the next—just like falling dominoes. The simplistic nature of the metaphor indicates how much room exists for differences between it and reality.

Discrediting the source of information and options is another means of reducing the complexity and resolving the contradictions with which policymakers have to deal. At first, President Johnson handled the critics of his war policy quite well, inviting them to his office and talking to them for hours. But as opposition increased and polls indicated a dip in his popularity, he responded to criticism by discrediting its source. He maintained that Senator William Fulbright (the chairman of the Senate Foreign Relations Committee) was upset at not being named secretary of state; the liberals in Congress were angry at him because he hadn't gone to Harvard, because the Great Society was more successful than the New Frontier, and because he had blocked Robert Kennedy from the presidency; the columnists opposed him to make a bigger splash and to follow James Reston and Walter Lippman; and the young were hostile because they were ignorant.

At other times presidents may simply avoid information they fear will force them to face disagreeable decisions that complicate their lives and produce additional stress. Richard Nixon is a classic example. In his memoirs he writes of putting off confronting his own attorney general, John Mitchell, because of his hypersensitivity and desire not to know the truth about Mitchell's involvement in Watergate in case it was unpleasant. He just could not bring himself to talk to Mitchell personally. Similarly, the president found it too painful to discuss Watergate with experienced officials he had brought back to the White House to help restore confidence in his administration. It was easier to rely solely on those personally close to him in dealing with the scandal. Referring to Nixon's ability to engage in self-delusion and avoid unpleasant facts, White House chief of staff H.R. Haldeman argues that the "failure to face the irrefutable facts, even when it was absolutely clear that they were irrefutable, was one of our fatal flows in handling Watergate at every step."[32]

Each of the cognitive processes that reduce uncertainty and complexity can be a reasonable response to a situation. The point is that people are likely to rely on them not by conscious choice but because of the human need for certainty and simplicity. In each of the examples cited above, the president and his advisers made use of an inference mechanism that diverted their attention from vital information and led them to ignore appropriate options. Potential actions that were considered disastrous would have been far less so than those that were taken, situations thought to be impossible actually occurred, hoped-for results from policies never materialized, inferences were based upon inappropriate analogies, and worthwhile criticism was rejected. Thus, the inference mechanisms that top decision makers employ to manage inconsistency clearly may jeopardize rational decision making.

INTERPERSONAL RELATIONS

Presidents are not the only ones in the White House whose social background, physical condition, psychological orientation, and cognitive framework affect their performance in office. The decisions and actions of their assistants are also affected by similar kinds of feelings, attitudes, and social conditioning. Moreover, the long hours assistants must work, the unrelenting pressures they are under, the complex issues with which they must deal, and the significant and often long-term implications of their decisions cannot help but condition their patterns of interaction, channels of communication, and performance of their staffing responsibilities.

The work is arduous. The hours are extensive. In addition, the ongoing demands of the job require physical presence in the White House. Large blocks of time are needed simply to get the tremendous amount of work done. This can result in some incredibly long and tiring workdays. For most aides a sixty- to eighty-hour week is standard. Arriving early in the morning and staying into the evening five days a week, senior and middle-level aides usually work a full day on Saturday, and frequently, a half day on Sunday either in the office or at home.

Group pressures also serve to reinforce the White House work ethic. Members of the presidential staff tend to be conscious of the hours that others work. "There's always a customary desire to be around when the phone rings," was the way one Carter aide put it.[33]

The long hours generate fatigue and lower tolerance. They make touching all bases a more burdensome chore. There is a tendency to circumvent those who might place obstacles in the way of decisions or actions. Thus in the Reagan administration, the secretaries of defense and state were not included in many Iran–Contra meetings when it became clear they opposed selling arms to the Iranian government.

In addition to the workload, the pressures of deadlines and crises are a significant and persistent part of the job. Combined with time constraints and high performance expectations, they contribute to staff anxiety. Not only is sufficient time often lacking to perform quality work, but the constant need to deal with a highly complex and politically divided governmental system—and often achieve a consensus—further complicates the task. Arthur Quern, an official in the Ford White House, contrasted his pre–White House expectations with the reality of the work he found:

> When I worked for the state of Illinois, I used to scream about the damn Feds. Why can't they do that . . . why can't they make a decision and get this whole thing straightened out? You're sure there is a button to push to get something done, but when you get here you find that it's not there. Rather, there's a flow chart telling you how many steps in the process you have to go through. It can be very frustrating.[34]

Richard Cheney, Ford's chief of staff and later defense secretary during the Bush administration, echoed a similar refrain:

> There is a tendency before you get to the White House or when you're just observing it from the outside to say, "Gee, that's a powerful position that person has." The fact of the matter is that while you're here trying to do things, you are far more aware of the constraints than you are of the power. You spend most of your time trying to overcome obstacles getting what the president wants done.[35]

Internal competition also tends to be heightened by these job-related pressures. The greater the work demands on staff, both in terms of quantity and quality, and the more severe the sanctions for shoddy or tardy performance, the more likely the environment will promote self-interested, competitive behavior.

Internal rivalries are not generated solely by the White House environment, however. The kinds of people who are attracted to jobs as presidential aides are also a proximate cause of their behavior. The White House tends to draw very ambitious people. Landon Butler, deputy assistant to President Carter, observed the intermix between ambition and service in a diary he prepared during the Carter transition:

> Our personal destinies get all mixed in with our work. The uncertainty of who gets invited into the government is bringing out the worst in people. They are overreaching. I'm getting angry. It's affecting my judgment. Will the White House be like this?[36]

Staff competition, of course, does not always adversely affect the running of the White House, although it does tend to make working there less pleasant. The Franklin Roosevelt White House, where a competitive staff structure reaped benefits for a president interested in maximizing his information, options, and influence, illustrates that some internal competition can be advantageous. On the other hand, infighting usually detracts from the efficiency of operations and lowers the morale of staff. When carried into the public arena, it can cause political embarrassment for the president.

A competitive environment also encourages self-interested behavior that can warp vision, overextend arguments, and lead to inaccurate or unbalanced presentations of issues, options, and their consequences for the president. All of this contributes to the dangers George Reedy saw and described in his book, *The Twilight of the Presidency.*[37]

Reedy was concerned with the isolation of the president, with his making of decisions and taking of actions in an environment that did not accord with reality. He saw the deference paid to the president by his aides, their propensity for telling him what he wanted to hear, and their obsession with satisfying his every whim as contributing to this potential danger. To make good decisions, Reedy contended, the president needs accurate information not pleasantries, wise recommendations not self-motivated advocacy, and intelligent support not blind loyalty.

The president's style of interacting with his aides, his attitudes and demeanor, his system of rewards and sanctions affect the way staff feel and influence how they work. While not necessarily eliminating the incentives or disincentives of the job, a president can either reduce or enhance their effect. In general, the more personable, accessible, and tolerant the president, the happier the staff. Efficiency, however, is not always promoted by the chief executive's being a nice guy.

Each White House has its style. During the Nixon years, especially during the Haldeman era, this style might be described as "macho." Aides had to prove how tough they were, how long they worked, how many sacrifices they made. There was little compassion from the president on down and no patience for poor work or tardy performance.

Presidents Ford and Carter were more tolerant, more open, and less imposing. They permitted a looser operation. Fewer sanctions were levied. Senior aides who did not produce quality staff work were circumvented rather than criticized or asked to leave.

President Reagan delegated operational authority to his senior aides. Thus it was their style, not his, that had a more direct and immediate impact on how others in the White House worked. With James Baker at the helm, assisted by Michael Deaver and Edwin Meese, there was a high degree of staff unity, political sensitivity, ideological loyalty, and public relations activity. Only the policy offices had difficulty and were marred by weak leadership. With Donald Regan at the helm, there was more infighting among presidential staffers, with turf battles, internal leaks, and open dissent characterizing relations between Regan and those who were appointed prior to his arrival. With

Howard Baker and Kenneth Dubberstein directing White House operations in Reagan's final two years, the internal friction decreased, and ideological conviction became less compelling than the political needs of the president.

The Bush White House initially reverted to a more centralized management style with the press and policy offices exercising more autonomy than other constituency-oriented units, such as congressional liaison and public liaison. All policy recommendations and political intelligence flowed through Chief of Staff John Sununu to the president.

White House work gives rise to a proclivity over time toward isolation. Not only do the long hours reduce the level of tolerance and aggravate personal ambition, but they also seem to encourage withdrawal tendencies in staff members. These tendencies heighten the temptation to see the world in terms of "we" and "they." They work to distance the president and his entourage from public criticism. Bad policy decisions and poor political judgments can result from the failure to consider the views of a significant portion of the population.

There are many incentives for staying in the White House: it is very comfortable; it provides luxurious services; it inflates egos; and it exaggerates personal power. To people who work hard, who may be frustrated by the difficulty of achieving specific political and policy goals in a pluralistic system, such an environment is apt to be seductive. There is a temptation to build a plastic bubble around the White House.

The White House also provides a sense of security, especially during periods of extreme public criticism. If the president and his aides are unable to convince others of their point of view, they can at least reinforce their own opinion by discussions among themselves. Under the circumstances, it is easy for presidential aides to rationalize working long hours in a pleasant, cozy, and protective environment.

The problem of losing touch tends to be worse toward the top of the White House hierarchy. The West Wing can resemble a closed shop. "West Executive Avenue [the street that separates the Old Executive Office Building from the West Wing of the White House] is the widest street in Washington," was the way that James Connor, Ford's staff secretary, put it.[38]

All of the pressures and deadlines, the internal competition, and the tendencies toward isolation cannot help but have an impact on the presidency. Presidents have no choice. They have to delegate since their tasks exceed their time, energy, and, often, their expertise. How their aides interact with them, with each other, and with their executive and congressional counterparts affects presidential performance in a direct and often immediate way. Presidents themselves can influence this pattern of interaction but they cannot control it. To some extent, all presidents are at the mercy of the organizational, operational, and personal proclivities of their staff. But this is particularly true for presidents who wish to direct change and thus tend to concentrate their advisory and decision-making structures in their White House staffs.

CONCLUSION

When all is said and done, *who* the president is matters. Social background, physical well-being, psychological makeup, cognitive views, and personal interaction all condition performance in office. How they affect that performance is difficult to measure with precision, but their impact must be considered when trying to explain presidential actions or predict presidential responses.

A case can also be made that some of these characteristics are better than others; that is, they are more desirable because they are more likely to lead to the president's achievement of his policy and political goals. James David Barber and others have argued that voters should take the character of the candidates into account when making their decisions on election day. They do, although most people do not have the kind and amount of information that may be necessary to render an informed, intelligent, psychologically oriented judgment.

Nonetheless, if socialization, physical condition, psychological orientation, and philosophical beliefs affect behavior, then they must have an impact on the president's capacity to lead. One would expect that those people who have demonstrated the most outstanding leadership skills in our democratic society will have a wide range of personal experience, particularly on the issues with which they must deal as president; will be physically and mentally healthy; will be stable, independent, and self-assured; will have a sophisticated understanding of domestic and international policy problems; and will relate easily and effectively to those around them. Some presidents have obviously demonstrated many of these tendencies and characteristics, but a surprising number of those presidents who have been highly evaluated did not.

As a group, the presidents who have been viewed as most successful have tended to come from the country's social and economic elite. Some of them have experienced serious health problems in office. Some have manifested psychological needs that seem to have influenced their desire for the nation's highest office as well as their conduct in it, energizing them or immobilizing them in different kinds of situations. The perspectives of some of the most accomplished presidents have also been limited or skewed. In contrast, some of the less accomplished presidents have had more humble origins, enjoyed better health, and have not been weighed down with heavy psychological baggage that made it difficult for them to separate their personal needs from their public policy decisions. Does this suggest that the norm is not the ideal for outstanding American presidents? It may, but it also points to the very complex environment in which presidents function—an environment that not only affects presidential decisions and actions but also influences personal tendencies and characteristics that, themselves, affect those decisions and actions.

Our conclusion is that leadership is not only a consequence of who the leader is but of how that leader interacts with others in the changing social, economic, and political milieu in which he must operate. Those who are better able to perceive change and adjust to it are apt to be more successful than those who do not and cannot. Moreover, not only does a great leader require the capacity to exercise significant leadership skills, but that leader also needs an environment in which his skills can be effectively exercised.

Returning to our distinction between two leadership types, we conclude that bad times, crises, or some cataclysmic event is probably necessary for leadership of the "director of change" variety, while good times in a politics-as-usual environment contributes to a president performing a "facilitator" role.

NOTES

1. E. Digby Baltzell and Howard G. Schneiderman, "Social Class in the Oval Office," *Society* 25 (September/October 1988): 45.

2. Ibid.: 44.

3. Ibid.: 49.

4. Ibid.: 44.

5. Jay Matthews, "Politics and the Height of Bias: And Now, a Short Word," *Washington Post*, June 12, 1988, p. F1a; Don Oldenburg, "Psyching Out the Presidential Candidates," *Washington Post*, May 13, 1988, p. D5a.

6. Jame E. Birren and K. Warner Schaie. Handbook of *The Psychology of Aging*, 2d ed. (New York: Van Nostrand, 1985); James F. Fries and Lawrence M. Crapo. *Vitality and Aging*, (San Francisco: Freeman, 1981); James N. Schubert, "Age and Active-Passive Leadership Style," *American Political Science Review* 82 (1988): 763–772.

7. See Robert E. Gilbert, "Personality, Stress and Achievement: Keys to Presidential Longevity," *Presidential Studies Quarterly* 15 (Winter 1985): 33–50.

8. Eric Goldman, *The Tragedy of Lyndon Johnson* (New York: Knopf, 1969), pp. 511–12.

9. Gilbert, "Personality, Stress, and Achievement": 35–36, 43–44.

10. Ibid.: 44.

11. Lyndon Johnson, *The Vantage Point* (New York: Holt, Rinehart and Winston, 1971), p. 425.

12. Dwight D. Eisenhower, *Mandate for Change* (New York: Doubleday, 1963), p. 267.

13. Alexander George and Juliette L. George, *Woodrow Wilson and Colonel House* (New York: John Day, 1956); Fawn Brodie, *Thomas Jefferson* (New York: W. W. Norton, 1974); Doris Kearns, *Lyndon Johnson and the American Dream* (New York: Harper & Row, 1976); Bruce Mazlish, *In Search of Nixon* (New York: Basic Books, 1972); and Betty Glad, *Jimmy Carter: In Search of the Great White House* (New York: W. W. Norton, 1980).

14. James David Barber, *The Presidential Character*, 3rd ed. (Englewood Cliffs, N.J.: Prentice-Hall, 1985).

15. Ibid., p. 5.

16. Ibid.

17. Ibid.

18. Ibid.

19. Ibid., p. 9.

20. Jeffrey Tulis, "On Presidential Character," in Joseph M. Bessette and Jeffrey Tulis, eds., *The Presidency in the Constitutional Order* (Baton Rouge, La.: Louisiana State University Press, 1981), pp. 292–301.

21. Alexander George, "Assessing Presidential Character," in Aaron Wildavsky ed., *Perspectives on the Presidency* (Boston: Little Brown, 1975) pp. 110–11.

22. James David Barber, *The Pulse of Politics* (New York: W. W. Norton, 1980), p. 3.

23. Ibid.

24. Ibid., pp. 3–4.

25. Ibid., p. 4.

26. Richard K. Betts, *Surprise Attack: Lessons for Defense Planning* (Washington, D.C.: Brookings Institution, 1982).

27. Leslie H. Gelb with Richard K. Betts, *The Irony of Vietnam: The System Worked* (Washington, D.C.: Brookings Institution, 1979), p. 190; see also pp. 353–54, 365–67.

28. Ibid., p. 365.

29. Hamilton Jordan, *Crisis: The Last Year of the Carter Presidency* (New York: Putnam, 1982), p. 250.

30. Warren G. Harding, quoted in William Allen White, *Masks in a Pageant* (New York: Macmillan, 1928), pp. 422–23.

31. Gelb with Betts, *The Irony of Vietnam*, p. 130.

32. H. R. Haldeman, *The Ends of Power* (New York: Times Books, 1978), p. 34.

33. Anonymous quotation appearing in Stephen J. Wayne, "Working in the White House: Psychological Dimensions of the Job" (paper presented at the Annual Meeting of the Southern Political Science Association, New Orleans, Louisiana, November 1977), p. 9.

34. Arthur Quern, as quoted in ibid., p. 10.

35. Richard Cheney, quoted in ibid.

36. Landon Butler, "Transition Diary," *Newsweek*, January 24, 1977, p. 29.

37. George E. Reedy, *The Twilight of the Presidency*, rev. ed. (New York: New American Library, 1987).

38. James Connor, quoted in Wayne, "Working in the White House," p. 25.

SELECTED READINGS

Baltzell, E. Digby and Howard G. Schneiderman. "Social Class in the Oval Office." *Society* 25 (September/October 1988): 42–49.

Barber, James David. *The Presidential Character*, 3rd. ed. Englewood Cliffs, N.J.: Prentice-Hall, 1985.

——————. *The Pulse of Politics*. New York: W. W. Norton, 1980.

Betts, Richard K. *Surprise Attack: Lessons for Defense Planning*. Washington, D.C.: Brookings Institution, 1982.

Buchanan, Bruce. *The Citizen's Presidency: Standard of Choice and Judgment*. Washington, D.C.: Congressional Quarterly, 1987.

——————. *The Presidential Experience: What the Office Does to the Man*. Englewood Cliffs, N.J.: Prentice-Hall, 1978.

Burke, John R. and Fred I. Greenstein. "Presidential Personality and National Security Leadership: A Comparative Analysis of Vietnam Decision-making." *International Political Science Review* 10 (1989): 73–92.

Cohen Jeffrey. "Presidential Personality and Political Behavior: Theoretical Issues and an Empirical Test." *Presidential Studies Quarterly* 10 (Summer 1980): 209–37.

George, Alexander. "Assessing Presidential Character." In Aaron Wildavsky, ed., *Perspectives on the Presidency*. Boston: Little Brown, 1975, pp. 91–134.

George, Alexander L. *Presidential Decisionmaking in Foreign Policy: The Effective use of Information and Advice.* Boulder, Colo.: Westview Press, 1980.

Gilbert, Robert E. "Personality, Stress and Achievement: Keys to Presidential Longevity." *Presidential Studies Quarterly* 15 (Winter 1985): 33–50.

Janis, Irving L. *Group Think.* Boston: Houghton Mifflin, 1982.

Lowi, Theodore. *The Personal President: Power Invested, Promise Unfulfilled.* Ithaca, N.Y.: Cornell University Press, 1985.

Reedy, George E. *The Twilight of the Presidency.* Rev. ed. New York: New American Library, 1987.

Whicker, Marcia Lynn, and Raymond A. Moore. *When Presidents Are Great.* Englewood Cliffs, N.J.: Prentice-Hall, 1988.

See also the psychobiographies listed in note 13.

9

The President and the Executive Branch

Public policies are rarely self-executing. They require a staff of experts, people who have an understanding of the substantive issues, institutional processes, and political implications involved in turning statutes, executive orders, and the like into services and benefits for the nation. These are the people who work in the executive branch. Some are civil servants, others are political appointees. Both are charged with the implementation of public policy.

The president sits atop the executive branch, the organization of which is pictured in Figure 9–1. As the title of chief executive implies, the president has responsibility for executing or implementing government policies. Implementation includes issuing and enforcing directives; disbursing funds; making loans; awarding grants; signing contracts; collecting data; disseminating information; analyzing problems; assigning and hiring personnel; creating organizational units; proposing alternatives; planning for the future; and negotiating with private citizens, businesses, interest groups, legislative committees, bureaucratic units, and even other countries.

In this chapter we examine the president's efforts, in conjunction with his subordinates in the executive branch, to implement public policies. A president who is a director will be able to dominate this process and ensure that policies are executed as he wishes; a president who is a facilitator will face just as great a challenge in leading the executive branch as in leading those who are not directly in his chain of command. We shall find that, despite the unquestioned importance of implementation, it receives relatively low priority in the White House. We shall also find that the president faces an uphill fight in implementing the policies for which he is responsible. Thus, we focus on the obstacles to effective policy implementation, including communication, resources, implementors' dispositions, bureaucratic structure, and executive follow-up, to understand better the difficulties the president faces.

Before we move on, we should clarify an important point. The president's role in implementation is not always as direct as in giving a

Figure 9-1. Organization of the Executive Branch

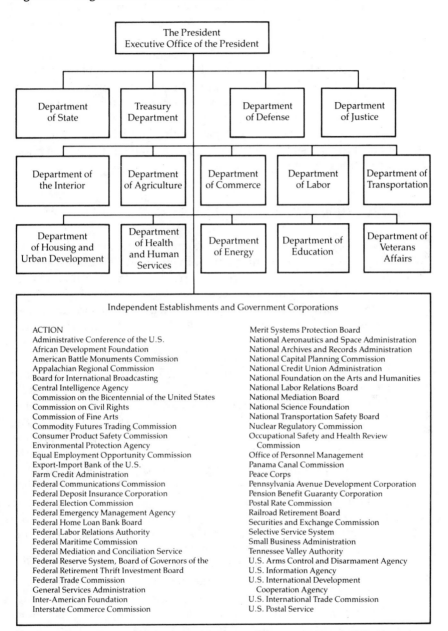

Source: Office of the Federal Register, *United States Government Manual, 1988–89* (Washington, D.C.: Government Printing Office, 1987), p. 21.

speech, negotiating with Congress, or making decisions. Moreover, implementation typically occurs over an extended period of time and far from the confines of the White House. In addition, the implementation of federal policy usually requires the efforts of many people, often thousands, at the federal, state, and local levels and in the private sector. As a result, many observers of the presidency mistakenly restrict their discussions of the president as chief executive to actions he personally takes. To avoid this error we cast our view more broadly in order to understand the problems with which the president must contend as he seeks to carry out his responsibilities for implementing policies, including those he initiates, those established in previous administrations, and those passed over his objections.

IMPLEMENTATION PROBLEMS

Since policy implementation is so complex, we should not expect it to be accomplished in a routine fashion. Even presidents cannot assume that their decisions and orders will be carried out. Indeed, their experiences in recent years would turn even the most optimistic observers into cynics. Once again we see the validity of Richard Neustadt's warning that presidents are rarely in a position to simply issue commands and have them obeyed.

In 1962 President John Kennedy ordered United States Army troops located in Memphis to the campus of the University of Mississippi at Oxford to control rioting that resulted from the attempts of a black, James Meredith, to enroll. As the hours passed after giving the order, the commander in chief saw no progress toward Oxford. Frustrated, he demanded of Secretary of the Army Cyrus Vance, "Where are the troops?" No one seemed to know. When he talked on the phone to the general who supposedly was leading the troops, the general indicated he was awaiting orders from the Pentagon.[1] This was hardly Kennedy's only frustration in policy implementation. Kennedy once told an aide not to abandon the minor project of remodeling Lafayette Park across the street from the White House. "Hell," the president exclaimed, "this may be the only thing I'll ever get done."[2]

President Ronald Reagan also had implementation troubles. For example, a potentially severe gap in our national defenses was created when several plants involved in producing the material for nuclear weapons had to be shut down when flaws in their design and operations endangered the public's health. Equally damaging, some White House aides took foreign policy into their own hands and funneled funds illegally from the sale of arms to Iran to the Contras in Nicaragua.

Given the frustration that presidents experience, we should not be surprised when President Carter complained, "Before I became president, I realized and I was warned that dealing with the federal bureaucracy would be one of the worst problems I would have to face. It has been even worse than I had anticipated."[3]

The experiences of recent presidents in implementation are summarized by Richard Cheney, President Gerald Ford's White House chief of staff:

> There is a tendency before you get to the White House or when you're just observing it from the outside to say "Gee, that's a powerful position that person has." The fact of the matter is that while you're here trying to do things, you are far more aware of the constraints than you are of the power. You spend most of your time trying to overcome obstacles to getting what the President wants done."[4]

LACK OF ATTENTION TO IMPLEMENTATION

Policy implementation has had a low priority in most administrations. Presidents have many obligations, of which implementing policy is only one. Policies must be developed, decisions made, legislation passed, controversies defused or contained, and the public courted, to name only the most obvious. Moreover, presidents often lack experience in administration and find other tasks more compatible with their skills and interests.

Foreign affairs are always a top priority of presidents because of the inherent importance of these issues and the unique constitutional responsibilities of presidents for them. Besides, presidents often feel they can accomplish more in the international arena than at home wrestling over domestic issues with an unresponsive Congress or a recalcitrant executive branch. Many presidents bring to office a strong interest in international relations. Ceremonial functions performed in the role of chief of state are traditions maintained by the president to broaden his public support. For example, within six weeks of George Bush's assuming office, he had traveled to Canada, Japan, China, and Korea and had trips planned to Europe and other parts of the world. All of these activities typically have priority over implementation.

In addition, the incentives to invest time in implementation are few. The president has only a short time in office and, at least in his first term, must constantly think about reelection. This encourages a short-run view in the White House, and presidents are more likely to try to provide the public with immediate gratification through the passage of legislation or the giving of speeches than with efforts to manage the implementation of policies. As one Office of Management and Budget official put it:

The people in the White House are there for such a short time. The pressure is on making some impact and getting some programs passed. There is not enough time or reward in thinking carefully about effectiveness and implementation. The emphasis is really on quantity, not quality. The President could never be reelected on the effectiveness theme. "We didn't do much, but it is all working very well." Do you think a President could win with that?[5]

Presidents know they will receive little credit if policies are managed well, because it is very difficult to attribute effective implementation to them personally. Moreover, to most people most of the time the functioning of government is not very visible. Both citizens and the press, when they pay attention to government at all, are most interested in controversial scandals, the passage of new policies, or ceremonial functions. Policies such as inflation or civil rights that have an immediate and direct effect on their lives attract their attention. Yet even here the press and public are mainly concerned with the impact of policies, not the process of their implementation. Although implementation directly influences the final results, this does not seem to be enough to entice the mass public and the press that caters to it to turn their attention to policy implementation.

As a result of these incentives, presidents direct a comparatively small amount of their time to policy implementation. Similarly, too little consideration is given to problems of implementation in the formulation of policies. Again, the proper incentives are missing. According to a Carter aide: "We all believe there should be more planning. The President has stressed the need for more caution. But when we fall behind, the President will impose a deadline. It is still a political system; and political systems are interested in results, not implementation."[6]

Thus, despite the president's clear responsibility for policy implementation, it typically receives relatively little attention from the White House. Although this may seem inevitable, given our discussion above, it is not without its costs. As an aide to President Reagan commented: "It's unfortunately true that the management of the bureaucracy becomes one of the lowest priorities of almost every administration that comes to this city. Every administration pays a heavy price for it before it's over."[7]

COMMUNICATION OF PRESIDENTIAL DECISIONS

The first requirement for effective implementation of presidential decisions or policies for which the president is responsible is that those who are to implement a decision must know what they are supposed to do. Policy decisions and implementation orders must be transmitted to the appropriate personnel before they can be followed. Naturally, these communications need to be accurate, and they must be accurately perceived by implementors. Implementation directives must also be clear. If they are not, implementors may be confused about what they should do, and they will have discretion to impose their own views on the implementation of policies, views that may be different from those of the president. Consistency in the communication directives is also crucial. Contradictory decisions confuse and frustrate administrative staff and constrain their ability to implement policies effectively.

Before subordinates can implement a presidential decision, they must be aware that the decision has been made and an order to implement it issued. This is not always as straightforward a process as it may seem. Ignorance or misunderstanding of decisions frequently occurs. Although the executive branch has highly developed lines of communication throughout the bureaucracy, this does not guarantee that communications will be transmitted successfully. The Bay of Pigs fiasco illustrates this point. On April 17, 1961, a force of 1,200 Cuban refugees, recruited, trained, and supplied by the Central Intelligence Agency (CIA), landed ninety miles south of Havana with the announced goal of overthrowing the Communist-oriented regime of Fidel Castro. Within three days the "invasion" had been crushed, inflicting a disastrous blow to American prestige, not to mention that of the new president, John F. Kennedy. The CIA never told the leader of the brigade sent to invade Cuba until it was too late that the president had ordered the soldiers to go to the mountains and fight a guerilla war if the invasion failed. The CIA disregarded the president's order, which it thought might weaken the brigade's resolve to fight or encourage the brigade to go to the mountains too quickly.

Sometimes aides and other officials ignore presidential directives with which they disagree primarily to avoid embarrassment for their chief. Such orders are generally given in anger and without proper consultation. President Nixon especially liked to let off steam by issuing outrageous orders. At one time he instructed Secretary of State William Rogers to "fire everybody in Laos," and he often told aides to "go after" reporters and once ordered that all reporters be barred from Air Force One. These and similar outbursts were ignored by H. R. Haldeman and the aides close to Nixon. They knew the president would view things differently when he calmed down.[8] In situations such as these, close associates of presidents have provided them safe outlets for their frustrations and protected them from their worst instincts.

In most instances, implementors have considerable discretion in interpreting their superiors' decisions and orders. Orders from the White House are rarely specific. Personnel at each rung in the bureaucratic ladder must use their judgment to expand and develop them. Obviously this process invites distortion of communications, and the further down in the bureaucracy presidential implementation directives go, the greater the potential for distortion. Moreover, as we shall see, subordinates do not always interpret the communications of superiors in a way that advances the goals of the president. Bureaucrats often use their discretion to further their personal interests and those of their agencies. Interest groups also take advantage of the discretion granted bureaucrats by pushing for their own demands at intermediate and low decision-making levels. It is for these reasons that observers of the federal bureaucracy often recommend that presidents and other high officials make every attempt to commit their directives to writing (in detail where possible), use personalized communications where appropriate, and show persistence in attempting to convey accurately their orders to those who actually implement policies.

In general, the more decentralized the implementation of a public policy, the less likely that it will be transmitted to its ultimate implementors accurately. Decentralization usually means that a decision must be communicated through several levels of authority before it reaches those who will carry it out. The more steps a communication must traverse from its original source, the weaker the signal that is ultimately received will be. A president can tell a secretary of state to go to another country and deliver a policy pronouncement to its prime minister, with little concern that his message will not be accurately transmitted. But he cannot have the same confidence about messages aimed at caseworkers in a social security office or soldiers in the field. The distance between the White House and the implementors is too great.

At times, executives and their staffs prefer *not* to transmit policy directives personally; they would rather get others to communicate for them. President Johnson wanted Secretary of the Treasury Henry Fowler to apply "jawboning," or powerful persuasion, to try to lower interest rates. Because Fowler opposed such efforts, Johnson decided not to communicate his wishes to the secretary directly. Instead he called House Banking Committee Chairman Wright Patman, a supporter of "jawboning," and asked him to pressure Fowler. Any time a step is added to the chain of communication, the potential for distortion is increased. Those who speak for others will have their own styles, their own views, and their own motivations. Not even presidents can depend upon other people to transmit directives exactly as they would desire.

Some presidents do not have personalities that are well suited to direct communication. This seems to have been particularly true of Richard Nixon. Fearing rejection and confrontation, he adopted an indirect administrative style to avoid possible unpleasantness. He even handed the phone to his chief of staff, Alexander Haig, so the latter could tell Gerald Ford he had been selected to become vice president. He spoke elliptically to those who disagreed with him to avoid being rebuffed and typically failed to issue unambiguous orders directly to his subordinates. He did not like to say no personally or to impose discipline on recalcitrant officials. When he found opposition within his administration, either he tried to accomplish his objectives without his adversaries' being aware of it or he had intermediaries take them written or verbal orders. The president shunned personal efforts at persuading or inspiring subordinates.[9]

Nixon's unwillingness to communicate directly with his subordinates fostered an environment in which discipline and cohesion were often low. It also revealed disunity in his administration that outsiders could exploit, further eroding cohesion. Officials in positions of power, such as Secretary of State Williams Rogers, could increase their discretion by implementing orders with which they disagreed only if they were transmitted personally to them by the president, which they rarely were.[10]

The press also may serve as a means of presidential communicating in more straightforward ways. Those in the White House often believe that since most high-level bureaucrats read *The New York Times* and the *Washington Post*, they can communicate with these officials about policy matters more rapidly through news stories than through normal channels. The White House also uses other media outlets such as television, newsmagazines, and specialized publications to send messages to government officials. Such messages may indicate a policy decision or position, or they may signal that an official White House statement was merely to appease special interests and should not be taken literally. On the other hand, the information provided in a story or as a response to a reporter's question is unlikely to be sufficient for guiding the implementation of a complex policy. Indeed, it may be in error. Yet it is to the nuances contained in such communications that ears in Washington are often most attuned.

If policies are to be administered as the president desires, his implementation directives must not only be received, but they also must be clear. Often the instructions transmitted to implementors are vague and do not specify when or how a program is to be carried out, however. Lack of clarity provides implementors with leeway to give new meaning to policies, meaning that sometimes inhibits intended change or brings about unintended change.

The lack of clarity in many implementation orders can be attributed to several factors. Perhaps the most important is the sheer complexity of policy making. When they establish policy, neither presidents nor members of Congress have the time or expertise to develop and apply all the requisite details for how it will be carried out. They have to leave most (and sometimes all) of the details to subordinates, usually in the executive branch. Thus, although it is the president's responsibility to implement policies of the national government, no matter who initiates them, he must delegate much of this responsibility to others.

The difficulty in reaching consensus on the goals of policies also inhibits clarity in implementation directives. In the United States we share wide agreement on the goals of avoidance of war, equal opportunity, and efficiency in government, but this consensus often dissolves when specific policy alternatives are under consideration. Lyndon Johnson once said, "If the full implications of any bill were known before its enactment, it would never get passed."[11] Clearly, imprecise decisions make it easier for presidents to develop and maintain winning coalitions. Different people or groups can support the same policy for different reasons. Each may hold its own conception of the goal or goals the program is designed to achieve. Ambiguous goals also may make it less threatening for groups to be on the losing side of a policy conflict, and this may reduce the intensity of their opposition.

The problems of starting up a new program may also produce confusion in implementation instructions. Often the passage of a new policy is followed by a period of administrative uncertainty in which there is a considerable time lag before any information on the program is disseminated. This period is followed by a second one in which rules are made but are then changed quickly as high-level officials attempt to deal with the unforeseen problems of implementing the policy and of their own earlier directives.

A cynical yet realistic explanation for lack of clarity in federal statutes is that Congress does not want them to be detailed. Congress would rather let executive branch agencies provide the specifics, not because of the latter's expertise, but in order to let the agencies take the blame for the rules that turn out to be unworkable or unpopular. Title IX of the Education Act Amendments of 1972 stated that "no person in the United States shall, on the basis of sex, be excluded from participation in, or be denied the benefits of, or be subject to discrimination under an education program or activity receiving Federal financial assistance." Such broad language allowed Congress to sidestep many touchy questions and leave their resolution to the president and his appointees. Moreover, individual members of Congress can gain credit with their constituents by intervening on their behalf regarding the application of regulations. In addition, if goals are not precise, Congress cannot be held accountable for the failure of its policies to achieve them. All of this only adds to the president's burden in guiding the bureaucracy.

Sometimes efforts are made to restrict the discretion of implementors. The Voting Rights Act of 1965 reduced the discretion of local voting registrars by limiting the use of literacy tests or similar voter qualification devices. In some cases the administration of voting registration was physically taken over by federal officials so that local officials could not inhibit voter registration. Another example of limiting implementors' discretion occurred in early 1973 when the Nixon administration issued new rules that restricted the way funds could be expended to aid the poor through social services. Funds could be used only for persons with specifically defined conditions of need and then only under a system of detailed accounting of the services provided. This was an attempt by the Nixon administration to restrict the options available to social workers.

It is generally easier for the president to reduce the discretion of officials with orders to stop doing something than to start doing something. For example, an absolute ban on providing funds for abortions for poor women is more likely to be unambiguous and more likely to be noticed if it is violated than an order to begin implementing a new policy. The implementation of most policies, however, requires positive actions, not prohibitions. Moreover, usually a series of positive actions extending over a long period of time and involving the technical expertise of numerous persons throughout a bureaucratic hierarchy is necessary to implement a policy. The complexity of such policy making makes it very difficult for a president to communicate and enforce rules that effectively reduce the discretion available to most policy implementors.

Vague policy decisions often hinder effective implementation, but directives that are too specific may also adversely affect implementation. Implementors sometimes need the freedom to adapt policies to suit the situation at hand. A myriad of specific regulations can overwhelm and confuse personnel in the field and may make them reluctant to act for fear of breaking the rules. Strict guidelines may also induce a type of goal displacement in which lower-level officials become more concerned with meeting specific requirements than with achieving the basic goals of the program. By rigidly adhering to the letter of a regulation, they may become so bogged down in red tape that the purpose of the rule is forgotten or defeated. Conversely, implementors sometimes simply ignore rigid regulations.

Inconsistency as well as vagueness in guidance from the president may provide operating agencies with substantial discretion in the interpretation and implementation of policy, discretion that may not be exercised to carry out a policy's goals. Environmental policy during the Nixon administration is an example. The president made a rhetorical commitment to supporting the National Environmental Policy Act (NEPA), but in practice his policy priorities were not significantly tied to environmental matters. Similarly, the Office of Management and Budget, the president's principal tool for controlling the federal bureaucracy, did not treat environmental policy goals as a major consideration in the evaluation of the activities of all federal agencies as NEPA intended. Federal officials received inconsistent signals from the White House concerning the importance of environmental policy and were left to resolve the question largely on their own.

Many of the factors that produce unclear communications are also responsible for inconsistent directives. The complexity of public policies, the difficulties in starting up new programs, and the multiple objectives of many policies all contribute to inconsistency in policy communications. Another reason that decisions are often inconsistent is that the president and top officials are constantly attempting to satisfy a diverse set of interests that may represent views on both sides of an issue. Policies that are not of high priority to the president may simply be left to flounder in a sea of competing demands.

RESOURCES

Implementation orders may be accurately transmitted, clear, and consistent, but if the president lacks the resources necessary to carry out policies, established at his discretion or by Congress, implementation is likely to be ineffective. Important resources include money, staff of sufficient size and with the proper skills to carry out their assignments, and the information, authority, and facilities necessary to translate proposals on paper into functioning public services.

Money

Sometimes the problem the president faces in implementing policy and delivering services is simply a lack of money. Elliot Richardson, when he was secretary of the Department of Health, Education and Welfare, discovered that the funds Congress appropriated for programs permitted his department to reach only very small percentages of those eligible for the benefits. When his staff estimated the cost of having the department's service-delivery programs reach each eligible person, it turned out to exceed the entire federal budget for that year!

Staff

Certainly an essential resource in implementing policy is staff. In an era in which "big government" is under attack from all directions, it may seem surprising to learn that a principal source of implementation failure is inadequate staff. Although about 5 million military and civilian personnel work for the federal executive branch (see Table 9-1), and therefore the president, there are still too few people with the requisite skills to do an effective job implementing many policies. We must evaluate the bureaucracy not only in terms of absolute numbers, but also in terms of its capabilities to perform desired tasks.

The federal government provides a wide range of services through its own personnel, such as national defense, immigration control, and maintenance of recreational facilities. Each of these and others like them are labor-intensive areas, and thus the services provided are directly

Table 9-1. Federal Executive Branch Employment

	Number of Employees
Executive Departments	
Agriculture	113,147
Commerce	42,936
Defense (civilian)	1,067,974
(military)	2,169,000
Education	4,554
Energy	16,657
Health and Human Services	133,842
Housing and Urban Development	11,843
Interior	73,980
Justice	65,529
Labor	17,487
State	25,325
Transportation	61,281
Treasury	135,628
Veteran Affairs	240,423
Larger Independent Agencies	
Environmental Protection Agency	14,021
Federal Deposit Insurance Corporation	8,708
General Services Administration	23,057
National Aeronautics and Space Administration	22,244
Tennessee Valley Authority	30,564
U.S. Information Agency	9,078
U.S. Postal Service	790,960

Source: U.S. Department of Commerce, *Statistical Abstract of the United States, 1988* (Washington, D.C.: Government Printing Office, 1987), pp. 310, 323.

related to the size and quality of the staff available to the relevant agencies over which the president presides. Yet there is substantial evidence that agencies and departments are woefully understaffed. For example, the air force and navy have too few experienced jet pilots, a shortage of staff at the Federal Drug Administration (FDA) has been responsible for delays in the testing of new drugs to combat AIDS, millions of illegal aliens elude our understaffed border guards every year, and some observers fear that the lack of maintenance of national parks will lead to permanent deterioration of such treasured American vacation spots as Yosemite and Yellowstone.

Although staff size can be critical for almost every policy, it is more so for some than others. Insufficient staff is especially critical to implementation when the policy involved is one that imposes unwelcome constraints on people, whether these be the requirements of grant policies, regulatory policies, or criminal law. Since such policies generally involve highly decentralized activities, a large staff is necessary if this behavior is to be monitored. It is much easier for the chief executive to implement a policy such as social security that distributes benefits recipients desire. More personnel are required to enforce limitations on people than to write checks to them.

The president's executive branch agencies do not even come close to meeting these needs. The fear of creating a totalitarian bureaucratic monster and the pressures to allocate personnel to more direct services, such as the provision of agricultural expertise to farmers, keep staffs that monitor implementation small. In addition, the scarcity of payroll funds coupled with the irresistible urges of policymakers to provide public services (at least in form) ensure that staffs will generally be inadequate to implement programs.

Because of lack of staff and because of traditional federal government deference to the states, federal programs rely heavily upon state agencies for their implementation. This, however, does not solve the president's problem of lack of staff at the federal level; it merely transfers the problem to the states. Since this shortage of personnel exists at every level of government, delegating the implementation of a policy to a lower level of government rarely alleviates the problem.

In addition to numbers, skill is an important characteristic of staff for implementation. One problem the president faces is the shortage of people with management skills among career executives. Personnel with substantive skills are also often in short supply in the executive branch. This is especially true when a government agency is carrying out or regulating highly technical activities. Inadequately trained inspectors for the Environmental Protection Agency were found to be missing more than half of the serious violations in their inspections of facilities handling and storing hazardous waste. Sometimes the necessary personnel are very difficult to hire because of the higher incomes and greater flexibility they can enjoy by working in the private sector. The military's problems in attracting physicians is a prime example. At other times, the needed staff may simply not exist even in the private sector, and a government agency must invest in developing expertise. The federal government's efforts to regulate energy prices and allocations in the 1970s illustrate both problems. No one really knew how to accomplish these tasks, and few people outside the energy companies had the background to understand the industry. Thus, employees of the Federal Energy Office relied upon "on the job training."

Information

Information is another essential resource in presidential policy implementation. This information comes in two forms. The first is information regarding how to carry out a policy. Executive branch officials need to know what to do when they are given directives to act. The second form of essential information is data on the compliance of others with governmental rules and regulations. Implementors must know whether other persons involved in implementing policies are complying with the law.

Program information is particularly critical for new policies or those involving technical questions, such as the abatement of air pollution or the development of a new weapons system, because implementors are asked to meet goals neither they nor anyone else knows how to accomplish, at least in the short run. Routine functions, such as dispersing funds, building roads, training troops, hiring typists, or purchasing goods, are relatively straightforward in their operation, and a wealth of information exists on how to carry them out. But the implementors of a new policy such as controlling hospital costs or developing a jet fighter do not share these advantages. They lack the necessary information to establish appropriate standards and guidelines. Thus, it is one thing for Congress or the White House to mandate a change in policy, but it is something quite different for the executive branch officials who work for the president to figure out how to do it.

The lack of knowledge of how to implement some policies has several direct consequences. Some responsibilities will simply not be met, or they will not be met on time. Inefficiency is also likely to characterize the implementation of such policies. Some efforts will prove to be mistakes, and implementors will have to try again. Moreover, regulations may be inappropriate, causing other government units or organizations in the private sector to purchase equipment, fill out forms, or stop certain activities unnecessarily. Ideally, for example, before an agency acts to implement a law by ordering costly changes in an industry or its products (such as automobiles), the agency should be able to predict the effects of the change on the economic health of the industry in question. Such information, however, is frequently lacking, and the president may be severely criticized as a result.

Implementation of policies often requires information on the compliance of organizations or individuals with the law. Compliance data, however, are usually difficult to obtain, in part because of the lack of staff. Thus, the president and his subordinates often have to rely upon information about compliance from those who are doing the complying. This occurs in a wide range of policies, including school desegregation, hospital care, and environmental protection. Quite naturally, this system of information raises questions about effective implementation. It should come as no surprise to us, then, when faulty welds are discovered in the trans-Alaskan pipeline, federal grants to state and local governments are misspent, or hazardous wastes are found to be polluting water supplies.

Authority

Authority is often a critical resource in policy implementation. The president actually has relatively little direct authority. Congress vests most authority in subordinate executive officials. Sometimes agency officials simply lack authority, even on paper, to implement a policy properly. For example, the policy being implemented may provide no sanctions against those violating the law, or the agency may lack authority to initiate administrative or judicial actions. When formal authority does exist, it is frequently mistaken by observers for effective authority. But authority on paper is one thing; authority effectively exercised is quite another.

One of the potentially most effective sanctions is the withdrawal of funds from a program. But there are many reasons why this authority is less than it seems. Cutting off funds is a drastic action. It may be embarrassing to all those involved and antagonize the implementors of a program whose active support is necessary for effective implementation. Cutting off federal funds from projects also alienates the members of Congress from the areas losing the money. Requiring states or cities to repay misspent funds can also have severe political consequences. In general, the White House does not even try to exercise this authority.

Executive branch officials may also be reluctant to exercise authority. Terminating a project or withdrawing federal funds may hurt most those whom the policy is designed to aid. Schoolchildren, the elderly, or the poor are often the real victims of cutbacks. If a company loses federal contracts because of racial or sexual discrimination, it may be forced to lay off workers. Those with the least seniority may be the minorities the policy is trying to help. Similarly, cutting off federal funds for the educationally disadvantaged because of misallocation is most likely to hurt students from poor families.

The desire for self-preservation keeps many of the president's agencies from withdrawing funds. Agencies like the Federal Highway Administration and the Department of Education are primarily involved in channeling grants to other levels of government. To survive they must give away money. If they fail to do so, they may look bad to Congress and superior executive officials. This may hurt them in their future quests for budgets and authority, resources of great significance for most bureaucrats. Thus, they may sacrifice the social objectives of a program to the "maintenance" objectives of the bureaucratic unit.

Although executive officials often lack effective authority over other public officials, this lack of control is small compared with their lack of authority over private individuals, groups, and businesses, upon whom the successful implementation of policies often depends. Therefore, they must make their policies attractive to the private sector. As a result of these efforts, the enforcement of policies such as those dealing with safety in the workplace, including coal mines, rarely results in serious penalties for noncompliance.

Facilities

Physical facilities may also be critical resources in implementation. Without the necessary buildings, equipment, supplies, and even green space, implementation won't succeed. National parks are overcrowded; military equipment, ranging from rifles to spare parts for airplanes, is often in short supply; those patrolling our borders lack the appropriate ships and planes to prevent the smuggling of illegal drugs; and we lack adequate storage facilities for our national oil reserves.

There is also often a shortage of sophisticated equipment. Computers are essential to the implementation of modern defense policy; they issue paychecks, assign personnel, navigate ships, and track missiles. Nevertheless, studies of the military's computers have found that the Defense Department has been saddled with thousands of obsolete machines that leave the military services ill prepared for a modern war. Similar problems have beset other agencies, such as the Internal Revenue Service, the Immigration and Naturalization Service, and the Social Security Administration.

Although the president can request funds for new or additional facilities, both the White House and Congress may hesitate to raise taxes to pay for them. Moreover, as was the case for staff, Congress often prefers to spread resources over many policies rather than to fund fewer programs adequately. Internal government procurement rules ("red tape") may add additional burdens to those trying to purchase expensive equipment such as computers.

DISPOSITIONS

If implementors are well disposed toward a particular policy, they are more likely to carry it out as the president intended. But when implementors' attitudes or perspectives differ from the president's, the process of implementing a policy becomes infinitely more complicated. Many policies fall within a "zone of indifference." These policies will probably be implemented faithfully because implementors do not have strong feelings about them. Other policies, however, will be in direct conflict with the policy views or personal or organizational interests of implementors. When people are asked to execute orders with which they do not agree, inevitable slippage occurs between policy decisions and performance. In such cases implementors will exercise their discretion, sometimes in subtle ways, to hinder implementation. As President Ford said:

> There are bureaucratic fiefdoms out in the states or in various regions, and the people who occupy those pockets of power want to do things in their own way. They are pros at it. They have been disregarding Presidents for years, both Democratic and Republican.[12]

Implementors may oppose a policy, and their opposition can prevent a policy option from even being tried. For some time there had been a policy debate over whether there should be a work requirement for those receiving welfare payments and able to work. During the Nixon administration, however, many top officials concluded that welfare administrators would not enforce a work requirement provision, even in the face of presidential exhortations and congressional demands. Thus, they had to turn to other alternatives, such as tax incentives, to encourage welfare recipients to work. On another occasion, Nixon ordered Secretary of Defense Melvin Laird to bomb a hideaway of Palestine Liberation Organization guerrillas, a move that Laird opposed. According to the secretary, "We had bad weather for forty-eight hours. The Secretary of Defense can always find a reason not to do something."[13] Thus, the president's order was stalled for days and was eventually rescinded. President Reagan's national security adviser explained that the United States could not employ a strategy of selective use of force in order to support diplomatic efforts to keep peace in Lebanon because of the lack of cooperation between the Departments of State and Defense.

The opposition of presidential subordinates to a policy may also defeat some of its immediate goals after it becomes law. President Carter ordered federal agencies to discourage the development of low-lying areas in danger of damage by flooding. Twenty-five months later only fifteen of the seventy-five agencies that had received the directive had issued regulations specifying how they were going to comply with the president's wishes. Forty-six of the agencies had not even taken the first step toward adopting regulations. The primary reason for this lack of action was not bureaucratic indolence. Instead, it was the opposition of agencies to the substance of the president's order.

Differences in organizational viewpoints may also impede the cooperation between agencies that is so often necessary in policy implementation. The army requires aircraft, all of which belong to the air force (at its insistence), to transport troops. Yet transporting troops is a low priority for the air force, which is more interested in strategic bombers and fighter planes. Thus, it typically does not fight for resources for troop transport planes or choose to allocate its scarce resources to that function, thereby undermining the ability of the army to carry out *its* function.

There may also be differences in viewpoints within an agency between presidential subordinates with different program responsibilities. There was intra-agency conflict over the implementation of the National Environmental Policy Act. Secretaries of transportation, for example, had a difficult time getting development-oriented agencies in the department, such as the Federal Highway Administration, to consider seriously the environmental consequences of their projects.

Bureaucratic units also resist vigorously the efforts of others to take away or share the resources deemed necessary to accomplish their missions. Feuding over responsibility for an activity has often hindered policy implementation. J. Edgar Hoover directed the Federal Bureau of Investigation with an iron fist from 1924 until 1972. According to Richard Nixon, Hoover "had always been rigidly territorial when it came to the functions and prerogatives of the FBI. He totally distrusted the other intelligence agencies . . . and, whenever possible, resisted attempts to work in concert with them."[14] At one point the director cut off all liaison activities with the other intelligence agencies, such as the Central Intelligence Agency, the Defense Intelligence Agency, and the National Security Agency. This hindered President Nixon's efforts to control dissension at home. Hoover didn't want to share his territory with anyone.

Staffing the Bureaucracy

Implementors' dispositions may pose serious obstacles to policy implementation. But if existing personnel do not implement policies the way top officials desire, why are they not replaced with people more responsive to leaders?

APPOINTMENTS.   The president has authority to appoint directly about six hundred leading members of the executive branch. This total includes the White House staff, between fifteen and twenty individuals in each of the cabinet-level departments, about ten persons in each of the major independent agencies (such as the National Aeronautical and Space Administration), the heads of some lesser agencies, and the commissioners of the independent regulatory agencies (as their terms expire). Of the roughly 5 million employees in the executive branch, far less than 1 percent are appointed by the president and his designees. This is an obvious constraint on the ability of any administration to alter personnel.

After being elected, a president has less than three months to search for a new team to take over the government. Moreover, this must be done by the president-elect and aides who are exhausted from the long, arduous election campaign and have many other demands on their time, such as preparing a budget and a legislative program. Members of the cabinet and other appointees usually have little advance notice of their selection and are busy wrapping up their other responsibilities and doing their homework on the issues relevant to their new positions prior to their confirmation hearings. Thus, they, too, often resort to haphazard recruiting techniques when they make their appointments.

Presidents are also constrained politically in their appointments. Usually they feel these appointments must show a balance of geography, ideology, ethnicity, sex, and other demographic characteristics salient at the time. Thousands of persons are urged upon an administration by themselves, members of Congress, or people in the president's party. Few of these persons are qualified for available jobs, but due to political necessity, more than a few are appointed. Political favors may please political supporters, but they do not necessarily provide the basis for sound administration. Moreover, such appointments may result in incompatibilities with the president that lead to politically costly dismissals.

The interest groups that appointments are designed to please keep a watchful eye throughout a president's tenure in office on who is appointed to what position. Not only is "balance" important at the beginning of a new administration, but it remains a constraint on recruiting personnel. Thus, in the middle of a term White House aides may be ordered to find a Mexican-American woman to serve as United States treasurer. A president also might desire to reward new groups. After the 1972 presidential election, Richard Nixon wanted his cabinet and subcabinet to represent more accurately his broadened electoral coalition. This led to a renewed emphasis on the demographic characteristics of appointees, delays in filling positions, and, most significantly, compromises in the quality of some appointees, such as many of those placed in top positions in the Labor Department to please the president's new "hard hat" constituency. It also led to a humorous incident in which Claude Brinegar was selected as secretary of transportation partly on the basis of his Irish Catholic background. The White House was in error, however. Brinegar was really a German Protestant.

A different type of "political" constraint may arise if a strong member of an administration opposes a person the president desires to appoint. Usually the president can overcome this opposition within the ranks, but sometimes the price may be too high. In his second term President Nixon wanted to appoint John Connally secretary of state but did not do so because of the opposition of his chief adviser on national security matters, Henry Kissinger. Instead, Kissinger was named secretary of state.

A surprising but nonetheless real limitation on personnel selection is that presidents often do not know individuals who are qualified for the positions they have to fill. Following his election in 1960, John F. Kennedy told an aide: "For the last four years I spent so much time getting to know people who could help me get elected President that I didn't have time to get to know people who could help me, after I was elected, to be a good

President."[15] Thus, presidents often appoint persons they do not know to the highest positions in the federal government.

Early in their terms recent presidents have typically not imposed their preferences for subcabinet level officials upon those whom they appoint to head departments and agencies. The reason has partially been the lack of organization in the personnel system. In addition, however, there has been a concern that since top officials will be held accountable for agencies' performances, they should be able to appoint subordinates whom they like and who will complement their own abilities and help them accomplish their jobs. Naturally, top officials generally request this freedom. High officials also fight to name their subordinates because if they lose to the White House on personnel matters, their standing within their departments will drop.

The Reagan administration, on the other hand, insisted on White House clearance of all subcabinet appointments. Although there is disagreement about the quality of the personnel appointed to high-level executive branch positions during this period, there is consensus on the view that Reagan's appointees were unusually loyal to the president and committed to his conservative ideology.

The Bush administration reverted to the more common practice of giving department and agency heads discretion in making political appointments. It has been more concerned with the competence and personal loyalty to the president of its political appointees than with their ideology.

As presidential terms extend from weeks into months and years, the White House's perspective sometimes changes. Frustrating problems in policy implementation often lead the president and his staff to take a more direct interest in personnel matters below the levels of department and agency heads. For example, in mid-1978 the Carter administration began a review of subcabinet officials with the object of weeding out those who were incompetent or disloyal. Tim Kraft was promoted to the position of assistant for political affairs *and* personnel (indicating an appreciation for the linkage between the two). Kraft and his staff began taking more interest in appointees: "We have told the personnel people in the departments that we want to be consulted on all appointments, whether they are presidential appointments or appointments to high GS [civil service] positions."[16]

Despite its frequent use, political clearance is often a crude process. Many policy views fit under a party label. Democrats range from very liberal to very conservative, and the range for Republicans is nearly as great. Moreover, political appointees may be motivated by materialistic or selfish aims and not necessarily be responsive to the president. A person may want an ambassadorship, or a young lawyer may seek experience in the Justice Department or a regulatory agency in hope of cashing in on it later for a high-paying job in the private sector. Political appointees may also remain loyal to their home-state political organizations, interest group associations, or sponsors in Congress—rather than to the White House.

Conversely, if political appointees are viewed as too close to the White House, they may be "shut out" in their departments and from their departments' client groups and thus be of limited usefulness to the president. No matter how loyal to the president appointees are, they need to know what to do and how to do it once they obtain their positions. People with these capabilities, as we have seen, are not easy to find. Moreover, too many political lieutenants in a department may separate the top executive from the bureaucracy and its services. They may also decrease the executive's opportunities to build personal support within the bureaucracy through communication, consultation, and access.

CIVIL SERVICE.   Below appointed officials in the federal hierarchy rank most executive branch employees. Almost all civilian employees are covered by the protection of personnel systems designed to fill positions on the basis of merit and protect employees against removal for partisan political reasons. The military has a separate personnel system designed to accomplish the same goals.

Political appointees often bring to office a distrust of the permanent bureaucracy, a suspicion fueled by presidential election campaigns such as those of Jimmy Carter and Ronald Reagan in which the winning candidate runs as a Washington outsider and engages in "bureaucrat bashing." (George Bush, however, abstained from the temptation to criticize the bureaucracy in his campaign in 1988.) Regardless of the attitudes they bring with them to government, most political appointees before they leave office come to regard members of the civil service as both competent and responsive to their leadership.[17]

If the president or a presidential appointee finds that a civil servant is obstructing implementation of the president's policies, he or she has some potential remedies. Those at the top of the civil service, those in the Senior Executive Service (SES), may be transferred and may be demoted more easily than in the past. Although members of the SES compose only a small percentage of the civil service (there are about 7,000 members of the SES), they are among the most powerful members of the career bureaucracy and the most crucial to implementing the president's policies.

Those below the SES are more difficult to move. It is possible for an incompetent or recalcitrant civil service employee to be dismissed, but this rarely happens. It takes more time, expertise, and political capital to fire a civil servant than most officials have or are willing to invest in such an effort. Transferring unwanted personnel to less troublesome positions is one of the most common means of quieting obstructive bureaucrats. In President Carter's words, it is "easier to promote and transfer incompetent employees than to get rid of them."[18] Transferring unwanted personnel is much easier when the civil servants in question opt not to use the technicalities and protections of the civil service system or their allies in Congress and interest groups. Ironically, these are the type of persons most likely to be dedicated to the notion of a civil service and therefore the ones an executive would probably least desire to replace. In addition, transferring personnel is not a panacea for the problems of implementors' dispositions, because it does not solve problems, it just relocates them.

As the size and scope of the federal government has grown since the 1960s, so has distrust, especially among Republican presidents. Over this period there has been a trend toward politicizing the bureaucracy, emphasizing the White House's operational control of the executive bureaucracy rather than traditional patronage. The number of political appointees at the top of the executive bureaucracy has increased substantially, as has the number of political appointees at lower ranks. Employing a related technique (developed by his predecessors), President Reagan made efforts to place political appointees in career positions just before leaving office.

Politicizing the bureaucracy has drawbacks, however. It is difficult to recruit high-quality political appointees to some of the lower sub-cabinet positions. In addition, layering political appointees at the top of

"I'm leaving, sir, to become a disgruntled former Administration official."

Source: Drawing by Dana Fradon; © 1983 The New Yorker Magazine, Inc.

bureaucratic units undermines the motivation of the career service and closes off career options to them. Finally, the short tenure in the same job of the typical political appointee (about two years) diminishes their ability to implement policy effectively.

The Nixon and Ford administrations were able to place many persons who had favorable attitudes toward the Republican administrations' domestic policies in top career and politically appointed managerial positions. Yet, the number of vacancies the Nixon and Ford administrations were able to fill was limited. After eight years of Republicans in the White House, nearly 70 percent of the existing top career and political executives had assumed their positions before the Nixon administration. (The figure for career executives alone was 85 percent.) Thus, filling vacancies is unlikely to be a sufficient strategy to alter the attitudes in the bureaucracy. The president must also influence those already holding their jobs.[19]

Incentives

Changing the personnel in government bureaucracies is difficult, and it does not ensure that the implementation process will proceed smoothly. Another potential technique the president can use to deal with the problem of implementors' dispositions is to alter the dispositions of existing implementors through the manipulation of incentives. Since people generally act in their own interest, the manipulation of incentives by high-level policymakers may influence their actions. Increasing the benefits or costs of a particular behavior may make implementors more or less likely to choose it as a means of advancing their personal, organizational, or substantive policy interests.

As we have seen, the ability of top officials to exercise sanctions is severely limited. Rewards are the other side of the incentive coin, but they are even more difficult for executives to administer than penalties. Individual performance is difficult to reward with pay increases. President Carter once complained that "more than 99 percent of all federal employees got a so-called 'merit' rating."[20] Raises are almost always given across-the-board, with everyone in the same category of employment receiving a similar percentage increase in salary regardless of differences in performance. The Civil Service Reform Act of 1978 created the potential for awarding merit pay increases or bonuses for many managers, supervisors, and top executives in the federal civil service, but Congress has appropriated little money for these raises and few civil servants have received them. Usually personal performance can be rewarded only by promotions, and they are necessarily infrequent. In addition, presidential subordinates who oppose or who are indifferent to a policy are unlikely to employ incentives to further its implementation.

THE BUREAUCRATIC STRUCTURE

Policy implementors may know what to do and have sufficient desire and resources to do it, but they may still be hampered in implementation by the structures of the organizations in which they serve. Two prominent characteristics of bureaucracies are standard operating procedures (SOPs) and fragmentation. Both may hinder presidential policy implementation.

Standard Operating Procedures

Standard operating procedures are routines that enable public officials to make numerous everyday decisions. They have many benefits for the chief executive. They save time, and time is valuable. If a social security caseworker had to invent a new rule for every potential client and have it cleared at higher levels, few people would be helped. So detailed manuals are written to cover as many particular situations as officials can anticipate. SOPs also bring uniformity to complex organizations, and justice is better served if rules are applied uniformly. This is true for the implementation of welfare policies that distribute benefits to the needy, as well as for criminal law policies that distribute sanctions. Uniformity also makes personnel interchangeable. A soldier can be transferred to any spot in the world and still know how to carry out a function by referring to the proper manual, a substantial advantage for the commander in chief.

Although designed to make implementing policies easier, at least in theory, SOPs may be inappropriate in some cases and function as obstacles to action. Presidents have had many a plan thwarted by standard government practices. They certainly frustrated President Franklin D. Roosevelt:

> The Treasury is so large and far-flung and ingrained in its practices that I find it is almost impossible to get the action and results I want. . . . But the Treasury is not to be compared with the State Department. You should go through the experience of trying to get any changes in the thinking, policy, and action of the career diplomats and then you'd know what a real problem was. But the Treasury and the State Department put together are nothing as compared with the Na-a-vy. . . . To change anything in the N-a-a-vy is like punching a feather bed. You punch it with your right and you punch it with your left until you are finally exhausted, and then you find the damn bed just as it was before you started punching.[21]

Standard operating procedures may hinder policy implementation by inhibiting change. Designed for typical situations, SOPs can be ineffective in new circumstances. In 1962 the United States discovered the presence of Soviet missiles in Cuba and reacted by blockading the island. President John F. Kennedy was very concerned about the initial interception of Soviet ships, and he sent Secretary of Defense Robert McNamara to check with Chief of Naval Operations George Anderson on the procedures being followed. McNamara stressed to Anderson that the president did *not* want to follow the normal SOP whereby a ship risked being sunk if it refused to submit to being boarded and searched. Kennedy did not want to goad the Soviet Union into retaliation. But Admiral Anderson was not cooperative. At one point in the discussion, he waved the *Manual of Naval Regulations* in the secretary's face and shouted, "It's all in here." To this McNamara replied, "I don't give a damn what John Paul Jones would have done. I want to know what you are going to do now."[22] The conversation ended when the admiral asked the secretary of defense to leave and let the navy run the blockade according to established procedures.

Sometimes SOPs cause organizations to take actions superior officials do not desire, as the Cuban missile crisis dramatically illustrates. Despite President Kennedy's explicit order that the initial encounter with a Soviet ship not involve a Soviet submarine, the United States Navy, according to established procedure, used its "Hunter-Killer" antisubmarine warfare program to locate and float above Soviet submarines within six hundred miles of the continental United States. Also following standard "Hunter-Killer" procedures, the navy forced several Soviet submarines to surface. This drastic action was not ordered by the president or the secretary of defense. It "just happened" because it was the programmed response to such a situation. The highest officials, who ostensibly had authority over the navy, never imagined standard procedures would supplant their directives. SOPs become deeply embedded in an organization and are difficult to control, even in times of crisis.

New policies are the most likely to require a change in organizational behavior and are therefore the most likely to have their implementation hindered by SOPs. In October 1983, 241 United States Marines were killed while they slept in a terrorist attack on their barracks outside Beirut, Lebanon. A presidential commission appointed to examine the causes of the tragedy concluded that, among other factors contributing to the disaster, the marines in the peacekeeping force were "not trained, organized, staffed or supported to deal effectively with the terrorist threat."[23] In other words, they had not altered their SOPs regarding security, basic to any military unit, to meet the unique challenges of a terrorist attack.

Fragmentation

A second aspect of bureaucratic structure that may impede implementation is fragmentation. Fragmentation is the dispersion of responsibility for a policy area among several organizational units.

The extent of governmental fragmentation is widespread. In the field of welfare, for example, more than one hundred federal human services programs are administered by ten different departments and agencies. The Department of Health and Human Services has responsibility for the Aid to Families with Dependent Children program; the Department of Housing and Urban Development provides housing assistance for the poor; the Department of Agriculture runs the food stamp program; and the Department of Labor administers training programs and provides assistance in obtaining employment. President Carter declared, "There are too many agencies doing too many things, overlapping too often, coordinating too rarely, wasting too much money—and doing too little to solve real problems."[24] The more actors and agencies involved with a particular policy and the more interdependent their decisions, the less the probability of successful implementation.

Over the years Congress has created many separate agencies and has favored categorical grants that assign specific authority and funds to particular agencies in order to oversee more closely and intervene more easily in the administration of policies. Dispersing responsibility for a policy area also disperses "turf" to congressional committees. In water resource policy, three committees in the House and three committees in the Senate have authority over the Army Corps of Engineers, the Soil Conservation Service, and the Bureau of Reclamation, respectively. None of these committees wants to relinquish its hold over these agencies. Thus, the agencies and programs that deal with a common problem remain divided among three departments.

Like congressional committees, agencies are possessive about their jurisdictions. Usually department or agency heads vigorously oppose executive branch reorganizations that encroach upon their sphere of influence. President Carter requested that funds for state drug abuse programs be divided into single, consolidated grants for mental health, drug, and alcohol abuse services. Congress refused to consent to this proposal, however. Professionals in the alcohol and drug abuse programs feared that their programs would be downgraded if they lost their separate legislative identities and were combined with mental health programs. They blocked the president's attempt to reduce program fragmentation.

Interest groups are a third force supporting fragmentation. When Lyndon Johnson tried to move the Maritime Administration from the Department of Commerce to the Department of Transportation, he was successfully opposed by the AFL-CIO. Although it made sense administratively to house the Maritime Administration with other transportation-related agencies, labor leaders feared a bureaucratic reorganization would jeopardize their close relationship with the Maritime Administration. Groups also develop close working relationships with congressional committees and do not want to lose their special access in a reorganization of committee jurisdictions that might follow an executive branch reorganization.

Often a combination of interest groups and legislative committees oppose reorganization. The Department of Education, proposed by President Carter, is composed almost exclusively of education programs from the old Department of Health, Education and Welfare. Head Start, Indian education, the school lunch program, GI bill benefits, job training, and some vocational and rehabilitation education programs remained where they were because of opposition to their being moved. For example, the Senate Argiculture Committee opposed change out of fear of losing oversight responsibility for child nutrition programs, and the American Food Service Association opposed change because it feared nutrition would not be a high priority with educators.

The nature of public policy also is a factor in producing fragmentation. Broad policies, such as those dealing with environmental protection, are multidimensional and overlap with dimensions of other policies, such as agriculture, transportation, recreation, and energy. Thus, presidents cannot easily organize government agencies around just one policy area.

Fragmentation implies diffusion of responsibility, and this makes coordination of policies difficult. The resources and authority necessary for the president to attack a problem comprehensively are often distributed among many bureaucratic units. For example, President Bush found that his high-priority efforts to interdict illegal drugs at the country's borders required coordination among the Treasury Department's Customs Service; the Department of Justice's Drug Enforcement Agency, the Federal Bureau of Investigation, and Border Patrol; and the Transportation Department's Coast Guard.

Duplication in the provision of public services is another result of bureaucratic fragmentation. President Carter complained, "There are . . . at least 75 agencies and 164,000 Federal employees in police or investigative work. Many of them duplicate or overlap state and local law enforcement efforts unnecessarily."[25]

Fragmentation may result in two or more agencies working at cross-purposes. According to Richard Nixon:

> One department's watershed project, for instance, threatens to slow the flow of water to another department's reclamation project downstream. One agency wants to develop an electric power project on a certain river while other agencies are working to keep the same area wild. Different departments follow different policies for timber production and conservation, for grazing, for fire prevention and for recreational activities on the federal lands they control, though the lands are often contiguous.[26]

Not only do such conflicts defeat the purposes of the programs involved, but they also force the president's highest-level aides and departmental executives to spend great amounts of time and energy negotiating with one another. This is wasteful, and it may result in compromises representing the lowest common denominators of officials' original positions. Unfortunately, bold and original ideas may be sacrificed for intragovernmental harmony.

Sometimes responsibility for a policy area is so fragmented that certain functions fall between the cracks. Some tasks do not fit neatly within an agency's formal authority. A former intelligence official writes of serving in a Scandinavian embassy and hiring someone to read the local Communist literature. From this a useful chart showing the hierarchy of the Communist party was developed. The project was cut from the budget, however, because coverage of the Communist movement was considered to be a CIA function, yet the CIA could not carry out this function because it was "overt," and the CIA was a clandestine organization.[27] Thus, the project fell between the divisions of organizational responsibility, and useful information was not available to the White House or others in government.

FOLLOW-UP

Because of all the hindrances to effective policy implementation, it seems reasonable to suggest that implementation would be improved if presidents followed up on their decisions and orders to see that they have been properly implemented. The following example illustrates the importance of follow-up.

President Nixon ordered the CIA to destroy its stockpile of biological weapons. CIA Director Richard Helms relayed the president's order to the deputy director for plans (the head of the covert action division), and he in turn relayed it to a subordinate. Fiver years later two lethal toxins were discovered in a secret cache. A middle-level official had disobeyed the president's order, later retired, and his successor had assumed that the storage of the toxins had official approval. When called before Congress, Helms testified that he had undertaken no follow-up check on his own order, and when asked who told him the toxins were destroyed, he replied, "I read it in the newspapers." Indeed, if the official who discovered the toxins had not received a directive from the new CIA director, William Colby, to be on the constant lookout for illegal action, he might not have checked on the legality of the toxins, and they would still be sitting there.[28]

The importance of follow-up was made apparent to Nixon at many other points in his administration. Once he ordered the demolition of two old Department of Defense buildings on the Mall near the White House, but it took more than a year to get them down. White House aide William Safire explains:

> Because the President of the United States took a continuing interest, because at least two of his aides were made to feel that its success was a crucial

test of their ability and because the President kept prodding, issuing orders, refusing to be "reasonable," a few miserable buildings were finally knocked down and their occupants reassigned.

After the demolition the president called together his aides. With "pride, relief, and wonderment," he told them, "We have finally gotten something done."[29]

Thus a president must constantly check up on his orders. Nevertheless, most recent presidents, including Nixon himself, have not followed this advice. Follow-up on the whole has been haphazard. They and their staffs have been too busy with crisis management, electoral politics, or getting legislation passed to delve into the details involved in monitoring policy implementation. Moreover, presidents lack systematic information about the performance of agencies.

One technique presidents could use to increase their capacity to follow up on their decisions is to enlarge the size of their personal staffs. This strategy can create additional burdens for the White House, however. Because chief executives can personally deal effectively with only a few people, they are forced to relay implementation orders and receive feedback through additional layers of their own staffs. This, in turn, increases both the possibility of communication distortion and the burden of administration, which the staff is supposed to lighten. The more authority is delegated to persons at the top of a hierarchy, the more possibilities there are for inadequate coordination, interoffice rivalries, communication gaps, and other typical administrative problems. Moreover, a large number of aides with limited access to a top official such as the president increases the chance of their carrying out orders given in anger. Those with limited access will be less likely to know the executive well enough or have enough confidence to hold back on implementing their supervisor's instructions.

A large staff for a president has another drawback. Only a few people can credibly speak for the president. If too many people begin giving orders in the president's name, for example, they will undermine the credibility of all those claiming to speak for him. This credibility is important for aides trying to help the president implement policies. As one Carter aide explained: "If you are perceived by people in a given agency as being close to the president because you have an office in the West Wing, your phone calls will be returned more rapidly and your requests for information or action will be taken more seriously."[30]

Presidential assistants carry the contigent authority of the president, authority that is essential to accomplish anything at all since under the law presidential assistants have no authority of their own. But presidential authority is undermined if numerous people attempt to exercise it.

Excessively vigorous staff involvement in implementation decisions may cause other problems. For example, some observers of recent presidential administrations have concluded that as larger numbers of bright, ambitious, energetic assistants probe into the activities of departments and agencies, they will bring more issues for decision to the president, issues that were formerly decided at lower levels in the bureaucracy. Bureaucrats will begin to pass the buck upward, and more and more decisions must then be made by the White House. This can easily make the Executive Office of the President top-heavy and slow. Involvement in the minutiae of government also may divert resources (including time) from the central objectives and major problems of a president's adminis-tration. In addition, if White House aides become intimately involved in the management of government programs, they may lose the objectivity necessary to evaluate new ideas regarding "their" programs.

Overcentralization of decision making at the highest levels may have other negative consequences. It may discourage capable people from serving in government posts where their authority is frequently undercut. It may lower morale and engender resentment and hostility in the bureaucracy. This may impede future cooperation; decrease respect for lower officials among their subordinates; reduce the time bureau-cratic officials have for internal management because they must fight to maintain access to and support of the chief executive; and weaken the capability of agencies to streamline or revitalize their management. Simi-larly, too much monitoring of subordinates' behavior may elicit hostility or excessive caution and lack of imagination in administering policy.

Another factor inhibiting follow-up is secrecy. Secretly executed poli-cies, such as those implemented by the CIA, require few reports to Congress or to superiors in the executive branch. Consequently, officials' actions are not routinely monitored. Since members of Congress risk criticism for violating national security if they make public any secret information, they are reluctant to do so and have incentives to forgo their responsibility for oversight and follow-up of certain secret policies. When President Johnson's fear of leaks regarding decisions on the Viet-nam War led him to restrict his direct communications to a few top officials (the Tuesday lunch group), he did without a prearranged agenda or minutes of the meetings which would have recorded deci-sions and made possible follow-up on them.

An organization's personnel may be aware of implementation prob-lems but fail to report them to the president or other administration officials. There are several reasons for this. An obvious one, which we noted earlier, is that subordinates may fear that reporting implementa-tion failures will reflect poorly on their own performance and also possi-bly anger their superiors. Employees may also have a natural loyalty to their organization or to others in the organization who might be hurt by their negative reports. Further, the informal norms against reporting negative information may be very strong. Thus, employees may with-hold information from their superiors to escape social ostracism in their peer groups. Finally, some bureaucrats may feel the president is simply too busy to bother with matters of policy implementation.

Even when information indicating poor policy implementation is available to the president and other top executive officials, they may fail to use it. Information coming from the field is often fragmentary, circumstantial, inconsistent, ambiguous, and unrepresentative—in sum, unreliable. In addition, we noted in the previous chapter that such information may be lost in the huge volume of information circulating in the executive branch. It is very difficult for the president to have a clear idea of how a complex policy is actually implemented.

Organizations may fail to report problems in policy implementation for political reasons, such as the fear of losing public or legislative support for their programs. Also, within some organizations rivalries between headquarters and field personnel make the latter reluctant to expose themselves to negative reactions to their implementation efforts.

Although there are limitations on performing follow-up properly, this does not mean follow-up cannot work. And we have seen substantial evidence that it needs to be done. One study found that the Nixon administration's efforts to monitor and evaluate the actions of welfare caseworkers, especially to review them for errors that allowed ineligible persons to receive funds under the Aid to Families with Dependent Children program, had a significant influence on reducing the number of persons receiving welfare. (Unfortunately, it appears that this approach also resulted in many eligible persons not receiving welfare payments.)[31]

The Reagan administration made headway in monitoring agency regulations when it required the Office of Management and Budget (OMB) to review all regulations proposed by executive agencies. This procedure allows the president to influence or block individual regulations more effectively than before. An additional requirement is that agencies inform OMB of upcoming regulations, which aids the White House in preempting the proposal of regulations it opposes or influencing them before they are proposed (when the political costs of opposition are less). Finally, the White House requires agencies to provide cost-benefit analyses of their proposed regulations. Since this type of analysis is often as much art as it is science, ideological preferences may determine the conclusions, which in turn may be used to resist regulations to which the administration is opposed.[32]

CONCLUSION

The president faces many obstacles in implementing public policies. Although he is the "chief executive," he typically is not in a position to command his own branch's bureaucracy. Moreover, he operates in an environment of scarce resources and few incentives to devote time and energy to implementation. The president emerges from this process as a facilitator rather than a director.

Improving implementation will be very difficult. The roots of most implementation problems are embedded deeply in the fabric of American government and politics, as we have seen. Moreover, as long as presidents remain more concerned with shaping legislation to pass in the Congress than with the implementation of the law after it is passed, as long as they persist in emphasizing public relations rather than policy, and as long as "crisis" situations continue to dominate their time, little progress is likely to be made in improving policy implementation. Moreover, until there are more political incentives for officials to devote more attention to policy implementation and to develop better administrative skills, these priorities probably will not change. Given both the low visibility of many policy implementation activities and the lack of interest in them, the prospects for a change in incentives are not very favorable.

NOTES

1. Lawrence F. O'Brien, *No Final Victories* (New York: Ballantine Books, 1974), p. 142.

2. John Kennedy, quoted in John Herbers, "Nixon's Presidency: Centralized Control," *The New York Times*, March 6, 1973, p. 20.

3. President Carter, quoted in G. Calvin Mackenzie, "Personnel Appointment Strategies in Post-War Presidential Administrations" (paper delivered at the Annual Meeting of the Midwest Political Science Association, Chicago, April 1980), introductory page.

4. Richard Cheney, quoted in Stephen J. Wayne, "Working in the White House: Psychological Dimensions of the Job" (paper delivered at the Annual Meeting of the Southern Political Science Association, New Orleans, Louisiana, November 1977), p. 10.

5. Quoted in Paul C. Light, *The President's Agenda: Domestic Policy Choice from Kennedy to Carter* (Baltimore: Johns Hopkins University Press, 1982), p. 145.

6. Quoted in ibid., p. 152.

7. David Gergen, quoted in "How Much Can Any Administration Do?" *Public Opinion* (December/January 1982): 56.

8. See, for example, William Safire, *Before the Fall: An Inside View of the Pre-Watergate White House* (New York: Doubleday, 1975), pp. 112–13, 285–87, 353, and 566–67; and H. R. Haldeman, *The Ends of Power* (New York: Times Books, 1978), pp. 58–59, 111–12, and 185–87.

9. See, for example, Henry Kissinger, *White House Years* (Boston: Little, Brown, 1979), pp. 26, 28–29, 45–46, 48, 141–42, 158–59, 264, 482, 729, 806, 879, 887, 900, 909, 917, and 994.

10. Ibid., pp. 28–29, 264, and 900.

11. Lyndon Johnson, quoted in Doris Kearns, *Lyndon Johnson and the American Dream* (New York: Harper and Row, 1976), p. 137.

12. Gerald R. Ford, "Imperiled, Not Imperial," *Time*, November 10, 1980, p. 30.

13. Melvin Laird, quoted in Seymour M. Hersh, *The Price of Power: Kissinger in the Nixon White House* (New York: Summit, 1983), pp. 235–36.

14. Richard M. Nixon, *RN: The Memoirs of Richard Nixon* (New York: Grosset and Dunlap, 1978), pp. 472–73, 513.

15. John F. Kennedy, quoted in Kenneth P. O'Donnell and David F. Powers, *Johnny, We Hardly Knew Ye: Memories of John Fitzgerald Kennedy* (New York: Pocket Books, 1972), p. 270.

16. Tim Craft, quoted in Dom Bonafede, "Carter Sounds Retreat from 'Cabinet Gov-

ernment,' " *National Journal,* November 18, 1978, pp. 1852–57; see also "Rafshoon and Co.," *Newsweek,* January 29, 1979, p. 23.

17. James P. Pfiffner, *The Strategic Presidency* (Chicago: Dorsey, 1988), p. 98.

18. Jimmy Carter, quoted in "Civil Service Reform," *Congressional Quarterly Weekly Report,* March 11, 1978, p. 660.

19. Richard L. Cole and David A. Caputo, "Presidential Control of the Senior Civil Service: Assessing the Strategies of the Nixon Years," *American Political Science Review* 73 (June 1979): 399–413.

20. Jimmy Carter, quoted in "Press Conference Text," *Congressional Quarterly Weekly Report,* March 11, 1978, p. 655.

21. Franklin D. Roosevelt, quoted in M. S. Eccles, *Beckoning Frontiers* (New York: Knopf, 1951), p. 336.

22. Quoted in Graham T. Allison, *Essence of Decision: Explaining the Cuban Missile Crisis* (Boston: Little, Brown, 1971), pp. 131–32.

23. *Report of the DOD Commission on Beirut International Airport Terrorist Act, October 23, 1983,* December 20, 1983, p. 133.

24. Jimmy Carter, quoted in "Carter Criticizes Federal Bureaucracy," *Congressional Quarterly Weekly Report,* June, 3, 1978, p. 1421.

25. Ibid.

26. Richard Nixon, "Government Reorganization—Message from the President," in Stanley Bach and George T. Sulzner, eds., *Perspectives on the Presidency: A Collection* (Lexington, Mass.: Heath, 1974), p. 257.

27. William Colby, *Honorable Men: My Life in the CIA* (New York: Norton, 1975), pp. 101–02.

28. Ibid., pp. 440–41; and "Intelligence Failures, CIA Misdeeds Studied," *Congressional Quarterly Weekly Report,* September 20, 1975, p. 2025.

29. Safire, *Before the Fall,* pp. 250–60.

30. Quoted in Wayne, "Working in the White House," pp. 16–17.

31. Ronald Randall, "Presidential Power versus Bureaucratic Intransigence: The Influence of the Nixon Administration on Welfare Policy," *American Political Science Review* 73 (September 1979): 795–810.

32. Joseph Cooper and William W. West, "Presidential Power and Republican Government: The Theory and Practice of OMB Review of Agency Rules," *Journal of Politics* 50 (November 1988): 864–95.

SELECTED READINGS

Aberbach, Joel D., and Bert A. Rockman. "Clashing Beliefs within the Executive Branch: The Nixon Administration Bureaucracy." *American Political Science Review* 70 (June 1976): 456–68.

Allison, Graham. *Essence of Decision.* Boston: Little, Brown, 1971.

Chambers, Raymond L. "The Executive Power: A Preliminary Study of the Concept and Efficacy of Presidential Directives." *Presidential Studies Quarterly* 7 (Winter 1977): 21–36.

Cole, Richard L., and David A. Caputo. "Presidential Control of the Senior Civil Service: Assessing the Strategies of the Nixon Years." *American Political Science Review* 73 (June 1979): 399–413.

Cooper, Joseph, and William W. West. "Presidential Power and Republican Government: The Theory and Practice of OMB Review of Agency Rules." *Journal of Politics* 50 (November 1988): 864–95.

Edwards, George C., III. *Implementing Public Policy.* Washington, D.C.: Congressional Quarterly, 1980.

Heclo, Hugh. *A Government of Strangers: Executive Politics in Washington.* Washington, D.C.: Brookings Institution, 1977.

Jones, Charles O. *Clean Air.* Pittsburgh: University of Pittsburgh Press, 1975.

Kaufman, Herbert. *Administrative Feedback.* Washington, D.C.: Brookings Institution, 1973.

Mackenzie, G. Calvin. *The In-and-Outers.* Baltimore: Johns Hopkins University Press, 1987.

Macy, John W., Bruce Adams, and J. Jackson Walter. *America's Unelected Government: Appointing the President's Team.* Cambridge, Mass.: Ballinger, 1983.

Malek, Frederic V. *Washington's Hidden Tragedy: The Failure to Make Government Work.* New York: Free Press, 1978.

Mazmanian, Daniel, and Jeanne Nienaber. *Can Organizations Change? Environmental Protection, Citizen Participation, and the Corps of Engineers.* Washington, D.C.: Brookings Institution, 1979.

Moore, Mark H. "Reorganization Plan #2 Reviewed: Problems in Implementing a Strategy to Reduce the Supply of Drugs to Illicit Markets in the United States." *Public Policy* 26 (Spring 1978): 229–62.

Nathan, Richard P. *The Administrative Presidency.* New York: Wiley, 1983.

Peterson, Paul E., Barry G. Rabe, and Kenneth K. Wong. *When Federalism Works.* Washington, D.C.: Brookings Institution, 1986.

Radin, Beryl A., and Willis D. Hawley. *The Politics of Federal Reorganization.* New York: Pergamon Press, 1988.

Rose, Richard. *Managing Presidential Objectives.* New York: Free Press, 1976.

Sapolsky, Harvey M. *The Polaris System Development: Bureaucratic and Programmatic Success in Government.* Cambridge, Mass.: Harvard University Press, 1972.

Williams, Walter, et al. *Studying Implementation: Methodological and Administrative Issues.* Chatham, N.J.: Chatham House, 1982.

Wood, Dan B. "Principals, Bureaucrats, and Responsiveness in Clean Air Enforcement." *American Political Science Review* 82 (March 1988): 213–34.

10

The President
and Congress

If one were to write a job description of the presidency, near the top of the list of presidential responsibilities would be that of working with Congress. According to Lyndon Johnson, "There is only one way for a President to deal with Congress, and that is continuously, incessantly, and without interruption."[1] Since our system of separation of powers is really one of *shared* powers, the president can rarely operate independently of Congress. Although he requires the cooperation of Congress, he cannot depend on it. Thus, one of the president's most difficult and frustrating tasks is trying to persuade Congress to support his policies.

The differences in our contrasting views of presidential leadership are perhaps most clear in the area of executive–legislative relations. The director president will dominate Congress, reliably obtaining its support for his policies and precluding legislative initiatives to which he is opposed. The facilitator, on the other hand, will find the going much tougher. He will often fail to achieve his legislative goals and almost always have to struggle to win at all. Congress may pass major legislation over his opposition. Frustration and stalemate will characterize such a presidency.

In this chapter we examine the president's leadership of Congress. Because it is important to understand the context of presidential–congressional interaction, we begin with a discussion of the president's formal legislative powers and the inevitable sources of conflict between the two branches. We then move to an examination of the potential sources of presidential influence in Congress, including party leadership, public support, and legislative skills. In our discussion we emphasize both how presidents attempt to persuade members of Congress and the utility of each source of influence.

FORMAL LEGISLATIVE POWERS

Presidents today have a central role in the legislative process. They are expected to formulate and promote policies. They are expected to coordinate them within the executive branch, to introduce them to Congress, and to mobilize support for them on Capitol Hill and, increasingly, with the general public.

These expectations suggest a broad scope of legislative authority for the president. In actuality, his constitutional powers are quite limited. Only four duties and responsibilities were designated by Article 2: (1) to inform Congress from time to time on the state of the union; (2) to recommend necessary and expedient legislation; (3) to summon Congress into special session and adjourn it if the two houses cannot agree on adjournment; and (4) to exercise a qualified veto.

With the exception of the veto, these responsibilities stem primarily from the president's unique position within the political system: the only official other than the vice president who was to have continuous tenure, a national perspective, and the ability to respond quickly and decisively to emergencies. As the framers of the Constitution saw it, these job-related qualifications placed the president in a unique position to inform Congress, to recommend legislation, and to summon it into session if necessary.

The rationale for the veto was different. Justified within the Constitutional Convention as a defensive weapon, it was proposed as a device by which the president could prevent his powers from being usurped by the legislature. The founders feared that the institutional balance would become undone and that the Congress would be the likely perpetrator. The extent to which their fears were justified and the use of the veto as a political and constitutional weapon are examined later in this chapter.

Over the years presidents have used their legislative responsibilities to enlarge their congressional influence. The State of the Union message is a good example. In the nineteenth century it was a routine message dealing primarily with the actions of the executive departments and agencies for the previous year. Beginning with Jefferson and continuing through Theodore Roosevelt, the address was sent to the Congress to be read by the clerk of the House and then distributed to the members. Woodrow Wilson revived the practice of the first two presidents and delivered the speech himself. Subsequently, presidents have timed the address to maximize its public exposure. Today it is an important vehicle by which presidents can articulate the legislative goals of their administrations, recite their accomplishments, present their agenda, and try to mobilize support for their programs.

Similarly, presidents have transformed their responsibility to recommend necessary and expedient legislation into an annual agenda-setting function. While nineteenth-century presidents formulated some legislative proposals and even drafted bills in the White House, it was not until the twentieth century that the practice of presidential programming developed on a regular basis. Wilson and Franklin Roosevelt submitted comprehensive legislative proposals to Congress. Truman packaged them in the State of the Union address. With the exception of Eisenhower in his first year in office, every subsequent president has followed the Truman tradition.

To some extent the Congress has found the president's legislative initiatives advantageous. In some cases it has insisted upon them. For example, the 1921 Budget and Accounting Act, the 1946 Employment Act, and the 1974 Budget Act require the president to provide Congress with annual reports and an annual executive budget.

The calling of special sessions by the president has fallen into disuse. The length of the current legislative year combined with changes in the calendar have made this function largely obsolete. The last special session occurred in 1948. In the past, however, presidents frequently would call special sessions after their inauguration to gain support for their objectives and to initiate "their" Congress. Until the passage of the Twentieth Amendment in 1933, Congress began its session on or about December 1. This made every other session of Congress "a lame duck" and forced a newly elected president to wait nine months for the newly elected Congress. Between the Lincoln and Franklin Roosevelt administrations there were nineteen special sessions.

SOURCES OF CONFLICT BETWEEN THE EXECUTIVE AND LEGISLATIVE BRANCHES

The president must influence Congress because he generally cannot act without its consent. Under our constitutional system of separation of powers, Congress must pass legislation and can override vetoes. The Senate must ratify treaties and confirm presidential appointments to the cabinet, the federal courts, regulatory commissions, and other high offices. Yet these overlapping powers do not explain the president's need to influence Congress. Theoretically, the two branches *could* be in agreement. In fact, the president and some members of Congress will always disagree because of their personalities or past histories. Yet these differences are not the source of systematic conflict. The source lies in the structure and processes of American politics.

In "The Federalist No. 46," James Madison focused on the greatest source of conflict between the president and Congress: their different constituencies.

> The members of the federal legislature will likely attach themselves too much to local objects. . . . Measures will too often be decided according to their probable effect, not on the national prosperity and happiness, but on the prejudices, interests, and pursuits of the governments and the people of the individual states.[2]

Only the president (and his vice presidential running mate) is chosen in a national election. Each member of Congress is elected by only a fraction of the populace. Inevitably, the president must form a broader electoral coalition in order to win his office than any member of Congress. Moreover, two-thirds of the senators are not elected at the same time as the president, and the remaining senators and all the House members seem to be increasingly insulated from the causes of presidential victories. In addition, the Senate overrepresents rural states because each state has two senators regardless of its population. Thus, the whole that the president represents is different from the sum of the parts that each legislator represents. Each member of Congress will give special access to the interests that he or she represents, but Congress as a body has more difficulty representing the nation as a whole.

The internal structures of the executive and legislative branches also cause differences between the president and Congress. The executive branch is hierarchically organized, facilitating the president's examining a broad range of viewpoints on an issue and then weighing and balancing various interests. This structure also helps the president to view the trade-offs among various policies. Since one person, the president, must support all the major policies emanating from the executive branch, he is virtually forced to take a comprehensive view of those policies.

On the other hand, each house of Congress is highly decentralized. The party structure is not a unifying force within the United States legislature, as we shall see later. Committee memberships are frequently unrepresentative of each chamber, and members of each committee may defer to members of the other committees. Thus, members representing special interests have a disproportionate say over policy regarding those interests.

One of the functions of decentralizing power and responsibility in Congress is to allow for specialization in various policy areas. However, because of specialization, legislators make decisions in form only about many of the policies with which Congress must deal. In actuality they tend to rely upon the cues of party leaders, state party delegations, relevant committee leaders of their party, and other colleagues to decide how to vote. These cue givers, however, are chosen because they represent constituencies or ideologies that are similar to those of the member who is consulting them. They do not represent a cross section of viewpoints.

Members of Congress are not generally in a position to make trade-offs between policies. Because of its decentralization, Congress usually considers policies serially, that is, without reference to other policies. Without an integrating mechanism, members have few means by which to set and enforce priorities and to emphasize the policies with which the president is most concerned, particularly when Congress is controlled by the opposition party. In addition, Congress has little capability, except within the context of the budget, to examine two policies, like education and health care, in relation to each other. Not knowing that giving up something on one policy will result in a greater return on another policy, members have little incentive to engage in trade-offs. Congress is also poorly organized to deal comprehensively with major policy domains. It distributes its workload among committees with jurisdictions that often do not cover entire policy areas such as welfare, national security, or economic stability.

Thus, while the structure of Congress ensures that a diversity of views will be heard and that many interests will have access to the legislative process, it does not follow that *each* member will hear all the views and see the proponents of each interest. Indeed, the decentralization of Congress almost guarantees that the information available to it as a whole is not a synthesis of the information available to each legislator. The Congress as a whole does not ask questions; individual members do. Thus, not all members receive the answers.

The hierarchical structure of the executive branch, with the president at the pinnacle, forces the president to take responsibility for the entire executive branch. Moreover, when the president exercises power, it is clear who is acting and who should be held accountable. Congress, on the other hand, is not responsible for implementing policies, and each member is relatively obscure compared with the president. Since Congress is so decentralized, any member can disclaim responsibility for policies or their consequences. Members of Congress, therefore, can and do make irresponsible or self-serving decisions and then let the president take the blame.

All of this can be very frustrating to the president. As Gerald Ford, who spent most of his adult life in Congress, wrote after leaving the White House:

> When I was in the Congress myself, I thought it fulfilled its constitutional obligations in a very responsible way, but after I became President, my perspective changed. It seemed to me that Congress was beginning to disintegrate as an organized legislative body. It wasn't answering the nation's challenges domestically because it was too fragmented. It responded too often to single-issue special interest groups and it therefore wound up dealing with minutiae instead of attacking serious problems in a coherent way.[3]

Another source of conflict between the president and Congress is the difference in information and expertise available to them. Despite the substantial increase in congressional staff in recent years, including the expansion or addition of analytic units such as the General Accounting Office, the Congressional Research Service in the Library of Congress, the Office of Technology Assessment, and the Congressional Budget Office, members of Congress rarely have available to them expertise of the quantity and quality that is available to the president.

Aside from the fact that the executive branch includes 5 million civilian and military employees plus hundreds of advisory committees while Congress employs only about 30,000 persons (including supporting agencies), the expertise of the two branches differs. Members of Congress tend to hire generalists, even on committee staffs. Some individuals develop great expertise in a particular field, but others may only be amateurs compared with their counterparts in the executive branch. Many are selected to serve legislators' needs and desires, which have little to do with policy analysis, and neither house has a merit system, a tenured career service, or a central facility for recruiting the best available talent.

Because the president and Congress have different information and expertise available to them, they may well see issues from different perspectives. The president's views will generally be buttressed with more data and handled more expertly. This may give him different views and more confidence in his views.

We have seen that the structure of American government exerts strong pressure on the two branches to represent different sets of interests and to view policies differently. This, in turn, sets the stage for conflict and virtually compels a president to try to influence Congress.

PARTY LEADERSHIP

"What the Constitution separates our political parties do not combine."[4] Richard Neustadt wrote these words three decades ago to help explain why presidents could not simply assume support from the members of their party in Congress. The challenge of presidential party leadership in Congress remains just as great and is just as important today as it was when Neustadt wrote his famous treatise on presidential power.

Party Support of the President

Representatives and senators of the president's party are almost always the nucleus of coalitions supporting the president's programs. As one White House aide put it: "You turn to your party members first. If we couldn't move our own people, we felt the opportunities were pretty slim."[5] No matter what other resources a president may have, without seats in Congress held by his party, he will usually find it very difficult to move his legislative program through Congress. Thus, leading his party in Congress is the president's principal task as he seeks to counter the tendencies of the executive and legislative branches toward conflict inherent in the system of checks and balances.

Tables 10-1 and 10-2 show the support given presidents by members of each party on roll-call votes on which the presidents took a stand. Clearly, there is a substantial difference between the levels of support

Table 10-1. Presidential Support by Party, 1953–1986 (in percentages)*

Year	President's Party	House		Senate	
		Democrats	Republicans	Democrats	Republicans
1953	R	45%	70%	42%	66%
1954	R	34	74	36	74
1955	R	42	52	37	70
1956	R	38	72	35	69
1957	R	48	52	44	69
1958	R	52	55	37	66
1959	R	34	72	28	73
1960	R	46	64	41	66
1961	D	73	26	68	31
1962	D	72	30	64	31
1963	D	75	21	63	37
1964	D	78	26	63	56
1965	D	75	24	64	44
1966	D	67	20	53	35
1967	D	70	28	56	42
1968	D	63	36	46	41
1969	R	48	57	42	65
1970	R	41	60	35	63
1971	R	41	71	33	65
1972	R	46	68	34	66
1973	R	31	65	24	64
1974	R	38	59	31	53
1975	R	37	68	36	67
1976	R	32	67	29	62
1977	D	61	32	62	39
1978	D	65	34	64	36
1979	D	64	26	67	39
1980	D	63	31	60	38
1981	R	39	72	33	81
1982	R	30	61	35	72
1983	R	28	71	39	73
1984	R	32	66	31	74
1985	R	28	68	27	76
1986	R	23	72	26	80

*On roll-call votes on which the winning side was supported by fewer than 80 percent of those voting.
R = Republican
D = Democrat

Source: George C. Edwards III, *At the Margins: Presidential Leadership of Congress* (New Haven, Conn.: Yale University Press, 1989), table 3.1.

presidents receive from members of the two parties, with the gap generally exceeding 25 percentage points. Four Republican and three Democratic presidents are covered by the tables, and although the presidents of each party varied considerably in their policies, personalities, and

Table 10-2. Partisan Support for Presidents, 1953–1986 (in percentages)*

	Presidents		
	Democratic	Republican	Difference
House			
Democrats	69%	28%	41†
Republicans	38	65	27
Senate			
Democrats	61	39	22
Republicans	35	68	33

*On roll-call votes on which the winning side was supported by fewer than 80 percent of those voting.
†Differences expressed as percentage points.

Source: George C. Edwards III, *At the Margins: Presidential Leadership of Congress* (New Haven, Conn.: Yale University Press, 1989), table 3.3.

political environments, their fellow partisans in Congress gave them considerably more support than they gave presidents of the opposition party.

With a president of their own in the White House, party members in Congress may alter their voting tendencies. For example, Republicans have a tendency to be more supportive of internationalist foreign policies when a Republican is president. They are also more likely to accept governmental economic activity under a Republican president. Democrats, on the other hand, have a tendency to move in the opposite direction when the opposition controls the presidency. In 1981, with a conservative Republican in the White House, many Republicans in Congress shifted to supporting foreign aid and increasing the national debt ceiling even though they had opposed these policies under the previous Democratic administration of Jimmy Carter. Similarly, many members of the president's party who voted for a bill when it was originally passed switch and vote against the same legislation if their party leader vetoes it.

Although the president receives more support from members of his party than from the opposition, this is not necessarily due to their shared party affiliation. It is difficult to tell whether a member of the president's party votes for the president's policies because of shared party affiliation, basic agreement with those policies, or some other factor. Undoubtedly, members of the same party share many policy preferences and have similar electoral coalitions supporting them. In 1981 President Reagan won several crucial votes in Congress on his taxing and spending proposals. He was immediately credited with extraordinary party leadership because nearly 100 percent of the Republicans in Congress supported his programs. If we examine voting on budget resolutions under Democrat Jimmy Carter, however, we find nearly the same degree of Republican party unity in the House. Thus, we should not necessarily ascribe Reagan's success to party loyalty. Republican members of the House had been voting a conservative line well before Ronald Reagan came to Washington.

Despite the proclivity of members of Congress to support presidents of their party, the White House also experiences substantial slippage in party cohesion in Congress. Table 10-2 shows that presidents can count on their own party members for support no more than two-thirds of the time (even on key votes). This forces them to adopt an activist orientation toward party leadership and to devote as much effort to converting party members to support them as to mobilizing members of their party who already agree with them.

Leading the Party

That members of the president's own party are more open to his influence is clear. Members of the president's party typically have personal loyalties or emotional commitments to their party and their party leader, which the president can often translate into votes when necessary. Thus, members of the president's party vote with him when they can, giving him the benefit of the doubt, especially if their own opinion on an issue is weak. Moreover, this proclivity for supporting the president increases the effectiveness of other sources of party influence.

One of these sources is the desire of members of the presidential party not to embarrass "their" administration. This attitude stems from two motivations. The first is related to the sentiments discussed above, but the second is more utilitarian. Members of the president's party have an incentive to make him look good because his standing in the public may influence their own chances for reelection. A president may also find it easier to obtain party unity behind his program if his party regains control of one or both houses of Congress at the time of his election. Many new members may feel a sense of gratification for the president's coattails. Moreover, the prospect of exercising the power to govern may provide a catalyst for party loyalty while the loss of power may temporarily demoralize the opposition party. All of the motivations to support the president are, of course, buttressed by basic distrust of the opposition party.

WORKING WITH CONGRESSIONAL LEADERS.   Each party has a set of floor and committee leaders in the House and Senate, and in theory they should be a valuable resource for their party's leader in the White House. The president needs both their advice and their resources for making head counts and other administrative chores. Because of their role perceptions, because their reputations for passing legislation give them a clear stake in the president's success, and because they are susceptible to the same sentiments and pressures toward party loyalty as are other members of Congress, floor leaders of the president's party in

Congress are usually very supportive of the White House. In the month before Ronald Reagan's inauguration, the new Senate majority leader, Howard Baker, declared, "I intend to try to help Ronald Reagan [carry out] the commitments he made during the campaign."[6]

Yet party floor leaders are not always dependable supporters. They certainly are not simply extensions of the White House. Senate Majority Leader Mike Mansfield broke with President Johnson over the war in Vietnam and sustained his opposition for the rest of Johnson's term in office. There is little the White House can do in such a situation. Presidents do not lobby for candidates for congressional party leadership positions and virtually always remain neutral during the selection process. They have no desire to alienate important members of Congress whose support they will need.

Similarly, committee chairpersons and ranking minority members are usually determined by seniority. Furthermore, the chairpersons always come from the majority party in the chamber, which often is not the president's. For all practical purposes, the president plays no role at all in determining the holders of these important positions. Moreover, the norm of supporting a president of one's party is weaker for committee leaders than for floor leaders.

Presidents and their staff typically work closely with their party's legislative leaders, meeting regularly for breakfast when Congress is in session. Sometimes these meetings include the leaders of the opposition party as well. These gatherings provide opportunities for an exchange of views and for the president to keep communication channels open and maintain morale. The significance of these efforts has varied, however. On one extreme, Nixon's meetings were often pro forma, serving more as a symbolic ritual than a mechanism for leadership. On the other, Johnson used them as strategy sessions, integrating congressional leaders into the White House legislative liaison operation.

Equally as important as the congressional party leaders' relations with the president are their relations with their party colleagues in Congress. Major changes have occurred in the past fifteen years that have weakened the ability of party leaders to produce votes for the president. According to Gerald Ford:

> Today a President really does not have the kind of clout with the Congress that he had 30 years ago, even in matters that affect national security. There is not the kind of teamwork that existed in the '50s, even if the President and a majority of the Congress belong to the same party.
>
> The main reason for this change is the erosion of the leadership in the Congress. Party leaders have lost the power to tell their troops that something is really significant and to get them to respond accordingly. The days of Sam Rayburn, Lyndon Johnson and Everett Dirksen are gone. That has adversely affected the Congress's ability to do things even in very difficult circumstances involving the national interest.[7]

One reason that party leaders have lost much of their power over their "followers" is the increased dispersion of power in Congress, especially the House. The face of Congress has changed over the past two decades. Seniority is no longer an automatic path to committee or subcommittee chairs, and chairpersons must be more responsive to the desires of committee members. There are also more subcommittees and more subcommittee chairpersons now, and these subcommittees have a more important role in handling legislation. While the power of subcommittees has increased, that of the southern oligarchies has declined. Members of both parties have larger personal, committee, and subcommittee staffs at their disposal as well as new service adjuncts such as the Congressional Budget Office. This new freedom and these additional resources, combined with more opportunities to amend legislation, make it easier for members of Congress to challenge the White House and the congressional leadership and to provide alternatives to the president's policies.

The president's program is also now subject to more cross-cutting demands within Congress as a result of split and joint committee referrals for some legislation. This further complicates the task of influencing members of Congress, because it is difficult to lobby several committees at once with the limited resources available to the president.

Yet other reforms have increased the burden of leaders. The increased number of roll-call votes and thus the increased visibility of representatives' voting behavior have generated more pressure on House members to abandon party loyalty, making it more difficult for the president to gain passage of legislation. Reforms that have opened committee and subcommittee hearings to the public have had the same effect. There has also been a heavy turnover in the personnel of Congress in recent years, and new members have brought with them new approaches to legislating. They are less likely to adopt the norms of apprenticeship and specialization than were their predecessors in their first terms. Instead, they have eagerly taken an active role in all legislation. They place a heavy emphasis on individualism and much less on party regularity.

Thus, congressional party leaders now have more decision makers to influence. They can no longer rely on dealing with the congressional aristocracy and expect the rest of the members to follow. According to one Johnson assistant:

> In 1965, there were maybe ten or twelve people who you needed to corral in the House and Senate. Without those people, you were in for a tough time. Now, I'd put that figure upwards of one hundred. Believe it, there are so many people who have a shot at derailing a bill that the President has to double his effort for even routine decisions.[8]

Although the party leadership at least in theory possesses sanctions that it can exercise to enforce party discipline, including exercising discretion on committee assignments, patronage, campaign funds, trips abroad, and aid with members' pet bills, in reality this discretion exists primarily on paper. Most rewards are considered a matter of right, and it is the leadership's job to see that they are distributed equitably. Party leaders do not dare to withhold benefits because they fear being overturned by the rank and file. Senate Majority Leader Robert Dole sometimes termed his position that of "majority pleader." Threats of sanctions in such a situation are unconvincing and thus rarely occur.

OBSTACLES TO PARTY UNITY.   The primary obstacle to party cohesion in support of the president is the lack of consensus among his party's members on policies, especially if the president happens to be a Democrat. This diversity of views often reflects the diversity of constituencies represented by party members. The frequent defection from support of Democratic presidents by the conservative southern Democrats, or "boll weevils," is one of the most prominent features of American politics. Under presidents Kennedy, Johnson, and Carter there was approximately a 25 percentage point difference between northern and southern Democrats in support of the presidents. When constituency opinion and the president's proposals conflict, members of Congress are more likely to vote with their constituencies, to whom they must return for reelection.

Republican presidents often lack stable coalitions as well. As we noted earlier, Ronald Reagan received nearly unanimous support from his party on his 1981 proposals to reduce taxes and expenditures. The next year, when he proposed legislation to increase taxes, to restrict abortions and forced busing for integration, and to allow school prayer, things were different. Republicans were in the forefront of the opposition to these policies.

The issues of the 1970s and 1980s, such as energy, welfare reform, social security financing, deregulation, containment of medical costs, and the social issues mentioned above lack either sizable constituencies, common underlying principles, or both. Yet these are necessary to provide the basis for consensus among party members.

A shift in the status of party members may present another obstacle to party unity. Just as regaining power may encourage party unity, having to share it may strain intraparty relations. When a party that has had a majority in Congress regains the White House, committee and floor leaders of that party will typically be less influential because they will be expected to take their lead on major issues from the president. This may cause tensions within the party, and make party discipline more difficult.

Yet other obstacles may confront a president trying to mobilize his party in Congress. If the president's party has just regained the presidency but remains a minority in Congress, its members need to adjust from their past stance as the opposition minority to one of a "governing" minority. This is not always easily done, however, as Richard Nixon found when he sought Republican votes for budget deficits.

Further difficulties may stem from the fact that the winning presidential candidate may not be the natural leader of his party. Indeed, as in the case of Jimmy Carter, he may have campaigned against the party establishment and not identified with whatever party program existed. Such a new president may arrive in Washington in an atmosphere of hostility and suspicion that is not conducive to intraparty harmony. Appeals for party loyalty under such conditions may fall on less than receptive ears.

MIDTERM ELECTION CAMPAIGNING.   Members of Congress who are of the president's party are more likely to support him than are members of the opposition party, and presidents do their best to exploit the potential of partisan support. Nevertheless, such actions are inevitably at the margins of coalition building, because they take place within the confines of the partisan balance of the Congress. To exploit fully the benefits of party leadership, a president needs as many of his fellow partisans in Congress as possible. Once members of Congress are elected, however, they almost never change their party affiliation, and the rare instances when they do have not resulted from presidential persuasion. Thus, if presidents are to alter the party composition of Congress, they must help to elect additional members of their party. One way to try to accomplish this goal is to campaign for candidates in midterm congressional elections.

Sometimes presidents are so unpopular that the candidates of their party do not want their support. President Johnson adopted a low profile during the 1966 campaign because of his lack of public support (below 50 percent in the Gallup Poll). In 1974, before he resigned, President Nixon wanted invitations to campaign for Republicans to prove that he wasn't political poison, but he had few offers as the Watergate crisis reached a head.

Nevertheless, modern presidents have often taken an active role in midterm congressional elections. In 1970, President Nixon was heavily involved in the congressional elections. He chose Vice President Agnew to carry the main burden of making speeches and offered him the services of several White House aides and speech writers. Nevertheless, behind the scenes Nixon was running the show, making strategic decisions such as selecting issues to raise and to avoid, labeling particular Democratic candidates as "radicals," encouraging people (mostly representatives) to run for the Senate, and deciding whom to support. He also made numerous campaign speeches. President Carter also was an active campaigner in 1978, speaking on behalf of Democratic candidates all across the country. Ronald Reagan did the same in 1982, although some candidates asked him to stay away because of the recession, with which many voters identified him. In 1986 he stumped the country in an unsuccessful effort to preserve the Republican majority in the Senate.

Presidential efforts in midterm elections have had quite limited success. As Table 10-3 shows, a recurring feature of American politics is the decrease in representation of the president's party in Congress in midterm congressional elections. We can also see this as far back as Woodrow Wilson's efforts in 1918, which were rewarded by the loss of both houses of Congress.

PRESIDENTIAL COATTAILS.   Another way in which the president may influence the partisan composition of Congress is through his coattails. Presidential coattails are part of the lore of American politics. Politicians project them in their calculations, journalists attribute them in their reporting, historians recount them, and political scientists analyze them. Yet we really know little about coattails. Most significantly, we have limited understanding of how they affect the outcomes in congressional elections. A coattail victory is a victory for a representative of the president's party in which presidential coattail votes provide the increment of the vote necessary to win the seat.

Coattail victories, whether they bring in new members or preserve the seats of incumbents, can have significant payoffs for the president in terms of support for the administration's programs. Those members of the president's party who won close elections may provide him an extra increment of support out of a sense of gratitude for the votes they perceive they received due to presidential coattails or out of a sense of responsiveness to their constituents' support for the president.

Yet research has found that the outcomes of very few congressional races are determined by presidential coattails—fewer than ten House seats in a typical election.[9] In 1988 George Bush won election while his

Table 10-3. Changes in Congressional Representation of the President's Party in Midterm Elections

Year	House		Senate	
	Losses	*Gains*	*Losses*	*Gains*
1954	18	0	1	0
1958	47	0	13	0
1962	4	0	0	3
1966	47	0	4	0
1970	12	0	0	2
1974	47	0	5	0
1978	15	0	3	0
1982	26	0	0	0
1986	5	0	8	0

party actually lost seats in both houses of Congress. Most House seats are too safe for a party, and especially for an incumbent, to have the election outcome affected by the presidential election.

Thus, presidents cannot expect personally to carry like-minded running mates into office to provide additional support for their programs. On the contrary, rather than being amenable to voting for the president's policies due to shared convictions, representatives are free to focus on parochial matters and to respond to narrow constituency interests. Similarly, although we cannot know the extent to which representatives have felt gratitude to presidents for their coattails and thus have given them additional legislative support in the past, we do know that any such gratitude is rarely warranted. The more representatives are aware of the independence of their elections from the president's, the less likely they are to feel that they must "thank" the president with an additional increment of support.

BIPARTISANSHIP.   On July 27, 1981, President Reagan delivered an exceptionally important and effective televised address to the nation seeking the public's support for his tax cut bill. In it he went to great lengths to present his plan as "bipartisan." It was crucial that he convince the public that this controversial legislation was supported by members of both parties and was therefore, by implication, fair. Thus, he described it as "bipartisan" *eleven* times in the span of a few minutes! No one was to miss the point. The president required the votes of Democrats in the House to pass his bill, and he wanted their constituents to apply pressure to them to support it.

Despite a president's advantage in dealing with members of his party in Congress, he is often forced to solicit bipartisan support. There are several reasons for this. First, the opposition party may control one or both houses of Congress. Even if the president received total support from all members of his party, he would still need support from some members of the opposition. Between 1953 and 1990 Republican presidents faced a Democratic House of Representatives for twenty-four years and a Democratic Senate for eighteen years.

A second reason for bipartisanship is that no matter how large the representation of the president's party in Congress, he cannot always depend upon it for support. Tables 10-1 and 10-2 show clearly that members of the president's own party frequently oppose him. As Jimmy Carter wrote, "I learned the hard way that there was no party loyalty or discipline when a complicated or controversial issue was at stake— none."[10] Southern Democrats support Democratic presidents less consistently than do Northern Democrats.

Not only do partisan strategies often fail, but they also may provoke the other party into a more unified posture of opposition. "Where there is confrontation, there can be no consensus," and consensus is often required to legislate changes on important issues. The president is also inhibited in his partisanship by pressures to be "president of all the people" rather than a highly partisan figure. This role expectation of being somewhat above the political fray undoubtedly constrains presidents in their role as party leader.

Despite the frequent necessity of a bipartisan strategy, it is not without costs. Bipartisanship often creates a strain with the extremists within the president's party as a Republican president tries to appeal to the left for Democratic votes and a Democratic president to the right for Republican votes. Although it is true that the Republican right wing and Democratic left wing may find it difficult to forge a coalition in favor of alternatives to their own president's policies, it is not true that they must therefore support their president. Instead, they may complicate a president's strategy by joining those who oppose his policies.

The ultimate limitation on a bipartisan strategy is that, as Tables 10-1 and 10-2 demonstrate, the opposition party is generally not a fertile ground for obtaining policy support. Liberal Democratic presidents have often been frustrated in their efforts to deal with Republicans. Republican presidents also face obstacles to obtaining bipartisan support. Only twenty-three House Democrats supported Ronald Reagan on both the important budget and tax votes in 1981, despite the president's persuasive efforts, the perception that the president had a mandate, and the pull of ideology. Nevertheless, a president cannot ignore the opposition party and even a few votes may be enough to bring him a majority.

PUBLIC SUPPORT

Although congressional seats held by members of the president's party may be a necessary condition for presidential success in Congress, they are not a sufficient one. The president needs public support as well. In the words of Eisenhower aide and presidential authority Emmet John Hughes, "Beyond all tricks of history and all quirks of Presidents, there would appear to be one unchallengeable truth: the dependence of Presidential authority on popular support."[11]

Public Approval

In his memoirs, President Johnson wrote, "Presidential popularity is a major source of strength in gaining cooperation from Congress."[12] Thus, following his landslide electoral victory, he assembled the congressional liaison officials from the various departments and told them that his victory at the polls "might be more of a loophole than a mandate" and that since his popularity could decrease rapidly, they would have to use it to their advantage while it lasted.[13]

President Carter's aides were quite explicit about the importance of public approval in their efforts to influence Congress. One stated that the "only way to keep those guys [Congress] honest is to keep our popularity high."[14] The president's legislative liaison officials generally agreed that their effectiveness with Congress ultimately depended upon the president's ability to influence public opinion. As one of them said, "When you go up to the Hill and the latest polls show Carter isn't doing well, there isn't much reason for a member to go along with him. There's little we can do if the member isn't persuaded on the issue."[15] The Reagan administration was especially sensitive to the president's public approval levels. According to one top aide, "Everything here is built on the idea that the president's success depends on grassroots support."[16]

Why is presidential approval or popularity such an important source of influence in Congress? According to a senior aide to President Carter:

> When the President is low in public opinion polls, the Members of Congress see little hazard in bucking him. . . . After all, very few Congressmen examine an issue solely on its merits; they are politicians and they think politically. I'm not saying they make only politically expedient choices. But they read the polls and from that they feel secure in turning their backs on the President with political impunity. Unquestionably, the success of the President's policies bears a tremendous relationship to his popularity in the polls.[17]

The public's evaluations of the president may be taken as indicators of broader opinions on politics and policy. Moreover, members of Congress must anticipate the public's reactions to their support for or opposition to the president and his policies. They may choose to be close to or independent from the president, depending upon his public standing, to increase their chances of reelection. Polls find that a significant percentage of voters see their votes for candidates for Congress as support for or opposition to the president.[18] Members of Congress may also use the president's standing in the polls as an indicator of his ability to mobilize public opinion against his opponents.

Public approval operates mostly in the background and sets the limits of what Congress will do for or to the president. Widespread support gives him leeway and weakens resistance to his policies. It provides a cover for members of Congress to cast votes to which their constituents might otherwise object. They can defend their votes as support for the president rather than on substantive policy grounds alone.

Lack of public support strengthens the resolve of those inclined to oppose the president and narrows the range in which he receives the benefit of the doubt. In addition, low ratings in the polls may create incentives to attack the president, further eroding his already weakened position. For example, after the arms sales to Iran and the diversion of funds to the Contras became a *cause célèbre* in late 1986, it became more acceptable in Congress and in the press to raise questions about Ronald Reagan's capacities as president. Disillusionment is a dangerous phenomenon for the White House.

The impact of presidential approval on presidential support occurs at the margins of coalition building, within the confines of other influences. No matter how low a president's standing in public polls or how close his election, he still receives support from a substantial number of senators and representatives. Similarly, no matter how high his approval levels climb or how large his winning percentage of the vote, a significant portion of the Congress still opposes his policies. Members of Congress are unlikely to vote against the clear interests of their constituents or the firm tenets of their ideology out of deference to a widely supported chief executive. Approval gives a president leverage, not control.

Thus, public approval is a necessary but not a sufficient source of influence in Congress. It is most useful in combination with party supporters in each house of Congress. If either approval or seats are lacking, the president's legislative program will be in for rough sledding. The consequences of the absence of each source of influence are described by two presidential assistants, the first to Nixon and the second to Carter:

> Nineteen seventy-two did not help us. It was similar to Eisenhower in 1956. We had tremendous public and electoral support. But that and a dime couldn't buy a cup of coffee. It was still a question of what we didn't have: what we didn't have was enough Republican congressmen.

> The 292 Democrats in Congress were potential supporters—that was only three fewer than LBJ had. But with the close election and the drop in approval, they remained that way: potential. We couldn't force them to be active supporters.[19]

As the most volatile leadership resource, public approval is the factor most likely to determine whether or not an opportunity for policy change exists. Public approval makes other resources more efficacious. The president's party is more likely to be responsive if he is high in public esteem, the public is more easily moved, and legislative skills become more effective. Thus, public approval is the resource that has the most potential to turn a typical situation into one favorable for change.

The fact that presidential approval is an important potential source of influence in Congress provides a strong incentive for the president to try to gain popular support. But, as we learned earlier, presidential approval is an effective source of presidential influence, but not one he can manipulate easily.

Mandates

Another indicator of the public's opinion of the president is the results of the presidential election. Electoral mandates can be powerful symbols in American politics. They accord added legitimacy and credibility to the newly elected president's proposals. Moreover, concerns for both representation and political survival encourage members of Congress to support the president if they feel the people have spoken.

More importantly, mandates change the premises of decisions. Following the 1932 election, the essential question became how government should act to fight the depression rather than whether it should act. Similarly, following the 1964 election, the dominant question in Congress was not whether to pass new social programs. Instead, it was over the issues of how many to pass and how much to increase spending. In 1981 the tables were turned. Ronald Reagan's victory placed a stigma on big government and exalted the unregulated marketplace and large defense efforts. Reagan had won a major victory even before the first congressional vote.

Although presidential elections can structure choices for Congress, merely winning an election does not give a president a mandate. Every election produces a winner, but mandates are much less common. Even large electoral victories such as Richard Nixon's in 1972 and Ronald Reagan's in 1984 carry no guarantee that Congress will interpret the results as mandates from the people to support the president's programs, especially if the voters also elect majorities in Congress from the other party.

The winners in presidential elections usually claim to have been accorded a mandate, of course, but in the absence of certain conditions few observers accept these assertions at face value. Conditions that promote the perception of a mandate include a large margin of victory, the impression of long coattails, hyperbole in the press analyses of the election results exaggerating the one-sidedness of the victory, a surprisingly large victory accompanying a change in parties in the White House, a campaign oriented around a major change in public policy, and the consistency of the new president's program with the prevailing tides of opinion in both the country and his party. Since it is unusual for these conditions to be met (George Bush's 1988 election was accompanied only by the last one), perceptions of mandates are rarely strong. Presidents can do little about these perceptions. Some are simply elected under more favorable conditions for legislative leadership than others. When mandates do occur or are effectively claimed, the issue becomes one of exploiting the special opportunities they provide.

PRESIDENTIAL LEGISLATIVE SKILLS

In this section of our discussion of presidential influence in Congress we examine other White House efforts to persuade members of Congress to support the president's legislative proposals. Some of these activities are aimed at building goodwill in the long run and others at obtaining votes from individual members of Congress on specific issues. Whatever the immediate goal, the nature of the legislative process in America demands that the president apply his legislative skills in a wide range of situations. In the words of one presidential aide:

> Senator A might come with us if Senator B, an admired friend, could be persuaded to talk to him. Senator C wanted a major project out of Chairman D's committee; maybe D, a supporter of our bill, would release it in exchange for C's commitment. Senator E might be reached through people in his home state. If Senator F could not vote with us on final passage, could he vote with us on key amendments? Could G take a trip? Would the President call Senator H?[20]

Congressional Liaison

Although the Constitution establishes separate institutions, the operation of the government requires those institutions to work together. The president is expected to propose legislation and to get it enacted into law. As our previous discussion suggests, he needs all the help he can get. To assist him in these efforts as well as with his other ongoing legislative responsibilities, a congressional liaison staff, based in the White House, has operated since 1953. The size of this staff and the duties it performs have expanded significantly in recent years.

The growth of the president's liaison mechanism has occurred in three stages. In its initial phase during the Eisenhower administration, the congressional relations office was small in size, adopted a low profile, and utilized a bipartisan approach in dealing with Congress. Wary of infringing on the legislature's prerogatives or of operating on its turf, the president's agents worked by telephone from the White House rather than in the halls of Congress, communicated mainly with and through the legislative leadership, and used gentle persuasion rather than arm twisting to achieve their goals. Eisenhower himself was not heavily involved in the details of legislation, although he did have contact with members of Congress, especially with the Republican leaders.

The congressional relations office assumed a more aggressive posture in its second phase, which occurred during the Kennedy–Johnson years. With a larger and more comprehensive legislative agenda to advocate, the staff expanded its size and its functions. In addition to pushing major White House policy initiatives, the president's liaison team began funneling legislative views into the executive decision-making process. The increasing development of policy by the White House made this input desirable from a congressional perspective.

Presidential assistants involved in legislation became more numerous, more visible, and more partisan. Attempts were made to organize executive department and agency liaison staffs more effectively behind the president's major priorities. Pressures were exerted on committee chairs, informal legislative groups, and in general, on more members on more issues. Rewards were also more generously bestowed. "The White House certainly remembers who its friends are," Lawrence F. O'Brien, head of the office, both warned and promised legislators early in the Kennedy administration.[21]

In an effort to improve the atmosphere for the administration on Capitol Hill and to meet an increasing need of Congress, the White House began providing casework services for members and their staffs. This care and feeding operation soon became a congressional expectation, one that subsequent White Houses could not shirk. Social lobbying increased as well.

By the end of the 1960s certain functions had come to be regarded as traditional liaison activities. In addition to catering to the constituency needs of members of Congress, these included gathering intelligence, tracking legislation, coordinating department and agency efforts, and working with the leadership on priority programs. These functions continue to be performed today, but the level of White House involvement and the scope of its activities have expanded even further. The principal reason for that expansion is the difficulty that contemporary presidents have had in mobilizing majority coalitions in support of their policy proposals.

Phase three in the evolution of the presidency's liaison mechanism began in the Carter administration. Frustrated by its inability to get Congress to enact its policy recommendations in the first year and a half of the administration, the Carter White House began to broaden its interaction with Congress and utilize outside forces to help build legislative support. The president increased the size of his congressional relations office despite his highly publicized reduction of White House personnel. Internal task forces on key initiatives were formed to coordinate the administration's congressional activities. A mechanism for setting priorities for highly visible issues was established. More sophisticated information retrieval systems and computerized mail logs were developed to process congressional mail and assess voting patterns. Even the president, a private person by nature, began to interact more regularly with members of Congress, particularly the leadership.

In conjunction with these changes, other presidential offices got more involved with Congress and the legislative process. Although it did not solicit congressional views, the president's domestic policy staff became more receptive to them. Members of Congress and their staffs were given opportunities to affect the development of proposed legislation *before* it was sent to Congress. A public liaison office was established to organize outside groups and community leaders into coalitions behind the administration's proposals. Once established, these coalitions, orchestrated by the White House, mounted grass-roots efforts and directed them toward Congress. They identified the positions of members on key issues, targeted those who were wavering, had them contacted by group representatives from their own constituencies, and supplemented these activities by organizing mass letter-writing and telephoning campaigns. These constituency-based pressures were designed to make it easier for members of Congress to vote with the president regardless of their party affiliation.

During the Reagan presidency, especially the first term, a legislative strategy group, consisting of senior presidential aides, operated out of the chief of staff's office to coordinate these "outreach" efforts and tie them to administrative lobbying on Capitol Hill. Other White House offices, in addition to congressional relations and public liaison, also got involved in congressional affairs. A newly constituted political office handled patronage and other party-related matters while an intergovernmental affairs office orchestrated state and local officials behind other administration initiatives.

In summary, congressional liaison has developed and expanded because it serves the needs of *both* executive and legislative branches. For the Congress, it helps integrate legislative views into executive policy making, it services constituency needs, it forces the president to indicate his legislative priorities, it provides channels for reaching compromises, and it helps the leadership to form majority coalitions. For the president, it enables him to gain a congressional perspective, to communicate his views to Congress, to mobilize support for his programs, and to reach accomodations with the legislature. Such efforts to bridge the constitutional separation have helped to overcome some of the hurdles in the formulation of public policy.

We now turn to the particular legislative techniques that the president and his liaison aides must utilize in their efforts to win support for the administration's proposals on Capitol Hill.

Personal Appeals

A special aspect of presidential involvement in the legislative process is the personal appeal for votes. According to presidential scholar Richard Neustadt, "When the chips are down, there is no substitute for the President's own footwork, his personal negotiation, his direct appeal, his voice and no other's on the telephone."[22] Members of Congress are as subject to flattery as other people and are impressed when the president calls.

Calls from the president must be relatively rare to maintain their usefulness. If the president calls too often, his calls will have less impact. Moreover, members might begin to expect calls, for which the president has limited time, or they may resent too much high-level pressure being applied to them. On the other hand, they may exploit a call and say that they are uncertain about an issue in order to extract a favor from the president. In addition, the president does not want to commit his prestige to a bill by personal lobbying and then lose. Also, his staff's credibility when speaking for him will decrease the more he speaks for himself.

Presidents become intensely involved only after the long process of lining up votes is almost done and their calls are needed to win on an important issue, a situation that arises only a few times a year. When presidents do call about a vote, they focus on key members of Congress, whose votes serve as cues for other members, and members who are uncommitted or weakly committed in either direction. They identify the latter by studying the head counts prepared by the White House congressional liaison office and the congressional whips of their party.

Despite the prestige of their office, their invocations of national interest, and their persuasiveness, presidents often fail in their personal appeals. President Eisenhower liked to depend heavily on charm and reason. In 1953 he tried to persuade Republican chairman Daniel Reed of the House Ways and Means Committee to support the continuance of the excess profits tax and to oppose a tax cut. "I used every possible reason, argument, and device, and every kind of personal and indirect contact," he wrote, "to bring Chairman Reed to my way of thinking." But he failed.[23] Lyndon Johnson was renowned for his persuasiveness but nevertheless failed on many issues, ranging from civil rights and education to Medicare and the Panama uprising. "No matter how many times I told Congress to do something," he wrote, "I could never force it to act."[24] If Eisenhower and Johnson often failed in their efforts at persuasion, we should not be surprised that other presidents did also.

Bargaining

It is part of the conventional wisdom that the White House regularly "buys" votes through bargains struck with members of Congress. There can be no question that many bargains occur and that they take a variety of forms. Reagan's budget director, David Stockman, recalled that "the last 10 or 20 percent of the votes needed for a majority of both houses [on the 1981 tax cut] had to be bought, period." The concessions for members of Congress included special breaks for oil-lease holders, real estate tax shelters, and generous tax loopholes for corporations. "The hogs were really feeding," he declared. "The greed level, the level of opportunism, just got out of control."[25] Nevertheless, bargaining, in the form of trading support on two or more policies or providing specific benefits for representatives and senators, occurs less often and plays a less critical role in the creation of presidential coalitions in Congress than one might think. For obvious reasons, the White House does not want to encourage the type of bargaining Stockman described.

The president cannot bargain with Congress as a whole because it is too large and decentralized for one bargain to satisfy everyone. Also, the president's time is limited, as are his resources—only so many appointive jobs are available and the federal budget is limited. Moreover, funding for public works projects is in the hands of Congress. In addition, if many direct bargains are struck, word will rapidly spread, everyone will want to trade, and persuasive efforts will fail. Thus, most of the bargains that are reached are implicit. The lack of respectability surrounding bargaining also encourages implicitness.

Fortunately for the president, bargaining with everyone in Congress is not necessary. Except on vetoes and treaties, he needs only a simple majority of those voting. A large part of Congress can be "written off" on any given vote. Moreover, as we have seen, the president generally starts with a substantial core of party support and then adds to this number those of the other party who agree with his views on ideological or policy grounds. Others may support him on the basis of goodwill that he has generated through his services, constituency interest, or because of public support for him or his policies. Thus, the president needs to bargain only if all these groups do not provide a majority for crucial votes, and he need bargain only with enough people to provide him with that majority.

Since resources are scarce, the president will usually try to use them for bargaining with powerful members of Congress, such as committee chairs or those whose votes are the most important. There is no guarantee that a tendered bargain will be accepted, however. The members may not desire what the president offers, or they may be able to obtain what they want on their own. This is, of course, particularly true of the most powerful members, whose support the president needs most. Sometimes members of Congress do not want to trade at all because of constituency opinion or personal views. At other times the president is unwilling to bargain.

Most of the pressure for bargaining actually comes from the Hill. When the White House calls and asks for support, representatives and senators frequently raise a question regarding some request that they have made. In the words of an Eisenhower aide, "Every time we make a special appeal to a Congressman to change his position, he eventually comes back with a request for a favor ranging in importance from one of the President's packages of matches to a judgeship or cabinet appointment for a 'worthy constituent.' "[26]

More general bargains also take place. In the words of Nixon's chief congressional aide, William Timmons: "I think they [members of Congress] knew that we would try our best to help them on all kinds of requests if they supported the President, and we did. It kind of goes without saying." His successor in the Ford administration, Max Friedersdorf, added his assurance that people who want things want to be in the position of supporting the president. This implicit trading on "accounts" is more common than explicit bargaining.[27]

For the White House, a member of Congress indebted to the president is easier to approach and ask for a vote. For the member, previous support increases the chances of a request being honored. Thus, office holders at both ends of Pennsylvania Avenue want to be in the other's favor. The degree of debt determines the strategy used in presidential requests for support. While services and favors increase the president's chances of obtaining support, they are not usually exchanged for votes directly. They are strategic and not tactical weapons.

Services and Amenities

Since a member of Congress who is indebted to the president is easier to approach and ask for a vote, the White House provides many services and amenities for representatives and senators. Although these favors may be bestowed on any member of Congress, they actually go disproportionately to members of the president's party. Personal amenities used to create goodwill include social contact with the president, flattery, rides on Air Force One, visits to Camp David, birthday greetings, theater tickets for the presidential box, invitations to bill-signing ceremonies, pictures with the president, briefings, and a plethora of others, the number and variety of which are limited only by the imagination of the president and his staff.

Also, the White House often helps members of Congress with their constituents. A wide range of services is offered, including greetings to elderly and other "worthy" constituents, signed presidential photographs, presidential tie clasps and other White House memorabilia, reprints of speeches, information about government programs, White House pressure on agencies in favor of constituents, passing the nominations of constituents on to agencies, influence on local editorial writers, ceremonial appointments to commissions, meetings with the president, and arguments to be used to explain votes to constituents. The president may also help members of Congress please constituents through patronage, pork-barrel projects and government contracts, and aid with legislation of special interest to particular constituencies.

Campaign aid is yet another service the White House can provide party members, and the president may dangle it before them to entice support. This aid may come in various forms, including campaign speeches by the president and executive officials for congressional candidates, funds and advice from the party national committees, presidential endorsements, pictures with the president, and letters of appreciation from the president. Some aid is more ingenious, as when Lawrence O'Brien, then postmaster general, held a stamp dedication ceremony, complete with parade and associated festivities, in Representative Stan Greigg's hometown in 1966.

All administrations are not equally active in providing services and amenities for members of Congress. The Johnson and Reagan White House fall on the "active" end of this spectrum while the Nixon and Carter presidencies fall on the other end. Yet the important point is that any such differences are relatively small in comparison to the efforts made by every recent administration to develop goodwill among its party members in Congress. Although this activity is to the president's advantage and may earn him a fair hearing and the benefit of the doubt in some instances, party members consider it their right to receive benefits from the White House and are unlikely to be especially responsive to the president as a result.

Pressure

In 1982 one of President Reagan's aides told of how he persuaded two Republican members of the House to vote for the president's budget cuts. The representatives feared the political repercussions in their constituencies of supporting the president, so the aide promised them the maximum campaign aid the law allows a party to give a candidate and won their votes. When asked what would have happened if the congressmen had not given in, the aide replied, "I would have nailed them to the wall."[28]

Thus, just as the president can offer the carrot, he can also wield the stick. Moreover, the increased resources available to the White House in recent years provide increased opportunities to levy sanctions in the form of the withholding of favors. As the deputy chairman of the Republican National Committee said, there is more money than ever "to play hardball with. We're loaded for bear."[29] The threats of such actions are effective primarily with members of the president's party, of course, because members of the opposition party do not expect to receive many favors from the president.

Although sanctions or threats of sanctions are far from an everyday occurrence, they do occur. These may take the form of excluding a member from White House social events, denying routine requests for White House tour tickets, and shutting off access to the president. Each of these personal slights sends a signal of presidential displeasure.

Heavy-handed arm twisting is unusual, however. More typical is the orchestration of pressure by others. The Reagan White House was especially effective in this regard. Operating through party channels, its Political Affairs Office, and its Office of Public Liaison, the administration was able to generate pressure from party members' constituents, campaign contributors, political activists, business leaders, state officials, interest groups, party officials, and, of course, cabinet members.

Despite the resources available to the president, if members of Congress wish to oppose the White House, there is little the president can do to stop them. This is true for those in his party as well as those in the opposition. The primary reason is that the parties are highly decentralized; national party leaders do not control those aspects of politics that are of vital concern to members of Congress: nominations and elections. Members of Congress are largely self-recruited, gain their party's nominations by their own efforts and not the party's, and provide most of the money and organizational support needed for their elections. Presidents can do little to influence the results of these activities, and usually they don't even try. As President Kennedy said in 1962, "Party loyalty or responsibility means damn little. They've got to take care of themselves first. They [House members] all have to run this year—I don't and I couldn't hurt most of them if I wanted to."[30]

Consultation

Consulting with members of Congress on legislation can be advantageous for the White House. Members of Congress appreciate advance warning of presidential proposals, especially those that affect their constituencies directly. No official, especially an elected one, wants to be blindsided. Politicians quite naturally want to be prepared to take credit or avoid blame. Moreover, when a policy fails, members of Congress are unlikely to support the president in the perilous landing of the policy if they are not involved in the take-off.

Consultation before announcing a bill may also be useful in anticipating congressional objections. It may, in fact, be possible to preempt some of the opposition with strategic compromises and to garner some advance commitments. At the very least, members of Congress will feel that they have had an opportunity to be heard. They take pride in their work and may be offended if they feel the White House has not taken them seriously.

Despite these advantages, presidential consultation with Congress has often played a modest role in presidential–congressional relations. It is not easy to do. Arriving at a common position within the executive branch may tax the resources and patience of the White House, particularly at a time when other exigencies press on the president and his staff. Extending the negotiations to the legislature (and thus the public) and broadening the conflict may render the process of policy formulation unmanageable and increase its costs significantly. White House officials often are also concerned with the nature of Congress, which they often view as parochial, sievelike, and prone to transforming important matters of state into pork-barrel issues.

An additional challenge is determining with whom the White House should consult. The decentralization of power within Congress presents a substantial burden to executive branch officials wishing to consult with all the relevant members of Congress, especially on jurisdictionally complex matters. In some cases even identifying the appropriate senators and representatives is difficult.

Time is an ever-present factor in White House operations, and it influences consultation with Congress as well. If severe deadlines are imposed on the production of a presidential initiative, such as the 1977 energy proposal, consultation may be difficult. In addition, a president with an extensive legislative agenda may send a large number of bills to Congress, restricting the time officials can devote to consulting on any one of them.

A president with firm ideas on policy is unlikely to relish consulting with Congress in order to make compromises to satisfy congressional desires. In addition, some presidential proposals are designed by the White House to assuage constituency groups or fulfill campaign promises, which significantly constrains the possibilities of modification of these bills in response to congressional consultation.

Some observers propose that the White House involve relevant members of Congress in the process of developing the president's legislative program, the rationale being that those who have been involved in formulating a bill are more likely to support it once it is sent to the Hill. This process is not typical however, because chief executives have found it too cumbersome to include members of Congress, especially those of the opposition party, in writing legislation, and most members of Congress prefer to protect their status as members of an independent branch.

Setting Priorities

An important aspect of a president's legislative strategy can be establishing priorities among legislative proposals. The goal of this effort is to set the congressional agenda. If the president is not able to focus the attention of Congress on his priority programs, members may become lost in the complex and overloaded legislative process. Congress needs time to digest what the president sends, time to come up with independent analysis, time to schedule hearings and markups of bills. Unless the president gives some indication of what is most important, Congress will simply put the proposals in a queue and they will compete with each other for attention.

This is especially likely to be a problem if much of the president's program must go through a single committee, as was the case for Jimmy Carter and the House Ways and Means Committee in 1977. Thus, it is wise to spread legislative proposals among committees so they can be working on different parts of the president's agenda at the same time.

Setting priorities is also important because presidents and their staff can lobby effectively for only a few bills at once. Moreover, the president's political capital is inevitably limited, and it is sensible to focus it on the issues he cares about most. In 1977 Jimmy Carter spent his political capital on ending pork-barrel water projects, not one of his priority items.

It is particularly important that priorities be clearly established in the first year in office when presidential influence in Congress is likely to be greatest. After the transition period more items are likely to be on the agenda. In 1981 Ronald Reagan focused attention on his priority programs and obtained passage of a large tax cut, a substantial increase in defense expenditures, and sizable decreases in spending for domestic policies. By 1982, however, the "honeymoon" was over and the legislative agenda was crowded.

The White House can put off dealing with the full spectrum of national issues for a period of months at the beginning of the term of a new president, but it cannot do so indefinitely. Eventually it must make decisions about them. By the second year the agenda is full and more policies are in the pipeline as the administration attempts to satisfy its constituencies and responds to unanticipated or simply overlooked problems. Presidents with large legislative agendas find it more difficult to set priorities than those, like Ronald Reagan, with only a small number of proposals.

Moreover, the president himself will inevitably be a distraction from his own legislative priorities. There are so many demands on the president to speak, appear, and attend meetings that it is impossible to organize his schedule for very long around focusing the attention of Congress and the public on his major goals.

Congress is also quite capable of setting its own agenda, providing competition for the president's proposals. Of the thirteen major legislative actions (as defined by *Congressional Quarterly*) of the Ninety-ninth Congress (1985–1986), the White House took the lead on only one of them. In 1987 President Reagan found Congress already working on the two primary domestic policy initiatives for his last two years in office, catastrophic health insurance and welfare reform.

Moving Fast

As noted, the president should move quickly to exploit the honeymoon atmosphere that typically characterizes this period. First-year proposals have a better chance of passing Congress than do those sent to the Hill later in an administration. Lyndon Johnson explained, "You've got to give it all you can in that first year. . . . You've got just one year when they treat you right."[31]

The danger, of course, is proposing a policy without thorough analysis in order to exploit the favorable political climate of the honeymoon. This appears to have occurred with the budget cuts Reagan proposed in early 1981. The departments, including cabinet members, and their expertise were kept at a distance in the executive decision-making process. Although taking time to draft proposals does not guarantee that they will be well conceived, it is by no means clear that rapid drafting of legislation is in the best interests of the nation.

It is easier for a president who has a small agenda and one that is essentially negative in character, such as Ronald Reagan's agenda of cutting taxes or spending, to exploit the honeymoon. It is much more difficult to draft complex legislation rapidly, a problem Jimmy Carter faced in his first year when he tried to deal with issues such as energy, welfare reform, and the containment of health costs. Kennedy and Johnson had the advantage of a party program that had been building up during the 1950s when the Democrats were not in the White House.

George Bush hit the ground coasting, not running, in 1989. Early in his term he neither projected a vision of public policy nor presented Congress with a clear agenda of priority legislation. Arguing that he required time to deliberate, he sent vague and disparate proposals to Capitol Hill. Whatever opportunity he had to exploit his honeymoon period was lost amid widespread criticism that his administration was suffering from a lack of focus.

The Context of Influence

In our discussion of the president's legislative skills, it is important that we keep in mind the general context in which he operates. Contemporary presidents serve during the post-Vietnam and post-Watergate period of congressional assertiveness. The diminished deference to the president by individual members of Congress and by the institution as a whole naturally makes presidential influence more problematical.

Current presidents also have the misfortune to preside during a period of substantial economic scarcity, whereas the Kennedy–Johnson years were characterized by stable prices, sustained economic growth, and general prosperity. The prosperity of the 1960s provided the federal government with the funds for new policies, with little risk. Taxes did not have to be raised and sacrifices did not have to be made in order to help the underprivileged. In the late 1970s, 1980s, and 1990s resources are more limited, helping to make the passage of new welfare or health programs, for example, more problematical. When resources are scarce, presidents are faced with internal competition for them and the break-down of supporting coalitions. They must choose between policies rather than building coalitions for several policies through logrolling.

In light of the above discussion, it is not surprising that the relations of recent presidents with Congress have been characterized often by stale-mate. The environment for presidential influence has been deteriorating.

Impact of Legislative Skills

In general, presidential legislative skills must compete, as does pub-lic support, with other, more stable factors that affect voting in Con-gress, including party, ideology, personal views and commitments on specific policies, and constituency interests. By the time a president tries to exercise influence on a vote, most members of Congress have made up their minds on the basis of these other factors.

Systematic studies have found that, once we control for the status of their party in Congress and their standing with the public, presidents renowned for their legislative skills, such as Lyndon Johnson, were no more successful in winning votes, even close ones, or obtaining congres-sional support than those, such as Jimmy Carter, who are considered to have been less adept in dealing with Congress.[32] The president's legisla-tive skills are not at the core of presidential leadership of Congress, at least not at the final stage of voting on the floor. Even skilled presidents cannot change the contours of the political landscape and create opportu-nities for change. Yet they can recognize favorable configurations of political forces, such as existed in 1933, 1965, and 1981, and effectively exploit them to embark on major shifts in public policy.

THE VETO

Sometimes not only does the president fail to win passage of his proposals but Congress passes legislation to which he is strongly op-posed. Since all bills and joint resolutions except those proposing consti-tutional amendments must be presented to the president for his ap-proval, the president has another opportunity to influence legislation: the veto.

When Congress passes an item that must be submitted to the presi-dent, the president has several options. Within ten days (Sundays ex-cepted) of its presentation the president may (1) sign the measure, in which case it becomes the law of the land; (2) withhold his signature and return the measure to the house in which it originated with a message stating his reasons for withholding approval; or (3) do nothing.

When the president returns a bill or joint resolution to Congress, he has *vetoed* the measure. It can then become law only if each house of

Congress repasses it by a two-thirds majority of those present. Congress may override the presidential veto at any time before it adjourns *sine die* (that is, before the end of that particular Congress).

Early presidents exercised their veto power sparingly and ostensibly for the purpose of voiding legislation they deemed to be unconstitutional in its content or sloppy and improper in design. The first six presidents vetoed a total of eight bills; the seventh president, Andrew Jackson, vetoed twelve. Jackson used his negative to prevent legislation he opposed from becoming law. His example was followed by others.

The president can veto only an entire bill. Unlike most state governors, he does not have an item veto, which allows just specific provisions of a bill to be vetoed. As a result of this constraint, members of Congress use a number of strategies to avoid a possible veto of a particular proposal. For example, Congress may add increased appropriations, or riders (i.e., nongermane provisions), that the president might not want to bills that the president otherwise desires. Thus, he must accept these unattractive provisions in order to gain the legislation that he wants. In most such cases, the president does not use his veto. For example, after President Carter vetoed a bill providing for increased salaries for Public Health Service physicians, Congress added the pay raise to mental health services legislation, a pet project of First Lady Rosalyn Carter. The president signed the bill.

In 1987 Congress passed the entire discretionary budget of the federal government in one omnibus bill. The president had to accept the whole package or lose appropriations for the entire government. President Reagan frequently called for a constitutional amendment giving the president an item veto, and President Bush has followed his example. They have argued that an item veto would allow the president to stop unnecessary spending within massive appropriations bills and thus help to bring the budget under control. Yet Congress is reluctant to give the president additional power, and there is reason to expect that the legislature could easily devise methods of protecting appropriations in danger of being vetoed.

If the president does nothing after he receives a measure from Congress, it becomes law after ten days (Sundays excepted) if Congress remains in session. If it has adjourned during the ten-day period, thus preventing the president from returning the bill to the house of its origination, the bill is *pocket vetoed*. A pocket veto kills a piece of legislation just as a regular veto does. Historically somewhat fewer than half of all vetoes have been pocket vetoes. Table 10-4 presents data on the vetoes by recent presidents.

Presidents have sometimes attempted to use the pocket veto by taking no action on measures sent to them just before Congress went into a temporary recess, claiming that the recess prevented them from returning their veto for congressional consideration. (In 1964 President

Table 10-4. Regular and Pocket Vetoes

President	No. of Regular Vetoes	No. of Pocket Vetoes	Total Vetoes
Eisenhower	73	108	181
Kennedy	12	9	21
Johnson	16	14	30
Nixon	26	17	43
Ford	48	18	66
Carter	13	18	31
Reagan	39	39	78

Johnson pocket vetoed a bill during a congressional recess and then recalled and signed it.) However, in 1976 after the Nixon and Ford White Houses had lost litigation on the issue, the Ford administration promised that the president would not use the pocket veto during congressional recesses as long as an official of Congress was designated to be on hand to receive his vetoes. Since Congress is in session nearly all year, most people thought only an adjournment *sine die* would provide the opportunity for a pocket veto. Ronald Reagan used the pocket veto during a recess at the end of the 1981 session without apparent problems, but thirty-three House Democrats filed suit in federal court to challenge his pocket veto during the congressional recess at the end of 1983 of a bill making aid to El Salvador dependent on human rights progress. In 1984 a federal appeals court ruled against the president.

The last column in Table 10-4 indicates that vetoes are rarely used. Not only are the absolute numbers low, but fewer than 1 percent of the bills passed by Congress (which number several hundred per session) are vetoed. The table also shows that presidents who faced Congresses controlled by the opposition party (Eisenhower, Nixon, Ford, and Reagan) used more vetoes, as we would expect. They were more likely to be presented with legislation that they opposed.

Table 10-5 illustrates another important fact about vetoes. Regular vetoes are generally sustained, but overriding does occur, especially when the president's party is in the minority in Congress. Some very important legislation has been passed over the president's veto. In the post-World War II era such legislation includes the Taft-Hartley Labor Relations Act (1947), the McCarran-Walter Immigration Act (1952), the McCarran-Wood Internal Security Act (1950), and the War Powers Resolution (1973).

Sometimes presidents choose not to veto a bill either because, as mentioned earlier, they feel the good in the legislation outweighs the bad or because they do not want their veto to be overridden. Thus, President Ford did not veto the 1975 food stamp legislation, which he

Table 10-5. Vetoes Overridden

President	No. of Regular Vetoes	No. of Vetoes Overridden	% Vetoes Overridden
Eisenhower	73	2	3%
Kennedy	12	0	0
Johnson	16	0	0
Nixon	26	7	27
Ford	48	12	25
Carter	13	2	15
Reagan	39	9	23

opposed, because only forty-six members of the House and Senate had supported his own proposal.

When a bill is introduced in either house of Congress, the chamber's parliamentarian classifies it as public or private. Generally, public bills relate to public matters and deal with individuals by classifications or categories, such as college students or the elderly. A private bill, on the other hand, names a particular individual or entity who is to receive relief, such as payment of a pension or a claim against the government or the granting of citizenship. Up until 1969 presidents usually vetoed more private than public bills. Recent presidents have vetoed very few private bills, however.

The veto is an inherently negative element in the president's arsenal, but sometimes it may be used as a threat to shape legislation. Presidents frequently threaten to veto legislation unless certain provisions are removed or altered. In a typical example, President Carter in 1978 threatened to veto any bill that provided for tuition tax credits. This encouraged Congress to drop such a provision, which had already passed the Senate. In a more unusual situation, President Reagan threatened to veto the omnibus appropriations bill in 1987, which contained the money necessary for running the government for the following year, if Congress did not include certain provisions that he favored. Fearing a shutdown of the government, Congress acquiesced.

Once exercised, the veto's usefulness as a threat ends and the chances of the president's obtaining positive action from Congress are substantially diminished. In 1988 Reagan vetoed the defense authorization bill because he objected to some funding provisions and restrictions on his discretion in procurement and arms control. Angered because it felt the president had violated an agreement on the bill and was grandstanding to aid George Bush's presidential campaign, Congress repassed the bill with essentially cosmetic changes. Moreover, the threat must be exercised with caution lest it be used too often and be too easily overcome. Thus, while a president's vetoes are normally successful in stopping legislation, they are less effective when used as inducements to pass his own legislation, and they are utilized in this way only in exceptional cases.

CONCLUSION

The president faces an uphill battle in dealing with Congress. His formal powers of recommending legislation to Congress and vetoing bills help set the legislature's agenda and prevent some of what he opposes from passing. Yet these prerogatives are of only marginal help. Conflict between the executive and legislative branches is inherent in our system of government. The overlapping powers of the two branches, their representation of different constituencies, the contrast of the hierarchical, expert nature of the executive and the decentralized, generalist Congress, and the different time frames within which they operate guarantee that, except in extraordinary circumstances, conflict between them will remain a central feature of American politics.

The chief executive's assets in dealing with Congress are unimpressive. Party leadership is a potential source of influence in Congress, and the president receives considerably more support from members of his party than from the opposition. Much, or even most, of this support is the result of members of the same party sharing similar policy views rather than the influence of the president's party leadership. Nevertheless, the president works closely with his party and its leaders in Congress and gains some increment of support as a result of party loyalty. Party support is undependable, however, as constituency interests, a lack of policy consensus, and other factors intervene and diminish the importance of the party label. Congressional party leaders are typically in weak positions to move their troops in the president's direction. Ideally, the president could influence the election of members of his party to Congress, but presidential coattails are very short and midterm campaigning seems to have limited payoffs. Thus, the president generally has to seek support from opposition party members, but his efforts at bipartisanship, although necessary, may strain relations with the less moderate wing of his own party.

The president is more likely to receive support in Congress when he has the public's approval than when he sits low in the polls. Unfortunately, as we have seen in Chapter 4, the president cannot depend on the public's support, nor can he be sure of being able to mobilize new support. Moreover, public approval is usually a necessary but not a sufficient source of influence. Even a president high in the polls will find it difficult to pass his program if his party lacks a substantial number of congressional seats.

The White House engages in a large-scale legislative liaison effort to create goodwill and influence votes on a more personal level. Bargains are consummated, services and amenities are provided, arms are twisted, presidential phone calls are made, and advance consultation is done. Yet there are severe limits on a president's time and resources. The president can also increase his chances of success if he moves his program early in his tenure and does not let it clog the legislative process. However, many presidents find it difficult or impossible to control the congressional agenda so neatly. Although presidential legislative skills are crucial in winning some votes, their importance can be exaggerated by those who focus more on the unique than the general. Thus, the president must constantly struggle to succeed in having his policies enacted into law.

Presidential leadership of Congress is at the margins most of the time. In general, successful presidential leadership of Congress has not been the result of the dominant chief executive of political folklore, who reshapes the contours of the political landscape to pave the way for change. Rather than creating the conditions for important shifts in public policy, the effective president is the less heroic figure of the facilitator, who works at the margins building coalitions to recognize and exploit opportunities presented by a favorable configuration of political forces.

The president remains an important influence on Congress, but he rarely dominates it. Ronald Reagan was considered a strong chief executive and began with a string of victories in Congress. But after the Democrats won control of the Senate in the 1986 elections and his approval ratings plummeted in the wake of the Iran–Contra scandal, he was successful only 44 percent of the time in 1987 and 47 percent in 1988. Budgeting was one of his principal tools for affecting public policy, yet the budgets he proposed to Congress were typically pronounced "DOA"—dead on arrival. Members of Congress truly compose an independent branch and in recent years have more often taken the lead in initiating major changes in public policy than the president.

NOTES

1. Lyndon Johnson, quoted in Doris Kearns, *Lyndon Johnson and the American Dream* (New York: Harper and Row, 1976), p. 226.

2. James Madison, "The Federalist No. 46," in *The Federalist* (New York: Modern Library, 1937), p. 307.

3. Gerald R. Ford, *A Time to Heal: The Autobiography of Gerald R. Ford* (New York: Harper and Row, 1979), p. 150.

4. Richard E. Neustadt, *Presidential Power: The Politics of Leadership from FDR to Carter* (New York: Wiley, 1980), p. 26.

5. Quoted in Paul C. Light, *The President's Agenda: Domestic Policy Choice from Kennedy to Carter* (Baltimore: Johns Hopkins University Press, 1982), p. 135.

6. Howard Baker, quoted in James L. Sundquist, *The Decline and Resurgence of Congress* (Washington, D.C.: Brookings Institution, 1981), p. 402.

7. Gerald R. Ford, "Imperiled, Not Imperial," *Time*, November 10, 1980, p. 30.

8. Quoted in Light, *The President's Agenda*, p. 211.
9. George C. Edwards III, *The Public Presidency* (New York: St. Martin's, 1983), pp. 83–93.
10. Jimmy Carter, *Keeping Faith: Memoirs of a President* (New York: Bantam, 1982), p. 80.
11. Emmet John Hughes, *The Living Presidency* (Baltimore: Penguin, 1974), p. 68.
12. Lyndon B. Johnson, *The Vantage Point: Perspectives of the Presidency, 1963–1969* (New York: Popular Library, 1971), p. 443.
13. Ibid., p. 323.
14. Quoted in "Run, Run, Run," *Newsweek*, May 2, 1977, p. 38.
15. Quoted in "Carter Seeks More Effective Use of Departmental Lobbyists' Skills," *Congressional Quarterly Weekly Report*, March 4, 1978, p. 585.
16. Quoted in Sidney Blumenthal, "Marketing the President," *The New York Times Magazine*, September 13, 1981, p. 110.
17. Dom Bonafede, "The Strained Relationship," *National Journal*, May 19, 1979, p. 830.
18. See, for example, *CBS News/The New York Times Poll*, October 30, 1986, tables 21, 27.
19. Quoted in Light, *The President's Agenda*, pp. 29, 31; see, more generally, pp. 28–31.
20. Harry McPherson, *A Political Education* (Boston: Little, Brown, 1972), p. 192.
21. Lawrence F. O'Brien, quoted in Neil McNeil, *Forge of Democracy* (New York: McKay, 1963), p. 260.
22. Richard E. Neustadt, "Presidency and Legislation: Planning the President's Program," in Aaron Wildavsky, ed., *The Presidency* (Boston: Little, Brown, 1969), p. 596.
23. Dwight D. Eisenhower, *Mandate for Change, 1953–1956* (New York: Signet, 1963), pp. 254–55.
24. Johnson, *The Vantage Point*, p. 40.
25. David Stockman, *The Triumph of Politics* (New York: Harper and Row, 1986), pp. 251, 253, 260–61, 264–65; see also William Greider, "The Education of David Stockman," *Atlantic Monthly*, December 1981, p. 51
26. Gary W. Reichard, *The Reaffirmation of Republicanism: Eisenhower and the Eighty-Third Congress* (Knoxville, Tenn.: University of Tennessee Press, 1975), p. 173.
27. William Timmons and Max Friedersdorf, quoted in "Turning Screws: Winning Votes in Congress," *Congressional Quarterly Weekly Report*, April 24, 1976, pp. 952–53.
28. Quoted in "Playing Hardball," *The Wall Street Journal*, August 18, 1982, p. 1.
29. Quoted in ibid.
30. John Kennedy, quoted in Theodore Sorensen, *Kennedy* (New York: Bantam, 1966), p. 387.
31. Lyndon Johnson, quoted in McPherson, *A Political Education*, p. 268.
32. George C. Edwards III, *At the Margins: Presidential Leadership of Congress* (New Haven: Yale University Press, 1989), chap. 9.

SELECTED READINGS

Davis, Eric. "Legislative Reform and the Decline of Presidential Influence on Capitol Hill." *British Journal of Political Science* 9 (October 1979): 465–79.
Edwards, George C., III. *At the Margins: Presidential Leadership of Congress.* New Haven: Yale University Press, 1989.
————. *Presidential Influence in Congress.* San Francisco: W. H. Freeman, 1980.
————. *The Public Presidency.* New York: St. Martin's, 1983.
Fisher, Louis. *The Constitution between Friends.* New York: St. Martin's, 1978.
Harmel, Robert, ed. *Presidents and Their Parties: Leadership or Neglect?* New York: Praeger, 1984.

Jones, Charles O. *The Trusteeship Presidency: Jimmy Carter and the United States Congress.* Baton Rouge, La.: Louisiana State University Press, 1988.

Light, Paul C. *The President's Agenda: Domestic Policy Choice from Kennedy to Carter.* Baltimore: Johns Hopkins University Press, 1982.

Neustadt, Richard E. *Presidential Power: The Politics of Leadership from FDR to Carter.* New York: Wiley, 1980.

Ragsdale, Lyn. "The Fiction of Congressional Elections as Presidential Events." *American Politics Quarterly* 8 (October 1980): 375–98.

Wayne, Stephen J. *The Legislative Presidency.* New York: Harper and Row, 1978.

11

The President and the Judiciary

The president's interactions with the Congress and the bureaucracy are constant and receive considerable attention. His relations with the third branch of government, the judiciary, are in many ways more intermittent and less visible. Nevertheless, the chief executive has important relationships with the courts. He has an opportunity to influence public policy for years to come through his nominations to the bench. The executive branch, operating through the solicitor general's office, is also a frequent litigant in the federal courts, especially at the Supreme Court level. Such litigation provides another opportunity for the president to influence judicial decisions. In addition, as chief executive the president may end up with responsibility for enforcing court decisions, even though he was not directly involved in them. Sometimes enforcing the law actually means complying with decisions directed at the White House. Although such instances are not common, they may provide moments of high political drama and have important consequences for our political system. Finally, the Constitution gives the president the right to exercise some judicial powers himself. He can grant pardons, amnesty, and clemency for those accused or convicted of federal crimes.

The distinction between the director and facilitator presidential types is less clear in relationships with the judiciary than with Congress. Both will take advantage of the opportunity to nominate compatible judges to the federal bench, but the director will be able to mold the courts in his image and move them to reach decisions of which he approves and to overturn previous decisions that he opposes. The facilitator will be constrained in placing his first choices on the bench and will not dominate judicial decision making. His victories will result from the views of the judges he nominates to the bench rather than from his influence over them once they don their judicial robes.

JUDICIAL SELECTION

The president's primary means of exercising leadership of the judicial branch is the nomination of federal judges. In this section we examine the process of judicial selection for the federal courts and the types of persons who become federal judges.

Selection of Lower-Court Judges

We begin with the federal district courts and the courts of appeals, which include most federal judges and which handle most federal cases. The president nominates persons to fill these slots for lifetime service. The Senate must confirm each nomination by a majority vote. Because of the Senate's role, the president's discretion ends up being much less than it appears.

Senatorial courtesy is the customary manner in which the Senate disposes of state-level federal nominations for such positions as judgeships and United States attorneys. Under this unwritten tradition, nominations for these positions are not confirmed when opposed by a senator from the state in which the nominee is to serve (all states have at least one federal district court) or, in the case of courts of appeals judges, the state of the nominee's residence if the senator is of the same party as the president. To invoke the right of senatorial courtesy, the relevant senator usually simply states a general reason for his opposition. Other senators then honor their colleague's views and oppose the nomination, regardless of their personal views or the candidate's merits.

The first instance of senatorial courtesy occurred in 1789, when President George Washington failed to have Benjamin Fishbourn confirmed as naval officer of the port of Savannah because of the opposition of Georgia's two senators. Since that time senatorial courtesy has become more and more established. By 1840, senators were virtually naming federal district court judges. In addition, at times senatorial courtesy has been successfully invoked by a senator not of the president's party.

A related practice began in the mid-1950s when the Senate Judiciary Committee initiated the practice of circulating a "blue slip" to the senators from the state in which a prospective judge was to serve, asking for permission to hold a hearing. Even those not from the president's party could object to a nominee by not returning the slip to the committee. Senators have not exercised this prerogative very often to defeat a nomination, however, and in 1979 the chairman of the Judiciary Committee, Edward Kennedy, announced that the committee would reserve the right independently to review and overrule a senator's failure to return a slip. After several years, the issue has not yet been pressed by a senator or the White House.

When a president fails to heed the tradition of senatorial courtesy, the results can be embarrassing. On April 1, 1976, President Ford nominated William B. Poff to a federal judgeship in Virginia. Virginia's Republican senator, William Scott, had previously given notice of his opposition to Poff and of his support for another candidate, Glenn Williams. It is important to note that Scott himself agreed that Poff was qualified for the position. He just felt Williams' philosophy was closer to his own. Thus, on April 15 Scott formally announced his opposition to Poff's nomination in a letter to the Senate Judiciary Committee, simply terming Poff "unacceptable." On May 5 the committee chairman, Senator James Eastland, moved to table the nomination, and it was tabled without objection.

The president is not without assets in such a situation, but he rarely will find it worthwhile to fight a senator over a district court judgeship. These judges seldom interfere with his policies. If he desires to do so, he can refuse to appoint anyone to the position in an attempt to pressure a senator into supporting his nominee in order to avoid a backlog of federal cases in the state. Or the president may make an appointment during a congressional recess at the end of a session. Although the nominee must still be confirmed in the next session of Congress, he may have had an opportunity to demonstrate his capabilities on the bench by then, and the Senate may be more deferential in its treatment of a sitting judge than of a more typical nominee.

Because of the strength of these informal practices, presidents usually check carefully with the relevant senator or senators ahead of time to avoid making a nomination that will fail to be confirmed. In many instances this is tantamount to giving the power of nomination to these senators. Typically, when there is a vacancy for a federal judgeship, the senator (or senators) of the president's party from the state where the judge will serve suggest one or more names to the attorney general and the president. If neither senator is of the president's party, the state's congressmen of the president's party or other state party leaders may make suggestions. Then the Department of Justice and the Federal Bureau of Investigation conduct competency and background checks on these persons, and the president usually selects a nominee from those who survive the screening process. It is very difficult for the president to reject the recommendation of a senator of his party in favor of someone else if the person recommended clears the hurdles of professional standing and integrity. Thus, the Constitution is turned on its head and the Senate ends up making nominations, which the president then approves.

The attorney general typically asks the Standing Committee on the Federal Judiciary of the American Bar Association (ABA) for its evaluation of potential nominees. Others have input in judicial selection as well. The ABA committee or the Department of Justice may ask sitting judges, usually federal judges, to evaluate prospective nominees. Sitting judges may also initiate recommendations to advance or retard someone's chances of being nominated. In addition, candidates for the nomination are often active on their own behalf. They have to alert the relevant parties that they desire the position and orchestrate a campaign of support on their behalf. As one appellate judge observed, "People don't get judgeships without seeking them. Anybody who thinks judicial office seeks the man is mistaken. There's not a man on the court who didn't do what he thought needed to be done."[1]

The president usually has more influence in the selection of judges to the federal courts of appeals than to federal district courts. Since the decisions of appellate courts are generally more significant than those of lower courts, the president naturally takes a greater interest in whom he appoints to these courts. At the same time, individual senators are in a weaker position to determine who the nominee will be because the jurisdiction of an appeals court encompasses several states. Although custom and pragmatic politics require that these judgeships be apportioned among the states, the president has discretion in how he does this and therefore has a greater role in recruiting appellate judges than district court judges. Even here, however, senators from the state in which the candidate resides may be able to veto a nomination.

Jimmy Carter attempted to alter the role of senators in the judicial selection process. Shortly after his election as president, Carter struck a deal with Senator James Eastland, chairman of the Senate Judiciary Committee, that the president would have a free hand in nominations to the federal courts of appeal but would continue to defer to senators in nominations to the federal district courts. The president then established the United States Circuit Judge Nominating Commission and appointed members to its thirteen panels. Each panel was composed of laypeople as well as lawyers and included women and minorities. When a vacancy occurred, the relevant panel interviewed potential nominees and recommended three to five persons to the president to fill the position, basing their evaluations on broad merit criteria. President Carter made his selection from this list of names.

In 1978 Congress added wording to an act creating new federal judgeships that asked the president to establish standards for selecting federal district court judges and emphasized the importance of merit selection and greater representation for women and minorities. President Carter subsequently requested senators to make special efforts to identify qualified women and minority candidates (although he had no authority to force them to comply). In response senators from most states adopted the use of nominating commissions to recommend candidates for federal district courts. The selection of members and the composition and operation of the commissions varied widely, as did the use of the names they produced. Nevertheless, states with these commissions produced judges with higher ratings by the ABA and a greater percentage of women and African-Americans than states without commissions, although there were notable exceptions on both sides.

Things changed once again following Ronald Reagan's election as president. He abolished the Circuit Judge Nominating Commission and invited the Republican senator(s) from the relevant state (or Republican House members if there was no senator) to identify prospective candidates for federal judgeships. Senators were encouraged to apply screening devices to ensure that their recommendations were based on merit, but he specified no particular type of mechanism.

Backgrounds of Lower-Court Judges

What kind of people are selected as judges as a result of this process? The data in Tables 11-1 and 11-2 show that federal judges are not a representative sample of the American people. They are all lawyers (although this is not a constitutional requirement), and they are overwhelmingly white males. Jimmy Carter is the only president who has appointed a substantial number of women and minorities to the federal bench. Federal judges have also typically held office as a judge or prosecutor, and often they have been involved in partisan politics. This involvement is generally what brings them to the attention of senators and the Department of Justice when they seek nominees for judgeships. As former United States attorney general and circuit court judge Griffin Bell once remarked:

> For me, becoming a federal judge wasn't very difficult. I managed John F. Kennedy's presidential campaign in Georgia. Two of my oldest and closest friends were two senators from Georgia. And I was campaign manager and special, unpaid counsel for the governor.[2]

Perhaps the most striking finding in Tables 11-1 and 11-2 is the fact that presidents rarely appoint someone to a judgeship who does not share their party affiliation. Merit considerations obviously occur after partisan screening. Judgeships are patronage plums that may serve as rewards for political service to either the president or senators of his party, as consolation prizes for unsuccessful candidates, or even to "kick upstairs" an official in order to remove him from an executive branch post. When the president nominates someone of the other party for a judgeship, it is usually because of ideological congruity with the nominee or to obtain support in a state where his party is weak.

Partisanship also plays a role in the creation of judgeships. Because of their keen interest in them, members of Congress are reluctant to create judicial positions to be filled by a president of the minority party in Congress. For example, Democrats in Congress rejected President

Table 11-1. Backgrounds of Recent Federal District Court Appointees

	Reagan*	Carter	Ford	Nixon	Johnson
Total number of appointees	290	202	52	179	122
Occupation (%)					
Politics/gov't	12.8	4.4	21.2	10.6	21.3
Judiciary	37.2	40.3	34.6	28.5	31.1
Large law firm	17.7	14.0	9.7	11.3	2.4
Moderate size firm	19.3	19.8	25.0	27.9	18.9
Solo or small firm	10.4	13.9	9.6	19.0	23.0
Professor of law	2.1	3.0	—	2.8	3.3
Other	0.7	0.5	—	—	—
Experience (%)					
Judicial	46.6	54.5.	42.3	35.2	34.4
Prosecutorial	44.1	38.6	50.0	41.9	45.9
Neither one	28.3	28.2	30.8	36.3	33.6
Party (%)					
Democrat	4.8	92.6	21.2	7.3	94.3
Republican	93.4	4.4	78.8	92.7	5.7
Independent	1.7	2.9	—	—	—
Past party activism (%)	58.6	60.9	50.0	48.6	49.2
Religious origin or affiliation (%)					
Protestant	60.0	60.4	73.1	73.2	58.2
Catholic	30.4	27.7	17.3	18.4	31.1
Jewish	9.3	11.9	9.6	8.4	10.7
Ethnicity or race (%)					
White	92.4	78.7	88.5	95.5	93.4
Black	2.1	13.9	5.8	3.4	4.1
Hispanic	4.8	6.9	1.9	1.1	2.5
Asian	0.7	0.5	3.9	—	—
Sex (%)					
Male	91.7	85.6	98.1	99.4	98.4
Female	8.3	14.4	1.9	0.6	1.6

*1981–1986.

Source: Sheldon Goldman, "Reagan's Judicial Legacy: Completing the Puzzle and Summing Up." Judicature 72 (April/May 1989): 321–22.

Eisenhower's efforts to create new judgeships in every year of his second term, 1957–1960, even though he offered to name Democrats to half the new positions. In 1962, however, a similar bill easily passed Congress with Democrat John Kennedy in the White House. This partisan behavior was nothing new. In 1801 the newly elected Jeffersonians repealed a law creating separate judges for the circuit courts of appeal that had been passed by the outgoing Federalists a few months earlier.

There is no doubt that various women's, racial, ethnic, and religious

Table 11-2. Backgrounds of Recent Federal Circuit Courts of Appeals Appointees

	Reagan	Carter	Ford	Nixon	Johnson
Total number of appointees	78	56	12	45	40
Occupation (%)					
Politics/gov't	6.4	5.4	8.3	4.4	10.0
Judiciary	55.1	46.6	75.0	53.3	57.5
Large law firm	12.9	10.8	8.3	4.4	5.0
Moderate size firm	10.3	16.1	8.3	22.2	17.5
Solo or small firm	1.3	5.4	—	6.7	10.0
Professor of law	12.8	14.3	—	2.2	2.5
Other	1.3	1.8	—	6.7	—
Experience (%)					
Judicial	60.3	53.6	75.0	57.8	65.0
Prosecutorial	28.2	32.1	25.0	46.7	47.5
Neither one	34.6	37.5	25.0	17.8	20.0
Party (%)					
Democrat	—	82.1	8.3	6.7	95.0
Republican	97.4	7.1	91.7	93.3	5.0
Independent	1.3	10.7	—	—	—
Past party activism (%)	69.2	73.2	58.3	60.0	57.5
Religious origin or affiliation (%)					
Protestant	55.1	60.7	58.3	75.6	60.0
Catholic	30.8	23.2	33.3	15.6	25.0
Jewish	14.1	16.1	8.3	8.9	15.0
Ethnicity or race (%)					
White	97.4	78.6	100.0	97.8	95.0
Black	1.3	16.1	—	—	5.0
Hispanic	1.3	3.6	—	—	—
Asian	—	1.8	—	2.2	—
Sex (%)					
Male	94.9	80.4	100.0	100.0	97.5
Female	5.1	19.6	—	—	2.5

Source: Goldman, "Reagan's Judicial Legacy": 324–25.

groups desire to have as many of their members as possible appointed to the federal bench. At the very least judgeships have symbolic importance for them. Thus, presidents face many of the same pressures for representativeness in selecting judges that they experience in naming their cabinet.

What is less clear is what policy differences result from presidents' appointing persons with different backgrounds to judgeships. The number of female and minority group judges has been too few and their service too recent to serve as a basis for generalizations about their decisions. There have been many members of each party appointed to the federal bench, however. It appears that, in general, Republican judges are somewhat more conservative than Democratic judges.

Selection of Supreme Court Justices

Like lower-court judges, justices of the Supreme Court must be approved by a majority of those voting in the Senate. There have been no recess appointments to the Court since the Senate voiced its disapproval of the practice in 1960. When the chief justice's position is vacant, the president may nominate either someone already on the Court or someone from outside it to fill the position. Usually presidents choose the latter course to widen their range of options, but if they decide to elevate a sitting associate justice, as President Reagan did with William Rehnquist in 1986, he or she must go through a new confirmation by the Senate.

The president operates under many constraints in selecting persons to serve on the lower federal courts, especially the district courts. Although many of the same actors are present in the case of Supreme Court nominations, their influence is typically quite different. The president is vitally interested in the Court because of the importance of its work and will generally be intimately involved in the recruitment process.

Unlike the case of federal judges, presidents have been personally acquainted with many of the people they have nominated to the Court, reflecting their involvement in the selection process, and it is not unusual for an administration official to receive a nomination. Presidents also often rely on the attorney general and the Justice Department to identify and screen candidates for the Court.

There are few matters as important to justices on the Supreme Court as the ideology, competence, and compatibility of their colleagues, and thus it is not surprising that they, especially chief justices, often try to influence nominations to the Court. Chief justice William Howard Taft, a former president, was especially active during his tenure in the 1920s, and Warren Burger played a prominent role in the Nixon administration. Nevertheless, although presidents will listen to recommendations from justices, they feel no obligations to follow them.

Senators play a much less prominent role in the recruitment of Supreme Court justices than in the selection of lower-court judges, especially for the district courts. No senator can claim that the jurisdiction of the Supreme Court falls within the realm of his or her special expertise, interest, or sphere of influence. Thus, presidents typically consult with senators from the state of residence of a nominee after they have decided whom to select. At this point senators are unlikely to oppose a nomination because they like having their state receive the honor and are well aware that the president can simply select someone from another state if he chooses to do so.

Candidates for nomination are also much less likely to play a significant role in the recruitment process. Although there have been exceptions, most notably William Howard Taft, people do not usually campaign for a position on the Court. Little can be accomplished through such activity, and, because of the Court's standing, it might offend those who do play important roles in selecting nominees.

The American Bar Association's Standing Committee on the Federal Judiciary has played a varied but typically more modest role at the Supreme Court level than for nominations to lower courts. Usually the committee is asked to evaluate candidates for the Supreme Court only after the president has nominated them. The committee prefers to screen potential nominees before they are nominated, however, so it will not be in the position of opposing the president's choice. Indeed, it has never found a nominee unqualified to serve on the Court.

Through 1988, 104 persons have served on the Supreme Court. Of the 143 nominees, 3 were nominated and confirmed twice, 8 were confirmed but never served, and 28 failed to secure Senate confirmation. The president, then, has failed 20 percent of the time to appoint the person of his choice to the Court, a percentage much higher than for any other federal position. Thus, although home-state senators do not play prominent roles in the selection process for the Court, the Senate as a whole does.

Six nominees have failed to receive Senate confirmation in this century (see Table 11-3). Their difficulties are instructive. Liberal and civil rights groups opposed John J. Parker, Clement Haynesworth, and G. Harrold Carswell, and organized labor was in active opposition against the first two as well. Abe Fortas (who was already on the Court and who had been nominated as chief justice) was opposed by conservative interests and was charged with ethical violations, as was Haynesworth. Carswell was the only one of this group whose competence was seriously questioned. Haynesworth's and Carswell's troubles were compounded

Table 11-3. Senate Rejections of Supreme Court Nominees in the Twentieth Century

Nominee	Year	President
John J. Parker	1930	Hoover
Abe Fortas*	1968	Johnson
Clement F. Haynsworth, Jr.	1969	Nixon
G. Harrold Carswell	1970	Nixon
Robert H. Bork	1987	Reagan
Douglas H. Ginsburg*	1987	Reagan

*Nominations withdrawn. Fortas was serving on the Court as an associate justice and was nominated to be chief justice.

because they were Republican appointees facing a Democrat-controlled Senate, while Fortas was nominated at the end of President Johnson's term and Senate Republicans refused to confirm him in the hope that a Republican president would be elected and have the opportunity to nominate a new chief justice.

On June 26, 1987, Justice Lewis Powell announced his retirement from the Supreme Court. President Reagan had already been able to elevate Justice William Rehnquist to be chief justice and also had appointed Sandra Day O'Connor and Antonin Scalia. With yet another appointee, he would have a solid bloc of conservative votes on the Court for years to come.

He nominated Judge Robert H. Bork to fill the vacancy. Everyone agreed that Bork was very intelligent and a distinguished legal scholar. Bork had also served in the Justice Department. (He was the one who had fired special prosecutor Archibald Cox in the famous Saturday Night Massacre of Watergate fame.) At this point agreement on his qualifications ended, however.

Bork testified before the Senate Judiciary Committee for twenty-three hours. At the end, his supporters portrayed him as a distinguished scholar who would practice "judicial restraint," deferring to Congress and state legislatures and adhering to the precedents of the Supreme Court. Conversely, his opponents saw him as an extreme judicial activist who would use the Supreme Court to achieve conservative political ends, reversing decades of court decisions. A wide range of interest groups entered the fray, mostly in opposition to the nominee, and in the end, following a bitter floor debate, the Senate rejected the president's nomination by a vote of 58 to 42.

Six days after the Senate vote on Bork, the president nominated Douglas H. Ginsburg to the high court. Just nine days later, however, Ginsburg withdrew his nomination after disclosures that he had smoked marijuana at parties while a law professor at Harvard. Not until the spring of 1988 did Reagan finally succeed in filling the vacancy with Anthony Kennedy.

These examples indicate that nominations are most likely to run into trouble under certain conditions. A president whose party is in the minority in the Senate or who makes a nomination at the end of his term faces a greatly increased probability of substantial opposition and defeat. Equally important, opponents of a nomination usually must be able to question a nominee's competence, temperament, or ethics in order to defeat a nomination. Such questions provide a rationale for opposition that can attract moderates and make ideological protests seem less partisan.

Characteristics of Justices

Competence and ethical behavior are important to presidents for reasons beyond merely obtaining Senate confirmation of their nominees to the Court. Skilled and honorable justices reflect well on the president and will likely do so for many years. Moreover, they are more effective advocates and thus can better serve the president's interests. In addition, presidents usually have enough respect for the Court and its work that they do not want to saddle it with a mediocre justice. Although the criteria of competence and character screen out some possible candidates, they still leave a wide field from which the president may choose. Other characteristics then play prominent roles.

Like their colleagues on the lower federal courts, Supreme Court justices share many characteristics that are quite unlike those of the typical American. All have been lawyers and all but two have been white males. Most have been in their fifties and sixties when they took office, from the upper-middle to upper class, and Protestants.

The only African-American (Thurgood Marshall) and woman (Sandra Day O'Connor) ever to sit on the Court are currently serving (as of 1990). Race and sex have become more salient criteria in recent years. In the 1980 presidential campaign Ronald Reagan even promised to appoint a woman to the first vacancy on the Court if he were elected.

Geography once was a prominent criterion for selection to the Court, but it is no longer very important. Presidents do like to spread the slots around, however, as when Richard Nixon decided that he wanted to nominate a southerner. At various times there has been what some have termed a "Jewish seat" and a "Catholic seat" on the Court, but these are not binding on the president. For example, after a half century of having a Jewish justice, there has been none since 1969.

Partisanship remains an important influence on the selection of justices; only 13 of 104 members were nominated by presidents of a different party. Moreover, many of the 13 exceptions were actually close to the president in ideology, as was the case in Richard Nixon's appointment of Lewis Powell. Herbert Hoover's nomination of Benjamin Cardozo seems to be one of the few cases where partisanship was completely dominated by merit as a criterion for selection. Usually over 90 percent of a president's judicial nominations are of members of his own party.

The role of partisanship is not really surprising, even at the level of our highest court. Most of the president's acquaintances are in his party, and there is usually a certain congruity between party and political views. The president may also use Supreme Court nominations as a reward, as when President Eisenhower nominated Earl Warren as chief justice. As leader of the California delegation to the 1952 Republican convention, Warren had played a crucial role in Eisenhower's obtaining the Republican nomination for president. Most justices have at one time been active partisans, which gave them visibility and helped them obtain the positions from which they moved to the Court.

Typically justices have held high administrative or judicial positions before moving to the Supreme Court. Most have had some experience as a judge, often at the appellate level, and many have worked for the Department of Justice. Some have held high elected office, and few have had no government service but have been distinguished attorneys. The fact that not all justices, including many of the most distinguished ones, have had previous judicial experience may seem surprising, but the unique work and environment of the Court renders this background much less important than it might be for other appellate courts.

PRESIDENT–SUPREME COURT RELATIONS

At the top of two complex branches of government stand the president and the Supreme Court. Each has significant powers. In a system of shared powers such as ours, it is not surprising that the president is interested in influencing the Court. In this section we examine efforts of the White House to mold the Court through filling vacancies, setting its agenda, and influencing and enforcing its decisions. We also look at interbranch relations involving advising and other services.

Molding the Court

As we have noted, one of the most significant powers of the president is molding the Supreme Court through his nominations. Since justices serve for life, the impact of a president's selections will generally be felt long after he has left office. Because of this, the policy preferences of candidates for the Supreme Court are important to most presidents, and they typically make substantial efforts to ascertain them. When they succeed, they can slow or alter trends in the Court's decisions. Franklin Roosevelt's nominees substantially liberalized the Court, while Richard Nixon's turned it in a basically conservative direction.

Presidents and their aides survey candidates' decisions (if they served on a lower court), speeches, political stands, writings, and other expressions of opinion. They also turn for information to people who know the candidates well. The most direct means of learning candidates' views on policy would be simply to ask them, but this must be done in a delicate manner. Most officials feel it is improper to question judicial candidates about upcoming judicial decisions, so conversations must be limited to broader discussions of issues. The Reagan administration was especially concerned about ideology and had each potential nominee fill out a lengthy questionnaire and be interviewed by a special committee in the Department of Justice.

As a result of all this effort, presidents are generally satisfied with the actions of their nominees, especially those who have prior judicial experience to examine. Nevertheless, it is not always easy to identify the policy inclinations of candidates, and presidents have been disappointed in their selections about a fourth of the time. President Eisenhower, for example, was displeased with the liberal decisions of both Earl Warren and William Brennan. Once when asked whether he had made any mistakes as president, he replied, "Yes, two, and they are both sitting on the Supreme Court."[3] Earlier, Woodrow Wilson was shocked by the very conservative positions of one of his nominees, James McReynolds. On a more limited scale, Richard Nixon was certainly disappointed when his nominee for chief justice, Warren Burger, authored the Court's decision calling for immediate desegregation of the nation's schools shortly after his confirmation. This did little for the president's "southern strategy."

Presidents make what in their views are errors in nominations to the Court for several possible reasons. They and their aides may have done a poor job of probing the views of candidates. Moreover, once on the court, justices may change their attitudes and values over time because of new insights gained in their position, the normal process of aging, or the influence of other members of the Court. (Virtually all justices between 1801 and 1835 were strongly affected by Chief Justice John Marshall.) Justices are also often constrained by their obligation to follow precedents (when they are clear).

Some presidents have been relatively unconcerned with ideology in their nominations. In a period of relative political and social calm or when there is a solid majority on the Court that shares his views and that is likely to persist for several years, a president might give less weight to policy preferences than to other criteria in choosing justices.

A president cannot have much impact on the Court unless he has vacancies to fill, of course. Although on the average there has been an opening on the Supreme Court every two years, there is a substantial variance around this mean. Franklin D. Roosevelt had to wait five years before he could nominate a justice. All the while he was faced with a Court that found much of his New Deal legislation unconstitutional. In more recent years Jimmy Carter was never able to nominate a justice. Indeed, between 1972 and 1984 there were only two vacancies on the Court. On the other hand, Richard Nixon was able to nominate four justices in his first three years in office.

Sometimes unusual steps are taken to enhance or limit a president's ability to fill vacancies. The size of the Supreme Court was altered many times between 1801 and 1869. In 1866 Congress reduced the size of the Court from ten to eight members so that Andrew Johnson could not nominate any new justices. When President Grant took office, Congress increased the number to nine, since it had confidence he would nominate members to its liking. This number has remained unchanged since then, and it now seems inviolate. Franklin D. Roosevelt attempted to "pack" the court in 1937, when he proposed to add a justice to the Court for every justice currently serving who was over seventy and had served

*"Do you ever have one of those days when every-
thing seems un-Constitutional?"*

Source: Drawing by Joe Mirachi; © 1974 The New Yorker Magazine, Inc.

ten years. This proposal was an obvious attempt to change the direction of Court decisions on his economic policies, and after a prolonged political battle Congress refused to approve it. The refusal, however, was given only after the Court made a strategic reversal and began approving liberal legislation. Thus, Roosevelt lost the battle but won the war.

The president's role in Supreme Court judicial selection is not limited to the nomination of justices. It extends to the creation of positions as well. Justices are typically not prone to retirement (in 1990 four of the justices were over seventy), but presidents sometimes are frustrated enough at Court decisions to attempt to accelerate the creation of vacancies. Thomas Jefferson and his supporters tried to use impeachment to remove justices and thus gain control of the judiciary that was largely Federalist (and thus anti-Jefferson). This strategy was abandoned, however, when the Senate in 1805 failed to convict Justice Samuel Chase, who had made himself vulnerable with his partisan activities off the bench and injudicious remarks on it.

More often, presidents have relied on indirect pressure. Theodore Roosevelt resorted to leaks in the press in an unsuccessful effort to induce two justices to resign. More recently, the Nixon administration orchestrated a campaign to force liberal justice Abe Fortas to resign after he was accused of financial improprieties.

Justices are not helpless pawns in the game of politics, of course, and may try to time their retirements so a president with compatible views will choose their successor. This is one reason that justices remain on the Court for so long, even when they are clearly infirm. William Brennan and Thurgood Marshall, the most senior justices on the Court in the 1980s, stayed through the Reagan years, because their liberal views contrasted sharply with those of the president. William Howard Taft, a rigid conservative, even feared a successor being named by conservative Republican Herbert Hoover!

Such tactics do not always succeed. In 1968 Chief Justice Earl Warren submitted his resignation to President Johnson, whom he felt would select an acceptable successor. When Johnson's choice of Abe Fortas failed to win confirmation, however, the opportunity to nominate the new chief justice passed to Warren's old California political rival, the newly elected president, Richard Nixon.

Arguments in the Courts

The president may influence what cases the courts hear as well as who hears them. The solicitor general is a presidential appointee who must be confirmed by the Senate and serves in the Department of Justice. It is he (not the attorney general) who supervises the litigation of the federal executive branch. In this position he plays a major role in determining the agenda of federal appellate courts. Although he exercises wide discretion, he is subject to the direction of the attorney general and the president, the latter of whom may play a role in major cases.

The solicitor general decides which of the cases lost by the federal government in the federal district courts or the courts of appeals will be appealed to the next higher court. The courts of appeals must hear properly appealed cases, but the Supreme Court, for all practical purposes, has complete control over its own docket. Thus, it is significant that the Court is far more likely to accept cases the solicitor general wants to be heard than those from any other party. Moreover, the amount of litigation involved is quite large. In recent years, the federal government has been a party to about half the cases heard in federal courts of appeals and the Supreme Court.

The executive branch also participates in cases to which it is not directly a party. The solicitor general files *amicus curiae* (friend of the court) briefs supporting or opposing the efforts of other parties before the Court. These cases range from school busing for racial integration to abortion rights to equal pay for women. Once again, the Court usually grants the government's request to participate in this way.

When a case reaches the Supreme Court, the solicitor general supervises the preparation of the government's arguments in support of its position, whether it is a direct party or an *amicus*. These arguments are often reflected in Court decisions and thus become the law of the land. Since the government has participated in almost every major controversy decided by the courts in the past forty years, the potential influence of the executive branch on public policy through the courts is substantial. Moreover, both as a direct party or as an *amicus,* the federal government wins a clear majority of the time.

The government's success is due to several factors. The solicitor general builds credibility with the Court by not making frivolous appeals and in a few instances even by telling the Court the government should not have won cases in lower courts. Equally important, the solicitor general and his staff (again, not the attorney general) develop more expertise in dealing with the Court than anyone else, since they appear before it more frequently, and they provide the Court with high-quality briefs.

On a very rare occasion the president may directly attempt to influence a Court decision. In a very unusual move in 1969 Department of Justice officials visited Justice Brennan and Chief Justice Warren to alert them that the administration was worried about the outcomes of some wiretapping cases that were on the Court's agenda. The administration was concerned that the Court's decisions would force the discontinuance of its surveillance of embassies or its prosecutions based on the information obtained from them. According to Warren, this visit had no influence on the Court's decision making.[4]

Enforcing Court Decisions

Another important relationship between the judicial and executive branches involves the enforcement of court decisions. Although the executive branch provides the federal courts with United States marshals, they are too few and lack sufficient authority to be of systematic aid, especially if a court order is directed against a coordinate branch of government. Thus, the courts often must rely on the president to enforce their decisions, especially their more controversial ones.

The Constitution is, not surprisingly, ambiguous as to the president's responsibility for aiding the judicial branch. Although it never explicitly discusses the point, the Constitution does assign the president the responsibility to "take care that the laws be faithfully executed." Typically, presidents have responded to support the courts, or at least the rule of law. On several occasions, such as during the efforts of presidents Eisenhower and Kennedy to integrate educational institutions, presidents have gone so far as to employ federal troops to ensure compliance with court orders.

Presidents may use the carrot as well as the stick to encourage others to comply with Court decisions. One of the most significant and controversial Supreme Court decisions of this century has been that of *Brown* v. *Board of Education* (347 U.S. 483, 1954), calling for an end to segregation in the public schools. Compliance with this decision was a long and tortuous process, but it was aided by the passage of laws that provide federal aid only for school districts that do not segregate and that provide schools with extra funds to help ease the process of desegregation.

There have been exceptions to presidential cooperation, however. In *Worcester* v. *Georgia* (6 Peters 515, 1832), the Court found that Georgia had no authority over Cherokee Indian lands and that missionaries arrested there by the state should be released. The Court also implied that it was the president's responsibility to enforce its decision. Georgia refused to comply with the decision, however, and President Andrew Jackson took no actions to enforce it. He is reputed to have stated, "Well, [Chief Justice] John Marshall has made his decision, now let him enforce it."

Other Relationships

In the earliest years of our nation the line of separation between the executive and judicial branches was vague and often crossed. President George Washington consulted with the chief justice on a range of matters and received written advisory opinions on matters of law. Washington even used the first two chief justices as diplomats to negotiate with other countries. The chief justice was also placed on a commission to manage the fund for paying off the national debt.

This interbranch cooperation did not last long, however. The diplomatic efforts of justices were criticized by many, the Court decided against providing further advisory opinions, and informal consultation between the White House and justices declined. The Court also refused to examine pension claims for the secretary of the treasury. The years of Jefferson's presidency were marked by hostility between the president and the judiciary, which was populated primarily by his Federalist political enemies.

The most notable formal exceptions in recent years to a strict separation between the two branches have been Justice Robert Jackson's service as chief American prosecutor at the Nuremberg trials of Nazi leaders following World War II and Chief Justice Earl Warren's chairmanship of the commission investigating the assassination of President Kennedy. Abe Fortas received a great deal of criticism for his activities as an informal adviser to President Johnson. This type of relationship has occurred from time to time, however, principally between justices and the presidents who appointed them, continuing a pattern established before the justice reached the Court. Felix Frankfurter continued to advise Franklin D. Roosevelt after he took his seat on the court, as did Chief Justice Fred Vinson for Truman, Louis Brandeis for Wilson, and a number of others throughout our history.

More striking perhaps is the fact that Chief Justice Warren Burger appears to have discussed issues pending before the Court with, and reported internal activities of the Court to, President Nixon and other top administration officials.[5] This would seem like a breach of the separation of powers. Burger also appears to have asked Nixon to use his influence with congressional Republicans to discourage them from proceeding with their attempt to impeach Justice William O. Douglas.

COMPLYING WITH THE COURT

It is one thing for the White House to enforce a court decision against someone else, and something quite different for it to comply with an order directed at the president when he has lost a case in the Supreme Court. At that point interesting constitutional questions arise that have the potential for substantial interbranch conflict. As we will see, however, presidents typically do comply with court orders, a task made easier by the general deference of the courts to the chief executive.

Presidential Compliance

The Constitution is ambiguous as to which branch shall have the final say in interpreting it. Jefferson, for example, argued that each branch has the authority to interpret the Constitution regarding its own actions. Thus, the president would be the final judge of his own conduct. Others disagreed and felt the Supreme Court should be the ultimate judge of the constitutionality of the executive's activities.

The Court made some progress in resolving this question in *Marbury* v. *Madison* (1 Cranch 137, 1803). The case involved the requests of Marbury and others to have the Supreme Court order Secretary of State James Madison to deliver their commissions as justices of the peace in the District of Columbia. Congress had created these positions at the end of President John Adams' term, and he had appointed Federalists to serve in them but had not gotten their commissions to them by the time he left office. The new president, Thomas Jefferson, wanted to appoint fellow party members to the positions and therefore refused to deliver the commissions after he took office.

The Court held that although Marbury and his co-plaintiffs were entitled to receive their commissions, the law that gave the Supreme Court original jurisdiction over the case was unconstitutional. Thus, the Court could not order the president or his secretary of state to act. It thereby avoided a confrontation with Jefferson. At the same time, the Court proclaimed the administration's actions to be unlawful and, more significantly, asserted its right to make the final judgment on the constitutionality of actions of the other branches of government.

Marbury did not really settle the question of the president's obligation to accept and follow the Court's interpretation of the Constitution, because the president could argue that the law the Court voided pertained directly to the judicial branch. It was not until *Dred Scott* v. *Sanford* (19 Howard 393, 1857) that the Court again declared an act of Congress unconstitutional, and this time the law was not directly related to the judiciary. In the meantime the question of the final arbiter of the Constitution remained open.

Several presidents, including Jefferson, Lincoln, and Franklin D. Roosevelt, have threatened privately to disobey Court decisions that went against them, but in each case defiance was unnecessary because the Court supported them. The most blatant instance of a president's threatening to disobey a Court order occurred in a case in which the Court was asked to enjoin President Andrew Johnson from administering military governments in southern states following the Civil War. In oral argument before the Court, the president, speaking through his attorney general, let it be known that he would not comply with a decision enjoining him from implementing the laws. The Court, in turn, found in *Mississippi* v. *Johnson* (4 Wallace 475, 1867), that it lacked jurisdiction to stop the president from performing official duties that required executive discretion. We should also note that Johnson had vetoed these bills when Congress passed them, but he faced impeachment if he failed to execute them.

Presidents typically have obeyed Court decisions, even if it were costly to do so. There are two prominent examples of this in recent years that we will briefly examine. Near the end of President Truman's tenure and during the Korean War, the United Steelworkers of America gave notice of an industrywide strike. Concerned about steel production during wartime, the president ordered the secretary of commerce to seize and operate the steel mills. The steel companies then asked the courts to find the president's actions unconstitutional, and in *Youngstown Sheet and Tube Co.* v. *Sawyer* (343 U.S. 579, 1952), the Supreme Court did so. It found that the president lacked inherent power under the Constitution to seize the steel mills and that Congress had chosen not to give him statutory power to do so. Thus, in a rare occurrence, the president was ordered to reverse his actions, and Truman immediately complied.

The Watergate scandal produced another important case involving presidential prerogatives. The special prosecutor, Leon Jaworski, subpoenaed tapes and documents relating to sixty-four conversations President Nixon had with his aides and advisers. Jaworski needed the material for prosecution of Nixon administration officials. The president claimed that executive privilege protected his private conversations with his assistants and refused to produce the subpoenaed material. The case worked its way quickly to the Supreme Court.

In *United States* v. *Nixon* (418 U.S. 683, 1974), the Court unanimously ordered the president to turn the subpoenaed material over to the special prosecutor. Although Nixon had threatened not to comply with anything less than a "definitive" decision, he obeyed the Court. The

Court held that a claim of executive privilege unrelated to military, diplomatic, or national security matters cannot be absolute and in this case must give way to considerations of due process of law in criminal proceedings. Moreover, the justices reaffirmed that it was they and not the president who must be the final judge in such matters. Nixon resigned the presidency about two weeks later.

Presidents have not always been responsive to court orders, however. For example, in *United States* v. *Burr* (25 Fed. Cas. 187, No. 14,964, 1807), President Jefferson was subpoenaed to appear at the treason trial of Aaron Burr and to produce a letter. Jefferson refused to appear at the trial, but he did provide the document, stressing that he did so voluntarily and not because of judicial writ. Similarly, President James Monroe was subpoenaed as a witness in a trial, but he sent a written response instead.

The Civil War raised many difficult constitutional questions for the Court and the president. One set of cases found President Abraham Lincoln simply ignoring court orders. The president had suspended the writ of habeas corpus, which requires the government to explain why a person has been detained, and in the most famous of these cases, a citizen held prisoner by the military sued for his freedom. Chief Justice Roger Taney ordered his release, but Lincoln refused to give him up to the United States marshal sent to bring him into court. The chief justice (on circuit court duty) then held in *Ex parte Merryman* (17 Fed. Cas. 144, No. 9,487, 1861), that the president had exceeded his constitutional authority (the Constitution gives only Congress the power to suspend habeas corpus), but Lincoln simply ignored the decision and Merryman remained under arrest. Lincoln argued that he had not violated the Constitution but that in any case it would be better for the president to violate a single provision to a limited extent than to have anarchy because of failure to suppress the rebellion in the South.

Another aspect of presidential compliance with Court decisions is the administration of laws that the Court has approved and that the president opposes. This issue has arisen most directly with the claims of some presidents to the right to decide not to execute laws they view as unconstitutional, even if they had received court approval. Jefferson's opposition to the Alien and Sedition acts passed under his predecessor, John Adams, and upheld by the courts, led him to stop all prosecutions and pardon all those convicted under these laws when he took office. Andrew Jackson dismantled the Bank of the United States although the Court had approved it as constitutional.

This issue has never been really resolved, and presidents have often been lax in administering laws that they oppose. In modern times the Nixon administration was ordered by federal courts to enforce more strictly laws to eliminate segregation and sex discrimination in public educational institutions. Such court orders are rare, however.

If presidents are dissatisfied with Supreme Court decisions, their first thought is usually directed toward appointing new members with views similar to theirs. There are some other options, however. They might join in congressional efforts to remove certain types of cases from the Court's appellate jurisdiction. Congress has succeeded in such an action only once, however—on jurisdiction to hear appeals on certain writ of habeas corpus cases following the Civil War—and in this case the president supported the Court.

The president might support efforts to pass a constitutional amendment to overturn a Court interpretation of the Constitution, as George Bush did when the Court held that burning the American flag was protected speech. President Reagan supported amendments to allow prayer in public schools and to prohibit abortions. Such efforts rarely succeed, however, and Reagan's did not. On the other hand, when the Court has made a statutory interpretation, it can be reversed by simply changing the law to clarify the intentions of those supporting the policy. In a notable example, in 1953 President Eisenhower supported legislation that deeded federal mineral rights on offshore lands to the states after the Court had held in 1951 that the federal government owned the rights.

Deference to the President

A principal reason that complying with judicial decisions has rarely posed a problem for the president is the small number of instances in which the courts have held presidential actions to be in violation of the Constitution. Rarely have even these decisions interfered significantly with the president's policies, the *Youngstown* case being a major exception. More typically these cases have dealt with matters such as presidential instructions to customs officials or the suspension of the writ of habeas corpus.

Most presidential actions are not based upon the president's prerogatives under the Constitution and therefore do not lend themselves to constitutional adjudication. Effective opposition to most presidential policies must focus on the broader political arena. Moreover, it is especially difficult to prevent the president from acting. Most challenges occur only after the fact. On some occasions it is possible to oppose the president through challenging the constitutionality of laws he supported and Congress passed. Such efforts are rarely successful, but they were important during the early years of the New Deal, as we have seen. In the end, however, President Roosevelt prevailed.

In the area of foreign and defense policy the Court has interpreted the Constitution and statutes to give the president broad discretion to act. In general the history of litigation regarding challenges to the president's actions in the field of national security policy has been one of avoidance, postponement of action, or deference to the chief executive. The judiciary has been content to find that discretionary actions of the executive branch were beyond its competence to adjudicate.

Since the Civil War, presidents have been allowed especially broad powers in wartime. In that conflict the Supreme Court approved President Lincoln's deployment of troops during hostilities in the absence of a declaration of war and gave the chief executive discretion to determine the extent of force the crisis demanded and when an emergency existed. Similarly, it upheld the president's blockade of the South, expansion of the army and navy beyond statutory limits, calling out the militia, and most of his suspensions of habeas corpus.

In World War I, Congress delegated President Woodrow Wilson broad authority to regulate commissions, transportation, and the economy; to draft soldiers; and even to censor criticism, all within the approval of the Court. Franklin D. Roosevelt exercised even broader economic powers during World War II: he relocated Japanese-Americans from the West Coast to relocation centers and confiscated their property, and he bypassed the courts to establish special military commissions to try Nazi saboteurs, again with the Court's okay.

During the period of United States military involvement in Vietnam, there was never a declaration or other formal congressional authorization for the war. Many people, including many legal authorities, felt that this country's participation in the war without a formal declaration by Congress was unconstitutional, and several dozen cases were brought in federal court by opponents of the war to challenge various aspects of its legality. Yet the Supreme Court simply refused to hear all but one of these cases and never issued a written opinion regarding the war. A combination of deference to the president and pragmatic politics (what would happen if the war were declared unconstitutional while troops were engaged in combat?) rendered the Court irrelevant to the issue.

It is interesting that in times in which presidents are most likely to stretch their power (that is, in wartime), the courts are the least likely to intervene. When they do, the war may be over. For example, following both the Civil War and World War II, the Supreme Court held that civilians could not be tried by military tribunals when the civilian courts were open. In each case, however, the president at which the decision was directed was no longer living.

Outside of war, the courts have found that the president also has substantial discretion to act in the areas of foreign affairs and defense. He has broad prerogatives to act in negotiating and executing international agreements, withholding state secrets from the public, allocating international airline routes, terminating treaties, making executive agreements, recognizing foreign governments, protecting American interests abroad with military activities, punishing foreign adversaries, and acquiring and divesting foreign territory.

In the domestic sphere the president's prerogatives are closely linked to maintaining order. Thus, the president has discretion to declare and terminate national emergencies and even martial law. He may also call out the militia or the regular armed forces to control internal friction and keep the peace.

Of course, the president does not always receive supportive decisions from the courts. President Nixon, for example, was told he could not impound funds appropriated by Congress, engage in electronic surveillance without a search warrant, or prevent the publication of the Pentagon papers. He also was forced to turn over the Watergate tapes. Yet Nixon's presidency was atypical. Most presidents operate under few constraints from the courts.

It is not unusual for actions of executive branch officials to be found in violation of statutes passed by Congress, usually for exceeding the discretionary limits in the law. In these situations the judiciary is finding that the law, not the Constitution, must be changed, or perhaps just clarified, before the president's agents can take certain actions. Depending on the prevailing view in Congress, this may pose little problem for the president. At any rate, rarely are the issues involved central to his program.

JUDICIAL POWERS

In addition to enforcing court orders, presidents have some judicial instruments of their own. They can issue pardons, grant clemency, and proclaim amnesty. These powers are exclusively theirs and theirs alone.

Over the years the exercise of this judicial authority by presidents has sparked controversy. Ford's unconditional pardon of his predecessor, Richard Nixon, in 1974 became a major political issue that adversely affected his electability two years later. Issued prior to a conviction or even an indictment of the former president, the pardon "for all offenses against the United States which Richard Nixon has committed or may have committed or taken part in during the period from January 20, 1969, through August 9, 1974," precluded any criminal prosecution. Although Ford was accused of subverting the legal process, his power to issue the pardon was not disputed.[6] Whether Nixon's acceptance of it amounted to an admission of guilt is also unclear.

In addition to the issuance of unconditional pardons, presidents can grant conditional ones. In 1974 the Supreme Court upheld President Eisenhower's commutation of a death sentence provided that the individual never be paroled. In 1972 President Nixon granted executive clemency to former labor leader James Hoffa on the condition that he refrain from further union activities.

Presidents may also issue general amnesty to those who have impeded war efforts. President Lincoln exercised this authority in 1863 in an effort to persuade southern deserters to return to the Union. His successor, Andrew Johnson, granted a universal amnesty in 1868 to all those who participated in the insurrection in order to heal the wounds of the Civil War. Twentieth-century presidents have used this power to pardon those convicted of crimes who subsequently served in the military and to prevent the imposition of wartime penalties (still on the books) on those who failed to register for the draft during peacetime.

The most sweeping and controversial amnesty proclamation in recent times occurred in 1977. Implementing one of his campaign promises, President Carter pardoned all Vietnam draft resisters and asked the Defense Department to consider the cases of military deserters during that war on an individual basis. Congress attempted to undercut Carter's general pardon by prohibiting the use of funds to execute his order. It was unsuccessful, however, because the president's directive to the Justice Department did not require a separate appropriation.

CONCLUSION

The president is involved in vital relationships with the judicial branch, especially the Supreme Court. He attempts to influence its decisions through the process of selecting judges and justices and the arguments of his subordinates before the courts. There are strong congressional constraints on him in the selection of judges, however, and presidents sometimes err in their choice of nominees. Although the executive branch has skilled litigators before the federal appellate courts and has a clear record of success, the chief executive is ultimately dependent upon the judgment of members of a branch of government much more independent of him than the legislature. The president is once again a facilitator, not a director, of change.

A judicial decision does not end the president's relationship with the courts on an issue. In the capacity as chief executive the president may be obliged to enforce decisions, a responsibility that sometimes conflicts with his policy goals. Moreover, although the judiciary is generally deferential to the president, he may be ordered to comply with a holding against an action of his. Such decisions do not touch most of what presidents do, but in some instances they do hamper their actions. Thus, the president's relations with the courts are characterized both by conflict and by harmony, and influencing judicial decisions remains an important, but at times frustrating, priority for the White House.

NOTES

1. Quoted in J. Woodford Howard, Jr., *Courts of Appeals in the Federal Judicial System: A Study of the Second, Fifth, and District of Columbia Circuits* (Princeton, N.J.: Princeton University Press, 1981), p. 101.

2. Griffin Bell, quoted in Nina Totenberg, "Will Judges Be Chosen Rationally?" *Judicature* 60 (August/September 1976): 93.

3. Dwight Eisenhower, quoted in Henry J. Abraham, *Justices and Presidents: A Political History of Appointments to the Supreme Court,* 2nd ed. (New York: Oxford University Press, 1985), p. 263.

4. Earl Warren, *The Memoirs of Chief Justice Earl Warren* (Garden City, N.Y.: Doubleday, 1971), pp. 337–42.

5. John Ehrlichman, *Witness to Power: The Nixon Years* (New York: Simon and Schuster, 1982), p. 133.

6. There were many allegations of a deal between the two men. Some observers accused Ford of having agreed to the pardon in exchange for his nomination as vice president by Nixon. Ford vehemently denied that such an agreement had been made in sworn testimony before the House Judiciary Committee in 1974.

SELECTED READINGS

Abraham, Henry J. *Justices and Presidents: A Political History of Appointments to the Supreme Court,* 2nd ed. New York: Oxford University Press, 1985.

Bond, Jon R. "The Politics of Court Structure: The Addition of New Federal Judges, 1949–1978." *Law and Policy Quarterly* 2 (April 1980): 181–88.

Danelski, David J. *A Supreme Court Justice Is Appointed.* New York: Random House, 1964.

Ducat, Craig R. and Robert L. Dudley. "Federal District Judges and Presidential Power During the Postwar Era." *Journal of Politics* 51 (February 1989): 98–118.

Goldman, Sheldon. "Reagan's Judicial Legacy: Completing the Puzzle and Summing Up." *Judicature* 72 (April/May 1989): 318–30.

Murphy, Bruce Allen. *Fortas.* New York: William Morrow, 1988.

O'Brien, David M. "The Reagan Judges: His Most Enduring Legacy?" In Charles O. Jones, ed., *The Reagan Legacy.* Chatham, N.J.: Chatham House, 1988. Pp. 60–101.

Rowland, C. K., Robert A. Carp, and Ronald A. Stidham. "Judges' Policy Choices and the Value Basis of Judicial Appointments." *Journal of Politics* 46 (August 1984): 886–902.

Schmidhauser, John R. *Judges and Justices: The Federal Appellate Judiciary.* Boston: Little, Brown, 1979.

Scigliano, Robert. *The Supreme Court and the Presidency.* New York: Free Press, 1971.

Segal, Jeffrey. "Senate Confirmation of Supreme Court Justices: Partisan and Institutional Politics." *Journal of Politics* 49 (November 1987): 998–1015.

Stidham, Ronald S., Robert A. Carp, and C. K. Rowland. "Patterns of Presidential Influence on the Federal District Courts: An Analysis of the Appointment Process." *Presidential Studies Quarterly* 14 (Fall 1984): 548–60.

Walker, Thomas G., and Deborah J. Barrow. "The Diversification of the Federal Bench: Policy and Process Ramifications." *Journal of Politics* 47 (May 1985): 596–617.

12

Domestic Policy Making

The framers of the Constitution gave the president a policy role, but they did not expect him to dominate the process. Yet that is precisely what has occurred. Seizing on the initiative which the Constitution provides—and which their central perspective, institutional structure, and political support facilitate—presidents have become chief policymakers. Today, the public expects the president to establish and achieve national goals. He is expected to redeem campaign promises, to respond to policy emergencies, and to propose solutions to the country's social, economic, and political ills on a regular basis. Failure to address critical issues and rectify national problems will likely result in public criticism and even electoral defeat the next time around.

The problem that the president faces in performing his leadership role is that public expectations often exceed his ability to meet them. He has at his disposal significant policy expertise, but the experts are not always in agreement on what to do or how to do it. He has considerable institutional resources in the presidential office and the executive branch, but he cannot control the behavior of those in other branches of government, much less those outside the government who affect that behavior. He has difficulty even overseeing the actions of those who are presumably subordinate to him. Finally, he has political clout but it varies with time and circumstances, and he cannot always exercise it effectively. Thus, the president's policy role is not an easy one, but it is a critical one for the success of his presidency. This chapter will focus on the problems inherent in presidential leadership of public policy.

The president's domestic policy role did not evolve gradually. It developed in response to severe policy problems during the twentieth century. To begin the chapter, we describe those responses, chronicling the growth of the president's role. Next we discuss the mechanism and processes that were established to help meet these enlarged responsibilities. Initially we focus on the work of the Office of Management and Budget (known as the Bureau of the Budget prior to 1970) in the clearance and coordination of presidential policy initiatives and regulations emanating from the executive departments and agencies. We then turn to the White House and to the development of a domestic policy office.

In this section we also examine the impact of differing organizational models, policy goals, and personal styles on policy making. Finally, we look at policy-making strategies: How can external forces be accommodated? How can internal agendas be constructed and accomplished? We place particular emphasis on the politics of agenda building—the content, packaging, and timing of domestic policy proposals.

THE DEVELOPMENT OF A POLICY ROLE

The framers of the Constitution did not envision the president as chief domestic policymaker. They did, however, anticipate that the institution would include a policy-making role. Within the framework of the separation of powers, the president was given the duty to recommend necessary and expedient legislation. He also had latitude in the execution of the law. Taken together, this duty and that discretion provided the constitutional basis upon which a substantial policy-making role could be built.

For the first one hundred years, presidents recommended measures, took positions, and occasionally even drafted bills, but they did not formulate domestic policy on a regular basis. Beginning with Theodore Roosevelt and continuing with Woodrow Wilson, presidential participation in the policy-making process expanded. Theodore Roosevelt developed a close relationship with Speaker of the House Joseph Cannon. The two consulted frequently on most major policy initiatives. Cannon's power as Speaker and party leader enabled him to gain support for proposals Roosevelt initiated or favored.

Woodrow Wilson expanded the president's role even further. Seeing his responsibilities as analogous to the British prime minister's—to propose an integrated set of measures which addressed social and economic problems and then to utilize his personal and political influence to get them enacted—Wilson personally supervised the development of policy in his administration. He chose priorities, helped formulate legislation, and exhorted his cabinet and members of Congress to support it. Wilson himself went to Congress on several occasions and was the first president since John Adams to use the State of the Union address to articulate his goals directly to Congress.

Wilson's program, known as the New Freedom, included labor measures, tariff reform, and consumer protection. He introduced legislation that led to the creation of the Federal Reserve system. Working primarily with the leaders of his party on Capitol Hill, he secured the passage of many of his domestic proposals, including the Adamson Act (which provided an eight-hour day for railroad workers), the Clayton Antitrust Act, and the act that established the Federal Trade Commission. He led the country into World War I but was unable to obtain Senate approval for the Treaty of Versailles, the agreement ending hostilities.

Wilson's Republican successors (Harding, Coolidge, and Hoover) did not expand the presidency's policy-making responsibilities. Their conservative philosophy undoubtedly influenced their conception of a limited role. This philosophy, combined with the dispersal of power in Congress, did not encourage extensive legislative activity or an aggressive presidential posture. From the perspective of the 1920s, the Republican interlude was a return to "normalcy," as Warren Harding termed it. From today's perspective it was a brief respite in the growth of the president's domestic role.

Institutionalizing Presidential Initiatives

Franklin Roosevelt, more than any other individual, enlarged the president's domestic role and shaped the contemporary expectations of the job. Coming into office in the throes of a depression, Roosevelt believed it absolutely essential for the president to take the policy initiative. In his first inaugural address, he stated:

> I am prepared under my constitutional duty to recommend the measures that a stricken Nation in the midst of a stricken world may require. These measures or such other measures as Congress may build out of its experience and wisdom, I shall seek within my constitutional authority to bring to speedy adoption.[1]

Having a sizable Democratic majority that was inclined to support his initiatives and being the kind of person who was not averse to using his personal influence to get them adopted, Roosevelt quickly and dramatically became deeply involved in the policy process.

During the first one hundred days of the New Deal, Roosevelt and his aides formulated a series of measures to address the nation's most pressing economic problems. Designed to regulate and stimulate financial, agricultural, and business sectors, these proposals, which Congress enacted into law, also created new executive and regulatory agencies. This expanded the bureaucracy, but it did not necessarily improve the president's ability to oversee the implementation of "his" laws.

In the period from 1934 to 1936 another series of programs, fashioned by the president and his aides, was subsequently passed by Congress. Known as the second phase of the New Deal, these proposals included labor reform, social security, soil conservation, and various public works projects. New administrative structures were also established to administer these programs.

By the end of the Roosevelt era, the president's role as domestic policymaker was firmly established. In fact, when Harry S Truman, Roosevelt's successor, asked Congress for legislation to combat inflation, he was criticized by the Republican majority for not presenting a draft bill. When Eisenhower failed to propose a legislative program during his first year as president, he was criticized from both sides of the aisle. "Don't expect us to start from scratch on what you people want," an irate member of the House Foreign Affairs Committee told an Eisenhower official. "That's not the way we do things here. You draft the bills and we work them over."[2]

Whereas Roosevelt extended presidential initiatives primarily into the economic sphere, presidents Kennedy and Johnson expanded them to include social welfare and civil rights measures.[3] Medical aid to the elderly, public housing, community health, minimum wages, and conservation and education programs plus a variety of civil rights policies were crafted during their administrations. By the end of the 1960s the domestic policy initiative was firmly established in the White House.

Presidents were expected to set their policy agendas and determine the contours of legislative debate; they were expected to draft legislation and to work for its enactment. As time went on, they were also expected to mobilize public coalitions in support of their legislative proposals. And where Congress was slow in acting or obstructionist in its response, presidents were expected to find other ways of fulfilling their policy promises. Executive orders and other administrative actions became vehicles by which they could accomplish some of their policy goals. Republican presidents in particular, when confronted by Democratic Congresses, resorted to their executive powers to achieve their policy goals.

Changing Policy Environment

That the decade of the 1960s was a period of unbridled prosperity, replete with low inflation and high employment, permitted the expansion of government services. Most elements of the society benefitted. Even the president reaped political advantage from his policy-making role. As the chief provider, he was charged with finding solutions to the country's domestic ills. These solutions took the form of federal programs to the disadvantaged. However, the weakening of the economy in the 1970s and early 1980s cast doubt about these programmatic solutions. It also placed increasing burdens on the president in the performance of his policy-making role.

Higher inflation, greater unemployment, declining productivity, increasing foreign competition, and decreasing natural resources limited the capacity of the federal government to respond to economic and social ills. Beginning with the Nixon administration and continuing through the Reagan years, presidents attempted to slow the federal government's involvement in the domestic sector. President Nixon initiated a program of New Federalism in which the national government's revenues were to be shared with the states in exchange for a larger state and local role in providing social services. President Reagan carried this initiative one step further. In an attempt to shrink the public sector and reduce the responsibility of the federal government, he proposed a swap in which the states would take over the welfare and food stamp programs while the federal government would run the Medicare program. Nixon's revenue-sharing policy was enacted. The Reagan program was not, although the revenue-sharing program was ended and the national government's share of domestic programs declined during his administration.

In addition to the devolution of federal responsibilities to the states, recent presidents have also supported a reduction or at least retrenchment of other domestic programs. Carter vetoed appropriations for nineteen water projects much to the dismay of their supporters in Congress. Reagan proposed user fees for those using federal facilities, including waterways. His budget cut spending for a variety of social services, thereby shrinking the domestic proportion of the total outlays. Social welfare expenditures as a percentage of the federal budget dropped from 54.4 percent in 1980 to 50.2 percent in 1984.

Consolidating and eliminating federal programs has been one response to changing economic conditions and shifting public moods. Less regulatory activity has been another. The Carter administration successfully pushed the deregulation of the airline, railroad, and trucking industries while the Reagan administration relaxed the enforcement of those regulations which conflicted with its policy, particularly in the areas of consumer protection, worker safety, and the environment. In addition, the administration created a new division in the Office of Management and Budget to review all executive regulations to make sure that they were necessary and cost-effective and conformed to administrative guidelines.

Reducing government programs, expenditures, and regulations has not been easy. Presidents have had to overcome countervailing pressures from various constituencies interested in protecting and promoting programs which benefitted them. The growing sophistication of interest groups has increased their ability to apply grass-roots pressure to their advantage. Moreover, presidents have found it necessary to pursue policies for which large constituencies have been lacking, such as raising social secuity taxes or cutting benefits for entitlement programs.

Contemporary presidents are in a bind. How can they meet public needs with existing economic resources and large budget deficits? How can they build political support for programs that lack organized national constituencies? How can they maintain their electoral and governing coalitions without being captive of the interests of those within these coalitions? These problems have led one astute observer, Paul C. Light, to conclude that domestic policy making places the president in a no-win situation: "The cost of presidential policy has grown, while the President's ability to influence outcomes has declined."[4]

How can presidents overcome this dilemma? How can they meet contemporary expectations of their policy-making role? In the next part of this chapter, we will explore this question by examining the mechanisms and processes which have been developed to aid the president in this increasingly difficult task.

THE OMB AND THE EXECUTIVE BRANCH

A president cannot make policy alone. He needs others to provide him with information and expertise, to coordinate and implement his decisions and actions, to articulate his positions publicly and privately, and to build coalitions in support of them on Capitol Hill and within the executive branch. Initially many of these functions were performed by the Bureau of the Budget, working in conjunction with a small White House staff.

Exercising Central Clearance

The Bureau of the Budget was originally established in 1921 to help the president prepare an annual budget and submit it to Congress. In performing this function the budget agency annually reviewed the requests for funds of the executive departments and agencies. Beginning in the 1930s, this centralized clearance process was extended to include all executive branch requests for legislation, regardless of whether or not money would be expended. In each case, the budget officials had to decide whether the proposal was in accord with the president's program, consistent with the president's objectives, or at the very least, not opposed by the president. Any proposal which the Bureau of the Budget believed conflicted with presidential policy could not be advanced by the departments and agencies.

In making their judgments, the analysts in the Budget Bureau used presidential campaign statements, major addresses and reports, and special messages to Congress. If there was a major issue about which the Budget Bureau was uncertain how the president's program applied or what the program actually was, the White House would be consulted. This situation was rare, however. As a consequence, the Budget Bureau's decision was usually final. Although an appeal could be made to the White House by the departments and agencies, the practice was not encouraged and was rarely successful. Presidents wanted the clearance procedure to work, and it did. In fact they extended it to include the positions that departments and agencies take on legislation, and the testimony their officials present to Congress.

The Congress also found the process useful. Beginning in 1947, standing committees of both houses requested that the Bureau of the Budget indicate the president's position on legislation that did not originate in the executive departments and agencies.

From the president's perspective, central clearance offered a number of benefits: (1) it provided a mechanism for imprinting a presidential seal of approval on those proposals that the administration supported and withholding it from those it opposed; (2) it made the departments and agencies more aware of each other's views; (3) it helped resolve interagency disputes and promote interagency coordination. One of its most important functions was the resolution of conflict. Rather than kill a proposal, the Budget Bureau tried to have the objectionable parts removed and mediate the differences between the agencies.

From the department's perspective, however, the clearance requirement was seen as a constraint and the Bureau of the Budget as the policing agency. The civil servants who worked in the budget agency were regarded as the people who said no.

The central clearance process continues to operate today in much the same manner as it did in the past. However, it has become more politicized in the sense that civil servants play a less important role and political appointees a more important one in making key clearance decisions.

It is a behind-the-scenes operation, but occasionally it engenders public controversy. A case in point occurred in May 1989 when the Office of Management and Budget, the successor to the Bureau of the Budget, altered the congressional testimony of Dr. James E. Hansen, director of NASA's Goddard Institute for Space Studies, weakening his conclusion that man-made gases were primarily responsible for the so-called "greenhouse effect," the warming of the earth's atmosphere by the depleting of the ozone layer. When congressional leaders found out about the change they went public, criticizing the administration for trying to repress scientific evidence that conflicted with its policy.

The controversy points to the increasing political role of the Office of Management and Budget (OMB). It is the political appointees in the OMB and in the White House who make the critical decisions on what does or does not accord with the program of the president. In the greenhouse controversy, it was White House and cabinet officials, in addition to those in the OMB, who participated in the decision.

Coordinating Executive Advice

In addition to applying the president's position on the policy proposals and the stands of the executive agencies, the Office of Management and Budget performs another coordinating function. It solicits and summarizes recommendations on enrolled bills, legislation which has passed both houses of Congress and is awaiting presidential action.

After Congress has enacted the legislation, the Office of Management and Budget circulates copies of it to all executive branch units that have been involved in its development, would be involved in its implementation, or have a substantive interest in the program itself. The departments and agencies have forty-eight hours in which to make a recommendation to the president. Their recommendations, accompanied by supporting arguments and frequently by drafts of signing and veto statements, are then summarized by the OMB, which adds a recommendation of its own and sends the entire file to the White House within the first five days of the ten-day period the president has to approve or disapprove the legislation. A similar process designed to solicit the views of key White House aides was also begun in 1965. A diagram of the enrolled bill process is shown in Figure 12-1.

Today, when presidents are ready to make decisions on pending legislation, they have the benefit of the advice of a large number of executive officials. And because they have limited time and expertise of their own, they usually follow it.

Of all the executive participants in the process, presidents seem to be most influenced by the OMB and secondarily by the principal agency into whose jurisdiction the legislation falls. An OMB recommendation to approve the bill is almost always accepted. As the agency that says no most often, its advice to the president to sign the legislation seems to be regarded as an all-clear signal by the White House. Rarely does a president disregard this opportunity to approve legislation. On the other hand, the OMB's advice to veto might be ignored if there is significant political pressure in favor of the legislation.

A study of executive recommendations and presidential actions on enrolled bills during the Nixon and Ford administrations revealed that the OMB's recommendation to veto was followed only about half the time.[5] If other executive agencies also urged the president to disapprove the legislation, the chances of his vetoing it increased. In general, the more unified the advice, the more likely it will be taken.

Reviewing Agency Regulations

The role of the OMB as policy overseer was extended during the Reagan presidency. This extension took the form of reviewing all regulations promulgated by the departments and agencies to implement new and existing legislation.

Within one month of assuming office, President Reagan issued Executive Order 12291, which required that all departmental regulations be subjected to a cost-benefit analysis. A new unit in the OMB was charged with performing this task. Known as the Office of Information and Regulatory Affairs, it had the authority to delay, change, or even prevent a

Figure 12-1. The Enrolled Bill Process

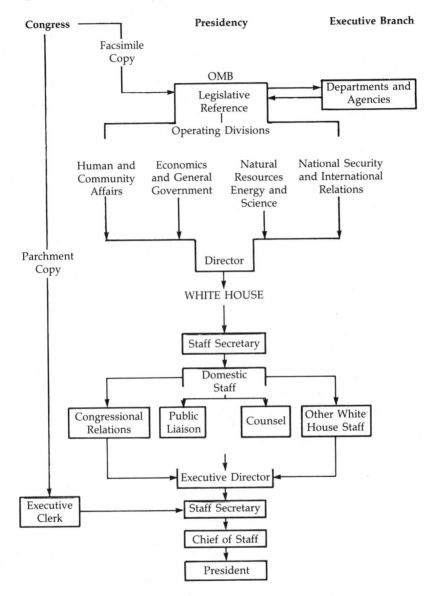

regulation from being issued if it did not meet the administration's cost-benefit criteria.

The insertion of the OMB into the policy implementation process had two principal effects. It decreased the number of regulations being issued and increased the OMB's influence within the government.

In order to conform to the new guidelines and protect their own autonomy, executive branch agencies reduced the volume of the new rules they promulgated. Figure 12-2 indicates the magnitude of this reduction. This decline in regulations was consistent with the Reagan administration's philosophy to reduce the role of the national government within the domestic arena and its campaign promise to try to eliminate governmental burdens on the private sector.

A second consequence of the OMB's additional functions in the regulatory review process was to extend its clout over the executive branch. Not only were departments and agencies discouraged from issuing new regulations, but those that they did propose were increasingly subject to modification by the OMB.[6] Moreover, an additional executive order issued by the president in 1984 required that even the proposal of a new regulation be justified. The agency had the burden of proof and the OMB made the final decision.

The OMB's stature with outside groups on the issuance of regulations was also enhanced. Business and professional organizations could appeal to the budget agency directly to remove or modify a regulation if

Figure 12-2. Departmental Rule Documents, 1977–1986

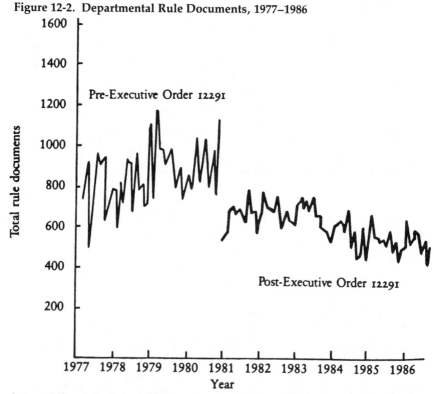

Source: Office of the Federal Register as reprinted in Peter M. Benda and Charles H. Levine, "Reagan and the Bureaucracy: The Bequest, the Promise, and the Legacy," in Charles O. Jones, ed., *The Reagan Legacy* (Chatham, N.J.: Chatham House, 1988), p. 118.

they were thwarted by the department. Moreover, Congress found its traditional relationship and influence with the bureaucracy undercut by the process. The OMB was in a position to negate political compromises made between legislative committees and executive branch agencies. Although Congress eventually was able to make the OMB's decisions more visible and thus subject them to public scrutiny, it was not able to reduce the OMB's decision-making authority. When that authority was supplemented by budget review and legislative clearance, the OMB was a force to be reckoned with in the formulation and implementation of domestic public policy.

Presenting an Annual Program

Since 1948, presidents have developed an annual legislative program and presented it to Congress in the form of special and required messages and addresses. This programming process developed out of the president's need to articulate his policy goals and to generate a record on which to appeal to voters. It also satisfied the need of Congress for an agenda upon which to focus its activities.

During the Truman and Eisenhower administrations, the Bureau of the Budget coordinated the mechanism that produced this program for the president. It did so initially as part of its annual budget review process. When departments and agencies were asked to submit their budgets for the next fiscal year, they were also asked to submit ideas for new proposals that would require funding. The Budget Bureau collected these ideas and forwarded them to the White House, which decided which of them to include in the president's program. The State of the Union address became the vehicle for announcing these policy proposals to Congress.

From the president's perspective, tapping a wide range of executive ideas and goals proved useful. It increased administration options. In the words of Clark Clifford, who as special counsel to Harry Truman initially directed the White House's programming operations:

> The purpose of obtaining this information was to have the background of the needs and also the opinions of the departments and agencies of government so that we would be able to extract from that voluminous source of information a legislative program. While much of it was self-serving, at least we felt that we had tapped knowledgeable and experienced people in government. Sometimes in that general request a real pearl would appear. It is like a diver swimming around and all of a sudden there would appear a pearl as large as a hen's egg. In my opinion, that alone would justify the effort.[7]

This departmental orientation to policy making ended in the 1960s. The desire of presidents Kennedy and Johnson to generate new initiatives, combined with their view of the bureaucracy as a pretty conservative place where innovative ideas were not likely to originate, resulted in a shift of focus from inside the executive branch to outside the government. In the words of President Johnson:

> I had watched this programming process for years, and I was convinced that it did not encourage enough fresh or creative ideas. The bureaucracy of the government is too preoccupied with day to day operations, and there is strong bureaucratic inertia dedicated to preserving the status quo. As a result, only the most powerful ideas can survive. Moreover, the cumbersome organization of government is simply not equipped to solve complex problems that cut across departmental jurisdictions.[8]

To generate new ideas, both Kennedy and Johnson set up task forces composed of campaign supporters, academicians, business and labor leaders, but not bureaucrats. Their job was to investigate a problem and present the president with a solution without regard to political considerations or costs. These factors were taken into account by the president and his aides when deciding which of the proposals to pursue.

Under Johnson the number of task forces increased, but their composition and their recommendations were secret. The purpose of the secrecy was to enable the president to take credit for ideas he liked but at the same time not be burdened by those he did not. The secrecy also permitted the president to ascertain the opinions of influential members of Congress without embarrassment to him or them. The Johnson aide who communicated with those in Congress would normally preface his remarks with the question, "The president hasn't decided to do this, but if he did, how would you respond?"

The high priority on new domestic policy proposals in both the Kennedy and Johnson administrations and the desire of both presidents to be personally involved in their development put an even greater burden for their initiation, coordination, and synthesis on White House aides. Moreover, the size of this effort and the number of task forces that were involved forced an expansion in the personnel who regularly dealt with domestic policy matters. By the mid-1960s, a separate White House staff was created to systematize the programming operation. This staff, although small and fairly general by contemporary standards, was the forerunner of the larger, more differentiated structure that has functioned as an operating arm of the presidency thereafter.

As a consequence of the growing White House role in policy making, the status and influence of the departments and agencies and the people who ran them declined. A two-track programming system eventually emerged with the departments and agencies on the second track. While they continued to submit proposals with their annual budget estimates, these submissions had less of an impact on the president's major domestic objectives. As power shifted to the White House, the Budget Bureau's influence in determining major presidential priorities also declined.

THE DOMESTIC POLICY OFFICE
AND THE WHITE HOUSE

The first domestic policy office was organized by the White House in 1965 to coordinate Lyndon Johnson's Great Society program. Charged with staffing Johnson's outside task forces and then reviewing their recommendations, the office developed policy initiatives for the president and then converted them into a legislative format, an executive order, or a departmental regulation.

President Nixon enlarged and institutionalized this White House policy-making operation. In 1970 he created a Domestic Council composed of his domestic cabinet secretaries and a supporting staff. Organized as a separate unit in the Executive Office of the President and directed by a senior White House aide, the staff quickly assumed dominance over the process. The council met infrequently. In fact, cabinet secretaries had difficulty even communicating with the president on an individual basis, much less as a group.

Since Nixon preferred a memorandum or option paper, the policy debate had to be in written form. Moreover, since he preferred a formal hierarchical mode of operation, proposals, memos, and option papers had to be sent through official channels. John Ehrlichman, Nixon's chief domestic adviser and executive director of the council, supervised staff operations. All domestic policy documents to and from the president passed through his office.

The council's work was done primarily by committees organized on the basis of projects or missions. Composed of subcabinet departmental officials but organized and run by Ehrlichman's staff, the committees operated as internal task forces. Their functions were similar to the Johnson external task forces—to examine issues, conduct studies, and prepare recommendations for the president. Once a course of action was chosen by the president, the committees reconvened for the purpose of implementing his decision.

The Domestic Council staff member who presided over the group had to make certain that recommendations to the president were in conformity with his basic goals and that the options he selected were properly translated into legislative proposals or executive actions. In this way a White House orientation was imposed on the policy-making process.

The Nixon council system was subsequently modified in 1972. Its staff was reduced in size. Senior personnel were reassigned to other departments and agencies. Some have contended that this was a thinly veiled attempt by the president to rein in the executive bureaucracy.[9]

As part of the policy reorganization, three cabinet secretaries were given additional responsibilities for coordinating domestic policy within three broad areas: human resources, natural resources, and community development. The events of Watergate, culminating first in Ehrlichman's resignation and eventually in Nixon's, ended this "super cabinet" experiment but did not deter future presidents from trying to exercise as tight control as possible over the domestic policy-making activities of their departments and agencies.

The domestic policy office has been continued in each subsequent administration. Its title, however, has changed, perhaps more for symbolic reasons than anything else. New administrations, not wanting their domestic proposals emanating from an office associated with their predecessor, changed its name. The Carter administration called it the Domestic Policy Staff, and the Reagan and Bush administrations titled it the Office of Policy Development. Although its principal functions have remained essentially the same—the development and coordination of major policy initiatives for the president—the degree to which the office has controlled policy making has varied. During its heyday in the Nixon administration, the Domestic Council was the principal policy unit. It ran the process by which major administration initiatives were developed, and its executive director was the president's main domestic adviser. In contrast, during the Ford period, the council played a much less important role. Weak leadership of its policy staff, an emphasis on economic matters, and Ford's desire for broader participation in key administration decisions helped shift power away from the White House and toward the departments and agencies.

Under Carter, the office was resuscitated, although it did not become the sole advisory body for domestic policy as it had been during the Nixon years. It did, however, become the principal coordinating mechanism for presenting and evaluating a range of opinions and options to the president.

Ronald Reagan's penchant for turning to his department secretaries for advice combined with his opposition to new and costly domestic programs once again reduced the influence and shifted the role of the White House's domestic policy staff. It performed largely administrative tasks, providing institutional support for the cabinet councils and helping the president with other policy matters that required his attention. The office's low status and limited impact generated considerable turnover among its staff.

Under Bush the policy staff has maintained a low profile. It has been most active in coordinating cabinet input into administration policy, particularly in response to emerging domestic issues.

The size of the domestic staff has varied from a high of approximately eighty at the end of Nixon's first term to about thirty to forty in other administrations. About half of the staff members have been professionals; the remainder have been supporting personnel. A senior presidential assistant has headed the office. Frequently, his deputy has coordinated the day-to-day operations.

In the course of their operation, the policy staffs have worked closely with the OMB. In general, priority policy making has been the prerogative of the president's domestic advisers while the clearance, coordination, and review of less important policy matters remain the job of the OMB. Conflict and cooperation have alternately characterized the relationship between these two presidential staffs. From time to time turf battles have also erupted between those responsible for economic advice and those charged with domestic policy making.

Structural Orientation

The relationship between the domestic policy staff and the executive departments and agencies has been critical to the success of the president's policy efforts. While most presidents-elect ritually promise to institute a cabinet government upon taking office, they often find this undesirable.

In general, contemporary presidents have adopted one of two approaches to policy making. They have either assumed a White House orientation in which their senior aides dominate the process or they have adopted a cabinet orientation in which department secretaries exercise greater influence. The Nixon, and to a lesser extent, Carter presidencies illustrate the first approach, and the Reagan and Bush presidencies exemplify the latter.

In the White House approach, strong, influential domestic advisers funnel recommendations to the president. They filter and broker ideas. Their influence stems primarily from their control over the information flow to and from the president and the analytic network upon which that information rests.

The senior advisers tend to be advocates as well as mediators. Presidents rely on them for advice. This enhances their status and provides them with greater influence, not only with the president but also with others who wish to affect his policy judgments.

In contrast, the cabinet approach is less centralized. Cabinet secretaries, individually and collectively, have a greater impact. The White House policy office functions as a liaison and secretariat rather than as a policy initiator. It coordinates executive branch activity rather than dominates it. The senior adviser is more of a broker than an advocate.

President Reagan utilized this approach in his cabinet council system. The councils, consisting of six to eleven department heads, were organized on the basis of substantive issues. Reagan established seven of them—economic affairs, commerce and trade, human resources, natural resources and environment, food and agriculture, legal policy, and management—in his first term but compressed them to three—economic affairs, domestic affairs, and national security—in the second.

In theory the councils were designed to provide a forum for cabinet members to discuss policy issues that crossed departmental lines. Each council was composed of six to eleven cabinet members, although its meetings were open to any department secretary who wished to attend. The president served as the official chair of each group. However, he attended only about 15 percent of the meetings, usually when an issue was in the final stages of consideration and recommendations for action were to be proposed. In the president's absence a cabinet member served as chair pro tempore with the power to convene sessions, propose agenda items, and designate interagency work groups to study specific issues. Naturally, the chair pro tempore's attitude toward using the council had a lot to do with its influence on administration policy.

How did the councils work? Ralph Bledsoe, executive secretary to the Domestic Affairs Council during most of the second term and a special assistant to the president for domestic policy, described their operating procedure as follows:

> Interagency working groups are still the primary means by which policy issues are identified and scoped. Working groups and task forces are responsible for preparation of the issues and options papers to be discussed by the councils. As with the cabinet councils, issues are usually discussed in one or more council meetings without the President in attendance. When an issue is ready to be forwarded to the President for discussion and/or a decision, the council directs that a paper be prepared reflecting the council's views. If the President is being asked for a policy decision, the paper is in decision memorandum format, usually including a statement of the issue, background information, a discussion of decision options with advantages and disadvantages of each, and a recommendation, if appropriate. Following a meeting with the President, at which council members present their advice and views, the President will usually make a decision that is then communicated to the appropriate departments and agencies for implementation.[10]

The cabinet councils were constructed with the president's delegatory style in mind. Patterned after a model Reagan had used when he was governor of California, the system was designed to involve him when necessary and in a relatively passive manner. Reagan could hear the issues debated, have points clarified, and then retire to make a decision.

It was hoped that the councils would generate broad discussion, help develop consensus, and provide a mechanism for implementing administration decisions in accordance with the president's wishes. To work, end-runs had to be avoided, an administrative structure tied to the White House had to be established, and decisions had to be made that were consistent with the general ideological perspective of the administration. Secretaries could not simply be departmental advocates.

These conditions were more prevalent during the first term of the Reagan administration than during the second. Cabinet secretaries in key policy areas, particularly economic affairs and administration and management, tended to work through the council structure and not around it. However, in other areas the influence of the OMB and the group that met regularly to plan the administration's legislative strategy reduced the role of the cabinet councils on key administration priorities.

Any policy-making apparatus has its limitations. A council system is no exception. It requires many hours of meetings and group discussions. It is prone to leaks and may also be subject to a "group-think" mentality, the emergence of a consensus that discourages careful and candid consideration. In Reagan's second term, these limitations, changes in personnel in the White House and cabinet, and the absence of clear and urgent policy objectives, effectively reduced the influence of the cabinet councils. While they continued to meet, increasingly they dealt with second-level issues.

President Bush initially chose to adopt the three-council system. However, he gave his department heads considerable discretion to develop policy in response to issues that emerged at the beginning of his administration. The White House policy staff helped coordinate the policy initiatives within the administration, solicited the views of others, organized work groups, and provided the president with a range of options and recommendations.

Stylistic Differences

In addition to the structural orientations presidents have adopted, their policy goals and personal styles have also affected White House policy making. The desire for innovative policy, particularly evident during the Kennedy–Johnson period, spurred the development of new sources for ideas and programs. The departments were supplemented by outside task forces. Similarly, the goals of retrenchment and consolidation, particularly evident during the Reagan administration, turned the focus back to executive officials appointed by the president who shared the president's ideological and policy perspectives.

While Kennedy and Johnson did not believe the bureaucracy could develop innovative policy, they were confident that civil servants would be able and willing to implement that policy once it had been initiated. Reagan lacked that confidence. He did not believe that career bureaucrats could be trusted to execute the demise of their own programs.

All recent presidents have tried to keep tabs on their principal policy objectives by using their staff to promote and protect their interests. How the staff worked and how much power it wielded related in part to the style of the president and his penchant for exercising central authority. Those presidents who wished to involve themselves in the details of decision making seemed to have more flexible staff structures. Johnson and Carter, in particular, had domestic policy offices that facilitated their reaching down the policy-making chain to make decisions. Both presidents had difficulty delegating authority to others. In contrast, Ford and Reagan were delegators who relied on their advisers for recommendations on what decisions to make and when to make them. Their policy operations were designed to relieve them of making the less important policy judgments. The difference was that Reagan had a more structured ideological perspective. It shaped the contours of his administration's decision making more than did Ford's pragmatic views.

Nixon, too, was a delegator. In contrast to Ford and Reagan, however, he did not enjoy or encourage oral debate among his subordinates. Rather he preferred a system that produced option papers from which he could make judgments. Like Carter, he desired detailed written analyses and ranges of alternatives from which he could choose.

STRATEGIES FOR POLICY MAKING

The organizational component is only one aspect of policy making. Presidents obviously need a mechanism to help them design and coordinate their program, but that mechanism alone cannot ensure their program's success. Policy must be strategically accomplished. External interests must be accommodated; agendas must be artfully constructed and packaged; and long-term national objectives must be maintained, despite the persistance of parochial perspectives and short-term goals.

Accommodating External Forces

Changes within the political and institutional environment, the decentralization of power in Congress, growth of single-issue groups, and weakening of partisan coalitions have increased and diversified pressures on the presidency. This has affected the policy-making process in two principal ways. It has made it more sensitive to outside interests, and it has required that the president devote more personal and institutional resources to the achievement of his domestic policy goals.

Prior to the 1970s the Bureau of the Budget and, to a lesser extent, the White House were relatively invulnerable to external groups seeking to influence their decisions. The Budget Bureau considered itself a presidential agency. It had only one principal constituent, the president. Civil servants, not political appointees, ran the process and made most of the decisions. They were expected to do so within the framework of the president's objectives but also on the basis of the merits of the issue.

Taking political factors into account was the job of senior presidential aides in the White House. They worked in a relatively closed environment. While leaders of the president's party, influential supporters, and friends could gain access, the general public, including most of the organized groups, were excluded. Congress and the bureaucracy were the principal turfs on which groups fought their political battles. The Bureau of the Budget and the White House were distanced from the fray.

This began to change in the 1970s. The reorganization of the Budget Bureau into the Office of Management and Budget and the creation of a number of political positions to oversee its operation, the increase in the size of the policy staffs in the White House and their growth in power and influence, and the need to mobilize interest groups behind the president's program all contributed to this increased receptivity to outside views and sensitivity to outside pressures. The reaction of presidents Ford and Carter to Watergate, particularly to Nixon's closed presidency, provided further impetus to open the White House to public view and political influence.

Lobbyists, who themselves were increasing in number, began to contact administration officials directly in the OMB and in the policy office to try to affect their judgments. The White House, in turn, began to utilize interest group and community leaders in building coalitions behind their programs. By the mid-1970s a separate unit within the White House had been established to accomplish this objective. Known as the Public Liaison Office, it became the primary link between the administration and interest group leaders.

The office functioned primarily as a conduit. It provided access for those outside the government who wished to affect administration policies. It also provided public relations opportunities for the president. Literally thousands of group representatives and community leaders have been invited to the White House to meet administration officials and hear them promote their programs. The effect of these activities has been to aid the president in getting his proposals through Congress and accepted by significant segments of the American people.

Another effect has not been nearly as beneficial. Such activities have also encouraged "revolving door politics," the practice of public officials leaving the government, obtaining jobs in the private sector, and cashing in on their political contacts. The key to interest group influence is access. Those individuals who, by virtue of their personal acquaintances, knowledge, and experiences, can provide such access, are extremely valuable to interest groups and will be well compensated for their ability to open doors and present positions. Several high officials of the Reagan administration were subsequently accused and convicted of violating a federal conflict-of-interest law that restricts (for a designated period) the contacts a former public official may have and the issues that the official may be involved with after returning to private life.

Recent administrations have worked hard to build political support on an issue-by-issue, constituency-by-constituency basis. They have used business, labor, and trade associations to ascertain congressional opinion and affect congressional decision making. They have encouraged letter writing and telephone campaigns; they have even gotten interest groups to contribute to the administration's electoral efforts. In doing this, they have not admitted to "lobbying" but to educating and providing channels of communication, since federal law prohibits the use of government funds to lobby for executive policies in Congress.

In addition to the work of the Public Liaison Office, other units have also been established to communicate with state and local governments and with party officials and political leaders around the country. A larger, more sophisticated White House communications operation has also been created to market the president and his policy objectives more effectively with the general population. By the 1980s more than one-third of the people who worked in the White House were involved in public relations activities of one type or another.

Building a Policy Agenda

The changing institutional and political environment for policy has also affected the content of agendas. In recent years their scope has become more modest while the policies within them have become more complex. Moreover, their promotion has become more closely tied to the cycle of presidential influence.

In the past, agendas tended to be laundry lists of proposals designed to appeal to as broad a segment of electoral supporters as possible. Franklin Roosevelt's New Deal, Truman's Fair Deal, Kennedy's New Frontier, Johnson's Great Society, even Nixon's New Federalism programs fit into this category. The depressed American economy of the 1930s, the increasing social consciousness of the 1960s, the democratizing of the nomination process in the 1970s, and the expansion of the electoral period during the past decade have all contributed to the demands for a large and diverse policy agenda.

The way in which presidents formulated their domestic programs also contributed to the same end. By soliciting proposals from a variety of sources and established interests, presidents have generated multiple pressures on their own programs. The most effective way to deal with these pressures had been to accommodate them in packages that included something for almost everyone.

While these pressures have persisted and even increased, the president's ability to achieve them has diminished. Resources have become more scarce; a huge national debt has developed. The government lacks the revenues to meet a plethora of policy demands. The system has become more pluralistic. Greater effort must be exerted to mobilize majority coalitions. This has increased the costs of domestic policy making for the president. More time, energy, and institutional resources have to be devoted to these activities.

One consequence of increasing costs and decreasing resources has been the need to limit items in the domestic agenda. Another has been to package and promote the proposals in such a way as to maximize their public appeal. A third imperative for the president is to effectively cycle them over the congressional calendar. Finally, he must avoid excessive involvement in the details of his administration's policy while maintaining a long-term national perspective.

LIMITING THE ITEMS.   The expansion of governmental activities has generated more groups with a stake in public policy. Today, there are more opinions to hear, more interests to balance, more agendas to combine. This has produced, in the words of Hugh Heclo, more "policy congestion."[11]

It has also increased the complexity of many issues with which contemporary administrations must deal. One policy decision affects another. Spheres of jurisdiction overlap. Distinctions between domestic and international concerns are no longer as clear-cut.

The task for the president and his aides is to sort out the relationships among the competing interests and complex issues and to integrate them into a single comprehensive program. One way to do this has already been discussed—use an institutional mechanism that imposes a presidential perspective as the Bureau of the Budget did prior to 1965 and the White House has done since then. Another tactic is to reduce the agenda to fewer critical items and bind them together in some fashion. The Reagan administration has employed this strategy as well.

Upon taking office, President Reagan translated his campaign stands—government is too large and costly, taxes are too high, defense is too weak, and regulations are too numerous—into two basic legislative initiatives, budget and tax reform, and two basic executive ones, a hiring freeze and a reduction of regulations. These items constituted the administration's primary agenda for its first two years in office. After that, it concentrated on maintaining the goals of its early policy through its budgetary requests and executive actions or, in some cases, inactions.

Limiting items helps the president set the pace and tone of public debate. It helps focus public attention on certain presidential activities. This contributes to the perception that the president is in command. It also enables the president to concentrate resources behind his administration's priorities rather than have them dissipated in accordance with numerous wish lists.

There is, of course, a negative side to limiting the agenda too much. Some people'e expectations will not be satisfied. For the Reagan administration it was the social objectives of the conservatives that were largely abandoned.[12]

PACKAGING AND PROMOTING LEGISLATIVE PRIORITIES.   In addition to limiting the items in the president's agenda, it is necessary to package them artfully. Presenting a few key proposals rather than a comprehensive set of policies reduces the number of instances in which supporters of the president can disagree. It encourages them to rally behind his policies, while it forces others to choose sides. Fewer positions and roll-call votes make it easier to concentrate resources and mobilize winning coalitions. Reagan followed this strategy in his 1981 and 1982 budget battles with the Democrats in Congress. By getting the House of Representatives to agree to an up or down vote on its final budget resolutions, the president improved his chances of obtaining the level of expenditures he desired. The packaging of the large personal and corporate income tax cut in 1981, the social security compromise in 1983, and the tax reform program in 1986 was key to their enactment into legislation.

The president must also promote his priorities within the Congress and among the general public. To gain congressional support, it is necessary to convince members of Congress that the proposed legislation is supported within their constituencies. Generating a constituency-based response is one way for the president to achieve that objective. Showing the economic benefit for the constituency is another. White House congressional liaison aides often present the administration's position, with the president telephoning wavering members before a critical vote.

CYCLING POLITICAL ISSUES.   Another strategic consequence of the increased costs of domestic policy making is that an administration's priorities must be cycled over the course of the congressional calendar. A president cannot wait several months before making his initial proposals nor should he inundate Congress with them.

Moving quickly on the most controversial items is important for two reasons. Electoral cycles, department pressures, and public moods tend to decrease presidential influence over time. As members of Congress position themselves for the next election, as bureaucrats and their clientele begin to assert their claims on political appointees, as segments of the winning coalition become disillusioned, as the outparty begins to coalesce in opposition to the incumbent, it is more difficult for a president to achieve domestic policy goals. Moreover, presidential reputations are built early and tend to persist longer than their ability to achieve policy successes.

Carter found this out the hard way. He used the first six months in office to develop policies to implement his election promises. By the time these proposals were readied for Congress, Carter's honeymoon had ended and his policies got stuck in a legislative labyrinth. George Bush, facing a similar problem, adopted a bipartisan approach in dealing with Congress to help surmount it with partial success.

The Reagan administration, in contrast, learned from the Carter experience. With its agenda in place prior to taking office, Reagan seized on his unexpectedly large electoral victory in 1980 to claim a mandate for his economic program and then moved quickly to obtain its enactment. Proposals that were developed later in the administration, such as the New Federalism and urban enterprise zone plans, met with considerably more congressional resistance. In general Reagan was less successful as his administration progressed. His congressional support declined even as his popularity increased.

The dilemma presidents often face is that their influence tends to be greatest when their knowledge of substantive policy issues is least. Not only do they not have sufficient time to educate themselves before making critical policy judgments, but they may not have time to develop innovative policy at all. According to Paul C. Light, declining influence requires presidents to look for available alternatives among existing options and take the first acceptable one. This may be the policy that raises the fewest objections, the one that has resulted in the most compromise, and consequently, the one able to muster the most support within the executive branch. That support makes it most acceptable to the largest number of decision makers even though it may not be the best solution.[13]

DISCERNING THE FOREST FROM THE TREES.   Constraints on time and energy suggest another lesson for contemporary presidents. They should not involve themselves too deeply in the details of decision making, although they must provide general policy guidance. Jimmy Carter is a case in point. Finding it difficult to delegate, he spent considerable time becoming an expert on the various policy issues in which he was interested or which came to his attention. At the beginning of his administration he read around four hundred pages of papers and memos a day! James Fallows, a former Carter speech writer, describes his boss as "the perfectionist accustomed to thinking that to do a job right you must do it yourself."[14] Fallows illustrated:

> He [Carter] would leave for a weekend at Camp David laden with thick briefing books, would pore over budget tables to check the arithmetic, and during his first six months in office, would personally review all requests to use the White House tennis court. . . . After six months had passed, Carter learned that this was ridiculous, as he learned about other details he would have to pass by if he was to use his time well. But his preference was still to try to do it all.[15]

Naturally, this prodigious effort took its toll, and Carter was eventually forced to cut back.

In contrast, Reagan took the opposite tack. While he articulated a strong ideological perspective, he left most of the details to senior White House and cabinet officials. This exposed him to the charge that he was manipulated by his staff and that he was overly dependent on key White House aides for the decisions he had to make, when he had to make them, and the range of options from which he had to choose. It also left him prey to his staff's misperceptions of what he wanted and its judgments of what was in his interest. The problems that developed in the White House national security staff and that culminated in the Iran–Contra affair demonstrate the dangers of a hands-off, disengaged approach to presidential staffing and decision making. (See Chapter 7 for a more detailed discussion of the Iran–Contra affair and its impact on presidential decision making.)

SUSTAINING A NATIONAL PERSPECTIVE.   Reagan's ideological perspective helped him tackle another policy-making problem that besets contemporary presidents—how to sustain a national perspective in the light of continuous parochial pressures. Ideology provides a rationale for including (and excluding) certain items in a policy agenda and linking them to one another in a way that makes sense to partisan supporters. It helps transform an electoral coalition into a policy one. It is also useful in overcoming the tendencies that frequently lead executive officials to adopt views and advocate interests that are at variance with the president's.

The Reagan administration employed ideology in converting electoral promises into tangible policy goals. It also used ideology as a criterion for appointment. Cabinet and subcabinet officials were nominated in part because they shared the president's views. They were expected to impose those views on their agencies rather than the other way around.

Ideology, in short, can be a unifying tool. It can build support by simplifying and focusing. It is not without its dangers, however. Rigid adherence to an ideological perspective makes compromise difficult. As it unites supporters so too can it unify opponents, thereby polarizing the policy positions. It can blind adherents to the nuances of proposals and the need for adjustment and change. Pragmatic solutions may be disregarded. Policy is apt to be more precipitous and extreme. Continuity between administrations of differing ideological perspectives is more difficult to achieve.

On the other hand, lack of an overarching ideological or conceptual framework can produce the same problem within an administration. Critics have contended that policy inconsistencies in the Carter administration were due in part to this problem. Again as James Fallows observed:

> I came to think that Carter believes fifty things, but no one thing. He holds explicit, thorough positions on every issue under the sun, but he has no large view of the relations between them, no line indicating which goals

(reducing unemployment? human rights?) will take precedence over which (inflation control? a SALT treaty?) when the goals conflict.[16]

In Reagan's case, the president's ideological perspective helped establish the goals and the initial programmatic components. The president subsequently deviated from these components when they appeared to be politically unattainable or economically or socially unfeasible.

MAINTAINING A LONG-RANGE VIEW.   Another problem related to promoting policy consistency is maintaining a long-range perspective. In making policy, everyday emergencies tend to drive out future planning. This limits the outlook of those involved in policy making to the short term and rarely beyond the next election.

Contemporary White Houses have attempted to design a longer-range domestic planning capability but without much success. In 1975 President Ford asked Vice President Rockefeller to provide leadership and direction for the establishment of social goals. However, Rockefeller's decision not to run for office one year later abruptly ended this effort.

The Reagan administration's attempt to create a long-range policy-making capability in the form of a new office of planning and evaluation met with a similar fate. Charged with developing strategic plans for the president's agenda and schedule, the office fashioned a series of early blueprints that consisted of possible responses to international and national crises, including an assassination attempt.

As the administration got underway and had to confront changing conditions and react to new problems, the office's futuristic planning became less relevant to contemporary presidential needs. Instead of being concerned with long-term goals, the White House became absorbed with day-to-day needs; instead of remaining on an ideologically generated calendar, the administration became more sensitive to changes in public moods. It depended increasingly on data from national surveys to discern shifts in public opinion and to anticipate the type and timing of actions that would most likely engender the necessary political support.

Although the planning and evaluation office was eventually disbanded, it left an impressive technological legacy in the form of an efficient information processing and retrieval system designed to serve the policy needs of the presidency. The Carter White House had begun to employ computers for tracking correspondence and grants, but the Reagan administration broadened their application to include the drafting, editing, and transmission of speeches and messages; the processing of presidential correspondence; and the scheduling of meetings, tracking of legislation, and monitoring of executive operations.

The White House has also expanded its access to commerical and governmental data bases. An electronic mail capability has been established within the Executive Office and between its various units and a growing number of executive departments and agencies. A portable electronic mail unit that travels with the president was also instituted. These advances in technology to make, communicate, and sell public policy will undoubtedly continue.

CONCLUSION

The president has become the nation's principal domestic policymaker. His role developed primarily in the twentieth century and largely as a consequence of social, economic, and political problems which required solutions by the federal government. With a national perspective, a large staff structure, and the ability to focus public attention and mobilize support, the president has been placed in a position to propose policy and get it adopted. The electoral process has provided him with further incentives to do so. Congress, the executive, and the public look to him for policy leadership.

The mechanism necessary to accomplish this leadership took form over two decades. Initially the Budget Bureau provided the resources and managed the processes, with its senior civil servants working closely with the White House to develop, coordinate, and clear policy proposals emanating from the departments and agencies. Once the president turned from departments and agencies to other sources for policy ideas, however, the budget agency's influence declined and the White House's increased.

Since the mid-1960s the president's chief policy aides have dominated the policy-making process. They, in turn, have depended on their assistants to monitor and integrate the input of others. The White House has also become more involved in building support for these priorities. Separate presidential offices charged with policy development and political liaison have now become institutionalized.

The development of these structures has enhanced the presidency's influence but not necessarily the president's. Although the incumbent's goals and style still shape domestic policy making, they cannot control it. A president is dependent on his staff for deciding when he should be involved, what options he should consider, how those options are presented to him, and how they should be articulated and promoted inside and outside the government.

Changes within the political system have made the president's tasks more burdensome. Competing demands, complex issues, and confrontational politics have made it more difficult for the chief policymaker to design programs and obtain support for them. His dilemma is that expectations of his role exceed his resources for achieving his goals. This has affected strategies for policy making.

Today, to exert policy leadership a president must accommodate external forces and mobilize them into a policy coalition. He must limit his priorities and carefully package, promote, and cycle them over the course of his administration. Finally, he must work to establish and maintain a long-term national perspective. It is important that key proposals be developed and enacted early. Addressing the national policy needs and contributing to the administration's political needs also serve the president's leadership needs.

These tasks are not easy. They require skillful personal and institutional leadership. A president cannot dictate policy outcomes but he can affect them. His reputation, his subsequent achievements, and ultimately the fate of his presidency may hinge on how well he does so.

NOTES

1. Franklin D. Roosevelt, "First Inaugural Address," March 4, 1933, as appears in the *Congressional Record*, 73rd Cong., Special Sess., pp. 5–6.
2. As quoted in Richard E. Neustadt, "Presidency and Legislation: Planning the President's Program," *American Political Science Review* 49 (December 1955): 1015.
3. The one previous exception was the social security program.
4. Paul C. Light, *The President's Agenda* (Baltimore: Johns Hopkins University Press, 1982), p. 217.
5. Stephen J. Wayne, Richard L. Cole, and James F. C. Hyde, Jr., "Advising the President on Enrolled Legislation," *Political Science Quarterly* 94 (Summer 1979): 303–17.
6. Peter M. Benda and Charles H. Levine, "Reagan and the Bureaucracy: The Bequest, the Promise, and the Legacy," in Charles O. Jones, ed., *The Reagan Legacy* (Chatham, N.J.: Chatham House, 1988), pp. 118–19.
7. Clark Clifford, quoted in Stephen J. Wayne, *The Legislative Presidency* (New York: Harper & Row, 1978), p. 104.
8. Lyndon B. Johnson, *The Vantage Point: Perspectives of the Presidency 1963–1969* (New York: Holt, Rinehart and Winston, 1971), pp. 326–27.
9. Richard P. Nathan, *The Plot That Failed* (New York: Wiley, 1975).
10. Ralph C. Bledsoe, "Policy Management in the Reagan Administration," in James P. Pfiffner and R. Gordon Hoxie et al., eds., *The Presidency in Transition* (New York: Center for the Study of the Presidency, 1989), pp. 60–61.
11. Hugh Heclo, "One Executive Branch or Many?" in Anthony King, ed., *Both Ends of the Avenue* (Washington, D.C.: American Enterprise Institute, 1983), p. 32.
12. Being a Republican and having a narrower constituency contributed to Reagan's ability to focus on economic matters. In contrast, Democratic presidents find themselves under greater pressures from a more heterogeneous group of supporters to involve the federal government in a greater range of social and economic programs.
13. Light, *The President's Agenda*, p. 219.
14. James Fallows, "The Passionless Presidency," *Atlantic*, May 1979, p. 38.
15. Ibid.
16. Ibid., p. 42.

SELECTED READINGS

Bell, Terrel H. *The Thirteenth Man: A Reagan Cabinet Memoir.* New York: Free Press, 1987.

Benda, Peter M., and Charles H. Levine. "Reagan and the Bureaucracy: The Bequest, the Promise, and the Legacy." In Charles O. Jones, ed. *The Reagan Legacy.* Chatham, N.J.: Chatham House, 1988. Pp. 102–42.

Bledsoe, Ralph C. "Policy Management in the Reagan Administration." In James P. Pfiffner and R. Gordon Hoxie, eds. *The Presidency in Transition.* New York: Center for the Study of the Presidency, 1989. Pp. 54–61.

Edwards, George C., III, Steven A. Shull, and Norman C. Thomas, eds. *The Presidency and Public Policy-Making.* Pittsburgh: University of Pittsburgh Press, 1985.

Heclo, Hugh. "One Executive Branch or Many?" In Anthony King, ed. *Both Ends of the Avenue.* Washington, D.C.: American Enterprise Institute, 1983. Pp. 26–58.

——————. "Reaganism and the Search for a Public Philosophy." In John L. Palmer, ed. *Perspectives on the Reagan Years.* Washington, D.C.: Urban Institute, 1986. Pp. 31–61.

Light, Paul C. *The President's Agenda.* Baltimore: Johns Hopkins University Press, 1982.

Newland, Chester. "A Mid-Term Appraisal—The Reagan Presidency: Limited Government and Political Administration." *Public Administration Review* 43 (January/February 1983): 1–20.

Pfiffner, James P. *The Strategic Presidency: Hitting the Ground Running.* Chicago: Dorsey, 1988.

Shull, Steven A. *Domestic Policy Formation: Presidential–Congressional Partnership?* Westport, Conn.: Greenwood, 1983.

Wayne, Stephen J. *The Legislative Presidency.* New York: Harper and Row, 1978.

Wyszomirski, Margaret J. "A Domestic Policy Office: Presidential Office in Search of a Role." *Policy Studies Journal* 12 (June 1984): 705–18.

13

Budgetary and Economic Policy Making

Presidents have always been concerned with the costs of government and the state of the economy, but that concern has never been greater than it is today. With a budget exceeding $1 trillion, with a national debt in the range of $3 trillion, with a sizable budget deficit, with federal revenues tied to economic conditions, with the private sector increasingly dependent on public expenditures, almost any substantive policy decision a president makes has significant budgetary and economic implications. Similarly, almost any major budget and economic decision has important political consequences.

Moreover, budgetary and economic decisions are interrelated. Budgetary problems are magnified by a weak economy and diminished by a strong one. A large and continuing budget deficit can have both long- and short-term effects on the economy, as can a surplus.

These factors make budgetary and economic policy making one of the most critical, complex, and persistent spheres for the exercise of presidential leadership. Like it or not, most things that presidents want to do cost money. Without sufficient financial resources they will be unable to achieve many of their most important policy objectives. But ironically *their* budgets are not theirs alone. Hampered by commitments made by their predecessors and previous Congresses; obligated to pay interest on the national debt and meet the statutory requirements of other ongoing legislative programs; and limited by the need to maintain payrolls, continue research and development, and ensure the production of items, particularly in the area of defense, that are vital to the national security, presidents today exercise decreasing influence over how their budgets will be allocated. And to make matters worse, the influence that they do exert is subject to congressional modification in the form of budget resolutions, authorization, and appropriation bills. Similarly, the revenue side is also conditioned by previous and current legislation and also fluctuates with the economy.

So presidents are placed in a dilemma. They are expected to redeem their campaign pledges, meet the country's changing needs, and do so in a manner that is both economic and efficient. Yet they often lack the resources to achieve these objectives and the discretion to obtain those resources. Directing change under these circumstances is extremely difficult although it is not impossible, as Franklin Roosevelt and Ronald Reagan demonstrated at the outset of their administrations. Nonetheless, being a facilitator rather than a transformer tends to be the order of the day as far as budget and economic policy making are concerned.

This chapter will explore the president's leadership dilemma in the area that has become so associated with his popularity, his reelectability, his reputation, and ultimately, his exercise of power. Beginning with a historic overview of the executive budget, we will look at the development of a presidential role in budgeting. The involvement of executive branch and congressional units in budgetary decision making is also examined, as are the various stages in the executive and legislative phases of the process. Similarly, we explore the evolution of economic policy making and the participation of presidential and other executive branch offices in decision making within this sphere. Throughout we describe the forces that affect presidential action and limit presidential discretion. The concluding section summarizes the recent trends in budget and economic policy making.

THE FEDERAL BUDGET

The budget is a document that forecasts revenue and estimates the expenditures of the federal government. It does so for a fiscal year, a twelve-month period beginning October 1 and continuing through the following September 30. Since the primary purpose of the budget is to allocate limited funds, that allocation is, by definition, highly political. Competition for limited resources is inevitable. Priorities have to be established. The budget is an instrument that reflects those priorities in a very concrete way.

A presidential budget has been required since 1921. The Budget and Accounting Act of that year made the president responsible for presenting a budget for executive departments and agencies to the Congress. Prior to that time agencies perfunctorily submitted their estimates to the secretary of the treasury, who passed them on to the legislature. The president played a relatively minor role in this process.

The 1921 act, a response to a series of budget deficits incurred at the beginning of the twentieth century and magnified by World War I, established a bureau within the Department of the Treasury to handle these new presidential responsibilities. Acting as a surrogate for the president, this division organized and ran a process that solicited yearly expenditure estimates from the departments and agencies, evaluated and adjusted them according to the president's goals, and finally combined them in a comprehensive executive budget. This budget review cycle has continued through the years.

The budget, however, has changed rather dramatically.[1] In its early years it was relatively small by contemporary standards, oriented toward the executive agencies, and utilized primarily as a vehicle for *controlling federal spending*. Since the primary object of the budget was to make the national government more economical, to eliminate the deficits, and to keep a lid on spending, federal outlays were substantially reduced during this initial period, 1921–1930.[2]

Total government expenditures were in the range of $2 billion to $3 billion. Most of the money went directly to the departments and agencies for the costs of running the government. There were relatively few public works projects that required direct funding.

The Great Depression of the 1930s had a major effect on the character of the budget. Increased demands for government intervention in the economy culminated in Franklin Roosevelt's New Deal programs. Followed by World War II and the cold war, this larger governmental role greatly accelerated spending in domestic and defense areas. Fortunately, the economic recovery, beginning in the late 1940s and continuing through the 1950s, provided increased revenues for these greater expenditures. These developments not only expanded the size of the budget but also moved it into an *incremental* phase, one in which existing programs continued to be maintained with a budget that included an increment to cover increased costs.

During this phase, which reached its zenith in the 1960s, the budget highlighted new programs and supported existing ones. Agencies assumed that the costs of their ongoing programs would be met in addition to whatever priority legislation the president wished to introduce.

While the departments continued to administer their programs, more and more of the outlays went to third parties. Programs designed to help the invalid and the poor, senior citizens, veterans, and others provided direct payments to individuals from the Treasury. Since the 1970s these so-called entitlement programs have consumed an ever-increasing proportion of government expenditures, expenditures that are not easily subject to presidential control. Today they constitute 43 percent of the total budget (see Figure 13-1).

The reason they are not under the president's control is that these programs and others like them legally entitle individuals to benefits as long as they meet stated eligibility requirements. These entitlements are independent of specific appropriations by Congress. (In 1974, Congress decided to peg social security payments to the consumer price index, forsaking decision making even on the levels of benefits. The president does not have the authority to change these payments.) Congress has obligated itself to provide whatever funds are required to those who qualify.

Figure 13-1. The Federal Budget for Fiscal Year 1990

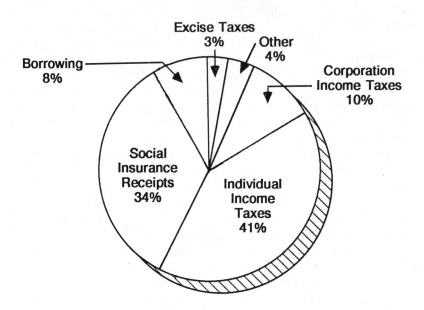

Where It Comes From ...

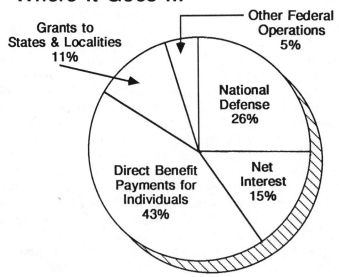

Where It Goes ...

Source: *Budget of the United States, Fiscal 1990* (Washington, D.C.: Government Printing Office, 1989), pp. 1–2.

From the president's perspective, the sad fact is that a smaller and smaller proportion of the total budget is subject to his discretion. Interest on the national debt, which constitutes about 15 percent of the total budget, must be met. Payments for agricultural commodities and government support programs are also required by law and usually not subject to presidential control. Many of the costs of national defense, such as personnel, weapons systems, and ships and aircraft, are "big-ticket" items and cannot be reduced or eliminated without basic changes in security policy and/or significant cost to the taxpayer. When these expenditures and the entitlement programs are considered, the result is that presidents can exercise effective discretion over about 23 percent of the budget. Thus, a president who wishes to reduce government expenditures substantially has little leverage to do so, at least on his own. (Percentages of federal receipts and expenditures are indicated in Figure 13-2.)

The increasing proportion of the budget devoted to direct benefit payments to individuals has important effects. In addition to decreasing presidential influence on the budget, these payments have increased the political ramifications of budget decisions. Instead of primarily affecting departments and agencies, the budget now has a direct impact on many outside the government. As a consequence, outside constituencies composed of veterans, senior citizens, farmers, labor, and others have organized to protect and extend their benefits. They regularly exert pressure on budget makers. This pressure makes it more difficult to use the budget as a device for controlling spending. By the late 1970s the budget demonstrated more of the president's weaknesses than his strengths; he was responsible for it yet controlled little of it.

The goal of presidential budgeting began in the 1980s. Seeds of this were sown in the economic problems of the previous decade: the decline in the nation's productivity and its industrial competitiveness and the rise in inflation and unemployment, especially during the 1970s. These factors, along with a steadily increasing national debt and sizable deficits, led those inside and outside the government to question the wisdom of ever-increasing government expenditures within the domestic sphere, particularly when the economy was weak.

Upon taking office, President Reagan took the lead in reordering national priorities and used the budget to achieve his objectives. *Incremental* increases gave way to *decremental* adjustments. The proportion of the budget devoted to domestic discretionary spending was cut; entitlement programs such as social security were adjusted; money for defense was increased.

These changes affected the budget's orientation more than they affected overall outlays. Instead of distributing an expanding base of resources, the budget redistributed a declining one. This increased the competition and division among the agencies and outside groups concerned with "their" expenditures. With different interests and groups

Figure 13-2. The Evolution of Receipts and Outlays in the Contemporary
              Federal Budget, 1940–1990

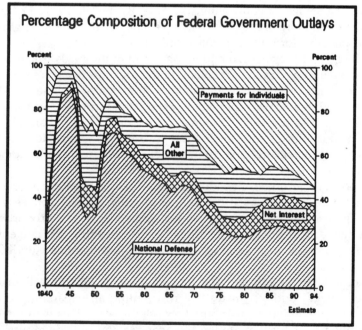

Source: *The United States Budget in Brief, Fiscal 1990* (Washington, D.C.: Government
Printing Office, 1989), p. iv.

vying to protect and promote their own programs, a consensus support-ing the budget was harder to achieve. Congress found it more difficult to enact budgetary policy. It spent more time on budget matters and had more votes on budget questions. Other issues were driven off the legisla-tive calendar as a result.

The president also had to devote more time and energy to his bud-get activities, not merely to formulating the budget but to obtaining congressional approval for it. As the principal policymaker and coalition builder, he had little option. His policy success and public approval were dependent, in large part, on his ability to get his budget proposals en-acted into law.

Differing budget priorities and policy proposals characterized presidential–congressional relations during the last six years of the Rea-gan presidency. With the president intent on increasing defense expendi-tures and decreasing personal and corporate income taxes, the Congress desirous of preserving popular domestic programs and maintaining the entitlements, and an increasing percentage of the total budget mandated by existing legislation and service of the national debt, the outcome was predictable—a growing federal deficit. By the end of the Reagan adminis-tration, the yearly deficits had almost tripled the national debt. They had also hindered business investment, contributed to a large, negative inter-national trade imbalance, and vastly increased United States, depen-dence on foreign capital as a means of financing its deficit. The United States moved from being the world's greatest creditor nation to the world's largest debtor nation. The figures are startling, as Table 13-1 attests.

During this period Congress and the president repeatedly clashed over the importance of the debt, its real and potential impact on the

Table 13-1. Budget Deficits and the National Debt (in billions of dollars)

Year	Deficit	Debt
1980	$ 73.8	$ 908.5
1981	78.9	994.3
1982	127.9	1,136.8
1983	207.8	1,371.2
1984	185.3	1,564.1
1985	212.3	1,817.0
1986	221.2	2,120.1
1987	149.7	2,345.6
1988	155.1	2,600.8
1989*	161.5	2,868.8
1990*	92.5	3,107.2

*Estimate.

Source: *The United States Budget in Brief, Fiscal 1990* (Washington, D.C.: Government Printing Office, 1989), table 1, p. 105.

economy, and how to deal with it. The president proposed substantial cuts in domestic programs and blamed Congress when the legislature failed to make them. Congress, in turn, reacted by reducing some of the defense spending the president requested, protecting the domestic programs it desired, and criticizing the president for the growing deficits.

In December 1985, the Congress went even further. It enacted the Balanced Budget and Emergency Deficit Control Act, known by the names of its original sponsors, Phil Gramm, Warren Rudman, and Ernest Hollings of the Senate. The act required a balanced budget within five years of its passage (subsequently extended to 1993), set specific deficit targets to be met over this period,[3] and authorized automatic cuts in some domestic and most defense programs (except primarily those involving personnel) to bring the deficit to the required levels if the targets were not met. By authorizing automatic cuts, Congress was acknowledging its own inability to make tough and potentially unpopular political decisions.

The General Accounting Office (GAO) was originally given the responsibility to determine the size of these cuts after receiving estimates from the Office of Management and Budget (OMB) and the Congressional Budget Office (CBO). However, the Supreme Court decided that the GAO's role violated the constitutional principle of separation of powers by involving a congressional agency in executive decisions. As a

Source: Reprinted by permission of United Feature Syndicate, Inc.

result, today it is the president who determines the magnitude of the cuts based on a joint report he receives from the OMB and CBO.

The Gramm, Rudman, Hollings (GRH) Act has not eliminated the deficit problem. In fact, sizable deficits are expected to continue. Moreover, the temptation to manipulate budget figures in order to reduce the apparent size of the deficit, or to manipulate the GRH targets so that automatic cuts are precluded or reduced has increased. The legislation has also failed to enhance the accountability of president or Congress. On the contrary, it has reduced that accountability and permitted each institution to continue to blame the other for the negative budget imbalance.

From the perspective of presidential leadership, the act demonstrates the limitations of using the budget as an instrument of change. Not only are presidents constrained by their predecessors' commitments, existing legislation, and their campaign promises, but they are also subjected to institutional forces, constituency pressures, and economic fluctuations. Accommodation, not domination, describes presidential budgeting most of the time.

We now turn to the roles of the major participants in the process in an attempt to define more precisely their influence on budgetary policy.

THE BUDGET MAKERS

The President

The president bears the primary responsibility for the executive phase of the budget. Increasingly, he is also expected to play a major role in the legislative phase as well. In each, he can exercise influence but cannot dictate the outcome.

There are various ways a president can affect the executive budget. His goals dictate its priorities and shape its initial guidelines; his policies determine the new big-item expenditures; his decisions resolve interagency disputes. He hears last-minute appeals and makes final judgments on them. The budget presented to the Congress must meet with his approval.

In shaping the budget, presidents can get involved in detailed decision making, if they desire. Some have done so. Ford and Carter spent considerable time on budget matters. Nixon and Reagan did not. Nixon took little interest in the budget and delegated considerable authority to his budget director while Reagan took a slightly different tack. Interested in setting broad budget policy, he was content to establish priorities and make decisions on items brought to his attention. By leaving the detailed evaluation of agency estimates to officials in the Office of Management and Budget, and by avoiding details, Reagan distanced himself from internal and external pressures to spend. This made it easier for him to propose budgets with substantial cuts in domestic spending but not easier to mobilize support for those cuts in Congress.

George Bush has taken a more active involvement in budget matters, particularly in the congressional phase of the process. Restricted in the executive phase during his first year by the obstacle every new president faces—the fact that his first budget is his predecessor's last—he reached a compromise with congressional leaders on the contours of the fiscal 1990 budget, one that was consistent with the target established by the Gramm, Rudman, Hollings legislation.

The Office of Management and Budget

When the Bureau of the Budget (BOB) was first created in 1921 as a unit within the Department of the Treasury, its initial charge was to "assemble, correlate, revise, reduce, or increase the estimates of the several departments or establishments."[4] In 1939 it was moved to the newly created Executive Office of the President, where it has remained ever since. In 1970 its title was changed from the Bureau of the Budget to the Office of Management and Budget and its functions broadened to include management responsibilities.

Despite the fact that the Budget Bureau was housed in the Treasury Department for its first eighteen years, it functioned as an important, powerful, and independent presidential agency. During this early phase of its existence, the bureau exercised central oversight over the budget. It operated according to a standard rule that departmental estimates equal to or less than the previous year's were automatically approved, while estimates for more money had to receive the authorization of the budget director, and in some cases, even the president.

The objectives of promoting economical government and controlling spending contributed to the bureau's power. Since most of the outlays prior to the mid-1930s went to the executive departments and agencies, there was little interest in the budget outside the government. The lack of public visibility and external pressure worked to the bureau's advantage. Its decisions were final unless overruled by the president, an infrequent practice in those days. Executive agencies were forbidden to circumvent the process by going directly to Congress for funds.

As the budget expanded, so did the size and functions of the budget agency and the interest in its decisions. In the 1920s and the 1930s, the bureau consisted of fewer than forty-five employees.[5] New responsibilities generated by World War II and the clearance of legislative policy matters enlarged the staff to more than five hundred by 1949 and created an institutional memory upon which the White House grew increasingly to depend.[6]

Most of the people who worked in the bureau were civil servants.

Initially, there were only two political appointees, the director and the deputy director. The latter, by tradition, was chosen from the ranks of the professionals who had worked their way up in the agency. As a consequence of its nonpartisan character, the Budget Bureau was particularly well suited to provide the president with "advice on the merits" as opposed to "advice on the politics." Moreover, its invulnerability to outside pressures, relative invisibility to the press, and accessibility to the president and his senior aides heightened its mystique and enhanced its clout.

Changes in the organization, influence, and roles of the BOB began to occur in the 1960s. These changes were a consequence of the increasing size of the White House staff, the increasing number of initiatives that emanated from it, and the increasing suspicion of the political loyalties of civil servants by new presidents and their staffs. Singularly and together, these factors decreased the agency's influence within the executive branch from 1961 through 1980. While it continued to run the budget review process and decide on routine budget matters, key issues became the more or less exclusive province of senior White House aides.

Changes in the character of the budget also worked to affect the bureau's role and ultimately its power. With less emphasis placed on limiting expenditures and more on highlighting programs, political policymakers, not career budget analysts, became the key players. With more requests emanating from the departments and agencies, budget review focused on the size of their increments rather than the merits of their existing programs. With an increasing percentage of the budget consisting of nondiscretionary spending, the Budget Bureau was limited in what it could cut and how much it could save. As a consequence of all these factors, the budget agency's influence declined while expenditures continued to expand. In the words of Allen Schick:

> Agencies became more vigorous (and successful) in pressing their claims for larger budget shares. The relationship (between the Budget Bureau and the executive agencies) became more a matter of bargaining, and less one in which high authority decided the outcome.[7]

Executive agencies acquired new allies and new bargaining chips in their efforts to maintain and increase spending. Outside groups, which benefitted from the programs, supported agency requests on Capitol Hill, thereby creating an environment that made it difficult for the president to sustain cuts in these programs. Prior to the 1970s these external political pressures were felt indirectly by the bureau. After 1970 the budget agency itself became more directly subject to outside influences. Changes in the organization and orientation of the agency were primarily responsible for its increased sensitivity to political matters.

A reorganization in July 1970 gave the Budget Bureau its new name,

Office of Management and Budget, a new structure, and more political appointees. Civil servants who had previously exercised policy judgments on budgetary and legislative matters were relegated to positions of lesser importance in the organizational hierarchy.

The politicization of the OMB has continued. Presidents Carter and Reagan added additional political positions and staffed them with people who shared their beliefs and perspectives. Today there are approximately three dozen senior political appointees in the OMB.

The functions of the office also expanded during this period. Nixon and Ford used it to improve management techniques and evaluate existing programs. Carter set up a division within the agency to oversee reorganization efforts. Reagan used the office to increase oversight of executive regulations, achieve sizable cuts in domestic programs, and institute a series of management reforms.

In recent times the OMB's political sensitivities and its expanded functions have contributed to its influence. The willingness of presidents to use the agency to promote their objectives has worked to the same end. The OMB's clout in the process has increased, allowing it (in conjunction with the White House) to shift major allocations from agency to agency in accordance with the president's budget priorities. To the extent that executive budgeting has become a top-down rather than bottom-up process, this has further contributed to the OMB's influence, particularly that of its top political appointees.

The OMB's ability to effect change does vary, however, over the course of an administration. In the beginning its institutional resources, particularly its access to information and expertise, are most valuable in overcoming departmental interests and congressional opposition to achieve new presidential goals. In the end its nay-saying abilities are apt to be most effective in maintaining the president's course.

How the Reagan administration obtained its 1981 budget cuts illustrates the advantage the OMB can give a president in his first year in office. In January 1981, before many of the departments were fully staffed and their secretaries had been fully briefed about their budget needs, the OMB proposed major reductions in domestic programs. Almost immediately, budget working groups were established. Composed of key White House personnel, budget officials, and appropriate department secretaries and their aides, the groups reviewed the proposed cuts and made recommendations to the president. In most cases the recommendations supported the cuts. Why? The president had stated his goals, the OMB had a near monopoly over budget information, and the composition of the groups was stacked against the departments. The secretaries were not in a position to advocate their departments' interests even if they wanted to. As a result, sizable reductions were proposed in twelve major entitlement programs and in much discretionary spending in only three weeks.[8] Although the Reagan administration attempted to maintain its centralized control over the budgetary process, it was not as successful in subsequent years.

Over time, however, the advantages which the OMB can give a president decline. The inevitability of pressure to maintain existing benefits, the relatively small amount of discretionary spending, and the tendency of departments to develop their own constituency-oriented programs limit the OMB's ability to effect major change over the course of an administration.

The Executive Departments and Agencies

While the OMB is the principal participant in the executive phase of the budgetary process, it is not the only one. In one way or another every single executive agency has an impact on the budget, mostly on its own.

Departments and agencies are asked to submit yearly estimates for their programs and operational costs. They are expected to defend these estimates before the OMB and the Congress. They may also have to appeal to the president if funding for a particular program is threatened.

Most agencies have a division that coordinates their budget preparation and another that facilitates their legislative activity. In deciding how much to request, agencies have limited discretion. A large percentage of their budget is required by existing legislation, either by formulas written into the law or by long-term commitments. Even within the discretionary portion there are presidential guidelines to follow, ceilings that cannot be exceeded, and administrative costs that must be met.

Nonetheless, the agencies have leeway when estimating their needs. They generally tend to request funds within an acceptable range but toward the top of that range, anticipating that the OMB will revise these requests downward. This expectation, in turn, contributes to their tendency to pad their estimates and the OMB's inclination to cut them. In general, the agencies that are most aggressive in requesting funds for their programs enjoy the greatest political support (which permits them to be most aggressive).

Budget decisions of an agency frequently have impact beyond that agency. In the 1980s the large increase in defense expenditures came at the expense of discretionary domestic programs. Even within the Department of Defense, the intense rivalry among the army, navy, and air force has a major impact on how that department allocates its requests.

The president and his advisers establish the guidelines; the departments and agencies make their estimates; the OMB evaluates those estimates; but Congress has the last word. Box 13-1 indicates the major steps in the executive phase of the budgetary process.

BOX 13-1.   THE EXECUTIVE BUDGETARY PROCESS

There are four principal stages in the executive phase of the process. In the first, the overall guidelines of the budget are established. They are conditioned by the objectives of the president, the state of the economy, and the commitments of legislation, past and present. In the second stage, the departments and agencies prepare their estimates in accordance with these guidelines. Personnel from the Office of Management and Budget examine these estimates in a formal review process in the third stage. The fourth stage begins with the president being briefed by the budget director, hearing appeals from the department and agency heads, and making the final decisions. The budget is then printed and sent to Congress in January. These stages of the budgetary process are detailed below.

Approximate Times	Actions
	Budget Policy Development
March, 1st year	Senior economic advisers review the outlook for the current and future fiscal years; they predict effects on revenues and spending programs and report to the president.
April–June	The OMB conducts spring planning review sessions, exploring funding implications of major issues or programs that will be considered in the fall budget review. The OMB sets overall guidelines for the executive agency budget submissions and sends these, along with instructions on preparing their proposed budgets, to the agencies.
	Agencies' Preparation of Proposed Budgets
July–August	Agencies develop their proposed budgets.
September	Agencies send the OMB their proposed budgets for the fiscal year that begins thirteen months later.
	OMB Review
September–October	The OMB staff analyzes proposed budgets and holds hearings with agencies.
October–November	Economic advisers again review the outlook for the fiscal year that begins the next October. The director holds agency-by-agency reviews at which he considers agency requests

BOX 13-1 *(continued).*

and staff recommendations and decides on
recommendations to the president.
The legislative branch and the judiciary submit budget requests to the OMB.
The OMB transmits the proposed budget and
economic advisers' findings to the president.
The OMB gives agencies their recommended
budget levels—also known as "the mark."

Presidential Decision

December

The president reviews OMB recommendations and decides on totals for agencies and
programs. Possible appeals by agencies to
the president are made. The OMB prepares
budget documents for transmittal to Congress.

January, 2nd year

The president delivers his proposed budget to
Congress.
The OMB sends an "allowance letter" to
each agency giving its total within the president's budget and also transmitting "planning
numbers" for the next two fiscal years.

Source: The Office of Management and Budget, as amended and updated by
the author.

The Congress

The Constitution requires that the Congress appropriate all funds
which the government spends and raise all revenues which it collects.
Congress meets this requirement by the passage of separate appropriation bills and revenue measures. During most of the nineteenth century,
policy committees of each house drafted the legislation which appropriated money for the departments and agencies within their jurisdiction.
There was no comprehensive national budget.

Following the passage of the Budget and Accounting Act of 1921, in
which Congress required the president to present such a budget, the
legislature centralized its own spending authority in two appropriation
committees. These committees, however, did not consider the budget as
a whole. Rather, using the president's executive estimates as guidelines,
they drafted individual bills for the separate departments. In many in-

stances, congressional appropriations did not match the president's budget estimates. Supplemental money bills, passed during the year, also magnified the difference between the president's requests and the appropriations made by Congress. The legislature's consideration of the budget was fragmented and highly political. Members could publicly support the president's goals yet push for exceptions for their own pet projects.

After several abortive attempts to pass a comprehensive budget rather than simply separate appropriation bills, Congress enacted legislation in 1974 that enabled it to do so. The Budget and Impoundment Control Act of that year established a congressional budget process, two congressional committees, and a Congressional Budget Office (CBO) to provide it with a budget capacity that rivaled the president's. The process set up a timetable for considering the budget; the committees were charged with drafting advisory and binding budget resolutions that the Congress could not exceed; and the CBO provided staff support for revenue and expenditure estimates.

While the Budget and Impoundment Control Act improved the capacity of Congress to consider a comprehensive budget, it did not force the legislature to abide by its own budget decisions. Separate appropriation bills still determined the actual expenditures; separate tax bills still determined the actual revenues. Thus, a gap between budget goals and appropriation and revenue measures was still possible, even probable. The 1974 act, however, did provide a procedure known as reconciliation by which Congress could direct its committees to legislate within the guidelines of its budget decisions. It was used for the first time in 1980.

Ronald Reagan took advantage of reconciliation in 1981 and 1982 by getting the Democratic House of Representatives to agree to a vote *without* amendments on a binding budget resolution that reconciled the differences between its budget estimates, appropriation bills, and revenue measures. In this way he was able to achieve many of his policy objectives through the mechanism of a budget. Today, a reconciliation provision is normally part of the binding budget resolution, which Congress is supposed to enact in the spring of every year.

The Budget and Impoundment Control Act (1974) and Gramm, Rudman, and Hollings Act (1985) have not lessened the importance of presidential involvement in the congressional phase of the budgetary process. Rather, they have increased it. The president's critical assessments of the economy and his targets for funding continue to provide the basis for initial deliberations by Congress. Over the course of the legislature's budget hearings, markup, and floor debate, the president may adjust his projections and requests. In fact, Congress requires a midyear update. At each stage presidential influence is important if the president's budget proposals are to prevail. Finally, if the deficit targets are not met, the sequestration process is triggered, and the president is forced to impose across-the-board cuts in many key federal programs. To avoid this "doomsday" mechanism, presidents need to work with Congress to reach permanent levels of spending.

The Budget acts of 1974 and 1985, in short, have reinstituted a joint process in which both president and Congress have important roles to play. The process involves many people, requires many reports, and extends many months over the course of the legislative calendar. It is a difficult one, which is dependent on the need for compromise but includes an automatic mechanism if that compromise fails.

The need for institutional cooperation but the difficulty of achieving it explains why presidents in recent times have been more successful in articulating their budgets than in getting them enacted into law. With over half of the Senate and a fourth of the House serving on budget, appropriations, or revenue committees, the task of achieving a consensus on a detailed list of expectations is often herculean. It requires significant political and legislative skills, although these skills in and of themselves may not be sufficient.

Ronald Reagan is a good example of a president who effectively mobilized a major coalition to achieve many of his budget priorities during the first two years in office but had difficulty doing so thereafter. Reagan's initial success was a product of several factors: his public appeal, his administration's lobbying skills, and the unity of congressional Republicans in contrast to the disunity of congressional Democrats. By 1983 he was in a much less favorable position with Congress. With his budgets ritually pronounced "dead on arrival," the president adopted a different tack, threatening to use his veto to deter the legislature from enacting appropriation bills that exceeded his requests in the domestic sphere and fell short of his requests in the areas of defense and national security. (Box 13-2 lists the principal steps in the congressional budget process and the target dates for completing them.)

PRESIDENTIAL LEADERSHIP AND THE BUDGET

The president has a leadership problem when it comes to the budget. The public expects and the Congress requires him to take the lead by providing a unified perspective and fashioning a budget for the entire nation. Moreover, in an age of decrementalism, he must use the budget to impose his policy objectives. His problem is that budgetary power is not centralized in the presidency. It is divided between executive and legislative branches and redivided within each. The various participants in the process bring to bear differing perspectives, goals, and political allegiances in making their decisions. They also encourage their external allies to get involved and exert pressure. As a consequence, the budgetary process is a continuous struggle and the budget a package of political

BOX 13-2.   THE CONGRESSIONAL BUDGETARY PROCESS

The congressional phase of the process begins with the budget committees of each house considering the president's request. In stage two the committees report their targets for revenue and expenditures and Congress enacts an advisory budget resolution. During the third stage the authorization and appropriation committees draft their legislation within the guidelines of the budget resolution. In the final stage Congress enacts a second budget resolution and has the power, if it desires, to reconcile differences among its revenue, appropriations, and budget committees.

These stages of the process are enumerated below:

January	Congress receives the president's budget.
February	The Congressional Budget Office reports to budget committees on the president's budget. Budget committees hold hearings as background for a concurrent resolution.
March	Each standing committee sends its budget estimates to House and Senate budget committees.
April 15	Congress passes a concurrent resolution in which the House and Senate agree on budget targets for receipts, budget authorities, and outlays.
May 15	The House may consider individual appropriation bills.
June	The House completes action on annual appropriation bills. The Senate must complete action by October 1.
July 15	The OMB sends Congress an update of the president's January budget.
June–September	Authorization and appropriation bills are considered and adopted by both chambers of Congress.
August	The OMB provides a "snapshot" of projected deficits. By August 20, the CBO issues its initial report on the projected deficit. By August 25, the OMB issues its initial report on the projected deficit and the president responds by issuing a sequestration order that reduces spending by the required amount to coincide with the GRH targets.
October	The fiscal year begins October 1, and the president's initial sequestration order takes effect. If Congress has not enacted appropriation bills, it must enact a resolution to continue spending at

BOX 13-2 *(continued).*

	the current rate or some other rate that coincides with the sequestration order. Failure to do so will deny money to the government and eventually force its closure. By October 15, the president issues his final sequestration order, which is effective immediately.
November	The comptroller general issues a compliance report.

compromises and economic judgments that has implications extending well beyond the fiscal year.

The Reagan experience illustrates the cycle of decreasing presidential influence on the budget. It suggests that presidents enjoy their greatest political leverage at the outset, particularly if economic problems were the principal campaign issues. Not only do presidents as chief budget makers gain discretion by virtue of the problems which their predecessors have been unable to resolve, but they also have leverage and flexibility by virtue of their election victory. The irony is that at the time at which their political influence is likely to be greatest, their budget expertise likely is not. Nor do they have much ability to make detailed changes in their first-year budget. The result is that a major reallocation of expenditures may occur without sufficient reflection or negotiation. In subsequent years this reflection and negotiation are more likely to occur and to inhibit rather than encourage major changes. As a consequence, reallocation tends to give way to incrementalism and presidents increasingly assume the role of facilitators rather than directors of change.

ECONOMIC POLICY MAKING

Presidents have been involved in the budget process since 1921, but not until the administration of Franklin Roosevelt in the 1930s have they been concerned on a regular basis with economic policy making. Prior to that time presidential activities were generally limited to initiating or supporting proposals to correct specific problems that had arisen within the economy. Theodore Roosevelt's trust busting and Woodrow Wilson's labor reforms are two examples of these early forms of presidential involvement.

The depth of the 1930s depression, the degree of public panic, and

Herbert Hoover's resounding election defeat signaled the beginning of a more comprehensive presidential role in the economy. No longer could presidents enjoy the luxury of standing on the sidelines. Franklin Roosevelt's activism became the model for his Democratic successors. Even Republicans found that there was no turning back.

Congress expected and even required this involvement. The Employment Act of 1946 obligated the president to prime the economy to maximize employment and production. The Taft-Hartley Act of 1947 gave the president the power to intervene in labor–management disputes that threatened the nation's security and well-being. In each case Congress not only acknowledged an expanded presidential role but created mechanisms to help the executive fulfill it.

Every president since Roosevelt has strived to meet these expanded expectations. Their policies, however, have differed. Truman, Kennedy, and Reagan desired to lower taxes to stimulate economic growth. Eisenhower and Ford tried to achieve savings by cutting government spending. Johnson obtained a surtax to help pay for the costs of the Vietnam War and his Great Society programs, while Nixon implemented wage and price controls to reduce inflation and stabilize the economy. Carter tried a variety of revenue and budget measures to deal with the high inflation and stagnant economy which plagued his presidency.

Differing fiscal approaches lay at the core of these presidential policies. A *fiscal* strategy is a plan to manipulate government revenue and expenditures to influence economic conditions. In contrast, a *monetary* approach regulates the supply of money to affect change. Presidents cannot affect monetary policy, generally the prerogative of the Federal Reserve Board, nearly as much as they can influence fiscal policy. However, even with fiscal policy, as pointed out in the previous section, it is the Congress which enacts appropriations and revenue bills. Although the president can influence the legislature's actions, he cannot control them.

Until the mid-1970s, fiscal strategies were predicated on Keynesian economics. John Maynard Keynes, an eminent British economist, argued that increases in government spending and reductions in government taxes would stimulate demand and invigorate the economy during periods of sluggish activity. The only trouble with adopting such a policy is that it also results initially in budget deficits. Keynes was not worried about these deficits, however, because he believed that in the long run a vibrant economy would generate greater revenues, reducing or eliminating the difference between expenditures and income. With the exception of Eisenhower, presidents Truman through Nixon subscribed to this belief.

An expanding economy coupled with relatively low unemployment and inflation during most of the 1950s and 1960s seemed to confirm the merits of the Keynesian approach. By the beginning of the 1970s, however, economic conditions began to change. Budget deficits increased, the rate of growth declined, and inflation rose dramatically throughout the decade. Keynesian economics did not contain satisfactory answers. Other theories began to command attention.

Monetarists, led by Professor Milton Friedman of the University of Chicago, contended that the supply of money was the key to sound economic growth, particularly to control the ravages of inflation. Increasing interest rates would reduce the amount of money in circulation, decreasing inflationary pressures and cooling the economy. Lowering interest rates, on the other hand, would have the opposite effect, stimulating demand and output by making borrowing cheaper and more money available. In periods of high inflation and an overheated economy, a tight money policy made sense. But when inflation was high and the economy stagnant, it did not. It was precisely this condition in the late 1970s that gave credence to still another economic strategy—supply-side economics.

The supply-side philosophy combined the Keynesian approach to generating demand with the monetarist's desire to regulate currency. Tax cuts stimulate spending while money supply controls inflation. Ronald Reagan, an advocate of this approach (and the first president to major in economics in college), sought to implement the fiscal component of this strategy as president. He proposed budgets that increased defense expenditures, cut domestic programs, and substantially reduced corporate and personal federal income taxes. Congress enacted the bulk of his requests during his first two years in office, although he was forced to modify his tax stand in 1982 because of the need for additional revenues and the desirability of closing tax loopholes.

While the tax cuts eventually stimulated the economy, they and the simultaneous increase in defense expenditures produced a large and growing federal budget deficit (which in the short run also acted as an economic stimulus). Reagan, who had promised to achieve a balanced budget during his 1980 campaign for the presidency (as had Franklin Roosevelt in 1932), and who had supported a balanced budget amendment while president, argued that the deficit was "institutional" and would be eventually reduced by a vigorous economy. He believed that a stimulated economy would increase growth and employment and produce greatly increased revenues for the government. When the latter did not occur, Reagan and Congress clashed repeatedly over the magnitude of the problem and which institution was to blame for it.

The success of Reagan's economic program, or any president's program, for that matter, is hard to measure. Mixed economic indicators, differing time frames, competing priorities, and changing world conditions make comparison and evaluation difficult. Nonetheless, the expectation today is that the president will be involved in economic policy making—that he will propose economic policy, and that he will mobilize support for it and consider its success critical to his administration. The issue is not whether the president will be a maker of economic policy but what kind of economic policies he will make. To help him with these efforts, an economic advisory mechanism within the presidency has been created.

ECONOMIC POLICYMAKERS

The Department of the Treasury

Most of the president's economic advisory structure has been established by Congress. The Treasury Department was the first executive branch agency to play a major role in the financial affairs of government. Charged with responsibility for collecting and dispersing federal funds, its functions have gradually expanded to include debt financing, import controls, and drug enforcement.

Representing the financial community, this department has exercised a conservative influence throughout the years on matters of economic policy. Its orientation is to promote stability and long-term growth. The secretary of the treasury has become the nation's chief economic spokesperson.

The secretary's role as an economic adviser to the president has been enhanced in recent years by the emergence of international and domestic problems of particular concern to the department. Stabilizing the value of the dollar in international financial markets, overseeing foreign investments of the United States, and conducting negotiations on the repayments of international loans have consumed much of the secretary's time in the 1980s. Similarly, within the domestic arena, tax policy and savings bank failures have thrust the Treasury Department into the center of political controversy. With no other presidential office or White House official charged with handling these matters, the secretary of the treasury has taken the lead as adviser and coordinator for the president. In this capacity the treasury secretary chaired the councils that fashioned and implemented major economic priorities in both the Reagan and Bush administrations.

The Federal Reserve Board

The second oldest government agency concerned with economic policy is the Federal Reserve Board (known as the "Fed"). However, it is not a presidential agency. Created by legislation in 1913, its principal function is to regulate monetary policy. It does so by adjusting the discount rate that commercial banks must pay when they borrow money from one of the member banks in the Federal Reserve System. The percentage of deposits that commercial banks must maintain is also regulated by the Fed. A third way the Federal Reserve Board can affect the money supply is by requesting its regional banks to buy or sell government securities on the open market. It also intervenes on the international market to increase or decrease the value of the dollar in accordance with the needs of the American economy.

In theory, the Fed operates with considerable autonomy from the president and Congress. Its members, nominated by the president and appointed with the advice and consent of the Senate, serve for fourteen years. Its chair, designated by the president from members of the board of governors, has a four-year term that does not coincide with the president's. This increases the chair's independence.

However, the Fed does not operate in a vacuum. It must be concerned with the impact that the fiscal policies of the president and Congress have on the economy. The Fed is sensitive to political pressures. One study indicates that it tends to refrain from making visible policy decisions in election years.[9] In contrast, the decisions to raise interest rates, which are obviously less popular than those to lower them, are made more frequently in nonelection years.[10]

The Council of Economic Advisers

The principal economic advisory units within the Executive Office of the President are the Council of Economic Advisers (CEA) and the Office of Management and Budget. Both have been established by statute. The Employment Act of 1946 created the CEA and charged it with advising the president on macroeconomic policy. This included analyzing economic conditions, forecasting trends, and preparing the president's annual economic report to Congress. In addition to providing the president with long-term advice, the council has become increasingly involved in short-term microeconomic issues such as trade policy, deregulation, even credit and housing programs. It has avoided operational responsibilities, however.

The council is small and specialized. It is composed of three members appointed by the president with the advice and consent of the Senate. They serve at the president's discretion. The council's chair is the principal link to the White House and to the president's other economic advisers. He participates in high-level economic policy meetings, supervises the operation of the CEA and the preparation of its annual economic report, and occasionally acts as an administration spokesperson on economic affairs.

The council is supported by a small staff, approximately twenty-five professionals, mostly economists, who come primarily from the academic community. Members of the council are also drawn from academia and frequently have worked on the council's staff prior to their appointment. All but two of those chairing the council have been university professors.

The academic orientation of the council has made it less subject to outside pressures than other economic advisory units. As a consequence, when strong political pressures are exerted, the chair of the council can take a longer-term, less partisan perspective than can some of the president's other advisers. This was particularly evident during the third and fourth years of the Reagan presidency, when council chairman Martin Feldstein frequently disagreed with the administration's public position on interest rates and the deficit. After two years in office, Feldstein returned to his academic position, and there was some question whether another chair would be appointed. Reagan waited until after his 1984 reelection to do so.

In general, the council has declined in influence as economic policy has become more political and as the number of academic advisers has proliferated. Nonetheless, the personal relationship of the chair and the president remains the key to the council's impact on economic policy making. Arthur Burns (Eisenhower), Walter Heller (Kennedy), and Alan Greenspan (Ford) were three chairmen who had their president's confidence and were able to exercise considerable influence on economic decisions. Others have not been as fortunate.

No longer enjoying the information advantage that it had when there were fewer economic policy units within the government and fewer economists to run them, the council's voice today is one among many. It has tended to deal primarily with microeconomic issues.

The Office of Management and Budget

The OMB also performs economic advisory functions for the president. Not only does its director participate in the initial forecasts for revenue and expenditures as budget planning gets under way, but he and his associates continually analyze and evaluate the merits of department and agency requests. Revisions of the initial budget forecasts are also the responsibility of the OMB. Since the orientation of the budget director is toward the bottom line—the differences between expenditures and revenues—the director must be concerned with tax policy and other revenue-producing measures. The director regularly meets with the president's senior economic advisers.

THE COORDINATION OF ECONOMIC ADVICE

In addition to using the Treasury Department, the Council of Economic Advisers, and the OMB in an advisory capacity, presidents have also concocted a number of other institutional arrangements for soliciting and coordinating recommendations and advice. The origins and organizations of these groups have varied.

Two political scientists, Erwin Hargrove and Michael Nelson, suggest that the pattern of economic advising since World War II can be described in stages.[11] In the first, 1946 to 1960, a broad, relatively unstructured relationship existed among the chair of the Council of Economic Advisers, the director of the Bureau of the Budget, and the secretaries of the treasury, commerce, and agriculture. These individuals, both collectively and individually, provided the president with advice, advocacy, and administration within the economic sphere.

Beginning in 1960 and continuing through the end of the Nixon administration, relationships among the president's primary economic advisers became institutionalized. A troika, consisting of the heads of three major advisory bodies—the Treasury Department, the OMB, and the CEA—met on a regular basis to coordinate policy. Within the group a rough division of authority emerged with the secretary of the treasury becoming the major spokesperson and revenue adviser, the chair of the council the principal forecaster and analyst, and the budget director the chief overseer of expenditures. Other cabinet secretaries, who had previously rendered economic advice, were generally excluded. This had the effect of reducing the impact of outside forces on the group and maximizing the range of presidential decisions.

The third phase of economic advising commenced in the 1970s and continues to the present. It is characterized by more participants, more external influences on policy judgments, and more formal advisory structures. With national economies more interdependent, foreign, defense, and national security affairs have greater impact on economic decisions and vice versa. As a consequence, the secretaries of state and defense, the president's national security adviser, and his special representative for trade negotiations all have legitimate concerns about the country's economic policy. Similarly, the explosion of federal programs in the 1960s, particularly entitlement programs, has created a large public constituency interested in and affected by economic decisions.

To cope with a policy-making process that has become more fragmentary, pluralistic, and political, recent administrations have had to devise mechanisms, consistent with their presidents' particular styles of decision making, that permit a range of views to be presented and a range of interests to be accommodated, yet at the same time, that work to coordinate these concerns, to promote consensus, to maximize the president's discretion, and to ensure the effective implementation of his decisions.

In the Ford administration an Economic Policy Board (EPB) performed these functions. The board, consisting of practically the entire cabinet, was run by an executive committee composed of the president's chief economic advisers and those domestic department heads who had an ongoing interest in a range of broad economic issues. Meeting three to four times a week, this executive committee functioned as a policy forum and conduit. The president attended its sessions on an average of once a week. The EPB was supported by a staff structure tied to the office of the president's assistant for economic affairs, a new position Ford had created. The head of this office presented the board's recommendations to the president and saw that the president's decisions were properly executed.

During the Carter presidency a more informal economic policy group emerged. While its composition was similar to Ford's EPB, Carter's organization lacked a staff back-up and a regular meeting schedule. Over time, key White House personnel, particularly domestic aide Stuart Eizenstat, became more involved in the details of economic policy decisions.

President Reagan reverted to the Ford model although he did not resurrect his Economic Policy Board. Rather, Reagan utilized cabinet councils as a forum for discussion, as a mechanism for providing recommendations, and as an institution for implementing presidential decisions. Meeting several times a week, with the president occasionally in attendance, the council discussed a range of policy issues from budgets and taxes to foreign investment, strategic reserves, and banking institutions.[12] Bush adopted the Reagan cabinet council model for his economic advisory structure. In addition, he appointed a principal assistant, Roger Porter, for economic and domestic policy.

The advantage of the more formal arrangement for Ford, Reagan, and Bush was that it relieved them of day-to-day decision making but still permitted them the opportunity to establish broad policy guidelines. In each administration economic groups developed a range of options from which the president made his decisions. In contrast, the Carter system maximized the president's personal involvement, but it also placed greater decisional responsibilities on his shoulders. Carter liked to make decisions and calculate their costs and benefits himself, but he did not possess an overarching economic philosophy to guide his choices. As a result, his policy appeared to lack consistency and coherence. Eventually, he lost interest in economic matters.

THE POLITICS OF ECONOMIC DECISION MAKING

Economic policy making has become more political, more pragmatic, and less stable. These changes have affected the advice the presidents receive as well as the accommodations they must make. They have also affected their involvement in economic matters.

The recommendation process is more sensitive to outside pressures from Congress, the bureaucracy, and organized interest groups, each of which has its own interests to protect and its own political axes to grind. Members of Congress must consider the economic impact on their constituencies, while department and agency heads must be responsive to their clientele, and organized groups must placate their supporters. To the extent that economic decisions require coalition building to become public policy, presidents must take these varied interests into account.

The politicization of economic decision making has made long-range planning more difficult. The election cycle must be considered when calculating the effect of policy change. Policymakers key recoveries to their own political benefit whenever possible.

Not only do short-run considerations such as elections tend to drive economic decisions, but they also enhance the pragmatic character of the decisions themselves. Presidents are more inclined to strive for what is politically feasible than what may be theoretically optimal or ideologically desirable. Perhaps this explains why presidents are more apt to pursue a policy of selective involvement in economic matters rather than to become a macromanager of the economy. This strategy has allowed them to claim credit for economic successes and share or, better still, avoid blame for economic failures.

The experience of the Reagan administration is a case in point. Coming into office with clear-cut views of how it wished to stimulate the economy, the administration was forced to compromise its initial budget and tax proposals in order to get them enacted into law.[13] The compromises became more extensive as the next presidential election approached and presidential influence in Congress declined. Pragmatic considerations, in short, muted the administration's ideological perspective but at the same time enhanced the chances for the passage of its legislative proposals.

The impact of politics on economic policy decisions has had another effect. It has made those decisions less stable over time. Unanticipated events and unintended consequences have forced presidents frequently to adjust their economic programs. President Ford was forced to abandon his Whip Inflation Now (WIN) program as economic conditions deteriorated and the country fell into a recession. President Carter had to recant a promise to provide taxpayers with a fifty dollar rebate as the budget deficit soared. President Reagan had to support the largest tax increase in the nation's history (referred to as a revenue enhancement plan) one year after getting his massive tax cut through Congress, and the large deficit President Bush inherited is likely to impose similar pressures on him to raise revenue despite his 1988 campaign pledge not to raise taxes.

Another factor that contributes to fluctuations in economic policy is the economy itself. Although presidents are ritually blamed for unfavorable conditions and are expected to improve them, many events and situations are beyond their immediate control. Existing laws establish levels of revenue and high percentages of expenditures. Interest rates dictate the cost of government borrowing while cost-of-living adjustments (COLAs) automatically raise federal outlays. Presidents must meet these obligations. Over time they can try to change them, but as recent presidents have discovered, change is not easy.

Similarly, international forces and events affect the American economy in ways that they did not prior to World War II. The rise in the price of imported oil in the mid-1970s contributed to the inflation in the United States at the end of the decade. The reindustrialization of West Germany and Japan and the growth of new industries in Asia have adversely affected American competition in steel, shipbuilding, textile, and automobile manufacturing. The weakness and strength of the dollar affect the flow of trade and tourism, the stability of financial markets, and the ability of countries to meet their foreign debts. All of these factors have short- and long-term consequences. All of them interfere with the president's ability to manipulate the economy along the lines he desires despite the fact that the president is ritually blamed for the economy's poor performance and lauded for its success.

These external factors also affect the process of making economic decisions. They have made that process more complex. They have produced more people inside and outside the government who are interested in economic policy. More interests must be balanced, more coordination is necessary, more time must be devoted to economic affairs. The burdens on the president and his advisers are greater; economic issues have more political impact; yet presidential control is more difficult to achieve. In no other policy area (except possibly the budget) are presidential limits more discernible. The increased complexity of the economic decision-making process compounds the president's leadership problem.

CONCLUSION

Presidential responsibility has been enlarged in budgetary and economic spheres. That enlargement has been a product of need, statute, and precedent. Acknowledging its inability to fashion comprehensive budget and economic policy, Congress has required the president to do so. This requirement, coupled with the expanded role of the federal government, has forced presidents and their staffs to devote increasing resources to these activities.

It has not been easy. Expectations of presidential performance have grown, but the president's capacity to affect budgetary and economic matters has not kept pace. Much of the budget is dictated by existing law and policy commitments. Presidents can affect discretionary funding, but even here political pressures often undercut their efforts to reorder spending priorities and revenue measures. Similarly, within the economic sphere, a myriad of forces from within the country and abroad are not easily subject to the president's control. These factors mute presidential efforts to stimulate the economy, but at the same time, make those efforts more important.

To help the president fulfill expectations of leadership within these areas, advisory mechanisms have developed and decision-making processes have evolved. The OMB continues to be the principal unit to provide the president with budget advice and oversee spending requests. However, the needs of the departments and agencies, the concerns of the House and Senate, and the interests of organized groups have involved many more participants in the budgetary and economic policy-making processes. This involvement has increased the complexity of these processes and has made them more political and less easily subject to presidential control. In both, power is decentralized and responsibility more difficult to pinpoint.

For the president this has meant that he must devote more attention to economic matters (including the budget), he must weigh more factors in making critical judgments, and he must use more skills in articulating and shaping an administration position. For the presidency these changes have placed greater stress on the organizational mechanism that coordinates and integrates the policy decisions and builds support for them inside and outside the government. For budgetary policy they have made it more difficult to control expenditures, although Reagan has demonstrated that priorities can be reordered. For economic policy they have produced a short-term perspective with more variation within and between administrations, a policy that places more emphasis on political feasibility.

In short, presidential roles have increased but presidential influence has declined within the budgetary and economic spheres. Leadership is more difficult to exert. Presidents have less ability to control the factors that affect their judgments. Yet those judgments are increasingly expected to solve national problems and promote national prosperity. Directing change under normal conditions is difficult. Presidents need crises as action-forcing and coalition-building mechanisms to do so. This raises the stakes, delays solutions, and frequently shortens the time frame in which those solutions are developed and implemented. During most of the time, the best presidents can do is facilitate. To do this effectively, they must devote more time to budgetary matters and selectively involve themselves in economic issues. They must coordinate support within the executive, build coalitions within Congress, balance interests, and maintain the confidence of the general public—a tall order to be sure.

NOTES

1. Our description of the evolution of the budget is based primarily on Allen Schick's discussion and analysis in his paper, "The Politics of Budgeting: Can Incrementalism Survive in a Decremental Age?" (paper presented at the Annual Meeting of the American Political Science Association, Denver, Colorado, September 2–5, 1982).

2. In 1920 federal expenditures totaled $6.357 billion. By 1930 they had been reduced to $3.32 billion.

3. The deficit targets are $100 billion for fiscal year 1990, $64 billion for fiscal year 1991, $28 billion for fiscal year 1992, and $0 for fiscal year 1993.

4. Louis Fisher, *Presidential Spending Power* (Princeton, N.J.: Princeton University Press, 1975), p. 35.

5. Larry Berman, *The Office of Management and Budget and the Presidency, 1921–1979* (Princeton, N.J.: Princeton University Press, 1979), p. 8.

6. Ibid., p. 102.

7. Schick, "The Politics of Budgeting," p. 7.

8. For a description of this process see William Greider, "The Education of David Stockman," *Atlantic*, December 1981, pp. 33–34.

9. John T. Woolley, *Monetary Politics: The Federal Reserve and the Politics of Monetary Policy* (New York: Cambridge University Press, 1984).

10. Ibid.

11. Erwin C. Hargrove and Michael Nelson, *Presidents' Politics and Policy* (New York: Knopf, 1984), pp. 186–89.

12. Task forces operating at the subcabinet level supplemented the council's deliberations with working papers and in-depth studies. An executive secretary from the president's Domestic Policy Office provided White House staff support and coordination [Murray L. Weidenbaum, "Economic Policymaking in the Reagan Administration," *Presidential Studies Quarterly* 12 (Winter, 1982): 95].

13. Hugh Heclo and Rudolph G. Penner, "Fiscal and Political Strategy in the Reagan Administration," in Fred I. Greenstein, ed., *The Reagan Presidency* (Baltimore: Johns Hopkins University Press, 1983); and Allen Schick, "How the Budget Was Won and Lost," in Norman J. Ornstein, ed., *President and Congress* (Washington, D.C.: American Enterprise Institute, 1982).

SELECTED READINGS

Anderson, James E., and Jared E. Hazleton. *Managing Macroeconomic Policy: The Johnson Presidency.* Austin, Tex.: University of Texas Press, 1986.

Berman, Larry. *The Office of Management and Budget and the Presidency, 1921–1979.* Princeton, N.J.: Princeton University Press, 1979.

Cutter, W. Bowman. "The Presidency and Economic Policy: A Tale of Two Budgets." In Michael Nelson, ed. *The President and the Political System.* Washington, D.C.: Congressional Quarterly, 1984. Pp. 471–93.

Genovese, Michael A. "The Presidency and Economic Management." *Congress and the Presidency* 14 (1987): 151–67.

Heclo, Hugh. "Executive Budget Making." In G. B. Mills and J. L. Palmer, eds. *Federal Budget Policy in the 1980s.* Washington, D.C.: Urban Institute Press, 1984. Pp. 255–91.

Peterson, Paul E., and Mark Rom. "Lower Taxes, More Spending, and Budget Deficits." In Charles O. Jones, ed. *The Reagan Legacy.* Chatham, N.J.: Chatham House, 1988. Pp. 213–40.

Pfiffner, James P., ed. *The President and Economic Policy.* Philadelphia: Institute for the Study of Human Issues, 1986.

——————. *Presidential Decision Making: The Economic Policy Board.* Cambridge, Eng.: Cambridge University Press, 1980.

Rose, Richard. "Can the President Steer the American Economy?" *Journal of Public Policy* 5 (1985): 267–80.

Schick, Allen. "How the Budget Was Won and Lost." In Norman J. Ornstein, ed. *President and Congress.* Washington, D.C.: American Enterprise Institute, 1982.

——————. *Reconciliation and the Congressional Budget Process.* Washington, D.C.: American Enterprise Institute, 1981.

Shuman, Howard E. *Politics and the Budget: The Struggle Between the President and the Congress.* 2nd ed. Englewood Cliffs, N.J.: Prentice-Hall, 1988.

Stein, Herbert. *Presidential Economics: The Making of the Economic Policy from Roosevelt to Reagan and Beyond.* New York: Simon and Schuster, 1984.

Stockman, David. *The Triumph of Politics.* New York: Harper and Row, 1986.

Tobin, James. "Reaganomics in Retrospect." In B. B. Kymlicka and Jean V. Matthews, eds. *The Reagan Revolution.* Chicago: Dorsey, 1988. Pp. 85–103.

Tomkin, Shelley Lynne. "Reagan OMB's 'Congress Watchers.' " *The Bureaucrat* 16 (Summer 1987): 55–59.

Weidenbaum, Murray L. "Economic Policy Making in the Reagan Administration." *Presidential Studies Quarterly* 12 (1982): 95–99.

——————. "The Role of the President's Council of Economic Advisers: Theory and Reality." *Presidential Studies Quarterly* 16 (1986): 460–66

Wildavsky, Aaron. *The New Politics of the Budgetary Process.* Boston: Little, Brown, 1988.

Woolley, John T. *Monetary Politics: The Federal Reserve and the Politics of Monetary Policy.* New York: Cambridge University Press, 1984.

14

Foreign and Defense Policy Making

Few would question the president's obligation to preserve and protect the nation. Few would deny him the constitutional and statutory authority to do so. Few would dispute his need to perform a variety of roles with the help of a responsive supporting staff. Still, the extent of the president's powers, the scope of his roles, and the nature of his advisory system have been subject to controversy.

These powers, those roles, and that advising system all contribute to his leadership capacities and successes. Powers are essential. Traditionally, executives have enjoyed a broad prerogative in foreign affairs, a prerogative that expands during crises that threaten the interests and security of the United States. That expansion, however, is limited in scope and time. One critical aspect of presidential leadership is how those limits are defined, both in legal and political terms.

Another component of the leadership equation in foreign affairs is the multiple roles presidents assume and the multiple forces that affect them. The roles derive from the Constitution, statute, and precedent. They have been more expansive in foreign affairs than in the domestic arena. The president's leadership problem stems from the fact that presidents do not exercise the roles exclusively nor do they control the environment in which it must operate. Congress is empowered to act in foreign affairs. Political parties and an increasing array of interest groups, private consultants and attorneys who represent corporations, associations, unions, and foreign governments seek to influence presidential judgments. The mass media regularly report on and evaluate presidential actions. Within the international arena the United States is one player among many. Its economy, its resources, its political and military positions are more interdependent with others than ever before. Moreover, presidents must deal with an increasing number of their own advisers who represent and present differing perspectives, organizations, and interests.

How all of these factors affect the president's capacity to lead will be the subject of this chapter. First we describe the president's formal authority in theory and in practice. Next we turn to the expansion of the president's policy-making role, identifying the factors which have contributed to that expansion and the success presidents have had in achieving their policy goals. Changes in the international and domestic environment, particularly within the last decade, have presented leadership problems. We discuss those problems and their impact on presidential policy making within the context of the "two presidencies" thesis and then go on to describe the advisory mechanism that has been created to help the president coordinate, formulate, articulate, and implement foreign and military policy. We examine this mechanism and assess its effect on policy, the presidency, and the governmental system. We conclude with a statement of how these factors singularly and together contribute to the kind of leadership a president can exert.

CONSTITUTIONAL AND STATUTORY AUTHORITY

The Original Design

The president's powers in foreign affairs and national defense have expanded significantly beyond their original design. The framers of the Constitution anticipated a policy-making role for the president, but they did not desire the executive to dominate that role. On the contrary, their fear that a president might pursue personal interests at the expense of the nation's welfare led them to divide and share responsibilities in such a way that the executive lacked the authority to conclude policy on his own. Whether or not to go to war was to be the decision of Congress. The president had discretion to react in times of emergency to repel attacks but presumably not to initiate hostilities or in any other way establish permanent war policy. The expectation was that he would summon Congress to do so. The president could, however, terminate hostilities.

Short of war, the executive was given considerable latitude in foreign affairs. He could initiate treaties in conjunction with the Senate; their approval required the concurrence of two-thirds of the upper chamber. Within foreign and military spheres the president was expected to exercise authority. This included nominating ambassadors and receiving them. Senate approval was required for the appointment to take effect. The performance of the ceremonial duties of a head of state was also seen as a presidential duty. Similarly, the president could nominate military officials and nominally, at least, command them. How command was to work in practice, however, was not enumerated.

In performing these executive responsibilities, the president would inevitably make decisions that had policy implications. The framers did not fear this. They anticipated that Congress by virtue of its power to appropriate money, authorize programs, and regulate commerce would establish the contours of that policy and would be able to check presidential initiatives adequately.

The Exercise of Powers

TREATY MAKING.   Treaty making was to be jointly exercised with the Senate. An incident that occurred early in the Washington administration, however, soured this arrangement and presaged the difficulties that the president would have in dealing with the upper chamber as both an advisory and consenting body. In August 1789, President Washington came to the Senate to request its advice on a treaty with the Indians of western Georgia. Armed with thirteen questions prepared by his secretary of war, General Knox, Washington desired the Senate's guidance in the negotiations. Instead, he was treated to a long, discursive discussion that reached no decision. Forced to return two days later for what turned out to be insipid advice, Washington did not personally go back to the Senate for its counsel. Instead, he and his successors turned to their principal department heads for advice and to the Senate primarily for its consent as required by the Constitution.

The experience had a profound effect on presidential–senatorial relations. It discouraged the president from involving the Senate in the negotiation phase of treaty making. While some consultation continued, presidents began to do more on their own. Woodrow Wilson's refusal to consider senatorial opinion in the negotiations on the Treaty of Versailles represents one of the most flagrant examples of chief executive's going it alone.

Historically, the Senate has approved without modification about 70 percent of the approximately fifteen hundred treaties that have been submitted to it by the president since 1789. Only sixteen of those that have come to a vote have been voted down (the most famous probably being the Treaty of Versailles ending World War I and establishing the League of Nations). However, many other proposed treaties have been withdrawn by the president because of opposition in the Senate and thus have never come up for a vote. About one hundred and fifty have been withdrawn since World War II, including the SALT (strategic arms limitation talks) II treaty proposed by President Carter and withdrawn to protest the Soviet Union's armed presence in Afghanistan.

Not only can the Senate approve treaties without modification (as it did with the Intermediate Range Ballistic Missile (INF) treaty with the Soviet Union in 1988) or reject them outright; it can also approve them with reservations or with amendments, thereby requiring changes or deletions. In early 1978 the Senate consented to two treaties dealing with the Panama Canal. It added a reservation to one of them stating that the

United States had a right to use military force, if necessary, to keep the canal open.

Once a change has been made to a treaty, it usually must go to the president and the other country or countries who are parties to the treaty for approval.[1] Additions and deletions are not always approved, however, and many treaties have failed for this reason.

From time to time the House of Representatives has also attempted to impose itself in the treaty-making process, but frequently without success. Arguing that the Congress as a body is empowered to deal with foreign commerce, military affairs, war, and international policy, it has proposed legislation and used its appropriations authority to this end. Both the president and the Senate have resisted the lower chamber's intrusion into their exclusive domain, however.

Whereas Senate consent is necessary for the ratification of treaties, it has not been considered essential for their termination. When President Carter ended a long-standing defense treaty with the Chinese Nationalists on Taiwan, he did not request the approval of the Senate. The legality of Carter's action, challenged by Senator Barry Goldwater, was upheld in court.

FORMULATING EXECUTIVE AGREEMENTS.   The need to obtain the Senate's consent has encouraged recent presidents to enter into executive agreements in order to avoid the formal treaty ratification process. The number of such agreements has mushroomed in recent years, as indicated in Table 14-1.

An executive agreement is concluded by the president on behalf of the United States with the head of government of another country. Unlike a treaty, it does not require a two-thirds vote of the Senate. Thus, when President Tyler failed to get the Senate to approve a treaty annexing Texas, he entered into an executive agreement to do so. Most executive agreements do not even need formal congressional approval, although some may require legislation to implement them. Such legislation is subject to a simple majority vote of both houses.

Unlike treaties, executive agreements do not supersede statutes. Otherwise, they are just as binding as treaties and have been used for such famous compacts as the destroyer bases deal with Great Britain in 1940, the Yalta and Potsdam agreements in 1945, and the Vietnam peace agreement of 1973.

Presidents have been careful in their choice of instruments for making international agreements. In recent years treaties have dealt with such diverse subjects as shrimp, the protection of Mexican archaeological artifacts, the dumping of wastes at sea, and the maintenance of lights in the Red Sea; executive agreements have also been used to end wars and to establish or expand military bases in other countries. In 1972, as a

Table 14-1. Treaties and Executive Agreements Approved by the United
          States, 1789–1986

Year	Number of Treaties	Number of Executive Agreements
1789–1839	60	27
1839–1889	215	238
1889–1929	382	763
1930–1932	49	41
1933–1944 (F. Roosevelt)	131	369
1945–1952 (Truman)	132	1,324
1953–1960 (Eisenhower)	89	1,834
1961–1963 (Kennedy)	36	813
1964–1968 (L. Johnson)	67	1,083
1969–1974 (Nixon)	93	1,317
1975–1976 (Ford)	26	666
1977–1980 (Carter)	79	1,476
1981–1986 (Reagan)	92	2,019

Note: Varying definitions of what comprises an executive agreement and their entry-into-force date make the above numbers approximate.

Source: Harold W. Stanley and Richard G. Niemi, *Vital Statistics on American Politics* (Washington, D.C.: Congressional Quarterly, 1988), p. 226.

result of SALT, President Nixon signed a treaty limiting the defensive weapons of the Soviet Union and the United States and an executive agreement limiting the offensive weapons of each country. Although most executive agreements are routine and deal with noncontroversial subjects such as food deliveries or customs enforcement, some implement important and controversial policies.

To influence executive agreements, Congress needs to know about them before they are finalized, while options are still open. Even more basic, it needs to know that the agreements even exist. In 1969 and 1970, the Senate Foreign Relations Committee discovered that presidents had covertly entered into a number of secret agreements with South Vietnam, South Korea, Thailand, Laos, Ethiopia, Spain, and other countries. In response to these actions Congress passed the Case Act of 1972, which requires the secretary of state to transmit to Congress within sixty days the text of any international agreement other than treaties to which the United States is a party. If the president feels publication of an agreement would jeopardize national security, he may transmit the text only to members of the Senate Foreign Relations and House Foreign Affairs committees under an injunction of secrecy that only he (or his successors) may remove.

Presidents Nixon and Ford did not fully comply with the Case Act, however. Some agreements were not submitted to Congress and others were submitted after the sixty-day period. Consequently, in 1977 Congress passed legislation requiring any department or agency of the United States government that enters into any international agreement on behalf of the country to transmit the text to the State Department within twenty days of its signing. Neither of these two laws actually limits the president's power to act without Congress in defense and foreign affairs. Yet their passage indicates that Congress is increasingly unwilling to defer blindly to the president's judgment.

In addition to concluding a formal agreement, presidents have also engaged in a form of diplomacy that recognizes "understandings" with other countries. A case in point is the SALT II treaty. Although the Senate never approved it, the Reagan administration abided by most of its provisions (as did the Soviet Union). Similarly, the Carter administration continued to observe the SALT I treaty for three years after it expired. Short of enacting legislation that requires a specific action, Congress can do little to prevent the president from making a unilateral policy declaration in concert with the leaders of other governments.[2]

RECOGNIZING AND NOT RECOGNIZING COUNTRIES.   In addition to negotiating treaties and formulating executive agreements and understandings, presidents can initiate or terminate relations with other countries. The right of recognition has traditionally been considered a presidential responsibility. George Washington exercised it when he received Citizen Genêt and thereby recognized the new French Republic in 1789. Presidents have even extended this to acknowledging the rights of a people who lack a state and to continuing to recognize a government that has been removed from power. The Senate has no role in this process other than to consent to the choice of an American ambassador.

Recognizing countries can be controversial. In 1933 Franklin D. Roosevelt recognized the government of the Soviet Union, fifteen years after it was constituted and functioning. In 1979 Jimmy Carter extended recognition to the government that controlled mainland China, the People's Republic, following a period of thirty years of nonrecognition. In 1984 Ronald Reagan announced the resumption of formal diplomatic relations with the Vatican. Each of these actions provoked criticism about the merits of the president's judgment, but not his right to make it.

Presidents can also end relations. Before war ensues it is customary to sever relations with adversaries. Similarly, events short of war can also result in a disruption of diplomatic activity. The revolutionary activities of Cuba and Iran led presidents Eisenhower and Carter to cut formal ties with these countries. However, some contact was maintained by an "interests section" that operated out of the embassy of a friendly country.

There are other actions that presidents can take to register their disapproval of the policies of other countries. Recalling an ambassador, instituting a trade embargo, reducing economic or military assistance, boycotting the Olympics, are all devices which contemporary presidents have employed to sanction the actions of others.

MAKING WAR.   The Constitution gives Congress the sole power to declare war, a power it has exercised only five times (in 1812, 1846, 1898, 1917, 1941). Such full-scale wars as those in Korea and Vietnam were not officially declared by Congress. In addition, presidents have employed a more limited use of force abroad without a declaration of war or statutory authority more than one hundred times. This presidential involvement of armed forces presents a conflict between constitutional theory and practice.

The roles as commander-in-chief, head of state, and head of government have undoubtedly contributed to the capacity of presidents to commit the nation to battle. Armed with a near monopoly of first-hand information, a potential for engaging public support, and an oath to provide for the common defense, they have used their prerogatives to broaden their constitutional powers. Jefferson ordered the navy and marines to retaliate against the Barbary pirates who threatened American shipping. Polk ordered the army into disputed territory with Mexico to protect Texas' claim to its borders. Lincoln instituted a blockade of the South and imposed other sanctions to put down the southern insurrection. Recent instances include the orders of President Eisenhower to send armed forces to Lebanon in 1958; of President Kennedy to blockade Cuba in 1962; of President Johnson to dispatch troops to the Dominican Republic in 1965; of President Nixon to bomb Cambodia in 1970; of President Ford to attack Cambodia in order to rescue the crew of the *Mayaquez* (a United States merchant ship seized by Cambodia in 1975); of President Carter to rescue the American hostages in Iran in 1980; and of President Reagan to send an armed force to the Caribbean island of Grenada and marines to Lebanon in 1983, bombers to Libya in 1986, and ships to the Persian Gulf in 1988.

Theoretically, Congress could have resisted many of these executive actions. In practice it has been unable and unwilling to do so. The House of Representatives condemned Polk, but after the Mexican War had been concluded. Congress forced Nixon to end bombing in Cambodia, but only after that action had been carried on for more than two years. During periods of crisis, Congress finds it difficult, if not impossible, to oppose the president.

The Vietnam War, which stirred up deep dissent at home, was the last straw. In 1973 Congress passed the War Powers Resolution over President Nixon's veto. It requires that the president consult with Congress "in every possible instance" involving the use of American troops in hostile or potentially hostile situations. The president must report to Congress in writing within forty-eight hours after ordering United States armed forces into hostilities. More significantly, the military action must

stop sixty days after the submission of this report unless Congress declares war, authorizes the use of force, extends the sixty-day period, or is
unable to meet because of an attack upon the United States. At any time
Congress can end the use of American armed forces by passing a concurrent resolution (which is not subject to a presidential veto).[3] The president may extend the use of force for thirty additional days if he deems it
necessary to protect departing American forces.

The law has aroused considerable debate about just what consultation means and whether the president could, in sixty days of hostilities,
place the United States in a position from which Congress could not
extract it. These issues were not resolved by the applications of the War
Powers Resolution since its passage: the evacuations from Southeast Asia
in April 1975, the rescue of the *Mayaquez* from Cambodia in May 1975, the
attempted rescue of the hostages from Iran in 1980, the Grenada invasion
of 1983, and the use of naval forces in the Persian Gulf in 1988.

In practically every administration there have been instances that
could have fallen under the purview of the act but were not reported to
Congress in accordance with its provisions (see Table 14-2). Why? What
is the problem?

Table 14-2. United States Troop Commitments, 1974–1986

Deployment	War Powers Application
Cyprus Evacuation (1974)	No Report
Cambodian Resupply (1974)	No Report
Cambodian Reconnaissance (1974)	No Report
Danang Sealift (1975)	Report/Sec. 4(a)(2)
Cambodian Evacuation (1975)	Report/Sec. 4(a)(2)
Vietnam Evacuation (1975)	Report/Sec. 4
Mayaguez Incident (1975)	Report/Sec. 4(a)(1)
Lebanon Evacuation (1976)	No Report
Korean Reenforcement (1976)	No Report
Zaire Airlift (1978)	No Report
Iranian Rescue Mission (1980)	Report/No section specified
Advisers in El Salvador (1981)	No Report
Sinai Multinational Force (1982)	Report/Sec. 4(a)(2)
Lebanon—PLO Evacuation (1982)	Report/No section specified
Lebanon—United States Evacuation (1982)	Report/No section specified
Chad Reconnaissance (1983)	Report/Sec. 4
Lebanon Peace-Keeping Force (1983)	Report/Sec. 4
AWACs to Chad (1983)	Report/Sec. 4
Grenada Invasion (1983)	Report/Sec. 4(a)(1)
Gulf of Sidra (1986)	Report/No statute cited
Libyan Retaliation (1986)	Report/No statute cited

Source: Daniel Paul Franklin, "War Powers in the Modern Context," *Congress and the
Presidency* (Spring 1987): 80.

Presidents believe the resolution unconstitutionally constricts their obligation to provide for the common defense by constraining their powers as commander-in-chief. Although they have not challenged the constitutionality of the legislation in court, they have narrowly interpreted its provisions, particularly its consultation and reporting requirements. Congress as a body has been reticent to impose these requirements on the president, much less start the clock running on the time limits contained in the legislation. Individual members, however, have raised and debated those issues with respect to specific presidential actions.

Is the resolution unworkable? Perhaps. Is it irrelevant? No. In theory it reasserts congressional authority while acknowledging expanded presidential powers; in practice, it does not prevent presidential initiatives but forces the president to consider the possibility that Congress, through action or inaction, could terminate those initiatives. This consideration presumably acts as a constraint on potentially unpopular presidential actions. However, the principal type of presidential initiatives that the War Powers Resolution seems designed to prevent, the long-term conventional limited wars similar to Korea and Vietnam, seem to be those that are least likely to occur if the political climate that has existed in the United States since the mid-1970s persists. If that climate were to change, the propensity of Congress to support military action begun by the president would probably increase as well. In general, the shorter the time frame and the quicker the needed response, the less likely Congress can play an important role.

Although Congress is not likely to oppose presidential involvement in emergency situations which threaten the national security or adversely affect American interests abroad, its propensity for influencing presidential policy in nonemergency situations has increased. Congressional power to authorize conscription or maintain an all-volunteer military, to appropriate money for defense, even to affect the sales of arms has been greater in peacetime. Since the Vietnam War, presidents can no longer count on bipartisan support for all military actions, alliances, and aid. In 1981 President Reagan had to use all of his persuasive powers to keep Congress from preventing a sale of special reconnaissance aircraft known as AWACS (Airborne Warning and Control Systems) to Saudi Arabia. Later in his presidency, he was forced to modify or abandon other arms deals because they faced certain defeat in Congress.

COMMANDING THE MILITARY.   The powers of the president as commander-in-chief have also been expanded. The initial concept of this role was unclear. Did the framers of the Constitution vest the president with a title—civilian head of the military—or empower him with operational authority? Over the years, presidents began to behave as if they had operational authority. Lincoln used the crisis of the Civil War to institute a series of military actions including a blockade of the South, the arrest of suspected traitors, activation of the state militia, establishment of military courts in areas of civil insurrection, and suspension of the writ of habeas corpus. Lincoln also got involved in the conduct of the war and the selection of field commanders.

Other presidents have also expanded the operational component of their commander-in-chief responsibilities. Franklin Roosevelt ordered the internment of persons of Japanese ancestry on the West Coast, chose the principal theaters of operations and points of invasion, and established a map room in the White House to keep abreast of developments in World War II. Harry Truman ordered the use of atomic weapons in that war, forbade American planes to cross the Chinese border during the Korean War, and dismissed his Pacific commander, Douglas Mac-Arthur. John Kennedy personally monitored the Bay of Pigs invasion and the blockade of Cuba during the missile crisis. Lyndon Johnson approved strategic and tactical military decisions in Vietnam, including the bombing of targets and mining of ports, while Richard Nixon extended the bombing to Cambodia.

Ronald Reagan was a particularly active military commander. In addition to his commitment of American forces in Lebanon and Grenada and approving their military actions, he ordered the bombing of military targets in Libya, sent United States warships and personnel to Central America, and dispatched a naval force to the Persian Gulf. He was the first president in twenty-five years to review a war game conducted by the Defense Department and national security staff. Moreover, Reagan initiated and later endorsed a National Security Council directive that developed strategic plans for fighting and winning prolonged nuclear and conventional wars.[4]

The destructiveness of nuclear weapons combined with this rapid deployment and delivery suggest that presidents can no longer leave war making to their military commanders. The ultimate responsibility for how war is to be conducted rests with the civilian commander, the president.

THE EXPANSION OF A POLICY-MAKING ROLE

Incentives for Presidential Leadership

The growth of the president's authority in foreign and military affairs has been the consequence of several factors: the increasing involvement of the United States within the international community; the public's desire for strong, personal leadership to direct that involvement; and the political ramifications of that leadership on the administration and its policy goals.

Since the end of World War II, the United States has been a dominant economic, military, and political power. It has tried to shape international developments, aiding its allies and resisting its adversaries, building its defenses yet promoting peaceful coexistence, fostering its interests yet supporting international cooperation. The industrial capacity, technological skills, and resource base of the United States were essential to the revitalization of the economies of countries in Western Europe and Asia following the destruction during World War II. The economic strength of the United States has also been an important source of technical, financial, and agricultural aid to the Third World, which needs the products and skills of an advanced technological society. The United States, in turn, has become increasingly dependent on the natural resources of developing countries, particularly those that produce energy. Today the economies of many nations, rich and poor, are more interdependent than ever before.

Resource dependency and economic interdependency have contributed to the incentives for American involvement. No longer can the United States afford to adopt an isolationist policy nor can the president avoid international affairs, at least not for long. Held accountable for the performance of the domestic economy, a president has no choice but to tackle international problems as well.

The technological advances in armaments, particularly nuclear weapons, and the continued competition and potential conflict with the Soviet Union have forced presidents to be continuously concerned about military preparedness, strategic planning, alliance building, and arms control. The vulnerability of all nations, the proliferation of nuclear weapons, and the persistence of armed conflict require the president to promote the common defense and peaceful coexistence at the same time.

Not only have world events forced the president to emphasize foreign and military affairs, but domestic political forces have also done so. The public looks to the president in times of crisis for leadership. He is the person around whom the country can rally, a unifying figure, the personification of the state.[5]

In the short run, crisis situations may increase the public's approval of the president. When American hostages were seized in Iran in 1979, public approval of Carter's performance rose. Over time, when he was unable to obtain their release, his approval level declined. This suggests that in the long run the persistence of the crisis works to the president's disadvantage. He is expected to resolve the problem in a manner favorable to American national interests.

In addition to the short-run support that crises can generate for a president, foreign policy leadership benefits the incumbent in other respects. It contributes to the image of strong national leadership. This is particularly useful during reelection campaigns when strength, assertiveness, will, and direction are seen as most desirable presidential traits.

The public wants to feel secure. People look to the president to satisfy that feeling. The nation's security in modern times has been a source of continuous concern and is a recurring campaign issue. The results of recent presidential elections testify to its importance. Candidates perceived as less competent in foreign affairs have lost.

The difficulties faced by presidents in formulating a policy agenda and in developing a consensus for it are not usually as arduous in foreign and military affairs as they are in domestic ones. Although partisanship has been increasingly evident in foreign and defense policy, presidential dependence on legislative enactments is still not as great as in the domestic area. Moreover, as the president's ability to effect domestic change decreases, his incentive to get involved in foreign affairs increases.

Taken together, these factors have encouraged the president to assume a dominant role in foreign affairs. They have also contributed to his ability to achieve his political goals. This emphasis and that success have led one political scientist, Aaron Wildavsky, to conclude that there are really two presidents: one domestic and one foreign.

Policy Goals and Presidential Success: The Two Presidencies Thesis

According to Wildavsky, presidents tend to get their way in the foreign policy realm far more often than in the domestic one. He added:

Although presidents have rivals for power in foreign affairs, the rivals do not usually succeed. Presidents prevail not only because they may have superior resources but because their potential opponents are weak, divided or believe that they should not control foreign policy.[6]

Wildavsky supported his argument with a study of congressional action on presidential proposals from 1948 through 1964. In this examination of congressional roll calls, he found that presidents had significantly better records in foreign and defense policy. He concluded:

When refugees and immigration—which Congress considers primarily a domestic concern—are removed from the general foreign policy area, it is clear that Presidents prevail about 70 per cent of the time in defense and foreign policy, compared with 40 per cent in the domestic sphere.[7]

Wildavsky wrote in the mid-1960s after an era of bipartisanship in foreign affairs. He wrote after the emergence of the United States as a world power, after presidents Roosevelt, Truman, Eisenhower, and Kennedy had established America's position as a leader of the Western world, container of communism, and promoter of international cooperation. He wrote before the Vietnam War.

The unpopularity of that war led to recriminations against the presidents who directed that effort and against the presidency itself. In an effort to deter future presidential action that lacked popular and congressional support, Congress passed a series of statutes designed to constrain executive discretion in hostile or potentially hostile situations. As a consequence, presidents still retain the policy initiative, but Congress has improved its capacity to modify that initiative and to say no.

Political and institutional changes during the 1970s have contributed to a more assertive posture in foreign affairs by Congress. The domestic impact of foreign policy has become more pronounced, blurring the old distinction between foreign and domestic affairs and creating new incentives for legislative involvement. The old adage that "politics stops at the water's edge" is no longer valid for noncrisis situations, a fact that George Bush lamented in his first inaugural address and has tried to reverse by adopting a bipartisan approach to foreign policy in the early stages of his administration.

With more committees and subcommittees dealing with international issues; more staff and better information facilities at their disposal; more foreign travel by legislators and their aides; more groups, governments, and individuals trying to affect policy judgments, members of Congress, individually and collectively, have become less disposed to acquiesce in the president's initiatives. Some have even taken matters into their own hands. At the height of the Iranian hostage crisis, Representative George Hansen went to Tehran to try to obtain the release of the hostages. In 1987 Speaker of the House James Wright went to Nicaragua to discuss efforts to halt fighting between government forces and their United States-backed opponents.

With presidential policy making subject to greater scrutiny, scholars have begun to reexamine Wildavsky's thesis. The results of that reexamination thus far have been mixed. In general, political scientists have found that presidents are still more likely to get their way in Congress on national security policy than on domestic policy but they are also more likely to lose than in the past. One recent study of congressional compliance with presidential requests in foreign affairs found that Congress gave the president all or part of what he wanted 65 percent of the time.[8] Another discovered that the typical member of Congress supports the president on foreign policy just over half the time.[9]

Although Congress has become more reluctant to ratify presidential policy, preferring instead to debate and modify it, the general public, party leaders, and elected officials continue to look to the president for guidance. The president provides the agenda and most of the specific policy initiatives. The difference is that today more members of Congress are interested in foreign policy, in large part because it has a more discernible domestic impact—many times directly on their own constituencies. With a growing number of interest groups concerned with international economic, defense, environmental, and human rights issues, foreign policy making has become more politically sensitive. The age of bipartisanship that occurred during and after World War II, when Congress dutifully followed the president's lead, seems to be over.

The increasing interest and involvement of Congress in foreign policy decisions places the president in a dilemma. How can he lead without followers? How can he be expected to make policy and be held accountable for it if he cannot be assured of its enactment? Presidents might desire to be strong policy leaders, but in normal times that leadership is often fragile. This is why they need a variety of policy experts and coalition builders to succeed. It is to that advisory mechanism that we now turn.

THE DEVELOPMENT OF AN ADVISORY SYSTEM

The Executive Departments

Throughout the nineteenth century and well into the twentieth, the secretary of state was the president's principal foreign policy adviser. He provided information and advice as well as implemented policy decisions. In performing this role, the secretary has been assisted by a staff of career officials, who were organized primarily on the basis of five regional bureaus.

Over the years the State Department has become more specialized. Functional divisions dealing with economics and business, international organization, environmental and scientific affairs, and public and congressional relations have supplemented the political bureaus. Nonetheless, the department remains relatively small. Its actual 1988 budget outlays of $3.4 billion pales by comparison to the Defense Department's $281.9 billion as does the size of its work force (25,482 compared to over 1 million civilians for the Defense Department). One reason that the State Department has not grown dramatically as American involvement in world affairs has increased is that a variety of old and new agencies now also participate in international activities.

There is an intelligence community. Consisting of almost forty separate agencies, it is dominated by the Central Intelligence Agency, National Security Agency, and the Defense Intelligence Agency. There is a United States Information Agency (USIA), which operates libraries; sponsors cultural, scientific, and educational programs; coordinates press relations; and runs the Voice of America, a worldwide radio and television network. There is a special trade representative, an Arms Control and Disarmament Agency, and a National Aeronautics and Space Administration (NASA). Many of the principal executive departments also have international divisions and ongoing interests in international affairs. The State Department no longer enjoys a monopoly.

The proliferation of agencies with international activities has presented the president with several problems: how to balance competing perspectives and interests within his administration; how to coordinate and integrate policy advice; how to articulate policy with a single voice; and how to do all of this within his time frame without jeopardizing his goals or sacrificing his discretion in the decision-making process. The resolution of these problems has proved difficult. Solutions have varied with the style and goals of the president and the institutional needs of his office.

President Franklin Roosevelt relied primarily on his White House staff. Presidential aides provided liaison with the military and State departments, acted as personal emissaries of the president to other governments, and funneled information and advice to Roosevelt. He, in turn, directed their activities.

Partially in reaction to the ad hoc nature of Roosevelt's advisory system and his reliance on personal aides rather than department heads, Congress enacted the National Security Act of 1947. This law, which combined the separate military departments into a single defense agency and established the Central Intelligence Agency, acknowledged presidential responsibilities within the national security sphere and provided a mechanism for meeting these responsibilities, the National Security Council (NSC).

The National Security Council

The National Security Council consists of four statutory members: the president, vice president, secretary of state, and secretary of defense. It also includes a number of advisory members such as the director of the CIA, the chairman of the Joint Chiefs of Staff, the director of the Arms Control and Disarmament Agency, and other advisers that presidents have added from time to time.[10] Beginning with Truman, presidents provided it with staff support.

The council's charge is advisory but its mandate is broad: to help define goals and priorities; to coordinate and integrate domestic, foreign, and military policies; and to suggest specific courses of action—all within the national security sphere.

In the Truman presidency, the council functioned as a forum for discussion. Truman used it only sporadically until the Korean War, when he began meeting with it on a regular basis. During this period the council performed an important advisory role. President Eisenhower expanded this role, converting the NSC into a policy-making body. It operated as a planning board for developing general policy positions. A White House secretariat, headed by a special assistant to the president for national security affairs, helped provide organizational support.

As an advisory body the council reached its zenith during the 1950s. Eisenhower's penchant for using formal organizations to establish broad objectives meshed well with the capacity of the National Security Council to provide an integrated set of policy recommendations. Beginning with Kennedy, however, the council's policy-making function was eliminated and its advisory role declined. Although it continued to meet, often for symbolic purposes, its principal responsibilities were assumed by a special assistant to the president for national security affairs and his staff.

The NSC enjoyed a mild resurgence during the Reagan administration. Functioning within a cabinet council system, it helped coordinate policy among the various agencies involved in national security issues. A major component of that job was to oversee the implementation of key presidential decisions. In doing so its staff provided coordination at the working-group level for various departments and agencies that were concerned with different aspects of national security policy. In the words of Colin Powell, the last national security adviser to hold office during the Reagan administration:

> We must make sure that all the relevant departments and agencies play their appropriate role in policy formulation. We must make sure that all pertinent facts and viewpoints are laid before the President. We must also make sure that no Cabinet official completes an "end run" around other NSC principals in pushing a policy line on which they too have legitimate concerns.[11]

The relative decline of the NSC's role as an advisory body has coincided with the development of a sizable staffing structure for the president's special assistant for national security affairs. Presidents have increasingly turned to that assistant for information, advice, and internal coordination.

The Special Assistant for National Security Affairs

Kennedy was the first president to create the position of special assistant for national security affairs. His purpose was to integrate the growing diversity of executive branch perspectives and views and to do so without the burden of a large support system. Moreover, his preferred style of decision making was to interact with a few key aides rather than preside over a cabinet-like body.

Kennedy's involvement in the management of foreign and defense policy enhanced the role of his national security adviser at the expense of senior officials in the State and Defense departments. Power shifted from these departments to the White House. This shift continued and accelerated in subsequent administrations. Increasing reliance by presidents on their national security adviser enhanced the prestige and influence of the adviser and in the process produced tension with the secretary of state.

The national security office grew. The staff approached one hundred and fifty policy experts and supporting personnel by 1972. The reach of the president's assistant expanded. Not only was he able to offer advice on a wider range of issues, but increasingly, he was able to act as the president's personal representative, negotiator, and spokesman. Henry Kissinger, who served in this position during the Nixon and Ford administrations, performed all of these roles. In addition, he presided over an elaborate system of interagency committees that fortified his position and undercut that of the department heads. In this way he controlled the flow of information and ideas to the president. Traditional departmental interests were muted.

Kissinger's personal relationships, particularly with President Nixon, prevented others from circumventing his authority. Moreover, his "closed" style of operating, combined with Nixon's penchant to consult primarily, sometimes exclusively, with his national security adviser, reduced the influence of others. Secretary of State William Rogers was not even informed of the president's China initiative until it was under way. For all intents and purposes, the traditional policy functions of the secretary of state had been eclipsed. After Rogers resigned in 1972, Nixon made it official. He appointed Kissinger to head the State Department yet allowed him to continue in his national security position.

Ford disengaged the positions in 1974, appointing Kissinger's principal assistant, Brent Scowcroft, to replace him. With this disengagement came a reversion of the adviser's responsibilities to those which were performed during the Kennedy period: briefing the president, acting as

"FIRST OF ALL I WANT YOU TO ISSUE A STATEMENT DENYING IT ."

Source: Pat Oliphant. Copyright 1971 Universal Press Syndicate. Reprinted with permission. All rights reserved.

a liaison to the departments, and coordinating presidential responses after decisions had been made. This reduced role was short-lived, however. The Kissinger model was restored during the Carter administration by one of Kissinger's former students, Zbigniew Brzezinski. Assuming functions of adviser, advocate, and sometimes spokesman, Carter's assistant for national security affairs clashed frequently with Secretary of State Cyrus Vance.

While Brzezinski did not retain the elaborate substructure of standing committees and working groups that characterized the Kissinger operation, most important studies, option papers, and memos to the president were still routed through his office. Of his own role, Brzezinski stated:

> I work very closely with the President. I'm his adviser in foreign policy and security matters. And I'm the coordinator for him of all the work that comes for his decision from the State Department, from Defense and from the CIA. Finally, and expressly so, the President wishes me and my staff to help him play an innovative role, that is to say, to try to look beyond the problems of the immediate and help him define a larger and more distant sense of direction.[12]

Still another attempt to change the relationship between the president, his adviser, and the secretary of state occurred during the Reagan administration. Desiring to have the department heads play a larger advisory role and to avoid the tension that had been created between the White House and other executive branch units, Reagan initially reduced the influence and visibility of his national security adviser and had him report to Edwin Meese, the person who was charged with policy coordination in both domestic and national security affairs during the early years of the administration. Not only did this reduce the influence of the national security adviser, but it also reduced that of his staff. Power shifted to the State Department, but tension between it and the White House remained high. Fueled by clashing personalities, policy perspectives, and institutional interests, these tensions eventually led to the resignation of the secretary of state, Alexander Haig, and the upgrading of the White House national security operation under a new director and with new personnel. In all, Reagan had six national security advisers in eight years.

Turnover in the White House and specifically on the national security staff combined with a lack of adequate presidential guidance and supervision contributed to the major foreign policy mishap of the Reagan administration—the Iran–Contra affair. The failure and unpopularity of the policy to sell arms to Iran in exchange for that country's help in obtaining the release of American hostages in Lebanon, combined with the illegal use of the profits from that arms sale to support the Contra forces fighting to overthrow the Nicaraguan government, prompted a reexamination of the role and procedures of the national security staff and its relationship to the president.

A presidential commission, headed by John Tower (former senator and Armed Services Committee chairman) and consisting of Edmund Muskie (a former senator and secretary of state during the Carter administration) and Brent Scowcroft (President Ford's national security adviser), criticized the actions of several national security aides and the president's failure to supervise them. It recommended an end to the staff's participation in covert operations and a return to its principal functions of coordinating national security advice for the president, but it did not recommend structural or procedural changes in the staff's mode of operation. In accepting the commission's findings and recommendations, President Reagan issued a directive that gave the State and Defense department secretaries primary responsibility for foreign and defense affairs, subject to interagency review, within the national security policy process. The national security adviser was charged with making that process work on a daily basis as well as briefing the president and providing him with the information and advice necessary to make decisions and take actions.

ASSESSING THE ADVISORY SYSTEM

As administration priorities shift and national security policy becomes more important, there is a tendency for the White House adviser to become more influential and for presidents to rely more on their national security adviser for policy advice. Why? For one thing, presidents seem to become more interested in making foreign policy. They see their ability to do so as more critical to their administration's popularity and to their own political success.

If policy matters become more important to presidents, it is natural for them to try to maximize their discretion when dealing with them, to exercise more central control, to act quickly and decisively and to do so in a manner that is consistent with their basic beliefs and their policy objectives. Naturally, presidents do not enjoy resistance to their policy from outside the administration much less within it (although the policy might benefit from such resistance). From the president's perspective reliance on *his* national security operation tends to facilitate these objectives.

There are several reasons for this. The national security adviser has one constituent, the president. The department secretaries have several: other governments, other departments, organized interest groups, and the department's own diverse bureaucracy. Second, the national security assistant is more apt to be on the president's wavelength with a staff of policy experts chosen in large part because of their acceptable political and ideological views. The secretaries are supported by a cadre of civil servants (and in the case of defense, career military officials) who have survived precisely because they do not enunciate partisan views or see the world primarily in ideological terms. The national security adviser and his staff can be ideological and partisan; the secretary of state must be pragmatic and diplomatic.

Moreover, the national security staff, unburdened by administrative responsibilities, can respond more rapidly and less visibly to presidential needs and requests, particularly emergencies. In contrast, the departments tend to move more slowly. They adhere to established procedures, utilize regular channels, and usually speak in carefully measured tones. Presidents often have become impatient with them and distrustful of them. Particularly fearful of leaks, some have even tried to avoid involving the departments entirely on very sensitive matters.

Not only does a White House office enjoy institutional advantages in responding to presidential needs, but the head of it also enjoys several personal advantages. He has better access to the president, including an office in the West Wing and a daily briefing with the president. He has fewer operational responsibilities, hence more time to focus on immediate problems that demand presidential decisions or actions. In contrast, the secretary of state must deal with a wider range of policy and administrative matters, including diplomatic and ceremonial functions.

It is easy to see why presidents have turned to their national security adviser. In addition to exercising more discretion within a supportive environment, they can more easily engage in top-down decision making and formulate policies that are consistent with their political beliefs and ideological convictions. Moreover, the policies themselves are apt to be more innovative and consist of fewer compromises than would result if a larger number of executive and legislative officials were involved.

These advantages, however, are offset by several major disadvantages, which were noted in a report prepared for President Bush by the National Academy of Public Administration. The report said, in part:

> The personal advice of the national security advisor, while not freighted with bureaucratic loads, is also less sensitive to the institutional apparatus necessary to build support and to implement policy decisions. Heavy reliance on informal processes may lead to inadequate communication and execution. . . . The departments provide greater institutional memory, continuity, professional experience, in-depth planning capability, and an orderly policy process. In negotiations with others, they also have the advantage of being once removed from the president so that mistakes are not likely to be as harmful, and changes of position can be made with less embarrassment to the president.[13]

The academy urged the president to clearly differentiate the roles of the department secretaries and the national security adviser at the beginning of his administration, which he did.

President Bush has opted for a system that maintains the roles of his cabinet secretaries as spokespersons, policy advisers, and operational chiefs but that enhances critical coordination, informational, and advisory responsibilities for his national security assistant and staff. Two committees—each composed of senior White House aides, cabinet secretaries, and military and intelligence officials—have been created to provide the national security process with coherence and compatibility. One of these groups is comprised of the secretaries, national security adviser, president, and vice president. It is a forum for high-level policy discussions. The other, known as the deputies committee because it is composed of the chief deputies of each of the appropriate agencies, meets daily to monitor issues, narrow options, and move them rapidly to the president's attention. Below the deputies group, policy-coordinating committees have been constructed on an issue-by-issue basis. They are tied to the national security staff by an executive secretary who provides White House staff support. In this way, the national security adviser and his staff remain at the center of the foreign policy decision-making mechanisms.

How a president organizes his national security operation ultimately depends on his own personality, policy goals, and institutional needs. There is no one right way to do it. As we have previously noted, style is an important influence on how a president interacts with his aides. Eisenhower thrived in group settings. Eliciting a team approach that emphasized consensus building from within, he set up a national security mechanism that provided internal coordination for a cabinet-based, advisory model. In contrast, Nixon's introverted personality, his secretive manner, and his need for power led him to adopt a hierarchical model in national security staffing. Jimmy Carter provided a third extreme. His desire to get involved in details, to evaluate a range of alternatives, but ultimately to make his own judgment caused him to utilize a variation of multiple advocacy—with undesirable consequences. His policy seemed to lack both direction and consistency.

A second component that affects the advisory structure is the goals themselves and the extent to which the president has made up his mind. Does he desire to reach a judgment or to exercise one he has reached? Lyndon Johnson's conviction about the Vietnam War cast him in the role of advocate. As a consequence, he wanted (although perhaps did not benefit from) a mechanism that supported his views.

Having a strong ideological bent shapes decision making. Reagan desired an advisory system that would produce a policy consensus *within* his conceptual framework and a mechanism for implementing his basic goals but one which relieved him of day-to-day decisional responsibilities. In contrast, Carter opted for a structure that processed information without filtering it too much. What he wanted from his advisers were choices not consensus.

Whereas style and goals explain differences in advisory systems, the institutional needs of the presidency have fostered some of the basic trends evident since the Eisenhower administration: the growth and specialization of a White House national security staffing structure, the increasing reliance on this structure over the course of an administration, and the advisory and advocacy roles of the national security adviser that often conflict with the secretary of state.

In short, presidents have to be comfortable with the system and the system has to work. It needs to generate information and ideas, to organize and manage competing viewpoints, and to help define and achieve a president's basic goals. It should provide *continuity* in policy and promote the *integration* of policies. It should enable the president to exercise strong and steady leadership.

CONCLUSION

The limited role that the framers of the Constitution envisioned for the president in foreign and military affairs has been expanded significantly. Today the president is expected to take the policy-making initiative in both spheres. He is expected to oversee the conduct of war and diplomacy. He is also expected to perform the symbolic duties of chief of state and commander-in-chief.

Although presidential expectations have increased, the ability of the president to meet these expectations has declined. That decline is a product of several factors: the interdependence of the United States on the economies, resources, and security of other countries; the increasing impact of foreign policy decisions on domestic affairs; the proliferation of groups and governments trying to affect policy decisions; and the more assertive role Congress has assumed. No longer does the legislature more or less automatically defer to presidential initiatives. As a consequence, presidents have had to devote more time and increasing resources to the performance of their policy-making responsibilities. They have had to make greater efforts at coordination within the executive branch and at consensus building outside of it. In this sense, their needs in foreign and national security affairs are not much different than in the domestic arena, although expectations—their own, and those of the American public and foreign government leaders—seem to be greater.

With foreign and defense policy so important, presidents have turned increasingly to their national security staff for help. Established in 1960 and expanded in size and specialization since then, this internal White House mechanism has provided a cadre of loyal policy experts to help presidents with the everyday problems with which they have to deal. The national security staff functions primarily to inform and advise the president and secondarily to handle his correspondence, speeches, and briefings. It has increased the president's information, maximized his discretion, and created the capacity for rapid and decisive responses. However, it has done all of this at a cost: an increase in tension between the White House and executive branch agencies, a decrease in the continuity of policy within and between administrations, and a constricting of vision and limiting of perspectives.

Despite the increasing obstacles they face, presidents continue to emphasize foreign policy matters, particularly as their administrations progress. There are psychological, political, and policy reasons for doing so. As foreign policy leaders they can act as unifying figures, overcome perceptions of partisanship, and work to achieve specific policy goals. Demonstrating leadership in this manner stands to increase their popularity, improve their reelectability, and enhance their place in history—all very desirable personal goals. Finally, there is that intangible but real desire to try to affect events, particularly to promote peace among nations. American presidents want and expect to be more than facilitators in international affairs. They want and expect to be directors of change and world leaders.

NOTES

1. Actually, all treaties approved by two-thirds of the Senate must be signed by the president before they go into effect.

2. Ryan J. Barilleaux, "Parallel Unilateral Policy Declarations: A New Device for Presidential Autonomy in Foreign Affairs," *Presidential Studies Quarterly* 17 (Winter 1987): 107–17.

3. The Supreme Court's legislative veto decision, *Immigration and Naturalization* v. *Chadha* (103 S. Ct. 2764) (June 23, 1983), calls into question the use of concurrent resolutions as a means of restricting executive activity.

4. Richard Halloran, "Reagan as Military Commander," *The New York Times Magazine*, January 15, 1984, p. 57.

5. Fred I. Greenstein, "Popular Images of the President," *American Journal of Psychiatry* 122 (1965):523–29.

6. Aaron Wildavsky, "The Two Presidencies," in Aaron Wildavsky, ed., *Perspectives on the Presidency* (Boston: Little, Brown, 1975), p. 452.

7. Ibid., p. 449.

8. Ralph G. Carter, "Congressional Foreign Policy Behavior: Persistent Patterns of the Postwar Period," *Presidential Studies Quarterly* 16 (Spring 1986): 333–34.

9. George C. Edwards III, "The Two Presidencies: A Reevaluation," *American Politics Quarterly* 14 (July 1986): 247–63.

10. Colin L. Powell, "The NSC System in the Last Two Years of the Reagan Administration," *Presidential Studies Quarterly, Proceedings*, 6 (1989): 205.

11. Ibid., p. 206.

12. Zbigniew Brzezinski, quoted in Dom Bonafede, "Brzezinski—Stepping Out of His Backstage Role," *National Journal* 9 (October 15, 1977): 1596.

13. National Academy of Public Administration, *The Executive Presidency: Federal Management for the 1990s* (Washington, D.C.: National Academy of Public Administration, 1989), p. 10.

SELECTED READINGS

Adler, David Gray. "The Constitution and Presidential Warmaking: The Enduring Debate." *Political Science Quarterly* 103 (1988): 1–36.

Barilleaux, Ryan J. "Parallel Unilateral Policy Declarations: A New Device for Presidential Autonomy in Foreign Affairs." *Presidential Studies Quarterly* 17 (1987): 107–17.

——————. *The President and Foreign Affairs: Evaluation, Performance, and Power.* New York: Praeger, 1985.

Berman, Larry. *Planning a Tragedy.* New York: Norton, 1982.

Bock, Joseph G., and Duncan L. Clarke. "The National Security Assistant and the White House Staff: National Security Policy Decision Making and Domestic Political Considerations." *Presidential Studies Quarterly* 16 (1986): 258–79.

Cleveland, Harlan. "Coherence and Consultation: The President as Manager of American Foreign Policy." *Public Administration Review* 46 (1986): 97–104.

Destler, I. M. "Reagan and the World: An Awesome Stubbornness." In Charles O. Jones, ed. *The Reagan Legacy.* Chatham, N.J.: Chatham House, 1988.

Edwards, George C., III. "The Two Presidencies: A Reevaluation." *American Politics Quarterly* 14 (1986): 247–63.

Fleisher, Richard, and Jon R. Bond. "Are There Two Presidencies? Yes, But Only for Republicans." *Journal of Politics* 50 (1988): 747–67.

George, Alexander. *Presidential Decision Making in Foreign Policy: The Effective Use of Information and Advice.* Boulder, Colo.: Westview, 1981.

Lord, Carnes. *The Presidency and the Management of National Security.* New York: Free Press, 1988.

Mulcahy, Kevin V. "Presidents and the Administration of Foreign Policy: The New Role for the Vice President." *Presidential Studies Quarterly* 17 (1987): 119–31.

Report of the Congressional Committees Investigating the Iran–Contra Affair. House Report No. 100-433. Senate Report No. 100-216. Washington, D.C.: Government Printing Office, 1987.

Rockman, Bert A. "America's Department of State: Irregular and Regular Syndromes of Policy Making." *American Political Science Review* 75 (1981): 911–27.

Rourke, John T., and Russell Farnen. "War, Presidents, and the Constitution." *Presidential Studies Quarterly* 18 (1988): 513–21.

Sigelman, Lee. "A Reassessment of the Two Presidencies Thesis." *Journal of Politics* 41 (1979): 1195–1205.

Wildavsky, Aaron. "The Two Presidencies." In Aaron Wildavsky, ed. *Perspectives on the Presidency.* Boston: Little, Brown, 1975.

Appendix A

Studying the Presidency

Although many people find the presidency the most fascinating subject in American politics, it unfortunately is not a topic that is easy to research. This overview of studying the presidency is designed to alert students to the implications, both positive and negative, of adopting particular research approaches and methodologies. Armed with this awareness, researchers should be able better to understand the advantages and limitations of various research designs. They can then more knowledgeably choose one that comes closest to meeting their needs.

APPROACHES

There are many approaches to studying the presidency, ranging from those concerned with the constitutional authority of the office to those dealing with the personality dynamics of a particular president. By approaches we mean orientations that guide researchers to ask certain questions and employ certain concepts rather than others. In this section we focus on some of the principal approaches employed by political scientists who study the presidency. The categories we use are neither mutually exclusive nor completely comprehensive. The goal here is to increase sensitivity to the implications of different approaches for what is studied, how a subject is investigated, and what types of conclusions may be reached rather than to create an ideal typology of scholarship on the presidency. Similarly, our focus is on approaches per se rather than on a critique of the work of individual authors or on a comprehensive review of the literature.[1]

Legal

The oldest approach to studying the presidency, what we shall term the legal perspective, concerns the president's formal powers. Legal researchers analyze the Constitution, laws, treaties, and legal precedents to understand the sources, scope, and use of the president's formal powers, including their legal limitations.[2] Since these have changed over time, there is typically a heavy historical orientation to the legal approach.

The legal perspective, with its emphasis on the historical development of the office and the checks and balances in the Constitution, also lends itself to discussion of the president's place in our system of government, both as it is and as scholars think it ought to be. Thus, there is often a clear prescriptive or normative element in these studies.

The range of issues involving presidential authority is great. Illustrations from the recent past include the right of the president to impound funds appropriated by Congress, the scope of the president's lawmaking power when he issues executive orders and proclamations, President Reagan's hiring freeze in 1981, the president's use of the pocket veto during brief congressional recesses, the constitutionality of the legislative veto, the role of the comptroller general in triggering budget reductions, and claims of executive privilege. Foreign policy issues have also reached the courts. These include the conduct of the Vietnam War by presidents Johnson and Nixon without explicit congressional authorization, President Carter's termination of the United States defense treaty with Taiwan and his settlement of the Iranian assets and hostage issues, and the president's use of executive agreements as substitutes for treaties.

Although the legal perspective is an important one and has an honored place both in political science and in a nation that prides itself on the rule of law, it also has limitations. A major one is that it neglects most of what the president does. Only a small portion of the president's behavior is prescribed by the wording of the Constitution, treaties, laws, or court decisions. Thus, most of the president's relationships with, for example, the public, the Congress, the White House staff, and the bureaucracy do not fall easily within the purview of the legal perspective. Instead, this behavior falls under the heading of informal or extraconstitutional powers. Similarly, since the focus of the legal perspective is on the presidency itself, topics such as press coverage of the presidency, the public's evaluation of the president, and other relationships that involve nongovernmental actors are largely ignored.

Equally significant, the legal perspective, although it requires rigorous analysis, does not lend itself to explanation. Studies focusing on the boundaries of appropriate actions do not seek to explain why behavior occurs or what its consequences are. Moreover, the fact that scholars employing this approach often rely heavily upon case studies inevitably makes the basis of their generalizations somewhat tenuous.

Thus, although studies adopting the legal perspective make important contributions to our understanding of American politics, they do not and cannot answer most of the questions that entice researchers to study the presidency. For this we must turn to alternative approaches.

Institutional

A second basic approach to the study of the presidency focuses on it as an institution in which the president has certain roles and responsibilities and is involved in numerous structures and processes. Thus, the structure, functions, and operation of the presidency become the center of attention. These concerns are broad enough to include agencies such as the Office of Management and Budget and units in the White House such as the legislative liaison operation. Scholars following this approach can move beyond formal authority and investigate, for example, the formulation, coordination, promotion, and implementation of the president's legislative program or the president's relationship with the media.[3] As with the legal perspective, scholars employing the institutional approach often trace the persistence and adaptation of organizations and processes over time. This gives much of the literature a historical perspective and also lends itself to evaluations of the success of institutional arrangements.

The institutional approach plays a crucial role in helping us to understand the presidency. Although at one time much of the work that falls under this heading emphasized formal organizational structure and rules, such as organization charts of the White House or procedures in the budgetary process, in more recent years the focus has moved to the behavior of those involved in the operation of the presidency. This has increased the utility of institutional research. By focusing on processes and behavior, scholars collect empirical data on a variety of activities. Quite clearly, without knowing what political actors are doing we cannot discuss the significance of their behavior, much less examine analytical questions of relationships such as those pertaining to influence. By seeking to identify patterns of behavior and studying interactions, such as those between the White House and the Congress, OMB, or media, institutional reasearch not only tells us what happens but, more significantly, starts us on the road toward understanding *why* it happens. When scholars examine, say, presidential efforts to influence the media, they are focusing on typical and potentially significant behavior that may explain patterns of media coverage of the White House. The question of taking the final step and *testing* for such a relationship leads us to a discussion of the limitations of this research.

There are two principal limitations to the institutional approach. First, it typically places a heavy emphasis on description at the expense of explanation. We know a great deal more about how presidents have organized their White House staffs, for example, than about the differences it makes for the kinds of advice they receive. In other words, we know more about the process per se than about its consequences. This, in turn, provides a tenuous basis for the prescriptive aspect of some institutional research. We cannot have confidence in recommendations about presidential advisory systems, for example, until we understand the impact of different arrangements on presidential decision making.

The second limitation is that in emphasizing organizations and processes, institutional studies may downplay or even ignore the significance of other factors such as political skills, ideology, and personality. Indeed, the implicit assumption that emerges from the often extensive attention scholars devote to structures and processes is that they are very significant. This may not always be the case, however. In the example above, it may be that the world view that a president brings to the White House is more important in influencing his decisions than the way he organizes his advisers. Similarly, ideology, party, and constituency views may be more important than the White House legislative liaison operation in influencing congressional votes on the president's program.

Political Power

In the political power approach, best represented by Richard Neustadt's *Presidential Power*,[4] researchers shift their focus from institutions to the people within them. The fundamental premise of this research is that the exploiting of political influence rather than the expanding of legal authority or the adjusting of institutional mechanisms is the key to the president's success. It rejects the assumption that the president effectively wields power or that he possesses enough power to meet his responsibilities.

Since researchers employing this approach view power as a function of personal politics rather than formal authority or position, they turn their attention to the internal dynamics of the presidency. They find the president operating in a pluralistic environment in which there are numerous actors with independent power bases and perspectives different from his. Thus, the president must marshal his resources to persuade others to do as he wishes.

Power is a concept that involves relationships between people, so this approach forces researchers to try to explain behavior and to seek to develop generalizations about it. Moreover, the necessity for the president to attempt to exercise influence in several arenas leads those following the power perspective to adopt an expansive view of presidential politics that includes both governmental actors (such as the Congress, bureaucracy, and White House staff) and those outside of government (such as the public, the press, and interest groups). In studying presidential interactions, the dependent variables, what authors are trying to explain, are many and may include congressional or public support for the president, presidential decisions, press coverage of the White House, bureaucratic policy implementation, or a set of policy options prepared by the bureaucracy for the president.[5] Because there are no assumptions of presidential success or the smooth functioning of the presidency, the effects of bureaucratic politics and other organizational factors in the executive branch are as important to investigate as behavior in more openly adversarial institutions such as Congress.

Although the power approach examines a number of questions left unexplored in other approaches, it also slights certain topics. With its focus on relationships, it does not naturally lend itself to investigation of questions of the president's accountability, the limitations of his legal powers, or the day-to-day operation of the institution of the presidency.

Some commentators are bothered by the top-down orientation of the power approach, that is, viewing the presidency from the perspective of the president.[6] They feel that it neglects the question of examining the presidency from the perspective of the American political system and that it carries an implicit assumption that the president should be the principal decision maker in American politics and that he should typically get what he wants. These critics argue that such premises are too Machiavellian and that an evaluation of the goals and means of presidents must be added to analyses of power.

Others feel that the depiction of the president's environment as basically confrontational, with conflicting interests of political actors creating centrifugal forces the president must try to overcome, is exaggerated. Moreover, the heavy emphasis placed on power or influence may lead analysts to underestimate the importance of ideology or other influences on behavior.[7]

Psychological

Perhaps the most fascinating and popular studies of the presidency are those that approach the topic from the perspective of psychological analysis. The most well known of these studies focus on psychopathology, essentially the negative manifestations of inner needs and ego defenses. They are based on the premises that personality is a constant and that personality needs may be displaced onto political objects and become unconscious motivations for presidential behavior. Some of these studies take the form of psychobiographies of presidents,[8] while others are attempts to categorize presidents on the basis of selected personality dimensions.[9]

Personality is an important factor in behavior and adds an important element to the study of the presidency. We need to take what goes on inside a president's head into account if we are to understand his behavior as president. Such a perspective forces us to ask why presidents behave as they do. It also forces us to look beyond external factors, such as advisers, Congress, the media, and interest groups, for answers to this question. If they were not strongly affected by their personalities, presidents would neither be very important nor merit such attention.

Psychological analysis is also applied to the study of the presidency in broader ways. Presidents and their staffs have cognitive processes through which they view the world and that affect their perceptions of why people and nations behave as they do, how power is distributed, how the economy functions, and what the appropriate roles are of government, presidents, and advisers. Their cognitive processes also function to screen and organize an enormous volume of information about the complex and uncertain environment in which they function. Objective reality, intellectual abilities, and personal interests and experiences merge with personal needs, such as those to manage inconsistency and maintain self-esteem, to influence the decisions and policies that emerge from the White House. Cognitive processes simplify decision making and lessen stress, especially on complex and controversial policies such as the Vietnam War. Group dynamics may also influence decision making, limiting the appraisal of alternatives by group members. Efforts to sort out the impact of these factors are only in their early stages, but there is little question that we cannot claim to understand presidential decision making until we do so.[10]

Although psychological studies can sensitize us to important personality factors that influence presidential behavior, they are probably the most widely criticized writings on the presidency. A fundamental problem is that they often display a strong tendency toward reductionism. That is, they focus very heavily upon the variable of personality to the exclusion of most other factors in their attempts to explain behavior. As a result, they convey little information about the institution of the presidency or the relationships between psychological and institutional variables. Alternative explanations for behavior are rarely considered in psychological studies.

A related drawback is that psychological studies have a tendency to focus on the negative aspects of a presidency. Scholars, like others, are quite naturally drawn to investigate problems. Thus, the principal focus often becomes the relationship between the personality flaws of the president and what the author feels to be some of the chief executive's most unfortunate actions. This reinforces the reductionist tendency because it is usually not difficult to find plausible parallels between psychological and decisional deficiencies.

The availability of data is also a problem for psychological studies. It is difficult to discern unconscious motivations or cognitive processes and to differentiate their impact from that of external factors. Often authors must rely upon biographical information of questionable validity about the behavior and environment of presidents, stretching back to their childhoods.

Summary

The legal, institutional, power, and psychological approaches have advantages and disadvantages for the researcher. Each is more useful for answering some questions than for answering others, each informs us about a different aspect of the presidency, and each focuses on certain variables at the expense of others. Moreover, although the power and psychological approaches are stronger on their concerns for explanation, the legal and institutional orientations are better at providing broad perspectives on the presidency.

Those thinking of doing research on the presidency should carefully determine what it is they want to investigate *before* selecting an approach, because not all approaches will be relevant to answering their questions. Selecting an approach is not the last decision one must make in deciding on a research project, however. Appropriate methods must be employed as well as the proper overall orientation.

METHODS

Although the American presidency has always been a prime topic of research interest for political scientists, our progress in understanding the institution has been very slow. One reason for this is that scholars have generally relied upon modes of analysis that do not easily lend themselves to examining basic questions about the presidency. In this section we explore some of the methods used by scholars to study the presidency, paying special attention to their advantages and limitations. This is not a "how to" discussion of methodology. Instead, our goal is to understand that some methods are more useful than others for investigating important questions regarding the presidency. Throughout, we should keep in mind that methods are not ends in themselves but rather techniques for examining research questions generated by the approaches discussed above.

Traditional Methods

The typical work on the presidency has focused on describing events, behavior, and personalities. Many studies, written by journalists or former executive branch officials, rely heavily upon personal experiences for data. Unfortunately, such anecdotal material is generally subjective, fragmentary, and impressionistic. When explanations of the causes and consequences of presidential actions do occur, the data base is typically composed of a single or a small number of examples. There is usually no possibility of controlling for alternative explanations. Thus, we must be very cautious about reaching generalizations based on this type of analysis, even when the anecdotes on which they are based come from eyewitnesses. In reading the memoirs of aides to Lyndon Johnson, Richard Nixon, or Ronald Reagan, one finds very different perceptions of the president and his presidency. As Henry Kissinger tells us about the Nixon White House staff, "It is a truism that none of us really knew the inner man. More significant, each member of his entourage was acquainted with a slightly different Nixon subtly adjusted to the President's judgment of the aide or to his assessment of his interlocutor's background."[11]

The commentary and reflections of insiders, whether participants or participant observers, are limited by their own perspectives, which may be rather narrow. Proximity to power can hinder rather than enhance one's perspective and breadth of view. The reflections of those who have served in government may be colored by the strong points of view they advocated or by a need to justify their decisions and behavior while in office. Faulty memories add a further element of uncertainty to such data. Moreover, proximity to power does not necessarily bring insiders insight or understanding of the process in which they have participated. Few insiders are trained to think in analytical terms of generalizations based on representative data and controls for alternative explanations.

Let us illustrate the problem with a few examples. One of the crucial decision points in America's involvement in fighting in Vietnam occurred during July 1965, when President Johnson committed the United States to large-scale combat operations. In his memoirs the president describes his decision-making process on this issue, and he goes to considerable lengths in interpreting this complex event to show that he considered all the options available at this time very carefully.[12] One of his aides later provided a detailed account of the dialogue between Johnson and some of his advisers.[13] It shows the president probing deeply for answers, challenging the premises and factual bases of options, and playing the devil's advocate. Yet a presidency scholar has argued persuasively that this "debate" was a charade, staged by the president to lend legitimacy to the decision he had already made.[14]

Another useful example, this one focusing on attributions of influence, is President Johnson's efforts at obtaining the support or at least the neutrality of the Senate Finance Committee chairman, Harry Byrd of Virginia, on the 1964 tax cut. Hubert Humphrey reported in his memoirs that Johnson cajoled Byrd into letting the tax bill out of committee, relying on Lady Bird's charm, liquor, and his own famous "treatment."[15] Presidential aide Jack Valenti tells a different story, however. He writes that the president obtained the senator's cooperation by promising to hold the budget under $100 billion.[16] Thus, we have two eyewitnesses reporting on two different tactics employed by the president and each attributing Senator Byrd's response to the presidential behavior that he observed.

To confuse matters further, Henry Hall Wilson, one of the president's congressional liaison aides, indicates that both eyewitnesses were wrong. According to Wilson, when the president proudly told his chief congressional liaison aide, Lawrence O'Brien, about his obtaining Byrd's agreement to begin hearings on the tax cut on December 7, O'Brien replied, "You didn't get a thing. I already had a commitment for the 7th."[17] In other words, according to O'Brien, Johnson's efforts were irrelevant and both eyewitnesses were wrong in attributing influence to him.

Even tapes of conversations in the Oval Office may be misleading. As Henry Kissinger explains regarding the Watergate tapes:

Anyone familiar with Nixon's way of talking could have no doubt he was sitting on a time bomb. His random, elliptical, occasionally emotional manner of conversation was bound to shock, and mislead, the historian. Nixon's indirect style of operation simply could not be gauged by an outsider. There was no way of telling what Nixon had put forward to test his interlocutor and what he meant to be taken seriously; and no outsider could distinguish a command that was to be followed from an emotional outburst that one was at liberty to ignore—perhaps was even expected to ignore.[18]

We have seen, then, that there are a number of limitations to the use of insider accounts. It does not follow that these are not useful. On the contrary, they often contain numerous insights that may guide more rigorous research, and they provide invaluable records of perceptions of participants in the process and events of the presidency. As long as the researcher understands the limitations of these works and does not accept them at face value, they can be a considerable asset.

Not all studies of the presidency that employ traditional methods are written by insiders. Some, such as Richard Tanner Johnson's *Managing the White House*,[19] are written by scholars, based primarily on the observations of others. Many of these observations are repeated and become the conventional wisdom. As a consequence, new studies based on old sources may add little to our knowledge of what happened or our understanding of why.

Problems also arise when researchers make assertions about the behavior of the public. They often fail to look at available systematic data. For example, most discussions of the president's relationships with the public include a section on the influence of "rally events," dramatic international events involving the United States that supposedly provide the president with a sudden surge of popular support. The problem with such discussions is that they are not based on examinations of relevant data. When we do examine the data (see Chapter 4) we find that sudden surges of, say, 5 percentage points in presidential approval are unusual, and the events that seem to generate them are highly idiosyncratic and do not differ significantly from similar events that were not followed by sizable surges in presidential approval. Moreover, most potential rally events fail to generate much additional approval for the president.[20]

Quantitative Analyses

Research on the presidency, then, has often failed to meet the standards of contemporary political science, including the careful definition and measurement of concepts, the rigorous specification and testing of propositions, the employment of appropriate quantitative methods, and the use of empirical theory to develop hypotheses and explain findings.

As we might expect, research on the presidency, taken as a whole, has not advanced our understanding of the institution very far. We lack a fundamental understanding of why things happen as they do. We have generally not focused on explanations, the relationships between two or more variables, but on descriptions. This situation presents a striking paradox: the single most important institution in American politics is the one that political scientists understand the least.

To increase our understanding of the presidency we need to move beyond the description of the institution and its occupants and attempt to explain the behavior we observe. In addition, we must seek to reach generalizations rather than being satisfied with discrete, often ad hoc analyses. To explain we must examine relationships, and to generalize we must look at these relationships under many circumstances. Quantitative analysis can be an extremely useful tool in these endeavors.[21]

There have been three principal constraints on using quantitative analysis to study the presidency. The first, the frequent failure to pose analytical questions, has already been discussed. The second constraint has been the small number of cases, or presidents. Viewing the presidency as a set of relationships, however, helps to overcome this problem. Although there may be few presidents, many persons are involved in relationships with each president, including the entire public, the membership of Congress, the federal bureaucracy, and world leaders. It is these relationships on which we can profitably focus, and because so many people interact with the president in one form or another, we are no longer inhibited by the small universe of presidents.

This leads us to the third perceived constraint on the quantitative study of the presidency: lack of data. Since scholars of the presidency have typically been more interested in description than analysis, they have often been primarily concerned with "inside" data on the president and the presidency. As we have seen, however, this usually is only one side of a relationship, and we need to be looking at both sides if we are to develop reliable explanations.

When we pose analytical questions, we are naturally led to search for data on the causes and consequences of presidential behavior. For example, we may ask what the president wants from other political actors, what he is trying to get people to do. Among other things, the president wants support from the public; positive coverage from the media; votes for his programs from Congress; options, information, and analyses from his advisers; and faithful policy implementation from the bureaucracy. Thus, we can look for data on these political actors, whose behavior is usually the dependent variable—that is, what we are trying to explain—in our hypotheses. Similarly, we can seek data on independent variables—that is, causes of behavior toward the president, such as the determinants of public opinion, congressional support, and bureaucratic faithfulness.

The proper use of quantitative analysis, like any other type of analysis, is predicated upon a close linkage between the methods selected and the theoretical arguments underlying the hypotheses being tested. A theoretical argument requires an emphasis on explanation—that is, *why* two variables are related. If closer attention is given to the use of theory in research on the presidency, our understanding of the institution will increase more rapidly than it has in the past.

Despite its utility for investigating a wide range of questions dealing with the presidency, quantitative analysis is not equally useful for studying all areas of the presidency. The research situations in which quantitative analysis is least likely to be useful are those in which there is a lack of variance in the variables under study. If the focus of research is just one president and the researcher is concerned not with the president's interactions with others but with how factors such as the president's personality, ideas, values, attitudes, and ideology influence his decisions, quantitative analysis will be of little help. The independent variables are unlikely to vary much during a term in office. Similarly, factors in the president's environment, such as the federal structure of this country's government or the basic capitalist structure of its economy, change little over considerable periods of time, and it is therefore difficult to employ quantitative analysis to gauge their impact on the presidency.

If we are able to move beyond case studies of a single president or a single country to make comparisons across different presidents and different nations, such studies would provide us a firmer basis for confidence in our conclusions. Whether all the necessary factors can be controlled to make such comparisons useful is an open question, however.

Quantitative analysis is also unlikely to be useful for the legal approach to studying the presidency. There are well-established techniques for interpreting the law, and scholars with this interest will continue to apply them.[22]

Normative questions and arguments have always occupied a substantial percentage of the presidency literature, and rightly so. Can quantitative analysis aid scholars in addressing these concerns? The answer is, partially. Let us illustrate this with the example of what has probably been the central normative concern regarding the presidency: its power.

To reach conclusions about whether the presidency is too powerful or not powerful enough requires a three-part analysis. The first is an estimation of just how powerful the presidency is. Quantitative analysis can be of utility in measuring and explaining the power in the presidency in a large range of relationships. For example, it can aid us in understanding the president's ability to influence Congress or the public. The significance of quantitative studies for the first part of this normative analysis, then, is clear.

The second step in answering the question of whether the presidency is too powerful or not powerful enough requires an analysis of the consequences of the power of the presidency. In other words, given the power of the presidency, as determined in part one, what difference does it make? Are poor people likely to fare better under a weak or a powerful presidency, for example? Are civil rights and civil liberties more or less likely to be abused?

To answer these and similar questions rigorously requires that we correlate levels of power with policy consequences. This does not have to be done quantitatively, of course, but such analyses will be more convincing if we have empirical measurements of economic welfare, school integration, wiretapping, military interventions, and other possible consequences of presidential power as well as measures of mediating variables.

Quantitative analyses will be of much less utility in arriving at conclusions to the third part of the analysis concerning presidential power: Do we evaluate the consequences of power levels determined in part two of the analysis positively or negatively? Whether we like or dislike the consequences will determine our ultimate answer to the question of how powerful the presidency should be. Our evaluation of these consequences will, of course, be determined by our values. Nevertheless, it is important to remember that quantitative analysis can be very useful in helping us to arrive at the point where our values dominate our conclusions.

In short, quantitative analysis leads us to examine theoretical relationships, and it has considerable utility in testing and refining them. While it cannot replace the sparks of creativity that lie behind conceptualizations, it may produce findings upon which syntheses may be built. Conversely, quantitative analysis may also reveal findings contrary to the conventional wisdom and thus prod scholars into challenging dominant viewpoints. To this extent it may also be useful in theory building.

No one should be under the illusion that quantitative analysis is easy to do or that there is consensus either on appropriate methods or on indicators. Some authors will inevitably employ indicators that lack validity and reliability and tests that are inappropriate. Their conclusions are likely to be incorrect. In addition, findings can and should be refined as our indicators and tests are refined. In essence, quantitative analysis poses methodological problems precisely because it attempts to measure concepts and to test for relationships carefully. Studies that do not involve such concerns are able to avoid methodological questions, but often at the expense of analytical potential.

Case Studies

One of the most widely used methods for studying the presidency is the case study. There are innumerable studies of individual presidents, presidential decisions, and presidential involvement in specific areas of policy and policy making.

The case study method offers the researcher several advantages. It is a manageable way to present a wide range of complex information about individual and collective behavior involving the presidency. Since scholars have typically found it difficult to generate quantitative data regarding the presidency, the narrative form often seems to be the only available option.

Conversely, case studies are widely criticized on several grounds. First, they have typically been used more for descriptive than for analytical purposes. As we shall note below, however, this failing is not inherent in the nature of case studies. A more intractable problem is the idiosyncratic nature of case studies and the failure of authors to employ common analytical frameworks. This makes the accumulation of knowledge difficult because scholars are often, in effect, talking past each other. In the words of a close student of case studies:

> The unique features of every case—personalities, external events and conditions, and organizational arrangements—virtually ensure that studies conducted without the use of an explicit analytical framework will not produce findings that can easily be related to existing knowledge or provide a basis for future studies.[23]

Naturally, reaching generalizations about the presidency on the basis of unrelated case studies is a hazardous task.

Despite these drawbacks, case studies can be very useful in increasing our understanding of the presidency. For example, analyzing several case studies can serve as the basis for identifying problems in decision making[24] or in policy implementation.[25] These, in turn, may serve as the basis for recommendations to improve policy making. Case studies may also be used to test hypotheses or disconfirm theories, such as propositions about group dynamics drawn from social psychology.[26] Some authors employ case studies to illustrate the importance of looking at aspects of the presidency that have received little scholarly attention, such as presidential influence over interest groups.[27]

On a broader scale, Richard Neustadt used several case studies to help generate his influential model of presidential power.[28] Graham Allison used a case study of the Cuban missile crisis to illustrate the utility of three models of policy making.[29]

Writing a case study that has strong analytical, as opposed to descriptive, content is difficult to do. It requires considerable skill, creativity, and rigor. It is very easy to slip into a descriptive gear. Those who embark on preparing case studies are wise to remind themselves of the pitfalls discussed earlier. It is especially important to have an analytical framework in mind before one beings to provide direction to data gathering and the line of argument.

CONCLUSION

Few topics in American politics are more interesting or more important to understand than the presidency. Researching the presidency is not a simple task, however. There are many reasons for this, including the relative sparsity of previous research that applied the approaches and methods of modern political science. There are fewer models to follow than we would like. The obstacles to studying the presidency may also be an opportunity, however. Few questions regarding the presidency are settled; committed and creative researchers have plenty of room to make important contributions to our understanding of this uniquely American institution. The prospects for significant research will be enhanced if investigators are aware of the implications of the approaches and methods they employ and choose those that are best suited to shedding light on the questions they wish to study.

NOTES

1. For a more extensive discussion of approaches to studying the presidency see Stephen J. Wayne, "Approaches," in George C. Edwards III and Stephen J. Wayne, eds., *Studying the Presidency* (Knoxville, Tenn.: University of Tennessee Press, 1983), pp. 17–49.

2. The classic work on the legal perspective is Edward S. Corwin's *The President: Office and Powers*, 4th rev. ed. (New York: New York University Press, 1957); an excellent more recent example is Louis Fisher, *Presidential Spending Power* (Princeton, N.J.: Princeton University Press, 1975).

3. See, for example, Stephen J. Wayne, *The Legislative Presidency* (New York: Harper and Row, 1978); and Michael Baruch Grossman and Martha Joynt Kumar, *Portraying the President: The White House and the News Media* (Baltimore: Johns Hopkins University Press, 1981).

4. Richard E. Neustadt, *Presidential Power: The Politics of Leadership from FDR to Carter* (New York: Wiley, 1980).

5. See, for example, George C. Edwards III, *At the Margins: Presidential Leadership of Congress* (New Haven, Conn.: Yale University Press, 1989); *The Public Presidency* (New York: St. Martin's, 1983); and *Implementing Public Policy* (Washington, D.C.: Congressional Quar-

terly, 1980). Other examples of the political power approach include Fred I. Greenstein, *The Hidden-Hand Presidency* (New York: Basic Books, 1982); and Bert A. Rockman, *The Leadership Question* (New York: Praeger, 1984).

6. See Bruce Miroff, "Beyond Washington," *Society* 17 (July/August 1980): 66–72.

7. See Peter W. Sperlich, "Bargaining and Overload: An Essay on *Presidential Power*," in Aaron Wildavsky, ed., *The Presidency* (Boston: Little, Brown, 1969), pp. 168–92.

8. See, for example, Alexander L. George and Juliette L. George, *Woodrow Wilson and Colonel House: A Personality Study* (New York: Dover, 1964).

9. The most notable example is James David Barber's *The Presidential Character: Predicting Performance in the White House*, 3rd ed. (Englewood Cliffs, N.J.: Prentice-Hall, 1985).

10. Some relevant studies include Alexander L. George, *Presidential Decisionmaking in Foreign Policy: The Effective Use of Information and Advice* (Boulder, Colo.: Westview, 1980); Bruce Buchanan, *The Presidential Experience: What the Office Does to the Man* (Englewood Cliffs, N.J.: Prentice-Hall, 1978); John D. Steinbruner, *The Cybernetic Theory of Decision* (Princeton, N.J.: Princeton University Press, 1974); Irving L. Janis, *Groupthink: Psychological Studies of Policy Decisions and Fiascoes*, 2nd ed. (Boston, Houghton Mifflin, 1982); and Richard E. Neustadt and Ernest R. May, *Thinking in Time* (New York: Free Press, 1986).

11. Henry Kissinger, *Years of Upheaval* (Boston: Little, Brown, 1982), p. 1182.

12. Lyndon B. Johnson, *The Vantage Point: Perspectives of the Presidency, 1963–1969* (New York: Popular Library, 1971), pp. 144–53.

13. Jack Valenti, *A Very Human President* (New York: Norton, 1975), pp. 317–19.

14. Larry Berman, *Planning a Tragedy: The Americanization of the War in Vietnam* (New York: Norton, 1982), pp. 105–21.

15. Hubert H. Humphrey, *The Education of a Public Man: My Life and Politics* (Garden City, N.Y.: Doubleday, 1976), pp. 290–93.

16. Valenti, *A Very Human President*, pp. 196–97. See also Russell D. Renka, "Bargaining with Legislative Whales in the Kennedy and Johnson Administration" (paper presented at the Annual Meeting of the American Political Science Association, Washington, D.C., August 1980), p. 20.

17. Transcript, Henry Hall Wilson Oral History Interview, April 11, 1973, by Joe B. Frantz, p. 16, Lyndon B. Johnson Library.

18. Kissinger, *Years of Upheaval*, pp. 111–12.

19. Richard Tanner Johnson, *Managing the White House* (New York: Harper and Row, 1974).

20. Edwards, *The Public Presidency*, pp. 242–47.

21. For a more extensive discussion of quantitative analysis of the presidency see George C. Edwards III, "Quantitative Analysis," in Edwards and Wayne, eds., *Studying the Presidency*, pp. 99–124.

22. For more on legal analysis of the presidency, see Louis Fisher, "Making Use of Legal Sources," in ibid., pp. 182–98.

23. Norman C. Thomas, "Case Studies," in ibid., pp. 50–78.

24. See, for example, Alexander L. George, "The Case for Multiple Advocacy in Making Foreign Policy," *American Political Science Review* 66 (September 1972): 765–81.

25. See, for example, Edwards, *Implementing Public Policy*.

26. See Janis, *Groupthink*.

27. See, for example, Bruce Miroff, "Presidential Leverage over Social Movements: The Johnson White House and Civil Rights," *Journal of Politics* 43 (February 1981): 2–23.

28. Neustadt, *Presidential Power*.

29. Graham T. Allison, *Essence of Decision: Explaining the Cuban Missile Crisis* (Boston: Little, Brown, 1971).

SELECTED READINGS

Edwards, George C., III, and Stephen J. Wayne, eds. *Studying the Presidency.* Knoxville, Tenn.: University of Tennessee Press, 1983.

Appendix B

Nonelectoral Succession, Removal, and Tenure

The Constitution and statutes provide for contingencies that might require the selection, removal, or replacement of a president outside the normal electoral process. In addition to the provisions of Article 1 (Impeachment) and Article 2 (Impeachment and Succession), there have been three amendments (numbers 20, 22, and 25) and three laws concerning succession and term of office. This appendix will examine these contingency arrangements. It will also briefly describe the impeachment process and the two most serious attempts to remove a sitting president. The Constitution and statutes provide for methods of succession and removal.

SUCCESSION

The principal reason for creating the vice presidency was to have a position from which the presidency would automatically be filled should it become vacant. Death, resignation, and impeachment constitute clear-cut situations in which this succession mechanism would work. Eight presidents have died in office and one has resigned. In each of the nine instances, the vice president became president.

One contingency the founders did not consider was temporary or permanent disability while in office. On a number of occasions, presidents have become disabled, unable to perform their duties and responsibilities. James Garfield, shot by a disappointed job seeker, lingered for almost three months before he died. More recently, Ronald Reagan was hospitalized twice, the first time following the attempt on his life and the other for an operation for cancer of the colon. During both hospital stays, he was unconscious for several hours and incapacitated for several months. Other presidents have also been incapacitated. Wilson suffered a stroke that disabled him for much of the last year of his administration, while Eisenhower's heart attack, ileitis operation, and minor stroke severely limited his presidential activities in 1955, 1956, and 1957 (see Chapter 8).

During none of these periods did vice presidents officially take over. In fact, Chester Arthur and Thomas Marshall, Garfield's and Wilson's vice presidents, respectively, avoided even the appearance of performing presidential duties for fear that their actions would be wrongfully construed. Vice President Richard Nixon did preside at cabinet meetings in Eisenhower's absence but did not assume the president's other responsibilities. George Bush, away from the capital at the time Reagan was shot, flew back to Washington immediately to be available if needed. However, to avoid any appearance of impropriety, he had his helicopter land at the vice president's residence even though he was scheduled to meet at the White House with senior presidential aides. By prearrangement with the vice president, President Reagan passed his powers and duties to Bush during the period when he was under the influence of anesthesia during his colon operation in 1985. He reassumed them when he declared himself able to do so several hours after his operation.

It was not until 1967 that procedures were established for the vice president to become acting president in the event of the president's disability. The Twenty-fifth Amendment to the Constitution permits the vice president to exercise the duties and powers of the presidency if the president declares in writing that he is unable to do so or if the vice president and a majority of the principal executive department heads reach that judgment. The president may resume his office when he believes that he is able unless the vice president and a majority of the principal executive department heads object. In that case Congress must make the final determination. The procedures, however, are weighted in the president's favor. Unless Congress concurs in the judgment that the president is disabled, the president is entitled once again to exercise the duties and powers of his office.

Another important provision of this amendment provides for filling the vice presidency should it become vacant. Prior to 1967, it had been vacant sixteen times. The procedures permit the president to nominate a new vice president, who takes office upon confirmation by a majority of both houses of Congress. Gerald Ford and Nelson Rockefeller were the only two vice presidents who assumed office in this manner. Ford was nominated by President Nixon in 1973 upon the resignation of Spiro T. Agnew. After succeeding to the presidency upon Nixon's resignation, Ford nominated Rockefeller.

While the presidency and vice presidency have never been vacant at the same time, Congress has provided for such a contingency should it arise by establishing a line of succession. The most recent succession law was enacted in 1947. It puts the Speaker of the House next in line to be followed by the president pro tempore of the Senate and the department heads in order of their seniority, beginning with the secretary of state. The provision for appointing a new vice president, however, makes it less likely that legislative and executive officials would ever succeed to the presidency, barring a catastrophe or an unlikely set of events that resulted in a president's death before a new vice presidential nomination could be made or confirmed.

REMOVAL

In addition to providing for the president's replacement, the constitutional framers also thought it necessary to provide for his removal. They believed that it was too dangerous to wait for the electors' judgment in the case of a president who had abused his authority. Impeachment was considered an extraordinary remedy but one that could be used against executive officials, including the president and vice president, who violated their public trust.

Article, 2, section 4, of the Constitution spells out the terms. The president, vice president, and other executive officials can be removed from office for treason, bribery, or other high crimes and misdemeanors. Precisely what actions would be considered impeachable offenses is left for Congress to determine.

The House of Representatives considers the charges against the president. If a majority of the House votes in favor of any of them, a trial is held in the Senate with the chief justice of the Supreme Court presiding. The House presents its case against the president. The latter, who may be represented by outside counsel, defends himself against the charges. A two-thirds vote of the Senate is required for conviction. If the president is convicted, he is removed from office. He may still be subject to civil or criminal prosecution.

Only one president, Andrew Johnson, has ever been impeached. The incident that sparked his impeachment was Johnson's removal of Secretary of War Edwin Stanton. Congress had passed a law over Johnson's veto that required appointees to remain in office until the Senate approved their successor. Known as the Tenure of Office Act (1867), it permitted the president some discretion during a congressional recess but required the Senate's advice and consent after Congress reconvened. In the absence of senatorial approval, the office reverted to its previous occupant.

During a congressional recess, Johnson removed Stanton. The Senate refused to concur in the removal upon its return. Under the law, Stanton was entitled to his old job. However, the president once again removed him. Upon his removal for a second time, the House of Representatives passed a bill of impeachment against the president. The Senate trial lasted six weeks. In its first vote the Senate fell one short of the required two-thirds. A ten-day recess was called by those favoring Johnson's removal. Extensive lobbying ensued, but when the Senate reconvened, no one changed his vote. Johnson was acquitted. The Tenure of Office Act was subsequently repealed during the Cleveland administration.

A second attempt to impeach a sitting president occurred in 1973. When Richard Nixon dismissed Archibald Cox, the special prosecutor who had been investigating charges of administration wrongdoing in the Watergate affair, members of Congress called for Nixon's removal. The Judiciary Committee of the House of Representatives began hearings on the president's impeachment. During the course of these hearings, the committee subpoenaed tapes of conversations which the president had held with aides in the White House, conversations that had been secretly recorded by the president. Claiming that these were privileged communications, Nixon refused to deliver the tapes, although he did send edited transcripts of them to the House committee. Not satisfied with this response, the House took its case to court and won. The Supreme Court ordered Nixon to release the tapes. When he did so, they revealed his early knowledge of the break-in and his participation in the cover-up. This information heightened calls for the president's ouster.

The House Judiciary Committee approved three articles of impeachment against Nixon. It looked as if the full House would vote to impeach him and that the Senate would vote to convict him. Faced with the prospect of a long trial and probable conviction, Nixon resigned on August 9, 1974.

TENURE

Electoral defeat and impeachment prematurely conclude a presidency—at least from the incumbent's perspective. Initially the Constitution imposed no limit on the number of times a president could be elected. Reeligibility was seen as a motive to good behavior. Beginning with Washington, however, an unofficial two-term limit was established. Franklin Roosevelt ended this precedent in 1940 when he ran for a third term and won.

Partially in reaction to Roosevelt's twelve years and one month as president, a Republican-controlled Congress passed and the states ratified the Twenty-second Amendment to the Constitution. It prevents any person from being elected to the office more than twice. Moreover, it limits to one election a president who has succeeded to the office and has served more than two years of his predecessor's term. Eisenhower was the first president to be subject to the provisions of the amendment, and Reagan was the second.

One of the consequences of this amendment is that it seems to weaken the president in his second term, particularly during his last two years in office. Not being able to run for the presidency again reduces a president's political power and his capacity to mobilize public backing for his programs and policies. On the other hand, it may improve his capacity to mobilize a bipartisan coalition because his motives may be less subject to suspicion. This might result in a weaker domestic presidency but a stronger foreign policy one. It would certainly affect his incentives for policy making in each of these spheres.

Appendix C

Provisions of the Constitution of the United States That Relate to the Presidency

ARTICLE I

Section 2. . . .

(3) [Representatives and direct Taxes[1] shall be apportioned among the several States which may be included within this Union, according to their respective Numbers, which shall be determined by adding to the whole Number of free Persons, including those bound to Service for a Term of Years, and excluding Indians not taxed, three fifths of all other Persons.][2] The actual Enumeration shall be made within three Years after the first Meeting of the Congress of the United States, and within every subsequent Term of ten Years, in such Manner as they shall by Law direct. The Number of Representatives shall not exceed one for every thirty Thousand, but each State shall have at Least one Representative; and until such enumeration shall be made, the State of New Hampshire shall be entitled to choose three, Massachusetts eight, Rhode-Island and Providence Plantations one, Connecticut five, New York, six, New Jersey four, Pennsylvania eight, Delaware one, Maryland six, Virginia ten, North Carolina five, South Carolina five, and Georgia three.

(4) When vacancies happen in the Representation from any State, the Executive Authority thereof shall issue Writs of Election to fill such Vacancies.

(5) The House of Representatives shall choose their Speaker and other Officers; and shall have the sole Power of Impeachment.

Section 3. . . .

(4) The Vice President of the United States shall be President of the Senate, but shall have no Vote, unless they be equally divided.

(5) The Senate shall choose their other Officers, and also a President pro tempore, in the Absence of the Vice President, or when he shall exercise the Office of President of the United States.

---

[1]The Sixteenth Amendment replaced this with respect to income taxes.
[2]Repealed by the Fourteenth Amendment.

(6) The Senate shall have the sole Power to try all Impeachements. When sitting for that Purpose, they shall be on Oath or Affirmation. When the President of the United States is tried, the Chief Justice shall preside: And no Person shall be convicted without the Concurrence of two thirds of the Members present.

(7) Judgment in Cases of Impeachment shall not extend further than to removal from Office, and disqualification to hold and enjoy any Office of honor, Trust or Profit under the United States: but the Party convicted shall nevertheless be liable and subject to Indictment, Trial, Judgment and Punishment according to Law.

Section 7. . . .

(2) Every Bill which shall have passed the House of Representatives and the Senate, shall, before it become a Law, be presented to the President of the United States; If he approve he shall sign it, but if not he shall return it, with his Objections to that House in which it shall have originated, who shall enter the Objections at large on their Journal, and proceed to reconsider it. If after such Reconsideration two thirds of that House shall agree to pass the Bill, it shall be sent, together with Objections, to the other House, by which it shall likewise be reconsidered, and if approved by two thirds of that House, it shall become a Law. But in all such Cases the Votes of both Houses shall be determined by Yeas and Nays, and the Names of the Persons voting for and against the Bill shall be entered on the Journal of each House respectively. If any Bill shall not be returned by the President within ten Days (Sundays excepted) after it shall have been presented to him, the Same shall be a Law, in like Manner as if he had signed it, unless the Congress by their Adjournment prevent its Return, in which Case it shall not be a Law.

(3) Every Order, Resolution, or Vote to which the Concurrence of the Senate and House of Representatives may be necessary (except on a question of Adjournment) shall be presented to the President of the United States; and before the Same shall take Effect, shall be approved by him, or being disapproved by him, shall be repassed by two thirds of the Senate and House of Representatives, according to the Rules and Limitations prescribed in the Case of a Bill.

Section 9. . . .

(2) The Privilege of the Writ of Habeas Corpus shall not be suspended, unless when in Cases of Rebellion or Invasion the public Safety may require it.

(8) No Title of Nobility shall be granted by the United States: And no Person holding any Office of Profit or Trust under them, shall, without the Consent of the Congress, accept of any present, Emolument, Office, or Title, of any kind whatever, from any King, Prince, or foreign State.

ARTICLE II

Section 1. (1) The executive Power shall be vested in a President of the United States of America. He shall hold his Office during the Term of four Years, and, together with the Vice-President, chosen for the same Term, be elected, as follows:

(2) Each State shall appoint, in such Manner as the Legislature thereof may direct, a Number of Electors, equal to the whole Number of Senators and

Representatives to which the State may be entitled in the Congress, but no Senator or Representative, or Person holding an Office of Trust or Profit under the United States, shall be appointed an Elector.

[The Electors shall meet in their respective States, and vote by Ballot for two persons, of whom one at least shall not be an Inhabitant of the same State with themselves. And they shall make a List of all the Persons voted for, and of the Number of Votes for each; which List they shall sign and certify, and transmit sealed to the Seat of the Government of the United States, directed to the President of the Senate. The President of the Senate shall, in the Presence of the Senate and House of Representatives, open all the Certificates, and the Votes shall then be counted. The Person having the greatest Number of Votes shall be the President, if such Number be a Majority of the whole Number of Electors appointed; and if there be more than one who have such Majority, and have an equal Number of Votes, then the House of Representatives shall immediately choose by Ballot one of them for President; and if no Person have a Majority, then from the five highest on the List the said House shall in like Manner choose the President. But in choosing the President, the Votes shall be taken by States, the Representation from each State having one Vote; A quorum for this purpose shall consist of a Member or Members from two-thirds of the States, and a Majority of all the States shall be necessary to a Choice. In every Case, after the Choice of the President, the Person having the greatest Number of Votes of the Electors shall be the Vice-President. But if there should remain two or more who have equal Votes, the Senate shall choose from them by Ballot the Vice-President.][3]

(3) The Congress may determine the Time of choosing the Electors, and the Day on which they shall give their Votes; which Day shall be the same throughout the United States.

(4) No person except a natural born Citizen, or a Citizen of the United States, at the time of the Adoption of this Constitution, shall be eligible to the Office of President; neither shall any Person be eligible to that Office who shall not have attained to the Age of thirty-five Years, and been fourteen Years a Resident within the United States.

(5) In case of the Removal of the President from Office, or of his Death, Resignation, or Inability to discharge the Powers and Duties of the said Office, the same shall devolve on the Vice-President, and the Congress may by Law provide for the Case of Removal, Death, Resignation or Inability; both of the President and Vice-President, declaring what Officer shall then act as President, and such Officer shall act accordingly, until the Disability be removed, or a President shall be elected.[4]

(6) The President shall, at stated Times, receive for his Services, a Compensation, which shall neither be increased nor diminished during the Period for which he shall have been elected, and he shall not receive within that Period any other Emolument from the United States, or any of them.

(7) Before he enter on the Execution of his Office, he shall take the following Oath or Affirmation:—"I do solemnly swear (or affirm) that I will faithfully

[3]This paragraph was superseded in 1804 by the Twelfth Amendment.
[4]Changed by the Twenty-fifth Amendment.

execute the Office of President of the United States, and will to the best of my Ability, preserve, protect and defend the Constitution of the United States."

Section 2. (1) The President shall be Commander in Chief of the Army and Navy of the United States, and of the Militia of the several States, when called into the actual Service of the United States; he may require the Opinion in writing, of the principal Officer in each of the executive Departments, upon any subject relating to the Duties of their respective Offices, and he shall have Power to Grant Reprieves and Pardons for Offenses against the United States, except in Cases of Impeachment.

(2) He shall have Power, by and with the Advice and Consent of the Senate, to make Treaties, provided two-thirds of the Senators present concur; and he shall nominate, and by and with the Advice and Consent of the Senate, shall appoint Ambassadors, other public Ministers and Consuls, Judges of the supreme Court, and all other Officers of the United States, whose Appointments are not herein otherwise provided for, and which shall be established by Law: but the Congress may by Law vest the Appointment of such inferior Officers, as they think proper, in the President alone, in the Court of Law, or in the Heads of Departments.

(3) The President shall have Power to fill up all Vacancies that may happen during the Recess of the Senate, by granting Commissions which shall expire at the End of their next Session.

Section 3. He shall from time to time give to the Congress Information of the State of the Union, and recommend to their Consideration such Measures as he shall judge necessary and expedient; he may, on extraordinary Occasions, convene both Houses, or either of them, and in Case of Disagreement between them, with Respect to the Time of Adjournment, he may adjourn them to such Time as he shall think proper; he shall receive Ambassadors and other public Ministers; he shall take Care that the Laws be faithfully executed, and shall Commission all the Officers of the United States.

Section 4. The President, Vice President and all civil Officers of the United States, shall be removed from Office on Impeachment for, and Conviction of, Treason, Bribery, or other high Crimes and Misdemeanors.

ARTICLE IV

Section 4. The United States shall guarantee to every State in this Union a Republican Form of Government, and shall protect each of them against Invasion; and on Application of the Legislature, or of the Executive (when the Legislature cannot be convened) against domestic Violence.

ARTICLE VI

(3) The Senators and Representatives before mentioned, and the Members of the several State Legislatures, and all executive and judicial Officers, both of the United States and of the several States, shall be bound by Oath or Affirmation,

to support this Constitution; but no religious Test shall ever be required as a Qualification to any Office or public Trust under the United States.

AMENDMENT XII[5]

The Electors shall meet in their respective states and vote by ballot for President and Vice-President, one of whom, at least, shall not be an inhabitant of the same state with themselves; they shall name in their ballots the person voted for as President, and in distinct ballots the person voted for as Vice-President, and they shall make distinct lists of persons voted for as President, and of all persons voted for as Vice-President, and of the number of votes for each, which lists they shall sign and certify, and transmit sealed to the seat of the government of the United States, directed to the President of the Senate;—The President of the Senate shall, in presence of the Senate and House of Representatives, open all the certificates and the votes shall then be counted;—The person having the greatest number of votes for President, shall be the President, if such number be a majority of the whole number of Electors appointed; and if no person have such majority, then from the persons having the highest numbers not exceeding three on the list of those voted for as President, the House of Representatives shall choose immediately, by ballot, the President. But in choosing the President, the votes shall be taken by states, the representation from each state having one vote; a quorum for this purpose shall consist of a member or members from two-thirds of the states, and a majority of all the states shall be necessary to a choice. [And if the House of Representatives shall not choose a President whenever the right of choice shall devolve upon them, before the fourth day of March next following, then the Vice-President shall act as President, as in the case of the death or other constitutional disability of the President.][6]—The person having the greatest number of votes as Vice-President, shall be the Vice-President, if such number be a majority of the whole number of Electors appointed, and if no person have a majority, then from the two highest numbers on the list, the Senate shall choose the Vice-President; a quorum for the purpose shall consist of two-thirds of the whole number of Senators, and a majority of the whole number shall be necessary to a choice. But no person constitutionally ineligible to the office of President shall be eligible to that of Vice-President of the United States.

AMENDMENT XV[7]

Section 1. The right of citizens of the United States to vote shall not be denied or abridged by the United States or by any State on account of race, color, or previous condition of servitude.

[5]Adopted in 1804.
[6]Superseded by the Twentieth Amendment, section 3.
[7]Adopted in 1870.

Section 2. The Congress shall have power to enforce this article by appropriate legislation.

AMENDMENT XIX[8]

The right of citizens of the United States to vote shall not be denied or abridged by the United States or by any State on account of sex.

Congress shall have power to enforce this article by appropriate legislation.

AMENDMENT XX[9]

Section 1. The terms of the President and Vice-President shall end at noon on the 20th day of January, and the terms of Senators and Representatives at noon on the 3rd day of January, of the years in which such terms would have ended if this article had not been ratified; and the terms of their successors shall then begin.

Section 2. The Congress shall assemble at least once in every year, and such meeting shall begin at noon on the 3rd day of January, unless they shall by law appoint a different day.

Section 3. If, at the time fixed for the beginning of the term of the President, the President elect shall have died, the Vice-President elect shall become President. If a President shall not have been chosen before the time fixed for the beginning of his term, or if the President elect shall have failed to qualify, then the Vice-President elect shall act as a President until a President shall have qualified; and the Congress may by law provide for the case wherein neither a President elect nor a Vice-President elect shall have qualified, declaring who shall then act as President, or the manner in which one who is to act shall be selected, and such person shall act accordingly until a President or Vice-President shall have qualified.

Section 4. The Congress may by law provide for the case of the death of any of the persons from whom the House of Representatives may choose a President whenever the right of choice shall have devolved upon them, and for the case of the death of any of the persons from whom the Senate may choose a Vice-President whenever the right of choice shall have devolved upon them.

Section 5. Sections 1 and 2 shall take effect on the 15th day of October following the ratification of this article.

Section 6. This article shall be inoperative unless it shall have been ratified as an amendment to the Constitution by the legislatures of three-fourths of the several States within seven years from the date of its submission.

---

[8]Adopted in 1920.
[9]Adopted in 1933.

AMENDMENT XXII[10]

Section 1. No person shall be elected to the office of the President more than twice, and no person who has held the office of President, or acted as President, for more than two years of a term to which some other person was elected President shall be elected to the office of the President more than once. But this Article shall not apply to any person holding the office of President when this Article was proposed by the Congress, and shall not prevent any person who may be holding the office of President, or acting as President, during the term within which this Article becomes operative from holding the office of President or acting as President during the remainder of such term.

Section 2. This article shall be inoperative unless it shall have been ratified as an amendment to the Constitution by the legislatures of three-fourths of the several States within seven years from the date of its submission to the States by the Congress.

AMENDMENT XXIII[11]

Section 1. The District constituting the seat of Government of the United States shall appoint in such manner as the Congress may direct:

A number of electors of President and Vice-President equal to the whole number of Senators and Representatives in Congress to which the District would be entitled if it were a State, but in no event more than the least populous State; they shall be in addition to those appointed by the States, but they shall be considered, for the purposes of the election of President and Vice-President, to be electors appointed by a State; and they shall meet in the District and perform such duties as provided by the twelfth article of amendment.

Section 2. The Congress shall have power to enforce this article by appropriate legislation.

AMENDMENT XXIV[12]

Section 1. The right of citizens of the United States to vote in any primary or other election for President or Vice-President, for electors for President or Vice-President, or for Senator or Representative in Congress, shall not be denied or abridged by the United States or any state by reasons of failure to pay any poll tax or other tax.

Section 2. The Congress shall have power to enforce this article by appropriate legislation.

---

[10]Adopted in 1951.
[11]Adopted in 1961.
[12] Adopted in 1964.

AMENDMENT XXV[13]

Section 1. In case of the removal of the President from office or of his death or resignation, the Vice-President shall become President.

Section 2. Whenever there is a vacancy in the office of the Vice-President, the President shall nominate a Vice-President who shall take office upon confirmation by a majority vote of both Houses of Congress.

Section 3. Whenever the President transmits to the President pro tempore of the Senate and the Speaker of the House of Representatives his written declaration that he is unable to discharge the powers and duties of his office, and until he transmits to them a written declaration to the contrary, such powers and duties shall be discharged by the Vice-President as Acting President.

Section 4. Whenever the Vice-President and a majority of either the principal officers of the Executive departments or of such other body as Congress may by law provide, transmit to the President pro tempore of the Senate and the Speaker of the House of Representatives their written declaration that the President is unable to discharge the powers and duties of his office, the Vice-President shall immediately assume the powers and duties of the office as Acting President.

Thereafter, when the President transmits to the President pro tempore of the Senate and the Speaker of the House of Representatives his written declaration that no inability exists, he shall resume the powers and duties of his office unless the Vice-President and a majority of either the principal officers of the executive departments or of such other body as Congress may by law provide, transmit within four days to the President pro tempore of the Senate and the Speaker of the House of Representatives their written declaration that the President is unable to discharge the powers and duties of his office. Thereupon Congress shall decide the issue, assembling within forty-eight hours for that purpose if not in session. If the Congress, within twenty-one days after receipt of the latter written declaration, or, if Congress is not in session, within twenty-one days after Congress is required to assemble, determines by two-thirds vote of both houses that the President is unable to discharge the powers and duties of his office, the Vice-President shall continue to discharge the same as Acting President; otherwise, the President shall resume the powers and duties of his office.

AMENDMENT XXVI[14]

Section 1. The right of citizens of the United States, who are 18 years of age or older, to vote shall not be denied or abridged by the United States or any state on account of age.

Section 2. The Congress shall have power to enforce this article by appropriate legislation.

[13]Adopted in 1967.
[14] Adopted in 1971.

Index